The Routledge Handbook of Social Care Work Around the World

The Routledge Handbook of Social Care Work Around the World provides both a comprehensive and authoritative state-of-the-art review of the current research in this subject. It is the first handbook to cover social care work research from around the world, including both low- and middle-income countries as well as high-income countries.

All of the 22 chapters are written by experts on long-term care services, particularly for older people, and cover key issues and debates, based on research evidence, on social care work in a specific country. They look at perspectives of social care work from the macro level: the structural conditions for long-term care, including demographic challenges and the long-term care policy; the meso level: the level of provider organizations and intermediaries; and the micro level: views of care workers, care users, and unpaid informal carers. Furthermore, they discuss a number of topics central to discussions of care work, including marketization, personalization policies, policy implementation under austerity, the provision of social care work, whether through public services, private arrangements, or mixed types, funding, the feminization of social care, and the new role that technology and robots can play in care work.

By drawing together leading scholars from around the world, this book provides an up-to-the-minute snapshot of current scholarship as well as signposting several fruitful avenues for future research. This book is both an invaluable resource for scholars and an indispensable teaching tool for use in the classroom, and will be of interest to students, academics, social workers, social policymakers and human service professionals.

Karen Christensen is Professor of Sociology at the Department of Sociology, University of Bergen, Norway. Her research and publications focus on welfare sociology based on her interests in social care, work, gender and migration. She has led or collaborated on a range of research projects, nationally and internationally, within areas such as elderly care, welfare and disability, comparative social policy, and the lives of migrant care workers.

Doria Pilling is a sociologist and Honorary Senior Research Fellow at the School of Health Services at City, University of London, UK. She has researched and published on a range of areas, including social disadvantage, case management, disability and employment, disability and technology, evaluation of service quality and comparative social policy.

The Routledge Handbook of Social Care Work Around the World

Edited by Karen Christensen and Doria Pilling

LONDON AND NEW YORK

First published 2018
by Routledge
2 Park Square, Milton Park, Abingdon, Oxon OX14 4RN

and by Routledge
711 Third Avenue, New York, NY 10017

Routledge is an imprint of the Taylor & Francis Group, an informa business

© 2018 selection and editorial matter, Karen Christensen and Doria Pilling; individual chapters, the contributors

The right of Karen Christensen and Doria Pilling to be identified as the authors of the editorial material, and of the authors for their individual chapters, has been asserted in accordance with sections 77 and 78 of the Copyright, Designs and Patents Act 1988.

All rights reserved. No part of this book may be reprinted or reproduced or utilised in any form or by any electronic, mechanical, or other means, now known or hereafter invented, including photocopying and recording, or in any information storage or retrieval system, without permission in writing from the publishers.

Trademark notice: Product or corporate names may be trademarks or registered trademarks, and are used only for identification and explanation without intent to infringe.

British Library Cataloguing in Publication Data
A catalogue record for this book is available from the British Library

Library of Congress Cataloging in Publication Data
Names: Christensen, Karen, 1959- editor. | Pilling, Doria, editor.
Title: The Routledge handbook to social care work around the world / edited by Karen Christensen and Doria Pilling.
Other titles: Handbook to social care work around the world
Description: Abingdon, Oxon ; New York, NY : Routledge, 2018. | Includes bibliographical references and index.
Identifiers: LCCN 2017035340| ISBN 9781472479457 (hardback : alk. paper) | ISBN 9781315612805 (ebook)
Subjects: | MESH: Health Services for the Aged | Long-Term Care | Cross-Cultural Comparison
Classification: LCC RA418 | NLM WT 31 | DDC 362.1—dc23
LC record available at https://lccn.loc.gov/2017035340

ISBN: 978-1-4724-7945-7 (hbk)
ISBN: 978-1-315-61280-5 (ebk)

Typeset in Bembo
by Swales & Willis Ltd, Exeter, Devon, UK

 Printed in the United Kingdom by Henry Ling Limited

In memory of our German and British caring mothers
Erika K.I.L. Christensen and Rose Arram
K.C. and D.P.

Contents

List of figures	*xi*
List of tables	*xiii*
List of contributors	*xv*

Introduction *Karen Christensen and Doria Pilling*	1

PART I

Nordic countries   13

1 Long-term care services in Norway: a historical sociological perspective *Karen Christensen and Kari Wærness*	15
2 Revisiting the public care model: the Danish case of free choice in home care *Tine Rostgaard*	29
3 Organizational trends impacting on everyday realities: the case of Swedish eldercare *Anneli Stranz and Marta Szebehely*	45

PART II

Northern and Western Europe   59

4 Long-term care reforms in the Netherlands: care work at stake *Barbara Da Roit*	61

vii

Contents

5 The English social care workforce: the vexed question
of low wages and stress 74
Shereen Hussein

6 The personalization and marketization of home
care services for older people in England 88
Kate Baxter

7 The development of an ambiguous care work sector
in France: between professionalization and fragmentation 102
Blanche Le Bihan and Alis Sopadzhiyan

8 Care provision inside and outside the professional
care system: the case of long-term care insurance in Germany 116
Hildegard Theobald

9 Employing migrant care workers for 24-hour care
in private households in Austria: benefits and risks for
the long-term care system 130
August Österle

10 Migrant care workers in Italian households:
recent trends and future perspectives 142
*Mirko Di Rosa, Francesco Barbabella, Arianna Poli,
Sara Santini and Giovanni Lamura*

PART III
Eastern Europe **157**

11 Post-socialist eldercare in the Czech Republic:
institutions, families, and the market 159
Adéla Souralová and Eva Šlesingerová

12 Imbalance between demand and supply of
long-term care: the case of post-communist Poland 171
Stanisława Golinowska and Agnieszka Sowa-Kofta

PART IV
Between Europe and Asia **185**

13 Long-term care in Turkey: challenges and opportunities 187
Sema Oglak

Contents

PART V
Asia 201

14 The emergence of the eldercare industry in China:
    progress and challenges 203
    Xiying Fan, Heying Jenny Zhan and Qi Wang

15 Challenges of care work under the new long-term care
    insurance for elderly people in South Korea 218
    Yongho Chon

16 Migrant live-in care workers in Taiwan: multiple roles,
    cultural functions, and the new division of care labour 228
    Li-Fang Liang

17 Has the long-term care insurance contributed to
    de-familialization? Familialization and marketization
    of eldercare in Japan 241
    Yayoi Saito

18 Care robots in Japanese elderly care: cultural
    values in focus 256
    Nobu Ishiguro

PART VI
North America 271

19 Long-term services and supports for the elderly in the
    United States: a complex system of
    perverse incentives 273
    Candace Howes

20 Complexities, tensions, and promising practices: work in
    Canadian long-term residential care 289
    Pat Armstrong and Tamara Daly

PART VII
Australia 301

21 Reforms to long-term care in Australia: a changing and
    challenging landscape 303
    Jane Mears

ix

Contents

PART VIII
Latin America 317

22 Facing the challenges of population longevity but
not being ready: the case of Argentina 319
Nélida Redondo

Index 332

Note: References are in the language of the first title, unless stated otherwise.

Figures

1.1	Number of service receivers during the year by type of service, 1965–1980	19
1.2	Places in institutions for older and disabled people, by type of section, 1970–1980	19
1.3	Work years in long-term care, percentage institutional and home-based care, 1980–2007	22
1.4	Receivers of home-based services per 31 December by type of service, 1992–2010	23
1.5	Receivers of home-based services, by age, 1992, 2002 and 2010	24
2.1	Home care recipients aged 65+ and percentage using for-profit providers in total and according to type of assistance, 2008–2015	32
2.2	Proportion of home care users 65+ who change provider type, annually, total and according to type of care, 2009–2015	34
2.3	Satisfaction and dissatisfaction with provider, by type of provider and service assistance, percentage of home care users, 2011 and 2015	35
2.4	Home care users' ranking of quality items according to provider type, practical care only, percentage satisfied and dissatisfied, 2015	37
2.5	Work content, percentage of home care workers carrying out different services, by sector of employment, 2015–2016	38
2.6	Organization of work, private–public distinction, 2015–2016	39
2.7	Information from and recognition by line manager, private–public distinction, 2015–2016	40
2.8	Skill formation and immediate support, private–public distinction, 2015–2016	41

Figures

2.9	Perceptions of quality, private–public distinction, 2015–2016	42
4.1	Employees and FTE in the LTC sector (2004–2014)	68
5.1	Trends of number of migrants working in the social care sector in England by year of entry to the UK and nationality, NMDS-SC, February 2016	77
10.1	Trend of care workers according to the areas of origin (2005–2014)	147
10.2	Value of public, informal and private care for dependent people (billion euros)	148
12.1	Factors of imbalance between demand and supply of LTC in Poland	180
14.1	Available services and amenities in the facilities	211
14.2	Amenities in residents' rooms	212
17.1	Number of home help users (Japan)	245
17.2	Number of the LTCI facility users (Japan)	246
17.3	The LTCI facility and home help users (Japan) percentage of the population 80+	246
19.1	Long-term services and supports industries	276
19.2	Elderly long-term recipients by service, 2014, 4.1 million	277
19.3	Total LTSS spending for elderly people by source, 2011, $191 billion	277
19.4	Number of employees and establishments, home health services, and SEPD (services for the elderly and persons with disabilities), 2001–2015	279
19.5	Average annual employment, home health and personal care aides (thousands)	282
19.6	Annual median hourly wage, home health and personal care aides (2016 dollars)	282
22.1	Percentage of people aged over 80 in the total population – Argentina – census dates 1947–2010	320
22.2	Percentage of elderly people put in geriatric homes by gender and age group, Argentina, 2010	325

Tables

3.1	Psychosocial working conditions in home care and residential care, 2005 and 2015, per cent	52
3.2	Reactions to working conditions in home care and residential care, 2005 and 2015, per cent	52
5.1	Karasek JCQ scales, decision latitude, psychological job demand, job insecurity and social support by social care staff individual characteristics, LoCS	80
5.2	Karasek JCQ scales, decision latitude, psychological job demand, job insecurity and social support by social care staff job characteristics, LoCS	82
6.1	Summary of research studies	91
7.1	Type of care work relationship and of tasks performed	109
7.2	Working conditions according to the care work relationship	110
8.1	LTCI design and use of benefits	120
8.2	Professional care system: situation and change	122
8.3	Indicators of the situation of care workers, comparing indigenous workers and those with migrant backgrounds	125
9.1	Cash-for-care and care services in Austria (31 December 2015)	133
9.2	Twenty-four-hour care workers by country of origin, age and gender (31 December 2013, 2015)	135
10.1	Families with at least one person aged over 65 years who received at least one type of help in the previous four weeks (percentage of total households with at least one person 65+) (2003–2009)	145
10.2	Families with at least one older person (65+) who received unpaid help from not cohabiting people in the past four weeks, by type of aid received (percentage of total households with at least one person 65+) (2003–2009)	145

Tables

13.1	Comparing total public social expenditures, 1990–2014 (% of GDP), Turkey and OECD	188
13.2	Life expectancy at birth in Turkey (1970–2015)	189
13.3	Actual and projected changes in elderly dependency ratio, Turkey, 1940–2075	189
13.4	Number of residential care facilities in Turkey (2016)	195
14.1	Characteristics of facilities	209
14.2	Characteristics of residents ($n = 241, 914$)	213
15.1	The main scheme of LTCI for Korea	222
17.1	Changes in home help providers (percentages)	249
17.2	Changes in facility care providers (percentages)	251
19.1	Employment in long-term services and supports, 2014 (thousands)	281
22.1	Percentage growth of the population of Argentina between censuses 1991–2001 and 2001–2010 by age groups	321
22.2	Country total, population of 65 and over in private homes (or households) by retirement or pension income, according to gender and age group, 2010	322
22.3	Country total, population of 65 and over in private homes (or households) by health	323

Contributors

Pat Armstrong is Professor of Sociology and of Women's Studies at York University, Toronto, Canada. Focusing on the fields of social policy, of women, work and the health and social services, she has published widely and is currently principal investigator of a seven-year Canadian SSHRC-funded project on reimagining long-term residential care, an international study into promising practices in nursing homes for older people.

Francesco Barbabella is a researcher at the Department of Health and Caring Sciences of the Linnaeus University, Sweden, and Research Fellow at the National Institute of Health and Science on Ageing (INRCA) in Italy. His main research interests concern long-term care systems and policies, the impact of migrant care workers and marketization on long-term care, and the role of ICTs in improving the health and social care of older people.

Kate Baxter is Research Fellow at the Social Policy Research Unit (SPRU), University of York, UK. She was previously a researcher/lecturer at the Centre for Primary Care Research at the University of Manchester, and at the Departments of Social Medicine and Primary Care at Bristol University. Her research focuses on social care for adults and older people, home care, personal budgets, and self-funders.

Yongho Chon is Assistant Professor at the Department of Social Welfare, Incheon National University, in South Korea. His main research interests lie in the areas of long-term care for older people, marketization of care, and service delivery systems. His main publications are based on a number of comparative studies on community-based long-term care systems in South Korea, Germany, and England.

Karen Christensen is Professor of Sociology at the Department of Sociology, University of Bergen, Norway. Her research and publications focus on welfare sociology based on her interests in social care, work, gender and migration. She has led or collaborated on a range of research projects, nationally and internationally, within areas such as elderly care, welfare and disability, comparative social policy, and the lives of migrant care workers.

xv

Contributors

Tamara Daly is Associate Professor at York University, Canada. Her scholarship and research grants focus on several areas, including: gender and health access; working, living and visiting conditions in long-term care facilities and systems; and promising practices and policies to improve access and health equity for diverse seniors, as well as for their paid and unpaid care providers.

Barbara Da Roit is Associate Professor of Economic Sociology at Ca' Foscari University of Venice, Italy. She previously worked at Utrecht University and the University of Amsterdam, both in the Netherlands. Her research focuses on the transformation of care policies and practices, on the relationships between formal and informal care, and on the intersections of care work and migration from a European comparative perspective.

Mirko Di Rosa is Research Fellow Expert at the Italian National Institute of Health and Science on Ageing (INRCA). While at INRCA, he has gained experience in international research projects in these fields: family care of older people; reconciliation of professional and caring responsibilities; migrant care workers; prevention of elder abuse/neglect; long-term care; older workers; and the role of technology in improving older people's quality of life.

Xiying Fan is Associate Professor and Director of the Department of Sociology at Shaanxi Normal University in Xi'n, China. Her research interests cover areas such as: the organization and operation of the nursing home sector for older people; the ageing of the population in China; and long-term care services for older people in China.

Stanisława Golinowska is Full Professor of Health Economics at the Medical College of Jagiellonian University in Krakow, Poland. Starting with a Humboldt Scholarship at Mannheim University, Germany, she later created several research institutes in Poland, including the Centre for Social and Economic Research (CASE). She has participated in and coordinated a number of projects on social/health aspects of ageing in Eastern Europe.

Candace Howes is Hogate-Ferrin Professor of Economics at Connecticut College, US. She earned her PhD from the University of California, Berkeley and began her career as an economist for the United Auto Workers. Her research interests for the last 15 years have focused on the low-wage female workforce generally and, more specifically, on workers providing long-term care to elderly and disabled people.

Shereen Hussein is Principal Research Fellow at the Social Care Workforce Research Unit, King's College London, UK. She is a demographer with a background in statistics and economics. Over the past two decades, she has worked, nationally and internationally, in the field of ageing and sociology of labour, including the complementary roles of formal and informal care, and issues relating to work, migration, care, and wages in the care sector.

Nobu Ishiguro is Associate Professor in Social Policy at the Graduate School of Language and Culture, Osaka University, Japan. Her research interests are comparative welfare state research focusing on long-term care policies, and most recently on care work, welfare governance and care technology in Nordic countries and Japan. Her publications include work on co-housing for senior citizens, working conditions, childcare policies, and care technology.

xvi

Giovanni Lamura is Head of the Centre for Socio-Economic Research on Ageing at Italy's National Institute of Health and Science on Ageing (INRCA). He has a background in economics, and his research interests include international research on family and long-term care, migrant care work, prevention of elder abuse, ICT-based support for informal carers, intergenerational solidarity, and interdisciplinary research on ageing.

Blanche Le Bihan is Assistant Professor at the French School of Public Health (EHESP) and Researcher at the Research Centre Arènes (UMR 6051), France. She has a background in political science, and her main research and publications concern social care and long-term care policies in France and in Europe, including issues about formal/informal carers and cash-for-care schemes. Her current research focuses on family carers and integrated care in Europe.

Li-Fang Liang is Assistant Professor at the Institute of Health and Welfare Policy, National Yang-Ming University in Taiwan. She is a feminist sociologist and interested in the 'invisible work' mostly done by women. Her current research examines how the Taiwan government considers migrant care workers as the solution for the deficits of local care labour through the enactment of its migrant labour and long-term care policy.

Jane Mears is Associate Professor in the School of Social Sciences and Psychology at Western Sydney University, Australia. She has been researching issues of concern to older people since the 1980s, having led research projects on long-term care, home care workers and violence against older women. Her publications concern policies and practices of relevance to ageing, caring, disability, and violence prevention.

Sema Oglak is Associate Professor at the Department of Labour Economics and Industrial Relations at the Adnan Menderes University, Turkey. Her main research interests include areas such as elderly long-term care policy and services, active ageing, health promotion, age-friendly environments, migrant care workers, and volunteering. She has been involved in several national and international projects related to long-term care services.

August Österle is Associate Professor of Social Policy at the Department of Socioeconomics, WU Vienna University of Economics and Business, Austria. His main research focuses on social policy and comparative welfare state analysis, especially in the fields of health and long-term care, on transnational social security, and on equity and social policy. Current activities focus on migrant care work and transnational access to social security.

Doria Pilling is a sociologist and Honorary Senior Research Fellow at City, University of London, UK. She has long-standing experience as a researcher and has led many research projects. Her main interests are in social disadvantage and disability, particularly social care, disability and employment, and disability and ICT. She has a number of publications, including several books.

Arianna Poli is a psychologist and PhD candidate at the Division Ageing and Social Change (ASC) at Linköping University, Sweden. Her main research interests concern: the role of informal and family care; migrant care workers in long-term care; the role of new technologies in supporting older people and their family carers; the availability of and access to healthcare services; and social exclusion and inequalities in old age.

Contributors

Nélida Redondo is Professor at ISALUD University, Buenos Aires, Argentina. She is currently working on research related to the sociology of ageing. Among several positions related to research, she is a consultant for international organizations that are conducting research projects on the social conditions of the elderly population in Argentina and other Latin American countries. She has coordinated several multi-centric research projects.

Tine Rostgaard is Full Professor at Vive – Danish Centre of Applied Social Research in Copenhagen, Denmark. She was previously Full Professor at Aalborg University, Denmark. Her field of research interests comprises comparative policy analysis of social care for children and older people. She has published widely, most recently in particular into the area of child and family policy, as well as about caring fathers in the Nordic welfare states.

Yayoi Saito is Professor at the Graduate School of Human Sciences, Osaka University, Japan. She has been a guest researcher at the University of Oslo, Norway and the University of Stockholm, Sweden. Her research and publications focus on areas such as Japanese eldercare policy, the long-term care insurance system in Japan, and eldercare in Sweden. Her central interests are international comparative studies of eldercare.

Sara Santini is a social gerontologist working at INRCA (Italian National Institute of Health and Science on Ageing) at the Centre for Socio-Economic Research on Ageing since 2000. She gained experience in national and international projects on family caregivers' quality of life; work-life balance; integrated care for older people; the use of ICTs as support for family caregivers; and intergenerational relationships. She is especially skilled in qualitative methodologies for data collection and analysis.

Eva Šlesingerová is Assistant Professor at the Department of Sociology (Social Anthropology Programme), Masaryk University in Brno, the Czech Republic. Currently, she is Marie Curie Fellow at the Institute of Sociology, Goethe University in Frankfurt, Germany. She lectures on subjects such as kinship and anthropology, and social and cultural theory, and she has published a book on *Imagination of Genes/Sociological*.

Alis Sopadzhiyan is Lecturer at the French School of Public Health (EHESP) and Researcher at the Research Centre Arènes (UMR 6051), France. She is a political scientist, currently developing her research in the field of healthcare policies in Central and Eastern Europe and long-term care policies in France and Europe. She has participated in several research projects/networks and is particularly interested in care professionals and integrated care.

Adéla Souralová is Assistant Professor at the Department of Sociology (Social Anthropology Programme), Masaryk University in Brno, the Czech Republic. In her research, she focuses on the issues of paid care, migration and the sociology of the family. She has published a book on mutual dependency in caregiving and has a range of other chapters and articles published, including publications on childhood.

Agnieszka Sowa-Kofta is Assistant Professor at the Institute of Labour and Social Studies and a member of the Supervisory Council at the Centre for Social and Economic Research in Warsaw, Poland. She is a sociologist and economist, with a background focusing on European social protection policy while at the Maastricht University in the Netherlands. Her research interests are social policy and, most recently, especially health and long-term care.

xviii

Contributors

Anneli Stranz is a researcher and lecturer at Stockholm University, Sweden. She has a background in social work studies, and has carried out research into the everyday life realities and working conditions of care workers. She is particularly interested in analysing how paid care work can be understood in relation to gender justice, and she uses comparative and feminist critical perspectives to investigate this.

Marta Szebehely is Professor of Social Work at Stockholm University, Sweden. She has been studying the gendered consequences of the decline in, and restructuring of, public care services for more than 30 years. Regarding research projects, she has been partnering and leading several Nordic and international comparative research projects on eldercare, including the NORDCARE study on care workers' working conditions in Nordic countries.

Hildegard Theobald is Professor of Organizational Gerontology at the University of Vechta in Germany. Her main research interests as well as many of her publications focus on international comparative research on the welfare state, including comparative research on long-term care policies, care arrangements, care work, professionalization and migration. She has a particular focus on gender-, class-, and ethnicity-based inequalities in these areas.

Kari Wærness is a sociologist and Professor Emerita at the Department of Sociology, University of Bergen, Norway. Within the field of social policy, family and care, she has been a leading social scientist in the Nordic countries since the 1980s and she has published widely. She made an important early contribution to bringing the Nordic model of welfare, care and care work to an international audience and debate.

Qi Wang is a PhD candidate in Sociology at Georgia State University in the US. Her research interests include environmental gerontology, cultural sociology, long-term care policies and services, immigration, and intergenerational relationships. She is currently working on a project that investigates the 'homemaking process' regarding settlement experiences and quality of life for Chinese elderly immigrants in the US.

Heying Jenny Zhan is Associate Professor at the Department of Sociology, Georgia State University in the US. She is conducting research in the field of social policy and social gerontology. In the last two decades, she has carried out several research projects on institutional elder care in China. She is actively involved in intellectual exchange between China and the US.

xix

Introduction

Karen Christensen and Doria Pilling

About the handbook

This is the first handbook covering care work research from around the world, including both low- and middle-income countries as well as high-income countries. The objective of this handbook is to provide a comprehensive and authoritative state-of-the-art review of current research in social care work – paid care work – around the world, with a specific focus on social care work towards older people.

Due to a worldwide demographic change towards ageing populations, currently much pressure is put on countries around the world to develop their long-term care services (WHO, 2015). Depending on country-specific social and historical circumstances, large variations can be found between regions and countries in different ways (cf. e.g. Muir, 2017; Ranci and Pavolini, 2013; Bettio and Verashchagina, 2004, 2010), in particular when related to the organizational distribution between what is seen as the main care providers constituting the 'care diamond': the state, the family or households, the market and non-profit organizations, including NGOs (e.g. Razavi, 2007, p. 21). However, there are also considerable similarities, these being stimulated by world-cross-country inspirations as well as different social historical circumstances sometimes leading to similar policy implementations. This handbook's topic is timely and highly relevant, because the ageing population is one of the greatest future social challenges, taking place in a globalizing world with rapid social changes, including increasing geographic mobility with many and different migration streams, women's increasing participation in the labour force, changing birth rates, new intergenerational relationships shifting earlier care obligation traditions, and changing attitudes towards ageing, including the (discriminatory) ageism dimension. Within this framework of social changes, there is currently a strong need for putting long-term care for older people on the agenda by making knowledge about it available. This handbook will make a contribution to this.

The handbook includes 22 chapters written by social sciences experts on long-term care and care work in their country. They have all carried out research into these areas themselves, being deeply involved and engaged in long-term care research. While some of these experts were recruited from our personal academic networks, most of them were selected based on long-term care networks, searches in a range of international journals publishing articles about care work, and finally also using the database EBSCOhost providing access to a huge number of worldwide research resources across many disciplines. Taking account of the impossible mission of covering 'the world', our principle became to select one expert, or expert team, per country, although we made two exceptions (for England and Japan). With a geopolitical unequal distribution of care work research in the world – unequal in the sense that, for example, less developed regions account for 62.4 per cent of people aged 65+, while their share of research published is only 4.5 per cent (Lloyd-Sherlock, 2014) – and ourselves as editors placed in the high-income part of the world, it was easiest to find contributors in Northern and Western European countries, while it was difficult to find contributors in Eastern European countries, Latin America and Africa. However, our extra work on this important matter resulted in the inclusion of Poland, the Czech Republic and Argentina in addition to a range of Nordic countries, countries from Northern and Western Europe, North America, Asia and Australia. In sum, the handbook provides a broad and qualified – in terms of research-based – insight into central issues and challenges related to long-term care work around the world.

In the following part, we will first introduce the key term of 'care work' as a concept and social phenomenon, then also defining 'social care work'. We will then give a concise overview of the issues emerging from the different world areas and countries, and finally briefly discuss the entire collection of chapters in this handbook as a contribution to the discussion of social sustainability.

Care, care work, and social care

Although being of high relevance today related to an ageing population and their ageing-related needs for help and support, that is, 'care', the phenomenon of care has been relevant across history, time and place, even though it has perhaps historically been most commonly thought of in relation to young children. The ongoing characteristic existence of care as a phenomenon has to do with 'care' being a profound part of human (interdependent) lives. This is probably also the reason why there exists a kind of common sense regarding what 'care' is, often implicating in a simple and positive sense concern and concentration on the situation and needs of other people. The theorization of care as a concept by scientists of different disciplines comprises various sets of dimensions and variations in a more complex picture. Our point of departure here is the understanding of care as a social practice, involving a social interaction between people (Tronto, 1993; Noddings, 1984) and representing in society the potential of a 'different voice' (Gilligan, 1982; see also Wærness, 1984); a voice related to the way of treating other people with respect and moral considerations, in a world increasingly stressing economic rationality and people's autonomy and independence. This different-voice perspective has later been explored further into an understanding of care as a 'good for social policy' (Daly, 2002), and is currently revitalized by the discussion of care as an alternative to neo-liberalism (Tronto, 2017). A classical sociological approach to 'care' points to the framing of this by the type of social relationship in which it takes place, with the power distribution of this relationship – as part of a wider welfare system – providing the conditions for the way care is practised, that is, caring (Wærness, 1984). Two basic and widely used dimensions of caring were also introduced early as the difference between 'caring for' and 'caring about', representing – simply said – work and love, respectively, in the 'labour of love' (see Graham, 1983; Ungerson,1983). An important point from this is that care concerns 'work', even when being family-like, but 'work' in this handbook context will involve some kind of love/emotional aspect too. Based on the power distribution explanation, Wærness (1984) suggested a distinction between 'care' when this is about helping, for example, older people needing support, as different from 'personal service' when the caregiver is subordinated to the one receiving help; she has also pointed to the possible tension between care (for dependence on help), treatment (for illness) and service (when the user role is more independent). However, historically, all these dimensions and distinctions are undergoing significant changes. Important in this matter are the current widespread long-term care policies of 'person-centred care' (WHO, 2015, pp. 134–5), aiming at older people's self-management, and the 'ageing in place' policies (WHO, 2015, p. 136), implying being able to remain in one's local community with established local networks. This often particularly means being able to stay at home as long as possible. These policies have contributed to intensifying the blurring boundaries, for example, between professional and informal family-like care (see e.g. Ayalon, 2009) and closely connected today also to the current increasing 'care mix' of different financial arrangements, types of services, service providers and settings (e.g. Daly, 2002, p. 260). It is this intensified blurred status that is an important point of departure for understanding today's care work, because – across the world – many new arrangements of care work are now arriving, crossing earlier more separated areas, such as private/public accountability, formal/informal care, home/institution, professional/non-professional work, regulated/unregulated settings, and in-house/external organizational models.

While care can be carried out for all age groups, whether young or old, disabled or abled, including thereby childcare, family care and care for people due to illness, the handbook's focus is on care work for older people, more specifically people above the age defined as retirement age in their respective countries, including older people with disabilities and other smaller groups. Furthermore, the focus is on 'social care', defined internationally as 'long-term care' when concerning people needing help due to ageing or disability. While 'social' here relates to a degree (lower or higher) of involvement of the state party (a welfare state role) in the care diamond, other parties may be very much or little involved too, including, for example, service providers, community groups, family carers (normally unpaid) and friends. 'Social' also implies that this is primarily about paid, not unpaid, care, although again unpaid parts may be involved; but social care work is someone's occupation, including different degrees of formal and informal qualifications. Furthermore, 'social' means that this is not including healthcare work, unless healthcare work is integrated with or otherwise related to social care work (e.g. home nursing services, or being part of important support for older people), or the care work includes, for example, semi-medical tasks, such as supervising medication. Similar to excluding pure healthcare work, we also consider domestic work on its own as being different from social care work, But again, in some settings, much care work can involve domestic household tasks. Finally, we see social care related to an everyday life setting, but it can take place in homes, institutions, or in one of the many in-between categories, for longer or shorter terms.

In the international language about long-term care work, and used in several of this handbook's chapters, a difference is made between which kind of needs care work is provided for: 'activities of daily living' (ADL) and 'instrumental activities of daily living' (IADL). ADL includes eating, bathing, dressing, getting in and out of bed, and using the toilet, while IADL covers activities that 'facilitate independent living', including using the telephone, taking medications, managing money, shopping for groceries, preparing meals and using a map (cf. e.g. WHO, 2015, but with some definition variations; see e.g. Muir, 2017, p. 44). When seen from the care work side, however, many other tasks can be involved – cf. the blurring boundaries – such as housework, including cleaning, laundering, washing up and tidying, particularly when this is taking place at home. Also, the work may not always only be for the care recipient, but may in practice include work for a whole family and household around the recipient, in particular in more unregulated private household arrangements. Finally, the ADL/IADL function approach overlooks that care work is not only about physical work, but in particular also involves communication as well as emotional work of some kind, with 'caring about' being one dimension.

While the everyday social setting is important and covers a micro level, with views of care workers, as well as their managers, care users, and informal carers, the handbook, overall, also covers a meso level, the level of provider organizations and intermediaries, and a macro level, consisting of the structural conditions for long-term care work, including demographic changes, legislation and long-term care policies, labour market characteristics, and migration policies, as well as general cultural traditions and orientations.

Nordic long-term care: still the ideal model for the future?

The handbook includes three of the Nordic countries: Norway, Denmark, and Sweden. This is an important group of countries to include as the Nordic model, for almost three decades now, has been presented as the forerunner organizing welfare assistance and services, including long-term care services, through the famous comparative welfare regime analysis by Esping-Andersen (e.g. Esping-Andersen, 1999). The Nordic model is in the foreground due to its comprehensive and generous services that are universal, allocated to all classes and based on needs rather than income. Many countries, and in this handbook many chapters, refer to the Nordic countries in this sense (see e.g. the first English chapter, and the chapter on the Netherlands), and politically this development has to do with long-standing social democratic influences as well as their status as rich countries in the world. However, in this handbook, the authors of these Nordic chapters present critical views on their countries as comprehensive and generous systems. Although using different approaches – the Norwegian chapter by Karen Christensen and Kari Wærness a historical-sociological approach, the Danish by Tine Rostgaard a policy-implementation analysis, and the Swedish by Marta Szebehely and Anneli Stranz an organizational analysis looking at everyday life impacts for workers and older people – they all problematize the Nordic model in terms of pointing out tendencies that clearly show a weakening of the main public (state) responsibility. In particular, this critical perspective has to do with the opening up and increasing use of private for-profit actors as service deliverers, mostly in Sweden, and with the softest version in Norway, with the way the services have been increasingly narrowed and bureaucratically standardized in the last decades, and with the increasing view of users as consumers of services. Particularly the latter has happened in Denmark with the implementation of the free-choice-of-provider model in all municipalities since 2003. All three chapters explicitly or implicitly point out that the earlier Nordic women-friendly welfare state (Hernes, 1987), which made care work paid and public, is now losing its glory due to the fact that care workers – with class and ethnicity being social factors – are facing less autonomy and weaker working conditions, and informal (female) carers are under pressure again. All this said, the Nordic countries are still at the top of those countries with the highest long-term care expenditures and still also have the highest proportion of public services (OECD, 2015).

Northern and Western European long-term care: towards marketization and personalization, combined with professionalism variants and household migrants

Many countries in the world are inspired by the Nordic model and are simultaneously very different (see e.g. the first Japanese chapter). However, those countries closest to the Nordic model are European. A few of these have had some kind of basic similarities with the Nordic model earlier and then changed radically in the 1980s or more recently, as is the case with the

Netherlands. The Netherlands implemented a universal long-term care model in the late 1960s, but during the 1990s – unsuccessfully – combined universalism with cost reductions, and since the mid-2000s radically strengthened the cost-reduction strategy parallel with decentralization implementation. Using an approach that understands the cost problem of long-term care as having direct implications on care employment and care workers' working conditions, the chapter by Barbara Da Roit about the Netherlands shows how this country has developed a hierarchy of care workers, with lower-level formal care provided by low-qualified workers close to the cleaning sector, outside the formal long-term sector. Da Roit also points out that while a large increase in informal family carers is not a likely scenario in a situation with more women participating in the labour market, the retrenchment currently seems to develop a niche for live-in migrant care workers from a care market as an alternative to family care in the Dutch system.

Probably the most central inspiration for developing a private market related to long-term care services comes from the UK, where the Thatcher government already in the late 1970s started the implementation of New Public Management ideas in terms of transferring private market ideas to the welfare sector. Between 1990 and 2010, there was a remarkable change in social care provision from being mainly provided by the local authorities to over two-thirds being purchased by local authorities from independent providers. In UK terms, the modernization of public services was first about marketization (e.g. Anttonen and Meagher, 2013), whereby private actors could take over tasks earlier delivered by the state, and later personalization (e.g. Christensen and Pilling, 2014), aiming at giving users more choice and control over their services, in particular implemented with the help of cash-for-care arrangements, whereby the user – with or without help from a support organization of some kind – buys his or her own care services in order to live an independent live. Both chapters on the English social care sector focus on the impact of the intersecting processes of marketization and personalization, including such tendencies as (higher) demands on care workers and (lesser) control of their work, and using migrant care workers to fill gaps, these workers being more willing than indigenous workers to accept lower wages, even below the UK minimum wage. In regard to older people, these processes may mean they are being pushed into making (forced) choices of which service provider – within a complex mix of for-profit and non-profit providers – to choose when often not interested nor able to manage this. Together, the two chapters by Shereen Hussein and Kate Baxter show how the intersecting processes of marketization and personalization change the role of the state and local authorities. It changes from funding *and* providing long-term care to becoming market facilitators, with mainly the independent for-profit sector providing the services. Simultaneously, the services are individualized towards consumer roles, also including older people. Hussein's chapter additionally touches upon the important classic discussion of low payments for (women's) caring work as 'natural' (see e.g. Nelson, 1999; Folbre, 1995).

Both the marketization and personalization processes, with various forms of cash-for-care arrangements as a central driver of these processes, are relevant in the rest of the European countries we have been able to include in the handbook, but in different ways. Starting with Germany and France, the main focus is on the implications of long-term care policies on professionalization, de-professionalization and new forms of care work in the borders between public and private care. Blanche Le Bihan and Alis Sopadzhiyan, the authors of the French chapter, show how the French long-term care system with its clear priority of home-based care from the 1960s first developed a professionalization of care work (including in this a professional identity of care workers), to avoid informal family care burden. They then show how this process was hindered, in particular from the mid-2000s, by a long-term care plan (Plan Borloo from 2005) that promoted a personal for-profit-based service sector, creating blurring boundaries between domestic care and care work. Stimulating for this development was also a cash-for-care scheme, developed in the late 1990s, that increasingly created blurring boundaries between professional care work and informal care by family, not least due to the available option of employing a relative as one's care worker. A somewhat similar situation is pointed out by Hildegard Theobald about the German long-term care system. She shows how the law on long-term care insurance in the mid-1990s is the starting point for developing a complex stratification of care work, following an opening up for a care market with competition between for-profit and non-profit providers. The stratification of care work takes place both inside the regulated professional German care system within the framework of the long-term care insurance system, and outside this. Inside, she points, in particular, to those without formal training, receiving lower security standards and discrimination in terms of doing more low-status cleaning work. Outside the formal system, there is an increasing recruitment of migrant care workers as part of a rather unregulated market.

While Austria and Italy are often categorized into different clusters of care strategies (see e.g. Bettio and Plantenga, 2004, p. 100), with Italy belonging to the Southern European countries, the two countries also recently appear to have similarities. As investigated by the authors August Österle (for Austria) and Mirko Di Rosa and his colleagues (for Italy), both countries are currently receiving migrant care workers, and mainly from Eastern European countries, Austria in particular from Slovakia and Romania. In both chapters, there is a focus on the implications of long-term care policies that make migrant care work a central part of long-term-care. With both countries having strong family-care traditions, a cash-for-care approach in long-term care has been a driver for developing in Italy what is called 'the-migrant-in-the-family-model' (van Hooren, 2012) and in Austria a '24-hour-care-in-private-households' system. While in Austria this developed (unintendedly) out of a grey economy, before it was formalized in 2007, and is today constantly increasing, in Italy this was related to a cash-for-care approach that was extended to older people (65+) already in 1988, and then grew into the highest long-term care expenditure in Italy in 2015 (with much less increase in community and residential care). Both chapter authors point out the significance of the migrant-in-household model when implemented in countries with such strong family traditions. This opens up risks related to privately hiring care workers for users (the families), risks regarding care drain issues in the migrant care workers' home country when leaving families behind and risks of devaluating care work; there are additionally risks of creating insecure working conditions for the migrant workers, as well as exploitation risks and challenges related to intimate relationships in private households.

Eastern European long-term care: remaining post-communist impact?

Rather than being receivers of migrant care workers, the overall picture of Eastern European countries is to 'export' workers, including care workers. While it is found in comparative analyses of Central and Southern Eastern European countries that they share many of the same trends and characteristics regarding long-term care as European countries in general, these countries also have some specific characteristics: family orientation and residualism with limited service provision (Österle, 2012). An important context for understanding the development of long-term care in Eastern European countries is their major transformation since 1989 from a communist regime with central planning to a society with a democratic free market economy strengthened by globalization processes. But Eastern European countries also have country-specific differences, and so is the case for Poland and the Czech Republic, included in the handbook. Although the authors of these cases use different approaches, Adéla Souralová and Eva Šlesingerová using a historical approach focusing in particular on the changes in family care in the Czech Republic as affected by the long-term care development, and Stanisława Golinowska and Agnieszka Sowa-Kofta a demand and supply analysis, differences between these post-communist societies appear. The Czech chapter provides insight into how under the communist regime in the 1950s, a discourse of liberalizing families in order to emancipate women was a communist ideology, though not met by adequate institutional care provision for older people. Therefore, later the country moves towards a familialism discourse, first explicit and then implicit in post-communist time. Then, the Czech Republic seems to move more clearly into commodification of care, developing marketization, particularly through the implementation of a cash-for-care arrangement in 2006. However, the provision of services by for-profit organizations is still very low compared to provision by municipalities, and the cash (for care) is often used as an income supplement rather than for buying care, implying that family members are providing the care. In Polish society, it is rather the very limited volume of public services that has brought some commercialism into (particularly) residential care, this being in practice only for those with high income. And central in the non-profit Polish long-term care institutional sector is the Catholic Church, still running many nursing homes, due to the weak public sector. Regarding use of migrant care workers, this seems to be more developed in Poland, although this mostly has been a sending country of migrant workers. In particular, workers from Ukraine, mainly recruited through informal networks, are now carrying out care work for older people in Poland, but so far limited to wealthy middle-class families. In the Czech Republic, hiring migrant care workers is rarely taking place, but Czech women have started doing care work on a rotational migration basis in Germany and Austria, and migrant care work in the Czech Republic is expected to arrive sooner or later, according to Souralová and Šlesingerová.

Between Europe and Asia: still admiring familialism?

As a country 'between' Europe and Asia, we have put the Turkish chapter by Sema Oglak into its own section. While sharing many of the same social changes as developing countries – a transition from extended to nuclear families and increasing numbers of older people living alone – its population is ageing much faster, and in a situation where Turkey belongs to middle-income countries. This may be one explanation for almost no developed long-term care system, with both home-based and institutional care extremely limited. Another explanation, indicated by Oglak, is that the country still relies intentionally on family care – the main support for disabled and older people in their homes consists of a means-tested allowance for a family member to provide care. This also implies inequality, as Turkish upper- and middle-class families solve their care needs by hiring migrant care workers, these being women and mainly from ex-communist countries.

Asian long-term care: between marketization and the filial piety

Our Asian selection includes four countries, with one of them not being a high-income country: China. The Chinese chapter, written by Xiying Fan, Heying Jenny Zhan and Qi Wang, uses an approach combining insight into demographic changes, policy priorities and cultural values to contextualize the Chinese long-term care situation. The important point of departure lies in the long-lasting family-planning policy, the one-child policy – although recently loosened – which, combined with the post-war Chinese baby boom, for decades has created a 4-2-1 family (four grandparents, two parents, one child). This is currently challenging the thousands of years of Confucian cultural tradition of filial piety, emphasizing childrens' duty of loyalty and care towards ageing parents. But this obviously becomes difficult with only one child, who not only has to work to provide for their own family, but also probably to migrate to another part of the country, to obtain work, thereby creating the old age problem of 'empty nests'. Recognizing the strong deficits of collective-run welfare for older people, the People's Republic of China's central government during the mid-1990s started decentralizing and privatizing former government-owned eldercare institutions. While in other countries, including Asian countries, the for-profit/ non-profit dimension is important, in China rather the government/non-government difference is vital because non-government facilities are poorly treated and in different ways put under financial pressure. Being the most promoted facilities, and at the same time not supported, implies that only better-off older people can afford these places; large numbers are therefore not in use, while the residential demand-supply gap is huge and rising. While Xiying Fan and colleagues point out how the new five-year plan stresses 'ageing at home', including family care in spite of the clearly weakened filial piety tradition, China also faces a big problem regarding care workers. Significant numbers of migrants from other parts of China show high turnovers due to weak working conditions, and qualified workers (nurses) are not finding care work attractive.

The three other Asian countries face many similar challenges, including the weakening conditions for filial piety. However, they are high-income Asian countries, and have developed their long-term care in different directions. In order to counter the problem of inadequate long-term care services, only available for the poorest, South Korea expanded its social care services for older people in the 2000s and introduced a long-term care insurance system in 2008, using marketization measures such as service provider competition and user choices to speed up the process. Yongho Chon, the author of this chapter, focuses on the implications of these changes for care workers, those directly working for older people. Although the new system did boost the numbers of care workers significantly, Chon points out new research observing difficulties in recruiting and keeping qualified young workers; due to demanding working conditions for low payments, when for-profit companies lower the wages because of the strong competition and for profit-increase reasons. Another explanation seems to be that the government supported the private sector in developing training organizations for care workers, using low entry requirements, and then also introduced a compulsory certification system, but with low requirements and poor training. Chon points to the care work challenge as a central problem that should be noticed in order to avoid poor quality due to particularly high turnover in South Korean long-term care.

Unlike South Korea (and also Japan, see below), Taiwan has not developed a long-term care insurance, and thereby did not develop a financial system for public services, these therefore being very limited. However, Li-Fang Liang, the chapter's author, shows how the government in practice encouraged another direction, by facilitating the flow of labour through bilateral agreements with sending countries, and how this resulted in a huge increase, now counting (at the end of 2016) almost a quarter of a million migrants. Many of them are hired directly by families, living-in and being paid less than other care workers. This development also implies a commodification of care development. Like the other Asian chapter authors, Liang also stresses the impact of culture on social care solutions. In Taiwan, this has resulted in an 'outsourced filial piety', realizing, in other words, the filial piety through a live-in migrant care worker in the household. However, Liang shows some important implications, including a blur between care work and domestic work, when the migrant in fact works for the whole family, the development of a care hierarchy between the female family employer concentrating on 'mind work' while the migrant does the 'body work', and in general the development of class and ethnic inequalities between women.

The Japanese chapter, written by Yayoi Saito, somehow summarizes the two important processes going on in Asian long-term care, namely marketization (including commodification) and (re-)familialization, the obligations of family to take on care for the older family members. Saito shows how Japan developed a long-term care insurance in 2000 to meet the country's demand of care due to ageing, the problem of social hospitalization (overly long hospital stays) and a decrease in three-generation families. However, although having the ambition of relieving the family burden, and also introducing a kind of voucher system for users in order for them to be able to make choices in a provider market with home care providers – now dominated by for-profit providers – the supply did not meet the demand. But in contrast to Taiwan, no domestic worker market, due to immigration policies forbidding the entrance of unskilled workers, has developed. Instead, a grey market of quasi-facilities and serviced housing has developed. This market is increasing but very little regulated, and threatens, according to Saito, the quality of long-term care in Japan. Another Japanese 'solution' is pointed out by the second Japanese author, Nobu Ishiguro, within the Japanese context of being the world's leading country of a robot industry and known for robot culture over many years. Framing the discussion with the help of four government-directed discourses – reducing care workers' burden, making older people more independent of help, wishing to get the domestic robot industry growing, and saving costs when care work is labour-intensive – Ishiguro concludes that the question is not whether robots can replace humans, but how humans use technology, and in some cases (using the case of transfer lifts) this can make a positive impact on the direct interaction with the older person. For the future of implementing robots in social care, Ishiguro, however, points to the risks for the quality of care, if robots are used for reducing the time for worker-user interaction, this being essential for understanding the specific needs in each situation and having enough freedom to develop a care dialogue with older people.

The North American way of approaching long-term care: through marketization and labour division

We have included two North American chapters: one by Candace Howes, who gives an overview of the US long-term care system, and one by Pat Armstrong and Tamara Daly, who use the case of food and laundry in Canadian nursing homes to discuss promising practices in residential care. Applying an economic perspective, Howes points to the characteristic roots of the US system of long-term services and support as a welfare system that always has been based on means-testing, and therefore only for the poorest people. The only publicly funded system providing long-term care for older people is the Medicaid programme, funded by state and federal tax revenue. However, the majority of older people do not qualify for this programme, and therefore are dependent on help from family and networks, unless they are wealthy people. Howes also points to the strong American tradition of fee-for-service reimbursement policies towards agencies. Recently, many states are using managed care schemes. Managed care organizations are paid a maximum or capitated fee for each Medicaid-eligible participant and have the flexibility to arrange services that are cost-effective and tailored to each client according to agreed quality standards, but there are also incentives to limit services and cut costs. Undervalued care work, low wages and inadequate training have always been part of the US system. Armstrong and Daly, from a feminist perspective, show possible consequences of these traditions, such as when food and laundry are outsourced services, and thereby carried out by workers – many of them migrants – separated from care work in the nursing home. Armstrong and Daly suggest that promising practices for nursing homes should include that one avoids a too flexible division of labour, that workers need more training and autonomy, and not least to be employed by the nursing home directly. They point out that this would be a contribution to making this women's work more visible and valued.

Australia: following the model of consumer-directed long-term care

The chapter about Australian long-term care is written by Jane Mears. She approaches this from a recent-history review and its implications for older people, informal carers, care workers and care providers. Taking its starting point in a system dominated by informal family care and care provided by non-profit organizations, with little government involvement, Australia during the 1980s became inspired by the international New Public Management reforms. While long-term care services were expanded, they were also increasingly becoming more consumer-directed. A characteristic Australian part of this expansion, however, is a pressure from stakeholders representing a voice of older people and informal carers and contributing to criticizing the consumer direction. As in many other countries of the world, implications of this development includes older people's difficulties with acting as consumers, care workers' greatest motivation for leaving the job being low payment, and much training for care workers being contracted out to an unregulated sector.

Argentina: facing an ageing society with no state, market or civil society involvement

Argentina has some characteristics in common with the welfare regimes in Southern European countries described as 'family regimes' (Esping-Andersen, 1999) regarding the strong family tradition. Although being an upper middle-income country, it faces large challenges regarding poverty and inequality, these being high in relation to OECD standards (OECD, 2017). Within this context, Nélida Redondo, the author of this chapter, approaches the Argentine long-term care problem as a social and gendered inequality problem. Fall in death rates due to more diseases being under control – large reductions in mortality in younger ages – has made Argentina one of the first Latin America countries currently experiencing demographic ageing. While both health coverage and old-age pensions are almost universal, practically no social care for older people is available, and therefore this is dependent on families. This challenges the burden of women (as family carers) and puts much stress and pressure on them to care for their parents. For those without family and network (also a majority being women), there is only the solution of the so-called 'geriatric homes', which are found, however, to violate basic human rights. On this research-based background, Redondo calls for future 'de-familialization' policies in order to counter gender inequalities and set public long-term care on the Latin American agenda.

The handbook: a contribution to the social sustainability discussion

At the last international long-term care conference, in Milan 2017 (Transforming Care Conference, 2017), gathering many of the world's long-term care experts, August Österle contributed with a keynote about sustainability related to the long-term care discussion. He pointed our attention to the worldwide high focus on economic sustainability and environmental sustainability, while often leaving out the discussion of social sustainability. With the worldwide demographic challenges of ageing populations – in low- and middle-income as well as high-income countries – the discussion of social sustainability should be highly prioritized too, and with long-term care issues at the centre of this discussion. This handbook is a contribution to this important future discussion, and it points overall to the following three main problems to be taken into serious consideration, if there is in fact a real intention of making long-term care sustainable.

First, with its historical roots in feminized, informal, unpaid, taken-for-granted family care, social care work within long-term care systems has been treated as inferior work – women's work – and even today, even in the forerunner Nordic countries, a gendered devaluation of this work takes place. With increasing migration, although differentiated across the world, the gendered dimension is often also combined with an ethnic dimension, creating thereby, continuously, new types of hierarchies between care workers, due also to the many new types of blurring boundaries towards domestic work and informal work, as well as professional healthcare work. Sustainability here would therefore need to include a priority of developing adequate working conditions, better payments and a higher degree of public involvement and concern in all care work arrangements, whether residential or home-based/household-based or in the broad in-between area. Second, long-term care, when this is specifically related to older people, has historically been placed 'behind' healthcare as well as economic pension systems; and when old age has been seen as a respectable dignified part of life, this has implied duties and burdens for mainly younger women to providing care for the family's older members, independent of their own life plans and careers. This all points at old age and old-age care as a second priority area. However, with a worldwide ageing population, this neglect or low priority is no longer a sustainable way forward. There is now a great need for long-term thinking about older people as participants of society, seeing social care work as supporting this social participation through the different old-age phases with different needs. Third, and finally, the chapters of this handbook clearly show the many overlapping, crossing and similar challenges, as well as policies accentuating these challenges, including marketization, commodification of care, personalization, particularly when related to market mechanisms, (de-)professionalization and not least (re-)familialization processes. Too little attention has been paid as to how comparisons can contribute to constructing processes of learning from each other across countries in the world. By providing long-term care knowledge from very different parts of the world, this handbook is also a contribution to this very important comparative element of developing sustainable long-term care services. We thank all the contributors to this handbook, including those who have supported the contributors on their chapters, for working together with us on this.

As editors, we thank the academic institutions we have been affiliated to during the time we worked together on this book: the University of Bergen, Department of Sociology, and City, University of London, School of Health Sciences.

References

Anttonen, A. and Meagher, G., 2013. Mapping marketization: concepts and goals. In G. Meagher and M. Szebehely, eds. *Marketisation in Nordic eldercare: a research report on legislation, oversight, extent and consequences.* Stockholm: Stockholm Studies in Social Work 30, pp.13–22.

Ayalon, L., 2009. Family and family-like interactions in households with round-the-clock paid foreign carers in Israel. *Ageing and Society,* 29, pp. 671–86. DOI: 10.1017/S0144686X09008393.

Bettio, F. and Pantenga, J., 2004. Comparing care regimes in Europe. *Feminist Economics,* 10(1), pp. 85–113. DOI: 10.1080/1354570042000198245.

Bettio, F. and Verashchagina, A., 2010. Long-term care for the elderly: provisions and providers in 33 European countries. European Commission. DOI: 10.2838/87307.

Christensen, K. and Pilling, D., 2014. Policies of personalisation in Norway and England: on the impact of political context. *Journal of Social Policy,* 43(3), pp. 479–96. DOI: 10.1017/S0047279414000257.

Daly, M., 2002. Care as a good for social policy. *Journal of Social Policy*, 31(2), pp. 251–70. DOI: 10.1017/S0047279401006572.

Esping-Andersen, G., 1999. *Social foundations of post-industrial economies*. Oxford: Oxford University Press.

Folbre, N., 1995. Holding hands at midnight: the paradox of caring labor. *Feminist Economics*, 1(1), pp. 73–92. DOI: 10.1080/714042215.

Gilligan, C., 1982. In a different voice: psychological theory and women's development. Cambridge, MA: Harvard University Press.

Graham, H., 1983. Caring: a labour of love. In J. Finch and D. Groves, eds. *A labour of love: women, work and caring*. London: Routledge and Kegan Paul, pp. 13–30.

Hernes, H., 1987. *Welfare state and women power: essays in state feminism*. Oslo: Norwegian University Press.

Lloyd-Sherlock, P., 2014. Beyond neglect: long-term care research in low and middle income countries. *International Journal of Gerontology*, 8, pp. 66–9. DOI: 10.1016/j.ijge.2013.05.005.

Muir, T., 2017. *Measuring social protection for long-term care*. OECD Health Working Papers, no. 93. Paris: OECD. Available at: www.oecd-ilibrary.org/social-issues-migration-health/measuring-social-protection-for-long-term-care_a411500a-en [accessed 14.07.2017].

Nelson, J.A., 1999. Of markets and martyrs: is it ok to pay well for care? *Feminist Economics*, 5(3), pp. 43–59. DOI: 10.1080/135457099337806.

Noddings, N., 1984. *Caring: a feminine approach to ethics and moral education*. Berkeley, CA: University of California Press.

OECD, 2015. *Health at a glance 2013*. Paris: OECD. Available at: http://dx.doi.org/10.1787/health_glance-2015-graph201-en [accessed 19.07.2017].

OECD, 2017. *Going for growth 2017: Argentina*. Available at: www.oecd.org/countries/argentina/Going-for-Growth-Argentina-2017.pdf [accessed 14.07.2017].

Österle, A., 2012. Long-term care financing in central Eastern Europe. In J. Costa-Font and C. Courbage, eds. *Financing long-term care in Europe: institutions, markets and models*. London: Palgrave Macmillan, pp. 236–53.

Ranci, C. and Pavolini, E., eds., 2013. *Reforms in long-term care policies in Europe: investigating institutional change and social impacts*. New York: Springer.

Razavi, S., 2007. *The political and social economy of care in a development context: conceptual issues, research questions and policy options*. Gender and development programme. Paper no. 3. United Nations Research Institute for Social Development. Available at: www.unrisd.org/80256B3C005BCCF9/(httpPublications)/2DBE6A93350A7783C12573240036D5A0 [accessed 14.07.2017].

Transforming Care Conference, 2017. Available at: www.transforming-care.net/ [accessed 14.07.2017].

Tronto, J.C., 1993. Moral boundaries: a political argument for an ethic of care. New York: Routledge.

Tronto, J., 2017. There is an alternative: *homines curans* and the limits of neoliberalism. *International Journal of Care and Caring*, 1(1), pp. 27–43. DOI: 10.1332/239788217X14866281687583.

Ungerson, C., 1983. Why do women care? In J. Finch and D. Groves, eds. *A labour of love: women, work and caring*. London: Routledge and Kegan Paul, pp. 31–49.

Van Hooren, F.J., 2012. Varieties of migrant care work: comparing patterns of migrant labour in social care. *Journal of European Social Policy*, 22(2), pp. 133–47. DOI: 10.1177/0958928711433654.

Wærness, K., 1984. The rationality of caring. In M. Söder, ed. *Economic and industrial democracy*. London: Sage, pp. 185–212. Available at: http://journals.sagepub.com/doi/abs/10.1177/0143831X8452003 [accessed 16.07.2017].

WHO (World Health Organization), 2015. *World report on ageing and health*. Geneva: WHO. Available at: www.who.int/ageing/publications/world-report-2015/en/ [accessed 07.07.2017].

Part I
Nordic countries

1

Long-term care services in Norway
A historical sociological perspective

Karen Christensen and Kari Wærness

Introduction

Norway is internationally known for providing one of the world's most universal and comprehensive long-term care services. According to an OECD report, Norway's expenditures on public long-term care services are 2.3 per cent of its GDP (OECD, 2013, p. 41), representing the third best position, after the Netherlands and Denmark. Part of this picture is the 90/10 percentage public/private share funding of long-term care services (Colombo et al., 2011, p. 231). This means that only a small part of these services are paid privately out of pocket, the public authorities thereby showing high responsibility. Another aspect adding to Norway's high standard reputation is the widespread use in international literature of Esping-Andersen's comparative analysis of welfare regimes (Esping-Andersen, 1999). This analysis places Norway in the Nordic social democratic regime, implying that the welfare state makes efforts to reduce people's dependence on the market to a minimum, and simultaneously seeks to reduce the dependence on family care. The Nordic countries thereby appear as general forerunners of the development of generous welfare states, although welfare researchers today also problematize this by revealing decreasing Nordic generosity (see e.g. Hooijer and Picot, 2015). However, without doubt, Esping-Andersen's analysis contributes to the high-welfare-standard picture of Norway, including the long-term care services that are the focus of this chapter.

The main target group of Norwegian long-term care services are older people, either 65+ or 67+ depending on the historical time, and increasingly today also (younger) disabled people and people with mental health problems. We only focus on older people and their main services here. Therefore, user-controlled personal assistance, the Norwegian version of cash-for-care, is not discussed as this is used particularly by younger disabled people as an alternative long-term care service (see Christensen, 2009). Currently, the long-term care services comprise home help in terms of domestic tasks and/or home nursing, institutional care in different variations, including nursing homes, old people's homes and sheltered housing. They also include new services such as meals on wheels and safety alarms. Our purpose in this chapter is to contribute to the efforts of moving beyond the high-welfare-standard picture by paying attention to the overall development and changes that have taken place 'behind' it, thereby aiming at making the nuances of Norwegian long-term care development more known internationally. Although a range of long-term care studies and reviews have presented important analyses of long-term care service provision in Norway (e.g Vabø et al., 2013; Jacobsen and Mekki, 2012; Vabø, 2012; Vabø, 2006; Christensen, 2004; Christensen and Næss, 1999; Næss and Wærness, 1995; Daatland, 1994), it more rarely accounts for the longer historical development, and if so it normally starts in late post-war Norway (see e.g. Christensen, 2005; Christensen, 2004). We will provide a historical sociological analysis inspired by Abrams (1982) of the development of today's Norwegian long-term care services, tracing it back to its roots in the nineteenth century. We will show how these roots play a role in linking action and structure (Abrams, 1982, p. 3), and how the development is then legitimized by political ideology (primarily about ageing), a development leading to an increasing gap between political ideals of old age and older people's everyday needs of long-term care services.

In the following, we briefly outline our historical sociological approach and present the main sources for our discussion. Then we will present our analysis, divided into four historical phases, and finally point out the main challenges of future long-term care services in Norway.

A historical sociological approach

Historical analyses have been a central part of the discipline of sociology since it originated, and they basically take their point of departure in the works of the founding fathers, Marx, Weber and Durkheim (see e.g. Ritzer, 2000). These works are all empirically based and focus on what Abrams calls 'the problematic of structuring' (Abrams, 1982, p. ix). Abrams suggests that rather than seeing history and sociology as two different disciplines, they should be understood as deeply connected in the sense that 'the world is essentially historical' (Abrams, 1982, p. 3). Taking this approach to the case of long-term care in Norway, it implies that, for example, the early roots of long-term care and legislation changes cannot be treated only as background, but are essentially part of the ongoing process of developing the services. Simply expressed, this is a social process perspective taking into account people and context. It is a perspective viewing the service development as a constant interaction and negotiation between structural and political national factors, organizational implementation directions and care workers' and welfare users' practices.

Scott (1986) argues that gender should be a part of the historical sociological analysis. While the minimum version of this is to include women in the analysis, the wider options are related to the alternative viewpoint a gender-sensitive perspective can bring into the analysis. This implies using gender as an analytical category (Scott, 1986, p. 1055). In the case of long-term care, a gender perspective is not only obvious to include, due to the fact that the major part of this work has always been carried out by women, but more important here is that the development of long-term care services is closely related to the changing roles of women over time (e.g. Christensen, 1998; Wærness, 1982). Part of the analysis will also be to use a groundbreaking concept grounded in empirical work within this research field: the concept of *rationality of caring* (Wærness, 1984). This internationally known concept was developed by the second author of this chapter, on the basis of the perspective of female workers practising care. It states that care work is based on a rationality opposing the dominant instrumental rationality and implies a 'sentient' actor (Hochschild, 1975) who combines emotions and rationality in care work. In a historical sociological analysis of long-term care in Norway, this is useful for a critical discussion of the extent to which the development takes into account women's practices and perspectives.

Both the authors being researchers with a specific interest in elderly care over several decades, our sources consist of our own and others' (mentioned above) empirical research into long-term care (our own including Wærness, 1992, 1998, 2010; Christensen, 1998, 1999, 2004,

2005, 2012). We also use welfare statistics showing development trends over time, based on national statistics (Statistics Norway, referred to in Otnes, 2015; Mørk et al., 2014; Borgan, 2012; Brevik, 2010) and to some extent also white papers (Meld. St. 29, 2012–2013; St. Meld. 25, 2005–2006), being aware of their political strategical functions rather than mirroring the status of welfare services.

As every historical analysis is complex, our analysis here will only provide a compressed picture of the development. We will use an analytical model comprising the main actors involved and relevant for grasping interactions and power shifts between them over time. Two main theories of ageing, representing contrasting views, are used: one focusing on *withdrawal and disengagement* from positions and roles in society (Cumming and Henry, 1961), and another focusing on *activity*, implying that norms for older people are the same as for middle-aged people (e.g. Atchley, 1977). Analytically, we will apply welfare 'triangles', one well known about the state, market and family (Esping-Andersen, 1999), and a less known earlier one (Seip, 1991) about the interaction between state, municipality and local associations and organizations. Our analysis of the early phase is based on Seip's model.

The roots of municipalization in Norway

The welfare triangle suggested by Seip (1991) includes two public actors – the municipality and the state – and a private actor or actors, primarily at this stage comprising local self-organized groups and associations. The historical role of Norwegian municipalities has its original point of departure in the Municipality Law of 1837 establishing local governments, that is, municipal self-government. This role is maintained until today and is the main reason for municipal variations. The municipalities therefore also play a central role in the development of welfare services, but – important in the Norwegian context – in interaction with the state and local voluntary organizations, the initiators. Seip describes this as 'almost a symbiosis' between private associations and the municipality (Seip, 1991, p. 26). That is a strong partnership; the role of the state, very similar to today, being to stimulate welfare activities by financially supporting municipalities. For example, the problem of too many older people in hospitals in cities forced the development of old people's homes, organized first by voluntary organizations (Seip, 1991, p. 30), then supported by the state through municipalities. This hospital-stay problem was also an important argument 100 years later in the 1950s for developing home-based services for older people (see Nordhus et al., 1986, p. 73). Also, taking place in towns, where the pressure was highest, home nursing initiatives were started in the 1870s by deaconesses (Wærness, 1982), primarily unmarried women, working voluntarily, motivated by God's calling and based in deaconess institutions. This was the historical beginning of what much later became and still is home nursing services, including personal care, bathing, and medical tasks such as wound care and handing out of medicine, provided by nurses or nurse assistants. However, until the 1960s, non-medical long-term care primarily consisted of institutional care in terms of old people's homes, the first central type of institution (Komitéen for eldreomsorgen, 1966). It covered older people without a safety net of family and kinship to take care of them, being also among the poorest. Overall, in the nineteenth century, elderly care included arrangements involving the church, charities and primarily the family; all were voluntary or informal unpaid work, based on family ties or moral principles. Municipalities cooperated with these voluntary and informal actors in order to develop local elderly care.

Summed up, the historically specific pattern here concerns the central role of the municipalities and the cooperation between the state, municipality and voluntary organizations in developing long-term care. Unlike the 'welfare state', this was an early period with a 'social assistance state' supporting only the poorest (Seip, 1979). The historical roots contain issues never leaving this field again: the close relation to women's work and unpaid voluntary work (associated with low social status), the dependence on informal support from family/networks, and the state option of controlling the costs by regulating what qualifies for state support in municipalities and for which groups of welfare receivers.

The historical development of home care services can illustrate these points. Comprising domestic tasks such as cleaning and laundry rather than nursing for sick bodies, the threshold for developing them was higher, explaining why they were first developed three-quarters of a century later. The high threshold had primarily to do with the family's responsibility for their older members, in other words closely related to women's role in society. Following industrialization, the family became the central unit for reproduction and care, and dependent on a wage earned by the father. A central part of women's lives until the 1950s was related to the domestic work tradition (Aubert, 1956). Domestic work in others' families was often a preparation for unmarried women, who then later became housewives in their own family, simultaneously caring for children and older family members in their own households. Due to the revelation of exploitation of domestic workers, a law on domestic work was introduced in 1948 requiring employers to improve working conditions (Aubert, 1956, p. 155). The numbers of domestic workers then decreased significantly, and parallel to this strong decline, the first initiatives to start home help services began.

In a white paper (St. Meld. 25, 2005–2006), the post-war development of long-term care services is divided into three phases: one from 1965 to 1980 called 'the public revolution', the next from 1980 to 1995 called 'consolidation and reorganization', and a final one from 1995 to 2010 called 'innovation and effectivization'. We find these phases meaningful, and therefore use them to point out central issues in each phase following the services into their future development.

Expansion 1965–1980: developing a tension between medical and social orientation

Public home help services for older people started in the 1960s, including first a few municipalities, later expanding to increasing numbers. The first state support for home help was provided in 1969, 17 years after the first voluntary initiative by two national female associations (Nasjonalforeningen for Folkehelsen and Norske Kvinners Sanitetsforening; see Wærness, 1982, p. 154). Compared to this, the first state support for home nursing was provided in the late 1950s, although only including a few municipalities, and from 1969 under the same directions as those regulating home help services (Wærness, 1982, pp. 116–17). The law requiring all municipalities to offer home-based services and institutional care came in 1964, with the Social Care Act. During the next 15 years, the number of older people receiving home help services increased from 13,000 in 1965 to 98,000 in 1980, while those receiving home nursing services increased from 24,000 to 75,000 (Borgan, 2012, p. 8). However, home nursing services were not legally required as separate municipal services before the Municipal Health Service Act of 1982. Interestingly, regarding this, overall expansion is also the development of the so-called housewife substitute services provided by professional (educated) housewife substitutes. These services started soon after the Second World War with the first state support as early as 1948. They were originally developed for supporting mothers in sickness periods, when they were not able to take care of their household and children themselves. In the expansion period for the main home-based services for elderly people, these housewife substitute services did not increase, even though they, particularly from the 1970s, increasingly included older people 67+ (Daatland, 1994, p. 27). Again, this development mirrors a gendered history: when women with young children started to participate in the labour market in the 1970s, the importance of the housewife role decreased, reflecting a change towards caring as paid work. It is also

Long-term care services in Norway

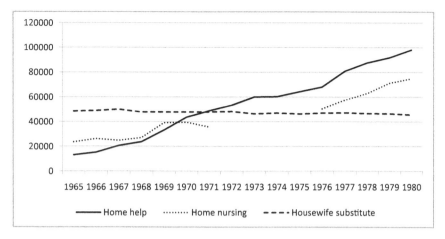

Figure 1.1 Number of service receivers during the year by type of service, 1965–1980
Source: Statistics Norway, figure based on Table B5 in Borgan (2012, p. 31).

interesting that while this housewife substitute position was professional, home help work (for older people) was made non-professional, unskilled labour. Middle-aged women with housewife experience therefore were attractive for this work in the expansion phase. This is also, and importantly here, different from the medical, professional nursing home services. See Figure 1.1 regarding the expansion of different home-based services.

A similar expansion characterizes places for older people in institutions, rising from 25,000 places in the mid-1960s to 40,000 15 years later (Borgan, 2012, p. 8). But this included at this stage two different types of institutions (see Figure 1.2): old people's homes (as mentioned) for those without family/network, and nursing homes for those with needs for medical treatment, inspired by the hospital model.

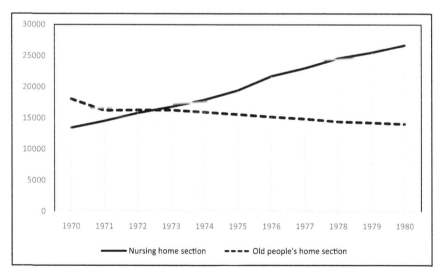

Figure 1.2 Places in institutions for older and disabled people, by type of section, 1970–1980
Source: Statistics Norway, figure based on Table B2 in Borgan (2012, p. 28).

As is clear from the two figures seen together, both revealing expanding services as the overall picture, is that a historical separation, and we will add potential tension, is created between practical everyday life assistance and nursing services (both can take place in homes or institutions). This social political separation is underlined, for example, by the legislation policy of two laws, one for social services (the Social Care Act of 1964, later replaced by the Social Services Act of 1991) and one for nursing services (the Municipal Health Service Act of 1982), a separation lasting until 2012, when the Municipal Health and Care Service Act of 2011 finally merged the laws. Another example is the unsuccessful attempt to realize the so-called 'small integration' between home help and home nursing services, for example due to different care work cultures and female care worker biographies (Christensen, 1998).

Summing up this expansion phase, it represents the last historical time where Seip's model is relevant. The municipalities expand the services, supported financially by the state, thereby representing a power shift towards local government. Due to municipalities taking over responsibility for an increasing number of services, voluntary organizations' role declines. The overall development is related to the change of women's roles, when women increasingly participate in the labour market – including the social care sector. An additional part of this development is the fact that the Social Care Act of 1964 loosened children's duty (mainly daughters) of caring for their parents. It was reduced to a duty between spouses regarding normal everyday life assistance. However, while representing a political change, such legislation has not had a direct impact on family duties. Historically, the family rather than voluntary organizations becomes an important actor in the further development of long-term care. While the importance of the family was first ignored by Esping-Andersen (1990), he later recognized the feminist critique and included the family in the welfare triangle (Esping-Andersen, 1999). The next historical phase requires the state-family-market model.

Reorganization 1980–1995: confronting traditional long-term care

Due to national long-term care figures showing overall the same tendencies as in the expansion period, this phase is also called a consolidation phase (St. Meld. 25, 2005–2006). The early historical local government policy (municipalization) now becomes manifested in three reforms (Romøren, 1991): the Municipal Health Care Act of 1982 requiring more decentralization and coordination; the so-called nursing home reform of 1988 requiring the municipalities to take over the accountability for nursing homes; and the reform closing down central institutions for people with intellectual disabilities and requiring municipalities to place them in home-like residences (Christensen and Nilsen, 2006). Together, these reforms now made municipalities accountable for offering and coordinating all long-term care services locally. The decentralization policies were marked by a change in state support, from 50 per cent and 70 per cent reimbursement costs for home-based and institutional care, respectively, in the expansion phase to a system of block grants from the mid-1980s (see e.g. Vabø, 2012, p. 284), thereby reducing the encouragement for expansion. The decentralization policies were also underlined by an ideology of staying home as long as possible, following the popularity of home-based services, with lower costs than institutional services. A concrete manifestation of this was the introduction of sheltered housing, starting in the mid-1980s, then strongly increasing between 1990 and 2000 (Borgan, 2012, p. 12). This again provided a way to postpone the need for institutional nursing home places, and simultaneously a more homelike version of traditional old people's homes. It also represents the beginning of targeting services to those with the greatest needs, all others being expected to want to stay at home as long as possible. The related new implicit pressure on families/women becomes very clear in the latest historical phase (see below).

However, even more important for the reorganization phase is the confrontation with traditional care, that is, care taking as its point of departure that older people – due to their ageing bodies – potentially need increasing help. In this reorganization phase, the view of older people was gradually changed. For example, the receivers of long-term care services were no longer called *clients* or *patients* (when involving nursing), but *users*, all of them. Slowly, the whole sector implemented this term and started encouraging older people to move away from the role as just *receivers of care* to become *active participants* in their care needs (cf. the different ageing theories). This was also taken further by the first policies of rehabilitation, expecting older people to be able to rehabilitate from needing a certain level of support back to less support (Næss and Wærness, 1995).

The confrontation with traditional care also involved classical modernization processes such as bureaucratization of the services and professionalization of care work (Christensen, 1998). Bureaucratization, for example, was strengthened by the Social Services Act of 1991 replacing the Social Care Act of 1964, now requiring the municipalities to make a formal legally based decision for each individual allocation, preferably supplemented with a detailed care plan for the content and duration of help (see Christensen, 1998, p. 517). This change was part of a more general increase in documentation and control of the services. They should not be figured out between the care worker and user – as in traditional care – but be foreseeable and controlled. And care work should no longer be based on informal care work experiences derived from the housewife role, but on modern working life. While, for example, the home helpers in the first phase typically had few clients, worked in small part-time jobs (supplementing their husband's main income) and were without colleagues due to isolated work in homes, the modernization of these characteristics followed the general development of women's changing roles into an increasing participation in working life on workplace premises. A vocational training, including two years practical and two years theory, was introduced in this phase (Høst, 1997), illustrating the thinking of professionalism as raising the quality of care. This was also related to a change in organizing the services into services provided not on a one-to-one basis, but by an increasingly diverse group of care workers, easily replaceable, an organization inspired by Taylorism ideas related to the industrial sector (Eliasson, 1992). These processes all represent a breaking away from care work practised by middle-aged women with housewife experience, the recruitment basis of the first home helpers (Wærness 1982). In other words, the rationality of caring women brought to the sector was increasingly replaced by an instrumental economic administrative thinking (Wærness, 2010, p. 133), keeping the voices from the field silent (Christensen, 2004). A from-below perspective was replaced by a from-above perspective, modernizing long-term care away from a rationality of caring.

At the end of this historical farewell to traditional care, New Public Management ideas inspired by the private sector were brought into long-term care, one key factor being the purchaser-provider model (see e.g. Vabø, 2006, p. 413). This model separates care planning from work performance (contrasting to a rationality of caring) and also makes it easier for municipalities to include new private for-profit actors in its care provision, if the municipality chooses to contract them. Although this has only developed into a soft version of marketization in Norway (Vabø et al., 2013), it still functions as a facilitator for developing marketization further.

Summing up this extremely important historical phase, one point is that while the state, and locally the municipalities, as well as the family, have been involved actors since the first development of long-term care services, the inclusion of the market represents a new direction, potentially also replacing voluntary organizations. Within the state-family-market model, the power of the state is strengthened. Even though local government is still very important, producing local variation, the changes in this mid-phase concern stronger public long-term care in terms of a state role governing the services away from their historical point of departure. From women's perspective, this represents a double-edged sword: on the one hand, it brings female care workers nearer modern working life; on the other, this is simultaneously a neglect of their experience-based knowledge, and the new positions do not change the status of their work. Their low status continues into the next phase.

Effectivization 1995–2010: confronting the welfare idea with individualization

As mentioned above, the ideology of staying home as long as possible was used to encourage the expansion of home-based services. It was presented as best for older people to postpone institutional care. The fulfilment of this plan occurred in the beginning of the 2000s, when measured by work years (see Figure 1.3): the percentage of work years of those employed in home-based care and institutional care exchanged position. However, this had specific historically related consequences for both institutional and home-based care, and for the latter particularly we suggest calling this a medicalization turn (Wærness, 1998), related to the social-medical difference developed earlier.

Regarding variations of institutional care, nursing home places were stabilized at around 40,000 places between 1991 and 2009, old people's homes were almost removed, while sheltered housing increased to 50,000 places in this period (Brevik, 2010). Clearly, nursing homes now are given the (institutional) function of being the last station when all other homelike attempts are unsuccessful, for example in the case of dementia. The rate of places in nursing homes, measured, for example, as beds per capita, is among the highest in Europe; around 80 per cent of Norwegian nursing home residents are dementia patients and around 40 per cent of the Norwegian population dies in a nursing home (Jacobsen and Mekki, 2012, p. 132; Meld. St. 29, 2012–2013, p. 101).

An even clearer separation of social and medical services took place within home-based services: while home help services decreased from the mid-1990s, home nursing services increased, crossing each other around 2004 (see Figure 1.4). Figure 1.4 also shows that between 1997 and

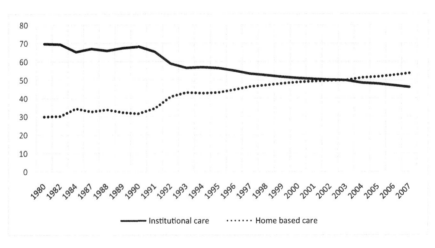

Figure 1.3 Work years in long-term care, percentage institutional and home-based care, 1980–2007

Source: Figure based on Table 6.1v. in Brevik (2010, p. 240).

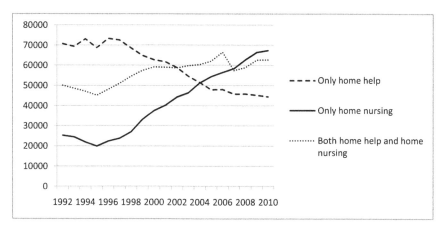

Figure 1.4 Receivers of home-based services per 31 December by type of service, 1992–2010
Source: Statistics Norway, figure based on Table B14 in Borgan (2012, p. 36).

2010, the number of those only receiving domestic services decreased from half of those receiving services to a quarter (Borgan, 2012, p. 16). So while the total number of home service users increase in this period, the increase favours those needing nursing/medical services.

The medicalization change gives priority to medical services rather than social work, displacing the services to those with the most severe (medical) needs, implicitly asking other people to manage with little support for as long as possible. This is underlined, for example, in the new view of users, as illustrated by this statement referred in a white paper by the Norwegian Association for Occupational therapists (St. Meld. 25, 2005–2006, p. 43, our translation):

> The challenges related to the demographic development and still more users of health and care services make it necessary to change focus in the view of users: from users only as passive receivers of care services and big spenders of public resources, to users as active participants and resources for families as well as society, who wish to live in their own homes and be independent as long as possible. With this point of departure, it will be important to ask: What is required by us, in order, to the greatest extent, to go through ageing as healthy, active, participating, self-helped, autonomic and safe individuals?

While occupational therapists as well as physiotherapists earlier played a minor but important role in the sector, they gradually play a more important role in the current focus on rehabilitation (reablement) schemes in some municipalities (Tuntland et al., 2015; Ness et al., 2012) and inspired by Danish elderly care (see Hansen and Kamp, 2016). The ideology now is home as long as possible with self care, implying an 'active' user and/or a user with family/network available for help, or a user with resources to buy private help. Regarding the care workers, this is a development taking another professionalizing direction (Hansen and Kamp, 2016), but again silencing the from-below perspective. It contrasts the rationality of caring by simply making 'caring' old fashioned, replacing it with joint responsibility between care workers and users (co-production), as is clear in the newest white paper (Meld. St. 29, 2012–2013).

We find that this expectation of more active and resourceful users is related to marketization thinking of users as individualized consumers. A striking example is the free-choice-of-provider arrangement, easy to implement with the purchaser-provider model established. After the assessment of needs, the user can choose between public and private providers, the latter being involved after having obtained a contract with the municipality. While 4 per cent of Norwegian municipalities implemented free-choice-of-provider in 2008 in home care services, this doubled to 8 percent in 2012 (Vabø et al., 2013, p. 174). Interesting for our argument is that this user choice first only comprised home help services. Even today, only the largest cities, Oslo and Bergen, have used free choice in home nursing. In contrast to the earlier intention of a 'small' integration, marketization separates home/domestic help from medical care, again hierarchically placing domestic help at the bottom. Historically, this also relates to the difference between home nursing services as free while home help is income-based and cost-shared (Vabø et al., 2013, p. 184). Marketization of nursing homes, in terms of including private for-profit providers, is complex, but there seems to be a tendency for voluntary organizations to lose the competition with for-profit actors (Meld. St. 29, 2012–2013, p. 71), particularly those being part of chains (Vabø et al., 2013, p. 182). While voluntary organizations once were the initiators of public elderly care, they now lose ground for market-inspired competition reasons.

An important change in this most recent historical phase is that more people below 67 are long-term care users (Brevik, 2010; Romøren, 2007). While around 24,000 people below 67 received home-based services in 1992, this rose to 66,000 in 2010 (see Figure 1.5). For the older age groups, the figures are decreasing, except for those 90+. However, although the figures for those 90+ increased, the percentage is still much lower than for those below 67. According to Romøren, younger users mainly comprise people with mental health problems, but also somatic diseases, including traffic victims (Romøren, 2007, p. 5). Looking at the mean weekly amount of hours of help, the same tendency appears: the older you are, the less help you receive, except to some degree, again for those 90+: for the age groups 18–49, 50–66, 67–79 and 80–89, the hours decrease from 16 to 11.5 to 5.2 to 4.2, and 5.4 for those 90+ (Otnes, 2015, p. 56, based on Statistics Norway).

A case study looking at these developments shows that the assessment of the needs of younger and older persons are different: when younger people are assessed, they are compared with non-disabled healthy people, seeking thereby to reach the same (normal) standard. But this equalizing normal-standard method is not used for older people, thereby potentially placing the allocation of services for them at a lower level (Hamran and Moe, 2012). In both quantitative and qualitative terms, long-term care services are increasingly taken away from older people and ageism is easily involved.

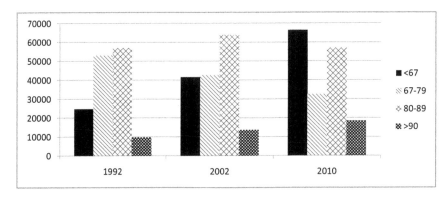

Figure 1.5 Receivers of home-based services, by age, 1992, 2002 and 2010
Source: Statistics Norway, selected years based on Table B15 in Borgan (2012, p. 36).

Summarizing this current historical phase, there is a tendency towards downgrading the services, although the sector's running expenses and the labour work years continue the increase established in the expansion phase (Borgan, 2012, p. 19), mainly due to more users (all ages included) and an increasing bureaucratization, for example related to more computer-based documentation work since the late 1990s (see Christensen, 1999). However, the number of receivers of institutional and home-based care in different population age groups has been decreasing since the beginning of the 1990s: in institutional care mostly for those 90+ (from 45 per cent to 30 per cent) and for home-based care mostly for those between 80 and 89 (from 38 per cent to 29 per cent; figures covering 1994–2013, cf. Otnes, 2015, pp. 53–4). This service downgrading makes the social-medical split from the earlier historical phase clearer, and the effectivization effect very much seems to come from the efforts to postpone institutional care as long as possible for older people, while avoiding it as much as possible for younger people, and rather allocating them sheltered housing or home-based care (Otnes, 2015, p. 55). Thus, while older people are still the majority population of long-term care services, the policies increasingly replace elderly care with 'younger care' (Romøren, 2007). Politically stressing at the same time the role of an independent participating welfare user furthermore implies that more will be dependent on informal care. Behind the generous public long-term care system therefore also lies the fact that in 2013, 53 per cent of all those being allocated long-term care services according to self-report say they are getting unpaid help from family and local network, this even rising to 70 per cent, surprisingly, among those in institutions (Mørk et al., 2014, p. 23). Informal help again increasingly plays a major role in today's long-term-care, also related to the increasing amount of everyday life online activities (social care application, banking, etc.) not manageable for many older people, and therefore often implying new informal help needs.

Concluding remarks

In a current book about the Norwegian fear of old age, discussing the historical changes in views of ageing, a cogent example is given about an old man in a nursing home. While he was having lunch, sitting at a table with others, he asked the staff present to help him get a slice of bread. Encouraged to do so by the policies of user activation, the answer the old man got was: go and get it yourself (Bakken, 2014, p. 133). The example points out the risk of activation ideology to turn into humiliation. Although Norway, internationally seen, holds high public standards, the country is also in a process of moving away from its basic social responsibility for covering the needs derived from old age, as illustrated by Bakken's astounding example.

We find that there are three important historical lines – challenges – revealed by our analysis of the historical development. One line concerns the change from understanding older people as people with potentially increasing care needs due to the ageing process to expecting – today longer than ever and encouraged by medical developments – them to be as active in older age as in their middle age. This is theoretically framed by the activation theory (Atchley, 1977) and today increasingly practised through reablement schemes, more or less successfully (Tuntland et al., 2015). Another line concerns care work. Following the historical change of women's role away from the private household, including paid domestic work, care work has moved into the labour market. Here, it has increasingly adopted its premises; these premises even derived from a quite different sector, first the industrialized, then the private market sector. Consequently, the 'female' practices are downgraded and separated from the more ('important') medical/professional services and carried out by those with the least education, often unskilled workers. The options of rationality of caring are thereby historically limited. The third line concerns the change in the role of local government, involving the municipalities and local voluntary organizations. From municipalities being encouraged to take rather full responsibility for long-term care services (legislation based on the Municipal Health Service Act of 1982), municipalities increasingly now move – with the largest cities first – in the direction of making their situation more dependent on private market actors. This way, the historical changes of the Norwegian long-term care sector discussed here is also a contribution to the literature increasingly questioning Esping-Andersen's (1999) Nordic welfare regime model. Although Norway has its own specific historical development, there are possibilities of learning about implications and consequences from other countries in the world, where this development has been part of their long-term care history much longer (see e.g. the English, American and Canadian chapters of this handbook).

References

Abrams, P., 1982. *Historical sociology*. Near Shepton Mallet, Somerset: Open Books.
Atchley, R. C., 1977. *The social forces in later life*. Belmont: Wadsworth.
Aubert, V., 1956. The housemaid: an occupational role in crisis. *Acta Sociologica*, 1(3), pp. 149–58.
Bakken, R., 2014. *Frykten for alderdommen. Om å eldes og leve som gammel* [The fear for old age: on ageing and living when old]. Oslo: Res Publica.
Borgan, J.-K., 2012. *Pleie- og omsorgsstatistikk 1962–2010* [Health and care statistics 1962–2010]. Report 10/2012. Oslo-Kongsvinger: Statistics Norway. Available at: www.ssb.no/helse/artikler-og-publikas joner/pleie-og-omsorgsstatistikk-1962-2010?fane=om [accessed 25.06.2017].
Brevik, I., 2010. *De nye hjemmetjenestene – langt mer enn eldreomsorg. Utvikling og status 'i' yngres bruk av hjemmebaserte tjenester 1989–2007* [The new home-based services – much more than elderly care: the development and status of younger people's use of home-based care services in 1989–2007]. NIBR Report 2/2010. Oslo: Norsk institutt for by og regionforskning (NIBR). Available at: https://evalueringsportalen.no/evaluering/de-nye-hjemmetjenestene-langt-mer-enn-eldreomsorg-utvikling-og-status-i-yngres-bruk-av-hjemmebaserte-tjenester-1989-2007 [accessed 25.06.2017].
Christensen, K., 1998. *Omsorg og arbejde. En sociologisk studie af ændringer i den hjemmebaserede omsorg* [Care and work: a sociological study of changes in home-based care]. Bergen: Department of Sociology, University of Bergen.
Christensen, K., 1999. Computerbruk og omsorgsarbeid – lar det seg forene? [Computer use and care work: is that compatible?]. In K. Thorsen and K. Wærness, eds. *Blir omsorgen borte? Eldreomsorgens hverdag i den senmoderne velferdsstaten.* [Is caring lost? Everyday elderly care in the late modern welfare state]. Oslo: Ad Notam Gyldendal, pp. 127–48.
Christensen, K., 2004. Silent voices: on gender-related power and public care services. In K. Wærness, ed. *Dialogue on care*. University of Bergen: Centre for Women's and Gender Research, pp. 119–45.
Christensen, K., 2005. The modernization of power in Norwegian home care services. In H.M. Dahl and T.R. Eriksen, eds. *Dilemmas of care in the Nordic welfare state: continuity and change*. Aldershot: Ashgate, pp. 33–47.
Christensen, K., 2009. In(ter)dependent lives. *Scandinavian Journal of Disability Research*, 11(2), pp. 117–30. DOI: 10.1080/15017410902830553.
Christensen, K., 2012. Towards a mixed economy of long-term care in Norway? *Critical Social Policy*, 32(4), pp. 577–96. DOI: 10.1177/0261018311435028.
Christensen, K. and Næss, S., 1999. *Kunnskapsstatus om de offentlige msorgstjenestene* [State of the art about the public care services]. Report 2. Bergen: Centre for Social Sciences Research.
Christensen, K. and Nilsen, E., 2006. *Omsorg for de annerledes svake. Et overvåket hverdagsliv* [Care for different vulnerable people: a controlled everyday life]. Oslo: Gyldendal Akademisk.
Colombo, F., Llena-Nozal, A., Mercier, J. and Tjadens, F., 2011. *Help wanted? Providing and paying for long-term care*. Paris: OECD. DOI: 10.1787/9789264097759-en.
Cumming, E. and Henry, W.E., 1961. *Growing old*. New York: Basic Books.
Daatland, S.O., 1994. *Hva skjer i eldresektoren? Status og utvikling av eldrepolitikkens tilbud og tjenester* [What happens in the eldercare sector? Status and development of the politics of services for older people] NGI-report 1/1994. Oslo: Norsk gerontologisk institutt (NGI).

Eliasson, R., 1992. Omsorg som lönarbete: om taylorisering of professionalisering [Care as paid work: on Taylorization and professionalization]. In R. Eliasson, ed. *Egenheter og allmänheter. En antologi om omsorg och omsorgens villkor* [Peculiarities and the general: an anthology into care and caring conditions]. Lund: Arkiv Förlag, pp. 131–42.

Esping-Andersen, G., 1990. *The three worlds of welfare capitalism.* Princeton, NJ: Princeton University Press.

Esping-Andersen, G., 1999. *Social foundations of post-industrial economies.* Oxford: Oxford University Press.

Hamran, T. and Moe, S., 2012. Yngre og eldre brukere i hjemmetjenesten – ulike behov eller forskjellsbehandling. Flerfaglig praksis i et interaksjonistisk perspektiv [Younger and older users of home-based care: different needs or discrimination. Multidisciplinary practice in an interactionist perspective]. Report Series 3/2012. Tromsø: Senter for omsorgsforskning. Available at: http://munin.uit.no/handle/10037/8975 [accessed 02.07.2017].

Hansen, A.M. and Kamp. A., 2016. From carers to trainers: professional identity and body work in rehabilitative eldercare. *Gender, Work and Organization.* DOI: 10.1111/gwao.12126.

Hochschild, A.R., 1975. The sociology of feeling and emotion: selected possibilities. *Sociological Inquiry,* 45(2–3), pp. 280–307. DOI: 10.1111/j.1475-682X.1975.tb00339.x.

Høst, H., 1997. *Konstruksjonen av omsorgsarbeideren – i spenningsfeltet mellom utdanningspolitikk, kommunalisering og interesseorganisering* [The construction of the care worker: in the tension between education-politics, municipalism and interest organization]. AHS Report Series A 2/1997. Universitetet i Bergen: Arbeidsliv – historie – samfunn, Gruppe for flerfaglig arbeidslivsforskning.

Hooijer, G. and Picot, G., 2015. European welfare states and migrant poverty: the institutional determinants of disadvantage. *Comparative Political Studies,* 48(14), pp. 1879–904. DOI: 10.1177/0010414015597508.

Jacobsen, F.F. and Mekki, T.E., 2012. Health and the changing welfare state in Norway: a focus on municipal health care for elderly sick. *Ageing International,* 37, pp. 125–42. DOI: 10.1007/s12126-010-9099-3.

Komitéen for eldreomsorgen [The committee on eldercare], 1966. *Innstilling I* [Proposal I]. National policy document, Norway.

Meld. St. 29, 2012–2013. *Melding til Stortinget. Morgendagens omsorg* [Report to the 'Storting': tomorrow's care]. Oslo: Helse- og omsorgsdepartementet. Available at: www.regjeringen.no/no/dokumenter/meld-st-29-20122013/id723252/ [accessed 02.07.2017].

Mørk, E., Sundby, Otnes, B. and Wahlgren, M., 2014. *Pleie- og omsorgstjenesten 2013. Statistikk om tjenester og tjenestemottakere* [Health and care services 2013: statistics about services and service receivers]. Report 33. Oslo-Kongsvinger: Statistics Norway. Available at: www.ssb.no/helse/artikler-og-publikasjoner/pleie-og-omsorgstjenesten-2013 [accessed 02.07.2017].

Ness, N.E., Laberg, T., Haneborg, M., Granbo, R., Færevaag, L. and Butli, H., 2012. *Hverdagsmestring og hverdagsrehabilitering* [Everyday life coping and everyday life rehabilitation]. Ergoterapeutene, Norsk Sykepleierforbund, Norsk fysioterapeut-forbund. Available at: http://ergoterapeutene.org/Ergoterapeutene/aktuelt/Nyhetsarkiv/Rapporten-Hverdagsmestring-og-hverdagsrehabilitering-overlevert-departementet [accessed 02.07.2017].

Nordhus, I.H., Isaksen, L.W. and Wærness, K., 1986. *De fleste gamle er kvinner – eldreomsorg fra et kvinneperspektiv* [Most older people are women: eldercare from women's perspective]. Bergen: Universitetsforlaget.

Næss, S. and Wærness, K., 1995. *Fra pasient til bruker. Utviklingen fra tradisjonell kommunal eldreomsorg til rehabiliteringsorienterte hjemmetjenester i Hurum kommune* [From patient to user: the development from traditional municipal eldercare to rehabilitation-oriented home services in Hurum municipality]. Bergen: Senter for omsorgsforskning.

OECD, 2013. A good life in old age? Monitoring and improving quality in long-term care. *Paris: OECD.* DOI: 10.1787/9789264194564-en.

Otnes, B., 2015. Utviklingen i pleie- og omsorgstjenestene 1994–2013 [The development of health and care services 1994–2013]. *Tidsskrift for omsorgsforskning,* 1(1), pp.48–61.

Ritzer, G., 2000. *Classical sociological theory.* Fifth edition. New York: McGraw-Hill.

Romøren, T.I., 1991. Tre reformer som endret det kommunale hjelpeapparatet [Three reforms changing the municipal support system]. In A.H. Nagel, ed. *Velferdskommunen. Kommunenes rolle i utviklingen av velferdsstaten* [The welfare municipality: the role of the municipalities in developing the welfare state]. Bergen: Alma Mater Forlag AS, pp. 152–64.

Romøren, T.I., 2007. Kommunale hjemmetjenester – fra eldreomsorg til 'yngreomsorg'? [Municipal home-based services: from eldercare to 'youngercare'?]. *Aldring og Livsløp,* 24(1), pp. 1–11.

Seip, A.-L., 1979. Velferdsstatens framvekst i Norge [The welfare state development in Norway]. *Historisk tidsskrift*, 1, pp. 43–69.

Seip, A.-L., 1991. Velferdskommunen og velferdstrekanten. Et tilbakeblikk [The welfare municipality and the welfare triangle retrospective]. In A.H. Nagel, ed. *Velferdskommunen. Kommunenes rolles i utviklingen av velferdsstaten* [The welfare municipality: the role of the municipalities in developing the welfare state]. Bergen: Alma Mater Forlag AS, pp. 24–42.

Scott, J., 1986. Gender: a useful category of historical analysis. *American Historical Review*, 91(5), pp. 1053–75.

St. Meld. 25, 2005–2006. *Mestring, muligheter og meninger. Fremtidas omsorgsutfordringer* [Coping, possibilities and meanings: care challenges of the future]. Oslo: Helse- og omsorgsdepartementet. Available at: www.regjeringen.no/no/dokumenter/stmeld-nr-25-2005-2006-/id200879/ [accessed 02.07.2017].

Tuntland, H., Aasland, M.K, Espehaug, B., Førland, O. and Kjeken, I., 2015. Reablement in community-dwelling older adults: a randomised controlled trial. *BMC Geriatrics*, 15(145), pp. 1–11. DOI: 10.1186/s12877-015-0142-9.

Vabø, M., 2006. Caring for people or caring for proxy consumers? *European Societies*, 8(3), pp. 403–22. DOI: 10.1080/14616690600821990.

Vabø, M., 2012. Norwegian home care in transition: heading for accountability, off-loading responsibilities. *Health and Social Care*, 20(3), pp. 283–91. DOI: 10.1111/j.1365-2524.2012.01058.x.

Vabø, M., Christensen, K., Jacobsen, F.F. and Trætteberg, H.D., 2013. Marketisation in Norwegian eldercare: preconditions, trends and resistance. In G. Meagher and M. Szebehely, eds. *Marketisation in Nordic eldercare: a research report on legislation, oversight, extent and consequences*. Stockholm University: Department of Social Work, pp. 163–202.

Wærness, K., 1982. *Kvinneperspektiver på sosialpolitikken* [Women's perspectives on social politics]. Oslo: Universitetsforlaget.

Wærness, K., 1984. The rationality of caring. *Economic and Industrial Democracy*, 5, pp. 185–211.

Wærness, K., 1998. The changing 'welfare mix' in childcare and care for the frail elderly in Norway. In J. Lewis, ed. *Gender, social care and welfare state restructuring in Europe*. Aldershot: Ashgate, pp. 207–28.

Wærness, K., 2010. Challenges for the future of public care: a lesson from Norway. In Y. Saito, R.A. Auestad and K. Wærness, eds. *Meeting the challenges of elder care: Japan and Norway*. Tokyo: Kyoto University Press, pp. 128–35.

2

Revisiting the public care model

The Danish case of free choice in home care

Tine Rostgaard

Introduction

Nordic long-term care (LTC) systems for older people are generally characterized by the specific features of generosity, universalism, formalism and not least by the statist approach (Anttonen and Zechner, 2011). The characteristic features of the Nordic model thus imply that all citizens have access to high-quality care regardless of income and means, that informal carers play a relatively marginal role in comparison with other welfare models, and that there is wide public responsibility for financing, organizing and delivering care.

Nonetheless, similar to the development in other European countries, the public model of the Nordic countries has also been affected by marketization reforms and the specific introduction of private for-profit providers in LTC. In Denmark, this has been encouraged by the idea that having an alternative to the public provision will give more freedom of choice for the individual as well as better quality of care through the development of a more effective and consumer-focused approach. Since 2003, all municipalities must ensure a choice between home care providers, and more than one-third of home care recipients now make use of a for-profit provider. With the obligation to introduce alternative providers, Denmark has been the Nordic country institutionally implementing marketization to the greatest degree. This also means that formal care work is increasingly carried out in the private, for-profit sector.

This chapter investigates the background to and implications of introducing consumer choice and marketization into a public care system. It briefly introduces the assumptions behind the politics and policies of free choice, and moves on to investigate the increasing involvement of for-profit providers in home care; what it is that characterizes the for-profit companies and those users who make use of a for-profit care solution. The chapter also looks at the implications of marketization and investigates both users and employees' perspectives, compares users' levels of satisfaction with public and for-profit providers, and investigates whether there are differences in work content and conditions between the two sectors. The analysis also looks into the concept of quality of care, and how this is perceived by staff working in the public versus the for-profit home care sectors. The chapter finally revisits Nordic care model characteristics, critically examining how marketization may have affected these.

Methodology

The chapter draws on a number of data sources, including satisfaction surveys among users of home care (Epinion, 2011, 2015; SFI, 2011). The satisfaction surveys are conducted for the Ministry of Social Affairs on a regular basis, with a representative sample of home care users. For instance, the 2015 survey includes 2,312 respondents, selected from a representative sample of home care users 65+ and interviewed over the phone. The response rate was 60 per cent. Some caution should be applied when interpreting such data as the frailest users are typically less well represented. Given that these users in Denmark are more likely to use a public provider of home care, caution should be taken when interpreting the total scores across public and for-profit sectors.

The main data source is a survey conducted in 2015–2016 as part of a larger Nordic survey among care workers, NORDCARE, where the author was the Danish investigator. It included unionized employees working in home care or nursing homes in the public and for-profit sectors and had an overall response rate of 59 per cent. In this chapter, we use only the data on home care workers in Denmark. The Danish sample included in total 361 home care workers and forms the basis for the analysis here. Of these, 13 per cent were working for a private, for-profit provider.

In addition to surveys among users and care workers, the chapter draws on public documents and statistics.

The Danish long-term care system and rationale for introducing free choice

Denmark is often described as belonging to the public service model, along with other Nordic countries (Anttonen and Sipilä, 1996). This applies to services in general, including LTC for older people. Public social care services are provided within a formally based care system, where the main responsibility for the organization, provision and financing of care traditionally lies with the public sector, not the family, nor the market.

One reason for the comprehensiveness in coverage and approach is that the Nordic countries – including Denmark – have all had economically efficient and politically stable democratic states for a number of years, and have thus been able to implement encompassing social policies, including care policies for children and older people. The Nordic countries have accordingly been labelled 'caring states' (Leira, 1992).

Access to benefits is, according to the principle of universalism, based on citizenship, not contributions nor merit, and, in the case of care services for older people, depending on need. Care services are available for and used by all classes, with no stigma associated. Vabø and Szebehely (2012) further argue that the Nordic service universalism is about more than issues of eligibility and accessibility; it also encompasses whether services are attractive, affordable and flexible in order to meet a diversity of needs and preferences.

The state and municipalities heavily subsidize care services financed through income and local taxes, and home care services for older people are free of charge. There is national legislation guiding the overall levels and quality of services. Responsibility for implementation, however, lies entirely with the municipalities, including needs assessment, entitlement to, and content of service delivery. Each of the 98 municipalities in Denmark ensures the organization, provision, and regulation of care services. Home care has become the main service for frail older people since the introduction of deinstitutionalization in the late 1980s. The main tasks have traditionally been personal care, (e.g. assistance with bathing, getting dressed, etc.)

and practical assistance (e.g. cleaning and shopping). As the municipalities in 2007 took over parts of healthcare, home care workers are now also assisting home nurses in performing simple healthcare-related tasks, such as changing dressings, giving injections and medication.

As mentioned, Denmark has taken the lead among the Nordic countries towards a more marketized model of LTC. The 2003 Law on Free Choice of Provider (Frit valg af leverandør) made every municipality obliged to ensure that users had a choice of more than one provider of home care, basically introducing a quasi-market in care giving users a choice between public and for-profit providers. Independent of the choice of provider, the service package is identical, with the same assessment procedure and no user fees involved. However, only those using a for-profit provider can purchase supplementary services through their service provider, something that the municipalities have argued leaves them in a poorer competitive situation. Overall, for-profit providers must within the same sum of money provide the same basic services, but can otherwise try to perform better in terms of communication, customer relations, time of delivery, continuity of staff, etc.

Along with competition, contracts, and cost control, free choice was an important component of the New Public Management (NPM) reforms that have affected the public sector in Denmark, as well as in many other countries, in recent decades (Vabø, 2009; Pollitt and Boucaert, 2000). The free choice of home care provider was the first real test case of introducing consumerism of public goods, and extraordinary in being a service directed at very frail people. Also, it was far from being advocated by any user groups. It has also stayed as a relatively unique example in Denmark of a nationally implemented choice option, with the free choice of hospital as the only other example. The Law on Free Choice was introduced by a Liberal-Conservative government, in order to improve user autonomy and care quality, cut costs, and, more implicitly, encourage the development of a market in care. The introduction of free choice in Danish home care was not least part of a strategy to respond to criticisms of what is generally called a welfarist approach, with standardized products, top-down decision-making and automatic acceptance of the judgement of professionals (Evers, 2003). The Liberal-Conservative government also saw free choice as a way of accommodating individual preferences, thereby empowering the users. The political assumption was that free choice would break with the former public monopoly of service provision, thereby ensuring more efficient and improved care provision. According to traditional assumptions about market mechanisms, quality of care should improve as providers compete and users gain influence over choice. Following a change of power to a centre-left government in 2011, there was less ideological support for contracting out and the free choice model in general. However, the instruments of marketization were by no means rolled back, and in fact new rules were introduced that simplified the process of outsourcing home care for the municipalities (Bertelsen and Rostgaard, 2013). With the advent of a Liberal government in late 2016, support for free choice in home care remains strong, and there are also new plans for introducing free choice into other welfare services.

Popularity and take-up of free choice of provider

Free choice quickly became popular among users, not so much in take-up of for-profit services, which was slow initially, but more as the appreciation of free choice as an additional social right – and popularity has only increased over time. In 2007, when the earliest figures were available, 61 per cent of a nationally representative sample of home care users 65+ indicated that such choice was important to them, while 25 per cent found it to be of no importance, and the remaining (14 per cent) were neither for nor against (SFI, 2007). As of 2015, supporters of free choice among home care users have risen to 70 per cent, while those finding little value in free choice have dropped to 14 per cent, and those indifferent stayed at almost the same level, 16 per cent. It should, however, be added that only around two-thirds of the home care users were aware of the existence of free choice, a similar number to that in 2011, the first year in which this question was posed (66 per cent in 2011 and 70 per cent in 2015) (Epinion, 2011, 2015). Nevertheless, as an inherent component in an otherwise public welfare model, introduction of the choice of home care provider apparently resonated and continues to resonate as something that is both acceptable and desirable for most home care users in this age group. The continued popularity is also interesting to observe as the users over time have changed profile, with eligibility for home care services increasingly being more targeted towards the frailest, those with need for personal care, and – as we document below – often most likely to use a public provider. Despite this, overall popularity of free choice persists. Free choice, as an idea as much as an actual realization, thus continues to be favoured, politically as well as among frail older people with a need for care.

Today, 12 per cent of older people 65+ receive home care in Denmark, a drop from 18 per cent in 2008 (see Figure 2.1). In addition to this, around 4 per cent of 65+ live in a nursing home. Among present home care users, one in three (36 per cent) use a for-profit provider, and a mixed market of care has thus been realized. Comparable data only go as far back as 2008, but show that only one in four used a for-profit provider then (26 per cent). Over time, it is consistently those using practical care only who choose a for-profit provider (from 35 per cent in 2008 of all home care users with this type of care to 46 per cent in 2015). However, over time, also the frailest users, and thus those using personal care, have increasingly favoured a for-profit provider. The proportion using a for-profit provider has risen among those using combinations of personal care and practical assistance (from 21 per cent in 2008 to 33 per cent in 2015), as well

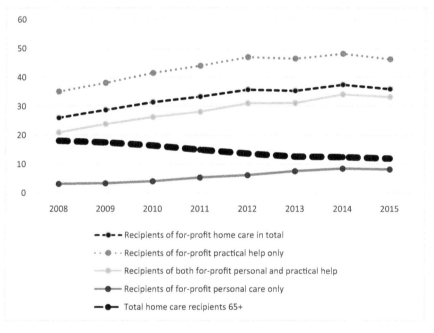

Figure 2.1 Home care recipients aged 65+ and percentage using for-profit providers in total and according to type of assistance, 2008–2015

Source: Danmarks Statistik (n.d., Tables AED12 and AED06).

as those using personal care only (from 3 per cent in 2008 to 8 per cent in 2015) (see Figure 2.1). The figures thus show an ongoing increase over time that, however, slows down somewhat from 2013, and then levels out. As we explain below, this is presumably related to a number of bankruptcies occurring in the for-profit sector in later years.

In regard to how this may have affected the number of care workers, it is obvious that the increase in take-up of for-profit home care services has stimulated the creation of jobs in the for-profit sector. There are, however, no comparable statistics over time. The most recent estimate shows 46,200 full-time equivalent care jobs (home helpers, hjemmehjælpere), social and healthcare assistants (social- og sundhedsassistenter), social and healthcare helpers (social og sundhedshjælpere), etc. in public LTC overall, thus also including nursing homes. In addition, there are 2,005 full-time equivalent jobs in the for-profit home care sector (Danmarks Statistik, 2008). A recent overview of the almost 10,000 home care workers organized in the main union representing this sector, FOA (Danish Union of Public Employees), shows that, among these, 5 per cent work with a for-profit provider (FOA, personal communication).

For-profit providers thus predominantly provide practical care where users typically receive 0.5–1.0 hours care or less per week, and less often provide the more time-intensive personal care. Therefore, the proportion of total hours of care provided by for-profit companies has so far been limited. Eighty-three per cent of total hours of home care were provided in 2015 for personal care, and only 17 per cent of hours went to practical assistance. In 2015, however, private providers gained an increasing share of the market, and also in the delivery of personal care. It has been estimated that for-profit providers delivered 15.1 per cent of all home care hours in total by 2015 (Dansk Industri, 2016). The total market share is growing for the for-profit providers, but is still relatively limited.

Danish rules require that municipalities either operate competition by procurement (udbudsmodellen) or competition by endorsement (godkendelsesmodellen). If municipalities use the former model, they invite public as well as for-profit home care providers to compete based on a written tender. Here, there is wide possibility for providers to compete on price and quality. If they use the latter model, which was by far the most popular model until 2013, municipalities retain the power to set prices and quality standards for tendering procedures with home care providers. Since changes in the Social Service Law of 2013, many municipalities now apply the procurement model and invite competition on price and quality. The intention was not only to introduce real competition, but also to decrease the number of contracted providers – which, for instance, in Copenhagen municipality alone, amounted to 37 different providers – and thus make the choice more manageable for the user and make administration easier and less costly for the municipality. The total number of for-profit providers has accordingly dropped from 459 in 2013 to the present 387 (as of 2016) (Dansk Industri, 2016). Unlike the tendency for market concentration as is the case, for instance, in Sweden, where for-profit provision of care is increasingly concentrated in the hands of a few multinational providers run by private equity firms (Erlandsson et al., 2013), the care market in Denmark is scattered among small and locally operating providers.

The recent change in the law has been accompanied by an increase in bankruptcies among for-profit home care providers, with subsequent failure to provide services to users. In 2015 alone, there were 10 bankruptcies, with eight the previous year (Dansk Industri, 2016), and the union representing the care workers, FOA, estimates that up to 23 major firms have had to close down since 2013 (Politiken, 2016). This indicates that since the introduction of the new rules, for-profit companies have competed on prices that were too low. FOA estimates that the bankruptcies since 2013 have affected more than 10,500 home care users and more than 1,000 care workers (FOA, 2016; Politiken, 2016). One indication of the many bankruptcies is the substantial number of users that have had to change provider, in 2015 nearly 7,000 home care users 65+, in comparison to the annual average of 3,800 people in the years 2009–2012 (Danmarks Statistik, n.d.). In comparison, 99,000 people 65+ received home care services in 2015. As Figure 2.2 indicates, this amounts to around 6 per cent of all home care users 65+ changing provider in 2015, compared to 3 per cent in 2009. Apart from an unusual increase among users of personal care only who changed provider in 2012, it is mainly users with practical care that change provider, but for all types of assistance we see an increase since 2013, especially high for those using practical assistance only and combinations of practical and personal care.

The statistics do not point at the direction of change, and could in principle involve users changing from a public to a for-profit provider. However, if matched with Figure 2.1, which shows a slight levelling out in users of for-profit providers in the years 2013–present, and especially among those who use personal care only, it indicates that the change of direction has been in favour of the public provider.

Because of the bankruptcies, municipalities have also had to take over service delivery, and at great costs. Every two out of three municipalities have accordingly responded by establishing emergency procedures in case they need to take over service delivery. Emergency delivery of services is most acute in the case of personal care, which for the user is hard to be without (KL, 2016). Additionally, employees have risked not being paid or losing their jobs.

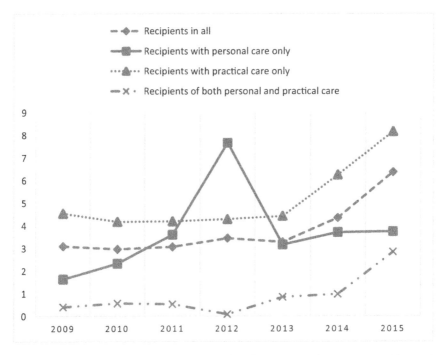

Figure 2.2 Proportion of home care users 65+ who change provider type, annually, total and according to type of care, 2009–2015

Source: Danmarks Statistik (n.d., AED14).

Note: The increase among users of personal care changing provider in 2012 mainly consists of users 80+. Change of provider between for-profit public providers, and vice versa. Only one change per year is included, regardless of number of subsequent changes.

Implications of the choice model for users

As one main idea behind the Danish free choice model was to improve quality of care through more individualized services, the model adheres to a consumer market logic based on the sovereignty of the individual (Kremer, 2006; Højlund, 2002). The consumerist approach obviously breaks with previous assumptions that professionals were the only ones who could define needs and suggest proper interventions. Accommodation of participation and empowerment of the user has thus gone hand in hand with increasing criticism of the previously unchallenged dominance of professionalism, giving users a stronger voice (Foster and Wilding, 2000). This was summed up in the following way by the Liberal-Conservative government behind the law: 'With free choice, the individual can better influence his or her own life, and at the same time citizens will experience a more attentive public sector, with focus on individual wishes and needs' (Regeringen, 2004, author's translation).

One way of approaching the users' perspectives and whether services have become more attentive to their needs is to look at how satisfied users are with service provision. Judging from the user satisfaction surveys, regularly conducted nationally (Epinion, 2011, 2015), regardless of provider type, home care users 65+ overall tend to be satisfied with the services received: 83 per cent of users of practical care were in 2015 satisfied or very satisfied, and among users with personal care the satisfaction was equally high, 88 per cent.

Looking more closely at satisfaction levels according to provider type reveals that satisfaction depends on both provider and type of care received: users receiving *practical assistance* in 2015 from a for-profit provider were slightly but not statistically significantly more satisfied than users with a public provider (86 versus 81 per cent) (Figure 2.3). Levels of satisfaction have decreased for both provider types since 2011. The proportion of users dissatisfied with services may equally reveal how well the services are received, and, as Figure 2.3 shows, dissatisfaction

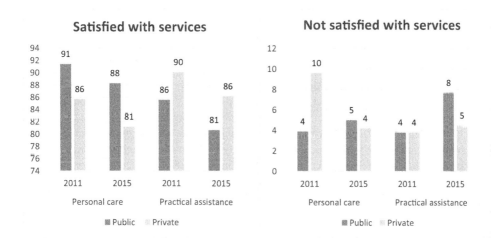

Figure 2.3 Satisfaction and dissatisfaction with provider, by type of provider and service assistance, percentage of home care users, 2011 and 2015

Source: Epinion (2011, 2015).

Note: Survey data. Satisfaction includes response categories 'satisfied' and 'very satisfied', dissatisfaction includes response categories 'dissatisfied' and 'very dissatisfied'. Not including the category 'neither-nor'.

with public provision of practical assistance rose disproportionally compared to that for the for-profit provider from 2011 to 2015.

In contrast, users of *personal care*, and thus the most frail, and those most unlikely to choose a for-profit provider, as seen in Figure 2.1, were in 2015 in general slightly more satisfied if they used a public provider than a for-profit provider (88 versus 81 per cent). This tendency was maintained from 2011, and again levels of satisfaction have gone down in general (Figure 2.3). Dissatisfaction with for-profit provision of personal care had, however, decreased relative to the public provision from 2011 to 2015.

While we cannot disentangle users experiencing bankruptcies and subsequent provider change, the figures nevertheless indicate a general lowered satisfaction with services over time and, equally interesting, regardless of provider type. However, there are also some important changes in satisfaction according to provider type: users seem over time, on the one hand, to be less dissatisfied with the for-profit provider providing personal care, and, on the other, they seem more dissatisfied with public providing of this service. Figure 2.3 also reveals a slight difference in preference among users for for-profit providers providing practical assistance and public providers providing personal care, as is indeed the traditional division of work.

The user satisfaction surveys also allow a closer look at how users of *practical care* (similar figures for personal care are not available) rate various quality items in regard to different provider types, and may thus give an indication of provider type preferences. Three 'traditional' quality items (Rostgaard, 2007) are explored: (1) *care continuity*, which covers whether care is provided more or less in the same way regardless of the different care workers coming to the home; (2) *care worker continuity*, covering whether the user finds the number of different care workers being neither too many nor too few; and (3) whether services are provided at the stated time. Here, for-profit providers seem in particular to be able to meet expectations in regard to care worker continuity. Care users are particularly satisfied with this provider type when it comes to ensuring that it is the same care worker that provides care most of the time (Figure 2.4). The importance for users of this quality item has been picked up by many for-profit providers, who accordingly promote themselves in their company slogans as being able to meet precisely these standards. The lack of performance on exactly this quality item has also been picked up by public providers in their scrutiny of why home care users increasingly prefer the for-profit option (e.g. Københavns Kommune, 2014).

Users also tend to indicate that they chose a for-profit provider because this allows them to negotiate the time given as well as the services provided. This suggests that for-profit providers are able to provide an overall flexibility that public providers are less likely to meet (Rostgaard, 2007). This alleged flexibility is despite the care package and the economic resources going along with it being identical across provider types. Any additional services or time provided thus needs to come from the for-profit companies saving money elsewhere.

Implications for care workers

Free choice caters for a model of care provision that, to an increasing degree, places the consumer at the centre of the service provision, and thus challenges the sovereignty of the professional care worker. The framework of free choice has constructed the for-profit sector as the service provider that best caters for the individual's needs. The service sector itself as well as the users thus hold an inherent expectation that employees will be able to provide more flexible and personalized services – something that employees may find rewarding or demanding. Employees in the for-profit sector may also have been affected by the above-mentioned interruptions of services. A recently conducted survey among care workers allows for a thorough investigation

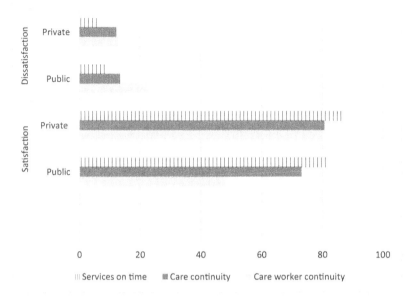

Figure 2.4 Home care users' ranking of quality items according to provider type, practical care only, percentage satisfied and dissatisfied, 2015

Source: Epinion (2015).

Note: Survey data. Satisfaction includes response categories 'satisfied' and 'very satisfied', dissatisfaction includes response categories 'dissatisfied' and 'very dissatisfied'. Not including the category 'neither-nor'.

of the work content and working conditions of employees working in the for-profit versus the public sector. Here, we use survey data from the NORDCARE study.

Care workers are, in general, employed based on their educational background, job experience, etc., regardless of which sector they work in. There is no indication that private for-profit providers systematically target, for instance, low-skilled, low-educated care workers.

Based on the survey data, we find, however, some significant differences in qualifications, in that publicly employed care workers are more likely to have obtained the highest care degree (social and healthcare assistant, social- og sundhedsassistent) and also have longer job experience. There are, though, no differences in the employment situation of the care workers working in the two sectors. They are equally likely to work part-time or full-time, to work in day, evening or night shifts, and tend to have permanent contracts to the same degree. There is also no difference in the number of users that they care for every day, evening or night. There is an equally high share of care workers with a migrant background (either born abroad themselves or having a parent born abroad), of 5.8 per cent in the public and 6.3 per cent in the private for-profit sector. However, and perhaps as a consequence of the number of recent bankruptcies, employees working in the for-profit sector are significantly more worried than those in the public sector about losing their job: 38 per cent of employees in the for-profit sector indicate that they have this worry very often/often, compared to 22 per cent of employees in the public sector.

Looking at the content of care that care workers provide, we also find some noteworthy differences. While for-profit providers predominantly provide practical assistance, it is no surprise that employees in this sector significantly more often provide cleaning services than

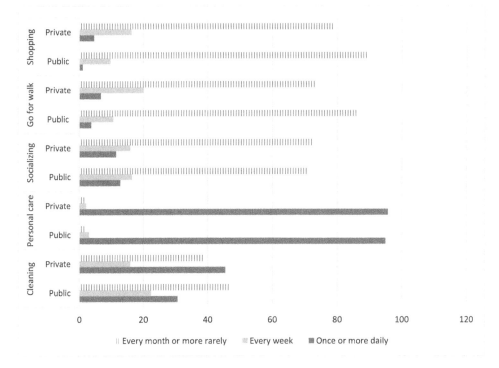

Figure 2.5 Work content, percentage of home care workers carrying out different services, by sector of employment, 2015–2016

Source: NORDCARE data, Danish sample of home care workers.

Note: Statistically significant public-private differences in cleaning, going for a walk and shopping, at 5 per cent level.

employees in the public sector (Figure 2.5). However, perhaps more surprising is that there are no statistically significant differences in the frequency of providing personal care, where the public provider is the dominant service provider. This indicates the aforementioned flexibility from the privately employed care worker side in providing services. There is additional indication of flexibility, as privately employed care workers are significantly more likely to report that they often assist the older person in shopping and going for a walk, services that today are less likely to find their way into care packages. However, publicly employed care workers also report providing such activities, although to a significantly less frequent extent.

An important difference is also that the organization of work places employees in the private sector in a more vulnerable position in a number of ways (Figure 2.6). A number of differences in work conditions of private and publicly employed care workers were also found to be statistically significant in a regression analysis controlling for education, age, work hours, gender, and urban or rural location. This found that privately employed care workers were more often working alone, and therefore had no immediate colleague to rely on for physical support, for example with heavy lifts. Nor could they rely on an immediate colleague for emotional support and professional interchange. Working alone more often may partly be explained by their more frequent provision of practical assistance such as cleaning, rather than personal care, compared to publicly employed care workers, personal care often requiring an extra hand with the physical work. However, privately employed care workers were also significantly more likely to report

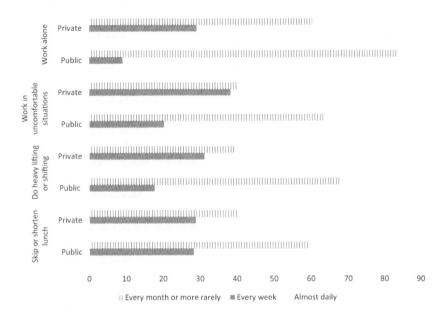

Figure 2.6 Organization of work, private–public distinction, 2015–2016

Source: NORDCARE data, Danish sample of home care workers.

Note: All significant at the 5 per cent level, apart from uncomfortable situations, which is, however, significant at the 10 per cent level. Controlled for education, age, work hours, gender, and urban or rural location.

that they worked in physically uncomfortable working situations, or did heavy lifts and shifted weights. Finally, privately employed care workers were significantly more likely to skip or postpone their lunch in order to manage a busy day and to be able to provide for users.

Another area where care workers in the for-profit sector stand out is in the relationship with the line manager. Not only were they more likely to work alone, but they also seemed to stand more alone in a number of other ways (Figure 2.7). As many as 21 per cent of employees working in the for-profit sector reported that they worried about not receiving information from their line manager compared to only 7 per cent in the public sector. A slightly but still significantly higher proportion of employees in the for-profit sector also felt a lack of recognition from their line manager compared with those in the public sector (26 per cent versus 20 per cent). In addition, and not shown in the figure, while one in two employees in the public sector said that they had team meetings with their manager almost every day or at least every week, this was only the case for one in six among those in the for-profit sector. Instead they had a meeting monthly (44 per cent) or even less often (40 per cent).

Privately employed home care workers also felt they had less access to skill formation and support from peers and line managers than their colleagues working in the public sector (Figure 2.8). Checking again for the influence of education, age, gender, work hours, and urban or rural location, only the private-public distinction turned out to be statistically significant, this being at a very high level, considerably less than 5 per cent. Privately employed home care workers thus less often felt supported by their line manager. They also less often felt that they had time to discuss their work with colleagues, this most likely being related to their more often working alone, as

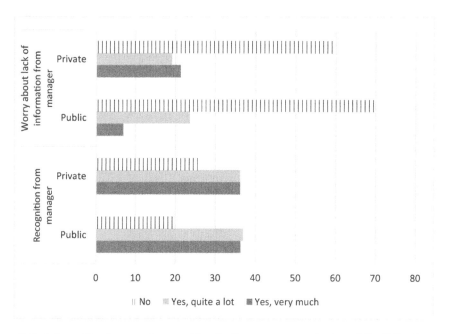

Figure 2.7 Information from and recognition by line manager, private–public distinction, 2015–2016

Source: NORDCARE data, Danish sample on home care workers.

Note: All significant on a 5 per cent level. Controlled for education, age, work hours, gender, and urban or rural location. Recognition not including 'don't know'.

previously indicated, but also possibly being an indication of time pressure. Finally, employees in the for-profit sector also seemed to do less well on skill formation in that they less often had the opportunity to improve their skills, either at the workplace or through further training.

The way the respondents reacted to a number of value statements may indicate their perception of quality of the care that they provide. One statement was whether the care workers themselves would like to receive the care they offer if they became frail in their older days. Here, there was no significant statistical difference in the way that care workers across sectors rated their services; one in three in both sectors would not like to receive such care services (Figure 2.9). There was also no difference related to sector on whether – or not – they agreed that the services were personalized, and thus accommodating to the needs of the individual user. Around one in four in both sectors disagreed with this statement.

Finally, a much higher proportion among care workers in the public sector felt confident that their colleagues had the necessary qualifications to carry out their work. As many as one in three in the for-profit sector questioned this. Care work is interpersonal work and requires communication skills, both verbally but also in writing, as the job entails providing written reports. One in four in the for-profit sector stated that it was a problem that their colleagues did not write or speak Danish sufficiently well, while this was the case for one in five in the public sector. This could be an indication in both sectors of a general lack of writing skills, but also of the increasing inclusion of migrants in both sectors. Today, an equally high proportion of home care workers have a migrant background (6 per cent in both sectors). Finally, and confirming perhaps the general perception of the public sector as being overly bureaucratic, employees in

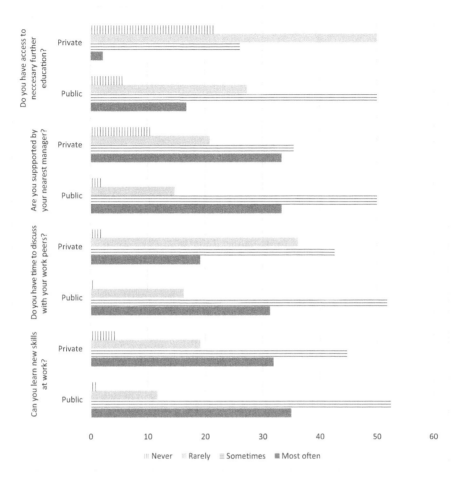

Figure 2.8 Skill formation and immediate support, private–public distinction, 2015–2016

Source: NORDCARE data, Danish sample on home care workers.

Note: All significant at the 5 per cent level. Controlled for education, age, work hours, gender, and urban or rural location.

the public sector were more likely to state that too much of their work time was spent not on providing care, but on documentation and other paperwork. While this may not indicate a difference in the actual time spent on paperwork, it nevertheless suggests that care workers in the for-profit sector felt less burdened by this.

Overall, given the poorer working conditions, it is not surprising that care workers in the for-profit sector are more likely to be looking for work elsewhere. As many as 57 per cent of privately employed care workers indicated in the survey that they had within the last year considered quitting their job, compared to 39 per cent in the public sector. This continued to be significant (below 5 per cent) in a regression analysis, and could not be further explained through the addition of gender, work location, education or work hours, although further analysis showed that the older the person, the less likely it was that they were interested in resigning.

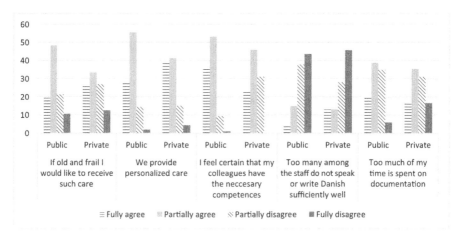

Figure 2.9 Perceptions of quality, private–public distinction, 2015–2016

Source: NORDCARE data, Danish sample on home care workers.

Note: Only questions about competences, Danish proficiency and need for documentation were significant at the 5 per cent level. Controlled for education, age, work hours, gender, and urban or rural location.

Conclusions: revisiting the public care model

With the requirement that municipalities must ensure that users of home care have a choice of provider, Denmark represents the Nordic forefront in the transition from a public to a quasi-market-based home care model among the Nordic countries. The introduction of the free choice has continued to prove popular among users. The public provider persists as the dominant provider on the market, providing for two out of three users, but for-profit providers have steadily increased their market share, although with a levelling out in the recent year (2015). Political support for the free choice model has also persisted over time, and recent changes made it more attractive for municipalities to introduce competition over price. A number of bankruptcies have unfortunately accompanied this change.

In regard to being an experiment of free choice in an otherwise public service model, free choice in home care thus stood its case as long as competition was over quality of care rather than price. The free choice excels in enabling the user to decide about the provider best catering for his or her needs, and thus adheres to the discourse of consumerism. The recent development has, however, exemplified the costs of introducing the price mechanism as a way to increase efficiency and quality, with disruption of services for users as a result, not to mention the additional cost for municipalities picking up for the number of users who were left without services. Also, a substantial number of employees have lost their job and wages.

Overall, the introduction of competition does not seem to have led to higher user satisfaction values over time, neither for those using a private nor a public provider. There is, however, an indication – and in compliance with traditional arguments for more competition – that the introduction of competition has sharpened providers' sense of what users find important, and that they have likewise improved services to become more attentive to users' needs. Some learning across sectors thus seems to have taken place.

The introduction of a quasi-market in home care, however, also means that public money finances the delivery of care services in a sector that performs more poorly than the public sector on a number of employee-related and service performance points, such as working in a vulnerable position and with fewer opportunities to achieve information and engage with line managers and colleagues. The analysis of work content and conditions is based on a sample of union members only. We would expect non-unionized care workers to have poorer working conditions in general. This means that, to the best of our knowledge, the interpretations based on the survey data may in fact underestimate the differences between public and privately employed care workers in general, with the likelihood that privately employed care workers in general have even poorer working conditions than documented here.

The question that remains is whether the change towards a more market-based system, and not least the poorer working conditions for for-profit care workers, is compatible with a public service model within the Nordic welfare regime? Returning to the characteristics of such a model, it is obvious that the introduction of a more mixed economy of care means that it is no longer the public sector only that holds responsibility for care provision. On the other hand, there is still public responsibility for organizing and financing home care and general universalism is upheld, as services are still available for all citizens regardless of means of income. It may also be argued that service universalism still applies as the introduction of the mixed economy of care has only increased the attractiveness and flexibility of the services and affordability is maintained. Nevertheless, the change towards the mixed economy of care is also supporting a development where service delivery in the for-profit sector depends on providing less good working conditions for their employees. Upholding consumer choice for the user thus comes at a price for the employee, at least under the present regulation and conditions of the free choice.

References

Anttonen, A. and Sipilä, J., 1996. European social care services: is it possible to identify models? *Journal of European Social Policy*, 6(2), pp. 87–100.

Anttonen, A. and Zechner, M., 2011. Theorizing care and care work. In B. Pfau-Effinger and T. Rostgaard, eds. *Care between work and welfare in Europe*. Houndsmills: Palgrave Macmillan, pp.15–34.

Bertelsen, T.M. and Rostgaard, T., 2013. Marketisation in eldercare in Denmark: free choice and the quest for quality and efficiency. In G. Meagher and M. Szebehely, eds. *Marketisation in Nordic eldercare: a research report on legislation, oversight, extent and consequences*. Stockholm Studies in Social Work; No. 30.

Dansk Industri (Danish Industry), 2016. *De ældre vil gerne de private*. [Older people are interested in the private for-profit sector provision]. Copenhagen: Dansk Industri. Available at: http://di.dk/Opinion/offentligprivatsamspil/analyser/Pages/Deaeldrevilgernedeprivate.aspx [accessed 16.07.2017].

Danmarks Statistik (Statistics Denmark), 2008. *103.000 arbejder i ældreomsorgen. Personale i ældreomsorgen. Nyt fra Danmarks Statistik* [103,000 work in the long–term care sector]. Available at: www.dst.dk/pukora/epub/Nyt/2009/NR064.pdf [accessed 16.07.2017].

Danmarks Statistik (Statistics Denmark), n.d. *Indikator 15 – Antal hjemmehjælpsmodtagere, der skifter leverandør* [Number of home care users changing provider]. Copenhagen: Danmarks statistik. Available at: www.dst.dk/da/Statistik/emner/tvaergaaende/de-kommunale-serviceindikatorer/aeldre#15 [accessed 17.07.2017].

Epinion, 2011. *Brugerundersøgelse om hjemmehjælp i eget hjem og plejebolig/plejehjem* [User satisfaction survey about home care and nursing home]. Copenhagen: Social – og Indenrigsministeriet.

Epinion, 2015. *Brugerundersøgelse om hjemmehjælp i eget hjem og plejebolig/plejehjem* [User satisfaction survey about home care and nursing home]. Copenhagen: Social – og Ældreministeriet. Available at: www.sum.dk/Aktuelt/Nyheder/Aeldre/2015/December/~/media/96887F842DE04B5CBC84E43CCBC5ADF8.ashx [accessed 12.07.2017].

Evers, A., 2003. *Current strands in debating user involvement in social services*. Discussion paper for the group of specialists on user involvement in Social Services (CS-US) – Council of Europe. September 2003. Giessen: Justus-Liebig-Universität.

Erlandsson, S., Storm, P., Stranz, A., Szebehely, M. and Trydegård, G-B., 2013. Marketising trends in Swedish eldercare: competition, choice and calls for stricter regulation. In G. Meagher and M. Szebehely, eds. *Marketisation in Nordic eldercare: a research report on legislation, oversight, extent and consequences*. Stockholm Studies in Social Work 30. Stockholm University: Department of Social Work.

Tine Rostgaard

FOA (Danish Trade Union for Public Employees), 2016. *Endnu en konkurs i den private for-profit hjemmepleje* [Another bankruptcy in the private, for-profit home care]. Press release. Available at: www.foa.dk/forbund/presse/seneste-pressemeddelelser?newsid=4B8FF874-CC86-4F68-8755-403DCB5104CA [accessed 12.07.2017].

Foster, P. and Wilding, P., 2000. Wither welfare professionalism? *Social Policy and Administration*, 34(2), pp. 143–59. DOI: 10.1111/1467-9515.00182.

Højlund, H., 2002. *Velfærdsforskydninger. Dokumentation, fleksibilitet og delagtiggørelse på ældreområdet* [Welfare transformations: documentation, flexibility and participation in long-term care]. Working Paper 12. Copenhagen: Copenhagen Business School (CBS).

KL (National Association of Danish Municipalities), 2016. *Undersøgelse af kommunale beredskabsplaner ved konkurs blandt private leverandører af hjemmepleje og/eller hjemmesygepleje* [Investigation of municipal emergency plans in case of bankruptcies among private for-profit providers of home care and/or home nursing]. Copenhagen: KL. Available at: www.ft.dk/samling/20151/almdel/suu/bilag/475/1613310/index.htm [accessed 12.07.2017].

Københavns Kommune (Copenhagen Municipality), 2014. *Hjemmepleje* [Home care]. Available at: www.kk.dk/sites/default/files/BRUS_Hjemmepleje_SUF_2014.pdf [accessed 12.07.2017].

Leira, A., 1992. Welfare states and working mothers: the Scandinavian experience. New York: Cambridge University Press.

Politiken, 2016. *Ældre er vilde med privat pleje på trods af konkursbølge* [Older people crazy about private for-profit care despite recent bankruptcies]. 15 September. Copenhagen: Politiken.

Pollitt, C. and Boucaert, G., 2000. *Public management reform: a comparative analysis*. Oxford: Oxford University Press.

Regeringen., 2004. *Frihed til at vælge* [Freedom to choose]. *Copenhagen:* Statsministeriet. Available at: www.stm.dk/multimedia/Frihed_til_at_v_lge.pdf [accessed 16.07.2017].

Rostgaard, T., 2007. *Begreber om kvalitet i ældreplejen* [Conceptualizations of quality in long-term care for older people] Copenhagen: SFI. Available at: www.sfi.dk/publikationer/begreber-om-kvalitet-i-aeldreplejen-5374 [accessed 12.07.2017].

SFI (Danish National Centre for Social Research), 2007. *Brugerundersøgelse om hjemmehjælp til beboere i eget hjem og i plejebolig / plejehjem* [User satisfaction survey among care users at home and in nursing homes]. Udarbejdet for Socialministeriet og KL. Copenhagen: SFI. Available at: www.kl.dk/ImageVaultFiles/id_36023/cf_202/SFI-rapport_om_brugertilfredshed_p-_-ldreomr-det.PDF [accessed 16.07.2017].

Vabø, M., 2009. Home care in transition: the complex dynamic of competing drivers of change in Norway. *Journal of Health Organization and Management*, 23(3), pp. 346–58. DOI: 10.1108/14777260910966762.

Vabø, M. and Szebehely, M., 2012. A caring state for all older people? In A. Anttonen, L. Häikiö and K. Stefánsson, eds. *Welfare state, universalism and diversity*. Cheltenham: Edward Elgar, pp. 121–43.

3

Organizational trends impacting on everyday realities

The case of Swedish eldercare

Anneli Stranz and Marta Szebehely

Introduction

In Sweden, as in all the Nordic countries, publicly funded care services for older persons constitute a part of the welfare state that many citizens experience personally – as care recipients, as family members of older people in need of care or as paid care workers. These encounters with eldercare as a welfare service and as employment have a major impact on the everyday life and welfare of large groups in the society – mostly women.

In this chapter, we describe the organizational and social policy changes of the eldercare sector in Sweden, and analyse how the changes have affected older people in need of care, their families and the paid care workers – with a focus particularly on the last group. The chapter is organized in five sections. The first section describes the data sources and methods used in the chapter; the second section gives the context for eldercare services in the Swedish welfare state; the third section summarizes three decades of organizational trends in Swedish eldercare; and the fourth section analyses how these changes have affected the everyday lives of care workers, and to some extent the users and their families. Finally, we conclude by discussing the women-friendly potential of the Swedish welfare state for care workers in light of the recent changes in eldercare services.

Methods and data sources

Sweden has a long tradition of social science research in care work inspired by feminist care theorists, in particular the Norwegian sociologist Kari Wærness (e.g. Wærness, 1984). The authors of this chapter both belong to this stream of research, which in Sweden was initiated by Rosmari Eliasson-Lappalainen, now a professor emerita in social work at Lund University. Already in the mid-1980s, she developed a framework programme on research into care for older people in which she stressed the need to combine an everyday life perspective with an analysis of the structural and organizational conditions under which care work takes place (Eliasson, 1986). Since 1992, research with this perspective has been generously funded by the Swedish research fund Forte through four six-year programme grants, the first two led by Eliasson-Lappalainen and the second two by Szebehely. Over the years, these programmes have been linking feminist-oriented research on care with social policy-oriented welfare state research and studies of organizational trends in care services, and how they affect the everyday lives of care workers, care users and families of frail older people.

This chapter is mainly based on research conducted within these programmes, utilizing a variety of methods: ethnographic studies with participant observations and in-depth interviews with care workers and care users; surveys with care workers; and historical and institutional document analysis, as well as analysis of public statistics.

A significant part of the section on how care workers are affected by cutbacks and recent organizational changes is based on the NORDCARE study, a survey of care workers carried out in 2005 and 2015 by Szebehely, Stranz and Nordic colleagues. In 2005, a mail questionnaire was distributed to 5,000 unionized care workers in home and residential care for older and disabled people in the Nordic countries (overall response rate 72 per cent). In 2015, a similar questionnaire was sent to 8,000 eldercare workers in the Nordic countries (response rate 55 per cent). Since approximately 8 out of 10 Swedish care workers are unionized, the sample is fairly representative of the care workforce, although those with the most precarious employment conditions are under-represented (Szebehely et al., 2017). The survey has been replicated in several other countries and the data have been used for cross-country comparisons of employment and working conditions (e.g. Meagher et al., 2016; Stranz, 2013; Banerjee et al., 2012; Daly and Szebehely, 2012; Trydegård, 2012; Elstad and Vabø, 2008).

Eldercare services in the Swedish welfare state

We take our starting point in the widespread image of the Nordic universal care regime: high coverage of generously funded, publicly provided services of high quality that are offered to and used by all social groups according to need rather than to purchasing power (Anttonen et al., 2012; Vabø and Szebehely, 2012).

It has been discussed whether this image of Nordic universalism is or ever has been accurate (see e.g. Anttonen, 2002). In a wider international comparison, however, Sweden is still one of the world's most generous countries when it comes to public spending on eldercare. In 2013, the public expenditure on long-term care (services for older or disabled people, health and social components taken together) corresponds to 3.2 per cent of GDP, considerably higher than in other OECD countries except for the Netherlands (OECD, 2015, p. 209).

This generosity is reflected in Swedish policy documents and social legislation that ensures the individual a right to assistance. However, eldercare is not carried out at the national level, but by 290 highly independent municipalities that are responsible for financing the services through municipal income tax and for organizing the service provision. Within the limits prescribed by legislation, the local authorities decide on tax rates, establish local guidelines, set budgets and organize services for older people, as well as for other groups in society. As a reaction to population ageing, financial crises and competition with programmes for other groups with stronger legal protection such as preschool children and disabled persons below retirement age, many municipalities have tightened the eligibility criteria for entering eldercare services (Szebehely and Trydegård, 2012). Measured as expenditure for eldercare services in relation to the population 80 years and older, the public spending has not kept pace with the ageing population since 1990, while the spending on disability services has increased considerably (SALAR, 2014, p. 19).

As a result, without changes in national eldercare policies or legislation, for decades the service coverage has declined: between 1980 and 2015, the proportion of the population 80+ receiving either home-based or residential care has dropped from 62 to 37 per cent (NBHW, 2016, Tables 6 and 8; Ulmanen, 2015, p. 21).

In the 1980s and 1990s, the decrease was sharpest in home care, but more recently it is residential care that has declined most drastically: between 2000 and 2015, more than one-quarter of residential care beds have disappeared and the proportion of the population 80+ in residential care has decreased from 20 to 13 per cent (SOU, 2017, p. 220). In the same period, the number of home care users has increased, but the increase has not compensated for deinstitutionalization as hardly any home care user receives the same amount of care as in residential care (Ulmanen and Szebehely, 2015, p. 84). Ageing-in-place policies are certainly not unique to Sweden, but the decline in residential care has been more dramatic than elsewhere, and while the coverage of both home care and residential care is still comparatively high, Sweden is no longer among the top five countries in Europe (Rodrigues et al., 2012, pp. 89–91).

Also important in this context is that the number of hospital beds in Sweden has declined rapidly since the early 1990s (Szebehely and Trydegård, 2012). Today, Sweden has significantly fewer hospital beds and shorter lengths of stays in hospital than almost all other OECD countries (OECD, 2015, pp. 105, 109). As a result, older people often leave hospital with remaining care needs, and the eldercare services are increasingly targeted to those with greatest needs. Those living in residential care have become older and frailer, their length of stay shorter (Schön et al., 2016), and a higher proportion of home care clients are very ill. In both arenas of care, the proportion with dementia is growing (NBHW, 2014).

As several scholars have argued, home care services have serious problems in meeting the large care needs; instead, the family or privately purchased help have to fill the gaps caused by ageing-in-place policies (Ranci and Pavolini, 2015). This offloading of services from the state to the family and the market is clearly visible in the case of Sweden: both family care and privately purchased care services, financed out of the pocket of the user, have increased (Ulmanen and Szebehely, 2015). This changing mix in the political economy of care is unevenly distributed from a social class perspective. In the 1980s and 1990s, family care, in particular help by middle-aged daughters, increased mainly for older people with fewer resources, while privately purchased care increased among those with more resources. However, more recently as a consequence of the drastic decline of residential care, family care provided by both women and men has increased in all social groups. This has had negative consequences for both women and men's well-being and working life, but the problems are more common among women (Ulmanen, 2015).

The care workforce in the Swedish welfare state

The Nordic model is often seen as being successful in recognizing caregiving work through a process of state responsibility and professionalization. The publicly financed social care system constitutes an important labour market primarily for low-educated women, and the eldercare sector employs a high proportion of care workers.

The gender-segregated labour market, and thereby women and men's different working conditions, is a prominent feature in Scandinavian countries (Borchorst, 2012). A typical care worker in the Swedish context has long been seen as a middle-aged white woman. Women still form the majority of eldercare workers (9 out of 10), but an increasing proportion of the care workforce are immigrants. One in three men care workers and one in five women workers are born outside the Nordic countries, the majority in countries outside Europe (Statistics Sweden, 2016a; see also Behtoui et al., 2016).

Part-time work is more common in eldercare than in other parts of the Swedish labour market, also compared to other women-dominated sectors. More than half of the eldercare workers work part-time, often involuntarily as they are not offered full-time work, or as a response to arduous working conditions (Meagher et al., 2016).

Even if the training levels have increased over time as a result of various state initiatives, still one in five residential care workers and one in four home care workers lack relevant training (NBHW, 2013, p. 148). Reflecting the increased health problems among older people in both residential and home-based care, present national guidelines stress that all care workers should have training as assistant nurses, but there is an obvious gap between policy ambitions and the actual situation when it comes to formal training.

Compared to all women in the labour market, the eldercare sector is characterized by high physical demands due to heavy lifting and work in uncomfortable positions, which is related to a high proportion of occupational injuries among care workers. Physical load injuries are three times more common in eldercare than the average in the labour market (Work Environment Authority, 2007). Both back pain and exhaustion are reported considerably more often by care workers than by the rest of the workforce, and these problems have increased significantly among care workers in recent years (Statistics Sweden, 2016b).

Also, the psychosocial working conditions are more problematic in care work than in the labour market in general: eldercare workers report four times more often than the rest of the workforce that they have been exposed to violence or the threat of violence at work, and almost twice as often that they find their jobs psychologically demanding. Eldercare workers also report more limited decision latitude and more stress at work – an unhealthy combination of high demands and low control (high-strain jobs) that has increased in the last two decades, and was reported twice as often by eldercare workers in 2015 as by the rest of the workforce (Statistics Sweden, 2016b).

Notifications of occupational disease due to social and organizational causes have increased by over 70 per cent between 2010 and 2014. These notifications are often related to psycho-social working conditions, in particular to relationships at the workplace such as demanding contacts with clients, threats and violence, and lack of support from managers and colleagues (Work Environment Authority, 2015). Thus, it is not surprising that sickness absence is high among eldercare workers – in particular among women workers: female eldercare workers have 50 per cent more sick days than women in the rest of the workforce (NBHW, 2015, p. 133).

A comparison of two public sectors (the women-dominated home care sector and the men-dominated technical sector) reflects the pattern of gender differences in working conditions. In the home care sector, the managers are responsible for much larger groups of employees, and thus have less time to support the workers; the workload is higher for both managers and workers, and the possibilities of influencing their own work situation are fewer (Work Environment Authority, 2014)

De-caring organizational trends in eldercare services

Home care

As in many other countries, care for older people was almost entirely confined to institutions until the early 1950s when home care services started to develop on a small scale, inspired by the British experience during the war. In all social groups, these services soon became very popular: between 1960 and 1980, the number of users increased from 60,000 to 250,000 (Szebehely, 2005). In the first decades, the home care services were characterized by personal and stable relationships between care workers and users. Each worker helped only a couple of clients per day, and each visit lasted for an hour or more. The way the services were organized left the worker with enough discretion, time and knowledge about the individual user. Therefore, the workers had the possibility to adapt their help *to the varying situations of different care recipients*. However, the work itself was not regarded as a proper job. In the beginning, housewives were employed by the hour, no formal educational requirements were demanded, and the pay was lower than in, for instance, cleaning jobs. Informal qualifications, such as the care worker's experience of homemaking and informal care, necessary for coping with the work, were not recognized (Vabø and Szebehely, 2012; Eliasson-Lappalainen and Motevasel, 1997).

Since the early days of home care, the employment conditions and the salaries have improved, but the hourly pay for a care worker is 79 per cent of the national average, and part-time work and employment by the hour are still more common than in most other occupations (Meagher et al., 2016). Further, the way care work is organized has not improved – rather the opposite. From the 1980s onwards, rationalization strategies aiming at cost-efficiency were introduced. A *Taylorization* of care work took place: the daily organization of home care became increasingly predetermined; the tasks to be carried out at each occasion were set in advance; a horizontal and vertical division of labour and a standardization and fragmentation of care into manageable 'care products' were introduced (Vabø and Szebehely, 2012; Eliasson-Lappalainen and Motevasel, 1997).

During the last decades, these 'de-caring' organizational trends have increased with the international wave of market-inspired reforms often labelled New Public Management (NPM). A central aspect of NPM is the introduction of a *purchaser-provider split*: a division between the purchaser/needs assessor and provider units that implied a significant change in the daily organization of home care services. It brought about an increased distance between the 'office' and the 'workshop', between the decisions and the actual provision of help. This resulted in new demands on exactness and clarity in the 'order'; increasingly often, the work task is connected to a standardized time frame such as 5 minutes to make a bed, 10 minutes to change incontinence pads or 15 minutes for a shower, and the number of visits carried out per day has increased (Meagher et al., 2016).

Another aspect of NPM is the increased reliance on private actors as providers of publicly funded services through the introduction of market-inspired measures such as competitive tendering and user choice models. Over the last two decades, the share of private provision of the publicly funded home care services has increased from less than 3 per cent in the beginning of the 1990s to 23 per cent in 2016. The entire increase has taken place in the for-profit sector: only 3 per cent is provided by non-profit organizations and 20 per cent by for-profit companies – a mix of large, international corporations and many small and often short-lived companies (NBHW, 2017, Table 9; Erlandsson et al., 2013).

Responsibility for controlling the quality of care services rests with the municipalities, even when care is provided by a private company. Partly as a reaction to the increasing number of private providers, there has been an increased focus on how to regulate and measure quality in eldercare, and how to monitor the quality of care. As a result, there are increased demands on staff to document the care they carry out. This trend is strengthened by the focus on individualized and person-centred care stressed in legislation and national policy documents. For each client, a care plan is to be set up where the individual's particular needs, habits and preferences are to be noted, and the care workers are supposed to regularly update these plans and to document all activities with and for a particular client in relation to the plan. Both care workers and their managers thus spend increasingly more time on documentation of various kinds.

Residential care

With the exception of the increased presence of care plans, documentation and for-profit providers (an increase between 1990 and 2016 from 0 to around 17 per cent of residential care;

NBHW, 2017, Table 10; Erlandsson et al., 2013), the organizational trends in residential care and home care are quite different. An important turning point was the introduction of the Ädel-reform in 1992, when the responsibility for nursing homes was shifted from the healthcare sector to the municipal social service sector. Since then, there is no legal distinction between nursing homes and other forms of residential care homes, and all forms of residential care are guided by a 'social care model', with a norm of small care units and a relatively high degree of privacy for residents.

Today, a typical residential care home consists of several units (floors) where 8–12 residents live, each in a private room or small apartment with their own furniture, and the resident is formally regarded as a tenant. More than 95 per cent of residents have a private bathroom, and more than 80 per cent have private cooking facilities, usually a kitchenette (NBHW, 2017, Table 2).

The staffing level is high in international comparisons. There is usually no specialized cleaning, laundry or housekeeping staff; instead, each care worker is responsible for most aspects of care (personal care, domestic work and social support) for a handful of residents. Compared with many other countries, there is less differentiation of care workers with different levels of training: care workers with no or shorter training (care aides) do more or less the same tasks as those with longer training (assistant nurses) (Daly and Szebehely, 2012).

It has been estimated that 70 per cent of all residents have dementia, with half of them living in specialized dementia units (NBHW, 2014, p. 25). These units, initially called 'group homes', started with the ambition to create a family-like setting in a small-scale stand-alone building in which staff would cook and do other household activities together with the residents (Wilson et al., 1993). Nowadays, these units tend to be part of larger facilities, and because of the residents' increasing frailty, joint domestic activities are much less prominent (Verbeek et al., 2009). More recently, insufficient staffing levels in dementia care, in particular at night, have led to intense political debate and media coverage, caused by the results from unannounced inspections in 2010 which found that 55 out of 94 dementia care units inspected had inadequate staffing at night (Choiniere et al., 2015). As a result, in 2016 new binding guidelines were implemented stating that in all residential care (including dementia units), personnel have to be available around the clock. Whether this will lead to increased staffing levels or a reallocation of staff from day to night shift is still to be seen.

Consequences of cutbacks and organizational changes for care workers

In line with international care research, Swedish scholars have highlighted the complexity of care work: the coexistence of negative and positive aspects related to care as relational and emotional work. These aspects are often stressed as making the work meaningful (e.g. Trydegård, 2012; Elwér et al., 2010), while organizational conditions or lack of resources that prevent the staff from giving the care the elderly person needs lead to feelings of inadequacy. Such feelings have been shown to be a risk for care workers' health and well-being, and are also strongly related to considerations to quit the job (Stranz, 2013; Trydegård, 2012). Thus, the encounters between caregivers and care recipients are a central source of motivation and job satisfaction as well as of stress and fatigue. Care research often underlines that the organization of care and the conditions under which it is performed have obvious impact on both the quality of work and the quality of care (Stranz and Sörensdotter, 2016; Stranz, 2013; Daly and Szebehely, 2012).

Early research on home care has illuminated an occupation and a work practice that had been quite invisible and unacknowledged in social science research and as a part of the welfare state. In the 1980s and 1990s, this research provided knowledge about the everyday care practices under different organizational conditions in Swedish home care (e.g. Eliasson-Lappalainen and Motevasel, 1997; Szebehely, 1995), giving a base for comparisons over time. In the 1980s, a home care worker usually helped four older persons during a full-time workday, and the workday was dominated by domestic tasks combined with social and emotional support. Twenty years later, a care worker would help twice as many users per day, the time for household tasks being significantly reduced. The focus of the work had shifted from care of the home to care of the body, with less time for the social aspects of work. This shift was a result partly of increased care needs among those deemed eligible for home care, and partly of the attempt to reduce public expenditure by shifting the responsibility for household chores from the state to the family or the market (Vabø and Szebehely, 2012).

There are fewer detailed descriptions of residential care work in earlier days, but it seems reasonable to state that nursing home care in the 1980s had more characteristics of assembly line care than 30 years later. After the Ädel-reform in 1992, the units became smaller, and each care worker became responsible for providing holistic care for a smaller number of residents rather than conducting a specific task for 20–30 residents. The care workers in the more medical model of nursing homes before 1992 had considerably less discretion in their workday than the care workers in the small-size social model residential care home. However, more recently, cutbacks and the process of marketization have had an impact on everyday care work in both residential and home-based care.

The *NORDCARE* survey 2005 and 2015: deteriorating working conditions

In this section, we analyse some of the structured and unstructured (open-ended) survey questions from the 2005 and 2015 NORDCARE surveys, based on responses from 378 home care workers and 819 residential care workers in Swedish eldercare.

The sharp decline of residential care beds has affected both residential and home-based services: in both arenas, the care needs of clients have increased radically. However, the care needs differ significantly between home care and residential care: according to the 2015 NORDCARE survey, 43 per cent of the residential care workers reported that all or most of their clients require help to move from the bed, compared to 7 per cent of the home care workers.

Another aspect of a heavier workload is the increase in the number of clients a care worker assists during a working day. Between 2005 and 2015, there has been an increase in both arenas of care, but particularly in home care: from 8.6 clients on average per day to 11.8, and in residential care from 8.6 to 10.1. In home care, the number of *visits* is even larger as often a care worker visits the same client several times a day; in 2015, a home care worker made 15 visits per day on average and more than half of these visits lasted 15 minutes or less (these questions were not asked in 2005).

In line with the more restrictive needs assessment in home care, and thus a raised threshold for entering the services, domestic tasks such as cleaning have declined and tasks focusing on bodily care have increased. Another, partly expected, change is that documentation of both medical and social activities is a rising task in everyday care practice due to policies on quality control. The proportion of respondents answering that they do administrative tasks such as documentation several times every day has more than doubled between 2005 and 2015 – up from 11 to 28 per cent in home care and from 16 to 37 per cent in residential care.

Table 3.1 shows the trends in some aspects of psychosocial working conditions related to demands and discretion at work. In home care, the most dramatic changes concern the reduced possibility for the care workers to plan the daily work and the reduced scope for discussing work-related difficulties with colleagues. In 2005, 39 per cent reported that they most often had the possibility to plan their daily work, compared to 16 per cent in 2015. In these respects, the residential care workers are much better off: they report more freedom of action in their daily work and more time to talk to their colleagues compared to staff in home care, and these aspects of working conditions have not deteriorated to the same extent. In contrast, in residential care, the work intensity has increased considerably: in 2005, 40 per cent of residential care workers reported that they most often had too much to do compared to half of the workers in 2015. In 2015, this is a central difference between the work arenas. The experience of having too much to do can contribute to the higher proportion of residential care workers reporting that they feel inadequate in relation to the care recipient, compared to home care workers (Table 3.1).

Research has shown that the eldercare sector is highly exposed to change – both reorganization and implementation of new work methods – and that frequent changes often influence the work situation in a negative way (Fläckman et al., 2009). The results from NORDCARE confirm this research in that an increased proportion of the residential care staff is worried that their work situation will change (Table 3.1).

When the staff's experiences of physical and mental exhaustion and back pain are compared between the years, we can see an increase in all three aspects, in particular in residential care settings (Table 3.2).

Table 3.1 Psychosocial working conditions in home care and residential care, 2005 and 2015, per cent

	Home care		*Residential care*		*2015: comparison of residential care/home care*
	2005	**2015**	**2005**	**2015**	
Most often too much to do	36	40 ns	*40*	*50* **	**
Most often possible to affect the daily planning of the work	*39*	*16* ***	47	41 $^\mathrm{T}$	***
Most often enough time to discuss difficulties in work with colleagues	*57*	*35* ***	59	51 ns	***
Most often feel inadequate	22	24 ns	32	38 $^\mathrm{T}$	***
Most often worried that the work situation will change	22	25 ns	*18*	*25* *	ns

Note: *** $p < 0.001$; ** $p < 0.01$; * $p < 0.05$; $^\mathrm{T}$ $p < 0.10$; ns not significant.

Table 3.2 Reactions to working conditions in home care and residential care, 2005 and 2015, per cent

	Home care		*Residential care*		*2015: comparison of residential care/home care*
	2005	**2015**	**2005**	**2015**	
Almost always feel physically tired after a working day	28	32 ns	29	41 ***	*
Almost always experience back pain after a working day	11	20 *	15	27 ***	*
Almost always feel mentally exhausted after a working day	14	24 *	16	26 ***	ns
Have during the last year seriously considered quitting the job	40	46 ns	40	50 **	ns

Note: *** $p < 0.001$; ** $p < 0.01$; * $p < 0.05$; $^\mathrm{T}$ $p < 0.10$; ns not significant.

There is also an increase between 2005 and 2015 in the proportion of care workers who seriously have considered leaving their job, particularly in residential care (50 per cent versus 46 per cent home care). In both arenas, the proportions are very high (Table 3.2). This measure does not reveal if workers will actually quit but it is an indicator of how the working situation is perceived. Obviously a large and increasing proportion of care workers find their situation at work problematic.

An analysis of comments to an open-ended question in the 2005 NORDCARE survey about reasons for considering quitting in the eldercare sector showed that these were strongly connected to physical and mental strain and worries about one's own health (Stranz, 2013). In a preliminary analysis of the comments to the same question in 2015, similar themes regarding a high workload, both mentally and physically, and how that affects one's health, are predominant.

As indicated in Table 3.1, the working situation in home care is characterized by decreased discretion and increased stress, while in residential care the higher workload is the most salient feature. Some quotes from the two groups of workers illustrate these different trends:

Home care:

> If things go on like this, that we have 13 or 14 clients per day, I don't think I can keep working until I retire.
>
> Physically and mentally demanding; afraid of forgetting things with users; feeling that you can't manage at an increasingly rapid speed.
>
> It is because I can't give the care that my care recipients or users deserve and because we are so controlled by the minute; stress, stress.

Residential care:

> Because we get new bosses and directives several times per year and because we document too much so the clients suffer (less time for walks, for instance) and that is hard.
>
> There are many more demands on care staff. Demands from residents and family. Sometimes it feels you'd have to be superhuman to live up to everybody's wishes and demands. We don't have enough staff for that. Also, all the documentation is exhausting.
>
> Because it gets worse and worse, both for the residents and for us staff.

When it comes to worries about health and fears that their own bodies will not manage the increased stress and workload, the care workers' statements are more similar across the two arenas of care work:

> My body is ageing; you get older and can't take it because of the workload and not enough staff (residential care).
>
> Because I won't make it until the end because the organization of home care tears us into pieces (home care).
>
> Bad pay, increased workload, stress, worn out body (residential care).

A common feature for the majority who responded to the survey in both years is that a high proportion (just over 70 per cent) found their tasks interesting and meaningful, and around half of the respondents agreed that they often get a lot back in meeting with the care recipient. The relational aspects, both with clients and colleagues and the feelings of doing meaningful work, were the main reasons for staying at work in 2005 (Stranz, 2013) and are also frequently mentioned in the 2015 survey.

The results from the NORDCARE surveys from 2005 and 2015 highlight the fact that it is the shortcomings in the organization of work that make staff consider quitting, and that it is the relational aspects that make them want to stay. However, even when the organizational and material resources are insufficient, care is still provided but at the expense of something – or someone – else. The care workers risk their health, both physically and mentally, and this is the most important reason why respondents consider leaving their work in the eldercare sector.

Concluding remarks

Both home-based and residential care have gone through major organizational changes over the last decades, and in both forms of care the organizational reforms have been implemented with hardly any consideration of the consequences for staff. Obviously, new organizational models have been introduced in stark opposition to the actual results of care research showing that time, continuity and discretion for care workers to meet the varying needs of different care recipients is crucial for good care.

Both national statistics on work-related injuries and the NORDCARE survey present a picture of worsening working conditions for the staff in eldercare, a trend that can be related to declining resources and organizational changes. Further, policy ambitions concerning the quality of care and the users' scope to influence their care have increased substantially in recent years with policies emphasizing an individualized approach to care. Thus, at the policy level, the welfare state's ambitions have increased while at the same time financial resources have decreased and organizational conditions have deteriorated, making it more difficult for care workers to actually carry out high-quality care.

Care workers become worn out and want to quit. As the care workers' bodies are their main working tool, it is their bodies that are bearing the cost of increasingly demanding working conditions. Care workers' needs for better working conditions are not recognized, which contributes to declining physical and mental health.

Care services are an essential part of the Nordic model. These services are often regarded as the embodiment of the women-friendliness of the Nordic welfare states (Hernes, 1987). Whereas care services certainly are empowering for groups of women as care users and family members of older persons in need of care – or at least were so before the cutbacks and 'de-caring' organizational trends – some researchers have problematized the notion of women-friendliness from the perspective of paid care workers. Those working in the care sector have a different class – and often also ethnicity position from the group of women usually in focus in the discussion of the women-friendly welfare state – the white middle class (Dahl, 2004; Borchorst and Siim, 2002).

From a social justice perspective, it is crucial that care workers are included in the equality ambitions of the welfare state. It would only be relevant to speak of a women-friendly welfare state if the workers' right to provide care that they find adequate is recognized and they have good pay and working conditions.

References

Anttonen, A., 2002. Universalism and social policy: a Nordic-feminist revaluation. *NORA-Nordic Journal of Feminist and Gender Research* , 10(2), pp. 71–80. Available at: www.tandfonline.com/doi/abs/10.1080/080387402760262168 [accessed 30.05.2017].

Anttonen, A., Häikiö, L. and Stefánsson, K., eds. 2012. *Welfare state, universalism and diversity*. Cheltenham: Edward Elgar.

Banerjee, A., Daly, T., Armstrong, P., Szebehely, M., Armstrong, H. and LaFrance, S., 2012. Structural violence in long-term residential care for older people: comparing Canada and Scandinavia. *Social*

Science and Medicine, 74(3) 390–8. Available at: https://doi.org/10.1016/j.socscimed.2011.10.037 [accessed 30.05.2017].

Behtoui, A., Boreús, K., Neergaard, A. and Yazdanpanah, S., 2016. Speaking up. Leaving or keeping silent: racialized employees in the Swedish elderly care sector. *Work, Employment and Society*. DOI: 10.1177/0950017016667042.

Borchorst, A., 2012. Reassessing woman-friendliness and the gender system: feminist theorizing about the Nordic welfare model. In A. Anttonen, L. Häikiö and K. Stefansson, ed. *Welfares state, universalism and diversity*. Cheltenham: Edward Elgar, pp. 106–20.

Borchorst, A. and Siim, B., 2002. The women-friendly welfare states revisited. *NORA-Nordic Journal of Feminist and Gender Research*, 10(2), pp.90–8. DOI: 10.1080/080387402760262186.

Choiniere, J.A., Doupe, M., Goldmann, M., Harrington, C., Jacobsen, F.F., Lloyd, L., et al., 2015. Mapping nursing home inspections and audits in six countries. *Ageing International*, 41(1), pp. 40–61. Available at: https://link.springer.com/article/10.1007/s12126-015-9230-6 [accessed 30.05.2017].

Dahl, H.M., 2004. A view from the inside: recognition and redistribution in the Nordic welfare state from a gender perspective. *Acta Sociologica*, 47(4), pp. 325–37. DOI: 10.1177/0001699304048666.

Daly, T. and Szebehely, M., 2012. Unheard voices, unmapped terrain: care work in long-term residential care for older people in Canada and Sweden. *International Journal of Social Welfare*, 21(2), pp. 139–48. DOI: 10.1111/j.1468-2397.2011.00806.x.

Eliasson, R., 1986. *Ramprogram för FoU-området Äldre* [Programme for research on older people]. Stockholm: Department of Social Services.

Eliasson-Lappalainen, R.E. and Motevasel, I.N., 1997. Ethics of care and social policy. *Scandinavian Journal of Social Welfare*, 6(3) 189–96. DOI: 10.1111/j.1468-2397.1997.tb00188.x.

Elstad, J.I. and Vabø, M., 2008. Job stress, sickness absence and sickness presenteeism in Nordic elderly care. *Scandinavian Journal of Public Health*, 36(5), pp. 467–74. DOI: 10.1177/1403494808089557.

Elwér, S., Aléx, L. and Hammarström, A., 2010. Health against the odds: experiences of employees in elder care from a gender perspective. *Qualitative Health Research*, 20(9), pp. 1202–12. DOI: 10.1177/1049732310371624.

Erlandsson, S., Storm, P., Stranz, A., Szebehely, M. and Trydegård, G-B., 2013. Marketising trends in Swedish eldercare: competition, choice and calls for stricter regulation. In G. Meagher and M. Szebehely, eds. *Marketisation in Nordic eldercare*. Stockholm University. Available at: www.normacare.net/wp-content/uploads/2013/09/Marketisation-in-nordic-eldercare-webbversion-med-omslag1.pdf [accessed 30.05.2017].

Fläckman, B., Hansebo, G. and Kihlgren, A., 2009. Struggling to adapt: caring for older persons while under threat of organizational change and termination notice. *Nursing Inquiry*, 16(1), pp. 82–91. DOI: 10.1111/j.1440-1800.2009.00434.

Hernes, H., 1987. Welfare state and women power: essays in state feminism. Oslo: Norweigan University Press.

Meagher, G., Szebehely, M., and Mears, J., 2016. How institutions matter for job characteristics, quality and experiences: a comparison of home care work for older people in Australia and Sweden. *Work, Employment and Society*, 30(5), pp. 731–49. DOI: 10.1177%2F0950017015625601.

NBHW, 2013. *Tillståndet och utvecklingen inom hälso- och sjukvård och socialtjänst. Lägesrapport 2013* [The status and development in health care and social services: status report 2013]. National Board of Health and Welfare (Socialstyrelsen). Available at: www.socialstyrelsen.se/publikationer2013/2013-2-2 [accessed 30.05.2017].

NBHW, 2014. *Demenssjukdomarnas samhällskostnader i Sverige 2012* [The societal costs of dementia in Sweden 2012]. National Board of Health and Welfare (Socialstyrelsen). Available at: www.socialstyrelsen.se/publikationer2014/2014-6-3 [accessed 30.05.2017].

NBHW, 2015. *Tillståndet och utvecklingen inom hälso- och sjukvård och socialtjänst. Lägesrapport 2015.* [The status and development in health care and social services: status report 2015]. National Board of Health and Welfare (Socialstyrelsen). Available at: www.socialstyrelsen.se/publikationer2015/2015-2-51 [accessed 30.05.2017].

NBHW, 2016. *Statistics on care and services for the elderly 2015*. National Board of Health and Welfare (Socialstyrelsen). Available at: www.socialstyrelsen.se/publikationer2016/2016-4-29 [accessed 05.04.2017].

NBHW, 2017. *Statistics on elderly and people with impairments: management form 2016*. National Board of Health and Welfare (Socialstyrelsen). Available at: www.socialstyrelsen.se/publikationer2017/2017-2-18 [accessed 17.04.2017].

OECD, 2015. *Health at a glance 2015: OECD indicators*. Paris: OECD. DOI: 10.1787/health_glance-2015-en.

Ranci, C. and Pavolini, E., 2015. Not all that glitters is gold: long-term care reforms in the last two decades in Europe. *Journal of European Social Policy*, 25(3), pp. 270–85. DOI: 10.1177/0958928715588704.

Rodrigues, R., Huber, M. and Lamura, G., eds., 2012. *Facts and figures on healthy ageing and long-term care*. Vienna: European Centre for Social Welfare Policy and Research. Available at: www.euro.centre.org/data/LTC_Final.pdf [accessed 30.05.2017].

SALAR (Swedish Association of Local Authorities and Regions), 2014. *Välfärdstjänsternas utveckling 1980–2012* [The development of welfare services 1980–2012]. Stockholm: Sveriges Kommuner och Landsting. Available at: http://webbutik.skl.se/bilder/artiklar/pdf/7585-042-9.pdf?issuusl=ignore [accessed 30.05.2017].

Schön, P., Lagergren, M. and Kåreholt, I., 2016. Rapid decrease in length of stay in institutional care for older people in Sweden between 2006 and 2012: results from a population-based study. *Health and Social Care in the Community*, 24(5), pp. 631–8. DOI: 10.1111/hsc.12237.

SOU (Swedish Public Investigation), 2017. *Läs mig! Nationell kvalitetsplan för vård och omsorg för äldre personer* [Read me! National quality plan for care of older people]. Report 20. Stockholm: Ministry of Health and Social Affairs. Available at: www.regeringen.se/4969b7/contentassets/9378aff4b35a427c99b77234 5af79539/sou-2017_21_webb_del1.pdf [accessed 20.07.2017].

Statistics Sweden, 2016a. *Employees 16–64 years at national level by occupation (4-digit SSYK 2012), region of birth and sex. Year 2014*. Available at: www.statistikdatabasen.scb.se/pxweb/en/ssd/START__AM__AM0208__AM0208E/YREG53/?rxid=0cc02e0b-c020-4bd2-bf11-a627b7b332e2 [accessed 21.07.2017].

Statistics Sweden, 2016b. *Arbetsmiljöundersökningen. Andel av de sysselsatta enl. arbetsmiljöundersökningen för vald arbetsmiljöfråga efter yrke SSYK. År 1997–2015* [Work environment survey: work environment of employed population by occupation 1997–2015]. Available at: www.statistikdatabasen.scb.se/pxweb/sv/ssd/START__AM__AM0501__AM0501A/ArbmiljoYrk2/?rxid=5c137e04-90b4-448e-8709-4a97c1ac1bf1 [accessed 17.04.2017].

Stranz, A., 2013. *Omsorgsarbetets vardag och villkor i Sverige och Danmark: ett feministiskt kritiskt perspektiv* [The everyday realities and conditions of care work in Sweden and Denmark]. PhD thesis. Stockholm University. Available at: http://su.diva-portal.org/smash/get/diva2:659124/FULLTEXT03.pdf [accessed 30.05.2017].

Stranz, A. and Sörensdotter, R., 2016. Interpretations of person-centered dementia care: same rhetoric, different practices? A comparative study of nursing homes in England and Sweden. *Journal of Aging Studies*, 38, pp. 70–80. DOI: 10.1016/j.jaging.2016.05.001.

Szebehely, M., 1995. *Vardagens organisering. Om vårdbiträden och gamla i hemtjänsten* [The organization of everyday life: on care workers and older people in home care]. Lund University: Arkiv Förlag.

Szebehely, M., 2005. Care as employment and welfare provision: child care and elder care in Sweden at the dawn of the 21st century. In H.M. Dahl and T.R. Eriksen, eds. *Dilemmas of care in the Nordic welfare state*. Aldershot: Ashgate, pp. 80–97.

Szebehely, M. and Trydegård, G-B., 2012. Home care for older people in Sweden: a universal model in transition. *Health and Social Care in the Community*, 20(3), pp. 300–9. DOI: 10.1111/j.1365-2524.2011.01046.x.

Szebehely, M., Stranz, A. and Strandell, R., 2017. *Vem ska arbeta i framtidens äldreomsorg?* [Who will work in eldercare in the future?]. Working Paper 1/2017. Stockholm University: Department of Social Work. Available at: www.socarb.su.se/polopoly_fs/1.320035.1486983623!/menu/standard/file/Slutversion%20rapport%20feb13.pdf [accessed 30.05.2017].

Trydegård, G-B., 2012. Care work in changing welfare states: Nordic care workers' experiences. *European Journal of Ageing*, 9(2), pp. 119–29. Available at: https://link.springer.com/article/10.1007/s10433-012-0219-7 [accessed 30.05.2017].

Ulmanen, P., 2015. *Omsorgens pris i åtstramningstid* [The cost of caring in the Swedish welfare state]. Stockholm University. Available at: www.diva-portal.org/smash/get/diva2:858835/FULLTEXT01.pdf [accessed 30.05.2017].

Ulmanen, P. and Szebehely, M., 2015. From the state to the family or to the market? Consequences of reduced residential eldercare in Sweden. *International Journal of Social Welfare*, 24(1), pp. 81–92. DOI: 10.1111/ijsw.12108.

Vabø, M. and Szebehely, M., 2012. A caring state for all older people? In A. Anttonen, L. Häikiö and K. Stefánsson, eds. *Welfare state, universalism and diversity.* Cheltenham: Edward Elgar, pp. 121–43.

Verbeek, H., Van Rossum, E., Zwakhalen, S.M.G., Kempen, G.I.J.M. and Hamers, J.P.H., 2009. Small, homelike care environments for older people with dementia: a literature review. *International Psychogeriatrics*, 21, pp. 252–64. DOI: 10.1186/1471-2318-9-3.

Wilson, N.L., Malmberg, B. and Zarit, S.H., 1993. Group homes for people with dementia: a Swedish example. *The Gerontologist*, 33(5), pp. 682–6. DOI: 10.1093/geront/33.5.682.

Work Environment Authority, 2007. *Belastningsergonomiska risker vid vårdarbete i enskilt hem* [Ergonomic risks in care work in private homes]. Korta sifferfakta no. 11. Stockholm: Arbetsmiljöverket. Available at: www.av.se/arbetsmiljoarbete-och-inspektioner/arbetsmiljostatistik-officiell-arbetsskadestatstik/faktablad-om-arbetsmiljostatistik/ [accessed 30.05.2017].

Work Environment Authority, 2014. *Inspections of female and male dominated municipal activities, home care services and technical administration.* Report 3/2014. Stockholm: Arbetsmiljöverket. Available at: www.av.se/globalassets/filer/publikationer/rapporter/inspections-of-female-and-male-dominated-municipal-activities-home-care-services-and-technicaladministration-report-2014-3-eng.pdf [accessed 05.04.2017].

Work Environment Authority, 2015. *Sociala och organisatoriska orsaker* [Social and organizational causes]. Korta arbetsskadefakta no. 6. Stockholm: Arbetsmiljöverket. Available at: www.av.se/globalassets/filer/statistik/arbetsmiljostatistik-sociala-och-organisatoriska-orsaker-faktablad-2015-06.pdf [accessed 30.05.2017].

Wærness, K., 1984. The rationality of caring. *Economic and Industrial Democracy*, 5(2), pp. 185–211. Available at: http://journals.sagepub.com/doi/pdf/10.1177/0143831X8452003 [accessed 30.05.2017].

Part II
Northern and Western Europe

4

Long-term care reforms in the Netherlands

Care work at stake

Barbara Da Roit

Introduction

The Dutch government introduced, as early as 1968, a compulsory insurance meant to finance healthcare costs deemed as 'uninsurable' under the regular healthcare insurance system. The Exceptional Health Expenditure Law (AWBZ, *Algemene Wet Bijzondere Ziektenkosten*), initially funding residential care costs, expanded over time to cover an increasing range of services (Van den Heuvel, 1997). Notwithstanding many institutional differences, the long-term care (LTC) system grew as generous and universalistic as those of the Nordic countries. The access to care was based on individual rights of residents and on (increasingly) standardized assessment procedures and resource allocation. Despite alternate phases of expansion and containment, the policy's coverage and expenditure grew considerably until the first half of the 2000s (Da Roit 2012a, 2012b). State intervention was based on funding and regulation. Care service provision was assured by a large non-profit sector (Meijer et al., 2000) growing out of the tradition of the Dutch 'pillarized' system: before the consolidation of the Dutch welfare state, a number of organizations existed with a confessional or political background (Protestant, Catholic, socialist or liberal) providing care, housing, education and leisure. Alongside the secularization of Dutch society since the 1970s, these original care organizations were often brought together into bigger service providers in the non profit sector. The market was hardly present in the sector until the 1990s.

Informal care in the Dutch context remained of great importance even after the development of LTC policies. However, similarly to the Nordic countries, the care provided by informal caregivers was hardly present in the form of bodily care, but rather focused on emotional and organizational support. It was widespread, but mainly voluntary, and 'light', entailing a few hours a week of support (Da Roit 2010; Haberkern and Szydlik, 2010; Brandt et al., 2009).

Therefore, care work in the Netherlands is increasingly understood since the 1960s and the 1970s as a (semi-)professionalized activity and offered ample employment opportunities, mainly to women, within a relatively well-regulated non-profit sector. Self-employment only concerned a minority of workers performing exclusively household chores (*alphahulpen*) and directly hired by the users. All other care workers would be employed by non-profit organizations at different levels of training and qualification (Arts, 2000), alongside nurses. As the Dutch

LTC sector integrated health, social and home help activities, care workers, besides *alphahulpen* and lower-qualified employees, often performed different types of tasks ranging from nursing, to caring, to support.

The 1990s inaugurated a season of LTC reforms that is not yet concluded. While the 1990s and early 2000s attempts to reduce costs while maintaining universalism did not produce sizeable changes, since the mid-2000s a more radical strategy has been implemented. The introduction of the Social Support Act (Wmo, *Wet maatschappelijk ondersteuning*) in 2007 and the new LTC legislation of 2015 (Wlz, *Wet langdurige zorg*) are the two landmarks of a process elsewhere labelled as the 'hollowing out' of the national LTC insurance (Da Roit, 2012a). This new strategy is based on a combination of vertical and horizontal decentralization of care responsibilities and budget cutbacks. First, alongside restricted access to residential care, families and other informal networks' members are asked to contribute more to care arrangements. Second, only the needs of people with severe limitations are being covered by a new and more limited in scope national LTC scheme, mostly but not necessarily in residential settings. Third, for those falling out of the new national LTC scheme, the funding and regulation of home nursing – including medical care and personal care with bathing, dressing, undressing, etc. – is being devolved to healthcare insurances and to municipal 'social' home care, that is, support with everyday activities and with housework. Fourth, the new configuration of responsibilities and functions rests on diminished resources.

These transformations have important consequences not only for people with LTC needs and their kin, but also for care workers. This chapter scrutinizes how care work has been framed and understood in the debate on the LTC reforms, and how the latter are likely to transform care employment, the meaning and boundaries of different forms of care work and the position of (different types of) care workers.

Analytical framework

Care policies play a large role in care employment and in defining the characteristics of care work. Social policies define the division of responsibilities between the public and private sphere impacting on the dimensions of the care sector. Moreover, they largely determine employment relations and paid care workers' professional profiles. The diverse development of social services in Europe and its impact on employment structure represents a core issue within welfare regime theory (Esping-Andersen, 1990). Given their labour-intensive character, care services are unlikely to benefit from productivity gains, and their cost increases rapidly relative to that of goods, giving rise to the 'cost-disease' problem (Baumol, 1967). This raises the question of who will pay for care services. The literature shows that three ideal-typical solutions to the cost disease may be found (Folbre and Nelson, 2000; Esping-Andersen, 1999; Skolka, 1977).

The first solution entails placing the burden of service production on the families through unpaid care. Care is here 'familialized', being both a responsibility of and provided by (female) family members. Familialization can be by default (i.e. the state takes for granted that family members will care) or supported (i.e. the state provides money to sustain informal care) (Saraceno and Keck, 2010). Within this configuration, the increasing care costs are 'hidden' within families. Limited public expenditure goes along with limited female employment because of the lack of employment opportunities and of chances for conciliating care and work. This solution is typical of the conservative/corporatist welfare regime (Esping-Andersen, 1990, 1999).

The second way out of the cost disease consists in limited public intervention and low regulation in the care sector that allows, thanks to low-waged and low-protected jobs, the creation of a care market accessible to a large population. While the responsibility of care remains with the individuals (and families), care delivery occurs in the market. This model shares with the previous one limited public expenditure. However, it displays higher female employment alongside unstable, low-end jobs and lower-quality services. This solution is typical of the liberal welfare regime (Esping-Andersen, 1990, 1999).

The third solution to Baumol's cost disease consists of high investment by the public sector, which fosters an extensive supply of social services and the growth of (public or publicly regulated) employment. In this model, care is de-familialized, de-marketized and professionalized. The main problem encountered by this configuration is the level and dynamics of public expenditure. This solution is associated with the social democratic welfare regime (Esping-Andersen, 1990, 1999).

Despite some fluctuations, Dutch LTC policies have known an exceptional development until recently. The configuration of care work approaches the social democratic solution to the cost-disease problem, where costs represent a constant challenge. In the Dutch case, this was reflected in a continuous attempt to strike a balance between universalism and cost control (Da Roit, 2012a). Since the early 1990s, the costs of LTC emerged as a policy issue in relation to the ageing of the population, alongside more restrictive economic and social policies.

Addressing rising care costs, LTC systems that resemble the social democratic model involve: (1) increasing productivity within the given set-up; (2) re-familializing care responsibilities and tasks; and (3) marketizing care provision.

While the use of technology remains limited in care, increasing productivity requires reducing to a minimum the labour needed to perform tasks. This goes under the umbrella term of Taylorization of care: the fragmentation of care activities into specific tasks, sequencing and timing (Knijn, 2001).

Re-familialization entails that functions taken up by the welfare state are no longer covered by public schemes and that a call on family members or other informal caregivers is made to take up more responsibilities. This strategy is expected to reduce the pressure on public budgets. The (re)development of informal care can be supported by the state through cash-for-care provisions, considered to be less expensive than services in kind (Da Roit and Le Bihan, 2010).

The marketization of care can be pursued in different ways. First, the private sector can be designated as the preferred provider of care within publicly funded services through subcontracting or quasi-markets (Le Grand, 1991). Second, final users can be provided with cash-for-care benefits to be spent in the market (Da Roit and Le Bihan, 2010). Third, families under the increasing pressure of needs and the decreasing availability of care may decide to purchase market services.

All three directions of change – widely undertaken by Dutch LTC reforms – are likely to have important consequences for the professionalization of care, for the dimensions and features of the care sector as an employer, and for working conditions in care. Care policy reforms are by no means the only reasons for the transformation of care work. More general changes in Dutch labour market regulation – the trend towards more flexible employment, activation, the role of collective national agreements – are very likely to affect work both in the care sector and in other areas. However, the changes that the Dutch LTC has recently undergone are likely to have profound impact on the social regulation of care and care work.

Aims, data and methods

The first objective of the chapter is to understand the rationale of the recent reforms and how care work has been framed in the debate. In order to place the recent reforms in the longer-term LTC transformation, the reform attempts enacted from the 1990s to the early 2000s and their consequences for care work are reconstructed based on the results of previous own research (Da Roit 2010, 2012a, 2012b). Furthermore, the ways in which the problem of care work has been framed in the debate surrounding the recent LTC reforms is based on analysis of policy documents (between 2005 and 2015). The analysis starts with scrutiny of the *Memorie van Toelichting* (MvT) of the two main reforms – the 2007 Social Support Act and the 2015 LTC reform. An MvT is an explanatory memorandum that accompanies bills offering an overview of the reform aims, of the choices made, of the debates about the proposal, the stakeholders' and government's standpoints. The MvT of the 2007 Social Support Act (Tweede Kamer – Second Chamber [TK], 2005) and of the 2015 LTC reform (TK, 2014) therefore represent a good basis for understanding the rationale of the reforms. Alongside MvTs, governmental and stakeholders' perspectives on care work are reconstructed based on governmental statements, ministerial letters to the parliament, parliamentary notes and Q&A sessions. These materials have been selected through a keywords search (care AND work, employment, professionals, labour market) in two publicly available databases (www.overheid.nl and www.rijksoverheid. nl). In addition, the five reports of an independent commission designated by the government to follow up the decentralization process in social policy at large (Transitiecommissie Sociaal Domein – Transition Committee on Social Domain [TSD], 2014, 2015a, 2015b, 2016a, 2016b) have been consulted.

The second objective of the chapter is to shed light into the transformations of care work as a consequence of the 2007 reforms onwards, by looking at policy evaluations, labour market data, analyses and forecasts. While the 2015 reform has not yet been fully evaluated, the Social Support Act was the object of extensive evaluations (Kromhout et al., 2014; De Klerk et al., 2010). The authoritative source on labour market developments in the Netherlands are reports by the Employee Insurance Agency (Uitvoeringsinstituut Werknemersverzekeringen, UWV), commissioned by the Ministry of Social Affairs and Employment (Ministerie van Sociale Zaken en Werkgelegenheid, SZW). The chapter makes use of the UWV report published on the care labour market (UWV, 2015). The report is based on different data sources, including that of the research programme *Care and welfare labour market* (*Onderzoeksprogramma Arbeidsmarkt Zorg en Welzijn* – AZW) (UWV, 2015, p. 6). AZW data have been directly consulted (at www. azwinfo.nl/jive/).

Cutting costs while maintaining universalism: shift from the early 1990s to the mid-2000s

Between the early 1990s and early 2000s, there have been continuous attempts to reduce LTC expenditure, increase users' choice, shift responsibilities from the state to families and communities, and increase efficiency in the provision of formal care. Neo-liberal and communitarian ideas and the calls of patients' organizations for more flexible, less bureaucratic and more tailor-made care converged with the urge for budget containment. However, consensus was created around cost-containment measures that should not endanger the LTC policy architecture. As shown elsewhere (Da Roit, 2012a, 2012b), these attempts were based on the tightening of eligibility criteria, the introduction of market principles, New Public Management ideas (Ferlie et al., 1996) and the emphasis on informal care.

First, the introduction of competition mechanisms allowed the entry of private providers into a newly created care quasi-market (Knijn and Verhagen, 2007), therefore diversifying employment conditions in the care sector (Da Roit, 2012a, 2012b).

Second, the Taylorization of care changed work organization (Knijn, 2001): the fragmentation of tasks into elementary units performed by different professionals working in a sequence reduced the complexity of tasks undertaken by individual workers and their degree of professionalism. The attempt here was to increase productivity and reduce costs.

Third, the introduction of the personal budget – a benefit alternative to services that could be used to hire informal caregivers or to purchase market care – further opened up the care sector to private entrepreneurs and self-employment, stimulated entrepreneurship among care workers, but also paved the way to new forms of care employment and to the de-professionalization of care work. In fact, the possibility to pay informal caregivers supported the idea that care is not necessarily a professional activity requiring specific knowledge, training, supervision, etc., but one that can be performed by anyone chosen by care users. Through the personal budget, a new profile of care worker emerged based on a contract between an individual user and an individual worker. While this construction allowed the recognition of informal care, it also entailed nonstandard and less protected forms of employment (Grootegoed et al., 2010).

The reforms adopted up to the first half of the 2000s played an important role in introducing new ideas about care work, but they did not structurally change Dutch LTC policies nor care employment. LTC expenditure kept rising (Eggink et al., 2008), even if the cost of labour was kept under control (Da Roit, 2012a). Despite some fluctuations, employment in the sector kept growing until the early 2000s (Eggink et al., 2010). Marketization happened to a much lesser extent than expected (Da Roit, 2012a, 2012b). The substitution of formal care with informal care through the personal budget was also limited: despite the personal budget growth, services in kind remained the backbone of the Dutch LTC system, cash-for-care benefits used to compensate informal caregivers were often paid to relatives who had already been caring for free (Grootegoed et al., 2010), and a considerable number of personal budget claimants were new LTC clients.

It was only in the mid-2000s that a more radical strategy emerged, more explicitly limiting the scope of the LTC national scheme and devolving part of its responsibilities to other sectors of social protection or directly to the individuals and their families. The first signs of this new direction emerged with the introduction of the new Social Support Act in 2007. The strategy was then completed with the overall reform of the LTC sector in 2015.

Rationale and (non-)debates around the 2007 Social Support Act and the 2015 long-term care reform: LTC back to basics

The MvT of the 2007 Social Support Act (TK, 2005) argues that due to socio-economic and demographic developments and to the rising costs of LTC insurance, 'a new balance in responsibility' is needed: 'social capital', 'participation', mutual support, voluntary work and informal care should be supported (TK, 2005, p. 2). According to the government, the existing LTC system expanded well beyond the funding of care costs that are 'uninsurable' – as meant by the 1968 Exceptional Health Expenditure Law – and therefore needs to be brought back to its initial purposes: taking support with housework out of the package insured under this law is explicitly a 'first step' towards a 'smaller' LTC scheme (TK, 2005, p. 3).

The 2007 reform can be seen as a turning point in the long-lasting transformation process of LTC. The explanatory notes for the 2007 Social Support Act already indicated that the target of the LTC scheme should be 'people with very serious and long-term care needs' (TK, 2005, p. 2). This view came to its climax with the abolition of the Exceptional Health Expenditure Law and its substitution by the new Long-Term Care Act (Wlz) in 2015. In fact, the new 2015 LTC scheme only covers care costs of people with round-the-clock care needs in institutions and at home, while all other care has been shifted to the healthcare insurance system (nursing at home) or to municipalities (social support). The government's motivation rests on three principles: (1) increasing quality, mainly meant as provision tailored to individual needs and client involvement; (2) fostering self-help and informal support before professional care is provided in order to increase solidarity in the community and save resources; and (3) reducing costs in order to ensure the long-term financial sustainability of the care system (TK, 2014, pp. 5–6). Two interrelated aspects in the debate on the LTC reforms since 2007 are striking: the high level of consensus on which the political and policy process rested, and the omission of a number of topics in the political and policy debate.

The entire debate about LTC reforms in the Netherlands has been surrounded by a sense of inevitability, shared by policymakers and stakeholders. Just as in the 1990s, neo-liberal and communitarian ideas were embraced by both the centre-right and the centre-left of the political arena (Kremer, 2006), and no opposition emerged against the decomposition of the Exceptional Health Expenditure Law. If in the 1990s the political consensus was on the need to reduce costs while maintaining universalism (Da Roit, 2012a), it then shifted to the need to change the system and reduce universalism in order to maintain solidarity towards the neediest. The sense of inevitability of the reform was shared not only by coalition parties, but also by client organizations, professional organizations and representatives of the Dutch municipalities. In reaction to the bill proposal, client organizations raised issues related to coordination, the centrality of the clients and their say (TK, 2014, pp. 89–90); professional organizations were concerned with administrative procedures, coordination and specific target groups' needs; and the municipalities raised concerns about the division of responsibilities in specific cases (TK, 2014, pp. 90–4). Even among care providers, directly affected by cutbacks, there was hardly any opposition, despite criticism about the abrupt pace of the reforms (e.g. Panteia-SEOR-Etil, 2013, p. 73).

The consensus built around the reforms was also the result of marginalization of two crucial issues. First, concerns about the diminished accessibility of care, the resizing of social rights and the rise of social inequalities remained, until recently, confined to an academic and media debate, hardly discussed in the political arena. While territorial inequalities have been occasionally touched upon (TSD, 2016c; Van Nijendaal, 2014, p. 91; Deelstra, 2008, p. 29), possible inequalities within municipalities have been only very recently addressed (Da Roit and Thomese, 2016; TSD, 2016c). Second, the reforms' consequences for care work were discussed at a rather late stage and considered as an inevitable by-product of the reform.

Job losses as 'inevitable evil'

The labour market consequences of the reform were hardly debated prior to the adoption of the 2007 Social Support Act. The trade unions did express their concerns about employment during the consultations and argued that the introduction of the Act should not lead to employment loss and decreasing quality (TK, 2014). On that occasion, the government declared that no cutbacks would accompany the introduction of the bill, and therefore no job losses could be expected. The point was therefore removed from the table.

The scenario, however, rapidly changed, when it became clear that further LTC reforms would indeed entail cutbacks. The foreseen job losses became then an 'inevitable evil'.

In a letter to the parliament, the Minister of Health, Well-Being and Sport and the State Secretary to Social Affairs illustrate their 'vision' on care work in relation to the LTC reform (Ministerie VWS, 2013):

> We are very much aware that these transformations will not be easy. Yet we consider them necessary for sustainable care. The entire Netherlands is liable for contributing to care costs. We have to deal thriftily and carefully with this. Even if this sometimes means uncertainty and job losses.
>
> *(Ministerie VWS, 2013, p. 2, own translation)*

The letter continues by saying that there is a need to balance between the necessary flexibility of the sector and employees' security. Yet the responsibility for managing this transition rests on the stakeholders in the field (municipalities, insurance companies, unions, providers). The care labour market projections presented would be useful for the stakeholders to 'prepare themselves' for the future (Ministerie VWS, 2013, p. 4). It was announced that there would be a loss of 22,000 full-time jobs (36,000 employees) between 2013 and 2015 (Ministerie VWS, 2013, p. 5). What the government could do was use temporary funds so that the job losses in the field had a more gradual character (see also Ministerie VWS, 2014, pp. 8–10). It was also made clear that the restructuring of the sectors would entail not only less employment opportunities, but also a reshaped composition of the labour force. The government expected an increase of the needed qualifications and the 'exit' of lower qualified workers. More autonomy and reliance on the informal network should reduce the need to provide simple and practical support, while there should be an increasing need of professionals able to solve problems, coordinate, support and perform more complex tasks (Ministerie VWS, 2013, p. 7).

The government's announcements over the reform plans and the consequences for care work and the adoption of the reform itself were accompanied by protests set up by trade unions: collection of signatures against the reform, demonstrations (e.g. the campaign '*red de zorg*' ['save the care'] of FNV [Federatie Nederlandse Vakbeweging – the Netherlands Trade Union Federation]) and requests to revise the government's plans (FNV, 2015).

However, the consequences of the reform for care work have never really entered the political debate. The MvT of the 2015 reform, for instance, does not address employment issues (TK, 2014). The focus has rather been on cases of care organizations' bankruptcy (e.g. Van Rijn, 2016), on occurrences of substitution of regular employment by self-employment (e.g. Van Rijn, 2015).

While employment in care has not become a crucial policy issue, there is evidence that the Dutch LTC reforms are drastically reshaping care work, both quantitatively and qualitatively.

A new configuration of care work?

The reforms have impacted on the dimension of the care sector, and therefore on employment opportunities, especially for women. Moreover, the content and boundaries of care work are being questioned and redefined.

LTC jobs: shrinking, flexibilizing, professionalizing

As shown by UWV (2015, p. 2) data, the Dutch care sector at large counted approximately 1.1 million employees and represented 15 per cent of all jobs in 2013. The largest sub-sector is the LTC one, identified as 'nursing, caring and home care' (VVT, *verpleeging, verzorging en thuiszorg*): it accounts for 38 per cent of all jobs in care (UWV, 2015, p. 2). While other sectors have suffered from the financial crisis since the late 2000s, employment in care and in LTC continued to grow between 2008 and 2013 by 13 per cent and 19 per cent, respectively. However, as a consequence of government policies, the number of employees stopped growing in 2012 and dropped by 32,000 positions (14,000 full-time equivalents) between 2012 and 2014 (Figure 4.1).

The UWV (2015) forecast is that of a shrinking LTC sector until 2017, and of very moderate growth thereafter.

Not only has employment in LTC been shrinking, it has also been changing. First, in the past few years, self-employment has expanded. In eldercare, where self-employment was traditionally marginal, the number of self-employed doubled between 2009 and 2013, reaching 11,000 positions (CBS, 2015). Even if the flexibilization of work is a general trend in the Netherlands

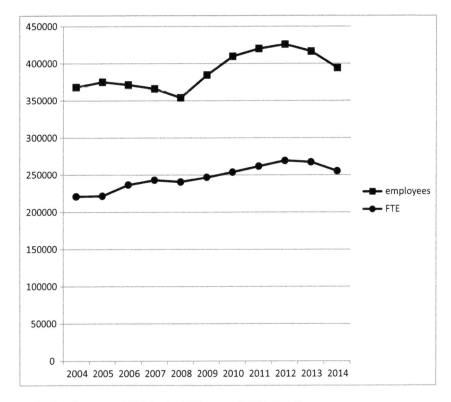

Figure 4.1 Employees and FTE in the LTC sector (2004–2014)

Source: Elaboration based on AZW data available at www.azwinfo.nl/jive/.

and flexible work remains relatively limited in care (cf. Van Echtelt et al., 2016, p. 32), the reforms did contribute to it. As a response to policy change and to related uncertainties, employers in the sector have adopted a flexibilization strategy. They reduced the number of 'stable' jobs by not replacing outgoing employees, and they often applied fixed-term contracts to the incoming personnel in order to maintain flexibility in the workforce (Panteia-SEOR-Etil, 2013, p. 73). Care employment at lower levels is particularly suffering from care organizations' policies (Panteia-SEOR-Etil, 2013, p. 75).

Also, the workers' perception of their conditions changed as a consequence of the reforms. While the employees' satisfaction in the care sector remains high, it has considerably diminished in the past few years. In 2015, around 70 per cent of the surveyed employees in the LTC sector found that work pressure had increased over the previous year, and 63 per cent had a similar expectation for the future (Evers et al., 2015, pp. 22–3). Of all respondents expecting increased pressure, 97 per cent consider this a direct consequence of government policies (Evers et al., 2015, p. 23).

Jobs pushed out of the core LTC sector: informalization and de-professionalization

Alongside changes in the quantity and quality of employment, the reform is having an effect on the boundaries of care work. This involves the redefinition of professional care as opposed to informal care, as well as the exclusion of jobs from the LTC sector.

One remarkable feature of care work in the 'old' Dutch LTC sector was its integration. Different jobs oriented to nursing, caring, cleaning and supporting were all considered part of the complexities of care. The recent reforms have split policy responsibilities between different levels of government and, in doing so, defined previously non-existing boundaries between care workers.

As shown above, the care work remaining under the newly defined national LTC sector consists of a core of selected higher-skilled professionals. The same can be said for the funding and regulation of home nursing now falling under the health insurers' responsibility. Housework and daily support, now falling under the responsibility of the municipalities, are being pushed out of the domain of professional care, towards marketized, informal, and de-professionalized forms of support. There is evidence, for instance, of the increasing importance of cleaning companies either as contractors of the municipalities or as subcontractors of care organizations as providers of home help (Research for Beleid, 2007). In other words, the pressure towards cost containment put on the municipalities paved the way to the contracting of services at lower prices outside the traditional care sector and within a commercial sector, that of cleaning companies, in which employment is less protected and paid. It should be noted that the national collective agreement of workers in the care sector is distinct from that of the cleaning sector.

Employment reduction and segmentation: discussion and conclusion

With the introduction of the Exceptional Health Expenditure Law in 1968, the Dutch LTC system developed based on principles very close to the ideal-typical social democratic response to the dilemmas of care services, even if with some oscillations: high and increasing public investments in care services, large and growing relatively protected and increasingly professionalized employment, and wide availability and accessibility of high-quality care services.

The recent reforms are likely to have a profound impact on care work, in three ways.

First, the 2007 Social Support Act and the 2015 LTC reform contribute to the segmentation of care employment. As a consequence of the decentralization process started with the 2007 Act, the devolution of home help to the municipalities marked the separation between the care sector in a strict sense and home help. The 'core' LTC sector newly defined in 2015 has further been shrinking and undergoing a process of professionalization. By contrast, home help, now excluded from 'proper' LTC, has become closer to the cleaning sector. The latter is an employment area where the lower-qualified care workers excluded from LTC as a consequence of cutbacks are expected to find employment. These developments are likely to have great impact on employment opportunities and conditions of lower-qualified women. Job losses and the reduced employability in care of lower-qualified (and older) women were considered as an inevitable 'evil'. This is particularly striking in a time of policies strongly oriented to work activation.

Second, the reform's attempts to shift responsibilities to the families are likely to lead to the informalization and marketization of care work, both intended and unintended. As mentioned above, the explicit rationale of the recent Dutch LTC reforms consists of restricting access to formal care in order to foster informal care. The emphasis on informal care and the de-professionalization of basic formal care – already started with the introduction of the personal budget in the 1990s – is subsequently being reinforced, especially in the non-core LTC sector, that is, jobs excluded from the new LTC national scheme and home healthcare, now falling under municipal responsibility. Yet the extent to which the shift from public to private care is going to be successful is still under scrutiny. A few existing qualitative studies underline that 'going back' to the family is not straightforward, owing to strong values of autonomy among older people and their children (Grootegoed, 2013; Grootegoed and Van Dijk, 2012).

Quantitative evidence suggests that in the past few years there has been a reduction in the number of informal caregivers and of the proportion of people receiving informal care (Swinkels et al., 2015; Van Houwelingen and De Hart, 2013; Oudijk et al., 2010), even if caregiving has become more intense (Cloïn et al., 2013; Oudijk et al., 2010). In addition, studies available from other countries suggest that the reduction of formal care for older people is associated with higher levels of involvement of family members among lower social classes, while middle and upper middle classes tend to resort more to paid care (Pickard, 2012; Rostgaard and Szebehely, 2012; Johansson et al., 2003; Sundström et al., 2002). One should therefore allow for the possibility that substituting formal with informal care is hard to reach, and another development is likely: the development of a bigger care market, especially in the field of home help. It is worth underlining that the household services market in the Netherlands is largely unregulated, also as an explicit policy choice made by the Dutch government. There is evidence that this sector largely employs, among others, many (undocumented) migrants (Van Walsum, 2013).

Third, a further possibility towards the marketization, informalization and de-professionalization of segments of care work is linked to a recent and still limited phenomenon in the Netherlands: that of migrant care work. Care markets based on migrant workers in continental and Southern European countries developed as substitutes for, or complements to, family care (Da Roit and Weicht, 2013). The phenomenon of live-in migrant care workers caring for older people was until recently unknown in the Netherlands. High levels of formal care provision, regulated cash-for-care benefits, labour markets and migration had so far protected the Netherlands from the development of live-in migrant care markets (Da Roit and Weicht, 2013; Van Hooren, 2012). However, the emergence of a niche for live-in migrant care workers in the Dutch context (Da Roit and Van Bochove, 2015) signals that the market represents an alternative to family care in times of retrenchment. Though very limited, this arrangement does exist, fostered by increasing home care demands, especially among older people in need of continuous supervision. It has been suggested that the still largely available formal care, and mistrust towards atypical forms of care, have until now prevented the expansion of the phenomenon (Da Roit and Van Bochove, 2015). However, the transformation of the meaning of care entailed by the recent reforms might give grounds for this solution.

This chapter has outlined the strong link between care employment and care policies in the Netherlands. Since the policy trajectory is far from being stabilized, the full effects of the reforms on care work needs to be assessed in the future.

References

Arts S.E.J., 2002. *Caring as an occupation: content and quality of working life among home helps*. Utrecht: Nivel – Universiteit van Maastricht. Available at: https://cris.maastrichtuniversity.nl/portal/files/760563/guid-b98a9c50-2712-4a63-85ee-a4242dbcfb7c-ASSET1.0 [accessed 18.05.17].

Baumol, W.,1967. The macroeconomics of unbalanced growth. *American Economic Review*, 57, pp. 415–26.

Brandt, M., Haberkern, K. and Szydlik, M., 2009. Intergenerational help and care in Europe. *European Sociological Review*, 25(5), pp. 585–601. DOI: 10.1093/esr/jcn076.

CBS (Centraal Bureau voor de Statistiek), 2015. *Minder werknemers, maar meer zelfstandigen in de zorg* [Less employees but more self-employed in the care sector]. Available at: www.cbs.nl/nl-nl/nieuws/2015/11/minder-werknemers-maar-meer-zelfstandigen-in-de-zorg [accessed 14.07.2017].

Cloïn, M. et al. 2013 *Met het oog op de tijd. Een blik op de tijdsbesteding van Nederlanders* [With an eye on time: a look on the time use of Dutch people]. The Hague: SCP.

Da Roit, B., 2010. Strategies of care: changing elderly care in Italy and the Netherlands. Amsterdam: Amsterdam University Press.

Da Roit, B., 2012a. Long-term care reforms in the Netherlands. In C. Ranci and E. Pavolini, eds. *Reforms in long-term care policies in Europe*. New York: Springer, pp. 97–115.

Da Roit, B., 2012b. The Netherlands: the struggle between universalism and cost containment. *Health and Social Care in the Community*, 20(3), pp. 228–37. DOI: 10.1177/0958928713499175.

Da Roit, B. and Le Bihan, B., 2010. Similar and yet so different: cash-for-care in six European countries' long-term care policies. *Milbank Quarterly*, 88(3), pp. 286–309. DOI: 10.1111/j.1468-0009.2010.00601.

Da Roit, B. and Thomese, G.C.F., 2016. Maakt lokale thuiszorg zorg (on)gelijker? Sociaaleconomische ongelijkheid in de toegang tot huishoudelijke zorg binnen Nederlandse gemeenten voor en na de invoering van de WMO [Is more local care more unequal? Socio-economic inequalities in the access to home help within Dutch municipalities after the implementation of the new Social Support Act]. *Mens en Maatschappij*, 91(4), pp. 381–403.

Da Roit, B. and Van Bochove, M., 2017. Migrant care work going Dutch? The emergence of a live-in migrant care market and the restructuring of the Dutch long-term care system. *Social Policy and Administration*, 51(1), pp. 76-94. DOI: 10.1111/spol.12174.

Da Roit, B. and Weicht, B., 2013. Migrant care work and care, migration and employment regimes: a fuzzy-set analysis. *Journal of European Social Policy*, 23(5), pp. 469–86. DOI: 10.1177/0958928713499175.

Deelstra, W.F., 2008. *Huishoudelijke verzorging en de Wmo* [Home help and the Social Support Act]. Houten: Bohn Stafleu van Loghum.

De Klerk, M., Gilsing, R. and Timmermans, J., eds., 2010. *Op Weg met de Wmo. Evaluatie van de Wet maatschappelijke ondersteuning 2007–2009* [On the way with the Social Support Act: evaluation 2007–2009]. The Hague: SCP. March 2010. Available at: www.scp.nl/Publicaties/Alle_publicaties/Publicaties_2010/Op_weg_met_de_Wmo [accessed 14.07.2017].

Eggink, E., Pommer, E. and Woittiez, I., 2008. *De ontwikkeling van AWBZ-uitgaven. Een analyse van awbz-uitgaven 1985–2005 en een raming van de uitgaven voor verpleging en verzorging 2005–2030* [The development of the AWBZ expenditures: an analysis of AWBZ expenditure 1985–2005 and estimates of care expenditures 2005–2030]. The Hague: Sociaal en Cultureel Planbureau.

Eggink E., Oudijk D. and Woittiez, I., 2010. *Zorgen voor zorg. Ramingen van de vraag naar personeel in de verpleging en verzorging tot 2030* [Caring for care: estimates of the demand of care personnel until 2030]. The Hague: Sociaal en Cultureel Planbureau.

Esping-Andersen, G., 1990. *The three worlds of welfare capitalism*. Cambridge: Polity Press.

Esping-Andersen, G., 1999. *The social foundations of postindustrial economies*. Oxford: Oxford University Press.

Evers, G., Jettinghoff, K. and Van Essen, G., 2015. *Effecten van beleidsmaatregelen op de arbeidsmarkt in de zorg en WJK, AZW: Onderzoeksprogramma Arbeidsmarkt, Zorg en Welzijn* [Policy effects on the care and welfare labour market: research programme Labour Market, Care and Welfare]. Available at: www.publicatiesarbeidsmarktzorgenwelzijn.nl/werkgeversenquete-2015-meting-april-juni-2015/ [accessed 14.07.2017].

Ferlie, E., Ashburner, L., Fitzgerald, L. and Pettigrew, A., 1996. *The new public management in action*. Oxford: Oxford University Press.

FNV (Federatie Nederlandse Vakbeweging), 2015. *Letter to the Ministry of Health, Wellbeing and Sport*, 15.04.2015. Available at: www.fnv.nl/site/nieuws/webassistent/a.zegers/FNV_wil_einde_aan_goed nieuwsshow_Kabinet_over_zorg_en_stelt_ultimatum/brief_fnv_aan_staatssecretaris_van_rijn_over_goede_zorg.pdf [accessed 14.07.2017].

Folbre, N. and Nelson, J.A., 2000. For love or money – or both? *The Journal of Economic Perspectives*, 14(4), pp. 123–40. DOI: 10.1257/jep.14.4.123.

Grootegoed, E., 2013. *Dignity of dependence: welfare state reform and the struggle for respect*. PhD thesis, Amsterdam Institute for Social Science Research (AISSR).

Grootegoed, E. and Van Dijk, D., 2012. The return of the family? Welfare state retrenchment and client autonomy in long-term care. *Journal of Social Policy*, 41(4), pp. 677–94. DOI: https://doi.org/10.1017/S0047279412000311.

Grootegoed, E., Knijn, B. and Da Roit, B., 2010. Relatives as paid care-givers: how family carers experience payments for care. *Ageing and Society*, 30(3), pp. 467–89. DOI: https://doi.org/10.1017/S0144686X09990456.

Haberkern, K. and Szydlik, M., 2010. State care provision, societal opinion and children's care of older parents in 11 European countries. *Ageing and Society*, 30(2), pp. 299–323. DOI: https://doi.org/10.1017/S0144686X09990316.

Johansson, L, Sundström, G. and Hassing, L.B., 2003. State provision down, offspring's up: the reverse substitution of old-age care in Sweden. *Ageing and Society*, 23(3), pp. 269–80. DOI: https://doi.org/10.1017/S0144686X02001071.

Knijn, T., 2001. Care work: innovations in the Netherlands. In M. Daly, ed. *Care work: the quest for security*. Geneva: ILO. pp. 159–74.

Knijn, T. and Verhagen, S., 2007. Contested professionalism: payments for care and the quality of home care. *Administration and Society*, 39(4), pp. 451–75. DOI: 10.1177/0095399707300520.

Kremer, M., 2006. Consumers in charge: the Dutch personal budget and its impact on the market, professionals and the family. *European Societies*, 8(3), pp. 385–401. DOI: 10.1080/14616690600822006.

Kromhout, M., Feijten, P., Vonk, F., de Klerk, M., Marangos, A.M., Mensink, W., et al. 2014. *De wmo in beweging. Evaluatie wet maatschappelijke ondersteuning 2010–2012* [The Social Support Act on the move: evaluation 2010–2012]. The Hague: SCP. May 2014. Available at: www.scp.nl/Publicaties/Alle_publicaties/Publicaties_2014/De_WMO_in_beweging [accessed 14.07.2017].

Le Grand, J., 1991. Quasi markets and care policies. *The Economic Journal*, 101(408), pp. 1256–67.

Meijer, A., Van Campen, C. and Kerkstra, A., 2000. Comparative study of the financing, provision and quality of care in nursing homes. The approach of four European countries: Belgium, Denmark, Germany and the Netherlands. *Journal of Advanced Nursing*, 32(3), pp. 554–61. DOI: http://dx.doi.org/10.1080/14616690600822006.

Ministerie VWS (Ministerie van Volkgezoindheid, Welzijn en Sport), 2013. *Kamerbrief: visie op de arbeidsmarkt in de zorg en ondersteuning* [Letter to the Second Chamber: vision on the care and support labour market]. 25.10.2013. Available at: www.rijksoverheid.nl/documenten/kamerstukken/2013/10/25/kamerbrief-over-visie-op-de-arbeidsmarkt-in-de-zorg-en-ondersteuning [accessed 14.07.2017].

Ministerie VWS (Ministerie van Volkgezoindheid, Welzijn en Sport), 2014. *Kamerbrief. Stand van zaken arbeidsmarkt in de zorg* [Letter to the Second Chamber: state of affairs on the care labour market]. 07.07.2014. Available at: www.rijksoverheid.nl/documenten/kamerstukken/2014/07/07/kamerbrief-stand-van-zaken-arbeidsmarkt-zorg [accessed 14.07.2017].

Oudijk, D., de Boer, A., Woittiez, I., Timmermans, J. and de Klerk, M., 2010. *Mantelzorg uit de doeken* [Informal care revealed]. The Hague: SCP. Available at: www.scp.nl/Publicaties/Alle_publicaties/Publicaties_2010/Mantelzorg_uit_de_doeken [accessed 14.07.2017].

Panteia-SEOR-Etil, 2013. *Arbeidsmarkteffecten maatregelen AWBZ en Wmo en stelselwijziging JZ* [Labour market effects of the Exceptional Health Expenditure Law and Social Support Act and system changes in youth care]. Zoetermeer, October 2013. Available at: www.etil.nl/wp-content/uploads/2014/03/eindrapport-AER-LZenO-okt-2013.ashx_.pdf [accessed 14.07.2017].

Pickard, L., 2012. Substitution between formal and informal care: a 'natural experiment' in social policy in Britain between 1985 and 2000. *Ageing and Society*, 32, pp. 1147–75. DOI: https://doi.org/10.1017/S0144686X11000833.

Research for Beleid, 2007. *Aanbesteding hulp bij het huishouden* [Tendering in home help]. Leiden: Eindrapport.

Rostgaard, T. and Szebehely, M., 2012. Changing policies, changing patterns of care: Danish and Swedish home care at the crossroads. *European Journal of Ageing*, 9(2), pp. 101–9.

Saraceno, C. and Keck, W., 2010. Can we identify intergenerational policy regimes in Europe? *European Societies*, 12(5), pp. 675–96. DOI: http://dx.doi.org/10.1080/14616696.2010.483006.

Skolka, J.V., 1977. Unbalanced productivity growth and the growth of public services. *Journal of Public Economics*, 7, pp. 271–80.

Sundström, G, Johansson, L. and Hassing, L.B., 2002. The shifting balance of long-term care in Sweden. *The Gerontologist*, 42(3), pp. 350–5. DOI: https://doi.org/10.1093/geront/42.3.350.

Swinkels, J.C., Suanet, B., Deeg, D.J.H. and Broese van Groenou, M.I., 2015. Trends in the informal and formal home-care use of older adults in the Netherlands between 1992 and 2012. *Ageing and Society*. DOI: https://doi.org/10.1017/S0144686X1500077X.

TK (Tweede Kamer), 2005. *Nieuwe regels betreffende maatschappelijkeondersteuning (Wet maatschappelijkeondersteuning). Memorie van Toeliching* [New rules concerning social support: explanatory memorandum]. 2004–2005, 30 131, no. 3. Available at: https://zoek.officielebekendmakingen.nl/kst-30131-3.html [accessed 14.07.2017].

TK (Tweede Kamer), 2014. *Memorie van toelichting. Wetvoorstel langdurige zorg* [Explanatory memorandum: law proposal for long-term care]. Available at: www.rijksoverheid.nl/documenten/kamerstukken/2014/03/10/memorie-van-toelichting-wet-langdurige-zorg [accessed 14.07.2017].

TSD (Transitiecommissie Sociaal Domein), 2014. *Eerste rapportage* [First report]. The Hague, 15.12.2014. Available at: www.rijksoverheid.nl/documenten/rapporten/2014/12/15/eerste-rapportage-transitiecommissie-sociaal-domein-tsd [accessed 14.07.2017].

TSD (Transitiecommissie Sociaal Domein), 2015a. *Tweede rapportage transitiecommissie sociaal domein 'duurzaam partnerschap en standaarden: basis voor transformatie'* [Second report transition committee social domain: 'sustainable partnership and standards: basis for transformation']. The Hague, 04.05.2015. Available at: www.rijksoverheid.nl/documenten/rapporten/2015/05/04/tweede-rapportage-transitie commissie-sociaal-domein [accessed 14.07.2017].

TSD (Transitiecommissie Sociaal Domein), 2015b. *Derde rapportage transitiecommissie sociaal domein 'mogelijk maken wat nodig is'* [Third report transition committee social domain 'making possible what is necessary']. The Hague, 03.09.2015. Available at: www.rijksoverheid.nl/documenten/rapporten/2015/09/03/derde-rapportage-transitiecommissie-sociaal-domein-mogelijk-maken-wat-nodig-is [accessed 14.07.2017].

TSD (Transitiecommissie Sociaal Domein), 2016a. *Vierde rapportage TSD: Eén sociaal domein* [Fourth report transition committee social domain: one social domain]. The Hague, 25.02.2016. Available at: www.rijksoverheid.nl/documenten/rapporten/2016/02/25/vierde-rapportage-transitiecommissie-sociaal-domein-tsd-een-sociaal-domein [accessed 14.07.2017].

TSD (Transitiecommissie Sociaal Domein), 2016b. *Vijfde rapportage TSD: Transformatie in het sociaal domein; de praktijk aan de macht* [Fifth report transition committee social domain]. The Hague, 30.09.2016. Available at: www.transitiecommissiesociaaldomein.nl/documenten/rapporten/2016/09/30/vijfde-rapportage-tsd-transformatie-in-het-sociaal-domein-de-praktijk-aan-de-macht [accessed 14.07.2017].

TSD (Transitiecommissie Sociaal Domein), 2016c. *De decentralisatie in het sociaal domein: wie houd er niet van kakelbont? Essays over de relatie tussen burger en bestuur* [Decentralization in the social domain: essays on the relationship between citizen and government]. The Hague, 21.01. 2016. Available at: www.transitiecommissiesociaaldomein.nl/documenten/publicaties/2016/01/21/transitiecommissie-sociaal-domein-essaybundel-spread [accessed 14.07.2017].

UWV, 2015. *Zorg. Sectorbeschrijving* [Care: sector description]. 16.06.2015. Available at: www.uwv.nl/overuwv/Images/Sectorbeschrijving%20Zorg%20def.pdf [accessed 14.07.2017].

Van den Heuvel, W., 1997. Policy towards the elderly: twenty-five years of Dutch experience. *Journal of Aging Studies*, 11(3), pp. 251–8.

Van Echtelt P., Croezen, S., Vlasblom, J.D., De Voogd-Hamelink, M. and Mattijssen, L., 2016. *Aanbod van arbeid 2016. Werken, zorgen en leren op een flexibele arbeidsmarkt* [Labour supply 2016: work, care and education in a flexible labour market]. The Hague: SCP. Available at: www.scp.nl/Publicaties/Alle_publicaties/Publicaties_2016/Aanbod_van_arbeid_2016 [accessed 14.07.2017].

Van Hooren, F., 2012. Varieties of migrant care work: comparing patterns of migrant labour in social care. *Journal of European Social Policy*, 22(2), pp. 133–47. DOI: http://dx.doi.org/10.1177 %2F0958928711433654.

Van Houwelingen, P. and De Hart, J., 2013. Maatschappelijke participatie: voor en met elkaar [Social participation: for and with each other]. In M. Cloïn, ed. *Met het oog op de tijd Een blik op de tijdsbesteding van Nederlanders* [With an eye on time: a look at the time use of Dutch people]. The Hague: SCP. Available at: www.scp.nl/Publicaties/Alle_publicaties/Publicaties_2013/Met_het_oog_op_de_tijd [accessed 14.07.2017].

Van Nijendaal, G.A., 2014. Drie decentralisaties in het sociale domein [Three decentralizations in the social domain]. In J.H.M. Donders and C.A. de Kam, eds. *Jaarboek Overheidsfinanciën 2014* [Yearbook of government's finances 2014]. The Hague: Wim Drees Stichting, pp. 85 100.

Van Rijn, M.J., 2015. Antwoorden op Kamervragen van het Kamerlid Siderius (SP) over thuiszorgorganisatie Vérian die zelfstandige thuishulpen vraagt na een massaontslag [Replies to questions of the Second Chamber's member concerning the home care organization Vérian seeking self-employed home help after mass redundancies]. Ingezonden 23.12.2014; 2014Z23916. Antwoord van de staatssecretaris van Volksgezondheid, Welzijn en Sport op Kamervragen [Answer from the Secretary of State for Public Health, Welfare and Sport on Chamber Questions], 05.04.2016. Available at: www.rijksoverheid.nl/zoeken?trefwoord=Antwoorden+op+Kamervragen+van+het+Kamerlid+Siderius+%28SP%29+over+thuiszorgorganisatie+V%C3%A9rian+die+zelfstandige+thuishulpen+vraagt+na+een+massaontslag [accessed 14.07.2017].

Van Rijn, M.J., 2016. *Stand van zaken na faillissement TSN Thuiszorg*. Brief van de staatssecretaris van Volksgezondheid, Welzijn en Sport aan de voorzitter van de tweede kamer, 05.04.2016 [State of the art after the bankruptcy of TSN Home care. Letter of the State Secretary for Health, Welfare and Sport to the President of the second chamber, 05.04.2016]. Available at: www.rijksoverheid.nl/documenten/kamerstukken/2016/04/05/kamerbrief-over-faillissement-tsn-thuiszorg [accessed 14.07.2017].

Van Walsum, S., 2013. Regulating migrant domestic work in the Netherlands: opportunities and pitfalls. In A. Triandafyllidou, ed. *Irregular migrant domestic workers in Europe: who cares?* Farnham: Ashgate, pp. 161–86.

5

The English social care workforce

The vexed question of low wages and stress

Shereen Hussein

Introduction

The UK developed its modern welfare state after the Second World War (Esping-Andersen, 1999); compared to other European countries, it is relatively more complex and much less universal, particularly when compared to Scandinavian countries. In England, the largest country in the UK, social care is funded through both public and private funds. The state only provides services to those deemed to be unable to meet the cost of care themselves, that is, through means-tested assessment. This is in sharp contrast with health services (National Health Service [NHS]), which are free and universal in coverage to all British and European Economic Area (EU plus Norway, Iceland and Liechtenstein) nationals. It is noticeable that in England, the gap between health and social care provision is greater for individuals with higher incomes who often have to pay their full costs for residential care (Roberston et al., 2014). There are no exact figures on the percentage of publicly funded social care provision in England, however there is evidence of a sharp decline in publicly funded care services for adults and older people since 2009 (Humphries et al., 2016).

Reducing social care state spending has been a policy adopted by successive UK governments with the rationale of coping with government deficits in the aftermath of the financial crisis in 2008. In the two or three decades before the financial crisis, many welfare states in Europe were going through processes that can be described generically as 'marketization', which could be defined as the measures by which the government authorizes, supports or enforces the introduction of markets to be responsible for functions previously carried out, at least in part, by the state. The UK was one of the first European countries to adopt this approach to welfare services, starting this process during the Thatcher government years in 1979–1983. Later on, the personalization agenda (since 2007) came into effect and was regarded as '*a cornerstone of the modernisation of public services*' (Department of Health [DoH], 2006). The ethos of personalization is regarded by the DoH as a means of enhancing service users' choice and control regardless of whether they are funded directly by the state or not. Further, personal budgets (a key component of personalization) later became a 'mainstream' part of care provision, the Care Act (2014) strengthening this policy

The English social care workforce

through its statutory guidance: 'Everyone whose needs are met by the local authority . . . *must* receive a personal budget as part of the care and support plan, or support plan' (DoH, 2014, p. 152, emphasis in original).

Some argue that the personalization agenda has assisted the progression of the marketization process and shifted some of the state's responsibilities onto individuals (Christensen and Pilling, 2014; Ferguson, 2007). Through the personalization agenda, individuals judged to be eligible to receive state support were given control of their own publicly funded budgets, through personal budgets, including, if they wished, direct payments (cash-for-care) with which to purchase for themselves the services they chose to use. The availability of personal budgets allowed users to buy their care from a wide range of providers, including private (for-profit) organizations. Marketization has thus increased the role of the private sector through various channels, as out-sourced providers who compete for local authority-funded care packages and as responders to a larger than before pool of 'clients' with purchasing power (self-funders and those in receipt of personal budgets) (Brennan et al., 2012).

The increased role of the private sector is perceived to have several implications on the social care workforce, including the levels of wages, the organization of work and contractual arrangements. This chapter provides detailed analysis of the work structure, wages and the role of gender and migration in the social care sector in England where marketization and personalization form key pillars of social care provision for adults and older people. The analysis is based on empirical studies on the English social care workforce spanning from 2010 to 2016. The chapter starts by providing an overview of the organization of social care in England and the characteristics of its workforce. It then provides detailed analysis of the extent of and perceived reasons for poverty-pay in the sector. Primarily quantitative and qualitative data obtained from front-line care workers, employers and service users are analysed to further understand the reasons behind persistent low wages in the sector. I then provide evidence of unresolved job stress in the care sector utilizing the Karasek control-demand model and explore subsequent moral distress among social care workers (Karasek et al., 1998a).

Data and methods

The findings draw on two research projects: secondary analysis of the National Minimum Dataset for Social Care (NMDS-SC) and the Longitudinal Care Work Study (LoCS), both funded by the English Department of Health.[1] I specifically draw on the analysis of the NMDS-SC, which is recognized as the main source of workforce information for the long-term care (LTC) sector in England. There is no sampling frame for the data; rather, there is an attempt to collect information from all care providers of older people and adults, completion being encouraged by incentives of training funds offered to care providers; it is assumed the sample is random for the most part.

The LoCS study adopts a longitudinal design aiming to achieve a locally representative sample of LTC workers in four different parts of England across the statutory, voluntary and private sectors. Nested samples of front-line staff and managers were drawn from care providers in these areas. The study gained ethical approval from King's College London and research governance agreement from the four participating local councils. The mixed-method design includes a repeated survey for staff ($n = 1,342$) and repeated interviews with employers/managers, front-line staff, and users and carers ($n = 300$). The current analysis uses the first two waves of LoCS (T1: 2010–2011 and T2: 2012–2013); a third wave of the survey and interviews were being undertaken in 2016. Both the NMDS and LoCS focus on social care for adults and older people in England, and the analysis presented here refers to this sector; any reference hereafter to social care will thus refer to the adult and social care sector, excluding social care provision for children and young people.

The LoCS survey included the standardized scales of Karasek's job content questionnaire (JCQ). JCQ is a self-completed instrument designed to identify two crucial aspects: job demands – the stressors existing in the work environment – and job decision latitude (control) – the extent to which employees have the potential to control their tasks and conduct throughout the working day (Karasek et al., 1998a). The control-demand (CD) model postulates that job strain is the result of an interaction between demand and control. The JCQ social support scale combines both co-workers' and supervisory support scales. Such support is theorized to moderate or buffer the impact of job-related stress (Karasek et al., 1998b); in particular, individuals in high-stressor jobs will have lower psychological strain in the presence of social support. JCQ also includes a separate indicator of job insecurity.

Both quantitative and qualitative data analysis methods were used to investigate trends in the contribution of migrant workers, wages in the sector, and stress and job demand. More specifically, the NMDS-SC was used to investigate trends in the contribution of migrant workers to the English social care sector according to nationality. JCQ obtained from LoCS were analysed using difference in means techniques to investigate associations between different elements of JCQ and various individual and work characteristics. In-depth interviews from LoCS were analysed thematically to investigate reasons for low wages and explanatory factors of stress in the sector.

The English social care workforce

The adult social sector is estimated to offer around 1.55 million jobs in England alone, with 1.2 million of these jobs involving hands-on provision of care ('front-line' jobs), spanning domiciliary (42 per cent), residential (43 per cent) and day and community (15 per cent) service types (SFC, 2016, pp. 14–18). These figures include between 110,000 and 160,000 personal assistant jobs in domiciliary care employed by direct payment recipients (service users who receive payments from their local authority to organize and purchase their own care). The latter figures are likely to underestimate the numbers of those directly employed by service users due to lack of data on this group.

The sector is characterized by persistent high turnover rates (Hussein et al., 2016a), with the independent sector (including private and voluntary) employing over three-quarters of the workforce (SFC, 2016, p. 17). Social care provision relies heavily on the human input of the workers, through hands-on support, provision of personal care, practical and emotional support. The workforce is predominantly female – around 83 per cent overall, rising to 85–90 per cent of those undertaking direct care-providing jobs. Men account for up to a quarter of the workforce in certain areas, notably day care, support roles and management (Hussein et al., 2016b). While women constitute the vast majority of this workforce, men remain significantly over-represented in managerial and supervisory roles, which have better wages and job conditions (Hussein and Manthorpe, 2014). However, not all men enjoy these advantages where ethnic group and nationality interact with gender (Hussein et al., 2016b).

Historically, the UK has relied extensively on immigration to fill labour shortages, first from Commonwealth states, formerly part of the British Empire (Hussein and Manthorpe, 2005). Following early waves of immigration, during the 1960s and 1970s, the UK gradually restricted migration from Commonwealth countries and began to closely link migration policies to economic imperatives such as redressing workforce shortages. However, the UK was one of a minority of EU states that permitted early access to the labour market from the A8 accession

The English social care workforce

countries (Czech Republic, Estonia, Hungary, Latvia, Lithuania, Poland, Slovakia and Slovenia; Portes and French, 2005) after they joined the EU in 2004. More recently, in 2011, the UK has introduced an 'immigration cap' on non-EU migrants with the help of a points system (Dobson and Salt, 2006) in order to reduce the number of migrants from this group, particularly those seeking to work in low-skilled jobs.

The marketization and personalization agenda has facilitated an increased role of migrant workers, particularly among those who have arrived from Eastern European countries and are already residents in England. This has been occurring within a context of high demand and increasingly competitive markets for social care that are associated with unattractive work packages, including low wages and zero-hours contracts. Such conditions are likely to attract vulnerable workers, including migrants who are looking for a foothold in the English labour market (Hussein, 2017; Rubery et al., 2015). Trends analysis utilizing the NMDS-SC, presented in Figure 5.1, clearly shows a significantly increased share of Eastern European countries, reflecting recent changes in UK immigration policies. While traditionally, migrants from outside the EU constituted the vast majority of migrant workers in the sector, the profile has changed significantly since 2003. Moreover, the analysis shows that from mid-2013, migrants from A2 countries (Bulgaria and Romania) have exceeded non-EU nationals working in the sector for the first time. However, the implications of the Brexit vote of June 2016 are not yet clear on

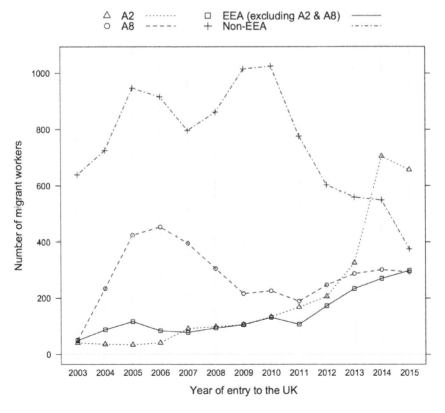

Figure 5.1 Trends of number of migrants working in the social care sector in England by year of entry to the UK and nationality, NMDS-SC, February 2016

77

the migrant social care workforce and the sustainability of care provision in general, given the persistent high vacancy and turnover rates and the sector's inability to recruit enough staff (Hussein et al., 2016a). It is interesting to note that gender dynamics seems to be different among British and migrant care workers. While the majority of migrant workers recruited to the sector are women, the share of men is higher than that of British workers (25 per cent compared to 17 per cent; see Hussein and Christensen, 2017).

Wages in the English social care sector

The English social sector is characterized by very low pay and difficult working conditions, and with fiscal cuts to local government, the social care sector has increasingly become fragmented and casual through outsourcing and other factors (Gardiner and Hussein, 2015; Hussein, 2011b; 2017). Evidence of low pay in the sector, particularly among direct care workers, is abundant, with the Low Pay Commission (2014) highlighting the care sector as one of most vulnerable sectors in terms of its workers being paid on or under national minimum wage (NMW) thresholds. The NMW came into effect in England during the last nine months of the twentieth century (April 1999), with the care sector arguably one of the main beneficiaries of its introduction. Nonetheless, social care was, and remains, one of the lowest-paying sectors in England.

Moreover, the sector has increasingly been suffering from fragmented working-time arrangements, including the widespread use of zero-hours contracts (Rubery et al., 2015), particularly in the home care sector, where migrant workers are over-represented (Hussein, 2011a). Wages are, in the majority, attached to actual face-to-face engagement with service users either in care homes or in their own homes, and almost no payment is given for other 'tasks', including being 'on call' and travel time between users for home-based care (Rubery et al., 2015; Hussein, 2011b; 2017). A recent HM Revenue & Customs (HMRC) campaign targeting employers of social care for adult and older people reflects growing concerns around non-compliance and highlights that inappropriate deductions from pay and accommodation offsets are further drivers of national minimum wage underpayment, as well as the lack of payment for travel time between clients. Nearly half of the care employers investigated were found to be non-compliant (HMRC, 2013).

The vast majority of participants in LoCS interviews indicated that low pay is the norm in the English social care sector, however explanations of the reasons underlying this 'fact' were mixed. Thematic analysis of LoCS in-depth interviews identified poor wages as a direct component of the nature of care work. Here, there was an implicit, and in some cases explicit, assumption that challenging poor wages or asking for better pay could be regarded as an indication of the unsuitability of an individual to work in the sector. Other determinants observed in the analysis were related to the value the wider society, and consequently the government, places on caring for older people. And the last theme highlighted the impact of current social care policies, particularly marketization and outsourcing, as well as wider fiscal challenges and austerity levels.

The intrinsic nature of front-line care work is often cited as an explanatory factor of the acceptance of low wages and poor working conditions. These intrinsic justifications were expressed by many front-line social care workers themselves, who repeatedly talked about money not being an important element in their decision to work in care. Some managers expressed views that those who would like to obtain a decent wage should not consider working in the sector, implying that those who are seeking fair wages may lack the right qualities to be a social care worker.

Many participants in the LoCS study highlighted 'positive' characteristics of the work, such as the ability to work flexibly, as a counter-response when asked about their level of pay. However, some participants struggled to convincingly make this argument as payment is attached to strict roles of contact time, leaving very little margins for changing circumstances, including illness. Yet social care workers seemed to view the problems only in relation to the arrangement of payments rather than the level of wages itself:

INT: What do you think about your pay and conditions?

RESP: Well pay, conditions? Oh well I think maybe conditions, 'cause if we don't work, we don't get pay, I suppose a lot of firms like that . . . Okay, yes I was supposed to be on duty today and I wasn't able to go to work, I was sick for whatever reason, then I wouldn't get pay, or if I was at work and I was taken ill a couple of hours after being at work, then I would only get paid for those two hours.

(Front-line staff 1033009; LoCS)

The analysis of LoCS interviews indicated general acceptance that poor wages have always been a feature of social care work and it is not likely to change. For some, this was concluded to be mainly associated with the wider norms of the society in terms of the value placed on social care work. That it is related to the old, disabled and the weak, and working in the sector is not seen as part of a wider 'career'. This theme was evident among a large number of managers and service users and reoccurred over time. Some managers explicitly linked low wages to ageism and the value the society places on looking after older people.

Most employers/managers spoke about the impact of funding cuts on front-line care workers, while acknowledging the fact that care work pay has always been very low. The amount of pay increases that employers and front-line staff spoke of were very marginal. All wages were governed by the NMW rate, but simultaneously working conditions were becoming more difficult, particularly in relation to offering sick leave or paying for time spent 'in attendance' between calls, or indeed travel time. The very marginal pay increases (5p or 10p) identified by managers were attributed to the austerity measures and progressive outsourcing and privatization in recent years. However, there was some scepticism about the reality of the inability of the private sector to pay a decent wage, and some managers questioned the influence of funding cuts on wages. This situation of pushing wages as low as possible is further influenced by the increased private sector share of the market due to the marketization agenda. Many managers argued instead that many private social care providers should be able to afford to pay better wages but they are keeping wages as low as possible to achieve their main goal of high profit margins.

Stress and social care work

Stress for staff has a direct impact on overall service quality and on the retention of good workers, which may affect the quality of service delivery and outcomes (Edwards and Burnard, 2003). Furthermore, previous research shows that such job strain is associated with several adverse health outcomes, most notably cardiovascular disease (Landsbergis and Theorell, 1999; Hallqvist et al., 1998). Social care work can be described as an emotionally taxing work; research demonstrates that moral distress is a serious issue for social care workers who deal with some of the most vulnerable groups in society, including older people with dementia and people with severe learning disabilities (Spenceley et al., 2015; Varcoe et al., 2012). Table 5.1 presents Karasek's JCQ scales by social care workers' individual characteristics as derived from the responses to the LoCS staff survey. On average, participants scored 71.04 on the decision latitude scale (control),

Shereen Hussein

34.96 on psychological job demand (demand), 6.00 on job insecurity and 24.33 on the social support scale. Scores of control and demand from the study resonate with that of Wilberforce et al. (2014), who used the same instruments among a sample of care/support workers providing care to individuals who were in receipt of personal budgets in England.

The analysis indicates that job demand, social support and job insecurity vary significantly by some individual characteristics. Table 5.1 shows that women and those who find their personal finances difficult or very difficult to manage, a proxy for poverty-pay, display significantly higher levels of job demand ($F = 4.105$, $p = 0.046$ and $F = 6.557$, $p < 0.011$), while workers from black and ethnic minorities have significantly lower social support. Workers who found their finances difficult to manage also displayed significantly lower job control ($F = 3.839$, $p = 0.004$).

Table 5.1 Karasek JCQ scales, decision latitude, psychological job demand, job insecurity and social support by social care staff individual characteristics, LoCS

Individual characteristics		Karasek JCQ scales			
		Job control	Job demand	Job insecurity	Social support
Gender			*		
	Male				
	Mean (μ)	70.81	34.19	6.17	24.23
	N	202	205	202	201
	Standard deviation (σ)	11.17	6.36	2.10	3.77
	Female				
	μ	71.11	35.16	5.94	24.33
	N	880	884	894	880
	σ	11.29	6.56	2.14	3.75
Nationality					
	British				
	μ	71.03	35.05	5.98	24.35
	N	912	917	924	909
	σ	11.38	6.42	2.12	3.79
	Migrant				
	μ	71.12	34.46	5.93	24.24
	N	179	181	182	181
	σ	10.60	6.98	2.05	3.53
Ethnicity					*
	White British				
	μ	71.24	35.01	5.93	24.43
	N	859	863	873	860
	σ	11.30	6.39	2.08	3.75
	Black and minority				
	μ	70.36	34.72	6.07	23.91
	N	204	207	205	203
	σ	11.06	7.11	2.08	3.52
Managing finances		***	*		**
	Living very comfortably				
	μ	75.06	34.78	5.34	25.10
	N	68	68	68	67
	σ	12.62	7.35	1.89	4.05
	Doing all right				

μ	72.61	35.31	5.84	24.53
N	425	433	437	434
σ	11.04	6.35	1.85	3.47
Just about getting by				
μ	70.11	34.57	6.09	24.14
N	360	359	362	356
σ	11.00	36.41	2.32	3.78
Finding it quite difficult				
μ	68.60	34.55	6.34	23.97
N	144	147	145	140
σ	11.10	6.94	2.26	4.143
Finding it very difficult				
μ	68.37	35.61	5.96	24.03
N	82	79	81	80
σ	11.19	6.51	2.15	4.08
Total‡	**μ**	**71.04**	**34.96**	**6.00**	**24.33**
	N	**1149**	**1156**	**1156**	**1143**
	σ	11.22	6.53	2.13	3.74

Note: * Significantly different at $p < 0.05$; ** $p < 0.005$; *** $p < 0.001$; ‡ Subgroups may not add to total number due to missing values.

Table 5.2 presents the summary statistics on job control, demand, insecurity and social support measures by some job characteristics. There are some significant variations by all job characteristics for both job demand and control. Care workers who were members of trade unions displayed higher levels of job control ($F = 3.390$, $p = 0.014$). Both job control and job demand were significantly lower among front-line workers whose job is 'all hands on care', referring to those who work directly with service users providing intimate and personal care ($F = 8.07$ and 37.00, $p < 0.001$). Job demand and control were significantly higher among workers who were members of any trade union ($F = 8.26$, $p = 0.004$; $F = 131.13$, $p < 0.001$). Job insecurity seemed to vary the most according to the nature of the job, with those in administrative posts or with little care responsibilities ($F = 3.27$, $p = 0.021$) and by sector, with those in the public sector having the highest levels of job insecurity ($F = 19.04$, $p < 0.001$).

It is surprising to note that those who indicated they belong to trade unions displayed significantly higher levels of job insecurity ($F = 23.07$, $p < 0.001$). These differences are likely to be related to austerity measures and public cuts, where workers employed in the public sector, who are more likely to be members of trade unions, feel higher levels of job insecurity. It is also likely that those who belong to trade unions are likely to have joined because they are not highly satisfied with various elements of their work, and thus represented a selected group who are already dissatisfied. Interestingly, the analysis shows that social support only varies according to ethnicity, union membership and sector of work, with those working in the voluntary sector reporting the lowest social support levels (which is a combination of co-workers' and supervisors' support).

The concept of 'moral distress' could be employed to understand the nature of stress experienced by long-term care workers. This concept can be identified as 'the pain or anguish affecting the mind, body, or relationships in response to a situation in which the person is aware of a moral problem, acknowledges moral responsibility, and makes a moral judgement about the correct action' (Nathaniel, 2004). Analysis of in-depth interviews from LoCS identified a number of situations when 'moral distress' could be experienced by social care workers. These include situations when a perceived tension between rights and protection occur; when workers

Table 5.2 Karasek JCQ scales, decision latitude, psychological job demand, job insecurity and social support by social care staff job characteristics, LoCS

Job characteristics		Karasek JCQ scales			
		Job control	Job demand	Job insecurity	Social support
Nature of work		***	***	*	
	All hands-on care work				
	μ	68.15	31.68	5.62	24.49
	N	204	209	212	203
	σ	11.38	6.05	2.51	4.08
	Mostly care work				
	μ	70.71	33.72	5.94	24.48
	N	261	263	264	261
	σ	10.07	6.77	2.00	3.52
	Mostly administration with some care work				
	μ	71.22	36.55	6.11	24.20
	N	384	382	378	378
	σ	10.89	6.04	1.96	3.70
	Little or no care work, mainly administration				
	μ	73.09	36.51	6.16	24.25
	N	292	294	294	293
	σ	11.96	6.12	2.06	3.82
Trade union member		**	***	***	***
	Yes				
	μ	71.98	36.92	6.27	24.01
	N	598	599	598	596
	σ	11.46	6.12	2.09	3.69
	No				
	μ	70.03	32.65	5.66	24.68
	N	496	502	510	497
	σ	10.81	6.21	2.12	3.76
Sector			***	***	**
	Private				
	μ	71.11	32.46	5.54	24.41
	N	368	381	385	371
	σ	11.22	6.29	2.24	3.91
	Public				
	μ	70.98	36.62	6.36	24.49
	N	614	615	608	610
	σ	11.21	6.31	2.09	3.70
	Voluntary				
	μ	71.89	34.59	5.77	23.45
	N	146	151	151	150
	σ	11.05	6.07	1.63	3.37
Total‡	μ	**71.04**	**34.96**	**6.00**	**24.33**
	N	**1149**	**1156**	**1156**	**1143**
	σ	**11.22**	**6.53**	**2.13**	**3.74**

Note: * Significantly different at $p < 0.05$; ** $p < 0.005$; *** $p < 0.001$; ‡ Subgroups may not add to total number due to missing values.

are faced with users' challenging behaviour; when there are discrepancies between the perceived right course of action and workers' ability to take such a decision; and when time and 'task' constrain their ability to provide the 'right' care. A specific tension occurred when workers' duty to 'protect' collided with what they felt to be tailored and personalized care. These tensions caused dilemmas for care workers that could be manifested in feelings of inability to provide high-quality care, which in turn could be a factor of distress to the workers:

> There is so much paperwork. If a resident falls or trips over a pair of steps, it's not because oh he's tripped up. They don't do that any more. Look where you are going. You can't say that. You have to write a risk assessment out . . . It does [she points to her heart], that's exactly how it makes you feel. They can't go out in the snow, because they might fall over and hurt themselves. The joy that I had when I was a kid of running in the snow and rolling in the snow and that sort of thing is lost for them.
>
> *(Older people care home worker, 2105008; LoCS)*

Challenging behaviour and use of restraints can also be a cause of moral distress to many social care workers. A particular stressor could be viewed in relation to how challenging behaviour, communication and workers' perception of best practice interact and influence workers' decisions about job quitting: 'People just resign . . . at times, after a year, even huge turnover in management, it's affected in that house as well, because of the workload, staff conflict. Staff not feeling they are supported enough' (Employer, 1072001; LoCS).

The fact that social care workers provide care to the most vulnerable people, some of whom may lack cognitive/mental capacity or suffer from extreme memory problems, can pose a number of challenges and impact on workers' stress. It is plausible that social care workers could be accused of abusive behaviour if it proved difficult to establish the exact circumstances surrounding an incident where service users are hurt, for example. Front-line care staff provided several examples when similar situations caused them unnecessary stress, when they either needed to defend themselves or wanted to protect the people they cared for. This residential care worker explains one of these situations:

> We took Paul to the doctors and again because of the autism in that communication obstacles, he couldn't translate the actual problem to the doctor very well and Paul had – with [specific] Syndrome they bruise easily. They can just accidentally walk into a table and they get a massive bruise or something like that. The doctor decided making investigative questions and enquiries about abuse. Paul only went there for like a cold or something. It's a whole thing that doctors and nurses just assume they know better.
>
> *(Residential care worker, 2105012; LoCS)*

Most participants identified training and support from supervisors and co-workers to be important in their ability to deal with these situations. However, many also mentioned talking to partners and family members about work stressors, which indicates a certain degree of stress spilling over to family life.

Discussion

The English social care system is less universal and more complex than in many other European countries, particularly social democratic welfare states such as Scandinavian countries. England was one of the first European countries to marketize care through progressive policies of privatization and outsourcing, leading to transforming care into a commodity that is governed by market forces with a large share of for-profit organizations. These dynamics create increasing pressures to maximize profit, in the main through reducing staff cost, which accounts for nearly 60 per cent of residential care and 80 per cent of domiciliary care total cost (Care Quality Commission, 2016). The result has been increasingly low wages, precarious working arrangements and fewer job security measures. Similar to many other countries, the English social care sector relies on women and migrants who are more likely to accept 'bad jobs' (Kalleberg, 2011) – that is, jobs that are low-paid, have weak contractual protection with little job security, and require low levels of qualifications.

Migrants have continued to form a significant part of the British social care sector; however, since 2003, there have been considerable changes in the profile of these migrants, particularly in relation to source country. The findings based on analysis of the NMDS-SC indicate that while 10 years ago migrants from outside the EU (mainly nurses from the Philippines) constituted the vast majority of migrant workers in the English adult social care sector, by 2014 the major group of migrants were from A2 countries (Bulgaria and Romania). The future UK immigration policies are currently very uncertain with the recent vote of British citizens to leave the EU. The implications of Brexit on adult and older people's social care provision and markets remain to be seen, but are likely to be significant given the continuous reliance of the English adult social care sector on migrants.

The evidence presented here indicates that the English low-skilled, low-status, adult social care work carries considerable wage penalties for a considerable part of its highly vulnerable workforce. Several authors explain low wages in social care by the intrinsic nature of care work itself and the vulnerability of those who choose and associate with this work (Duffy et al., 2013). It is argued that the reward gained from the inherent nature of working with vulnerable individuals in need of care can increase front-line workers' job satisfaction and feelings of self-worth to a certain degree to compensate for the bad qualities of the job, including very low wages (Morgan et al., 2013; Rakovski and Price-Glynn, 2010). Some argue that the acceptance of poor working conditions can relate to a concept of self-sacrifice adopted by some workers as a way of affirming their own identity at work, where they are seen, by others and themselves, as placing their values ahead of their own needs (Baines and Cunningham, 2011). The analysis presented here confirms these arguments to a certain extent, and thus poses several questions on how to enable the sector to re-evaluate the worth of its work, taking into account the wider social and economic costs of poverty-pay, stress and potential health outcomes. This process needs to consider the particular vulnerability associated with many individuals working in this workforce, especially in relation to gender and migration status.

In addition, the value a society places on the act of caring for older people and those who are 'weak', such as disabled people and those with mental health problems, can also be considered as an explanatory factor of consistently low wages in the social sector, where ageism and discrimination not only affect those individuals, but also those working with them (Stone and Harahan, 2010). The analysis shows that this is a view shared by many managers and service users who participated in the LoCS study. Moreover, marketization of care presents a situation where care providers operate within a tight public funding structure, meaning that private companies have to enhance their profits through higher fees for self-funding care users, maintaining low wages and increasing workers' productivity through shorter visits to perform more tasks or by increasing the ratio of care recipients per worker (Folbre, 2012).

Persistent low wages and increasingly difficult working conditions carry a heavy penalty for social care workers, particularly those who could be considered as vulnerable workers. Prime among this group of social care workers are women and migrants who may lack other employment options or who have other responsibilities and constraints that prevent them from seeking alternative work. Thematic analysis of the in-depth interviews of LoCS shows that moral distress among front-line workers can occur in a number of situations, particularly when there is lack of job authority to ensure that the perceived appropriate actions can be undertaken. Training and support from co-workers and supervisors was identified as important in reducing the effect of stress. However, the majority of participants indicated that lack of time and increased workload impact negatively on their ability to manage work-related stress.

Conclusion

Migrants and women continue to form a significant part of the English social care workforce; the findings presented here show that many of those workers, particularly those who find their finances difficult to manage, are more prone to higher levels of stress that are associated with various risks to individual workers, as well as to the sector as a whole, including high turnover rates and reduced quality of care. With escalating demands on the formal social care sector, it is crucial to implement both policy and practice measures to reduce poverty-pay, job demand and insecurity among social care workers. These need to be viewed as preventative strategies to maintain the well-being of workers as well as the quality of care to the most vulnerable in society. Such strategies should acknowledge the stressful nature of care work and address possible situations where many workers are subjected to various forms of 'moral distress'. These are likely to impact not only on workers' ability to complete their work to the highest quality, but also have potential negative impact on their own well-being and the likelihood of job quitting.

Note

1 The analysis presented in this chapter was funded by the English Department of Health, Policy Research Programme (DH/035/0095). The views expressed are those of the author alone and do not necessarily represent that of the Department of Health. I am grateful to all those who participated in the interviews or completed the survey. I thank colleagues at the Social Care Workforce Research Unit.

References

Baines, D. and Cunningham, I., 2011. 'White knuckle care work': violence, gender and New Public Management in the voluntary sector, *Work Employment and Society*, 25(4), pp. 760–76. DOI: 10.1177/0950017011419710.

Brennan, D., Cass, B., Himmelweit, S. and Szebehely, M., 2012. The marketization of care: rationales and consequences in Nordic and liberal care regimes. *Journal of European Social Policy*, 22(4), pp. 377–91. DOI: 10.1177/0958928712449772.

Care Quality Commission, 2016. *The state of health care and adult social care in England 2015/16*. London: House of Commons. Available at: www.cqc.org.uk/sites/default/files/20161019_stateofcare1516_web.pdf [accessed 15.07.2017].

Christensen, K. and Pilling, D., 2014. Policies of personalisation in Norway and England: on the impact of political context. *Journal of Social Policy*, 43(3), pp. 479–96. DOI: 10.1017/S0047279414000257.

DoH (Department of Health), 2006. *Our health, our care, our say: a new direction for community services*. London: The Stationery Office. Available at: www.gov.uk/government/publications/our-health-our-care-our-say-a-new-direction-for-community-services [accessed 15.07.2017].

DoH (Department of Health), 2014. *Care and support statutory guidance issued under the Care Act 2014*. London: Department of Health. Available at: www.gov.uk/government/publications/care-act-2014-statutory-guidance-for-implementation [accessed 15.07.2017].

Dobson, J. and Salt, J., 2006. Foreign recruitment in health and social care: recent experience reviewed. *International Journal of Migration, Health and Social Care*, 2(3/4), pp. 41–57. DOI: 10.1108/17479894200600026.

Duffy, M., Albelda, R. and Hammonds, C., 2013. Counting care work: the empirical and policy applications of care theory. *Social Problems*, 60(2), pp. 145–67. DOI: 10.1525/sp.2013.11051.

Edwards, D. and Burnard, P., 2003. A systematic review of the effects of stress and coping strategies used by occupational therapists working in mental health settings. *British Journal of Occupational Therapy*, 66(8), pp. 345–55. DOI: 10.1177/030802260306600803.

Esping-Andersen, G., 1999. *Social foundations of post-industrial economies.* Oxford: Oxford University Press.

Ferguson, I., 2007. Increasing user choice or privatizing risk? The antinomies of personalisation. *British Journal of Social Work*, 37(3), pp. 387–403. DOI: https://doi.org/10.1093/bjsw/bcm016.

Folbre, N., 2012. *Love and money: care provision in the United States.* New York: Russell.

Gardiner, L. and Hussein, S., 2015. *As if we cared: the costs and benefits of a living wage for social care workers.* London: Resolution Foundation. Available at: www.resolutionfoundation.org/app/uploads/2015/03/As-if-we-cared.pdf [accessed 15.07.2017].

Hallqvist, J., Diderichsen, F., Theorell, T., Reuterwall, C. and Ahlbom, A., 1998. Is the effect of job strain on myocardial infarction risk due to interaction between high psychosocial demands & low decision latitude? Results from Stockholm Heart Epidemiology Program (SHEEP). *Social Science & Medicine*, 46(11), pp.1405–15. DOI: 10.1016/S0277-9536(97)10084-3w.

HMRC (HM Revenue & Customs), 2013. National minimum wage compliance in the social care sector: an evaluation of national minimum wage enforcement in the social care sector over the period 1st April 2011 to 31st March 2013. London: HMRC. Available at: www.gov.uk/government/uploads/system/uploads/attachment_data/file/262269/131125_Social_Care_Evaluation_2013_ReportNov2013PDF. PDF [accessed 15.07.2017].

Humphries, R., Thorlby, R., Holder, H., Hall, P. and Charles, A. (2016) *Social care for older people: home truths.* The King's Fund and Nuffield Trust. Available at: www.kingsfund.org.uk/publications/social-care-older-people [accessed 20.07.2017].

Hussein, S., 2011a. Migrant workers in long-term care: evidence from England on trends, pay and profile. *Social Care Workforce Periodical*, 12, March 2011. Available at: www.kcl.ac.uk/sspp/policy-institute/scwru/pubs/periodical/issues/scwp12.pdf [accessed 15.07.2017].

Hussein, S., 2011b. Estimating probabilities and numbers of direct care workers paid under the national minimum wage in the UK: a Bayesian approach. *Social Care Workforce Periodical*, 16, December 2011. Available at: www.kcl.ac.uk/sspp/policy-institute/scwru/pubs/periodical/issues/scwp16.pdf [accessed 15.07.2017].

Hussein, S., 2017. 'We don't do it for the money' . . . The scale and reasons of poverty-pay among frontline long term care workers in the United Kingdom. *Health and Social Care in the Community*. 12.06.2017. DOI: 10.1111/hsc.12455.

Hussein, S. and Christensen, K., 2017. Migration, gender and low-paid work: on migrant men's entry dynamics into the feminised social care work in the UK. *Journal of Ethnic and Migration Studies*, 43(5), pp. 749–65. DOI: 10.1080/1369183X.2016.1202751.

Hussein, S. and Manthorpe, J., 2005. An international review of long-term care workforce: policies and shortages. *Journal of Aging and Social Policy*, 17(4), pp. 75–94. DOI: 10.1300/J031v17n04_05.

Hussein, S. and Manthorpe, J., 2014. Structural marginalisation among the long-term care workforce in England: evidence from mixed-effect models of national pay data. *Ageing and Society*, 34(1), pp. 21–41. DOI: 10.1017/S0144686X12000785.

Hussein, S., Ismail, M. and Manthorpe, J., 2016a. Changes in turnover and vacancy rates of care workers in England from 2008 to 2010: panel analysis of national workforce data. *Health and Social Care in the Community*, 24(5), pp. 547–56. DOI: 10.1111/hsc.12214.

Hussein, S., Ismail, M. and Manthorpe, J., 2016b. Male workers in the female-dominated long-term care sector: evidence from England. *Journal of Gender Studies*, 25(1), pp. 35–49. DOI: 10.1080/09589236.2014.887001.

Kalleberg, A., 2011. Good jobs, bad jobs: the rise of polarised and precarious employment in the United States, 1970s–2000s. New York: Russell Sage Foundation.

Karasek, R., Brisson, C., Kawakami, N., Houtman, I., Bongers, P. and Amick, B., 1998a. The job content questionnaire (JCQ): an instrument for international comparative assessments of psychosocial job characteristics. *Journal of Occupational Health Psychology*, 3, pp. 322–55. Available at: http://citeseerx.ist.psu.edu/viewdoc/download doi=10.1.1.515.1283&rep=rep1&type=pdf [accessed 26.10.2017].

Karasek, R., Triantis, K. and Chaudhry, S., 1998b. Coworker and supervisor support as moderators of associations between task characteristics and mental strain. *Journal of Occupational Behavior*, 3(2), pp. 181–200.

Landsbergis, P. and Theorell, T., 1999. Measurement of psychosocial workplace exposure variables: self-report questionnaires. *Occupational Medicine*, 15, pp. 163–71.

Low Pay Commission, 2014. *National minimum wage: Low Pay Commission report 2014.* London: Low Pay Commission. Available at: www.gov.uk/government/publications/national-minimum-wage-low-pay-commission-report-2014 [accessed 15.07.2017].

Morgan, J., Dill, J. and Kalleberg, A., 2013. The quality of healthcare jobs: can intrinsic rewards compensate for low extrinsic rewards? *Work Employment and Society*, 27(5), pp. 802–22. DOI: 10.1177/0950017012474707.

Nathaniel, A.K., 2004. A grounded theory of moral reckoning in nursing. *The Grounded Theory Review*, 4(1), 45–58. Available at: http://groundedtheoryreview.com/2004/11/29/1599/ [accessed 15.07.2017].

Portes, J. and French, S., 2005. *The impact of free movement of workers from central and Eastern Europe on the UK labour market: early evidence.* Working Paper 18. London: Department for Work and Pensions.

Rakovski, C. and Price-Glynn, K. 2010. Caring labour, inter-sectionality and worker satisfaction. *Sociology of Health and Illness*, 32(3), pp. 400–14. DOI: 10.1111/j.1467-9566.2009.01204.x.

Robertson, R., Gregory, S. and Jabbal, J., 2014. *The social care and health systems of nine countries.* London: The King's Fund.

Rubery, J., Grimshaw, D., Hebson, G. and Ugarte, S.M., 2015. 'It's all about time': time as contested terrain in the management and experience of domiciliary care work in England. *Human Resource Management*, 54(4), pp. 753–72. DOI: 10.1002/hrm.21685.

SFC (Skills for Care), 2016. *The state of the adult social care sector and workforce in England.* Leeds: SFC. Available at: www.nmds-sc-online.org.uk/Get.aspx?id=980099 [accessed 15.06.17].

Spenceley, S., Witcher, C., Hagen, B., Hall, B. and Kardolus-Wilson, A., 2015. Sources of moral distress for nursing staff providing care to residents with dementia. *Dementia*. DOI: 10.1177/1471301215618108.

Stone, R. and Harahan, M.F., 2010. Improving the long-term care workforce serving older adults. *Health Affairs*, 29(1), pp. 109–15. DOI: 10.1377/hlthaff.2009.0554.

Varcoe, C., Pauly, B., Storch, J., Newton, L. and Makaroff, K., 2012. Nurses' perceptions of and responses to morally distressing situations. *Nursing Ethics*, 19(4), pp. 488–500. DOI: 10.1177/0969733011436025.

Wilberforce, M., Jacobs, S., Challis, D., Manthorpe, J., Stevens, M., Jasper, R., et al. 2014. Revisiting the causes of stress in social work: sources of job demands, control and support in personalised adult social care. *British Journal of Social Work*, 44, pp. 812–30. DOI: 10.1093/bjsw/bcs166.

6

The personalization and marketization of home care services for older people in England

Kate Baxter

Introduction

This chapter focuses on the personalization and marketization of home care services for people aged 65 years or older in England. Personalization is an approach to arranging social care that enables people to have choice and control over the shape and location of their care. This chapter draws on research undertaken by the author and colleagues on developments in the market for home care and personalization of services for older people over the last decade. It comprises a brief background on personalization and marketization in the home care sector and the mechanisms used to facilitate personalization, known as personal budgets. This is followed by an overview of the methods and data used in the studies discussed. The next two sections summarize the research evidence from these studies, covering, first, the shifting role of local councils from providing services to facilitating the market and, second, the opportunities for older people to engage with personalization and become active consumers. The chapter finishes with a short conclusion.

Background

In England, the organization, funding and delivery of social care is devolved to local councils (also termed local authorities). Overall spending on home care is considerable; the combined value of expenditure by councils, the voluntary sector and private spending on non-residential care for people aged over 65 is estimated at £8.8 billion a year (IPC, 2014a, p. 16). Substantial changes to the system in the last three decades have seen the introduction of a market structure and personal budgets (see below) as mechanisms for achieving personalization of care.

The introduction of a market structure

For many years, social care, including home care, was both funded and provided by local councils. Today, councils still fund the majority of formal (paid-for) home care but provide very little; the main providers – also referred to as agencies – are independent organizations, both for- and not-for-profit.

These changes in the provision of care can be traced back to the NHS and Community Care Act 1990 and the community care reforms that followed (Lewis and Glennerster, 1996). Implemented in 1993, the NHS and Community Care Act provided the framework for a 'mixed economy' of care whereby local councils were encouraged to purchase services from independent providers, in competition for contracts with their own 'in-house' services (DoH, 1989). Contracts were put out to tender. Local council 'care managers' arranged service users' packages of care from providers that won contracts. These changes stemmed from the New Public Management movement of the 1980s that advocated a shift towards systems associated with the private sector, such as budgetary transparency, the separation of purchaser and provider functions, and competition between public and independent agencies (Dunleavy and Hood, 1994).

Local councils purchased around 2 per cent of home care for older people from independent providers in 1992, increasing to 73 per cent in 2005 (CSCI, 2006, p. 4) and 89 per cent in 2011–2012 (IPC, 2014a, p. 15). Most providers are small, providing care to fewer than 50 people (CSCI, 2009, p. 56). Sixty-four per cent employ less than 10 people (Skills for Care, 2015, p. 6). Market composition changes constantly, with a significant minority of registered providers entering and exiting each year (CSCI, 2006). From 2011–2012 to 2012–2013, the number of registered home care agencies increased by 9 per cent to 7,420 (IPC, 2014a, p. 16).

Local councils use a mix of contract types to purchase home care from independent providers. Initially, the most common was the 'block' contract, typically covering hundreds of hours of care a week, over a defined period of time, for a prearranged payment. These large contracts gave financial security to providers, enabling them to invest in training and staff, and were associated with provider price discounts and other economies of scale (Forder et al., 2004). However, they offered little flexibility, with providers taking on packages of care across large geographical areas, resulting in time-consuming journeys between clients. 'Sophisticated block' and 'cost and volume' contracts were subsequently developed to offer some flexibility in pricing and delivery around the margins. Specialist services or additional hours over and above those covered in the various forms of block contract were purchased using spot contracts; these were one-off contracts with the price and quantity of care agreed at short notice as needed.

Personal budgets as mechanisms for achieving personalization

Changes to the demand side of the market have run in parallel with those on the supply side. Until 20 years ago, people eligible for local council-funded home care were, in the main, provided with services over which they had little choice or control. Following the development in the 1980s of the UK's independent living movement (which helps disabled people live in mainstream communities) and debate and pressure from disabled people about the inflexibility of, and their lack of control over, conventionally provided services, direct payments were introduced in 1997.

Direct payments are cash payments given to eligible people to purchase services and support of their choice within agreed boundaries and with a range of checks and balances. They were initially introduced for working-age disabled people, but later extended to older people, carers and parents of disabled children. Direct payments were intended to create greater choice and control for their users and to enable them to tailor (personalize) the support they received. Direct payments meant people could make arrangements themselves and buy services from any provider rather than relying on local council care managers to buy services on their behalf from a limited range of contracted providers. However, concerns have been raised about the impact of direct payments on the make-up of the care workforce and collective provision of care, for example, in day centres (Sawyer, 2008; Ferguson, 2007; Scourfield, 2005).

Direct payments accounted for 8 per cent (£1.4 billion) of councils' expenditure on adult social care in 2013–2014, compared to 4 per cent in 2008–2009 (Adult Social Care Statistics Team, 2014, p. 6). Most older people have retained services purchased on their behalf by local councils through managed personal budgets (explained below); only 15 per cent of eligible older people used direct payments in 2014, compared with 37 per cent of younger adults (ADASS, 2014).

Alongside direct payments, successive governments have introduced other forms of individual and personal budgets. These developments have been influenced in part by the perceived success of the 'In Control' scheme, which began as a small project in 2003 to facilitate disabled people, predominantly with learning disabilities, to have more control over their lives through self-directed support (personalization).

Between 2005 and 2007, the Labour government piloted individual budgets in 13 local councils in England (Glendinning et al., 2008). Individual budgets brought together several funding streams in addition to social care, for example, funds to help disabled people live independently, or to access work or equipment. One main purpose was to be transparent about resources available for spending on care needs and remove barriers between different funding streams; it was anticipated that this would assist people in planning and controlling their care. The evaluation showed that, for some people, individual budgets offered choice and control and were cost-effective, but integrating different funding streams was problematic. Such was the strength of political interest in transparent budgets as mechanisms to achieve personalization that individual budgets were superseded by 'personal budgets' following an announcement in December 2007 (HM Government, 2007), before publication of the final report on individual budgets. Personal budgets covered social care only.

Personal budgets are similar to direct payments and individual budgets in that they are an allocation of funding offered to people following a care needs assessment. Again, the idea is that a transparent process for assessing needs and allocating a budget, with recipients aware of its value, will facilitate personalization. Personal budgets can be taken as a direct payment (a cash budget held in a personal account) but they can also be held in local council or other third-party accounts, in which case they are known as 'managed personal budgets', or taken as a combination of the two.

The implementation of personal budgets for all eligible adults was prioritized by the coalition government between 2010 and 2015; the intention was to reach 30 per cent coverage by April 2011 (Care Quality Commission, 2010, p. 3), increasing to 100 per cent by 2013 (DoH, 2010, p. 19). This target was reduced in October 2012 to 70 per cent. Take-up has been variable and was initially low. In 2009–2010, 13 per cent of eligible service users held a personal budget, but by 2014 this had risen to 80 per cent (ADASS, 2014). In 2015, new legislation in the form of the Care Act (2014) was implemented, making it compulsory for councils to assign personal budgets to all people eligible for support.

Broadly speaking, these budgets in their various forms have become synonymous with the umbrella term 'personalization'.

Methods and data

This chapter draws on findings from four studies that took place between 2007 and 2014, covering various aspects of the personalization and marketization of home care services for older people in England. Table 6.1 gives an overview of the studies. Findings from

Table 6.1 Summary of research studies

Study topic, dates and aims	Data and analysis
Study 1 topic: Response of home care agencies to increased user choice	Setting: Four local councils with range of take-up of DPs, deprivation scores and rural/urban settings
Dates: 2007–2008	Data: Semi-structured interviews Four council commissioners
Aims: To examine the threats, barriers and opportunities as seen by home care agency managers for responding to increased user choice through personal budgets	• Thirty-two managers of home care agencies (large/small, with/without DP users, council contracts, for-/not-for-profit) Analysis: Thematic analysis of a priori and emergent themes – flexibility of services, experiences with personal budget users, perceived threats and opportunities, workforce issues, wider home care market
Publications: Baxter et al. (2008, 2011a, 2011b)	
Study 2 topic: Personalization of home care for older people using managed personal budgets	Setting: Three councils with high percentages of older people using personal budgets
Dates: 2011–2012	Data: Semi-structured interviews
Aims: To explore factors affecting the delivery of personalized support to older service users who opt for managed personal budgets	• Three council commissioners/contract managers • Fifteen managers of home care agencies • Eighteen older service users • Three focus groups with support planners[1]
Publications: Baxter et al. (2013); Rabiee and Glendinning (2014); Rabiee et al. (2016)	Analysis: Thematic analysis of a priori and emergent themes – commissioning and contracting arrangements, market developments, communication issues, training and resources

(continued)

Table 6.1 (continued)

Study topic, dates and aims	Data and analysis
Study 3 topic: Small follow-up to 'Personalization of home care for older people using managed personal budgets' *Dates*: 2013–2014 *Aims*: To follow up on changes in commissioning methods, numbers of providers, and functioning of brokers *Publications*: Baxter and Rabiee (2015)	*Setting*: Three councils (as above) *Data*: Semi-structured interviews • Three council commissioners/contract managers • Three brokers[2] *Analysis*: Thematic analysis of a priori and emergent themes – challenges of commissioning and contracting arrangements, matching needs to available care
Study 4 topic: People who fund their own social care *Dates*: 2014 *Aims*: To scope the research evidence on people who pay for their own social care (known as self-funders or private payers) *Publications*: Baxter (2016); Baxter and Glendinning (2015)	*Setting*: n/a *Data*: Seventy-one publications *Analysis*: Descriptive analysis under following headings – size of evidence base, characteristics of population, information issues, provider experiences

1 Support planners: social work or other trained staff, employed by local councils to work with older people to help them think about their care and support needs and the best ways of meeting them. Together, they develop a support plan that sets out the outcomes people want to achieve through care and support.

2 Brokers: trained staff employed by local councils to work with support planners and providers to identify the most appropriate home care provider(s) to deliver a care package. This is essentially a procurement role.

study 1 were also combined with selected findings from the national evaluation of the pilot programme of individual budgets (Glendinning et al., 2008) to compare workforce issues (Baxter et al., 2011b).

The transformation of local council adult social care departments from monopsony purchasers to market facilitators

The last three decades have seen a transformation of local council adult social care departments from powerful, sole purchasers of home care services, using large contracts to purchase care, to commissioners of care, with weaker purchasing power but a growing market-shaping and enabling role (Christensen and Pilling, 2014). Thus, the organization of adult social care in England has shifted from being predominantly local council-funded and provided in the 1980s and 1990s to being provided today, in the main, by the independent sector (IPC, 2014a), often commissioned by local councils but purchased to a growing extent by people using personal budgets, direct payments or their own funds.

Contracting by localities

In the early 2000s, councils began to award home care contracts by geographical localities, known as zones. Zone-based contracts covered smaller areas than typical block/cost and volume contracts. Thus, rather than, say, four providers being contracted to cover home care anywhere across a city, four zones would be set up with all the care in each zone being provided by the agency that won the contract for that zone; this meant all the business from one zone was guaranteed to one provider, but also that all service users in that zone who relied on the council to arrange their care had no choice of provider.

Care was contracted in zones for two main reasons: (1) to address the high turnover of agency care workers by encouraging locally based agencies to employ local care workers; and (2) to reduce the costs of care by reducing the travel time and expense associated with moving between clients that, without zones, might be located some distance apart (Baxter et al., 2008). For home care agencies, zone-based contracting had mixed impacts. High turnover of agency care workers was not alleviated, mainly because competition came from other service and retail sectors such as supermarkets, not only other care agencies. Agency managers also actually felt restricted because they could not offer to provide care to a potential client living just outside their zone. However, because of simultaneous (albeit small) increases in the number of direct payment users, care agencies hoped to gain flexibility by attracting direct payment clients outside their zone if the package of care was large enough to make it financially viable, and also by refusing direct payment clients within their zone if they did not have sufficient capacity to offer high-quality care (Baxter et al., 2008). Interestingly, in our 2011–2012 study on managed personal budgets, agency managers made very similar comments about the new framework agreements, discussed below.

The development of framework agreements

Framework agreements were introduced from 2006 following a European directive aimed at simplifying procurement arrangements in the single market (European Parliament and the Council of the European Union, 2004). A framework agreement is a contract that sets out the price, quality and other terms on which a council will purchase services. Unlike block or cost and volume contracts, framework agreements do not guarantee any business to a provider.

Instead, whenever packages of care are needed, all providers on the framework can bid to deliver it. If more than one provider bids, the one preferred by the service user is selected. Providers tender to be on the framework and councils can purchase care only from providers on the framework. Framework agreements are intended to reduce contract management time and increase competition, in part by enabling smaller providers to compete. However, it is believed that tendering processes disadvantage small providers lacking expertise or capacity (National Market Development Forum, 2010).

In our 2011–2012 study on managed personal budgets for older people using home care services, all three study councils had introduced framework agreements so managed personal budget holders would have a choice of home care provider, rather than being restricted to the provider for their zone (Baxter et al., 2013). Two councils limited the number of home care providers on their frameworks to about 10 to ensure a stable market and reduce the risk of providers becoming financially unviable with a very small share of the market. The other, a large rural council, had around 40 providers on the framework, offering not only conventional personal care, but also other services such as live-in care or domestic help. This council felt they needed a large number of providers to cover their geographical area, as well as to offer a diverse range of services.

Home care provider and council commissioning managers felt framework agreements gave providers more freedom to choose which service users they wished to provide care to, and in what geographical area (Baxter et al., 2013). Both provider and commissioning managers felt this was an improvement over the previous zone-based contracts; providers also felt they had more control over workload, but worried travel times and costs would increase through no longer being able to group clients geographically – this being one reason for introducing zone-based contracts. However, as anticipated, with greater freedoms came concerns that a large number of providers on a framework would mean intense competition and overcapacity; in fact, there was no evidence that overcapacity was an issue, and even in the council with 40 framework providers it was often difficult to source providers (Baxter et al., 2013).

By the time of our follow-up study in 2013–2014, the study councils had noted some additional, unanticipated impacts of framework agreements (Baxter and Rabiee, 2015). First, they had realized that a large number of providers on a framework did not necessarily indicate a wide choice of provider because not all providers offered care in all geographical areas (they preferred to cluster their care packages together for efficiency) and some never bid for any care packages. Both these issues arose because framework providers were not obliged to provide any care at all, unlike the old zone-based contracts. In addition, it was reportedly easier for providers to 'hand back' packages of care than it was under the previous system, for example if providers had capacity or recruitment problems. Second, framework agreements were typically retendered every three to four years. If it became apparent that there were insufficient providers on the framework, there was no opportunity to add new providers until the next retender. Indeed, it was suggested that this was a reason some providers gained places on the framework but never took any packages of care; they gained places 'just in case' they had capacity to take on council-funded packages of care in the next three to four years. Third was the rise in the number of zero-hours contracts for care workers and the subsequent reduced capacity of providers during school holidays. With zero-hours contracts, employers are not obliged to provide a minimum number of work hours to employees and employees are not obliged to accept any hours offered. Zero-hours contracts increased because, in effect, framework contracts were zero-hours contracts at the provider level; providers passed the uncertainty on to their care workers. Gaps in capacity therefore arose as care workers with young children opted not to work during school holidays because they were unsure whether their (unpredictable) income would cover the costs of childcare. To solve these problems, councils were considering a return to locality-based working and abandoning framework contracts in favour of any suitable provider, thus increasing councils' choice of provider.

Market shaping

As local councils reduced the amount of care they purchased directly from providers and began instead to experiment with different contracts to facilitate greater competition and choice for service users, they developed a parallel market-shaping role. The term 'place-shaping' emerged following an independent inquiry (Lyons, 2007) into the future role, function and funding of local government. Lyons felt that local councils should use their purchasing power and long-term perspective to shape markets and involve service users in the design and delivery of services, in order to respond better to local needs and expectations. Although referring to all community services, his idea of place-shaping is apt for adult social care.

Later, the 2012 government policy document *Caring for our future* made it mandatory for local councils to promote diversity and quality in service provision to facilitate choice for service users, and support was offered in developing market position statements (DoH, 2012). A market position statement is a 'market-facing' document bringing together material to inform providers' plans (IPC, 2011).

None of the three 2011–2012 study councils had a market position statement. However, some council activities to provide market intelligence and encourage innovation were the kind of initiatives they later encompassed. For example, one council created 'market development' posts. Their purpose was to interrogate support plans and talk to support planners to gather information about local demand for home care and related services, for example the type of care and support people wanted, especially if different to conventional care or not available locally (Baxter et al., 2013). They disseminated this information to local providers, encouraging them to fill any gaps. Although these were newly created posts at the time of the first study, the follow-up study showed they had developed into roles concentrating on prevention, procurement and market intelligence (Baxter and Rabiee, 2015). Regular learning events had been introduced, bringing together key players. For example, home care providers met with support planners to present details of the types of care and support they offered; support planners then offered reasons why they would or would not recommend those services to managed personal budget holders. Thus, the supply and (proxy) demand sides of the market were brought together.

Another council in the 2011–2012 study took a hands-off approach, introducing innovation grants awarded through open competition. The purpose was to encourage home care providers to develop new services by sharing financial risk with the council. The council wanted to be seen to offer financial support at a time when providers' guaranteed income was being eroded by reductions in council-purchased care packages and the ending of block contracts (Baxter et al., 2013). Similar grants had been introduced in another council by the time of the study follow-up in 2013–2014.

As a further way of shaping care markets, each of the study sites was in the early stages of introducing e-market websites to link current and potential service users with providers and encourage more active engagement. These websites were reportedly aimed at people using direct payments or purchasing care from their own funds, but the long-term intention was for them to be used by people with managed personal budgets as well (Baxter and Rabiee, 2015). At the time of the research, the websites acted as information hubs but were not interactive; there was no facility for potential service users to see whether providers had care workers available at the times required, or for providers to see and monitor the types of care people wanted or the areas where there was most demand. Interestingly, none of the brokers we interviewed (see below) used the e-market websites as sources of information or ways of engaging with potential care providers.

Many councils now have some form of e-market website for social care; one example with an element of interactivity is 'shop4support', which is described as 'similar to an online supermarket but [. . .] dedicated to social care' (Connect to Support, 2017). It provides an online platform for people to search for care providers, including personal assistants, arrange initial meetings and pay for the care they want. These sites are usually not restricted to care work, but include other forms of help such as home repairs or gardening.

Opportunities for older people to become active consumers

The personalization and marketization agendas have resulted in a shift from large-scale contracting of services by local councils to individualized arrangements in which service users are expected to exercise greater choice and control, either directly or indirectly, over services. In effect, people have been encouraged and, in theory, enabled to become active consumers.

Practitioners as facilitators of choice

Many older people use council-managed personal budgets to purchase home care. Compared to people using direct payments, they depend more heavily on assistance from council and care agency practitioners to help facilitate choice and control. Our evidence suggests that the extent to which practitioners actually facilitate choice and control is variable.

For example, the role of support planners is to facilitate choice by helping people think about what types of care and support will best meet their needs. In our research, support planners all had some form of training in adult social care, but not necessarily person-centred assessments or planning. We found some support planners were very good at encouraging older people to 'think outside the box' about what care they wanted, suggesting novel solutions to meeting needs and encouraging people to be active consumers (Rabiee et al., 2016). However, novel solutions were not routinely offered by providers, leading to concerns that people's expectations were being raised then dashed. To avoid this, other support planners framed people's expectations within available local services, thus limiting choice from the outset.

A new role of local council-based 'broker' was introduced alongside framework agreements. The role is essentially administrative and not to be confused with 'support brokers' who help disabled/older people plan and arrange their care. Brokers liaise with support planners, but do not usually have direct contact with service users. They send service users' basic support plans to providers on the framework and request expressions of interest to provide the care. Details of interested agencies are then sent to support planners to discuss options, if any, with the service user with a view to selecting their preferred provider. In theory, brokers facilitate choice by sourcing a range of potential providers; in practice, they match agreed needs with available providers, and there is very little, if any, active involvement on the part of the older person.

Brokers were usually provided with only a summary support plan and felt this was insufficient to create a full picture of a person's support needs; home care agency managers and support planners agreed (Baxter and Rabiee, 2015; Baxter et al., 2013). As a result, there could be lengthy exchanges between the various parties (but not necessarily the service users) before agreeing arrangements for meeting care needs. There were also differences in opinion over the extent to which brokers *should* facilitate choice of provider. Support planners felt that only providers in the area close to a service user should be asked to provide care. Brokers, on the other hand, typically offered new packages of care to all framework providers, regardless of location. They felt that while geographical proximity to clients may reduce travel time, the purpose of framework agreements was to offer choice to service users, not convenience to providers.

In relation to providers, our research suggests a shift in the attitudes of care agency managers from being fearful of personal budgets resulting in over-demanding clients to being frustrated at councils for limiting the freedom of personal budget users to practise choice and control. Our early research showed home care agency managers felt self-funding clients were overly demanding because they were spending their own money and so had higher expectations than council-funded clients; this resulted in concerns that direct payment users might also be more demanding because they too would be dealing with visible levels of cash (Baxter et al., 2008). Agency managers at the time wanted councils to continue acting as intermediaries between them and service users. More recently, agency managers have expressed frustration at the inflexibility of managed personal budgets with even small changes to service arrangements, such as merging two short visits to create one longer visit, having to be approved by the council (Rabiee et al., 2016).

Consumer activity and workforce changes

Our early evidence suggested that home care agency managers expected the types of services and support older people using direct payments wanted to purchase would change, this in turn impacting on the home care workforce. However, these initial expectations do not appear to have materialized.

Home care agency managers suggested the skill mix of the care workforce may change with increased use of direct payments (Baxter et al., 2008). For example, they expected people to start asking for help with types of support not covered in local council contracts, such as social outings and companionship visits, or help with cleaning and domestic chores, leading to demand for a greater number and variety of care workers and more diverse support. However, national minimum standards for the quality of personal care (DoH, 2003) placed increasing pressure on care workers to gain professional qualifications, pushing them towards providing skilled care rather than companionship or support with household tasks. Some agency managers felt care workers were deterred by the requirement to gain formal qualifications and pushed into the less regulated personal assistant market (Baxter et al., 2011b).

The less regulated personal assistant market (for people employed directly by service users) was a concern. Managers felt it was a form of unfair competition, because direct payment users often paid personal assistants more per hour than agencies paid care workers (Baxter et al., 2008). Agency managers anticipated a more fluid care worker market, with care workers leaving agencies to become personal assistants and returning periodically, perhaps between personal assistant jobs (Baxter et al., 2011a). Some had introduced 'anti-poaching' clauses into care worker and client contracts; these set out the right of agencies to charge clients a substantial 'finder's fee' if they made private arrangements with a care worker met through an agency (Baxter et al., 2011a).

Running in parallel with these expectations of new forms of support and a more fluid workforce, care agency managers were concerned there might be a loss of professional distance between care workers and service users if the latter began to request companionship-style care and develop relationships more akin to friendships (Baxter et al., 2011b). When employing personal assistants privately, these relationships can become very close and risk the service user feeling guilty for taking actions that adversely affect the personal assistant, for example cutting hours or ending the employment relationship (Arksey and Baxter, 2012). These concerns led some agencies to move care workers between clients regularly, to stop close relationships developing or service users becoming too reliant on specific workers. The downside is that this has a potential negative impact on continuity of care and runs counter to personalization.

Overall, despite expectations, the types and range of support that home care agency workers offer now appear very similar to the support offered when personal budgets were in their infancy. As well as the reasons discussed above, cuts in social care funding have resulted in tighter budgets and higher eligibility criteria for council-funded care, meaning that there is little room within personal budgets for older people to cover any support beyond personal care.

The relationship between information and active consumerism

For a market in social care to develop and thrive, providers need to be willing and able to offer good-quality accessible information, and consumers need to be willing and able to engage in an active way (IPC, 2014a; Baxter and Glendinning, 2011). There is evidence, however, that older people are not as active as expected and that providers struggle to offer quality information to the right audience.

One major issue affecting opportunities for older people to be active is that searching for and arranging care usually takes place at a point of crisis with little time or desire to look for information or shop around (IPC, 2014b; Glendinning, 2008). Even when time is not an issue, evidence suggests older people using managed personal budgets are reluctant to make choices about providers as they find it difficult to judge the quality of care in advance of receiving it; much depends on the relationship between the care worker and the care recipient, and that can only be judged *ex poste* (Baxter et al., 2011a). Instead of making choices about providers, older people prefer to exercise choice over daily events such as what a care worker makes them for lunch or how they provide care (Rabiee and Glendinning, 2014). These choices are about personalizing care, but rarely result in switching between providers. There is also evidence that older people gain little in the way of choice and control from using direct payments compared to managed personal budgets (Woolham et al., 2016), suggesting that the mode of arranging care has little influence on the level of consumer activity.

Our research with providers shed limited evidence on these issues, but showed they struggled over what information to advertise and who to target. In our early work, agency managers were enthusiastic about advertising the wide range of services they could offer. They were keen to make people using direct payments and managed personal budgets aware of services such as shopping or companionship on trips out, in addition to personal care. Managers hoped that personal budget users would engage and have choices similar to self-funders. However, at the time, many older people still used the less flexible council-commissioned services rather than personal budgets, so to avoid confusion about what was available to whom, care agencies typically used a single set of advertising materials for all clients (Baxter et al., 2008). As a result, they advertised only help that was available to everyone, in effect, personal care and help with activities of daily living. They also struggled to identify potential customers to target, having to rely instead on leafleting large areas in the hope of reaching new clients (Baxter et al., 2011a). Council support planners and brokers acted as central points or conduits for passing information to managed personal budget users, but agencies still struggled to identify appropriate routes for advertising to self-funders or direct payment users.

Since our study, e-market websites have become a routine offer from local councils. However, making information available does not necessarily mean it is sought or used; for example, self-funders (who might be expected to be model active consumers) are not well informed about care options (Baxter and Glendinning, 2015) and older people do not practise switching providers. This raises the question of how well the model of active consumerism fits the home care market for older people.

Conclusion

This chapter has brought together findings from four research studies and considered them longitudinally. As such, it has offered a chronological perspective on the marketization and personalization of home care for older people in England.

Three issues have arisen from the empirical analyses presented. First, the transition from large block contracts through zone-based to framework contracts has seen councils' direct involvement in purchasing decrease in favour of stronger market-shaping activities. Second, personalization, or at least the use of personal budgets in various forms, has become more widespread for older people, but the care and support options available to them, or their interest in exercising choice over providers, do not appear to have developed at the same pace. Third, agency managers' fears about the impact of budgetary freedoms and the choice afforded to direct payment users and self-funders appear to have been replaced with frustration at the boundaries imposed by councils on how older people can use personal budgets.

There have been enormous changes in the structure and organization of home care services; the market now comprises many independent providers competing to deliver care to many individual consumers. However, the market is heavily regulated, and older people using home care services still have limited choice and are only minimally engaged as active consumers.

Recent legislation in the form of the Care Act (2014) has given all eligible people the right to a personal budget, thus confirming the personalization and marketization agenda for the foreseeable future. Councils are tasked with shaping the market, but have some way to go to ensure it is diverse and dynamic. Self-funders will become an increasing proportion of the consumer side of the market, driving demand alongside direct payment and managed personal budget users. The structures are, at least in part, in place to facilitate the market, but there is scant evidence to suggest that personalization in the form of personal budgets is the most appropriate way to ensure older people's care and support needs are met.

References

ADASS (Association of Directors of Adult Social Services), 2014. *ADASS personalisation survey 2014: national overview report.* Available at: www.adass.org.uk/media/4692/adasspersonalisationsurveyreport 03102014.pdf [accessed 15.03.2017].

Adult Social Care Statistics Team, 2014. *Personal social services: expenditure and unit costs, England 2013–14 final release.* Health and Social Care Information Centre. Available at: http://content.digital.nhs.uk/ catalogue/PUB16111/pss-exp-eng-13-14-fin-rpt.pdf [accessed 15.05.2017].

Arksey, H. and Baxter, K., 2012. Exploring the temporal aspects of direct payments. *British Journal of Social Work*, 42(1), pp. 147–64. DOI: 10.1093/bjsw/bcr039.

Baxter, K., 2016. Self-funders and social care: findings from a scoping review. *Research Policy and Planning*, 31(3), pp. 179–93.

Baxter, K. and Glendinning, C., 2011. Making choices about support services: disabled adults' and older people's use of information. *Health and Social Care in the Community*, 19(3), pp. 272–9. DOI: 10.1111/j.1365-2524.2010.00979.x.

Baxter, K. and Glendinning, C., 2015. *People who fund their own social care: a scoping review.* London: School for Social Care Research. Available at: https://pure.york.ac.uk/portal/files/33313357/sscrSelf FundSR11.pdf [accessed 15.07.2017].

Baxter, K. and Rabiee, P., 2015. Council-managed personal budgets for older people: improving choice through market development and brokerage? *Journal of Care Services Management*, 7(4), pp. 136–45. DOI: http://www.maneyonline.com/doi/abs/10.1179/1750168715Y.0000000002.

Baxter, K., Glendinning, C., Clarke, S. and Greener, I., 2008. *Domiciliary care agency responses to increased user choice: perceived threats, barriers and opportunities from a changing market.* York: University of York, Social Policy Research Unit

Baxter, K., Glendinning, C. and Greener, I., 2011a. The implications of personal budgets for the home care market. *Public Money and Management*, 31(2), pp. 91–8. DOI: http://dx.doi.org/10.1080/095409 62.2011.560702.

Baxter, K., Wilberforce, M. and Glendinning, C., 2011b. Personal budgets and the workforce implications for social care providers: expectations and early experiences. *Social Policy and Society*, 10(1), pp. 55–65. DOI: 10.1017/S1474746410000382.

Baxter, K., Rabiee, P. and Glendinning, C., 2013. Managed personal budgets for older people: what are English local authorities doing to facilitate personalized and flexible care? *Public Money and Management*, 33(6), pp. 399–406. DOI: http://dx.doi.org/10.1080/09540962.2013.835998.

Care Act, 2014. Chapter 23. Available at: http://services.parliament.uk/bills/2013-14/care.html [accessed 21.07.2017].

Care Quality Commission, 2010. *Putting people first: policy briefing.* Available at: www.thinklocalactpersonal. org.uk/_assets/Resources/Personalisation/Personalisation_advice/Putting_people_first_briefing1.pdf [accessed 15.05.2017].

Christensen, K. and Pilling, D. 2014. Policies of personalisation in Norway and England: on the impact of political context. *Journal of Social Policy*, 43, pp. 479–96. DOI: 10.1017/S0047279414000257.

CSCI (Commission for Social Care Inspection), 2006. *Time to care? An overview of home care services for older people in England, 2006.* Available at: www.ukhca.co.uk/pdfs/timetocare.pdf [accessed 15.05.2017].

CSCI (Commission for Social Care Inspection), 2009. *The state of social care in England 2007–08.* Available at: www.housinglin.org.uk/_assets/Resources/Housing/Support_materials/Other_reports_and_guid ance/The_state_of_social_care_in_England_2007-08.pdf [accessed 15.05.2017].

Connect to Support, 2017. *About shop4support.* Available at: www.connecttosupport.org/s4s/CustomPage/ Index/15 [accessed 15.03.2017].

DoH (Department of Health), 1989. *Caring for people: community care in the next decade and beyond.* London: The Stationery Office.

DoH (Department of Health), 2003. *Domiciliary care: national minimum standards. Regulations, Care Standards Act 2000.* Available at: www.age-platform.eu/images/stories/uk_minimumcarestandarts_athome.pdf [accessed 15.05.2017].

DoH (Department of Health), 2010. *A vision for adult social care: capable communities and active citizens.* Available at: www.cpa.org.uk/cpa_documents/vision_for_social_care2010.pdf [accessed 15.05.2017].

DoH (Department of Health), 2012. *Caring for our future: reforming care and support.* Available at: http:// webarchive.nationalarchives.gov.uk/+/www.dh.gov.uk/health/files/2012/07/2900021-CaringFor Future_ACCESSIBLE-10.07.2012.pdf [accessed 15.05.2017].

Dunleavy, P.J. and Hood, C., 1994. From old public administration to New Public Management. *Public Money and Management*, 14(3), pp. 9–16. DOI: http://dx.doi.org/10.1080/09540969409387823.

European Parliament and the Council of the European Union, 2004. Directive 2004/18/EC of the European Parliament and of the Council of 31 March 2004 on the coordination of procedures for the award of public works contracts, public supply contracts and public service contracts. *Official Journal of the European Union*, L 134, pp. 114–240. Available at: http://data.europa.eu/eli/dir/2004/18/oj [accessed 15.07.2017].

Ferguson, I., 2007. Increasing user choice or privatizing risk? The antinomies of personalization. *British Journal of Social Work*, 37(3), pp. 387–403. DOI: https://doi.org/10.1093/bjsw/bcm016.

Forder, J., Knapp, M., Hardy, B., Kendall, J., Matosevic, T. and Ware, P., 2004. Prices, contracts and motivations: institutional arrangements in domiciliary care. *Policy and Politics*, 32(2), pp. 207–222. DOI: https://doi.org/10.1332/030557304773558152.

Glendinning, C., 2008. Increasing choice and control for older and disabled people: a critical review of new developments in England. *Social Policy and Administration*, 42(3), pp. 451–69. DOI: 10.1111/j.1467-9515.2008.00617.x.

Glendinning, C., Challis, D., Fernandez, J.-L., Jacobs, S., Jones, K., Knapp, M., et al., 2008. *Evaluation of the individual budgets pilot programme: final report.* York: University of York, Social Policy Research Unit.

HM Government, 2007. *Putting people first: a shared vision and commitment to the transformation of adult social care.* Available at: http://webarchive.nationalarchives.gov.uk/20130107105354/http:/www.dh.gov. uk/prod_consum_dh/groups/dh_digitalassets/@dh/@en/documents/digitalasset/dh_081119.pdf [accessed 15.05.2017].

IPC (Institute of Public Care), 2011. *Developing a market position statement for adult social care: a toolkit for commissioners. Final report*. South West Regional Improvement and Efficiency Partnership. Available at: https://ipc.brookes.ac.uk/publications/Toolkit_for_Developing_MPS.pdf [accessed 15.05.2017].

IPC (Institute of Public Care), 2014a. *The stability of the care market and market oversight in England*. Care Quality Commission. Available at: www.cqc.org.uk/sites/default/files/201402-market-stability-report.pdf [accessed 15.05.2017].

IPC (Institute of Public Care), 2014b. *DCMQC (Developing Care Markets for Quality and Choice) briefing paper 1: the basics of market facilitation*. Oxford: Oxford Brookes University. Available at: https://ipc.brookes.ac.uk/publications/DCMQC_paper_1_Basics_of_market_facilitation.pdf [accessed 12.05.2017].

Lewis, J. and Glennerster, H., 1996. *Implementing the new community care*. Buckingham: Open University Press.

Lyons, M., 2007. *Lyons inquiry into local government. Place-shaping: a shared ambition for the future of local government*. Final report. London: The Stationery Office.

National Market Development Forum, 2010. *How will 'personalisation' change the way services are procured?* Discussion Paper 3. London: Think Local Act Personal, pp. 20–6. Available at: www.marketshaping.co.uk/wp-content/uploads/2011/06/NMDF_Briefing_Paper_Merged.pdf [accessed 15.05.2017].

Rabiee, P. and Glendinning, C., 2014. Choice and control for older people using home care services: how far have council-managed personal budgets helped? *Quality in Ageing and Older Adults*, 15(4), pp. 210–19. Available at: https://pure.york.ac.uk/portal/files/31127247/PRqaoaNov2014.pdf [accessed 20.07.2017].

Rabiee, P., Baxter, K. and Glendinning, C., 2016. Supporting choice: support planning, older people and managed personal budgets. *Journal of Social Work*, 16(4), pp. 453–69. Available at: https://pure.york.ac.uk/portal/files/44308362/PRjsw23april2015.pdf [accessed 20.07.2017].

Sawyer, L., 2008. The personalisation agenda: threats and opportunities for domiciliary care providers. *Journal of Care Services Management*, 3(1), pp. 41–63. Available at: www.adass.org.uk/adassmedia/stories/L%20Sawyer%20Personalisation.pdf [accessed 20.07.2017].

Scourfield, P., 2005. Implementing the Community Care (Direct Payments) Act: will the supply of personal assistants meet the demand and at what price? *Journal of Social Policy*, 34(3), pp. 469–88. DOI: 10.1017/S0047279405008871.

Skills for Care, 2015. *The size and structure of the adult social care sector and workforce in England*. Available at: www.skillsforcare.org.uk/Documents/NMDS-SC-and-intelligence/NMDS-SC/Analysis-pages/The-size-and-structure-Report-2015.pdf [accessed 15.05.2017].

Woolham, J., Daly, G., Sparks, T. and Ritters, K., 2016. Do direct payments improve outcomes for older people who receive social care? Differences in outcome between people aged 75+ who have a managed personal budget or a direct payment. *Ageing and Society*, 22 January. Available at: https://doi.org/10.1017/S0144686X15001531. [accessed 15.07.2017].

7

The development of an ambiguous care work sector in France

Between professionalization and fragmentation

Blanche Le Bihan and Alis Sopadzhiyan

Introduction

The French system for caring for older people was traditionally based on home care (Jenson, 1997; Anttonen and Sipilä, 1996) with the significant involvement of family members (partners or children) as informal care providers. This system has evolved since the 1990s with the implementation of a specific policy for older people aimed at meeting the needs of those families not covered by the healthcare system. It is based on the creation of a specific cash-for-care allowance (Le Bihan and Martin, 2010; Frinault, 2009; Martin, 2001) and has brought about the development of a formalized sector of care work. The overall public cost for dependent elderly people in 2011 was around €21 billion (60 per cent of which corresponds to the healthcare social security cost) (Renoux et al., 2014, p. 5), representing a little over 1 per cent of GDP, more or less the same as in the UK and Germany, but less than in Scandinavian countries. Estimations for the next 20 to 25 years are that the overall cost of long-term care (LTC) policies in France could reach 2.0–2.5 per cent of GDP. As in many European countries, helping elderly people to live at home is presented as a priority in France. The objective is both to contain the cost of the care system, as care in residential homes appears to be very expensive, and to satisfy the wish of many elderly people to continue living at home for as long as possible. Indeed, more than 90 per cent of people aged 75 and over live at home, and three out of four aged over 85 (FNORS, 2008, p. 14). Estimates show that in France, 75 per cent of dependent elderly people in need of care receive support from relatives, who on average spend twice as much time with their parents as professionals.

This chapter investigates the 'elderly care work at home' sector in France and analyses the objectives and impact of the various policy measures related to its development. It argues that though formalization of care work appears to be a major trend in elderly care policy, this process does not usher in the development of a homogeneous professionalized care sector. On the

An ambiguous care work sector in France

contrary, the home care sector is characterized by various tensions: both between the distinct profiles of professional workers and between different forms of care work. This is blurring the traditional distinction between formal (professional) and informal (family) care (Le Bihan, 2012; Pfau-Effinger, 2005). Exploring two main notions – formalization defined as the process leading from informal forms of care activities to more structured forms of care activities, and professionalization implying precise conditions of work that correspond to the achievement of this formalization process – the chapter exposes two main findings. First, it highlights the complexity of the formalization process of the care work sector in France and demonstrates that formalization, which facilitates the recognition of care as work, does not necessarily mean professionalization. Second, it outlines the diversity of the resources available to support families in caring activities: heterogeneous professional care, and semi-formal forms of care work with the possibility to employ a relative and informal family carer.

The first part of this chapter outlines the main axes of the policy measures in favour of the formalization of care work, and the key role of both elderly care policy and employment policy. The second part exposes those characteristics of the care work sector in France that underpin its fragmentation and diversity. Finally, the last section discusses the impact of the various measures, concluding that no coherent care work sector exists in France and identifying high levels of tension.

Methods and data

This chapter is based on two sources of information. First, a detailed analysis was made of various policy documents and public reports over a period that begins with the introduction in the 1990s of a specific policy for older people, and runs through to the 2015 reform of the French LTC system (the Act on Adapting Society to an Ageing Population, *loi d'adaptation de la société au vieillissement*), together with a review of existing policy and sociological studies. Second, statistics on home-based care were collected – a complicated undertaking (Aldeghi and Loones, 2010), since home care services to elderly people in France are part of a larger unclear professional sector called 'personal services' (*services à la personne*) created in 2006. It includes all activities performed on a professional basis at people's homes in three broad areas: childcare, care for vulnerable people, and domestic services. The personal services sector covers 21 activities, ranging from cleaning, ironing, shopping and cooking, meal delivery, help with administrative tasks, and personal help and care, to gardening, small repairs, home lessons, babysitting and pet-sitting. The home care workers belonging to this personal services sector support both older and disabled people mainly with personal care and household tasks. Care delivered excludes all forms of nursing and healthcare activities, which are performed by nurses or nurse assistants (*aides soignantes*), who belong to the healthcare sector.

Quantitative data referred to in this chapter concern home care workers delivering care to both elderly and disabled people. Note that as care to older people accounts for 84 per cent of the activities performed (Marquier 2010a, p. 2), these figures are representative of care delivered to elderly people. These data are mostly based on the home-based workers survey (*IAD survey*) led by the DREES (Research, Statistics and Survey Direction) in 2008 and analysed by Marquier (2010a, 2010b). Besides, when available, analysis of the 2011 INSEE employment survey (see Devetter and Lefebvre, 2015; Jany-Catrice, 2015) are mentioned. Finally, where data concerning home care workers are missing, figures related to the larger personal services sector will be used, with an explicit reference to this fact.

103

The development of the home care work sector: a formalization process related to different policy issues

The development of a home care work sector in France cannot be analysed as a policy measure in its own right. It is related to different issues put onto the political agenda at different times; it refers to various rationales in terms of funding and measures that have contributed – in different ways – to the formalization of the French home care work sector. Two main dimensions of the formalization process will be identified: the professionalization of a care work sector related to the elderly care policy and the reduction of informal care work in relation to the employment policy.

The elderly care policy and the development of a professional care work sector

In France, the prioritization of home care was already being presented as the best solution for meeting the care needs of older people back in the 1960s, and the idea has regularly been confirmed since then. Recalled in the recent Act on Adapting Society to an Ageing Population (December 2015), this prioritization of home care is based on the investment of family carers (who remain major actors in the care arrangements), as well as on the involvement of professional carers from both the health and the social care sectors.

Although the number of people receiving social care services at home increased steadily from 280,000 in 1979 to 600,000 in 1993, state financial support for these services remained insufficient until the 1990s (Ennuyer, 2014, pp. 114–15). At that time, the system was based on social assistance – that is, focused on the poorest older people in need of care who could not pay for services – and could only provide up to 30 hours of home care per month. The financial contribution made by families, and their involvement in delivering care, was the major source of support at home. Consequently, the introduction at the end of the 1990s of a specific policy for older people in need of care, based on the creation of a cash allowance to meet the needs not covered by the healthcare system, was an important turning point in the organization of care.

Care is linked to activities and relationships involved in looking after older people, young children, and those who are in poor health (Daly 2002, p. 252). It is strongly related to affection and feelings, but, as underlined by feminist analysts, it is also defined as a task-oriented activity, and as such assimilated to 'work' (Ungerson, 1997, 2005). The formalization of a care work sector can be analysed as a process of commodification of care (Ungerson, 1997) understood as the externalization of care tasks traditionally performed by women on an informal basis towards the market. It is based on the recognition of care as work, which implies payment for the tasks involved in caregiving and delivered by care workers. Contributing to the personal funding of home care services, the creation in the elderly care sector of a cash-for-care scheme in the late 1990s plays a major role in this process. Launched in 1997, the specific dependency allowance (*Prestation spécifique dépendance, PSD*, which in 2002 became the current personal allowance for autonomy, *Allocation personnalisée d'autonomie, APA*) is delivered to older people aged 60 and over, according to their income and level of dependency. It finances a specific care plan defined by health and social care professionals in consultation with recipients, and can be used to pay for care delivered at home or an institution on a professional basis or by a relative (with the exception of the spouse).

The creation of a new allowance (APA) in 2002, marked a step further in the process of formalization of care work. It officially designated workers delivering care to older people at their homes as professional care workers. It was combined with a number of other initiatives contributing to the professionalization of the care sector – such as the creation of a national diploma, a collective agreement and a new job classification – as well as the introduction, in some social care services, of a fixed monthly wage and of salary increases.

The link with employment policy

Although the measures implemented to formalize a care work sector are part of elderly care policy, they are also an instrument of employment policy, aimed at reducing unemployment (Martin, 2001). The quantitative objective – increasing home care services – is a major dimension of the formalization process of the care work sector in France. Morel and Carbonnier, in their work on household services in Europe, state that the employment potential of such services has been a decisive argument in many countries, but 'nowhere has this argument been driven as forcefully as in France where the promotion of the domestic services sector became a cornerstone of the government's employment policy' (Morel and Carbonnier, 2015, p. 13). From this perspective, home care work is defined as 'employment in the home' and is associated with domestic services and considered a major source of employment.

Two main periods can be identified in the achievement of this employment objective. The first period – between the 1980s and the beginning of the 2000s – is characterized by the implementation of several measures aimed at encouraging employment in the home. In this perspective, the introduction of financial incentives in the early 1980s, with exemption of the payment of social charges for elderly people, disabled people and parents of young children employing someone, were followed by the creation of a tax deduction system in 1991. It had a major impact and made services accessible to the middle classes. Finally, to facilitate home employment, 'service employment vouchers' (*chèque emploi service*) were also created in 1994 – simplifying the procedure for paying people working within the home. With the objective of reducing undeclared work, and support of female professional activity, these measures contributed to increasing the number of people employed within the whole services sector from 551,000 at the end of 1991 to 771,000 at the end of 1996 (Le Bihan and Martin, 2007, p. 40).

The second period corresponds to the implementation of the Social and Cohesion Plan (known as the *Plan Borloo*). Launched in 2005, it pursued the previous objective of curbing informal care work delivered by the family or by undeclared home carers, and a new voucher (universal services voucher – *chèque emploi service universel*) was introduced to further simplify the administrative procedures for employers. Above all, the *Plan Borloo* sets job creation as a priority, and from this perspective it established a new economic sector – the personal services sector – which brought together two distinct activities, domestic workers and care workers, within a single socio-professional category. The merger was made on the basis that both activities are performed at home – without taking into account their distinct institutional trajectories. French analyst Jany-Catrice identifies different strategies developed with the aim of 'creating homogeneity out of diversity' (Jany-Catrice, 2015, p. 67): the reference to personal services as a specific economic sector; the creation of a specialized National Personal Services Agency (*Agence nationale de services à la personne*) devoted to the promotion of this sector; the reorganization of statistical and occupational categories; and the launch of a major advertising campaign introducing this new economic sector of services.

With regard to the job creation objective, these various incentives had an immediate positive impact and facilitated the development of the so-called personal services sector: the number of workers rose from 1,182,000 in 2006 (Gallois, 2008) to 1,320,000 in 2008 (+4 per cent) (Ould Younes, 2010, p. 1). Nevertheless, the overall impact of the plan is called into question in recent official reports (Jany-Catrice, 2016; Cour des Comptes, 2014, pp. 59–98) given its high public cost and its effect on the deterioration of job quality within the home care sector.

As stated, the development of a formalized home care sector via the externalization towards the market of care tasks traditionally performed on an informal basis, is a major objective of policies implemented since the 1990s. Yet there are different dimensions to that formalization process linked to the policies' goals. Though the objective of curbing unemployment through the creation of a personal services market is a permanent preoccupation, other policies also aimed at developing a home care services sector on a professional basis. In contrast, since the mid-2000s, the focus is quantitative, and little accent is put on the quality of the jobs created or the level of qualifications of the professionals employed.

A care work sector characterized by fragmentation, diversity and material insecurity

The French care work sector is characterized by a lack of unity regarding both the way it is regulated and the profiles of the care workers within this sector. This complexity is a significant source of fragmentation, affecting both the type of tasks care workers perform and their working conditions.

The complex regulation of a fragmented sector of care

In France, the home care services sector is fragmented in terms of its legal framework, the nature and status of service providers and the type of care work relationships they are involved in. Public and private sectors coexist, with three types of service providers – public social services, non-profit organizations, and private companies – each having specific regulations. The home care sector for elderly people has long been characterized by the prevalence of non-profit associations and public providers. Within the wider personal services sector, the number of private companies has increased from 500 in 2005 to 20,000 at the end of 2013 as a consequence of the 2005 *Plan Borloo* (Cour des Comptes 2014, p. 37). This trend has only partially impacted the home care sector, since the activities offered by private companies mainly concern domestic services, with fewer than one in three offering services for disabled and elderly people. A study led by Marquier shows that in 2008, a large majority of home care professionals (78 per cent) declare working within a non-profit organization, 20 per cent within public municipal services and only 4 per cent for for-profit private organizations (Marquier, 2010b, p. 2). Furthermore, home care services in urban areas appear to be impacted more by the development of the private market than in rural areas. The absence of a unique regulatory framework is seen as an obstacle to structuring both service provision and employment within the sector. Different (often overlapping) collective agreements coexist, with the collective agreement referring to the private sector being less protective of employee rights than that of non-profit organizations or public services (Devetter and Lefebvre, 2015).

The complexity of the French home care sector is exacerbated by the coexistence of three different forms of care work relationship, associated with three different hourly rates: the *prestataire* system (service provision), the *mandataire* system (partial delegation) and the system of formal direct employment (see Table 7.1). Within the *prestataire* system, the care user and their family are not required to carry out any administrative tasks, since the services are managed by the care worker's employer. The hourly rate associated with the *prestataire* system is also the highest. At the opposite end of the scale is the direct employment system, which is the cheapest solution as directly employed care workers earn 12 per cent less than those employed under the *prestataire* regime (Marquier, 2012b, p. 8). In direct employment, the care user is responsible for both recruiting and managing the working relationship with the care worker. The *mandataire* system is an intermediate approach where the care user remains the employer of the care professional, but most of the administrative tasks are supported by the organization providing the services. This type of care work relationship is also the most ambiguous, since care users are often unaware that they remain the employer of the care professional.

The existence of three different care work relationships reflects policymakers' determination to introduce flexibility and facilitate home care employment. The care user decides on the type of solution, as well as on the care provider – yet in all cases, the care work relationship is an employer-employee one, defined through a legally binding employment contract. In practice, the choice of one of these options also corresponds to different user needs. Direct employment is often used when needs are limited, and concern mainly cleaning and other domestic tasks. The type of care work relationship evolves to become a *mandataire* or *prestataire* type of employment as the care needs of the older person become more intensive.

It is not uncommon for care workers to cumulate several employers, making them simultaneously dependent on different collective agreements, different forms of care work relationships and different hourly rates in the course of a single working day (Devetter and Lefebvre, 2015). This results in administrative difficulties for both employers and employees.

Professional care workers: diversity of profiles and tasks

It is difficult to estimate the number of care professionals working within the sector, as it is hard to distinguish professionals having more than one employer, those working part-time, cumulating a care worker job with other activities, or not declared by their employers. Moreover, the statistics generally include other workers providing personal services: 1,320,834 people in 2008 (Ould Younes, 2010, p. 4, Graph 2), though some estimations specific to the home care sector do exist. In a survey of the 7,000 services providing help in the home performed in 1999 (80 per cent of care users are older people), there were 220,000 home care workers, 93 per cent of whom provided personal care for older people (Bressé, 2003, p. 126). According to later estimations, their number had increased to 515,000 home care workers in 2008, 494,000 of whom worked with older people (Marquier, 2010b, pp. 1–2), and to 535,000 in 2011 (according to the 2011 INSEE employment survey; see Devetter and Lefebvre, 2015, p. 154, Table 7.2). Although each of these three surveys use different methodologies and include different types of professionals in their data (the personal services sector did not exist in 1999), it is clear that the number of workers providing care for older people increased between 1999 and 2011. The sector is also characterized by strong feminization and a relatively large proportion of immigrant workers in comparison with other sectors: 97.5 per cent of home care workers in elderly people's homes are women (Marquier, 2010b, p. 3, Table 2). According to statistics concerning the broader personal services sector, the average age of care workers is also high. Twenty-four per cent of employees are aged 55+, compared to 11 per cent of employees across all employment sectors. Twelve per cent are born in other countries (Cour des Comptes, 2014, p. 98), against 5 per cent among all the employed labour force (Aldeghi and Loones, 2010, p. 59).

A further characteristic of the French home care sector is the diversity of profiles of care workers and the range of caring tasks performed. This diversity stems from heterogeneity – both in terms of the home care workers' professional trajectories, and in terms of the reasons leading them to home care work. As underlined by Avril (2014, p. 92), a majority of home care workers (70 per cent) already had a job before being recruited as workers within the home care sector, and only 22 per cent of them had no professional occupation. In 2011, 60 per cent of the active home care workers had previously worked in other professional sectors such as office, commercial or domestic employees, and 30 per cent had been employed as factory or farm workers. Entering the home care sector thus appears to be a way to remain in the labour market after having lost a previous job, or a way of accessing a permanent job. This is often the case for women belonging to disadvantaged social classes having cumulated long and frequent periods of unemployment, or for immigrant care workers whose diplomas are not recognized in France. Finally, for 13 per cent of home care workers, their activity remains a complement to a parallel professional activity. This proportion rises to 25 per cent where the care worker is directly employed (Marquier, 2010b, p. 7, Graph 3).

This diversity also concerns the type of caring tasks performed by care workers (Ennuyer, 2014; Bressé, 2003). Though the tasks related to daily living activities constitute a central part of home care worker workloads, a survey conducted in 2008 showed that most (97 per cent) also do cleaning tasks (including dishwashing), 71 per cent do laundry, and 73 per cent prepare meals (Marquier, 2010a, p. 3). Above all, Marquier shows that the type of activities home care workers perform most frequently depends on the type of care work relationship in which they are engaged, with the highest proportion of tasks related to daily living activities for those employed under the *prestataire* and *mandataire* regimes (see Table 7.1). Three different profiles of employees at home can be defined according to activities performed (Campéon and Le Bihan, 2006, pp. 8–10): domestic cleaners (*aides ménagères*), who in practice often also provide personal care and have no formal qualifications; home carers (*aides à domicile*), who provide personal care as well as domestic cleaning, and consider their jobs to cover a wide range of activities; and personal care assistants (*auxiliaires de vie à domicile*), who have specific qualifications and present themselves as professional carers having specific skills. These people often object to being referred to as 'domestic cleaners' (Dussuet, 2005).

Precarious working conditions and low levels of training

The majority of care workers are employed under a permanent contract, which appears to be a secure form of employment. But this employment stability is only apparent because of the high prevalence of undeclared work, part-time work and situations in which the care worker has several employers (Devetter and Lefebvre, 2015). Despite the move towards formal care work, delivering care services still does not provide full-time work, with fewer than 30 per cent of home care workers working full-time (Marquier, 2010b; see also Table 7.2). This proportion goes up to 44.4 per cent in the public sector, as against 19.8 per cent in the private sector (Nahon, 2014, p. 2, Table 1). Thirty-eight per cent of home care workers declare themselves willing to work more hours. The average length of the working week is 26.1 hours over 4.9 days, with home care workers working with 6.5 different people within a week – 5.4 of whom are elderly people.

Significant differences in working conditions remain for care workers employed under different care work regimes – regarding the length of the working week or the prevalence of atypical working hours or split shifts (see Table 7.2). Furthermore, the number of working hours a day does not reflect the time effectively devoted to work, especially for *prestataire*-employed care workers. Their working day is split into three different shifts corresponding to three key moments during the day (morning, lunchtime and evening). The time necessary to go from one workplace to another is not included in the individual private employers' collective agreement, and is taken into account for only 41 per cent of workers employed by service provider companies (Devetter and Lefebvre, 2015, p. 158). The multiplication of short visits within a day for home care workers willing to complete a full-time schedule is another factor that increases the temporal pressure and impairs the working conditions of professional care workers (Devetter et al., 2012).

Table 7.1 Type of care work relationship and of tasks performed

Type of care work relationship[1]	Care work regulation		Type of tasks performed on a weekly basis[2]			
	Home care worker's employer	Employment-related administrative tasks	User's care needs	Activities of daily living[**]	Instrumental daily activities (IDA)[***]	Part of IDA linked to administrative tasks, indoor and outdoor leisure activities
Prestataire (service provision) 37.1%	Service provider organization	Service provider organization	Very intensive	33.6%	53.6%	10.3
Mandataire (partial delegation)[*] 39.5%	Care user	Most of the tasks performed by service provider	Intensive	33.5%	54.2%	9.4
Direct employment 23.5%			Limited	22.3%	64.5%	10

Source: Adapted from: (1) Marquier, 2010b (p. 3, Chart 1) and (2) Marquier, 2010a (p. 5, Table 2).

Note: [*] Mandataire or mixed type of employment; [**] Activities of daily living concern essential everyday activities such as getting dressed, eating, etc.; [***] Instrumental daily activities refer to domestic tasks related to the person's direct environment, such as cleaning, doing the laundry and the groceries, preparing the meals, etc.

Table 7.2 Working conditions according to the care work relationship

| | Full-time work[1] | Full-time monthly wage[2] | Working days a week[3] | Atypical working hours | | | |
				Work on Sundays[1]	Night work[1]	Overtime hours[1]	Same working schedule every week[1]
Prestataire (service provision)	37%	€1,100–1,300	5.1	59.5%	2.8%	51.1%	66.8%
Mandataire (partial delegation)*	32.3%*	€1,000–1,400		63.2%	11.6%	47.1%	65.2%
Direct employment	16.9%	€880–1,500	4.4	36.1%	12.7%	25.8%	76.9%
All	30.4%	-	-	55.5%	8.6%	43.6%	68.6%

Source: Adapted from: (1) Marquier (2010b, p. 6, Table 4); (2) Marquier (2010b, p. 7, Graph 4); and (3) Marquier (2010b, p. 3).

Note: * *Mandataire* or mixed type of employment.

The same differences are observed with regard to care worker pay. The average wage is €832 per month, but monthly earnings vary significantly when care workers are employed full-time (€1,190) or part-time (€717), depending on the type of care work regime and applicable hourly rates negotiated in the collective agreements, as well as to whether they work in the public or private sector (Marquier 2010b, p. 7, Graph 4). In all cases, the monthly salary within the home care sector remains one of the lowest, in comparison with other sectors (Nahon, 2014).

Lastly, the sector is characterized by the low level of training received by care workers. According to statistics (Marquier, 2010b, p. 3, Table 1), 62 per cent of them have no diploma from either the health or the social sector. The least-qualified carers are directly employed, with only 3 per cent having a specific training qualification, as against 33 per cent for the *prestataire* regime. As data from the broader personal services sector show, access to training remains low, although it is more frequent for employees of service provider companies (9 per cent) than for directly employed workers (0.5 per cent) (Devetter and Lefebvre, 2015, p. 165). The complex and fragmented regulation is a significant barrier to the development of continuous training for care workers as each occupational sector develops its own training action (Cour des Comptes, 2014). Consequently, there is a lack of clarity concerning the available training programmes, which are numerous but fragmented, often featuring overlapping competences. This reinforces the weak appeal of the sector, where difficulties are experienced in 65 per cent of recruitment initiatives (Cour des Comptes, 2014, p. 86). Thus, development opportunities within the sector remain low due to limited opportunities to accumulate service seniority, low wage growth assigned for cumulated experience, and scarce access to continuous training.

The ambiguous formalization of the care work sector

Despite the formalization of a home care sector over the past 30 years, the privatization trend induced by the policies implemented since the mid-2000 have contributed to blurring the boundaries of care work at two levels: between the two activities (care work and domestic work) merged within the personal services sector and between formal (associated with care delivered by professionals) and informal care (associated with care provided by relatives), as discussed below. In this sense, the formalization process has also hindered professionalization of the sector.

The blurring of boundaries between care work and domestic work

Bringing together domestic services and care activities, the *Plan Borloo* launched in 2005 introduced confusion to the professionalization of a home care sector. Each of the two activities corresponded to a different logic, identified by Morel and Carbonnier (2015) as a needs-based logic for care services and consumer-based logic for domestic services. This last is at the core of the *Plan Borloo*, which was oriented towards the development of employment through the promotion of domestic services. The emphasis is on household demand rather than on service providers, incentivizing the emergence of a private personal services market characterized by competition between employers (with the development of different statuses: private households, non-profit organizations, private enterprises) and between qualified workers and unskilled workers. As analysed by Jany-Catrice (2015), the development of a single personal services sector has therefore contributed to the redefinition of the ideal of welfare state, with an emphasis on an individualist approach to welfare.

The promotion of competition and individualization has resulted in a confusion between the occupations of domestic workers and home care workers, impacting on 'the types of skills associated with these services, with both a symbolic and an effective devaluation of the profession of home caregiver' (Morel and Carbonnier, 2015, p. 19). Indeed, whereas the policy measures implemented in the 1990s and early 2000s contributed to establishing home care work as a qualified activity, complementary to care delivered by nurses and part of what might be referred to as the 'welfare sector', the *Plan Borloo* assimilated it to an unskilled job, such as domestic cleaner. In this sense, and as analysed by Jany-Catrice, the homogeneity of the personal services sector appears 'fictional' and 'marks a break with previous modes of regulation in the social sphere' (Jany-Catrice, 2015, p. 73).

As a consequence, it can be argued that the recent formalization policies based on the objective of job creation, rather than on the development of a professionalized home care sector, led instead to the creation of a multilevel professional care market characterized by various tensions (Le Bihan, 2012). The gap (in terms of working conditions and training opportunities) between directly and *prestataire*-employed workers has continued to widen; this is the case for care workers within both public and private sectors (Devetter and Lefebvre, 2015). Also, competition between home care workers and domestic workers has been reinforced, since the employment measures implemented from the 2000s have opened up the possibility of displacing care for elderly people to more unskilled jobs. This contributes to blurring the frontier between specific tasks relating to elderly people and domestic tasks. It can be considered as a major obstacle to the creation of a uniform sector of activity and to the definition of the level and type of skills required by care workers to perform their work (Devetter and Lefebvre, 2015; Ennuyer, 2014; Ribault, 2008). Furthermore, it deskills care work and contradicts the necessity of its professionalization as there is an implicit idea that skills required for care work remain attached to women. All these tensions constitute a barrier to the improvement of job quality and to the social recognition of care work. They show the importance of maintaining the distinction between domestic workers and home care workers.

The need to reconsider the distinction between formal and informal care work

The introduction in the late 1990s of a cash-for-care scheme that can be used to pay either for a care worker or a relative also had an ambiguous impact in terms of marketization of intimacy and commodification of care (Ungerson, 1997), and entailed reconsideration of the traditional distinction between formal and informal care work (Le Bihan, 2012). The French cash-for-care scheme demonstrates the need for further consideration, to reach beyond the simple distinction of unpaid informal care provided by family members, and paid care provided on a formal basis by workers from outside the family. It confirms the redefinition of the boundaries between formal and informal care, as defined by Pfau-Effinger et al. (2009). The authors suggest consideration of a wider definition of formal care that goes further than equating formal care with professional care. This includes 'forms of care work which are carried out on the basis of gainful employment' (Pfau-Effinger et al., 2009, p. 6), as well as care work provided by family members in return for payment.

Informal care concerns all forms of activities that are provided outside of a statutory employment framework. It can be paid or unpaid, income-oriented (grey care market), or based on mutual help or obligation (unpaid family care). But this is not sufficient. And the French cash-for-care system illustrates this process of defining new forms of care work – neither completely formal, nor completely informal – particularly with the option of paying a relative to perform the care activities defined by the social services. As mentioned above, this cannot be considered conventional formal employment. Although it is, in theory, subject to statutory working conditions, and therefore matches the definition of formal care work proposed by Pfau-Effinger et al. (2009), it illustrates the emergence of 'semi-formal' forms of care work arising out of the regulation of informal care activities. Considering the various characteristics of French cash-for-care scheme regulations, this notion of 'semi-formal' care seems particularly appropriate. Yet its definition remains ambiguous. Payment of a relative through an employment contract might be considered a step towards formalization, but the situation is more complex. Care activities, even when unpaid, are far from being informal in the sense that they often constitute structured, organized and skilled work. A further ambiguity concerns the notion of affection and feeling, which is strongly related to care practices (Daly, 2002), and can in fact characterize both family (paid or unpaid) and professional paid care.

Conclusion

In France, the formalization of home care work is the result of different policies having various, and sometimes contradictory, goals. At the end of the 1990s, the initial idea of enabling older people to buy care services on the market, and externalize care tasks traditionally performed by women within the family, is an important step towards formalization of the home care sector by achieving its professionalization. This was part of both elderly care policy – with priority given to home-based care – and employment policy – with the objective of curbing informal work. The APA reform of 2002 confirmed this movement, with recognition of the specific professional identity of 'care workers'. Although the 2005 *Plan Borloo* was also based on the employment potential existing in the services sector, it marked a break with previous policy orientation. Focusing on the promotion of household services and on competition, it has led to the development of a private, for-profit market, referred to as the personal services sector.

But the combination of both domestic and care workers within the single personal services sector has resulted in confusion between the two activities, contributing to a blurring of the traditional boundary between formal care and informal care. It has hindered the professionalization process initiated in earlier years and led to the creation of a multilevel care market characterized by poor working conditions and poor career development opportunities.

More recently, the ambitious Act on Adapting Society to an Ageing Population (2015) has revived the importance of the professionalization of the care work sector. Focusing on home-based care and suggesting increasing the amounts of the cash-for-care allowance, the law also proposes a new funding for the training of social care workers. Considering the failure of the formalization of a coherent personal services sector, other ideas high on the political agenda – such as the coordination of health and social care services for older people, or the targeting of public support on care-related activities (as recommended in a recent report from the Cour des Comptes, 2014) – could contribute to better distinguishing them from domestic activities. Nevertheless, without a clear move away from the employment-oriented policy that fosters competition between employees and between employers, and in the absence of a real strategy aimed at improving the working conditions of low-skilled workers, it is unlikely that these measures will significantly break the trend towards privatization and enhance both the quality and the appeal of home care jobs.

References

Anttonen, A., and Sipilä, J., 1996. European social care services: is it possible to identify models? *Journal of European Social Policy*, 6(2), pp. 87–100.

Aldeghi, I. and Loones, A., 2010. *Les emplois dans les services à domicile aux personnes âgées* [Jobs in the home care sector for elderly people]. CREDOC [Centre de Recherche pour L'Etude et L'Observation des Conditions de al Vie – Research Centre for the Study and Observation of Conditions of Life]. Cahier de recherche 277. Available at: www.credoc.fr/pdf/Rech/C277.pdf [accessed 19.05.2017].

Avril, C., 2014. *Les aides à domicile: un autre monde populaire* [Home carers: another working-class world]. Paris: La Dispute.

Bressé, S., 2003. L'enjeu de la professionnalisation du secteur de l'aide à domicile en faveur des personnes âgées [The issue of professionalization in the home care sector for elderly people]. *Retraite et Société*, 39(2), pp. 119–43.

Campéon, A. and Le Bihan, B., 2006. Les plans d'aide associés à l'allocation personnalisée d'autonomie. Le point de vue des bénéficiaires et de leurs aidants [The personal plans associated with the personal autonomy allowance: the point of view of the recipients and their carers]. *Etudes et Résultats, DREES*, 461. Available at: http://drees.social-sante.gouv.fr/IMG/pdf/er461.pdf [accessed 24.05.2017].

Cour des Comptes, 2014. *Le développement des services à la personne et le maintien à domicile des personnes âgées en perte d'autonomie* [The development of personal services and the support at home for elderly people in need of care]. Available at: www.ccomptes.fr/Publications/Publications/Le-developpement-des-services-a-la-personne-et-le-maintien-a-domicile-des-personnes-agees-en-perte-d-autonomie [accessed 24.05.2017].

Daly, M., 2002. Care as a good for social policy. *Journal of Social Policy*, 31(2), pp. 251–70. DOI: https://doi.org/10.1017/S0047279401006572.

Devetter, F.-X. and Lefebvre, M., 2015. Employment quality in the sector of personal and household services: status and impact of public policies in France. In C. Carbonnier and N. Morel, eds. *The political economy of household services in Europe*. Basingstoke: Palgrave Macmillan, pp. 150–71.

Devetter, F.-X., Messaoudi, D. and Farvaque, N., 2012. Contraintes de temps et pénibilité du travail: les paradoxes de la professionnalisation dans l'aide à domicile [Time constraints and difficult working conditions: the paradoxes of the home care professionalization]. *Revue Française des Affaires Sociales*, 2–3, pp. 244–68.

Dussuet, A., 2005. *Travaux de femmes: enquêtes sur les services à domicile* [Working women: investigation in home care services]. Paris: Editions L'Harmattan.

Ennuyer, B., 2014. *Repenser le maintien à domicile. Enjeux, acteurs, organisation* [Rethinking support at home: concerns, actors, organization], 2nd ed. Paris: Dunod.

FNORS (Fédération nationale des observatoires régionaux de la santé – National Federation of the Regional Health Observatories), 2008. *Vieillissement des populations et état de santé dans les régions de France* [Ageing of the population and state of health in the French regions]. Available at: www.fnors.org/uploadedFiles/vieillissement.pdf [accessed 19.05.17].

Frinault, T., 2009. *La dépendance: un nouveau défi pour l'action publique* [Dependency: new issue for public actions]. Rennes: Presses Universitaires de Rennes.

Gallois, F., 2008. *Les chiffres clés des services à la personne. Activités, emplois, acteurs* [Personal services' key figures: activity, jobs, actors]. Paris: Centre national d'animation et de ressources. Available at: www.uniopss.asso.fr/resources/trco/pdfs/2009/01_janvier_2009/chiffres_cles_SAP_dec2008.pdf [accessed 19.05.17].

Jany-Catrice, F., 2015. Creating a personal services sector in France. In C. Carbonnier and N. Morel, eds. *The political economy of household services in Europe*. Basingstoke: Palgrave Macmillan, pp. 60–81.

Jany-Catrice, F. 2016. Les 'services à la personne' en France? L'impasse de stratégies univoques de croissance économique [The 'personal services' in France: the impasse of a unequivocal strategy for economic growth]. *Revue Française des Affaires Sociales*, 1(5), pp. 263–78.

Jenson, J., 1997. Who cares? Gender and welfare regimes. *Social Politics: International Studies in Gender, State and Society*, 4(2), pp. 182–7. DOI: http://dx.doi.org/10.1093/sp/4.2.182.

Le Bihan, B., 2012. The redefinition of the familialist home care model in France: the complex formalization of care through cash payment. *Health and Social Care in the Community*, 20(3), pp. 238–46. DOI: 10.1111/j.1365-2524.2011.01051.x.

Le Bihan, B. and Martin, C., 2007. Cash for care in the French welfare state: a skilful compromise? In C. Ungerson and S. Yeandle, eds. *Cash for care in developed welfare statesy*. Basingstoke: Palgrave Macmillan, pp. 32–59.

Le Bihan, B. and Martin, C., 2010. Reforming long-term care policy in France: private–public complementarities. *Social Policy and Administration*, 44(4), pp. 392–410. DOI: 10.1111/j.1467-9515.2010.00720.x.

Marquier, R., 2010a. Les activités des aides à domicile en 2008 [Home carers' activities in 2008]. *Etudes et Résultats, DREES*, October (741), pp. 1–8. Available at: http://drees.social-sante.gouv.fr/IMG/pdf/er741.pdf [accessed 24.05.2017].

Marquier, R., 2010b. Les intervenants au domicile des personnes fragilisées en 2008 [Home care workers for fragile people in 2008]. *Etudes et Résultats, DREES*, June (728), pp. 1–8. Available at: http://drees. social-sante.gouv.fr/IMG/pdf/er728-2.pdf [accessed 24.05.2017].

Martin, C., 2001. Les politiques de prise en charge des personnes âgées dépendantes [Long-term care policies for dependent elderly people]. *Travail, Genre et Sociétés*, 6(2), pp. 83–103.

Morel, N. and Carbonnier, C., 2015. Taking the low road: the political economy of household services in Europe. In C. Carbonnier and N. Morel, eds. *The political economy of household services in Europe*. Basingstoke: Palgrave Macmillan, pp. 1–36.

Nahon, S. 2014. Les salaires dans le secteur social et médico-social en 2011. Une comparaison entre les secteurs privé et public [Wages in the social care sector in 2011: comparison between the public and the private sectors]. *Etudes et Résultats, DREES*, April (879), pp. 1–6. Available at: http://drees. social-sante.gouv.fr/etudes-et-statistiques/publications/etudes-et-resultats/article/les-salaires-dans-le-secteur-social-et-medico-social-en-2011 [accessed 24.05.2017].

Ould Younes, S., 2010. *Les services à la personne: une croissance vive en 2007, Atténuée en 2008* [Personal services: serious growth in 2007 slowed down in 2008]. 20. Paris: DARES Analyses. Available at: http:// dares.travail-emploi.gouv.fr/IMG/pdf/2010-020-2.pdf [accessed 19.05.17].

Pfau-Effinger, B., 2005. Development paths of care arrangements in the framework of family values and welfare values. In B. Pfau-Effinger and B. Geissler, eds. *Care and social integration in European societies*. Bristol: Policy Press, pp. 21–46.

Pfau-Effinger, B., Flaquer, L. and Jensen, P.H., 2009. *Formal and informal work: the hidden work regime in Europe*. New York and London: Routledge.

Renoux, A., Roussel, R. and Zaichman, C., 2014. *Le compte de la dépendance en 2011 et à l'horizon 2060* [Dependency accounts in 2011 and in 2060]. Dossier Solidarités et Santé, no. 50. Available at: www. argusdelassurance.com/mediatheque/5/0/8/000025805.pdf [accessed 19.05.17].

Ribault, T., 2008. Aide à domicile: de l'idéologie de la professionnalisation à la pluralité des professionnalités [Home care: from ideology in favour of professionalization to a plurality of professionalities]. *Revue Française de Socio-Économie*, 2(2), pp. 99–117. DOI: 10.3917/rfse.002.0099.

Ungerson, C., 1997. Social politics and the commodification of care. *Social Politics: International Studies in Gender, State and Society*, 4(3), pp. 362–81. DOI: 10.1093/sp/4.3.362.

Ungerson, C., 2005. Care, work and feeling. *The Sociological Review*, 53, pp. 188–203. DOI: 10.1111/ j.1467-954X.2005.00580.x.

8

Care provision inside and outside the professional care system

The case of long-term care insurance in Germany

Hildegard Theobald

Introduction

In 1995–1996, long-term care insurance (LTCI) was introduced in Germany, which provides universal but capped benefits based on social rights in a situation of care dependency. Within the framework of LTCI, beneficiaries may choose between home-based and residential care services or a cash benefit. The new policy scheme reinforced the prevalent family-oriented care model, but also triggered a considerable expansion of the professional care system embedded in a care market based on competition between registered for-profit and non-profit providers on equal terms. Due to the capped service benefits, care gaps emerged that were filled either by informal, family care or by services or assistance purchased by private means or the unregulated cash benefit. These services or assistance concern, first, additional privately financed services delivered by registered providers within the framework of LTCI, that is, inside the professional care system. Second, outside the professional care system, beneficiaries purchase different types of services such as, for example, meals on wheels by service providers not registered within the framework of LTCI, or employ domestic or care workers within the household context.

The expansion and restructuring of paid care work inside and outside the professional care system was accompanied by a corresponding expansion and restructuring of care employment and the increasing employment of care workers with migrant backgrounds, both inside and outside the professional care system. The processes resulted in a stratification of the female work field by migration status and training levels.

The chapter's analysis is based on the assumption that the interaction among distinct social policy approaches impact on the emerging patterns of care arrangements, the expansion and (re)structuring of paid care work inside and outside the professional care system, and the patterns of stratification among care workers. This chapter draws on neo-institutionalist approaches used within international comparative research on long-term care to systematically analyse the interrelationship between policy approaches, care arrangements, the development of paid care work inside and outside the professional care system, and the impact on the situation of care workers. LTCI is viewed as the most relevant social policy approach for the development, but the effects of employment, professionalization, and migration policies are also included in the analysis (for the relevance of further policy fields, see van Hooren, 2014; Williams, 2012; Theobald, 2011; Simonazzi, 2009). Empirically, this chapter draws on LTCI policy regulations, representative statistics, a literature review, and findings from our own representative research project in Germany with professional care workers in home-based and residential care provision within the framework of LTCI. This research project replicates in 2010 the NORDCARE survey of care workers that was first conducted in Sweden, Finland, Norway, and Denmark in 2005. The German survey was distributed to a random sample of 1,517 care workers in home-based and residential care provision in the entire country (response rate = 43 per cent). The services are available to all age groups, but predominatly used by older people.[1] A country-wide inquiry based on interviews and questionnaires with 1,500 members of private households, 759 managers in home-based services and 2,829 managers and main responsible care workers in residential care facilities is an important source for representative statistics in this chapter. This was carried out by a private research institute on behalf of the Federal Ministry of Health in 2010 (see TNS Infratest Sozialforschung, 2011).

This chapter is organized into four sections. In the following section, the conceptual background is developed. In the empirical part, the basic institutional and cultural dimensions of LTCI in Germany are outlined before care arrangements and their mix of different types of paid and informal family care work are shown. Based on this mixture, the situation of care workers in different types of paid care provision dependent on training levels and migration status is compared. In the final section, the conceptual framework and empirical findings are discussed to reveal the interrelationship between social policies, the construction of paid care work inside and outside the professional care system, and the situation of the different groups among care workers.

Construction and stratification of care work and the interaction of policy fields

Daly's (2000) framework on the interrelationship between care policies and the effects on social care workers is used as a starting point for the development of my own conceptual framework. In her approach, Daly (2000) distinguishes between structures, processes and outcomes to reveal the interrelationship between patterns of inequalities and care policies. Structures are defined as institutional designs of care policies, that is, the risks covered by policies and the design of entitlements and underlying values. As a fundamental gendered and classed process, Daly (2000) teases out the social construction of care work across the private–public border. Finally, outcomes are defined as the gendered and classed stratifications in care work. Concepts and findings created within international comparative research on care, professional approaches, selected employment and migration policies are used to elaborate the basic approach.

Long-term care policies

The involvement of different societal sectors – family, state, market, welfare associations – in policy arrangements and care responsibilities is characteristic for long-term care as a societal activity (see e.g. Lyon and Glucksman, 2008). Since the 1990s, universal and market-oriented long-term care policies have been introduced in several continental European countries – including Germany – with far-reaching effects on the societal organization of care responsibilities. The policy approaches show country differences with regard to the definition of universalism and market-oriented policies. As a common characteristic, the term 'universal' concerns the coverage of the whole population without means-testing within the framework of a policy scheme, while further institutional dimensions differ widely. Three characteristics are necessary for a systematic comparative analysis of the institutional dimensions and underlying cultural values in continental European countries: eligibility criteria (i.e. universalism versus selectivism), the level of generosity (i.e. comprehensiveness of public support) and the type of support (i.e. money, services or time). Two basic approaches can be distinguished within market-oriented policies: first, a market-oriented restructuring of the professional care system – that is, the establishment of a care market and/or the transfer of approaches of work organizations from the private service sector to the publicly financed sector and, second, the introduction of cash-for-care schemes, which may enable the purchasing of services or assistance even outside the professional care system (for greater detail, see Theobald, 2015).

Employment policies and professionalization

While long-term care policies are decisive for the allocation of distinct care activities, employment policies, such as labour laws or the definition of social security standards, and professionalization policies contribute to the construction of care work (Williams, 2012; Theobald, 2011; Simonazzi, 2009). Professional approaches to care work define training levels, related care tasks and development paths in care work. Kuhlmann and Larsen (2014) distinguish between three types of professional developments in (nursing) care work: (1) an elitist model with an emphasis on bachelor or masters programmes, orientated towards a highly qualified care or nursing staff, and neglecting training of further groups among care workers (e.g. the UK); (2) a model of constrained professionalization (e.g. Germany) focusing on qualified occupational training programmes; and (3) a model of integrated professionalism (e.g. Finland) in which professionalization is undertaken at different levels and related to more integrated professionalization paths.

Migration policies

Migration policies determine the rules for the entrance and exit of non-nationals into a country, including access to the formal labour market. Different types of policies have emerged to regulate entrance in the area of long-term care. General migration policies define non-national populations' access to all areas of the labour market, for example distinct policies related to the single market within the European Union (EU). Finally, specific national regulations or agreements with selected countries define criteria and conditions for access to certain labour market areas, such as employment in long-term care. The different migration approaches create opportunities but also vulnerabilities, and contribute to the development of patterns of stratification based on distinct migration status (see van Hooren, 2014).

According to the basic assumption of Daly's (2000) conceptual approach, the significant dimensions of policy design provide the framework for *processes* – the social construction of care work across the private-public border. Research has proven the influence of long-term care rights. At least a medium level of public funding and an emphasis on either care service provision and/or strictly regulated cash payments are a prerequisite for the formalization of care work as a regular employment activity (cf. e.g. Simonazzi, 2009). Processes differ further based on the role of different societal sectors. In particular, a market-dominated formalization impedes the social construction of care work on lower levels as a qualified, autonomous activity, while within private households, a blurred border to unpaid family work impedes the formalization of care work as regular employment activity (Knijn and Verhagen, 2007; Henriksson et al., 2006).

With the term *outcomes*, Daly (2000) defines patterns of stratification of care work in the care workforce based on gender and socio-economic class. Within long-term care, market- and family-oriented restructuring has resulted in an increasing precariousness of care work based on elements such as (involuntary) fixed-term contracts and part-time employment, employment with lower levels of social security, low or even declining wages, and (un)regulated activities within the household context (Theobald, 2012; Williams and Brennan, 2012). As a traditional female activity, care work is clearly gendered, with further stratifications visible, based on socio-economic class and increasingly also ethnicity or migrant backgrounds. Basic assumptions created within intersectional analysis are used to elaborate on this interplay. Analogous to unitary approaches, the intersection of inequalities is assumed to be socially constructed in a distinct historical and social context in which contemporary power relations operate (Becker-Schmidt, 2007). To reveal the patterns of stratification in the female work field, the analysis draws on the approach of Walgenbach (2007), who defines gender as a heterogeneous social category that combines different forms of inequalities and is constructed within a specific social context. Processes of social construction include both macro levels – including social policies – as well as meso and micro levels – for example, employment situations and work practices embedded in daily care work (for greater detail, see Theobald, 2017).

Long-term care insurance in Germany

Basic features of LTCI: institutional dimensions and underlying cultural values

With the introduction of LTCI, a mix of social and fiscal goals was intended to be achieved. Before its introduction, long-term care needs were mainly viewed as a family responsibility. Only when the family was not available and after a means test could costs for care provision be covered by the Federal Law on Social Assistance (BSHG). The emphasis on family care and the availability of only means-tested social assistance benefits created severe social and fiscal difficulties. From a social policy perspective, means-tested benefits resulted in high private costs for most users of residential care services, underdevelopment of home-based care services and a lack of support for informal, family care. From a fiscal perspective, the reliance on social assistance benefits put severe fiscal strains on the local levels responsible for these payments. The money provided by the introduction of LTCI aimed to reduce fiscal strains on the local levels.

Against this background, LTCI in Germany is characterized by three basic cultural values: (1) an emphasis on universal benefits covering the whole population without means-testing to reduce the risk of impoverishment; (2) an emphasis on state support for care within the family framework to promote family care provision; and (3) an emphasis on the superiority of markets with regard to a cost-effective and user-oriented expansion of the professional care system. These cultural values are reflected in the LTCI law (see Table 8.1). Federal law on LTCI stipulated three levels of increasing care dependency based on the amount of care provison needed and related benefits. With the reform in 2016, instead of levels of care dependency, care grades have been stipulated by LTCI law, which assesses care dependency by the level of autonomy in relevant areas. LTCI provides capped benefits at a medium level of generosity and enables user choice between different types of benefits, that is, residential and home-based care services, as well as an unregulated cash benefits or a mix of home-based care services and cash benefits to maintain family care provision (see Table 8.1).

Furthermore, embedded within the framework of LTCI, a professional care system was expanded but also marketized. A regulated care market was introduced based on equal

Hildegard Theobald

competition between the formerly dominating non-profit providers and for-profit providers with regard to care prices and quality. Access to the regulated care market was opened up for every provider meeting the criteria of (limited) qualification requirements. These were: nurses or elder carers in managerial positions should have had permanent responsibility as a nurse or an elder carer for at least two years, as well as further training; the principle of economic efficiency; and the availability of internal quality management. Care offers and related prices are negotiated between care provider organizations, experts of care insurance funds at regional levels, and representatives of social assistance authorities. Oriented towards a customer choice model, beneficiaries may choose between registered care providers and care offers.

Care arrangements: a mix of different types of care work

Since the introduction of LTCI, a recently slightly increasing proportion of 11–14 per cent of adults aged 65+ receive benefits (Federal Statistical Office, 2017) (see Table 8.1 for figures for 2015). Amounting to 1.0 per cent of GDP in 2013, public expenditure related to long-term care support (health and social care component) for older adults (65+) is below the OECD average (OECD, 2015, Table 11.21).

Within the framework of LTCI, a largely family-oriented care arrangement strategy has emerged. It is characterized by a dominant use of the unregulated cash benefit only (44 per cent of beneficiaries 65+ in 2015), whereas 26 per cent used home-based care services and 30 per cent received institutional care benefits (Federal Statistical Office, 2017). Private costs represent a share of 33 per cent of total costs (Rothgang, 2010). In contrast to the family orientation of LTCI, the restrictive public support, that is, the limited support of informal family carers and high private costs related to service use, are strongly criticized by beneficiaries and the general public alike (Carrera et al., 2013; Zok, 2011).

For beneficiaries to be cared for at home with the support of either service and/or cash benefit, the use of benefits is embedded in a complex care arrangement combining family caregiving and a mix of different types of paid care work inside and outside the professional care system. In 2015, 33 per cent of beneficiaries 65+ living at home chose the service benefit or a mix of

Table 8.1 LTCI design and use of benefits

Institutional dimensions	LTCI – design	Outcomes beneficiaries 65+ in 2015
Eligibility criteria		
Universalism versus selectivism	Universal	Coverage: 13.7% (total)
Generosity		
Range of care types	Personal care, household-related services, social services	Mainly personal care only
Public costs in % of GDP		1.0%
Private costs within the framework of LTCI		33% (2010)
		Home-based services: 3.6%
Type of benefit available	Cash benefit, home-based, (semi-) residential care services – choice	Cash payments only: 5.9% Residential services: 4.1%

Source: Federal Statistical Office (2017); OECD (2015).

the service and cash benefit and received professional LTCI care services, mainly for personal care and rarely for household-related activities (Federal Statistical Office, 2017). Based on their economic situation, living situation and cultural values, care services are more often used by beneficiaries who live alone (more often women) and belong to the higher socio-economic strata, and they are more likely to be German nationals (Schwinger et al., 2016; Heusinger and Klünder, 2005).

Capped benefits for professional home-based care services are not intended to cover needs-oriented care provision. They are meant to be complemented by either family care or different types of paid care work. The latter concerns, first, services delivered by the professional LTCI care system. Within this framework, beneficiaries may top up publicly financed services based on private means. Second, beneficiaries may purchase private services such as meals on wheels or assistance within the private household outside this professional care system based on the unregulated cash benefit and/or private means. Informal, mainly (female) family care is comprehensive and significant for maintaining care at home. According to representative statistics on beneficiaries living at home in 2010, main informal carers work 37.5 hours per week on average, while only 7 per cent of beneficiaries in general and 1 per cent at the highest care dependency level (III) are cared for only by professional LTCI care services (TNS Infratest Sozialforschung, 2011).

Two different types of private services or paid assistance outside the professional care system include regular support with some care- or household-related assistance, and comprehensive 24-hour care services. According to a 2010 representative inquiry among beneficiaries living at home, 17 per cent regularly purchased private services or assistance within the private household related to bodily care or household activities at least once a week (TNS Infratest Sozialforschung, 2011). This type of support is most often purchased by beneficiaries choosing a mix of the home-based service benefit and the LTCI cash benefit (29 per cent of these beneficiaries), followed by beneficiaries who opt for professional services only (20 per cent), and most rarely by beneficiaries receiving the cash benefit only (14 per cent). Since the end of the 1990s, a new type of care arrangement has emerged, namely the provision of comprehensive care work within private households by live-in migrant carer workers. Due to the often-irregular work situation, there are only estimations available, with 300,000 to 400,000 migrant live-in care workers in the most recent estimation (Satola and Schywalski, 2016) (for greater detail, see the section below).

Professional care system: expansion, restructurings and ethnic diversification

With the introduction of LTCI, a professional care system expanded and was simultaneously marketized. This affected the structuring of the professional care system and the situation of care workers (see Table 8.2 for an overview). Between 1991 and 2015, the number of home-based care providers more than tripled, from 4,000 to 13,323, followed by a strong increase in the share of for-profit providers (65 per cent in 2015) who served about 50 per cent of the users in the formerly predominantly non-profit care infrastructure (Federal Statistical Office, 2017; Slotala, 2011). With regard to residential care, the inroad of for-profit providers was less pronounced; in 2015, non-profit providers continued to cover the majority of providers and beds (Federal Statistical Office, 2017).

The expansion and restructuring of the professional care system are reflected in the changing situation of the care workforce. Concurrent with the expansion, the care workforce almost quintupled, followed by a rise in part-time working arrangements from about 40 per cent in 1993 to about 70 per cent in 2015 (Federal Statistical Office, 2017; Schölkopf, 1998).

Hildegard Theobald

This expansion included both an increase of qualified and assistant or untrained labour (Oschmianski, 2010). In 2015, 35 per cent of care workers had completed a qualified occupational-related training of mainly two to three years as elder carers or nurses, while 50 per cent had no care-related/assistant training, and there were considerable differences between home-based and residential care provision (Federal Statistical Office, 2017) (see Table 8.2).

The employment of trained and assistant staff clearly indicates a hierarchization of employment conditions based on training levels and working tasks. Part-time arrangements with lower social security standards (20.0 per cent in home-based care and 9.2 per cent in residential care in 2015 in total) are particularly widespread among care workers with non-care-related training, who more often provide household-related assistance in home-based care (Federal Statistical Office, 2017; TNS Infratest Sozialforschung, 2011). Beginning with for-profit providers and followed by non-profit providers, the hierarchization includes a lowering of wages for care workers at lower training levels (Kühnlein, 2007). The introduction of a statutory care minimum wage scheme in August 2010 (initially intended to run until December 2014, but amended in 2015 to run until 2017) successfully established a certain wage level for care workers employed by providers and conducting mainly personal care tasks. The minimum hourly wage was set at €8.50 for 2010 (rising in several steps to €10.20 in 2017) in the former West Germany and at €7.50 for 2010 (rising in several steps to €9.50 in 2017) in the former East Germany. Since the amendment in 2015, even care workers mainly involved in social care activities are included.

Table 8.2 Professional care system: situation and change

	1991–1993		2015	
	Home-based providers	Residential beds	Home-based providers	Residential beds
Number of providers/beds	4,000 (1991)		13,323	
Agency of the providers		682,220 (1993)		855,733
Non-profit	Dominant		34%	
For-profit		Dominant	65%	56%
Public			1%	38%
				6%
	1993		*2015*	
Number of care workers	49,808	174,051	355,613	730,145
full-time equivalent			238,846	525,205
Part-time work arrangements	46.0%	35.3%	72.8%	68.8%
on lower social security level*				
Training levels			20.0%	9.2%
Elder carers/nurses				
Further care-related training			45.5%	31.5%
Non-care-related training/assistants			6.9%	6.3%
Trainees			44.3%	55.0%
			3.3%	7.2%

Source: Federal Statistical Office (2017): data on 2015; Slotala (2011): home-based care providers 1990; Schölkopf (1998): number of beds in residential care 1993; care workers in residential/home-based care 1993 in non-profit organizations only.

Note: * Part-time work on lower social security level, that is, employment contracts with wages up to €450 per month or for short-term employment (up to three months and no more than 70 days per year) does not include statutory healthcare insurance, long-term care insurance, or unemployment insurance. Statutory pension insurance schemes are included, but can be declined by employees.

In addition, with the reform of LTCI in 2017, regional care insurance funds are obliged to accept wage levels based on wage agreements during the negotiation of the contracts.

The contradictory developments of the employment of both trained and untrained staff, an increase in part-time work arrangements, partly even with lower social security standards, and a hierarchization between different groups of care workers can be explained by the interplay of training regulations, a market-oriented reorganization of care work embedded in a cost containment framework, and employment policies. LTCI law only defines limited qualification requirements. The employment of trained staff is due to regulations outside LTCI law. Within home-based care, this employment is based on the combined provision of long-term care and home nursing services financed via healthcare insurance with regulated training requirements. With regard to residential care provision, qualification requirements stipulated by federal law are in place prescribing a 50 per cent quota of care workers with at least a qualified two- to three-year occupational training. According to a representative inquiry in 2010, this quota is mainly fulfilled by nursing homes (TNS Infratest Sozialforschung, 2011). In particular, since the introduction of a new type of assistant care worker – dementia carer – in 2008, training levels are gradually declining (cf. data on training levels in 2015 in Table 8.2).

Against the background of regulated training levels, the increase of partly involuntary part-time employment (above all at lower security levels), a lowering of wages, and hierarchization among care workers can be seen as cost-reduction strategies by care providers. This is intended to meet price competition in the care market, to generate profits, and to correspond to the principle of economic efficiency demanded during negotiations with the financiers (regional care insurance funds and social assistance authorities). Furthermore, employment at lower social security levels is promoted by changing labour market policies that emphasize this type of employment to reduce unemployment levels in general for the labour market (Oschmianski, 2010).

In addition to the hierarchization of the care workforce dependent on training levels, the employment of care workers with migrant backgrounds has increased. According to a representative inquiry in 2010, managers of home-based care providers estimated a proportion of 11 per cent of care workers with migrant backgrounds, while the proportion for residential care staff ranged from 23 per cent estimated by supervisors down to 15 per cent when estimated by general managers (TNS Infratest Sozialforschung, 2011). The term 'migrant backgrounds' includes both foreign-born care workers and second-generation migrants. Findings from our research project on the situation of care workers in home-based and residential care services are used to compare the differences between indigenous care workers and those with migrant backgrounds. In our sample, 10.2 per cent of home-based care staff have a migrant background, corresponding with the figures of the representative inquiry of 2010. The proportion in residential care provision is 14.0 per cent, which seems to be a bit too low according to the representative inquiry of 2010 (different estimations: 15 per cent versus 23 per cent) (see above).

In our study, about 79 per cent of care workers with migration backgrounds were foreign-born, and 21 per cent were second-generation migrants. About two-thirds of them were migrants with German ancestors who lived in the former Soviet Union or in Eastern European countries and had the right to migrate to Germany and to obtain German citizenship status. The remaining third came mainly from Western European EU member countries (17.7 per cent) and from outside Europe (16.5 per cent). For the most part, it can be assumed that these care workers have access to the labour market in general either based on German citizenship status or as residents of EU member states. Because there are no differences with regard to the presented research findings between first- and second-generation migrants, we do not distinguish between the groups. For the comparison, significant indicators of the employment and work situation (i.e. training levels, working time arrangements, and information on working tasks) have been selected.

The comparison of the situation between indigenous care workers and care workers with migrant backgrounds reveals a mixed picture of positive and negative indicators (for the findings, see Table 8.3). Care workers with migrant backgrounds are more (albeit not significantly) likely to have completed a two- to three-year occupational training programme as a nurse or elder carer than indigenous care workers. While there is no additional research available on the situation within home-based care, further studies available for residential care have found equal training levels for indigenous and care workers with migrant backgrounds (for an overview, see Stagge, 2016). The slightly higher proportion of trained care workers in residential care services (39.6 versus 31.4 per cent) may reflect lower participation rates among non-trained/ assistant staff with migrant backgrounds due to language difficulties. The comparable training levels among both groups of care workers can be explained by the demand for trained care workers based on training regulations and corresponding active German labour market policies emphasizing training possibilities related to care work to promote labour market participation.

In general, working time arrangements also paint a positive picture for care workers with migrant backgrounds. Compared with indigenous care workers, they are significantly more often employed on full-time contracts (61.9 versus 39.1 per cent) and more rarely by precarious, short part-time working contracts (9.6 versus 17.2 per cent). Indigenous care workers are more often employed on short part-time working contracts within home-based care (31.8 versus 11.8 per cent), while there is not much difference between the groups in residential care provision in general. However, care workers with migrant backgrounds and without formal care-related training in residential care provision are more often employed on this type of contract (26.7 versus 8.5 per cent).

A comparison of caring tasks reveals one difference between the groups in residential care services, which indicates discriminatory work practices in daily care delivery on the organizational level: care workers with migrant backgrounds are significantly more often involved in additional (low-status) daily cleaning activities. While this concerns all care workers with migrant backgrounds, it is particularly pronounced for those without formal care-related training. The latter confirms a disadvantaged situation already visible in working time arrangements for this group.

Care- and household-related work outside the professional care system

For the development of care- and household-related work outside the professional care system, we focus on domestic and care activities with private households as employers. Here, two types of domestic activities can be singled out: household-related services delivered on an hourly basis and comprehensive 24-hour care services provided by live-in migrant care workers. According to statistics, in 2010, 12 per cent of people aged 65+ regularly or occasionally purchased household assistance mainly on a grey market (own calculations based on the German Socio-Economic Panel GSOEP).[2] Since the 1990s, several efforts have been undertaken to promote regular household-related assistance instead of grey-market activities based on income tax deductions for the private household as employers. As part of the labour market reform in 2003 (amended in 2006 and 2008), a new category, 'mini-jobs in private households', was created, characterized by low wages and limited social entitlements (see Shire, 2015). Despite an increase of people employed in mini-job arrangements by private households from approximately 30,000 in 2003 to more than 280,000 in 2014, about 90 per cent of

Table 8.3 Indicators of the situation of care workers, comparing indigenous workers and those with migrant backgrounds

Training levels	Nurses/elder carers			Further-trained staff			Assistant/non-care-related training		
	Migrant	Indigenous	All	Migrant	Indigenous	All	Migrant	Indigenous	All
Total	49.2%	37.2%	38.6%	15.4%	15.2%	15.3%	35.4%	47.5%	46.1%
Home-based care	76.5%	50.6%	53.1%	5.9%	15.2%	14.3%	17.6%	34.2%	32.5%
Residential care	39.6%	31.4%	32.5%	18.7%	15.3%	15.8%	41.7%	53.2%	51.8%

Working time arrangements	Full-time (35+ hours)			Part-time (21–34 hours)			Part-time (−20 hours)		
	Migrant	Indigenous	All	Migrant	Indigenous	All	Migrant	Indigenous	All
Total**	61.9%	39.1%	41.6%	28.6%	43.6%	42.0%	9.5%	17.2%	16.4%
Home-based care	47.1%	26.6%	28.7%	41.2%	41.6%	41.5%	11.8%	31.8%	29.8%
Residential care**	67.4%	44.4%	47.0%	23.9%	44.7%	42.3%	8.7%	10.9%	10.6%
Without formal care training (residential care)*	45.7%	33.9%	35.0%	26.7%	57.6%	55.0%	26.7%	8.5%	10.0%

Care tasks: cleaning tasks	Daily			More rarely					
	Migrant	Indigenous	All	Migrant	Indigenous	All			
Total**	30.0%	15.2%	16.9%	70.0%	84.8%	83.1%			
Home-based care	20.0%	16.6%	16.9%	80.0%	83.4%	83.1%			
Residential care**	31.8%	14.6%	16.7%	68.2%	85.4%	83.3%			
Without formal training (residential care)**	50.0%	14.2%	17.3%	50.0%	85.8%	82.7%			

Source: Own study on home-based and residential care workers.

Note: * $p < 0.05$; ** $p < 0.01$ (chi-square tests). Rarer response alternatives: weekly, monthly, rarely, never (mainly rarely).

household assistance is estimated to still be delivered by the grey market (Shire, 2015). Women with German citizenship (90 per cent of employees) are the primary users of mini-job arrangements, while a large segment of grey-market-based migrant labour remains within private households (see Gottschall and Schwarzkopf, 2010).

A more recent development concerns comprehensive care support within the family context, that is, 24-hour care provision based on live-in arrangements. Since the end of the 1990s, a market has emerged with migrant care workers mainly from neighbouring Eastern European countries. Typically, two care workers provide 24-hour care on a two- or three-month rotational basis. Migrant care workers provide both domestic services and care services for frail, often elderly females with extensive care needs, who cannot draw on comprehensive informal family care provision (Neuhaus et al., 2009). Care recipients and their families appreciate being able to stay in their own homes without comprehensive family care, despite considerable care needs and the lower costs of this solution compared with 24-hour professional home-based care provision. The costs for 24-hour care arrangements are estimated to amount on average to between €1,000 and €2,000 per month, including accommodation (Satola and Schywalski, 2016).

Since 2000, some efforts have been undertaken to regulate the status of migrant care workers within the family context. In 2002, a legal but only very rarely used care worker recruitment scheme was introduced to hire domestic workers from Eastern European countries on regular working conditions for families with care-dependent members (Frings, 2011). In addition, regulations related to the EU single market – the Free Movement of Services and the Posting of Workers Directive – are used by private placement agencies to constitute a legal framework for a type of employment that is below German labour market standards. Objections are raised that 24-hour care work does not correspond with the regulations. Finally, there are also 24-hour care provision arrangements available, completely organized on a grey-market basis (Satola and Schywalski, 2016). Due to the existing power relations in private households, it is difficult even for regularly employed migrant care workers to enforce labour market standards. Independent of the employment situation, long working hours in addition to non-regulated working hour schemes and work breaks are very common in this area (see Neuhaus et al., 2009).

Conclusion

This chapter has focused on the social construction of care work inside and outside the professional care system, and the impact on the situation of care workers dependent on their intersected socio-economic and migration status. The chapter proceeded on the assumption that the development is strongly affected by social policies at the macro level (i.e. long-term care policies, LTCI in Germany), and further mediated by employment, professionalization and migration policies.

The law on LTCI provides the starting point for the allocation of care work into different societal sectors. LTCI is characterized first by a universal orientation, second by only a medium level of public support (capped benefits), and third by the choice between unregulated cash benefits and market-oriented professional services. This design of LTCI resulted in the emergence of significant care gaps that have had to be filled either by additional privately paid care services inside or outside the professional care system and/or by extensive family care. The design and underlying values have triggered a distinctive construction of care work across different societal sectors. The expansion of care employment was followed by an aggravation of the situation of care workers and the emergence of complex patterns of stratification between different care worker groups related to training levels and/or migration backgrounds.

Patterns of stratification inside the professional care system can be explained by inter-related effects of regulations with regard to training levels, employment conditions, and the care market embedded in a cost-containment framework. The opening up of a care market for for-profit and non-profit providers on equal conditions based on competition in care quality and prices and the principle of economic efficiency has resulted in considerable efforts by providers to reduce costs mainly related to care employment, that is, by the intro-duction of part-time working arrangements based partly on lower social security standards and lower wages. This introduction was followed by a hierarchization of care work based on training levels. At the same time, state regulations on training levels with regard to home nursing and residential care services impede cost reductions based on reducing training levels among staff. The more recent definition of a new type of assistant care worker – the demen-tia care worker – in residential care services and the simultaneous regulation of wage levels for care work will probably increase the employment of less costly assistant care workers and strengthen the hierarchization.

The increasing recruitment of migrant care workers changes stratification patterns. Within the professional care system, indicators of a positive employment situation (e.g. training levels, working time arrangements) can be explained by the interaction of training regulations, labour market policies, and citizenship status or general work permits of care workers with migrant backgrounds. Nevertheless, one indicator of discriminatory practices stands out: they perform daily cleaning tasks significantly more often in residential care services, indicating discriminatory practices at an organizational level.

Patterns of care employment differ markedly outside the professional care system, with high levels of precariousness and ethnic diversification. Levels of precariousness range from regu-lar household-related work with fewer social security benefits (mainly conducted by German nationals) to irregular (grey-market activities) or quasi-regular household-related assistance and care work considerably below German labour market standards (mainly carried out by migrant care workers). Here, EU regulations with regard to the single market are drawn on as a legal framework for constructing care activities.

The findings reveal the social construction of care work across the private-public border in a complex interplay of training levels and migration backgrounds based on the interaction of long-term care, employment, professionalization and migration policies. Inside the profes-sional care system, the development of more precarious employment conditions is dependent on training levels as an indicator of socio-economic level, while the division of work tasks (primarily cleaning tasks) reveals discriminatory work practices based on migrant backgrounds at the organizational level. Outside the professional care system, the situation is characterized by a high level of precariousness of the employment and working situation. Here, migrant care workers dominate the most precarious situations, such as employment as live-in carers providing 24-hour care within private households.

Notes

1 We would like to thank the Hans-Böckler Foundation, Düsseldorf, for the funding of the German part of the research project (PI for the German part Prof. Hildegard Theobald, University of Vechta).

2 GSOEP is a longitudinal survey of approximately 11,000 private households in the Federal Republic of Germany since 1984, which is produced by the Deutsches Institut für Wirtschaftsforschung (DIW) (for further information, see www.eui.eu/Research/Library/ResearchGuides/Economics/Statistics/DataPortal/GSOEP.aspx).

References

Becker-Schmidt, R., 2007. 'Class', 'gender', 'ethnicity', 'race': Logiken der Differenzsetzung, Verschränkung von Ungleichheitslagen und gesellschaftliche Strukturierung ['Class', 'gender', 'ethnicty', 'race': the logic of differentiation, the interrelationship of inequalities, and societal structures]. In C. Klinger, G -A. Knapp and B. Sauer, eds. *Achsen der Ungleichheit. Zum Verhältnis von Klasse, Geschlecht und Ethnizität* [Axes of inequality: the interrelationship between class, gender and ethnicity]. Frankfurt/Main: Campus, pp. 56–83.

Carrera, F., Pavolini, E., Ranci, C. and Sabbatini, A., 2013. Long-term care systems in comparative perspective: care needs, informal and formal coverage, and social impacts in European contexts. In C. Ranci and E. Pavolini, eds. *Reform in long-term care policies in European countries*. Heidelberg, NY: Springer, pp. 23–52.

Daly, M., 2000. *The gender division of welfare*. Cambridge: Cambridge University Press.

Federal Statistical Office, 2017. *Pflegestatistik: Pflege im Rahmen der Pflegeversicherung. Deutschlandergebnisse* [Long-term care statistics. Care within the framework of LTCI: findings for Germany]. 1999, 2007, 2009, 2011, 2013, 2015. Available at: www.destatis.de/DE/Publikationen/Thematisch/Gesundheit/Pflege/PflegeDeutschlandergebnisse.html [accessed 15.07.2017].

Frings, D., 2011. Sexistisch-ethnische Segregation der Pflege und Hausarbeit im Zuge der EU-Erweiterung [The sexist-ethnic segregation of care and housework in the course of the EU enlargement]. In K. Böllert and C. Heite, eds. *Sozialpolitik als Geschlechterpolitik* [Social policy as gender policy]. Wiesbaden: VS-Verlag für Sozialwissenschaften, pp. 81–104.

Gottschall, K. and Schwarzkopf, M., 2010. *Irreguläre Arbeit in Privathaushalten* [Irregular work in private households]. Arbeitspapier 217. Arbeit und Soziales. Düsseldorf: Hans-Böckler Stiftung. Available at: www.boeckler.de/pdf/p_arbp_217.pdf [accessed 15.07.2017].

Heusinger, J. and Klünder, M., 2005. *'Ich lass mir nicht die Butter vom Brot nehmen!' Aushandlungsprozesse in häuslichen Pflegearrangements* ['I stand up for myself!' Negotiation processes in domestic care arrangements]. Frankfurt/Main: Mabuse.

Henriksson, L., Wrede, S. and Burau, V., 2006. Understanding professional projects in welfare service work: revival of old professionalism? *Gender, Work and Organization*, 13(2), pp. 174–92. DOI: 10.1111/j.1468-0432.2006.00302.x.

Knijn, T. and Verhagen, S., 2007. Contested professionalism payments for care and the quality of home care. *Administration and Society*, 39(4), pp. 451–75. DOI: 10.1177/0095399707300520.

Kuhlmann, E. and Larsen, C., 2014. Care, Governance und Professionsentwicklung im Europäischen Vergleich [Care, governance and professional development in European comparison]. In B. Aulenbacher, B. Riegraf and H. Theobald, eds. *Sorge: Arbeit, Verhältnisse, Regime* [Care: work, relations, regime]. Soziale Welt, Sonderband 20. Baden-Baden: Nosmos, pp. 235–51.

Kühnlein G., 2007. Auswirkungen der aktuellen Arbeitsmarkt und tarifpolitischen Entwicklungen auf die Arbeits-und Beschäftigungsverhältnisse von Frauen in der Sozialen Arbeit [Effects of current labour market and collective bargaining policies on the work and employment situations of women in social work]. In H.-J. Dahme, A. Trube and N. Wohlfahrt, eds. *Arbeit in sozialen Diensten: flexibel und schlecht bezahlt?* [Social service work: flexible and badly paid?]. Baltmannsweiler: Schneider-Verlag Hohengehren, pp. 35–45.

Lyon, D. and Glucksman, M., 2008. Comparative configurations of care work across Europe. *Sociology*, 42(1), pp. 101–18. DOI: 10.1177/0038038507084827.

Neuhaus, A., Isfort, M. and Weidner, F., 2009. *Situation und Bedarfe von Familien mit mittel- und osteuropäischen Haushaltshilfen* [The situation and care needs of families with domestic assistance from Central and Eastern Europe]. Cologne: Deutsches Institut für angewandte Pflegeforschung e.v. Available at: www.dip.de/fileadmin/data/pdf/material/bericht_haushaltshilfen.pdf [accessed 15.07.2017].

OECD, 2015. *Health at a glance 2013*. Paris: OECD. DOI: http://dx.doi.org/10.1787/health_glance-2015-graph201-en [accessed 19.07.2017].

Oschmianski, H., 2010. Wandel der Erwerbsformen in einem Frauenarbeitsmarkt. Das Beispiel 'Altenpflege' [Changing forms of employment in a female labour market: the example of 'eldercare']. *Zeitschrift für Sozialreform*, 56(1), pp. 31–57. DOI: 10.1515/zsr-2010-0103.

Rothgang, H., 2010. Social insurance for long-term care: an evaluation of the German model. *Social Policy and Administration*, 44(4), pp. 436–60. DOI: 10.1111/j.1467-9515.2010.00722.x.

Satola, A. and Schywalski, B., 2016. 'Live-in-Arrangements' in deutschen Haushalten: Zwischen arbeitsrechtlichen/-vertraglichen (Un)-Sicherheiten und Handlungsmöglichkeiten [Live-in arrangements in German households: between labour law and employment-contract (in)securities and possibilities for action]. In K. Jacobs, A. Kuhlmey, S. Greß, J. Klauber and A. Schwinger, eds. *Pflegereport 2016. Die Pflegenden im Fokus* [Care report 2016. Focus on care workers.]. Stuttgart: Schattauer, pp. 127–38.

Schölkopf, M., 1998. Die Altenpflege und die Daten. Zur quantitativen Entwicklung der Versorgung pflegebedürftiger Menschen [Eldercare and data: the quantitative development of care for frail elderly people]. *Sozialer Fortschritt*, 47(1), pp. 1–9.

Schwinger, A., Tsiasioti, C. and Klauber, J., 2016. Unterstützungsbedarf in der informellen Pflege – eine Befragung pflegender Angehöriger [Support requirements in informal family care: a survey of family carers]. In K. Jacobs, A. Kuhlmey, S. Greß, J. Klauber and A. Schwinger, eds. *Pflegereport 2016. Die Pflegenden im Fokus* [Care report 2016. Focus on care workers.]. Stuttgart: Schattauer. pp. 189–216.

Shire, K., 2015. State policies encouraging the outsourcing of personal and household labour in Germany: familialism and women's employment in conservative welfare states. In C. Carbonnier and N. Morel, eds. *The political economy of household services in Europe*. Basingstoke: Palgrave Macmillan, pp. 102–26.

Simonazzi, A., 2009. Care regimes and national employment models. *Cambridge Journal of Economics*, 33, pp. 211–32. DOI: https://doi.org/10.1093/cje/ben043.

Slotala L., 2011. *Ökonomisierung der ambulanten Pflege* [The marketization of professional home-based care services]. Wiesbaden: Verlag für Sozialwissenschaften.

Stagge, M., 2016. *Multikulturelle Teams in der Altenpflege* [Multicultural teams in eldercare]. Wiesbaden: Springer VS.

Theobald, H., 2011. Migrant carers in long-term care provision: interaction of policy fields. In B. Pfau-Effinger and T. Rostgaard, eds. *Care between work and welfare in European societies*. Basingstoke: Palgrave Macmillan, pp.155–76.

Theobald, H., 2012. Combining welfare mix and New Public Management: the case of long-term care insurance in Germany. *International Journal of Social Welfare*, 21, pp. 61–74. DOI: 10.1111/j.1468-2397.2011.00865.x.

Theobald, H., 2015. Marketization and managerialization of long-term care policies in a comparative perspective. In E. Pavolini and T. Klenk, eds. *Restructuring welfare governance: marketization, managerialism, and welfare state professionalism*. Aldershot: Edward Elgar, pp. 27–45.

Theobald, H., 2017. Care workers with migrant backgrounds in formal care services in Germany: a multilevel intersectional analysis. *International Journal of Care and Caring*, 1(2), pp. 209–26. DOI: https://doi.org/10.1332/239788217X14944099147786.

TNS Infratest Sozialforschung, 2011. *Abschlussbericht zur Studie 'Wirkungen des Pflege-Weiterentwicklungsgesetzes'*. [Final report on the study 'The effects of the Long-Term Care Further Development Act']. Berlin: Bundesgesundheitsministerium. Available at: www.tns-infratest.com/sofo/_pdf/2011_abschlussbericht_wirkungen_des_pflege-weiterentwicklungsgesetzes.pdf [accessed 04.07.2017].

Van Hooren, F., 2014. Migrant care work in Europe: variety and institutional determinants. In M. Leon, ed. *The transformation of care in European societies*. Basingstoke: Palgrave Macmillan, pp. 62–82.

Walgenbach, K., 2007. Gender als interdependente Kategorie [Gender as an interdependent category]. In K. Walgenbach, G. Dietze, A. Hornscheidt and K. Palm, eds. *Gender als interdependente Kategorie* [Gender as an interdependent category]. Opladen, Farmington Hills: Barbara Budrich, pp. 23–64.

Williams, F., 2012. Converging variations in migrant work in Europe. *Journal of European Social Policy*, 22(4), pp. 363–76. DOI: 10.1177/0958928712449771.

Williams, F. and Brennan, D., eds., 2012. Care, markets and migration in a globalising world: introduction to the special issue. *Journal of European Social Policy*, 22(4), pp. 355–62. DOI: 10.1177/0958928712449777.

Zok, K., 2011. Erwartungen an eine Pflegereform. Ergebnisse einer Repräsentativbefragung [The expectations of a long-term-care reform: the findings of a representative inquiry]. *WiDO-monitor*, 8(2), pp. 1–8. Available at: www.wido.de/fileadmin/wido/downloads/pdf_wido_monitor/wido_mon_pflegereform_0711.pdf [accessed 15.07.2017].

9

Employing migrant care workers for 24-hour care in private households in Austria

Benefits and risks for the long-term care system

August Österle

Introduction

Migrant care work in private households has become an important element of Austria's long-term care system. But it is an element that is not well integrated into the long-term care system and one that is viewed as highly controversial by stakeholders and experts. Following an analysis of the development of the Austrian long-term care system, and migrant care work more specifically, this chapter studies the impact of migrant care work on the Austrian long-term care system. The discussion differentiates between the macro level (the long-term care policy level), the meso level (the level of provider organizations and intermediaries), the micro level (care workers and care users) and the interrelationship between these different levels. The chapter is based on a systematic analysis of research papers and statistical information. The author's own studies on the developments, the determinants and the implications of migrant care work draw on empirical data from a series of qualitative interviews with migrant care workers and experts (undertaken between the early 2000s and 2014) and a survey of the online presence of intermediaries acting as placement organizations.

The following section provides an overview of the Austrian long-term care system. It shows how it has shifted from a largely social assistance-oriented approach to a more universalistic approach. The development of migrant care work, or – as commonly termed in Austria – 24-hour care work, from an irregular phenomenon to a regular element of the Austrian long-term care system, is analysed in the next two sections. These also highlight the dimensions of migrant care work and its relative contribution to covering long-term care needs. This then leads to the discussion of the impact of migrant care work on the Austrian long-term care system and a brief conclusion.

The Austrian long-term care system

In the literature into welfare states from a comparative perspective, Austria is characterized as a corporatist and conservative welfare state where access to social rights is closely linked to employment status and family status (Österle and Heitzmann, 2016). The social insurance principle applies to pension, accident, health and unemployment policies. Childcare policies are tax-funded and characterized by a dominance of universal cash benefits over services. Provisions in the case of long-term care needs, up until the early 1990s, were rather fragmented and, to a large extent, social assistance-oriented. This was only changed with a comprehensive reform in 1993. Rather than following the strong social insurance tradition of this country, long-term care followed the family policy tradition with an important role for cash benefits and tax funding of public support. Austria became part of a group of European countries that have moved from residualism in long-term care to a more comprehensive approach characterized as 'restricted universalism' (Ranci and Pavolini, 2013, 2015). 'Restricted universalism' indicates that access to the cash-for-care benefit is open to the entire population in need of care without means-testing, but at the same time is intended to provide a contribution to care-related costs, but not to fully cover these costs (Österle, 2013).

With the 1993 reform, the Austrian long-term care system builds on three pillars: cash-for-care, services and family care (Österle, 2013). At the core of the new public long-term care policy is a cash-for-care benefit (*Pflegegeld*). This cash benefit is not means-tested, and is paid to people in need of long-term care according to seven levels of care needs. In 2017, the respective benefit ranges between €157.30 in level 1 and €1,688.90 in level 7 per month (see Table 9.1). It is paid to people in need of long-term care of all age groups, 82 per cent of whom are 61 years of age and older. Women represent 65 per cent of recipients. In terms of personal coverage, the Austrian cash-for-care system is one of the most generous in Europe. The benefit was paid to 5.3 per cent of the total population in 2015. However, 25 per cent of all recipients fell into benefit level 1 (the lowest level), and another 26 per cent into benefit level 2 (Statistik Austria, 2017a). When the benefit system was introduced in 1993, it found broad political support, though for different reasons, including support for informal caregivers, the empowerment of those in need of care, the strengthening of choice or the support for market-driven developments (Österle, 2013). Compared to other cash-for-care schemes in Europe, the Austrian approach at least implicitly follows a conservative familialistic logic (Da Roit et al., 2016). It is intended to provide financial support for long-term care-related uses, but recipients are free in the actual use. There is no limitation to some predefined packages of care. This leaves it to the user or the family whether the money is spent on paid care services, whether it is transferred to an informal caregiver or whether it just becomes part of the household income.

The social service infrastructure for long-term care prior to the 1993 reform was very much focused on residential care, home care services being well developed in a few provinces, but scattered and often non-existent in others. As the second pillar of the 1993 long-term care reform, the responsibility of the nine Austrian provinces for the development of care services was reinforced in a state-provinces treaty. But this was done without defining nationwide targets for infrastructure development. Still, there have been major changes and extensions in the 1990s and 2000s (Österle and Bauer, 2012). There has been a considerable extension in home care services and a stricter orientation of residential care towards those with more intense care needs. This went along with a substantial increase in staff numbers, growing professionalization and efforts to improve quality management. There is a considerable heterogeneity across Austria in terms of welfare mix. Overall, the public sector dominates the residential care sector (followed by the non-profit and the for-profit sector), while the vast majority of providers in home care are non-profits. Users, in principle, are free to choose services. In reality, however, there are considerable limitations. The extent of the potential choices depends on a variety of factors, including the availability of alternative providers (which is more limited in rural areas), regional differences in co-payment regulations, but also the ability and willingness to pay out of pocket for those services that are not publicly co-funded.

Despite the development of a more comprehensive long-term care policy, the family is still a core pillar of the long-term care system. Family orientation is strong in people's valuations and expectations (European Commission, 2007) and the family is strong in the actual caregiving practices. The 1993 reform was not just about relieving families from informal caregiving obligations, but about providing support for informal caregiving and preserving informal care resources. The cash-for-care system was intended as a programme that provides financial recognition and financial support for informal care work. Additional support for family caregivers includes pension insurance coverage, counselling services or a financially supported long-term care leave programme for employees introduced in 2014 (BMASK, 2016; Österle, 2013). The changes have significantly improved the situation of family caregivers, but a familialistic orientation with traditional gender roles is upheld (Appelt and Fleischer, 2014; Österle and Bauer, 2012).

Besides these three pillars, a growing number of households started to hire migrant long-term care workers from Central Eastern European countries to provide care in the private household of the user, commonly termed as 24-hour care. This was not part of the public long-term care policy agenda. It was a grass-roots development in the regions close to the Austrian eastern border that started in the second half of the 1990s (Österle and Hammer, 2007). In the early 2000s, it became an increasingly important but, up until 2006, an irregular source of long-term care provision. The respective developments are discussed in more detail in the following sections.

According to national statistics, public long-term care expenditure (including expenditure for the care allowance, for services and the 24-hour care-related benefit) accounts for 1.35 per cent of GDP in Austria (Statistik Austria, 2017a, 2017b). This is a level significantly below Northern European countries, but substantially larger than that in most Southern or Eastern European countries (OECD, 2015). By the end of 2015, the long-term care allowance was paid to 452,601 individuals (see Table 9.1). By the end of the same year, 55,000 people living in residential care settings, and 92,000 using home care services, received public financial support. Over the entire year 2015, 76,000 people were living in residential care settings, and 146,000 received at least some kind of home care service (Statistik Austria, 2017b). In addition, by the end of 2015, about 28,000 people in need of care were using 24-hour care provision (see below). While there is at least a partial overlap between users of traditional home care and 24-hour care, this implies that a large proportion of those receiving a cash-for-care benefit fully depend on informal, mostly family care work.

Total public expenditure on long-term care was €4.6 billion in 2015. Expenditure for the cash-for-care system was €2.5 billion (55 per cent), while total net expenditure for services amounted to €2.1 billion (45 per cent of total expenditure, including €1.43 billion for residential care, €0.39 billion for home care services, plus expenditure for other services such as day-care centres or financial support for 24-hour care) (Statistik Austria, 2017b). Important to note, net expenditure for services does not include substantial co-payments to be made by users from the cash benefit. In terms of funding services, residential care requires residents to use their pensions or other regular income and the cash-for-care benefit (up to some pocket money). Provinces are contributing if these sources do not cover the respective fees, but they have an opportunity of recourse to the assets of the user. Home care services require co-payments by users that are determined by the income of the user and the cash-for-care benefit. In addition, depending on care needs, provinces usually apply a certain maximum number of hours of services that are publicly co-funded.

Table 9.1 Cash-for-care and care services in Austria (31 December 2015)

Cash-for-care	Care services
Recipients of cash-for-care by benefit level (end of 2015):[1]	Residential care
Level 1 (€157.30): 112,788	Users (end of 2015):[2] 54,687
Level 2 (€290.00): 118,882	Users (total 2015):[2] 75,632
Level 3 (€451.80): 79,919	Care workers (FTE):[3] 32,176
Level 4 (€677.60): 64,479	Public net expenditure:[4] €1,432,000,000
Level 5 (€920.30): 48,121	
Level 6 (€1,285.20): 19,212	Home care
Level 7 (€1,688.90): 9,200	Users (end of 2015):[2] 91,613
Recipients in total: 452,601	Users (total 2015):[2] 145,723
Public expenditure: €2,530,000,000	Care workers (FTE):[3] 11,864
	Public net expenditure:[4] €386,000,000
	24-hour care
	Users (end of 2015): about 28,000
	Care workers: 55,801
	Public expenditure:[5] €139,000,000

Source: Statistik Austria (2017a, 2017b); BMASK (2016); Österle (2016)

Notes:

1 The benefit is for 2017, the number of recipients for 2015 (to allow for comparison with service users).
2 Users for whom services are publicly (co-)funded.
3 FTE: full-time equivalents.
4 Public net expenditure: public gross expenditure minus user contributions from cash-for-care benefits, from income-related co-payments and revenues from recourse to users.
5 Public expenditure for the means-tested 24-hour care benefit (see below).

Taken together, public coverage for long-term care has substantially increased since 1993, both in terms of personal coverage and in terms of the range of services. At the same time, individual financial contributions and family care provision remain very substantial. This confirms the initial characterization as restricted universalism. But similar to other countries, pressures on public long-term care systems and informal care resources continue to grow. Various socio-demographic factors, mobility, or employment and retirement patterns will make it more difficult for family members to provide long hours of care work informally, even more so when ageing leads to a growing number of people in need of long-term care (European Commission, 2015). One response to these challenges in the Austrian context is the employment of migrant care work in private households.

The emergence of 24-hour care work

Migrant care workers are employed throughout Europe to provide long-term care. In some European countries, the employment of migrant care workers by users or their families, often staying in the respective household as live-in workers, has reached significant levels (e.g. Da Roit and Weicht, 2013; van Hooren, 2012; Williams, 2012). Austria is one example. Here, the employment of migrant care workers in private households started in the mid-1990s, and became increasingly prominent in the 2000s. What was first a development in the border regions between Austria and neighbouring Central Eastern European countries, based on personal ties and word of mouth across borders, developed into a more organized system of migrant care work. Intermediaries started to expand the approach beyond word-of-mouth recommendations. Soon, what is commonly called 24-hour care in Austria became a widely known approach. The fact that it was a grey economy of care was silently accepted. Compared to the situation in other countries, migrant care work arrangements in Austria have some distinctive features. First, migrant care workers are almost exclusively from Central Eastern European countries. Second, all the arrangements are based on rotational migration between the respective home country and Austria as the destination country. Third, two care workers usually replace each other in one household in a two-weekly or more interval. Fourth, all migrant care workers are live-in care workers, having board and lodgings in the home of the user. Fifth, after the regularization, the dominant employment mode is self-employment.

In the summer of 2006, prior to a national election, the illegality of migrant care work became a major political issue. The continuing public debate, a consensus about the illegality of the practice but also about not making users of migrant care work responsible for this illegality, paved the way for a reform. The reform debate was then driven by two objectives: creating a legal framework for 24-hour care, but without endangering the specific characteristics and the affordability of the existing arrangements (Bachinger, 2010). This was achieved by allowing a self-employment option for migrant care work and by creating a new means-tested benefit for users of migrant care work (for details, see Österle and Bauer, 2016). For the employment of care workers, the reform allowed for three options: users or their families as employers, social service providers as employers of 24-hour care workers, or self-employment. Only the latter option allowed continuing with the common 24-hour care arrangement of two care workers replacing each other for two or more weekly shifts in the private household. An employer-employee relationship – because of work and wage regulations – would be a less flexible and more expensive option. Hence, today, 24-hour care workers are almost exclusively working as self-employed. Their earning perspective ranges considerably, depending on previous experience or specific qualifications in nursing, German-language skills or required tasks. Typically, the net income ranges between €600 and €1,000 for a two-weekly stay per month, plus the provision of board and lodging (Österle and Bauer, 2016).

Regular self-employment includes coverage in health, accident and pension insurance. Unemployment insurance, however, is a voluntary option in the case of self-employment. As it was imagined that these contributions would lead to an increase in the cost of now regular migrant care work, a means-tested benefit was introduced as a second major element of the reform. Apart from the means-testing, eligibility criteria include a certain level of care needs (dependency level 3 or above) of the user of 24-hour care work and some very basic qualification requirements for the care worker (one option to fulfil these criteria is proof of hands-on experience for at least six months). In addition to these core measures, further revisions and adaptations to the law were made. At the time of regularization, workers from Central Eastern European EU member states were still excluded from the Austrian labour market. To allow for regular employment, 24-hour care workers were therefore exempt from this rule. In addition, there were adjustments to the nurse and medical professional law on the delegation of tasks to 24-hour care workers. Overall, the reform was comprehensive and – largely because of the self-employment option and the financial benefit – very successful in terms of take-up.

After the regularization, there has been a constant and continuing increase in the number of 24-hour care workers. By the end of 2013, there were more than 44,000 24-hour care workers, and by the end of 2015 their number increased to almost 56,000 (see Table 9.2). Following the arrangement of two care workers replacing each other in one household in a two-weekly or more shift, this implies about 28,000 users of 24-hour care work. Compared to the number of around 453,000 individuals receiving a cash benefit, this seems a moderate level. But their role becomes quite important when comparing the number of migrant care workers with long-term care workers in home care and in residential care. By the end of 2015, in full-time equivalents, there were 32,300 care workers in residential care homes and 11,700 care workers in home care (in full-time equivalents), but almost 56,000 24-hour care workers.

Typically, 24-hour care workers are women from Slovakia or Romania, and mostly of middle or advanced age (see Table 9.2). About 95 per cent of 24-hour care workers are women, compared to 92 per cent in home care and 85 per cent in residential care (Statistik Austria, 2017b). Two-thirds are aged between 41 and 60 years of age. The group aged below 30 years of age is smaller than that aged 61 and older. The share of migrant care workers with dependents (children or adults in need of care) is not known. For Slovakia, Bahna (2015) indicates that care workers mostly have grown-up children, and only a few have older family members that need long-term care. For Romania, also a major source country of migrant care workers in Southern European countries, studies indicate that having younger children, but also having care obligations towards older family members, is more common (e.g. Bauer and Österle, 2016; Piperno, 2012). In terms of countries of origin, Slovakians still represent almost half of all 24-hour care workers in Austria, but their respective share is decreasing. By the end of 2015, 37 per cent were Romanians, and almost 6 per cent were Hungarians. All other countries of origin account for a maximum of 2.3 per cent of all 24-hour care workers.

Table 9.2 Twenty-four-hour care workers by country of origin, age and gender (31 December 2013, 2015)

	31 December 2013	*31 December 2015*
24-hour care workers[1]	44,143	55,801
24-hour care workers by nationality (% of all)		
Slovakia	56.0%	47.1%
Romania	30.1%	36.9%
Hungary	5.4%	5.6%
Bulgaria	2.0%	2.1%
Poland	1.9%	1.7%
Austria	1.9%	1.6%
Czech Republic	1.1%	0.9%
Croatia		2.3%
Other countries or unknown	1.6%	1.8%
24-hour care workers by gender		
Female	95.2%	94.7%
Male	4.8%	5.3%
24-hour care workers by age		
Up to 30 years	8.7%	6.9%
31–40 years	19.6%	17.6%
41–50 years	33.7%	34.2%
51–60 years	31.9%	33.7%
61 years and more	6.1%	7.7%

Source: Österle (2016)

Note:

1   24-hour care workers with an income beyond the threshold that requires them to pay social insurance contributions.

The development of rotational migration for 24-hour care in private households

The intersection of care regime, migration regime and employment regime has been identified as key for the emergence and institutionalization of migrant care work, and of the specific national patterns (Da Roit and Weicht, 2013; van Hooren, 2012; Williams, 2012). The factors that contributed to the emergence and growth of 24-hour care in Austria are manifold. Unlike Southern European countries, there was no strong tradition of employing migrant care workers in private households in Austria. In the case of household tasks, many families do employ workers, and many of them have a migration background, but usually they are employed on an hourly basis; live-in arrangements are the exception (Bauer et al., 2014). Twenty-four-hour care started to develop as a grass-roots phenomenon; it developed as a grey economy and was only later regularized, without, however, questioning the main features of the arrangements. It was a grass-roots development driven by individual factors. But these are rooted in the particular institutional context of the sending and receiving countries.

The demand for a 24-hour service is linked to the family orientation in the Austrian care regime. Caring in the family context, in the private home of the user, is the preferred care arrangement (Weicht, 2010; European Commission, 2007). Twenty-four-hour care allows long hours of care work in the private home when families are unable to provide the required care and when traditional services are either not available or not affordable to provide long hours of care every day. In addition, the use of traditional social services often implies multiple visits from different care workers specializing in specific tasks. Twenty-four-hour care instead is perceived as something close to traditional family care, ensuring continuing support in the private home without overburdening family members. However, even with the means-tested benefit, 24-hour care is not affordable for everyone, due to the substantial private costs to be covered or the lack of lodging opportunities for the care worker in the home of the care user.

From the care worker perspective, typical economic push and pull factors are important determinants of migration (Österle and Bauer, 2016). The income from employment, resulting in opportunities for improving living standards of the family back home, and investing in children's education are emphasized as key reasons for migration. In addition, the specific features of 24-hour care work attract women into this sector. Rotational migration allows access to the Western European labour markets and respective wage levels while still keeping the centre of private life in their home country. Twenty-four-hour care has extended the radius of what is usually possible only with commuting, and it does so without establishing a household in Austria.

From a care policy perspective, family orientation, low public expenditure and unregulated cash-for-care systems have been identified as major factors supporting the development of migrant care work. While public expenditure on long-term care is on an average European level in Austria, both family orientation and the availability of a relatively generous cash-for-care system have pushed the emergence of migrant care work (Da Roit and Weicht, 2013). When the benefit was introduced, it was an explicit goal that decisions should be left to the users, that it should help provide care in the private home of the user, and that such a benefit could contribute to market-driven developments in the care sector. Twenty-four-hour care was one – unintended – answer to long-term care needs fitting these ideas very well. From a migration policy perspective, open borders first facilitated free travel across borders, while largely limiting labour market access. Until 2011 and 2013 (for Romania and Bulgaria, respectively), regular employment for citizens from Central Eastern EU member states in Austria was limited to a few professions. The regularization of 24-hour care in 2007 therefore required that these workers were exempt from the limitations before labour markets were generally opened only years later. Anyone from outside the EU requires a specific approval for work in 24-hour care. As a consequence, all 24-hour care workers are from Central Eastern and South Eastern European EU member countries. From an employment perspective, the literature usually discusses labour market divisions that channel migrant workers into specific jobs (Williams, 2012). More important for the Austrian case (after the regularization) is the possibility to provide 24-hour care on the basis of self-employment. Self-employment helped to maintain the key features that existed before the regularization while still providing an affordable option to those who could afford 24-hour care before the regularization. Traditional employer-employee relationships, because of work time, wage and other regulations, would not allow for the traditional 24-hour care work arrangement, and would make respective arrangements unaffordable for most current users.

To sum up, with the regularization in 2007, 24-hour care work became a regular pillar of the Austrian long-term care system. At the same time, the integration into the traditional service system remained limited. This leads the discussion to an assessment of the benefits and the risks of migrant care work for the long-term care system in Austria.

Benefits and risks for the long-term care system

Twenty-four-hour care has become an important part of the Austrian long-term care system, but it remains very controversial. This section explores the benefits and risks involved. It does so by differentiating between the long-term care policy level, the level of provider organizations and intermediaries, and the level of care workers and care users and their families, and by considering the interrelationship between these levels and the effects 24-hour care produces. The discussion mainly focuses on the situation in Austria as destination country. The source country perspective will also be touched upon, but it is not at the centre of the discussion. Respective issues, for example brain drain and care drain, the reorganization of migrant care workers' care obligations, the impact on children left behind, or the role of financial and social remittances, are discussed in more detail elsewhere (e.g. Bauer and Österle, 2016; Boccagni, 2014; Lutz and Palenga-Möllenbeck, 2012; Piperno, 2012).

On the micro level, benefits for care workers, care users and their families have already been addressed when discussing the push and pull factors for care work migration. For care workers, 24-hour care work offers an attractive income and employment option. Not least, it is the rotational migration mode with work in Austria, but without establishing a household in this country, that makes it an economically attractive option. Since the regularization, migrant care workers also have access to social rights in Austria, including health insurance coverage, pension rights and family benefits (Österle and Bauer, 2016). On the negative side, three dimensions are of particular importance. First, care workers report a lot of strain related to living apart from family, from children or other family members in need of care and support, but also stress related to regular long-distance commuting (Bauer and Österle, 2013). Second, while the income perspective is the main driver of care work migration, particularly younger 24-hour care workers also expect that the job will help their professional career development (Österle and Bauer, 2016). But because of a lack of clearly defined qualification requirements that are embedded in the overall structure of care and nursing qualifications, and because of the often-isolated context in which many provide care work, respective career aspirations are difficult to realize. Third, work relations and work conditions are highly precarious and involve considerable risks for care workers (Bauer et al., 2014). This is determined by the self-employment mode that does not provide the same preventive measures that would apply for an employer-employee relationship.

In addition, because of the intimate character of the household as workplace and place of stay, and because of the 'emotional work' character, the enforceability of basic rights is limited (Christensen and Manthorpe, 2016). However, despite these risks, Bahna (2015) has shown a very positive job evaluation among Slovakian migrant care workers, a level even above that of the average female worker in Slovakia.

For care users and their families, the main benefit of the 24-hour care arrangement – for those who can afford 24-hour care – lies in having an option to ensure long hours of care work, a level of coverage that traditional care services can either not fulfil or that would not be affordable. It enables the person in need of care to stay in the private home and to have someone to be there for 24 hours a day, seven days a week, an arrangement that comes close to the 'ideal' of family care (Weicht, 2010). For family members, it implies a reduction of informal caregiving obligations and reduces the pressures on potential informal caregivers to limit or even quit their own employment. Balancing employment and caregiving is high on the agenda in the European employment rhetoric, even though mostly with a focus on childcare rather than long-term care for older people. A long-term care leave programme, introduced in 2014 in Austria, addresses the issue of balancing work and care by providing financially supported leave for between one and three months (BMASK, 2016). This can help for a transition period, but not for months or years of long-term caregiving. Twenty-four-hour care offers such a response, but with considerable private costs. Risks for users and their families mainly arise as quality risks. Regularization has created some very basic mechanisms of quality assurance, including the definition of professional competences and the need for written contracts and documentation of care work. This implies important improvements compared to the previous grey economy. At the same time, given that there is very little regulation of qualifications of care workers and of intermediaries, and no systematic policy to supervise quality, whether and how quality is taken into consideration is still largely left to users, families and intermediaries (Schmidt et al., 2016). Indeed, a survey of intermediaries in Austria has shown that existing offerings include the entire continuum from agencies that take quality issues very seriously to highly problematic offerings (Österle et al., 2013).

In a meso-level perspective, intermediaries are the main actors. In the early years of the development of 24-hour care, individuals started to act as intermediaries; some of these later turned into 'agencies' with a growing network of care workers. Today, many intermediaries not only offer a matching service; they support care users and care workers in administrative requirements, they organize short-term training courses and language courses or cooperate with respective institutions, and they organize travel between the home country and the destination in Austria. Acting as an intermediary requires no qualifications. The only requirement, as for care workers, is registration with the Austrian Chamber of Commerce. An accreditation has been proposed to institutionalize at least some quality control, but has not been installed so far, not even as a voluntary process. A novel development after the regularization was that traditional social service providers started to enter the 24-hour care market as intermediaries, usually via separate organizational units. In this segment, quality management is taken up in a more systematic way, for example by involving qualified home care professionals in assessing the need for 24-hour care or in the parallel use of traditional home care services and 24-hour care (Schmidt et al., 2016). But in general, as mentioned before, it is left to the intermediary how quality concerns are addressed. Only in 2015, newly established rules define some general basic professional requirements, including, for example, standards for information, contracting and documentation. This might help improve transparency and quality, but enforceability is still in question. Overall, the potential to use the role of intermediaries as a vehicle to introduce some more systematic approaches to quality assurance has not been taken up by the legislator.

From a macro-level long-term care policy perspective, 24-hour care is an option that was not intended with the 1993 reform. But it is now delivering a substantial share of the long-term care work needed in private households. With the 2007 reform, 24-hour care became a regular part of the long-term care system, but little effort was made to make it an integral part of existing provisions. Those in need of care or their families can use 24-hour care without ever getting in contact with a social service provider. Only in case of the means-tested 24-hour care benefit, there are very basic qualification requirements, which can also be met by proving at least six months of hands-on experience. In terms of the definition of tasks, however, 24-hour care workers can provide services that for traditional service providers would in fact require proof of qualification. This creates a couple of areas of conflict. While long-term care policies, after the 1993 reform, emphasized a professionalization in the care sector and made various efforts to improve and ensure the quality of services, 24-hour care opened up an option that is not touched by these efforts. Professionalization in the traditional social services is thwarted by opening up an option that leaves the judgement about quality and qualifications almost entirely to the user, the family of the user or the intermediary. Additionally, self-employment is not bound by work regulations, making it a more flexible but also more precarious arrangement. Twenty-four-hour care is still expensive and not affordable to all (even when receiving the specific 24-hour care benefit), but it offers a cheaper option compared to the use of traditional care services for long hours, given that usually only a limited number of hours are publicly co-funded. Hence, there is currently a highly unequal competitive situation between the traditional social services and 24-hour care. Efforts of professionalization and quality assurance on the side of the traditional social services are undermined by an acceptance and even support (via the 24-hour care benefit) of provisions that leave quality considerations largely to the user, their families and the intermediaries.

Conclusion

In 1993, Austria started a major reform of its long-term care system, including a novel universal cash-for-care benefit, initiatives for a substantial growth in the social service infrastructure, and policies supporting family caregivers and addressing quality issues. Alongside these policy changes, as an unintended development, 24-hour care became an increasingly attractive option for the coverage of long-term care needs in private households. What originally developed and grew as a grey economy of care was transformed into a regular and constantly growing element of the care system in 2007. Users appreciate that it allows long hours of care provision in the private home without having several care workers involved and an arrangement that comes closer to the traditional family ideal than traditional social services that are under increasing pressure of minute-by-minute service. The self-employment mode provides the flexibility to continue with the arrangements that existed before the regularization and remains less costly than the alternative of an employer-employee relationship.

But there are also considerable risks attached. The risks identified by Christensen and Manthorpe (2016) for migrant care workers in England – insecurity of care workers' employment conditions and rights, emotionalized relationships and the intimacy of employer-employee relationships – also apply to 24-hour care in Austria. Twenty-four-hour care and the underlying self-employment mode is an example of new deregulated work arrangements that are praised for flexibility, for the entrepreneurial approach, and cost-effectiveness. Specific requirements, including written contracts and documentation, have increased the formality of the arrangements. But public regulation to ensure quality of work and work relations are still limited. Arrangements remain precarious for care workers, but also users. It is left to the relative powers of the users, their families, the care workers and the way in which intermediaries are intervening in this relationship. And beyond the individual risks involved, this also entails risks for de-professionalization and devaluation of care work in a broader care regime perspective (Bauer et al., 2014). The character of care work as emotional work and the isolation and the intimacy of the private household – which is not just the workplace for care workers, but also the place where they stay for a regular two-week or more shift – makes it even more difficult to escape from the aforementioned risks and creates specific additional risks.

Limited existing research does not allow us to quantify the benefits and risks dimensions, but qualitative research discussed in this chapter confirms that 24-hour care involves benefits and risks for users and their families, for workers and the long-term care system in general. Twenty-four-hour care can lead to mutual beneficial relationships, but can also lead to enormous pressures and burdens on care workers, to distress in work relations and quality problems. It is a public responsibility to address these risks in an adequate way, even more so when 24-hour care is not just a regular option to provide care work, but an option that is financially supported by the public. In addressing the risks, it is of key concern to consider the particularities of the private household as a workplace and the transnationality of the arrangement and its implications for formal and informal care systems not only in the destination country, but also in the country of origin of care workers.

References

Appelt, E. and Fleischer, E., 2014. Familiale Sorgearbeit in Österreich: Modernisierung eines konservativen Care-Regimes? [Family care work in Austria: modernization of a conservative care regime?]. In B. Aulenbacher, B. Riegraf and H. Theobald, eds. *Sorge: Arbeit, Verhältnisse, Regime* [Care: work, relations, regimes]. Baden-Baden: Nomos Verlag.

Bachinger, A., 2010. 24-Stunden Betreuung: Gelungenes Legalisierungsprojekt oder prekäre Arbeitsmarktintegration? [24-hour care: successful legalization or precarious labour market integration?]. *SWS-Rundschau*, 50(4), pp. 399–413.

Bahna, M., 2015. Victims of care drain and transnational partnering? Slovak female elder care workers in Austria. *European Societies*, 17(4), pp. 447–66. DOI: http://dx.doi.org/10.1080/14616696.2015.1051 074.

Bauer, G. and Österle, A., 2013. Migrant care labour: the commodification and redistribution of care and emotional work. *Social Policy and Society*, 12(3), pp. 461–73. DOI: https://doi.org/10.1017/S1474746413000079.

Bauer, G. and Österle, A., 2016. Mid and later life care work migration: patterns of re-organising informal care obligations in Central and Eastern Europe. *Journal of Aging Studies*, 37, pp. 81–93. DOI: 10.1016/j.jaging.2016.02.005.

Bauer, G., Haidinger, B. and Österle, A., 2014. Three domains of migrant domestic care work: the interplay of care, employment and migration policies in Austria. In B. Anderson and I. Shutes, eds. *Migration and care labour: theory, policy and politics*. Basingstoke: Palgrave Macmillan, pp. 67–86.

BMASK (Bundesministerium für Arbeit, Soziales und Konsumentenschutz – Austrian Ministry of Labour, Social Affairs and Consumer Protection), 2016. *Österreichischer Pflegevorsorgebericht 2015* [Austrian long-term care report 2015]. Vienna: BMASK. Available at: https://broschuerenservice.sozialministerium.at/Home/Download?publicationId=366 [accessed 16.05.17].

Boccagni, P., 2014. Caring about migrant care workers: from private obligations to transnational social welfare. *Critical Social Policy*, 34(2), pp. 221–40. DOI: https://doi.org/10.1177/0261018313500867.

Christensen, K. and Manthorpe, J., 2016. Personalised risk: new risk encounters facing migrant care workers. *Health, Risk and Society*, 18(3–4), pp. 137–52. DOI: http://dx.doi.org/10.1080/13698575.2016.1182628.

Da Roit, B. and Weicht, B., 2013. Migrant care work and care, migration and employment regimes: a fuzzy-set analysis. *Journal of European Social Policy*, 23(5), pp. 469–86. DOI: https://doi.org/10.1177/0958928713499175.

Da Roit, B., Le Bihan, B. and Österle, A., 2016. Cash for care: an international perspective. In C. Gori, J.-L. Fernandez and R. Wittenberg, eds. 2016. *Long-term care reforms in OECD countries*. Bristol: Policy Press, pp. 143–66.

European Commission, 2007. *Health and long-term care in the European Union*. Special Eurobarometer 283/ Wave 67.3. Brussels: European Commission. Available at: http://ec.europa.eu/commfrontoffice/publicopinion/archives/ebs/ebs_283_en.pdf [accessed 17.07.2017].

European Commission, 2015. *The 2015 ageing report: economic and budgetary projections for the 28 EU member states (2013–2060)*. Brussels: European Commission. Available at: http://ec.europa.eu/economy_finance/publications/european_economy/2015/pdf/ee3_en.pdf [accessed 17.07.2017].

Lutz, H. and Palenga-Möllenbeck, E., 2012. Care workers, care drain and care chains: reflections on care, migration and citizenship. *Social Politics*, 19(1), pp. 15–37. DOI: https://doi.org/10.1093/sp/jxr026.

OECD, 2015. *Health at a glance 2015: OECD indicators*. Paris: OECD. Available at: www.oecd-ilibrary.org/social-issues-migration-health/health-at-a-glance-2015/long-term-care-expenditure_health_glance-2015-79-en [accessed 17.07.2017].

Österle, A., 2013. Long-term care reform in Austria: emergence and development of a new welfare state pillar. In C. Ranci and E. Pavolini, eds. 2013. *Reforms in long-term care policies in Europe: investigating institutional change and social impacts*. New York: Springer, pp. 159–77.

Österle, A., 2016. 24-Stunden-Betreuung und die Transnationalisierung von Pflege [24-hour care and the transnationalization of care]. In B. Weicht and A. Österle, eds. *Im Ausland zu Hause pflegen. Die Beschäftigung von MigrantInnen in der 24-Stunden-Betreuung?* [Caring at home abroad: the employment of migrants in 24-hour care]. Vienna: LIT Verlag, pp. 247–69.

Österle, A. and Bauer, G., 2012. Home care in Austria: the interplay of family orientation, cash-for-care and migrant care. *Health and Social Care in the Community*, 20(3), pp. 265–73. DOI: http://doi.org/10.1111/j.1365-2524.2011.01049.x.

Österle, A. and Bauer, G., 2016. The legalization of rotational 24-hour care work in Austria: implications for migrant care workers. *Social Politics*, 23(2), pp. 192–213. DOI: https://doi.org/10.1093/sp/jxv001.

Österle, A. and Hammer, E., 2007. Care allowances and the formalization of care arrangements: the Austrian experience. In C. Ungerson and S. Yeandle, eds. *Cash for care in developed welfare states*. Basingstoke: Palgrave Macmillan, pp. 13–31.

Österle, A. and Heitzmann, K., 2016. Reforming the Austrian welfare system: facing demographic and economic challenges in a federal welfare state. In K. Schubert, P. de Villota and J. Kuhlmann, eds. *Challenges to European welfare systems*. New York: Springer, pp. 11–35.

Österle, A., Hasl, A. and Bauer, G., 2013. Vermittlungsagenturen in der 24-Betreuung [Intermediaries in 24-hour care work]. *WISO*, 36(1), pp. 159–72.

Piperno, F., 2012. The impact of female emigration on families and welfare state in countries of origin: the case of Romania. *International Migration*, 50(5), pp. 189–204. DOI: 10.1111/j.1468-2435.2010.00668.x.

Ranci, C. and Pavolini, E. eds., 2013. Reforms in long-term care policies in Europe: investigating institutional change and social impacts. New York: Springer.

Ranci, C. and Pavolini, E., 2015. Not all that glitters is gold: long-term care reforms in the last two decades in Europe. *Journal of European Social Policy*, 25(3), pp. 270–85. DOI: https://doi.org/10.1177/0958928715588704.

Schmidt, A., Winkelmann, J., Rodrigues, R. and Leichsenring, K., 2016. Lessons for regulating informal markets and implications for quality assurance: the case of migrant care workers. *Ageing and Society*, 36(4), pp. 741–63. DOI: http://dx.doi.org/10.1017/S0144686X1500001X.

Statistik Austria, 2017a. *Bundespflegegeld* [Cash-for-care]. Available at: www.statistik.at/web_de/statistiken/menschen_und_gesellschaft/soziales/sozialleistungen_auf_bundesebene/bundespflegegeld/index.html [accessed 17.07.2017].

Statistik Austria, 2017b. *Betreuungs- und Pflegedienste* [Long-term care services]. Available at: www.statistik.at/web_de/statistiken/menschen_und_gesellschaft/soziales/sozialleistungen_auf_landesebene/betreuungs_und_pflegedienste/index.html [accessed 17.07.2017].

Van Hooren, F., 2012. Varieties of migrant care work: comparing patterns of migrant labour in social care. *Journal of European Social Policy*, 22(2), pp. 133–47. DOI: http://dx.doi.org/10.1177/0958928711433654.

Weicht, B., 2010. Embodying the ideal carer: the Austrian discourse on migrant carers. *International Journal of Ageing and Later Life*, 5(2), pp. 17–52. DOI: http://dx.doi.org/10.3384/ijal.1652-8670.105217.

Williams, F., 2012. Converging variations in migrant care work in Europe. *Journal of European Social Policy*, 22(4), pp. 363–76. DOI: https://doi.org/10.1177/0958928712449771.

10

Migrant care workers in Italian households

Recent trends and future perspectives

Mirko Di Rosa, Francesco Barbabella,
Arianna Poli, Sara Santini and Giovanni Lamura

Introduction

This chapter focuses on the role played by migrant care work within the Italian long-term care (LTC) system. Italy is a country where the informal sector, and in particular the family, has traditionally represented the bulk of care provision, with public policies and interventions tending to perpetuate and take for granted this constellation. In order to understand the interdependence and complementarity between public, private, family and migrant care, the following analysis will start by providing first a schematic overview of the formal LTC system, and of its main components: residential and home care as well as the cash-for-care schemes.

It will then consider the informal care provided by family caregivers, that is, those who provide help to a family member (generally spouses, parents, parents-in-law, grandparents) to perform the basic activities of daily living (ADLs, e.g. eating, dressing, going to the toilet) or the instrumental ones (IADLs, e.g. cleaning, shopping, preparing meals, transportation), as well as in the management of care and other support activities. In Italy, as in other Southern European countries, there is indeed a cultural preference for the family being entrusted with the care of older people (over 65 years old) (Da Roit et al., 2007; Special Eurobarometer, 2007).

The analysis will then move to examine the increasingly important pillar of the Italian LTC system represented by care workers who are directly employed by Italian households, usually called in Italian *assistenti familiari* or – in a partly pejorative informal term – *badanti* ('those who look after someone'). Their number has been estimated to reach over 830,000 people across the country (Pasquinelli, 2013, p. 43), including those – many – who are hired on an undeclared basis (i.e. without a contract) to provide care and social assistance, as well as housework, for seniors with ADL or IADL needs. This phenomenon has been growing over the years due to the fact that many older Italians receive an attendance allowance, a non-means-tested monetary benefit absorbing almost half of the public expenditure on LTC, which currently reaches 1.6 per cent of GDP (INPS, 2016, p. 75). These resources are meant to support families in everyday care provision. The lack of any restriction on how to spend them, however, leads many households to use this money to hire a care worker (Barbabella et al., 2016). As shown in more detail below, this phenomenon has radically changed the traditional approach to eldercare in

Italy into a 'migrant in the family model', rather than a simply familistic welfare regime (van Hooren, 2012). Within this context, several challenges are raised in terms of care quality, possible undeclared work, exploitation and abusive situations, as well as care drain risks. In the following paragraphs, after briefly presenting the methodology, the different care types are analysed in detail, starting with an overview of how Italy's formal LTC system basically works.

Methods

In order to provide an up-to-date framework of the LTC interventions for frail older people in Italy, secondary data analyses were carried out, based on existing institutional sources. The attempt made in drafting this chapter, therefore, has been not only to contribute to overcome the fragmentation traditionally characterizing these specific data in Italy, but also to provide a clear and concise set of core figures on the complex phenomenon of migrant work in LTC for dependent older people. In the following sections, the most recent data available for each source are analysed in detail, and used to build a comprehensive and in-depth picture of the main aspects of this phenomenon.

Long-term care provision in the Italian context: an overview

Italian society is among those worldwide that are most extensively affected by the phenomenon of population ageing, due to its long-standing very low birth rates (1.35 children on average per woman in 2015) and increasing life expectancy (84.7 years of life expectancy at birth for women and 80.3 for men)[1] (ISTAT, 2016). Furthermore, Italy is facing the challenge of addressing the complex care needs of older individuals for a long time. Among the European Union (EU) countries, it is just above the EU average of healthy life years (in 2014: 62.3 versus 61.8 for women; 62.5 versus 61.4 for men) (Eurostat, 2016). On the whole, currently over 21 per cent of the Italian population is over 65 years (13.2 million people), with circa 2.5 million (19 per cent of older adults) estimated to have functional limitations and to be in need of care (Barbabella et al., 2015, p. 15).

The impact of demographic trends on the Italian LTC system is exacerbated by a traditional lack in the coverage of formal LTC services, and more recently by the deepest economic recession since the Second World War. Historically, Italy's LTC provision has relied on the in-kind and financial contribution of families (Ferrera, 1996). However, in the near future it will be harder for households to be able to deliver the amount of care needed by their older members, as the ratio between adults (45–64 years) and older people (75+) is expected to halve by 2050 (Cangiano, 2014, p. 142), and the number of family caregivers needed to maintain current care levels to double (Colombo et al., 2011, p. 77).

Compared to most developed EU welfare states, the amount of LTC provided by Italian formal services is relatively limited. Residential care remains largely marginal (Gori et al., 2016), serving just 1.3 per cent of the over-65 population in 2012 (Barbabella et al., 2015, p. 24). Home-based care is more developed, but still largely insufficient to meet existing care needs. This has two causes. One is the lack of integration affecting LTC in the community, which is split into health and social sectors, each of them managing their own services with limited coordination. The second is that the coverage, especially the intensity of single services, remains low and geographically unequal.

The main public home care service (providing medical, nursing and rehabilitation care) is the *Assistenza Domiciliare Integrata* (ADI – Integrated Home Care) provided by local health authorities, very rarely including some more basic municipal home help. This reached just

4.3 per cent of older Italians in 2012, with large differences between regions, as highlighted by the fact that Tuscany and Emilia-Romagna, two neighbouring regions in Central Italy, reported, respectively, 2 per cent and 11.8 per cent (Barbabella et al., 2015, p. 21). The intensity of such a service is particularly low, since older users received on average 21 hours of home care per year, far away from the standards of other European countries (Garms-Homolová et al., 2012, p. 63). In addition to ADI, for less severe cases, a social care service is provided by municipalities, that is, the *Servizio di Assistenza Domiciliare* (SAD – Home Help Service) in relation to different daily tasks (such as personal hygiene, meals on wheels and home management), reaching only 1.3 per cent of the 65+ population (Barbabella et al., 2015, p. 22).

Compared to in-kind provision, cash-for-care represents the most important pillar of the Italian LTC system, whose mostly used support measure among older people is the *Indennità di Accompagnamento* (IA – Attendance Allowance). This is a state-based cash payment of a fixed amount – about €500 per month – granted to those needing continuous assistance for ADLs and/or mobility. It constitutes a universal measure, that is, not means-tested, and can be spent without accounting, with a strong incentive for using it to buy private care work. It was first introduced in 1980, with the aim of supporting adult people (up to 65 years) with limitations in performing ADLs and considered to be disadvantaged in accessing the labour market. Only in 1988 was this measure extended to 65+ citizens, in order to address the needs of this increasing population group. In 2013, circa 12 per cent of the older population was receiving IA, that is, a slightly lower share than in previous years, due to a re-centralization of needs assessment procedures and monitoring measures to combat misuse at local level. Its amount and the large number of recipients make it the most substantial public resource Italian families can count on to provide LTC, as also shown by the fact that, while in 2011–2013 both community and residential care expenditure did not increase, spending for IA increased by half a billion euros, up to a total of over €10 billion per year (Barbabella et al., 2015, p. 27). Furthermore, in addition to the state attendance allowance, many municipalities and regions offer local cash-for-care schemes to older people with LTC needs, which can be alternative or additional measures to the national benefits, depending on the selection criteria set by each municipality.

If we try to capture the developments in this field in a longitudinal perspective, the forms of public, informal and private care seem to have slightly changed over time. According to estimates by Italy's National Institute of Statistics (ISTAT, 2011a, p. 179), in 2009 about 30 per cent of Italian households with at least one person aged over 65 received one or more forms of care (Table 10.1). In one-third of cases, this was represented by informal care alone, including support provided by families and informal networks, whereas 8.7 per cent of cases relied only on private sources (services privately paid by households). The comparison between 2003 and 2009 reveals that the number of families who have received help has increased, but also that fewer families receive only informal care, with significant increases instead in private help, public help and mix.

Completing the overall picture, it should be mentioned that, despite the recent economic crisis, the out pocket costs by Italian households to meet their own care needs have been recently growing. Available data on consumption in the healthcare sector (ISTAT, 2015a, p. 6) suggest that the private expenditure borne by older people's households for health services (including, for instance, expenses for goods and services for personal care, social services, insurance and financial services) has reached about 6 per cent of total expenses (higher than the average reported by the general population: 4.4 per cent), but these figures do not include the possible employment of care workers. Not surprisingly, the purchase of private LTC insurance policies to cover the risk of a (temporary or permanent) disability condition is also growing, although 90 per cent of older Italians still do not have any kind of insurance (ISTAT, 2015b).

Table 10.1 Families with at least one person aged over 65 years who received at least one type of help in the previous four weeks (percentage of total households with at least one person 65+) (2003–2009)

	Only informal help (within and/or from outside the family)	_Source of help_			
		Only private help	_Only help from local and public institutions_	_Mix of help_	_No help_
2003	12.4	6.0	2.0	6.2	73.5
2009	10.0	8.7	3.0	7.5	70.8

Source: Our elaboration based on ISTAT data (ISTAT, 2011a).

The stable contribution of family caregivers over time

The Italian national survey on _reconciliation of work and family_ (ISTAT, 2011b, p. 1) estimated that there are about 3.3 million people aged between 15 and 64 who care for a dependent adult (including older people, sick and disabled), two-thirds of them being in the age group 45–64. On average, 8.6 per cent of the adult Italian population is engaged in unpaid care activities, with the number of female caregivers almost double that of men (2.1 million and 1.2 million, respectively).

Another indicator estimating the 'effort' of Italian family caregivers is provided by ISTAT's _fourth report on social cohesion_ (ISTAT, 2013, Table II.2.3.3). According to it, 78 per cent of all employed people who in 2012 benefited from the work permits granted by Law 104/1992 (law regarding the rights of persons with disabilities and their families) were represented by family caregivers. Such permits may consist of up to three days of paid leave per month (a maximum of 36 days yearly), or of two hours per day of paid leave.

ISTAT (2011a) also provides some estimates on the number of households with older members who receive unpaid support from other people (Table 10.2). Considering most recent data (2009), the largest amount of help is in housework activities, followed by the areas of bureaucracy (paperwork needed to acquire services and/or benefits from the public administration) and social activities (company, transportation, shopping). Over time, the share of households with older people benefiting from help remained stable in some areas (care and social activities), decreased in housework activities, and increased in all other areas (especially bureaucracy).

Table 10.2 Families with at least one older person (65+) who received unpaid help from not cohabiting people in the past four weeks, by type of aid received (percentage of total households with at least one person 65+) (2003–2009)

	Financial help	_Healthcare activities_	_Care for older people_	_Housework_	_Social activities_	_Bureaucracy_
2003	6.3	33.8	27.3	50.1	37.1	33.6
2009	7.9	33.2	30.7	46.6	38.3	40.1

Source: Our elaborations on ISTAT data (ISTAT, 2011a).

Mirko Di Rosa et al.

Summarized, we can say that the role of unpaid family care of older people in Italy has largely remained unchanged, confirming that it is mainly a women-based activity delivered primarily in mature age and regarding a large variety of tasks in everyday life (Di Rosa et al., 2015).

Household-based care workers: a silent care 'revolution' from the bottom of the Italian LTC system

The combined impact of a relatively weak role of formal in-kind LTC provision both in terms of coverage and intensity, a widespread use of substantial attendance allowances, and the presence of a still strong family network allowing most older people to 'age in place' have stimulated an increasing reliance on home-based, privately hired care workers (Lamura et al., 2010). Among the approximately 830,000[2] workers (mostly women), 90 per cent are migrants, and two-thirds are without a regular contract, and often without any professional training in care or nursing (Pasquinelli and Rusmini, 2013).

The legal and employment position of migrant care workers (MCWs) plays a crucial role in shaping their living and working perspectives, and indirectly affects the whole LTC sector (Pasquinelli, 2013; Pasquinelli and Rusmini, 2013). A particularly weak position characterizes the MCWs who have no or expired residence permits – since they have no possibility of training and professional development nor access to public services – as well as those who, while having a legal residence permit, work without a regular contract, thus making their social, employment and pension status precarious. To some extent, this is due to seeking short-term benefits by both sides: by the families, who try to pay less and are free from legal constraints, and by MCWs themselves, who renounce guarantees and safeguards for a higher salary, as this does not include (actually mandatory) social and fiscal contributions (Mesini et al., 2006).

Data referring to regularly employed care workers, while unable to capture the condition of those working under undeclared circumstances, still allow us to highlight some peculiar characteristics of this phenomenon (Figure 10.1). The main MCW region of origin is Eastern Europe, in particular Romania, which represents circa one-quarter of the total migrant labour force employed in LTC, all other major nationalities being outside the EU, including the Philippines and South America (Foundation Leone Moressa, 2011). The number of MCWs has steadily increased over the past 10 years, and it is likely to continue growing in the near future due to the increasing demand for LTC and the higher level of female participation in the labour market, with a consequent lower availability of family caregivers (Lamura et al., 2010). Also, the economic crisis, until 2012, only partly stopped this trend of increasing MCW numbers; from 2009 on, the number of Italian care workers also started to increase, showing that this activity became attractive for the autochthonous population too.

The negative, significant role of the economic crisis was also highlighted by a recent countrywide survey (Paolisso, 2013, p. 28), conducted on a sample of 1,500 75+ citizens, showing that, in order to pay for a care worker, three-quarters of respondents reduced the quality and quantity of food, and almost half had to ask for children's help. Often these sacrifices were insufficient, as 55 per cent of respondents had to resize the help provided by the care worker, and 25 per cent had to completely give it up. The reduction or renunciation of employing a care worker also increased the risk of a deterioration in the health and quality of life of older people, increasing their hospital readmissions, while shifting back the care burden partly or totally on family caregivers' shoulders.

MCWs are employed primarily to carry out housework, preparation and administration of meals (e.g. cutting up food or feeding the recipient), companionship and personal care, while less often carrying out tasks concerning the management of finances, the organization of care

146

Migrant care workers in Italian households

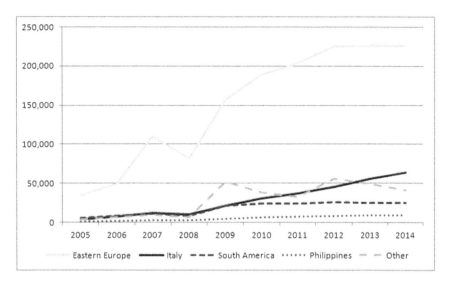

Figure 10.1 Trend of care workers according to the areas of origin (2005–2014)
Source: Our elaborations on INPS data (INPS, 2005–2014).

and transportation. Cohabiting in the same household as the care recipient is a condition that deepens the MCWs' involvement in all activities, except those that the family wants to continue to keep control of, such as finance management, organization of care and transportation (IRS-Soleterre, 2015).

The cohabitation pattern often influences the overall MCW model (Santini et al., 2011), also in relation to the cared-for person's disability level and to the care worker's working hours, with three main patterns emerging: half-day (normally the morning); morning and afternoon; and day and night (this being the case when the MCW lives together with the older care recipient). Two 'innovative' cohabitation approaches, which are less frequent but increasingly reported, concern, first, some women who migrated to live in the care recipient's home together with their own families (generally the MCW's husband and one or two children). Another solution refers to those MCWs who – unlike the first waves of MCWs, usually came alone – are supported by their own family network, already in Italy, allowing them to have a good private life or even to study. In both cases, a new combination of solidarity and work ties could potentially benefit all parties involved, although especially the first of these new solutions was not without conflicts and difficulties of cohabitation.

When the family employs a live-in MCW, the role of formal home care services decreases substantially for most tasks, up to a complete replacement (Di Rosa et al., 2012). The only two activities that continue to be delegated to a considerable extent to formal home care services are personal care and transportation, for which MCWs do not always have the necessary conveyances or skills.

In terms of *policy*, there have been no innovative interventions by the central government in recent years to regulate the employment of private care workers. From about a decade ago, tax incentives have been granted to care recipients and their families when employing care workers with a regular contract (Laws 342/2000 and 296/2006). This strategy aims at promoting the regularization of those MCWs who are employed without a regular contract or a residence permit, especially if coming from a non-EU country, enabling them and their employers to legalize their position without penalizing consequences.

The fundamental importance of MCWs in today's Italian landscape can be observed in Figure 10.2, which compares the estimated economic value of the main components of LTC provision in Italy (public, informal and private), drawing from different sources. Beyond the methodological limitations and the caution that must be used in performing such comparisons, this graph allows us to grasp the overall composition of LTC sources in Italy. The two most substantial components are those relating to the 'healthcare system' costs for LTC (including care in the community, as well as the semi-residential and residential care facilities for dependent people) and the expenditure for the state-funded 'cash allowance' (IA). Together with the 'social care system' spending (borne by municipalities to deliver home help, including SAD) and the benefits granted to promote the 'work-care reconciliation' (mainly in the form of paid care leaves and absences for assisting a relative with LTC needs), they form the overall public spending for both LTC in-kind services and cash transfers, estimated to reach a yearly amount of over €31 billion.

The availability of public and private care provision, however, does not prevent Italian households from providing LTC informally in everyday life. As shown in Figure 10.2, 'family caregivers' contribution to LTC (in-kind caring activities) has an economic value of around €10 billion, calculated by using cautious assumptions that might actually underestimate this figure. As for private spending, the estimated overall expenditure for 'care workers' privately paid by Italian households reaches €9.4 billion per year, of which only €2.6 billion are estimated to be regular contracts (our elaborations on INPS data; INPS, 2015a, 2015b). Their employment is fostered by the availability of IA among people with LTC needs (Barbabella et al., 2016), but is necessarily supplemented by pensions and families' financial resources. According

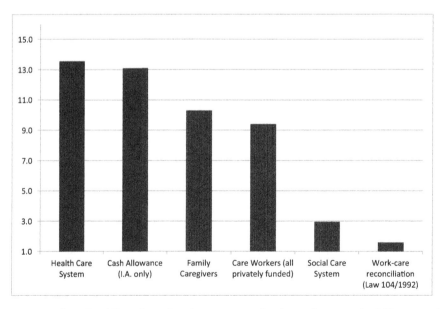

Figure 10.2 Value of public, informal and private care for dependent people (billion euros)

Source: Our elaborations on data from De Sario et al. (2010), RGS (2014), Spandonaro (2014) and Welfare Italia (2014).

to these estimates, therefore, more than one-third of all resources flowing into LTC provision comes from care recipients and their families, both in the form of in-kind informal care and as out-of-pocket spending for purchasing in-kind services.

The caregiving triad of migrant care worker, older person and family caregiver in the home environment

In order to understand how MCWs could become such a crucial pillar of the 'Italian way' of providing LTC, it is useful to analyse more in-depth the special meaning the 'home' has for many older people (and not only in Italy), as well as the relationships that are established between them, the family caregivers and the MCWs.

Generally speaking, there is a strong link between the home and the (older) person's identity, since home is the 'projection' of what one is and has been, representing a sort of 'ecological niche' (Scassellati Sforzolini, 2013) and the 'place of memory' (Taccani, 2013). The 'place attachment' concept (Low and Altman, 1992) might also explain older people's preference for ageing in place (Abramsson and Andersson, 2016). Ageing at home affords in this regard privacy, sustains self-identity, and gives purpose to life (Stones and Gullifer, 2016). At home, a triangular caring relationship takes place involving the frail older person, the MCW and the family caregiver, challenging some of the positive home and identity links.

Although older persons in need of care would like to keep their own privacy and autonomy, they see the MCW moving into their private space, cooking in their kitchen, touching their objects and even their body, despite the lack of any kin tie (the key to intimate relations among older Italians). While many would prefer to be cared for by a family member and might not cooperate with the MCW up to feeling frightened by his or her presence, other older care recipients are friendly hosts to the MCW at home, accepting being helped and touched.

The MCWs, mostly women, were often forced to leave their own country due to poverty or political reasons. They often have a 'heavy' past, including broken family ties, difficult love relationships or left-behind young children looked after by grandparents in the home country (Deluigi, 2013). They are asked to become familiar with the care recipient's home environment, adapting to unknown domestic and caregiving practices, possibly quite different from those characterizing their own cultures, and which they are not necessarily trained for. Especially in cases of a severe disability, they live night and day with the person they care for, handling emergencies due to the older person's unstable health condition, and, day by day, might end up setting aside their own emotions and personal relations and interests (Sgritta, 2009).

Family caregivers are the triad's third component, often being spouses, sons and especially daughters between 15 and 64 years old, and thus of working age. Twenty-two per cent of employed women caring for an older adult with a disability have part-time work (ISTAT, 2011b, p. 8), while only 8.4 per cent of men are in the same position. The increased number of women in the labour market and the increase of the statutory retirement age following the recent pension reform (Law 214/2011) may aggravate the condition of family caregivers, who are already challenged by current working and living conditions to properly reconcile work and family life. The double role of worker and caregiver might indeed affect the quality of life in multiple realms, including work (Principi et al., 2014), social relationships and health.

The relationship between a frail older person and an MCW is the meeting of two persons living in a situation of weakness, who chose 'the lesser evil' in order to survive (Taccani, 2013). In this delicate relationship, the family caregiver often has the responsibility to hold the balance (Hoff and Hamblin, 2011). This starts with the decision to hire an MCW, not always an easy one for a child, who often lives with a sense of guilt – especially in the case of daughters – for delegating the care of their parents. This decision can be followed by a long phase of search, mainly through word of mouth, and of testing different persons, until the 'right' MCW is found, whom the caregivers (and care recipients who are cognitively fit) feel they can trust. Many working caregivers consider the MCW as an irreplaceable support, especially where a supportive family network is unavailable (e.g. when the caregiver is an only child). Not surprisingly, the MCW may become a trouble for them when, for example, a frequent turnover of MCWs occurs, forcing them to replan the daily care management. This happens in particular when MCWs from near countries (e.g. Ukraine or Romania) plan a rapid profit in a short time, returning home as soon as possible, sometimes leading to such severe misunderstandings that the intervention of lawyers and trade unions is required.

The arrival of an MCW questions the family balance and often generates strong changes in family members' daily life and in relationships among them. Families can take the chance to open up to new care and living solutions and create human capital, or they can isolate and shut down any positive possibility in the caregiving triad. Taking the first path rather than the second depends primarily on creating good bonds within the triad. Nevertheless, the responsibility of this choice cannot be left totally to family caregivers and MCWs. In order to avoid the home turning from a place of care, memory and affection into a place of pain and isolation (Lazzarini and Santagati, 2008), regular and planned relationships between those living in the caregiving relationship at home and those who live outside (e.g. care professionals, social workers, volunteers) should be more strongly endorsed by local administrations and care providers. Social and health services, indeed, would ideally have the responsibility to create additional support to home care, promoting a more 'widespread sociality' (Iori, 2002), involving in the everyday care delivery relevant community stakeholders such as voluntary associations, trade unions, and parishes in a more integrated partnership between public and private (both for-profit and non-profit) service providers.

However, this is far from being the case in Italy. The massive presence of MCWs, representing the 'migrant in the family' model, strongly facilitated by the core traditional role played by the Italian family in daily eldercare provision (van Hooren, 2012), represents simultaneously a solution and a cause of potential tensions. These can be observed within the triad – as analysed in more detail in the next section – but also in structural terms, due to the prevalence of privately organized, semi-legal or even illegal working conditions, not to speak of the problems arising in the home countries, including the left-behind children and other frail relatives of the MCWs (Lamura et al., 2010).

Migrant care work and its impact on burden within the caregiving triad

While family caregivers' burden – defined as 'the physical, psychological or emotional, social, and financial problems' (George and Gwyther, 1986) – has been largely studied, much less empirical evidence is available on how the presence of MCWs is impacting on it. Some recent evidence from the Italian context has demonstrated that employing an MCW to care for an older dependent person can result in a decrease of the family caregiver's burden (Chiatti et al., 2013a; Da Roit, 2010). This is true even if the family caregiver remains a crucial actor constantly negotiating the caring tasks with the MCW, as the latter would relieve the family from most of the everyday care responsibilities, instrumental but partly also emotional ones, possibly also assuming a central role within the caregiving triad. This is consistent with studies carried out in other countries, demonstrating that MCWs are key actors defining the overall satisfaction in the caregiving triad (Ayalon and Roziner, 2016). Care recipients can benefit from dedicated and good-quality care, increasing their quality of life (Bilotta and Vergani, 2008) and, accordingly, reducing institutionalization as well as mortality.

However, the handover of care responsibilities to an MCW does not always lead to positive outcomes. For example, an inverse dyad reciprocity can develop between the family caregiver and the MCW, and a lower level of burden reported by a family caregiver can correspond to a higher level of burden experienced by the MCW (Ayalon, 2015; Della Puppa, 2012). For the MCW, the lack of proper qualifications, the degree of dependence of the care recipient, the emotional connotation of the daily tasks, the unpredictability of the care situation and needs, the demands for high levels of interactive work, as well as the difficulties in communicating with both family members and the older person, can further expose or even exacerbate the MCW's burden of care, impacting negatively on care and the development of a good care relationship (Bauer and Österle, 2013; Rosa et al., 2013). The presence of a high level of MCW burden has been revealed as a predicting factor of elder neglect (Ayalon and Roziner, 2016; Chiatti et al., 2013b). Within the caregiving triad, the MCW's burden of care thus seems to be even more relevant than that reported by family caregivers.

In summary, MCWs play a crucial role within the caregiving triad, being responsible for addressing most of the care recipient's needs, ensuring an overall balance within the triad, co-determining the overall quality of care, as well as contributing to the care recipient's quality of life.

Concluding remarks

Italy's LTC system relies heavily both on the traditional care provided by older people's family caregivers and, increasingly, on the more recent contribution granted by the MCWs privately hired by Italian households to support them in daily care tasks. Given the invisibility characterizing MCWs in private homes, the role played by this relatively new actor first went unnoticed. Only at a later stage, when the presence of MCWs became massive – showing its feature of a 'care revolution from the bottom' – was this role acknowledged and then even supported. This occurred by means of a series of direct and indirect policy measures, including the implementation of local cash-for-care schemes (in addition to the already existing state attendance allowance), tax deductions of costs related to the private employment of care staff, and training and accreditation programmes.

The strategic role of this relatively new actor within the Italian LTC context is certainly related to several advantages made possible by the presence of MCWs in terms of more tailored home care and reduced institutionalization at an apparently reasonable price for all involved parties, including a refocusing of formal home care services towards the most severe cases (Lamura et al., 2010). However, several challenges are raised simultaneously by this phenomenon in terms of care quality, possible undeclared work, exploitation and abusive situations, as well as care drain risks, especially with regard to the multidimensional consequences for both migrant women and their left-behind children suffering from depression, neglect and other disadvantages related to their separation (IRS-Soleterre, 2015; De Luigi, 2013). The most appropriate approach to analyse such a complex phenomenon would therefore include the consideration of pros and cons at micro (individual), meso (family/organizational) and macro (societal) levels, in source, transit and destination countries (Lamura et al., 2013). Until this is the case, we will run the risk – common to other Western European countries– of looking at migrant care work only as a means of solving the needs of our ageing societies, as a cost-effective way of complementing the scarce offer of public LTC services, and without reflecting side effects in the long term in both destination countries (including low quality of care, high private expenditure) and source countries (including implications for family care and demographics in migrants' countries of origin). This would be a short-sighted approach, not sustainable in our globalized world, as the current European migrant crisis clearly shows.

Notes

1 This is true in the long term, although there are very occasional fluctuations in the trend.
2 This estimate is based on a process, refined over the years, combining official and informal data sources, and consists of a calculation using social welfare (INPS) data relating to domestic workers, the data on foreign citizens (ISTAT) and those on irregular migrants (Institute for the Study of Multiethnic, ISMU), as well as the evidence provided by other stakeholders.

References

Abramsson, M. and Andersson, E., 2016. Changing preferences with ageing: housing choices and housing plans of older people. *Housing, Theory and Society*, 33(2), pp. 21–241. DOI: http://dx.doi.org/10.1080/14036096.2015.1104385.

Ayalon, L., 2015. A triadic perspective on elder neglect within the home care arrangement. *Ageing and Society*, 36(4), pp. 811–36. DOI: https://doi.org/10.1017/S0144686X14001512.

Ayalon, L. and Roziner, I., 2016. Satisfaction with the relationship from the perspectives of family caregivers, older adults and their home care workers. *Ageing and Mental Health*, 20(1), pp. 56–64. DOI: http://dx.doi.org/10.1080/13607863.2015.1020412.

Barbabella, F., Chiatti, C. and Di Rosa, M., 2015. La bussola di NNA 2015: lo stato dell'arte basato sui dati [The NNA 2015 compass: a data-driven state of the art]. In NNA (Network Non Autosufficienza), ed. 2015. *L'assistenza agli anziani non autosufficienti in Italia. 5° Rapporto* [Care for frail older people in Italy: 5th report]. Santarcangelo di Romagna: Maggioli, pp. 15–32. Available at: www.maggioli.it/rna/2015/pdf/V-rapporto-assistenza_anziani.pdf [accessed 24.05.17].

Barbabella, F., Chiatti, C., Rimland, J.M., Melchiorre, M.G., Lamura, G. and Lattanzio, F., 2016. Socioeconomic predictors of the employment of migrant care workers by Italian families assisting older Alzheimer's disease patients: evidence from the Up-Tech study. *Journal of Gerontology: Social Sciences*, 71(3), pp. 514–25. DOI: http://lup.lub.lu.se/record/e98734e8-3417-470b-9f0e-c8be72455399.

Bauer, G. and Österle, A., 2013. Migrant care labour: the commodification and redistribution of care and emotional work. *Social Policy and Society*, 12, pp. 461–73. DOI: 10.1017/S1474746413000079.

Bilotta, C. and Vergani, C., 2008. Quality of private personal care for elderly people with a disability living at home: correlates and potential outcomes. *Health and Social Care in the Community*, 16, pp. 354–62. DOI: 10.1111/j.1365-2524.2007.00746.x.

Cangiano, A., 2014. Elder care and migrant labor in Europe: a demographic outlook. *Population and Development Review*, 40(1), pp. 131–54. DOI: 10.1111/j.1728-4457.2014.00653.x.

Chiatti, C., Di Rosa, M., Melchiorre, M.G., Manzoli, L., Rimland, J.M. and Lamura, G., 2013a. Migrant care workers as protective factor against caregiver burden: results from a longitudinal analysis of the EUROFAMCARE study in Italy. *Ageing and Mental Health*, 17(5), pp. 609–14. DOI: http://dx.doi.org/10.1080/13607863.2013.765830.

Chiatti, C., Di Rosa, M., Barbabella, F., Greco, C., Melchiorre. M.G., Principi, A., et al. 2013b. Migrant care work for elderly households in Italy. In J. Troisi and H.-J. von Kondratowitz, eds. *Ageing in the Mediterranean*. Bristol: Policy Press. pp. 235–56. DOI: 10.1332/policypress/9781447301066.003.0011.

Colombo, F., Llena-Nozal, A., Mercier, J. and Tjadens, F., 2011. *Help wanted? Providing and paying for long-term care*. Paris: OECD. Available at: www.oecd-ilibrary.org/social-issues-migration-health/help-wanted_9789264097759-en [accessed 24.05.2017].

Da Roit, B., 2010. Strategies of care: changing elderly care in Italy and the Netherlands. Amsterdam: Amsterdam University Press.

Da Roit, B., Le Bihan, B. and Österle, A., 2007. Long-term care reforms in Italy, Austria and France: variations in cash-for-care schemes. *Social Policy and Administration*, 41(6), 653–71. DOI: 10.1111/j.1467-9515.2007.00577.x

De Sario, B., Sabbatini, A. and Mirabile, M.L., 2010. *Il capitale sociale degli anziani. Stime sul valore dell'attività non retribuita* [The social capital of older people: estimates of the value of unpaid activities]. Rome: IRES. Available at: http://old.spi.cgil.it/LinkClick.aspx?fileticket=qI7WwhzEe7Q%3D&tabid=1639 [accessed 24.05.2017].

Della Puppa, F., 2012. Being part of the family: social and working conditions of female migrant care workers in Italy. *Nordic Journal of Feminist and Gender Research*, 20(3), pp. 182–98. DOI: 10.1080/08038740.2012.685494.

Deluigi, R., 2013. L'invecchiamento, il lavoro di cura migrante e la questione degli 'orfani Bianchi': legami e dinamiche familiari in transito [Ageing, migrant care work and the problem of 'white orphans': family bonds and dynamics in transition]. *Rivista Italiana di Educazione Familiare*, 1, pp. 7–14.

Di Rosa, M., Melchiorre, M.G., Lucchetti, M. and Lamura, G., 2012. The impact of migrant work in the elder care sector: recent trends and empirical evidence in Italy. *European Journal of Social Work*, 15(1), pp. 9–27. DOI: http://dx.doi.org/10.1080/13691457.2011.562034.

Di Rosa, M., Barbabella, F., Poli, A. and Balducci, F., 2015. L'altra bussola: le strategie di sostegno familiare e privato. [The other compass: family and private support strategies]. In NNA (Network Non Autosufficienza), ed. *L'assistenza agli anziani non autosufficienti in Italia. 5° Rapporto* [Care for frail older people in Italy: 5th report]. Santarcangelo di Romagna: Maggioli, pp. 33–52. Available at: www.maggioli. it/rna/2015/pdf/V-rapporto-assistenza_anziani.pdf [accessed 24.05.2017].

Eurostat, 2016. *Population and social conditions*. Available at: http://ec.europa.eu/health/dyna/echi/datatool/ index.cfm [accessed 24.05.2017].

Ferrera, M., 1996. The 'southern model' of welfare in social Europe. *Journal of European Social Policy*, 6, pp. 17–37.

Foundation Leone Moressa, 2011. *Quali badanti per quali famiglie?* [Which private carers for which families?]. Mestre: Foundation Leone Moressa. Available at: www.fondazioneleonemoressa.org/newsite/ wp-content/uploads/2012/06/Quali-badanti-per-quali-famiglie_completo.pdf [accessed 24.05.2017].

Garms-Homolová, V., Naiditch, M., Fagerström, C., Lamura, G., Melchiorre, M.G., Gulácsi, L. et al., 2012. Clients in focus. In N. Genet, W. Boerma, M. Kroneman, A. Hutchinson and R.B. Saltman, eds. *Home care across Europe: current structure and future challenges*. European Observatory on Health Systems and Policies, pp. 55–70. Available at: www.euro.who.int/__data/assets/pdf_file/0008/181799/ e96757.pdf?ua=1 [accessed 24.05.2017].

George, L.K. and Gwyther, L.P., 1986. Caregiver well-being: a multidimensional examination of family caregivers of demented adults. *The Gerontologist*, 26, pp. 253–9. DOI: https://doi-org.pva.uib. no/10.1093/geront/26.3.253.

Gori, C., Barbabella, F., Campbell, J., Ikegami, N., D'Amico, F., Holder, H., et al., 2016. How different countries allocate LTC benefits to users: changes over time. In C. Gori, J.-L. Fernandez and R. Wittenberg, eds. 2016. *Long-term care reforms in OECD countries: successes and failures*. Bristol: Policy Press, pp. 77–115.

Hoff, A. and Hamblin, K., 2011. *Carers between work and care: conflict or chance? International report*. Available at: www.carersatwork.tu-dortmund.de/download/VW20CarersAtWork%20Comparative%20Report. pdf [accessed 24.05.2017].

Iori, V., 2002. Per una fenomenologia della domiciliarità [For a homecare phenomenology]. *Animazione sociale*, 8(9), pp. 37–42.

INPS (Istituto Nazionale di Previdenza Sociale), 2005–2014. *Osservatorio sul lavoro domestic* [Observatory on domestic work]. Available at: www.inps.it/webidentity/banchedatistatistiche/domestici/index.jsp [accessed 24.05.2017].

INPS (Istituto Nazionale di Previdenza Sociale), 2016. *XV Rapporto Annuale* [15th annual report]. Rome. INPS. Available at: www.camera it/temiap/2016/12/20/OCD177-2620.pdf [accessed 24.05.2017].

IRS-Soleterre, 2015. *Lavoro domestico e di cura: pratiche e benchmarking per l'integrazione e la conciliazione della vita familiare e lavorativa* [Housework and care work: best practices and benchmarking for the integration and reconciliation of family and working life]. Available at: www.soleterre.org/sites/soleterre/ files/soleterre/dettaglio/pubblicazioni/RAPPORTOLAVORODOMESTICOeDICURA_2015_ SOLETERRE_IRS.pdf [accessed 24.05.2017].

ISTAT (Istituto Nazionale di Statistica), 2011a. *Rapporto annuale. La situazione del Paese nel 2010* [Annual report: the state of the country in 2010]. Rome: ISTAT. Available at: www3.istat.it/dati/catalogo/20110523_00/ rapporto_2011.pdf [accessed 24.05.2017].

ISTAT (Istituto Nazionale di Statistica), 2011b, *La conciliazione tra lavoro e famiglia* [The reconciliation of work and family]. Rome: ISTAT. Available at: www.istat.it/it/files/2011/12/stat-report-Conciliazione-lavoro-famiglia.pdf?title=Conciliazione+tra+lavoro+e+famiglia+-+28%2Fdic% 2F2011+-+Testo+integrale.pdf [accessed 02.05.2017].

ISTAT (Istituto Nazionale di Statistica), 2013. *Quarto rapporto sulla coesione sociale. Volume II* [Fourth report on social cohesion. Volume II]. Rome: ISTAT. Available at: www.istat.it/it/files/2013/12/ Volume_II_2013.pdf?title=Rapporto+sulla+coesione+sociale+-+30%2Fdic%2F2013+-+Volume+II. pdf [accessed 24.05.2017].

ISTAT (Istituto Nazionale di Statistica), 2015a. *La spesa per consumi delle famiglie* [Spending for household consumption]. Rome: ISTAT. Available at: www.istat.it/it/files/2015/07/COMUNICATO-CONSUMI.pdf?title=Consumi+delle+famiglie+-+08%2Flug%2F2015+-+Testo+integrale.pdf [accessed 24.05.2017].

ISTAT (Istituto Nazionale di Statistica), 2015b. *Aspetti della vita quotidiana. Anno 2013* [Aspects of daily life: year 2013]. Rome: ISTAT. Available at: www.istat.it/it/archivio/129956 [accessed 24.05.2017].

ISTAT (Istituto Nazionale di Statistica), 2016. *Indicatori demografici. Anno 2015* [Demographic indicators: year 2015]. Rome: ISTAT. Available at: www.istat.it/it/files/2016/02/Indicatori-demografici_2015.pdf [accessed 24.05.2017].

Lamura, G., Chiatti, C., Di Rosa, M., Melchiorre, M.G., Barbabella, F., Greco, C., et al., 2010. Migrant workers in the long-term care sector: lessons from Italy. *Health and Ageing*, 22, pp. 8–12.

Lamura, G., Chiatti, C., Barbabella, F. and Di Rosa, M., 2013. *Migrant long-term care work in the European Union: opportunities, challenges and main policy options*. EU-Peer Review on 'Filling the gap in long-term professional care through systematic migration policies'. Vienna: ÖSB Consulting. Available at: http://ec.europa.eu/social/BlobServlet?docId=11116&langId=en [accessed 24.05.2017].

Lazzarini, G. and Santagati, M., 2008. *Anziani, famiglie e assistenti. Sviluppi del welfare locale tra invecchiamento e immigrazione* [Older people, families and caregivers: local welfare developments between ageing and immigration]. Milan: Franco Angeli.

Low, S.M. and Altman, I., 1992. Place attachment: a conceptual inquiry. In I. Altman and S. Low, eds. *Place attachment*. New York: Plenum Press, pp. 1–12.

Mesini, D., Pasquinelli, S. and Rusmini, G., 2006. *Il lavoro privato di cura in Lombardia* [Private care work in Lombardia]. Milan. Available at: www.qualificare.info/upload/Il%20lavoro%20privato%20di%20cura%20in%20Lombardia.pdf [accessed 24.05.2017].

Paolisso, G., 2013. *Gli Anziani over 75 e le Badanti* [Over 75-year-old people and private care workers]. Rome: Datanalysis. Available at: www.sigg.it/public/doc/congresso/58/28-11-2013/AUDITORIUM/10.00%20-%2011.30/17-Giuseppe%20Paolisso/Giuseppe-Paolisso.pdf [accessed 24.05.2017].

Pasquinelli, S., 2013. Le badanti in Italia: quante sono, chi sono, cosa fanno [Private care workers in Italy: how many they are, who they are, what they do]. In S. Pasquinelli and G. Rusmini, eds. *Badare non basta. Il lavoro di cura: attori, progetti, politiche* [Caring is not enough. Care work: actors, projects, politics]. Rome: Ediesse, pp. 41–55.

Pasquinelli, S. and Rusmini, G., 2013. *Quante sono le badanti in Italia* [How many care workers are in Italy]. Available at: www.qualificare.info/home.php?list=archivio&id=678 [accessed 26.05.2017].

Principi, A., Lamura, G., Sirolla, C., Mestheneos, L., Bien, B., Brown, J., et al., 2014. Work restrictions experienced by midlife family care-givers of older people: evidence from six European countries. *Aging and Society*, 34, pp. 209–31. DOI: 10.1017/S0144686X12000967.

RGS (Ragioneria Generale dello Stato), 2014. *Le tendenze di medio-lungo periodo del sistema pensionistico e socio-sanitario* [The medium- to long-term trends of the pension and social health system]. Report no. 15. Rome: RGS. Available at: www.rgs.mef.gov.it/_Documenti/VERSIONE-I/Attivit--i/Spesa-soci/Attivita_di_previsione_RGS/2014/Le-tendenze-di-m_l-periodo-del-s_p_e-s_s-Rapporto_n15.pdf [accessed 24.05.2017].

Rosa, E., Massaia, M. and Zanetti, O., 2013. Determinanti del burden of care delle badanti di pazienti affetti da demenza [Determinants of the burden of care in private care workers of patients suffering from dementia]. *Giornale di Gerontologia*, 61(2), pp. 103–6.

Santini, S., Principi, A. and Lamura G., 2011. *Carers between work and care: conflict or chance? Results of interviews with working carers*. Available at: www.carersatwork.tu-dortmund.de/en/publikationen.php [accessed 24.05.2017].

Scassellati Sforzolini, M., 2013. Pensare al futuro e alla bellezza della domiciliarità. Le strutture residenziali si aprono alla domiciliarità [Thinking of the future and the beauty of home care: residential facilities opening to home care]. In F. Aglì, ed. 2013. *Domiciliarità e residenzialità. La struttura residenziale, un'opportunità per garantire il diritto alla domiciliarità* [Home and residential care: the residential facility as an opportunity to guarantee the right to home care]. Torre Pellice: La Bottega del Possibile, pp. 9–13.

Sgritta, G.B., 2009. *Le famiglie possibili. Reti di aiuto e solidarietà in età anziana* [Possible families: help and solidarity networks in older age]. Rome: Edizioni Lavoro.

Spandonaro, F., 2014. *10° Rapporto Sanità. Investimenti, innovazione e selettività: scelte obbligate per il futuro del SSN* [10th health report. Investments, innovation and selectivity: mandatory choices for the future of the IT-NHS]. Rome: CREA Sanità. Available at: https://art.torvergata.it/retrieve/handle/2108/108808/291392/10-RAPPORTO-SANITA-CREA-TV.pdf [accessed 24.04.2017].

Special Eurobarometer, 2007. *Health and long-term care in the European Union*. N. 283, Wave 67.3. European Commission. Available at: http://ec.europa.eu/public_opinion/archives/ebs/ebs_283_en.pdf [accessed 24.05.2017].

Stones, D. and Gullifer, J., 2016. At home it's just so much easier to be yourself: older adults' perceptions of ageing in place. *Ageing and Society*, 36(3), pp. 449–81. DOI: https://doi.org/10.1017/S0144686X14001214.

Taccani, P., 2013. Da mani familiari a mani altre [From familiar hands to other hands]. In S. Pasquinelli and G. Rusmini, eds. *Badare non basta. Il lavoro di cura: attori, progetti, politiche* [Caring is not enough. Care work: actors, projects, politics]. Rome: Ediesse, pp. 76–92.

Van Hooren, F., 2012. Varieties of migrant care work. *Journal of European Social Policy*, 22(2), pp. 133–47. DOI: 10.1177/0958928711433654.

Welfare Italia, 2014. *Integrare il welfare, sviluppare la white economy* [Integrating welfare, developing white economy]. Rome: CENSIS-UNIPOL. Available at: www.sanita24.ilsole24ore.com/pdf2010/Sanita2/_Oggetti_Correlati/Documenti/Dibattiti-e-Idee/CENSISBUONO.pdf?uuid=AbZaC60J [accessed 24.05.2017].

Part III
Eastern Europe

11

Post-socialist eldercare in the Czech Republic

Institutions, families, and the market

Adéla Souralová and Eva Šlesingerová

Introduction

All European countries are facing long-lasting profound demographic changes characterized mainly by ageing populations. The phenomenon of demographic ageing is the result of the decline in the birth rate and the simultaneous prolongation of life expectancy. The problems arising from this situation have affected more or less all European countries, including the Czech Republic, since the mid-twentieth century. The increasing proportion of senior citizens within the population has become a big social issue in contemporary Czech society (Kubalčíková and Havlíková, 2016; Svobodová, 2008; Vidovičová and Rabušic, 2003). Model projections created by the Czech Statistical Office (CZSO) indicate that by 2050, about 33 per cent of the entire population will be people over 65, which means more than 2.5 million people. People over 70 and over 80 will also increase significantly (CZSO, 2013). This transformation of the demographic structure of the population has brought an increasing need for eldercare, as most older people do not live in conditions sufficient for their well-being, adequate quality of life, and self-reliance to their end of lives (based on their life expectancy). A significant number of older people spend the end of their lives partly or totally dependent on care assistance. Moreover, various Czech social actors construct ageing as a form of illness. Growing older, and even dying, is medicalized and treated as a diagnosis. Care service actors predominantly view the elderly as dependent and ill (Dudová, 2015; Kubalčíková et al., 2015).

Senior care services take place within institutional and non-institutional environments, and care providers are usually women. Family unpaid caregivers are confronted with an increased risk of poverty, burdened with responsibilities, and faced with a lack of effective alternative care facilities and support. Expectations involved in various types of normativity are often in contradiction and mutual conflict (Dudová, 2015). In fact, those normative expectations and contradictory claims have intensified expectations to take the responsibility for eldercare from the public to the private sphere, even though the Czech Republic has the largest percentage of informal senior home care in Europe, according to data from the cross-national database SHARE – the *Survey of Health, Ageing and Retirement in Europe* (Börsch-Supan, 2017). Regarding the situation of ageing relatives, the family is still expected to bear most of the responsibility, and formal services are used mainly in cases of the absence, deficiency or exhaustion of the family (Svobodová, 2007).

In this chapter, recent research on developments in the organization of eldercare in the Czech Republic is reviewed. We have analysed the existing literature on developments in eldercare services before and after the fall of communism. We describe the main topics addressed by research on care services, outline the historical developments in eldercare organization, and investigate the shifts in social services during the post-1989 transformation process. We are particularly interested in how the communist legacy is inscribed in contemporary ideals and practices of how eldercare should be provided. Our analysis of existing research shows that since the early 1990s, there have been several changes in how eldercare is organized, how the normative idea(l)s of eldercare are constructed, and how the care recipients' problems are perceived in social policy discourse. Using secondary analysis and statistical data, this chapter provides a macro-analysis of recent developments in the Czech eldercare system, with an emphasis on the heterogeneous processes and dimensions that are part of the general development of care services. We identify three main trends in current academic debates: (1) negotiations between collective care and family or individualistic responsibilities; (2) the deinstitutionalization of the eldercare system; and (3) the shift from state-organized care to market services.

The development of eldercare organization: playing with familialism

The historical heritage of the Czech Republic radically differs from that of Western European or Nordic countries, and this history still shapes the daily reality of eldercare provision. Taking into consideration the development of these specificities, we ask two questions in an effort to grasp eldercare system development: (1) How has this situation developed in the specific context of the Czech Republic? (2) Are there any specific issues relating to the process of transformation from a communist to a post-communist society?

The development of eldercare services has not been a homogenous and direct process in Czechoslovakia. Taking advantage of Leitner's typology of familialism, Maříková and Plasová (2012) write about the changes in the care system that developed in three historic periods under state socialism between 1948 and 1989. They argue that the assumed role of the family in eldercare policies changed over the decades of communist rule and developed from certain de-familializing tendencies in the 1950s, to a return to the family in the 1960s, towards an explicit familialism in the 1970s and 1980s, and finally to an implicit familialism in the post-socialist era (Maříková and Plasová, 2012, p. 93).

1950s: the new family and de-familialism under communism

This period is characterized by the ideological struggle for a new society in Czechoslovakia, including a new kind of family. The Communist Party tried to combat familialism and the ideas of the 'petty bourgeois' (Možný, 1991). The traditional and conservative idea of family consisting of a husband as the breadwinner and a wife as the family caretaker and homemaker was meant to be extinguished in the 1950s in Czechoslovakia. The official ideology of the Communist Party aimed to reconceptualize and reconstruct that idea of the family as a middle-class and bourgeois form of patriarchal and class dominance. The new communist regime was grounded in a critique of bourgeois values, including the figures of a breadwinning father and caregiving mother. This type of family was conceived to be 'reactionary' and destabilizing for the new regime. The emancipation of women from household and domestic work and their liberation from financial dependence on men was to be accomplished by introducing or pushing women into the labour market, paid work opportunities, and participation in the public sphere. All these efforts were meant to result in women being released from caring for dependent family members – including children and elderly people. These ideological expectations and the reasoning behind the shift to institutional and state forms of eldercare had even more pragmatic aims, such as to solve the housing crisis by providing a number of flats for young people when seniors have been settled in institutions (Maříková and Plasová, 2012). The communist state also insisted on its own parental role, as state/father and homeland/mother. State institutions were represented as symbolic 'parental caretakers' under the official ideology (Verdery, 1996).

1960s and 1970s: variability of caregiving modes? Between family and state

According to Maříková and Plasová (2012), the first half of the 1960s was characterized by the diversification of care services in Czechoslovakia. At this time, the failure of the ideological ideas and claims of the communist regime relating to the construction of a new social and economic order, as well as a new family, was becoming apparent. State socialism was not able to offer enough effective institutional care for all people in need. Still, in the first half of the 1960s, institutional residential services were more available than home-based care. The legal framework stressing social care only for elderly people without a family or a community network was influenced by §100 Social Services Act No. 102/1964. Kalinová (1998) argues that this Act expresses a focus on the family in eldercare; it was the political reaction to the beginning of demographic ageing. The tendency towards missing or decreasing opportunities for institutional residential care for people over 80 years of age was apparent at this time. Another shift to explicit familialism resulted from the regulation of the Federal Ministry of Labour and Social Affairs No. 128/1975, in which a monthly recurring financial benefit was introduced for persons caring for close dependent relatives (Niederle, 1996, p. 5).

The 1980s offered no significant changes in the legal framework concerning eldercare. The state (not very effectively) extended offers for combinations of family and state forms of care, for example nursing homes and day-care centres (Rendlová, 1982, p. 634). Families were expected to be the 'desired' as well as 'indispensable' sources of eldercare (Maříková and Plasová, 2012). This kind of familialism thus did not stem from voluntary choice, but from the insufficiency of the care system and the low quality of institutional care services and home nursing that were only available with difficulty (Wolfová, 1987). In contrast to the official ideology of the freed household and liberated women, pressure was applied for informal care in families.

Facing the changes after 1989: legacy and trends

According to Maříková and Plasová (2012), the tendency to increase the expectation of the family to be the primary caregiver for its dependent members continued after the fall of communism in 1989. That the family bears the responsibility is still more or less openly expected in the situation of population ageing and with the need to reach necessary levels of dignity of care for elderly people. The situation is the same in other countries in Central and Eastern Europe (Theobald and Kern, 2009). Österle (2012, p. 241) describes how the organizational structure of eldercare shifted from the communist legacy of state-run provision and state responsibility to regional and local authorities. This shift was not unproblematic: 'a lack of experience in social care development and a lack of funding that would have supported decentralized responsibilities, however, have for years limited the modernization and extension of infrastructure and delayed the emergence of a broader welfare mix'.

The 'cash-for-care' programme, which provides cash benefits directly to (paid at the national level) those who need care, and not to their relatives or 'close persons', and which was introduced in Western European countries in the 1990s, did not appear in the Czech Republic until 2006. As part of a huge reform of social service, Act No. 108/2006 Coll., on Social Services, the new care allowance system introduced a tax-funded universal cash benefit paid directly to those who need care, at four different levels of dependence (Barvíková, 2011). Recipients of the benefits are free to decide on how they want to use the benefit and what services they want to buy for the money they receive. Barvíková and Österle (2013, p. 250) conclude the aims of this policy as follows:

> The concept of social services aims to ensure a wider supply of services provided primarily in households of clients to enable them to lead an independent life and to co-decide the amount and type of services they receive. From a general perspective, developments in social services reflect the trend away from institutional care toward care in the community, in line with the idea of individualizing care and coming close to ordinary life in a domestic environment. This places emphasis on an individual approach toward users and their human rights. With the introduction of care allowances directed at care users, the emphasis of individual autonomy was further strengthened.

Generally, it can be argued that the process of transformation is heterogeneous and there are still a variety of discourses even when the norms of caregiving in the context of eldercare are standardized. Mainly, there is an emphasis on the deinstitutionalization, decentralization, professionalization, and plurality of care service modes (Kubalčíková et al., 2015; Österle, 2012). The ambivalent relationship, or rather practical coexistence, of state care and family care was accompanied by a multiplicity of organizations, municipal, civic, non-governmental organizations, and commercial bodies that provided care after the fall of communism. The existing commodification and marketization of eldercare has intensified during the post-communist transformations.

Recent trends in the organization of eldercare

The previous regime, the disruption in 1989, and the subsequent transition of Czech society to a market economy and democracy brought profound changes in the organization of (not only) eldercare. The political and historical circumstances motivated restructuring of the social services. Although this restructuring occurred in Czechoslovakia during the same period as in Western countries, the restructuring mechanisms were not motivated by the end of the 'golden age' of the welfare state, but by political changes. For this reason, the 1990s and the beginning of the new millennium brought 'a radical transformation from one social services regime to another' (Kubalčíková and Havlíková, 2016, p. 182). This transformation required the rejection of the old regime and the establishment of a new one; it took more than 15 years (1989–2006). Kubalčíková and Havlíková (2016, p. 181) observe that 'the transition to the modern conception of eldercare provision on the local and regional level has been rather slow and not very straightforward'. In addition, they argue that the Czech Republic is 20 years behind Western countries in adopting such trends, and so it can be seen as a 'latecomer in respect to the restructuring trends'. We focus on three important issues that we identified in contemporary research on eldercare in the Czech Republic: the role of family, deinstitutionalization and decentralization, and commodification of eldercare.

Omnipresent family: the perennial star

From a European perspective, as Österle (2012, p. 240) notes, long-term care systems in Central and Eastern European countries are characterized by 'family-orientation, residualism, social assistance orientation and comparatively low levels of service provision'. If there is a constant in the organization of eldercare that survived the collapse of the regime in 1989, it is 'the family'. Intergenerational solidarity became a prominent issue in the Czech sociology of the family in the 1990s, especially thanks to Ivo Možný, a founder and important figure in post-1989 Czech sociology. Writing about the fall of communism in his book *Proč tak snadno* (*Why So Easy?*), Možný (1991) analyses the communist legacy and various reasons for the smooth course of the 'velvet revolution'. He presents the social institution of the family and the orientation towards family life as one of the main structural causes of the fall of communism. Whereas in the early 1950s the communist regime characterized the family and familialism as a bourgeois and anti-modernist social institution, by the late 1960s and early 1970s the family had become a very important source of solidarity and it compensated for the failing state. Možný says that under communism, the state seemed to be strong and to have control over everything, but it was an illusion. The mutual interconnections, groups and clans, including party technocrats, local elites and police apparatuses, held real control and power. In fact, the state itself failed under communism, which become apparent in the non-functioning bureaucracy and care systems. The family became the 'foundation of the state' because it fulfilled many of the state's roles.

Current sociologists argue that intergenerational solidarity is at a high level in the Czech Republic and family members continue to be the key source of support in later life (Sýkorová, 2007). Intergenerational solidarity seems to be the guarantor of intergenerational care, above all of grandparental care for grandchildren. Hasmanová Marhánková (2010) argues that in the Czech Republic, motherhood is seen as a continuous commitment to care, as grandmothers are expected to take care of their grandchildren. A study by Souralová (2015a) shows the normative ideal of how 'correct' motherhood and grandmotherhood should look, and suggests that the feeling of not achieving this ideal leads some women to become nannies after retirement.

Grandparents care, but does anybody care about them? The answer to this question can be divided into two levels: the level of ideals and attitudes, and the level of practice and real care strategies. Shortly after the fall of communism, in 1991, 81 per cent of Czechs agreed with the statement presented in the European Values Study, a large scale, cross-national, longitudinal study, that 'Regardless of what the qualities and faults of one's parents are, one must always love and respect them'; in 2008, the number had dropped to 65 per cent (Rabušic and Hamanová, 2009). In 2008, half of Czechs replied that children should provide care for their elderly parents; 29 per cent believed that the children should have their own lives. In the Czech Republic, as in other countries, we can therefore find two discourses about the role of family in provision of eldercare – the discourse about family care, and the discourse of liberating the family from such care (Jeřábek, 2009).

When we come to the level of daily care provision, a survey conducted by Jeřábek in 2006 shows that 22 per cent of people had experience with caring for an elderly person in the last 5–10 years and 8 per cent were actively caring for one (Jeřábek, 2009). Sowa (2010, p. 13) estimates that as much as 80 per cent of eldercare for people older than 65 years is provided by family members, reaching the following conclusion:

> This translates into approximately 100,000 elderly who need assistance in basic activities of daily living and 300,000 elderly who are not able to perform instrumental activities of daily living. Assuming that every elderly person is provided with help by at least one

person means that there are about 400,000–500,000 informal care providers in the Czech Republic. These are mostly women (63 per cent) of working age, most of whom (80 per cent) have a regular full-time job.

Despite the fact that the family and intergenerational solidarity are prominent normative forms of expectation, and that the family is the most desired source of eldercare, a non-negligible number of people in the Czech Republic prefer various types of formal care facilities.

Deinstitutionalization, decentralization, and localization of care services

A core characteristic of current eldercare organization is its deinstitutionalization and decentralization. Barvíková and Österle (2013, p. 255) observe that since the early 1990s, long-term care has been characterized by a shift from a general institutional care system towards a system in which the emphasis is on the accessibility of social services at the local level. These new principles, unknown before 1989, entered the debate in 2006 with the new Social Service Act, and the discussion about eldercare in the Czech Republic was on the same lines as in the 1980s and 1990s in Western European countries (Kubalčíková and Havlíková, 2016).

The path to *deinstitutionalization* was a departure from the situation in which residential care was the major approach to organizing eldercare throughout the Central and Eastern European countries with a similar pre-1989 political history (Österle, 2012). As Österle critically adds, despite the changes, however, residential care is still the 'major public response towards the need for care if individuals and families are unable to take care of a relative' (Österle, 2012, p. 240). The stay in residential care is paid and it is not income-related. The fee for the stay varies according to the services, and in a few cases it can be twice as high as the average pension. In 2013, there were 491 nursing homes for seniors with altogether 38,000 clients (CZSO, 2014). The numbers started increasing in the 1990s: in 1995, there were 290 homes with a capacity for 32,000 people (Červenková et al., 2006); the number reached its peak in 2007, when the capacity was 41,600 (Jeřábková, 2009). Then, as a result of the new Social Services Act, the numbers stabilized around 38,000. What is quite interesting is that the capacity is increasing, but so are the numbers of unaccepted applicants – and the waiting lists are getting longer. For example, in 1995, when the capacity was 32,000, there were 18,500 people on the waiting list; in 2005, there were 38,000 occupied places and 43,000 candidates (Červenková et al., 2006); and in 2013, there were 36,600 clients and 61,000 waiting candidates (CZSO, 2014). Simply put, there are more candidates than actual clients accommodated in nursing homes. The waiting time varies between a couple of months to a couple of years.

Given the role of the family in eldercare, nursing homes are generally considered the last possible choice (Sowa, 2010; Barvíková, 2005), as the ideal situation is to live in one's own home with the support of family members (Barvíková and Österle, 2013; Možný et al., 2004; Veselá, 2002). Barvíková (2005) notes that many family members are interested in sharing the care for their elder parents or grandparents even after their placement in an institution and beyond the regular visits. Veselá (2002) produced another finding relating to family care: although a large percentage of respondents claim that they would take care of their parents, they also concede that there are obstacles that could challenge this preference and lead them to decide not to provide this care. The three most prominent obstacles are limits in employment caused by providing care, inability to provide the necessary qualified care, and the time demands of care.

Nursing homes are not the only institutions providing long-term eldercare, although they are the largest. Long-term care is provided within the social service system (nursing homes) and within the healthcare system – including selected hospital departments, aftercare, and long-term care homes (Barvíková and Österle, 2013; Horecký, 2010; Sowa, 2010). The role of healthcare in the organization of eldercare is not negligible, and it is a sign of the medicalization of later age and eldercare that we mentioned above. In the healthcare system, there are around 14,000 places in hospitals for elderly people in the Czech Republic (Horecký, 2010). Both of these types of care are organized differently – they are subject to the regulations of two different ministries (the Ministry of Labour and Social Affairs and the Ministry of Health), with separate criteria for accessibility and quality and different financing methods for clients. The lack of cooperation in the approach of these two ministries and the systems of care has been criticized (Barvíková and Österle, 2013). Horecký (2010, p. 2), for example, sees the strong division of competences and responsibilities between the two ministries as an obvious problem preventing the 'successful realization of any concept of long-term care'.

Hand in hand with deinstitutionalization, the need for community care and for *decentralization* already existed in the 1990s, but the systematic development of these services has only happened in the last few years (Österle, 2012). Community care services (including home-based care) are unequally distributed within the Czech Republic, and there are huge interregional differences in the accessibility of care (Barvíková and Österle, 2013; Österle, 2012; Průša, 2011). While the supply of this service is quite suitable in urban areas, the same cannot be said about less populated or mountain areas (Průša, 2011). Barvíková and Österle (2013, p. 253) identify many shortages in the current community care services: night services, all-day supervision, and 'other activities to secure the care primarily of the least independent senior citizens'. In summary, although there was a radical shift towards the decentralization of care services, a shift from institutional care to a form of community care that reflects the individual needs of each elderly person, this aim has not yet been fully accomplished. The decentralization was more successful in terms of how the services are financed – previously state-run care services passed into the responsibility of the municipalities, which currently provide 85 per cent of the capacity of all nursing homes (CZSO, 2014).

From state-organized care system to marketized and then commodified services

Marketization – the use of market mechanisms and for-profit delivery of care – is a key process in the current provision of social care services across Europe and across the different welfare regimes; however, the integration of this principle varies at the national level (Kubalčíková and Havlíková, 2016; Lehmann and Havlíková, 2015). The first step towards intensifying the marketization and commodification of social care services in the Czech Republic was the passage of the law (Act No. 108/2006 Coll., on Social Services) in 2006 after which people were given money to buy services on the care market. The second step was that the market itself had to change and be pluralized, both in the spectrum of care services that are sold and in the sellers of these services. Among these sellers, the municipalities are the most prominent, providing the majority of social care services for elderly people (87 per cent). They are followed by non-governmental organizations and churches (10 per cent) – here, the municipalities take part in funding the activities performed by non-governmental organizations and churches. The participation of for-profit organizations is the smallest portion, estimated to be 3 per cent (Pfeiferová et al., 2013; Sowa 2010). The private for-profit sector is rather sporadic and rare. Jeřábková (2009) notes that the marginal role of non-municipal actors is quite understandable as trade in social services generates losses, and is thus unattractive for investors.

The new law in 2006 was meant to lead to a big boom in new care services – especially those at the local level – and to the improvement in the quality of all care services (Barvíková and Österle, 2013; Horecký, 2010). The initial idea, however, was not met, and the care allowances are very often used for improving the recipients' income and not for buying care services. Although the numbers of recipients of the care allowances have been rising, the relative number of those who use this allowance for buying any services has risen quite slowly (Jeřábková and Průša, 2013). In the majority of cases, then, the care was provided informally by family members. Despite the changes in policy, the continuation of pre-2006 behaviour, when the benefits were 'designed or understood as either an income supplement or an income replacement' (Österle, 2012, p. 248), remained. Making elderly people consumers of social services and giving them the choice to use their cash benefit the way they want was not as straightforward, simple and fast as it was thought to be at the beginning of 2007. The right to choose the right services was hindered and marked by several limits and constraints. Some of these limits have been mentioned, such as the accessibility of service, and are external to the care receiver. The rather more internal constraints include insufficient knowledge about the options and available care possibilities (Kubalčíková and Havlíková, 2016) and the insufficient self-confidence of seniors (Barvíková and Österle, 2013).

Today's generation of seniors are people who spent most of their life in the communist regime and state socialism. Their cultural memory shapes the way they understand the care services and their own role in care relations and the care process. Very often they are not aware of their rights, and it can be quite hard for them to accept the role of consumers of social care. As a result, they 'find themselves in the role of sufferers and passive recipients of low-quality services rather than acting as service "consumers"' (Barvíková and Österle, 2013, p. 260). The state as a paternalistic and overwhelming caregiver (Verdery, 1996), and the idea that selling care is somehow inappropriate (in terms of love and attention), as it could not be part of the communist rhetoric of equality and contradicted the class ideology, influenced their habitus – socially and culturally coded ways of acting and making decisions (Bourdieu, 1977) – as not being self-confident and active care receivers within the care service market. For example, as Sedláková and Souralová (2017) show, some seniors feel that they should not 'bother' the personnel in nursing homes with their problems, requirements or even complaints. This attitude is far from consumer-like; rather, the current seniors who pay for these services could be described as 'grateful passive recipients' of social care services.

For-profit sector issues are particularly interesting in the Czech Republic. While many European countries rely on the migrant labour force in the care sector, this is not the case in the Czech Republic. Migrant women are rarely employed in the childcare or eldercare sectors, and hiring a private eldercare worker is not a common strategy in Czech families (see Souralová, 2015b, 2017). The Czech Republic continues to be a country that sends its care workers to Western countries. In recent years, a model has emerged in which Czech women from areas bordering Germany and Austria circularly migrate to care for German and Austrian seniors in their own homes (Kuchyňková and Ezzeddine, 2015). Although it is still not common to pay for private care workers – or to employ migrants in private households – according to Válková et al. (2010), the arrival of migrant labour to this sector is only a question of time, arguing that immigrants have already found their place in auxiliary construction work and in trade, and so they can in the near future be expected to appear in the care sector. So far, in 2017, however, we cannot observe any big changes in eldercare provision by the migrant care workers.

In recent years, a new private for-profit actor entered the field of eldercare – eldercare placement agencies (Souralová, 2017). The for-profit agencies offer home-based care, which includes help with daily tasks or small housework. They organize their service as 'the help for family members' and claim that their services can postpone the placement of elderly people in nursing homes. The agencies operate with no relation to the public care services and they are quite expensive in comparison with other eldercare services. One hour of services costs, on average, 120 CZK, which is slightly more than the average hourly wage in the Czech Republic and twice the minimum hourly wage. The average pension in 2016 was 11,400 CZK (approximately €425) – 12,500 CZK for men and 10,300 CZK for women monthly. The cash benefits for care in the same year were 880 CZK, 4,400 CZK, 8,800 CZK and 13,200 CZK, according to the four levels of dependence. It is obvious that the agencies are not for everyone – due to the cost, their service can be used neither by those seniors who live in poverty (and do not have money at all to pay for private care workers) nor by those who need 24/7 care as the cost would be four times higher than their total income (counted as the average pension + cash benefit for the fourth level of dependence, 120 CZK per hour, 24 hours per day, 30 days in a month). For these reasons, the typical model is for the agencies to be used for several hours per week, the care worker coming from the agency not replacing the caring family member/s, but rather making it possible to organize shifts/changes with the family member/s (Souralová, 2017).

Conclusions

Eldercare service issues relating to demographic ageing have recently become the subject of significant public debate and media coverage in the Czech Republic. We are witnessing efforts to move the Czech social care system out from the legacy of the previous regime and towards the systems found in Western countries. The public debates about the changes were discursively framed in the dichotomy between the 'bad/pre-modern pre-1989 system' and the 'good/modern system' that should have been established after 1989. We used a historical overview to demonstrate in our text how the legacy of the communist regime has influenced the contemporary character of eldercare in the Czech Republic. Focusing on the most significant current trends and shifts within the eldercare system, we identified three main areas: (1) the sphere of family; (2) the process of deinstitutionalization; and (3) the commodification and marketization of eldercare. Surprisingly enough, all of these aspects of eldercare (including state and grey economy and market) provision appeared even before 1989; however, their meanings changed with the new regime.

Historically, the Czech eldercare system developed from a phase of de-familialism through explicit familialism to implicit familialism and hybrid possibilities offering various types of eldercare from the state, the family, the marketplace, and medical services. There were a variety of discourses presenting different types of expectations, norms and standards from various stakeholders in eldercare under communism. At the beginning, the communist ideology stressed emancipation of women and institutionalization of eldercare instead of family responsibilities. Failure of the state economy caused the turn from institutions to family care and informal networks.

In the last decade, a new approach to eldercare emerged in the Czech context that intensified the processes of commodification and marketization of care. Drawing upon our review of existing research, we observed that the adaptation to the market style of care organization was quite difficult for the current generation of seniors as their habits and cultural memory were shaped under a radically different regime that practically prevented people from considering themselves as consumers. The lack of a systematic conception of eldercare and its dispersion between two non-communicating ministries represents a challenge. As a result, many eldercare services, especially those provided by for-profit organizations, are only available for seniors who can afford them or for those who have family members who are willing to invest their money and buy the services for them. Often, families decide to care for their family members themselves. Both paying for professional care and providing informal care can easily lead to the growing poverty of seniors and of their informal caregivers, and to an understanding of care as a burden, leading to precarious situations.

This chapter has illuminated the family as a steady rock in eldercare provision in the Czech Republic, across decades and regimes. The position of the family does not seem to have been very much affected by the marketization of eldercare as the 'Czech way' of marketization is marked by a poorly developed market (in terms of the pluralization of services and their geographic and economic accessibility) and by the slow adaptation of the older generation to the market principles of care. This is apparent in two aspects of current demand for eldercare. First, among different institutions (day-care centres, institutional care or private home-based care) that provide eldercare, only the nursing homes are known from the period before 1989, and nowadays they are the most often in demand, and for them demand outnumbers the supply. The cultural memory and relative poverty of seniors disqualifies other options, especially the private care workers, and paying for home-based care is still not so common a way of organization of eldercare in the Czech Republic. And second, for the generation that lived a majority of their life under communism, the role of consumers who cannot only select their services from diverse options, but also influence their character, is unaccustomed. Consequently, their scope of action is quite limited and they find themselves in the role of passive recipients rather than active actors in the market with care. Time will tell if the situation with long-term care will change with a new generation in the role of care recipients who will be confident enough to communicate their requirements and change the system in their own way (Barvíková and Österle, 2013; Válková et al., 2010).

References

Barvíková, J. 2005. Rodinná péče a profesionální péče [Family care and professional care]. In H. Jeřábek, ed. *Rodinná péče o staré lidi* [Family care for elderly people]. Prague: CESES FSV UK, pp. 58–70.

Barvíková, J., 2011. Long-term care in the Czech Republic: on the threshold of reform. In A. Österle, ed. *Long-term care in Central and South Eastern Europe*. Frankfurt am Main: Lang, pp. 81–103.

Barvíková, J. and Österle, A., 2013. Long-term care reform in Central-Eastern Europe: the case of the Czech Republic. In C. Ranci and E. Pavolini, eds. *Reforms in long-term care policies in Europe: investigating institutional change and social impacts*. New York: Springer, pp. 243–65.

Börsch-Supan, A., 2017. *Survey of health, ageing and retirement in Europe (SHARE).* Wave 6. Release version: 6.0.0. SHARE-ERIC. Data set. DOI: 10.6103/SHARE.w6.600.

Bourdieu, P. 1977. *Outline of a theory of practice*. Cambridge: Cambridge University Press.

Červenková, A., Bruthansová, D. and Pechanová, M., 2006. Sociálně zdravotní služby poskytované klientům na ošetřovatelských odděleních domovů důchodců a v léčebnách dlouhodobě nemocných se zřetelem k jejich sociální situaci a zdravotnímu stavu [Social and health services provided to clients in healthcare departments of nursing homes and in long-term care homes with regard to their social situation and health status]. Prague: VÚPSV. Available at: http://praha.vupsv.cz/Fulltext/vz_211.pdf [accessed 18.07.2017].

CZSO (Czech Statistical Office), 2013. *Projekce obyvatelstva ČR do roku 2100* [Population projection CR till 2100]. Available at: www.czso.cz/csu/czso/projekce-obyvatelstva-ceske-republiky-do-roku-2100-n-fu4s64b8h4 [accessed 18.07.2017].

CZSO (Czech Statistical Office), 2014. *Senioři v ČR – 2014* [Seniors in the CR – 2014]. Available at: www.czso.cz/csu/czso/seniori-v-cr-2014-2gala5x0fg [accessed 18.07.2017].

Dudová, R., 2015. *Postarat se ve stáří. Rodina a zajištění péče o seniory* [Care during old age: family and ensuring senior care]. Prague: SLON.

Hasmanová Marhánková, J. 2010. Proměny prarodičovství v kontextu představ aktivních stáří [Changes in grandparenthood in the context of ideas about active ageing]. In D. Ryšavý, ed. *Sociologica – andragogica Problémy ohrožených skupin, mezigenerační vztahy v rodině* [Problems of Endangered Groups, Intergenerational Relationships in the Family]. Olomouc: Univerzita Palackého, pp. 11–26. Available at: http://oldwww.upol.cz/fileadmin/user_upload/Veda/AUPO/Sociologica-Andragogica_2009.pdf [accessed 18.07.2017].

Horecký, J., 2010. *Current situation in quality of residential care*. Available at: www.horecky.cz/images/1330002273_current-situation-in-quality-of-residential-care.pdf [accessed 18.07.2017].

Jeřábek, H., 2009. Rodinná péče o seniory jako 'práce z lásky': nové argumenty [Family care for seniors as a 'labour of love': new arguments]. *Sociologický časopis* [Sociological Magazine], 45(2), pp. 243–65. Available at: http://sreview.soc.cas.cz/uploads/b02650d7a75e5ebccff13c37a521b65c39a7d028_Jerabek2009-2.pdf [accessed 18.07.2017].

Jeřábková, V., 2009. Zdravotně-sociální péče o seniory v České republice [Health and social care for seniors in the Czech Republic]. In J. Langhamrová, ed. *Reprodukce lidského kapitálu: vzájemné vazby a souvislosti* [Reproduction of human capital: mutual relations and connections]. Prague: Oeconomica. Available at: http://kdem.vse.cz/resources/relik09/Prispevky_PDF/Jerabkova.pdf [accessed 18.07.2017].

Jeřábková, V. and Průša, L. 2013. *Příspěvek na péči* [Care allowances]. Prague: VÚPSV. Available at: http://praha.vupsv.cz/Fulltext/vz_377.pdf [accessed 18.07.2017].

Kalinová, L., 1998. Transformace sociálního systému v Československu po únoru 1948 [Transformation of the social system in Czechoslovakia after February 1948]. *Acta Oeconomica Pragensia*, 8(5–6), pp. 129–46.

Kubalčíková, K. and Havlíková., J., 2016. Current developments in social care services for older adults in the Czech Republic: trends towards deinstitutionalization and marketization. *Journal of Social Service Research*, 42(2), pp. 180–98. DOI: http://dx.doi.org/10.1080/01488376.2015.1129014.

Kubalčíková, K., Havlíková, J., Hubíková, O. and Dohnalová, Z., 2015. *Sociální práce se seniory v kontextu kritické gerontologie* [Social work with seniors in the context of critical gerontology]. Brno: Masaryk University Munipress. Available at: https://is.muni.cz/do/fss/kspsp/knihy_esf/Kubalcikova-e-kniha.pdf [accessed 18.07.2017].

Kuchyňková, A. and Ezzeddine, P., 2015. 'Ještě nepatřím do starého železa' aneb paradoxy migrace péče z ČR do Rakouska ['Not ready to be thrown on the scrap heap' or the paradoxes of care migration from the Czech Republic to Austria]. *Gender, rovné příležitosti, výzkum* [Gender Equality Research], 16(2), pp. 16–40. DOI: http://dx.doi.org/10.13060/12130028.2015.16.2.218.

Lehmann, Š. and Havlíková, J., 2015. Predictors of the availability and variety of social care services for older adults: comparison of Central European countries. *Journal of Social Service Research*, 41(1), pp. 113–32. DOI: http://dx.doi.org/10.1080/01488376.2014.959150.

Maříková, H. and Plasová, B., 2012. Kontinuita anebo změna v systému zajištění péče o seniory v České republice od roku 1948 vzhledem k genderovanosti politik péče [Continuity or change in the senior care system in the Czech Republic after 1948, considering gendered care policies]. *Fórum sociální politiky* [Social Policy Forum], 6(3), pp. 2–7. Available at: http://praha.vupsv.cz/Fulltext/FSP_2012-03.pdf [accessed 18.07.2017].

Možný, I., 1991. *Proč tak snadno?* [Why so easy?]. Prague: SLON.

Možný, I., Přidalová, M. and Bánovcová, L., 2004. *Mezigenerační solidarita, výzkumná zpráva z mezinárodního srovnávacího výzkumu Hodnota dětí a mezigenerační solidarita* [Intergenerational solidarity, research report from the international comparative research project: the value of children and intergenerational solidarity]. Prague: VÚPSV. Available at: http://praha.vupsv.cz/Fulltext/vz_155.pdf [accessed 18.07.2017].

Niederle, P., 1996. Příspěvek při péči o blízkou a jinou osobu [Contribution to the care of a relative or other person]. *Sociální politika*, [Social Policy] 6, pp. 5–6.

Österle, A., 2012. Long-term care financing in Central Eastern Europe. In J. Costa-Font and C. Courbage, eds. *Financing long-term care in Europe: institutions, markets and models*. London: Palgrave Macmillan, pp. 236–53.

Pfeiferová, S., Lux, M., Dvořák, T., Havlíková, J., Mikeszová, M. and Sunega, P., eds., 2013. *Housing and social care for the elderly in Central Europe: WP 3 main findings report*. Prague: Institute of Sociology, Academy of Science of the Czech Republic. Available at: www.central2013.eu/fileadmin/user_upload/Downloads/outputlib/HELPS_Main_Findings_Report.pdf [accessed 18.07.2017].

Průša, L. 2011. *Model efektivního financování a poskytování dlouhodobé péče* [Model of effective financing and provision of long-term care]. Prague: VÚPSV. Available at: http://praha.vupsv.cz/Fulltext/vz_340.pdf [accessed 18.07.2017].

Rabušic, L. and Hamanová, J., eds., 2009. *Hodnoty a postoje v České republice 1991–2008* [Values and attitudes in the Czech Republic, 1991–2008]. Brno: Masarykova univerzita.

Rendlová, E. 1982. Způsob života starých lidí a rodinné vztah [Old people's ways of life and family relationships]. *Sociologický časopis* [Czech Sociological Review], 18(6), pp. 625–41.

Sedláková, T. and Souralová, A., 2017. Emerging age asymmetries in the research relationship. *Ageing and Society*.DOI: 10.1017/S0144686X17001040

Souralová, A. 2015a. Můžeš prostě říct, že máš babičku: Vietnamské děti, české babičky a význam prarodičovství v jejich biografiích ['That's the lady I call Grandma!' Vietnamese children, Czech grandmothers and the meaning of grandparenthood in the biographies of both]. *Sociologický časopis* [Czech Sociological Review], 51(5), pp. 815–44. DOI: https://doi.org/10.13060/00380288.2015.51.5.215.

Souralová, A., 2015b. An employer sui generis: how placement agencies are changing the nature of paid childcare in the Czech Republic. In A. Triandafyllidou and S. Marchetti, eds. *Employers, agencies and immigration: paying for care*. Farnham: Ashgate, pp. 151–67.

Souralová, A., 2017. *Péče na prodej. Jak se práce z lásky stává placenou službou* [Care for sale: how labours of love turn into paid service]. Brno: MUNI Press.

Sowa, A. 2010. *The long-term care system for the elderly in the Czech Republic*. ENEPRI Research Report. No. 72. Available at: www.ancien-longtermcare.eu/sites/default/files/ENEPRI%20RR%20No%20 72%20ANCIEN%20Czech%20Republic.pdf [accessed 18.07.2017].

Svobodová, K. 2007. Gender a poskytování péče starším osobám [Gender and eldercare]. *Právo a rodina* [Law and Family], 9(2), pp. 20–3.

Svobodová, K., 2008. *Analýza: Dostupnost institucionální péče o seniory z regionálního pohledu* [Analysis: accessibility of institutional care for seniors from a regional view]. Available at: www.demografie. info/?cz_detail_clanku&artclID=569 [accessed 18.07.2017].

Sýkorová, D., 2007. *Autonomie ve stáří. Kapitoly z gerontosociologie* [Autonomy in later life: the chapters from gerontosociology]. Prague: SLON.

Theobald, H. and Kern, K., 2009. Elder care systems: policy transfer and europeanization. In A. Cerami and P. Vahuysse, eds. *Post-communist welfare pathways: theorizing social policy transformation in Central and Eastern Europe*. Basingstoke: Palgrave Macmillan, pp. 148–63.

Válková, M., Kojesová, M. and Holmerová, I., 2010. *Diskusní materiál k východiskům dlouhodobé péče v České republice* [Discussion materials concerning solutions for long-term care in the Czech Republic]. Prague: MPSV. Available at: www.mpsv.cz/files/clanky/9597/dlouhodoba_pece_CR.pdf [accessed 18.07.2017].

Verdery, K. 1996. *What was socialism, and what comes next?* Princeton, NJ: Princeton University Press.

Veselá, J., 2002. *Představy rodinných příslušníků o zabezpečení péče nesoběstačným rodičům* [Attitudes of family members about organizing care for their dependent parents]. Prague: VÚPSV. Available at: http://. vupsv.cz/Fulltext/detsen.pdf [accessed 18.07.2017].

Vidovičová, L. and Rabušic, L., 2003. *Senioři a sociální opatření v oblasti stárnutí v pohledu české veřejnosti* [Seniors and social measurements in the field of ageing in the Czech public view]. Prague: VÚPSV. Available at: http://praha.vupsv.cz/Fulltext/vidrab.pdf [accessed 18.07.2017].

Wolfová, M. 1987. Domovy důchodců [Homes for seniors]. *Sociální politika* [Social Policy], 13(12), pp. 268–70.

12

Imbalance between demand and supply of long-term care

The case of post-communist Poland

Stanisława Golinowska and Agnieszka Sowa-Kofta

Introduction

Poland belongs to a group of nations that, after gaining independence following the First World War (1918), were constantly undergoing rapid changes and shocks due to internal and external causes. Integration of the country, previously divided between three empires (Austro-Hungarian, German and Russian), was easier in political than it was in economic and social terms. Differences in development between regions belonging to those three empires are still visible today.

The Second World War brought extermination of large parts of the population and tremendous damage to previously rebuilt economic resources and infrastructure. Over 40 years of communist rule, imposed after the war, was characterized by an accelerated industrialization and – on average – a moderate improvement of living conditions, with equalized standards.

Population changes were as rapid as institutional and economic development. The fertility rate in Poland was the highest in Europe after the Second World War. High population growth was mitigated by a negative migration balance.

Poles were leaving the country for political, economic and family reasons (family reunification). In the main host countries of the United States, Germany and lately Great Britain, the diaspora of Polish migrants has been created with vibrant migration networks involved in provision of support for the new migrants. Further emigration tendencies present in independent Poland are related to more unfavourable labour market conditions than in Western Europe. Transformation from a centrally planned to a free market economy (from 1989), together with competition strengthened by globalization processes and the shutting down of traditional industry, resulted in job destruction rather than job creation (Rutkowski, 2002). Thus, today's emigration is often treated as an 'export of unemployment'.

Population changes of the transformation period in Poland are characterized by a dramatic decline in fertility. The total fertility rate of 2.1 in 1989 had declined to 1.3 in 2006, becoming one of the lowest in European countries. In parallel, mortality was declining and the average life expectancy was improving, leading to population stabilization, but also fears of a shrinking in the future (Eberhard, 2014; Kotowska, 1999). In post-communist countries, the dynamic of population transition is much sharper and faster than it has been in Western European countries (Frątczak, 2004).

Demographic changes are accompanied by cultural changes in care function of the family towards older people. Although most care needs are still satisfied within the family, the ability to provide care is slowly decreasing. Today's family, while being the main source of care, is often searching for assistance externally. The state policy response to the growing demand for care in the ageing population is weak. Also, the response from private care institutions is limited as the real incomes of older people are low in comparison with the commercial cost of care services.

This chapter discusses imbalances between the rapidly growing demand for care services and its insufficient supply in Poland. The first section is dedicated to discussing factors that have an impact on the demand for care. The second section presents the supply of long-term care (LTC) services in Poland. Further, factors for imbalances between demand and supply of care and its policy and societal changes context are discussed. The last words of the chapter are devoted to the authors' short commentary on the uncertain future of LTC development due to changes in social policy towards a conservative policy model, with strong family obligations in care provision.

The background for this chapter is a comprehensive assessment of LTC performance in Poland and other Central and Eastern European countries prepared by the authors in numerous projects supported with different funds, mainly from the European Commission. These include the *Assessing Needs for Care in European Nations* (ANCIEN) project, (Golinowska, 2012; Golinowska and Styczyńska, 2012), the *Mobilizing the Potential of Active Ageing in Europe* (MoPAct) project (Golinowska et al., 2016, Sowa et al., 2016a), the *Health Promotion and Prevention of Risk – Action for Seniors* (ProHealth 65+) project, coordinated by Stanisława Golinowska (Golinowska, 2016), and the NEUJOBS project (Golinowska et al., 2013). The role of the local community in provision of care services for older people in Poland was assessed by the authors in a qualitative study prepared for the Ministry of Labour and Social Policy in Poland (Golinowska and Sowa, 2010). Financial aspects of long-term care were assessed in two reports prepared for the World Bank Office in Warsaw (World Bank, 2015; Golinowska et al., 2013).

A number of in-depth interviews with local authorities, managers of social assistance centres and residential care facilities were performed and analysed in order to identify barriers and opportunities for community care development and management.

Demand for care of older dependent people

Poor health and disability of older people in longer life

The demand for care among older people depends on the number of older people in the population, their health status and functional limitations, which together drive the need for care services, either received at home or in institutions.

Poland is still a relatively young European country, with 11 per cent of the population aged 65–79 and 3.9 per cent of the population above 80 years of age, which is below the average for the 28 European Union countries (13.4 per cent and 5.1 per cent of the population, respectively) in 2014 (Eurostat 2016, Tables code tps00010). However, the population is entering an ageing phase, with the proportion of older people foreseen to more than double in the decades to come. The share of people above the age of 65 in the Polish population is foreseen to increase from 14.9 per cent in 2014 to 32.9 per cent by 2060. Most importantly from the perspective of the rising care needs, the share of the oldest people, aged 80 years or more, is foreseen to triple (European Commission 2015, Table code proj_13ndbims).

In 1991, Polish women were expected to live on average 75.1 years and men 65.6 years (GUS, 2015). By 2014, the expected longevity increased to 81.7 years for women and 73.7 years for men. Also, the expected average longevity of people aged 65 has improved. In 2014, men aged 65 were expected to live more than three years longer and women more than five years longer than in 1991.

Despite the longevity improvement, on average about one-fifth of one's life is still spent in poor health, with chronic and often coexisting illnesses or disability. In the population above 65 years of age in Poland, about 40–46 per cent of life is foreseen to be spent in good health and without disability. In the *European Survey of Income and Living Conditions* (EU-SILC) for 2013, more than 85 per cent of Poles above the age of 60 reported suffering from some long-term illness, and at the age of 80 this rose to 90 per cent (GUS, 2016). For every third person above the age of 65, limitations in everyday activities due to health problems are severe (GUS, 2016). In their seventies, almost every second person has limitations in activities, and this share rises to 75 per cent above the age of 85 (Wizner et al., 2012, Table 4), resulting in a relatively high share of limitations (as defined in the International Classification of Functioning) compared to other countries (Berger et al., 2015, Table 1). With a growing proportion of people facing long-term illnesses and functional limitations, the need for some sort of care becomes evident, especially for people over 70 or 80 years of age (GUS, 2016).

Social perception of disability in Poland is determined by legal assessment of disability, for the purpose of establishing a right to social protection, and especially disability benefits. Reforms of medical disability assessment in the social security system, strongly influenced by fiscal measures, resulted in limitations of entitlement to disability benefits and, at the same time, to limitations in statistical analysis of the data on work disability, showing decrease in the number of disabled people. This has been used as a justification for decreasing expenditures on social benefits for disabled people.

The problem of poorer health status and disability advancing with age has not yet been perceived in public policy in terms arising from the concept of *healthy ageing*, imposing actions in the field of healthcare and health promotion for older people in Poland. There has been, however, policy emphasis, on *active ageing* and motivating the older population to an extension of working life and a greater involvement in family and social life (Golinowska, 2016).

Extending working life is not, however, a process fully socially accepted in Poland, and political authorities are not acting consistently in this field. Public opinion pressure has resulted in withdrawal of the 2012 decision to increase and equalize the retirement age for men and women to the age of 67. According to the new law, retirement is set again as 60 for women and 65 for men.

Limitation of traditional family obligation to care for older people

Traditionally in Poland, care for people with illnesses and limitations in activities has been provided at home, informally. In a conservative traditional society, especially in rural areas, there is support for and an expectation of family care perceived as a moral obligation. Provision of care to family members in need has been an obvious and for years undisputable, though lately more and more often questioned, family obligation. Various studies provide different estimates of the volume of informal care provided to older people, but it is indisputably an overwhelming majority of the older dependent population who receive informal care: from over 80 per cent (Wóycicka and Rurarz, 2007, p. 299) to even 93 per cent (Łuczak, 2013, p. 16; Błędowski, 2012, pp. 451–2).

The high level of informal care is often explained in relation to the traditional family situation and frequent co-residence of older people with their children. The need for family care is, in most cases, related to grandmothers' care of a grandchild/ren in the case of working mothers. According to the results of the AZER (Aktywność Zawodowa i Edukacyjna a Obowiązki Rodzinne – Professional and Educational Activity and Family Obligations) study, over three-quarters of care needs in families is related to care of children (Kotowska et al., 2007).

Care is also provided to dependent parents/parents-in-law and spouses, often combined with childcare. A typical caretaker is a woman aged 50 (Wóycicka and Rurarz, 2007). Statistics show that women this age often leave the labour market due to caring responsibilities, resulting, together with the retirement age of 60, in one of the lowest employment rates of females aged 50–64 in Europe (37 per cent compared to 49 per cent in the EU-28 in 2015) (Eurostat, 2016 [lfsi_emp_a]). During the economic transformation period, employers have not been willing to support older female employees. In such cases, women do not necessarily stay with the family, or even in the country. Searching for other employment opportunities, they move abroad, often undertaking informal care provision for older people in Germany, Italy or Great Britain.

Family limitations in care provision, resulting in a growing demand for formal care services, are especially important in families of young people who have emigrated. In some communities (e.g. in the Opolskie voivodship, due to emigration of people with double Polish-German citizenship), there are many solitary older people, whose care needs are growing, creating pressure to establish affordable formal care institutions.

In general, the growing population of older people with poor health and disabilities, along with family changes, and especially changes in the labour market and the processes of economic migration, question the sustainability of informal care provision in the future.

Ageism and loneliness

Arguments in favour of the development of formal LTC are also related to the presence of two phenomena: ageism and loneliness of older people.

The phenomenon of ageism occurs more strongly in Western civilization compared to other regions of the world, although even in European countries there are differences here. The *European Social Survey* (EURAGE, 2011) and Grześkowiak (2012) point out that worse treatment of older people is the most frequent in post-communist countries. This is most likely related to the fact that they come from a different – communist – era, which is negatively valued by younger people.

The occurrence of ageism in Poland is also explained in relation to the persistence of values associated with peasants' approach to health and physical fitness. Older men are useless as they cannot work, and become a burden on the family. The reflection of this is found in Polish proverbs (Woźniak, 2013). As a result, older people in current Polish society are not enjoying the traditional respect that should be associated with their life experience and wisdom.

Examples of hostile attitudes towards older people in Poland can be found in institutions and among individuals. Both manifest a disregard for the needs of older people, patronizing treatment, fraud and the occurrence of the most drastic form of disregard – violence (Woźniak and Brzeska, 2009). Recently, this problem has been addressed in journalism, as well as in research and reflection.

European data show that loneliness is more prevalent in post-communist than in other countries (Fokkema et al., 2012). Reasons include emigration of young people while parents remain in the country, and a fundamental change of lifestyle of the younger generation, with no place or time left for older people, unless they are caring for grandchildren.

Supply of care services for older people

Although family care is still dominant, public care for dependent people is also provided, though LTC has never been separated and defined by law. In fact, various LTC services are situated in the two sectors: healthcare and social assistance. In the health sector, a range of medical services is provided to people with nursing needs due to serious health problems. In the social sector, care and assistance is provided to dependent people in poor social and economic standing, living alone or coming from a dysfunctional environment. These different target groups cover children and youth with disabilities, adults with functional limitations, physical and mental health problems, as well as seniors.

According to the results of the PolSenior survey among older Poles, approximately 40 per cent of the population 65+ is in need of daily care, but less than 10 per cent receives support in the form of formal care services (Błędowski and Maciejasz, 2013, p. 62). There are various estimates of the coverage of the dependent population with formal care services. The Ageing Working Group estimates that only 4.6 per cent of the dependent population (i.e. of any age, with severe functional limitations) in Poland receive community (home) care and 3.4 per cent receive formal residential care (European Commission, 2015, Graph II.3.7). Regardless of the source of information, the proportion of recipients is low, and the need for care is not being met within the formal care settings.

Additionally, there are several types of cash transfers available to different types of beneficiaries: older people, dependent disabled people, families and caretakers of disabled children. Universal benefits are granted to all people above the age of 75. Benefits, however, are low, hardly allowing for satisfying any needs related to the provision of care.

Shortages in spending public money on LTC

The situation of public finances in Poland has become very tense since the introduction of the four modern social reforms of Prime Minister Buzek: education, healthcare, the pension system and the decentralization of the state in 1999. The high budgetary costs of the greatest reform – pensions – limited opportunities for increasing resources for other areas, particularly healthcare. A relatively high portion of the pay-as-you-go social security contribution was diverted into a private pension fund for the payee for investment. As a result, public spending on healthcare for many years was lower than before the reform. Only a programme of systematic increase in the social health insurance (SHI) contributions equalized the gap, although it has not balanced the system (Golinowska et al., 2012). Public expenditures on healthcare account for only 4.7 per cent of GDP. It is about a third lower proportion than on average in the European countries, which was the main reason for not having a serious debate on building a system of LTC, despite preparation of a project aimed at introducing care insurance in Poland, similar to the German model (Augustyn, 2010).

The situation in public finances became even more tense in the period of economic crisis. Tightening the budget had an impact on LTC services. Eligibility criteria for the use of care in the health sector were tightened, and access to social assistance homes (domy pomocy społecznej – DPS) was restricted by an introduction of payment for accommodation costs.

Barriers to formal home care development

In the health sector, care services are awarded based on the decision of a primary care physician to people with the most severe health problems and functional limitations, mostly related to age.

Care services are provided by community nurses and financed from the health insurance fund (Narodowy Fundusz Zdrowia – NFZ).

In the social sector, home care services are provided to dependent people in poor economic circumstances, who live alone and whose family cannot assure adequate assistance. Home care services have developed since amendment to the law on social assistance in 2004. They are granted based on an interview conducted by a social worker and provided at home by the so-called non-specialized caretakers employed by social assistance centres. There is a fee for care services depending on the scope and the volume of care provided.

For social assistance centres, provision of care to dependent older people is a marginal type of activity while the main field is related to the prevention of material poverty, income being the most important criterion to qualify for social assistance benefits.

The biggest barriers to home care provision are the financial constraints of people with care needs due to the obligatory fee that social assistance beneficiaries in need of care are often unable to meet. Other barriers to home care development are insufficient funds of gmina (local self-governments) and missing labour resources for care.

Care services can be provided in semi-residential facilities as well, such as day-care centres for older people. This type of activity, arranged by local governments for many years, remains underdeveloped with a low number of facilities (slightly over 300 across the country in 2016) (MRPiPS, 2016, Section 6, Table 9). However, with policy priorities oriented at active ageing, the Polish government is investing in day care, stimulating facilities' development, although their long-term sustainability, with low-level funding mainly from the local governments' budgets, is questionable.

Insufficient development of public residential care

Public residential care in Poland exists only for poor and solitary older people and people medically recognized as dependent, in need of professional full-time care.

The main institution of public residential care for older and chronically ill people in Poland has been social assistance homes (DPS), which were created and developed on the basis of the Social Welfare Act of 1923 in the health sector, integrated with the social care sector at that time, this continuing under the communist regime. They were perceived as institutions for bedridden, 'lying' persons. There were over 500 institutions throughout the country (data from 1980 – Grabusińska, 2013, p. 9). In the 1970s, other types of facilities – so-called senior homes – came into existence. They offered stay for older but functionally independent people. Senior homes were operated by housing cooperatives not related to the health sector (similar to sheltered housing in the UK). There were about 100 of these facilities (Grabusińska, 2013).

When an inventory of social assistance homes was performed in the 1990s in order to place them under the responsibility of the social sector (Ministry of Labour and Social Policy) and – in time – local governments, facilities were found to be highly neglected, with low quality standards. A recovery plan was prepared and was implemented for over 20 years (until 2012). Many facilities were closed and new – mostly non-public – facilities came into existence.

Currently, residential care services are provided in the social sector and partly still in the health sector, with different eligibility criteria, financing rules and types of services provided in both sectors. Separation of social care from the health sector and its inclusion in the social sector took place at the beginning of the 1990s, following the introduction of the Law on Social Assistance (1991).

In the health sector, there are three types of nursing residential long-term care homes: care and treatment facilities (zakład opiekuńczo – leczniczy – ZOL), nursing and care facilities (zakład pielęgnacyjno – opiekuńczy – ZPO) and palliative care homes. Some of the care facilities in the health sector were created as a result of hospital restructuring processes undertaken in 1999 when a development programme of residential care homes for dependent people was created and functioning standards were defined. The local self-governments participated in the process of establishing the residential LTC system and the NFZ contracted out the newly established homes. The establishment of these homes contributed to the reduction of the average length of stay in hospitals in Poland. Currently, the health sector operates about 501 of the two types of nursing homes (ZOL and ZPO) and 82 hospices and 72 palliative care units (GUS, 2017a, pp. 106–7). Half of these facilities were established by non-public organizations or individual persons. Their services are financed by the social health insurance (SHI). The SHI premium is paid from most employment types, and most types of fixed-term contracts. The coverage by SHI is high – about 98 per cent of the population (WHO and NFZ, 2011, p. 55). Family members, children, students, retirees, registered unemployed and social assistance beneficiaries are covered with the SHI. The SHI system was introduced in 1999, while currently the government is preparing to withdraw from the insurance-based system to a universal system funded from the central budget (general taxation).

Eligibility criteria for nursing home care are set with a reference to the Barthel scale of functional assessment of 40 points or less. Accommodation and boarding fees are paid by care recipients or their families.

In the social sector, there are traditional social assistance residential homes organized mainly through the social assistance (welfare) system. A residential home can accommodate full-time residents, providing protection as well as supportive services for persons in need who cannot receive care in their family or community. There are several kinds of residential homes, separated according to the kind of persons provided with care, that is: older people, chronically ill, mentally ill, intellectually disabled adults, intellectually disabled children and youth, and physically disabled people. Overall, the number of DPS amounts to slightly over 800 (MRPiPS, 2016, Table 2P).

The quality of care in DPS is evaluated as relatively good. An improvement of equipment standards took place in accordance with the standards required by the EU over the past decade. Study of service quality shows that care recipients have access to medical care, which is the most important feature perceived by residents, guaranteeing safety of residence (Millward Brown, 2015).

In the social assistance system, family care homes have also recently been developed. Families meeting appropriate conditions and qualifications undertake full-time care over a small number of care recipients (typically three to eight people) and receive remuneration for care provision. This is a newly established form of care that – besides ranking on some Internet websites – has not undergone a comprehensive evaluation.

Formal and informal commercialized care services

The highest increase in LTC facility development is observed in the private, fully commercial sector. Limited access to public services contributed to the development of private residential care. Facilities for seniors created in private homes were coming into existence one after another, often offering very modest or even poor standards, but also low fees. Homes for seniors with high or even luxury standards have also been developing, particularly in the period of 2010–2013, but since then slowing down (Krzemiński, 2014). However, persons willing to use private residential care often perceive their incomes (retirement pensions) as insufficient to cover the high costs (CBOS, 2012). According to the opinion of some investors in care facilities, if there is no public financial support for care recipients to buy private services (e.g. in the form of care insurance or care vouchers), the market for LTC services will remain limited.

Charity and religious organization of care for older dependent people

Traditionally in Poland, residential nursing homes for solitary and chronically ill people were run by the Catholic Church, care being provided by nuns of different orders. Such care homes are still operating, and even dominating in some more traditional regions such as Małopolska. It is estimated that nuns run over 100 homes for older and chronically ill people across the country (Rogaczewska, 2005, p. 13). Typically, nuns are well qualified, often being professional nurses, and one-fifth of them are highly educated (Rogaczewska, 2005).

Over the political and economic transformation period from communism to the democratic market-oriented state, the Caritas organization was also brought into existence and involved in care provision. They run 170 institutions for older, chronically ill and disabled people throughout the country, and constantly develop their activities in this field. These organizations have the status of public benefit organizations, so they can make use of the 1 per cent of their income tax liability that individuals can assign to such organizations (organizacja pożytku publicznego – OPP). Only about 10 per cent of all NGOs in Poland have OPP status (GUS, 2017b, p. 1). About three-quarters of the transfers are sent to associations and foundations providing support in health and care services (GUS, 2017b, p. 2).

Church and religious organizations form the backbone of care facilities for older people run by non-profit organizations. Their importance is not only an expression of the strong institutional tradition of the Catholic Church, but also the weakness of the public sector, especially related to difficulties in reconstruction of local self-government after many years of a highly centralized state. Religious organizations can also receive money from 1 per cent of income tax, if they obtain OPP status. Voluntary contributions to religious organizations accounts to about 3 per cent of the whole OPP charity transfers (GUS, 2017b, p. 2).

Migrant care workers

Although Poland has traditionally sent migrants abroad for work, over the last two decades it has become a migrant-receiving country for citizens of Eastern Europe. About half of the immigrants are Ukrainians undertaking jobs in agriculture and the building industry as well as home and care services. They do it legally (based on authorization received from the regional authorities) or illegally, without registration of employment (see Sobiesiak-Penszko, 2015). Care workers for older people are recruited mainly from Ukrainian women. Employees operate via organized informal networks of Ukrainians, working in turns. These networks cover potential informal workers on the one side and potential employers on the other side, who search for workers based on information from other – often former – employers. These networks operate in large cities and sometimes also cover Germany. Qualitative studies on care services provided by Ukrainians show that both sides – employers and employees – belong to the middle class in their home countries. Polish employers are mainly working women with a high professional position, or housewives whose wealth is attributable to their husbands' earnings (Racław, 2015). Ukrainian care workers are persons with at least a secondary education, with economic and social ambitions.

Even though the work of caring for an older person is demanding, immigrant care workers have a relatively good salary, satisfactory relations with families and typically good relations with the dependent persons, although the latter is not always obvious. Dependant and ill people, very often with mental disorders, can be difficult to be cared for. In turn, the family employing a care worker perceives that it is in control of the situation as the worker is cross-checked by the informal network.

Sobiesiak-Penszko (2015) suggests that the network of Ukrainian care workers fulfils the needs of a traditional and wealthy middle class, lessening the pressure for formal care, which is also desirable in less well-off families.

Insufficient education and employment of health and care professionals

Reduction (and rationalization) of expenditure on the health system in 1999 resulted in lowering expenditures for training medical staff, especially nursing personnel. Nursing schools at the secondary level were liquidated and implementation of the programme of nursing education at the tertiary level began, complementing qualifications of nurses already working towards a university degree. Nurses who did not decide to enrol in higher education left employment or emigrated, undertaking carer jobs abroad, which caused a deficit of nursing and care staff.

Actions aimed at introducing new medical professions oriented towards satisfying the needs of a dependent population were undertaken, including legal regulations for medical professions involved in LTC, requirements for competencies and education, including LTC nursing qualifications and the profession of medical worker.

As a result of these actions, the structure of employed nurses in terms of qualifications improved (Golinowska et al., 2013), however the low density of nursing and care staff in comparison with other countries remains a problem. Nurses still have low wages, strike relatively often, and continue to emigrate to care work in Western EU countries.

Parallel activities related to the education of care workers were undertaken in the social assistance system. Since 2011, the education of care workers has included a post-secondary level (2–4 semesters). Consequently, the following professions were introduced: caretaker of older persons, care worker in residential care (DPS), and community care worker and assistant of disabled persons. Also, standards of care were developed (Staręga-Piasek et al., 2011). Employment in care professions in social assistance is slowly increasing.

The imbalance between demand and supply of LTC services

The imbalance between supply and demand for care, especially in the older population, is a result of a complex process of transformation of Polish society over the past quarter-century. Social issues and needs were pushed aside by the agenda oriented to building a modern democratic state based on a liberal market. Only those social needs that were crucial for legitimacy of the systemic transformation were selectively satisfied. Initially vulnerable groups exiting the labour market were supported (early retirements, disability pensions, support for unemployed). In time, the policy was oriented towards support of entrepreneurship and the middle class (low taxes, tax deductions). Reforms of social institutions (pension, healthcare, education and administration), with the aim of introducing private market mechanisms into the public administration, were not always successful and are now being withdrawn (liquidation of private pensions, return to the traditional education structure, withdrawal from health insurance).

In the 25 years of the transition period (1989–2014), social policy did not respond sufficiently to the societal changes Polish society was undergoing as a result of the reforms and external changes: the fall of the Iron Curtain, globalization, EU accession, emigration and increasing mobility, as well as new information technologies. Polish society began to rapidly age and become more individualistic. Social inequalities arose and social ties weakened.

Stanisława Golinowska and Agnieszka Sowa-Kofta

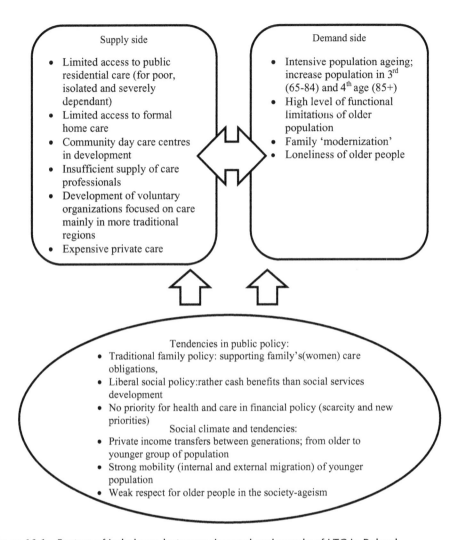

Figure 12.1 Factors of imbalance between demand and supply of LTC in Poland

The solution to social problems, often thanks to the support of a resourceful family (especially by women working on 'two jobs' – professionally and as housewives), is no longer an effective response to the challenges connected with ageing and globalization. In Figure 12.1, we present the main elements of imbalance between the demand and supply of care together with social and policy trends that have an impact on the provision of care.

The question arises: has the system of care services provision for the growing older population which has developed in Poland – characterized by the following characteristics – a chance to balance demand for care and supply of care in the coming years?

(1) dominant but decreasing family involvement;
(2) limited but improving quality of services within the public sector;
(3) limited but more educated professional nursing and care staff;
(4) stable commitment of the Church and other religious organizations in care provision; and
(5) still young but growing commercial services

Public sector development, it seems, will be crucial to tip the balance. It would require a clear statement of the state's obligations with respect to care services and definition of their quality standards, their designation and monitoring. Also, co-payment rules should be clearly defined.

A defined public sector would create space for the development of non-public care institutions and would be a reference for them in terms of quality standards.

The public sector in care service establishments enjoys a better reputation than the private sector. Research on the personal experiences of older people with disabilities carried out by Ostrowska (2015) over two decades (1993–2013) suggests progressive acceptance and normalization of disability and other perceptions of vulnerability in the public sphere. In the private sphere, the progress was significantly smaller, which was a disappointing finding of this research.

Final word: uncertain future

Polish society has been relatively young, and for years the most important task was job creation for the younger generation, the problem of dynamic ageing not being given much attention by politicians or public opinion. A survey by the Public Opinion Research Centre indicated that only half of respondents were aware that society ages (CBOS, 2012).

The consequences of rapid population ageing were discussed mainly by experts, initially internationally, and further nationally, by opinion-making institutes and *think tanks*. As a result, development of the LTC system is not yet being prioritized on the political agenda, despite the growing care needs of ageing baby boomers.

Currently, halfway through the second decade of the twenty-first century, the problem of demographic disproportion revealed its dramatic consequences. On the labour market, rapid decrease of unemployment, increase in demand for work and the lack of 'manpower', twofold activities were undertaken. An active ageing policy in line with the EU concept, referred to as senioral policy, was undertaken (Samoliński et al., 2015; Kosiniak-Kamysz, 2014). Its main points were related to the extension of working life (postponing retirement) and motivating older people to participate in decision-making processes in issues related to respecting their needs, supporting social work and voluntary activities in care facilities. However, only three years later, a policy of de facto deactivation was formulated. Child benefits were strongly raised and the policy of increasing and equalizing retirement age was withdrawn, possibly resulting in professional deactivation of women. Care services for older people are clearly indicated as a family domain, particularly for women. Only the governmental programme of supporting community day-care centres for older people (Senior-Wigor) might ease the family burden related to care obligations. Overall, one could say that the thesis of the book by Mariola Racław (2011), 'public concern, private care', will remain valid.

References

Augustyn, M., 2010. *Opieka długoterminowa w Polsce. Opis, diagnoza, rekomendacje* [Long-term care in Poland: description, diagnosis, recommendation]. Report of Grupa Robocza ds. przygotowania ustawy o ubezpieczeniu od ryzyka niesamodzielności przy Klubie Senatorów Platformy Obywatelskiej [Working group for preparation of the regulation on dependents insurance at the Civic Platform Senators Club]. Warsaw. Available at: http://rszarf.ips.uw.edu.pl/kierunki/ODzielona.pdf [accessed 15.07.2017].

Berger, N., Van Oyen, H., Cambois, E., Fouweather, T., Jagger, C., Nusselder, W., et al. 2015. Assessing the validity of the Global Activity Limitation Indicator in fourteen European countries. *BMC Medical Research Methodology*, 15(1). DOI: 10.1186/1471-2288-15-1.

Błędowski P., 2012. Potrzeby opiekuńcze osób starszych [Care needs of older people]. In M. Mossakowska, A. Więcek and P. Błędowski, eds. *Aspekty medyczne, psychologiczne, socjologiczne i ekonomiczne starzenia się ludzi w Polsce* [Medical, psychological and economic aspects of ageing in Poland]. Warsaw: Termedia Medical Publisher, pp. 449–66. Available at: www.pcpr-limanowa.pl/images/pdf/monografiaPol Senior.pdf [accessed 10.07.2017].

Błędowski, P. and Maciejasz, M., 2013. Rozwój opieki długoterminowej w Polsce – stan i rekomendacje. [Development of the long-term care in Poland. status and recommendations]. *Nowiny Lekarskie* [Medical News], 82(1), pp. 61–9. Available at: www.medicalnews.ump.edu.pl/uploads/2013/1/61_1_82_2013. pdf [accessed 10.07.2017].

CBOS (Centrum Badania Opinii Społecznej – Public Opinion Research Centre), 2012. *Społeczna solidarność z osobami w starszym wieku* [Social solidarity with older people]. BS/83/2012. Warsaw: CBOS. Available at: www.mpips.gov.pl/gfx/mpips/userfiles/_public/1_NOWA%20STRONA/Aktualnosci/seniorzy/ badania%20aktywne%20starzenie/2Spoleczna%20solidarnosc%20z%20osobami%20w%20starszym%20 wieku%20CBOS%202012.pdf [accessed 10.07.2017].

Eberhardt, P., 2014. Fazy rozwoju demograficznego Polski [Phases of demographic change in Poland]. *Roczniki Nauk Społecznych* [Annals of Social Sciences], 6(42), no. 2, pp. 136–60.

EURAGE (European Research Group on Attitudes to Age), 2011. *Ageism in Europe: findings from the European Social Survey.* London: Age UK. Available at: www.ageuk.org.uk/Documents/EN-GB/For-professionals/ageism_across_europe_report_interactive.pdf?dtrk=true [accessed 10.07.2017].

European Commission, 2015. *The 2015 ageing report: economic and budgetary projections for the 28 European Member States (2013–2060).* Available at: http://ec.europa.eu/economy_finance/publications/euro pean_economy/2015/ee3_en.htm [accessed 10.07.2017].

Eurostat, 2016. *Share of population in a certain age group compared to the total population data* [tps00010], Avaiable at: http://ec.europa.eu/eurostat/tgm/refreshTableAction.do?tab=table&plugin=1&pcode=t ps00010&language=en [accessed 30.03.2016].

Fokkema, T., de Jong-Gierveld, J. and Dykstra, P.A., 2012. Cross-national differences in older adult lone-liness. *Journal of Psychology*, 146(1–2), pp. 201–28. DOI: 10.1080/00223980.2011.631612.

Frątczak, E., 2004. Very low fertility: the patterns and their implications. European Population Committee. *The European Population Paper Series*. No. 21.

Golinowska, S., 2012. *The long-term care system for the elderly in Poland.* ENEPRI Research Report No. 83. Available at: www.ancien-longtermcare.eu/sites/default/files/ENEPRI%20RR%20No%2083%20 (ANCIEN%20-%20Poland).pdf [accessed 30.03.2016].

Golinowska, S., 2016. Promocji zdrowia dla osób starszych wśród europejskich koncepcji działań wobec starzenia się [Health promotion for older people, the European active ageing concept]. *Problemy Polityki Społecznej* [Problems of Social Policy], 34(3), pp. 27–51. Available at: www.problemypolitykispolecznej. pl/index.php/wzory-dokumentow/8-czasopismo/135-spis-tresci-34-3-2016 [accessed 15.05.2017].

Golinowska, S. and Sowa, A., 2010. *Działania samorządów lokalnych w opiece i integracji niesamodzielnych osób starszych* [Actions of territorial self-governments in care and integration of dependent older people]. Report for the Ministry of Labour and Social Policy. Warsaw: IPiSS.

Golinowska, S. and Styczyńska, I., 2012. *Quality assurance policies and indicators for long-term care in the European Union. Country report: Poland.* ENEPRI Research Report No. 109. Available at: www.ancien-longtermcare.eu/sites/default/files/RRNo109_Poland_%20ANCIEN_%20Golinowska&Styczynska QualityAssurancePolicies-Final.pdf [accessed 30.03.2016].

Golinowska, S. in association with Sowada, C., Tambor, M., Dubas, K., Jurkiewicz-Świętek, I., Kocot, E., Seweryn, M. and Evitovits, T., 2012. *Równowaga finansowa oraz efektywność w polskim systemie ochrony zdrowia. Problemy i wyzwania* [Sources of inefficiency and financial deficits in Poland's healthcare system]. Kraków: Vesalius – University Medical Publishing.

Golinowska, S., Kocot, E. and Sowa, A., 2013. *Health care and long term care sectors and their workforce. Country Report: Poland.* Neujobs Working Paper, EU FP7 Project. Available at: www.neujobs.eu/sites/default/ files/publication/2014/02/LTC_workforce_Poland_final_D12.2_D.pdf [accessed 16.07.2017].

Golinowska, S., Sowa, A., Deeg, D., Socci, M., Principi, A., Rodrigues, R., et al., 2016. Participation in formal learning activities of older Europeans in good and and poor health. *European Journal of Ageing*, DOI: 10.1007/s10433-016-0371-6.

Grabusińska, Z., 2013. *Domy pomocy społecznej w Polsce* [Social assistance homes in Poland]. Warsaw: Centrum Rozwoju Zasobów Ludzkich. Available at: http://irss.pl/wp-content/uploads/2013/12/ domy_pomocy_spolecznej_w_polsce.pdf [accessed 15.07.2017].

Grześkowiak, A., 2012. Analiza wybranych aspektów zjawiska ageizmu w Europie z wykorzystaniem wykresów typu biplot [Analysis of selected aspects of the ageism phenomenon in Europe using biplot charts]. *Ekonometria* [Econometrics], 3(37), pp. 71–82. Available at: www.dbc.wroc.pl/Content/18893/ Grzeskowiak_Analiza_wybranych_aspektow_zjawisk.pdf [accessed 15.07.2017].

GUS (Główny Urząd Statystyczny – Central Statistical Office), 2015. *Trwanie życia – tablice* [Life tables]. Available at: http://stat.gov.pl/obszary-tematyczne/ludnosc/trwanie-zycia/trwanie-zycia-tablice,1,1. html [accessed 15.05.2016].

GUS (Główny Urząd Statystyczny – Central Statistical Office), 2016. *Zdrowie osób starszych w świetle badań statystyki publicznej* [Health of older people in the light of public statistics]. Available at: http://stat.gov. pl/obszary-tematyczne/zdrowie/zdrowie/zdrowie-i-zachowania-zdrowotne-mieszkancow-polski-w-swietle-badania-ehis-2014,10,1.html [accessed 15.05.2016].

GUS (Główny Urząd Statystyczny – Central Statistical Office), 2017a. *Zdrowie i ochrona zdrowia w 2015* [Health and healthcare in 2015]. Available at: http://stat.gov.pl/obszary-tematyczne/zdrowie/zdrowie/ zdrowie-i-ochrona-zdrowia-w-2015-roku,1,6.html [accessed 15.07.2017].

GUS (Główny Urząd Statystyczny – Central Statistical Office), 2017b. *Organizacje pożytku publicznego i 1%* [Public benefit organizations]. Available at: http://stat.gov.pl/obszary-tematyczne/gospodarka-spoleczna-wolontariat/gospodarka-spoleczna-trzeci-sektor/organizacje-pozytku-publicznego-i-1,4,3. html [accessed 11.07.2017].

Kosiniak-Kamysz, W., 2014. The adaptation of society with an aging population. *The European Files*, No. 33, July 2014.

Kotowska, I.E., 1999. Drugie przejście demograficzne i jego uwarunkowania [The second demographic transition and its determinants]. In I.E. Kotowska, ed. *Przemiany ludnościowe w latach dziewięćdziesiątych w Polsce w świetle koncepcji drugiego przejścia demograficznego* [Population transformation in Poland in the 1990s in the light of the concept of the second demographic transition]. Warsaw: Monografie i Opracowania SGH, pp. 11–33.

Kotowska, I.E., Sztanderska, U. and Wóycicka, I., 2007. *Między domem a pracą. Rekomendacje dla polityków* [Between home and work: recommendations for politicians]. Gdańsk: Instytut Badań nad Gospodarką Rynkową and Scholar.

Krzemiński, J., 2014. *Niespokojna przyszłość domów spokojnej starości* [Insecure future of senior homes]. Available at: www.obserwatorfinansowy.pl/forma/rotator/niespokojna-przyszlosc-domow-spokojnej-starosci [accessed 10.07.2017].

Łuczak, P., 2013. Long-term care for the elderly in Poland. In P. Michoń, J. Orczyk and M. Żukowski, eds. *Facing the challenges: social policy in Poland after 1990*. Poznań: University of Economics Press, pp. 167–79.

Millward Brown, 2015. *Evaluation of the quality of care for older people in Poland*. Pilot study for the World Bank Office, Warsaw.

MRPiPS (Ministerstwa Rodziny Pracy i Polityki Społecznej – Ministry of Family Labour and Social Policy), 2016. *Statystykza rok 2015* [Statistics for 2015]. Available at: www.mpips.gov.pl/pomoc-spoleczna/ raporty-i-statystyki/statystyki-pomocy-spolecznej/statystyka-za-rok-2015/ [accessed 15.07.2017].

Ostrowska, A., 2015., *Niepełnosprawni w społeczeństwie 1993–2013* [Disabled persons in society 1993–2013]. Warsaw: IFiS PAN Publishing.

Racław M. ed., 2011., *Publiczna troska, prywatna opieka. Społeczności lokalne wobec osób starszych* [Public concern, private care: local communities and older people]. Warsaw: ISP & ZUS Publishing. Available at: www.isp.org.pl/publikacje,226,455.html [accessed 19.09.2017].

Racław, M., 2015. Opiekunowie rodzinni jako pracodawcy migrantek – 'nowi tradycjonaliści' z klasy średniej. [Family carers as employers of migrant workers: 'the new traditionalists' of the middle class]. In P. Sobiesiak-Penszko, ed. *Niewidzialna siła robocza. Migranci w usługach opiekuńczych nad osobami starszymi* [Invisible workforce: migrants in care services for the elderly]. Warsaw: Institute of Public Affairs Publishing, pp. 115–48. Available at: www.isp.org.pl/uploads/pdf/71482711.pdf [accessed 10.07.2017].

Rogaczewska, M., 2005. *Obrzeża Sektora. Organizacje Kościoła katolickiego* [On margins of the sector: Catholic Church organizations]. Warsaw: Klon-Jawor. Available at: http://wiadomosci.ngo.pl/files/ wiadomosci.ngo.pl/public/korespondenci/obrzeza_org_Kosciola_kat.pdf [accessed 15.07.2017].

Rutkowski, J., 2002. *Job destruction and job creation in Poland 1993–1999*. National Bank of Poland Conference: Monetary Policy in the Environment of Structural Change. Available at: https://ssl.nbp. pl/Konferencje/Falenty2002/pdf_en/rutkowski.pdf [accessed 16.07.2017].

Samoliński, B., Raciborski, F., Bousquet, J., Kosiniak-Kamysz, W., Radziewicz-Winnicki, I., Kłak, A. et al., 2015. Development of senioral policy in Poland: analysis. *European Geriatric Medicine*, 6(4), pp. 389–95. DOI: 10.1016/j.eurger.2015.01.009.

Sobiesiak-Penszko, P., ed., 2015. *Niewidzialna siła robocza. Migranci w usługach opiekuńczych nad osobami starszymi* [Invisible work force: migrant workers in care services for older people]. Warsaw: Institute of Public Affairs Publishing.

Sowa, A., Golinowska, S., Deeg, D., Principi, A., Casanova, G., Schulmann, K., et al., 2016a. Predictors of religious participation of older Europeans in good and poor health. *European Journal of Ageing*, 13(2), pp. 145–57. DOI: 10.1007/s10433-016-0367-2.

Staręga-Piasek, J., Balon, K., Rutkiewicz, G., Stec, K., Szmaglińska, I. and Zielony, I., 2011. *Standard usług opiekuńczych dla osób starszych świadczonych w miejscu zamieszkania* [Standards of home care services for older people]. Report of the project: Tworzenie i rozwijanie standardów usług pomocy i integracji społecznej. [Development of social services and social integration standards]. Warsaw: CRZL i Wrzos.

WHO and NFZ, 2011. Poland: health system review. *Health System in Transition*, 13(8). Available at: www.euro.who.int/__data/assets/pdf_file/0018/163053/e96443.pdf [accessed 16.07.2017].

Wizner, B., Skalska, A., Klich-Rączka, A., Piotrowicz, K. and Grodzicki, T., 2012. Ocena stanu funkcjonalnego osób starszych [Assessment of functional capabilities of older people]. In M. Mossakowska, A. Więcek and P. Błędowski, eds. *PolSenior. Aspekty medyczne, psychologiczne i ekonomiczne starzenia się ludzi w Polsce* [Medical, psychological and economic aspects of ageing in Poland]. Poznań: Termedia Medical Publisher, pp. 81–94. Available at: www.pcpr-limanowa.pl/images/pdf/monografiaPolSenior.pdf [accessed 10.07.2017].

World Bank, 2015. *The present and future of long-term care in ageing Poland*. Available at: https://das.mpips.gov.pl/source/opiekasenioralna/Long%20term%20care%20in%20ageing%20Poland_ENG_FINAL.pdf [accessed 10.07.2017].

Wóycicka, I. and Rurarz, R., 2007. Świadczenie opieki [Delivery of care]. In I.E. Kotowska, U. Sztanderska and I. Wóycicka, eds. *Aktywność zawodowa i edukacyjna a obowiązki rodzinne w Polsce w świetle badań empirycznych* [Professional and educational activities and care obligations in Poland: empirical studies]. Warsaw: Wydawnictwo Naukowe Scholar, pp. 282–305.

Woźniak, Z. 2013. Oblicza starości – między mitami a rzeczywistością [Different faces of old age: between myths and reality]. *Studia Kulturoznawcze* [Cultural Studies], 2(4), pp. 9–23.

Woźniak, B. and Brzyska, M., 2009. Przemoc wobec ludzi starszych – przegląd badań prowadzonych w Polsce [Violence against older people: review of Polish research]. In B. Tobiasz-Adamczyk, ed. *Przemoc wobec osób starszych* [Violence against older people]. Kraków: WUJ Publishing, pp. 70–80.

Part IV
Between Europe and Asia

13

Long-term care in Turkey
Challenges and opportunities

Sema Oglak

Introduction

Although Turkey's population is younger than that of European countries, the ageing population is growing rapidly and elderly people have an increasing need for long-term care services. The ageing of Turkey's population reflects a combination of declining birth rates, leading to fewer young people, and increasing life expectancy. The ageing of the population will have major implications for the long-term care sector, and in Turkey there is no long-term care insurance system. Elderly people are usually taken care of within their own family.

The aim of this chapter is to explain the current situation regarding the inadequate long-term care infrastructure, particularly of home care services, and to indicate the challenges posed. The next section briefly describes the background situation in Turkey and the present state of public social spending compared with other OECD countries. This is followed by a section indicating the sources on which the chapter is based. Next, the demographic outlook is set out: the rapidly rising ageing of the population, the expected changes in dependency ratio of older people, and their health. Changes in family structure are briefly described next. Following this, the major reform of health insurance and the social assistance available for older and disabled people are explained. Recent government policies for older people are next described. Then the long-term care situation is set out. The concluding section sums up the current situation of long-term care, and the challenges faced.

Context

Turkey, a country that has undergone rapid urbanization, is a middle-income country, with the 18th largest economy in the world (World Bank, 2017). According to the World Bank, its economic performance has been impressive since 2000, its poverty incidence being halved between 2002 and 2012, and extreme poverty falling even faster. A number of important social reforms have taken place since 2000, including that of the previously occupationally related health insurance system into a national health insurance programme with near universal health coverage. However, growth has slowed since 2012, and the outlook is uncertain (World Bank, 2017).

Sema Oglak

Table 13.1 Comparing total public social expenditures, 1990–2014 (% of GDP), Turkey and OECD

	1990 %	2000 %	2005 %	2010 %	2011 %	2012 %	2014 %
Turkey	5.5	7.7	10.3	12.8	12.5	13.0	13.5
OECD	16.9	18.0	18.8	21.1	20.7	21.0	21.1

Source: Adapted by author from OECD *Social Expenditure Database (SOCX)* (OECD, 2016a).

Turkish public social spending of 13.5 per cent of GDP in 2014 is much below the average of 21.1 per cent (Table 13.1). It has increased from less than 8 per cent in 2000 (Uckardesler, 2015, p. 151). In Turkey, most social spending is related to pension payments and healthcare expenditure (Uckardesler, 2015, p. 152). However, compared to the OECD average for income support, which amounts to 5 per cent of GDP, Turkey spends only 1.1 percent of its GDP to support the disadvantaged population via social assistance and social services. The amount was an even lower 0.30 per cent of GDP in the early 2000s (Uckardesler, 2015, p. 152). Figures are unavailable for expenditure on long-term health and social care.

Methods

This chapter is mainly based on secondary data from various Turkish government sources, including the Turkish Statistical Institute (Turkstat), Ministry of Family and Social Policies (MoFSP) and Ministry of Health (MoH). Data from international sources such as Eurostat and OECD were also used.

An important research source drawn upon in the chapter are analyses of the social implications of changes in the family in Turkey (MoFSP, 2014a, 2014b, 2014c). These analyses are mainly based on data from two surveys using representative samples of families in Turkey, termed *Research on Family Structure in Turkey* (TAYA) conducted by MoFSP in 2006 and 2011. Data were collected on family structure, lifestyles and values of family life. In TAYA 2006, 12,208 households were included, demographic information of 48,235 individuals belonging to these households was collected, and face-to-face interviews were conducted with 23,279 individuals over the age of 18, 2,213 of these individuals being aged 65+. In TAYA 2011, 12,056 households were included, the demographic information of 44,117 individuals belonging to these households was collected, and face-to-face interviews were conducted with 24,647 individuals over the age of 18, 2,455 individuals being aged 65+. A further *Research in Family Structure* survey was conducted in 2016 (Turkstat, 2017a). The author's own research on long-term care in Turkey is also a source for the chapter.

Demographic outlook

Ageing and emerging issues of care are generally more apparent in developed countries. Yet ageing is also becoming more and more important for developing countries, and Turkey is not an exception. Although Turkey is known for its young population, it is now becoming known as one of the fastest-ageing countries in the world (He et al., 2016, p. 11; Apakan, 2012, p. 2).

The percentage of the older population (65+) was around 3.9 per cent in 1935 and remained at under 6 per cent until the 2000s, rising rapidly to 8.3 per cent by 2016 (Turkstat, 2017b,

Table 1). According to population projections by Turkstat, this demographic shift will continue into the future. It is expected that the proportion of the elderly population will rise to 10.2 per cent in 2023, 20.8 per cent in 2050 and 27.7 per cent in 2075 (Turkstat, 2013). In absolute terms, Turkey's 6.7 million older adults in 2016 (Turkstat, 2017b) already outnumber the total populations of several European countries, such as Denmark (5.7 million) and Norway (5.2 million) (Eurostat, 2015). In the next 20–30 years, both the number of those aged 65+ as well as their share in the total population are expected to increase at an extraordinary rate (He et al., 2016, p. 11).

It is noteworthy that Turkey's ageing process is different from that of the developed countries. There are two reasons for this. First, Turkey is ageing faster than the developed countries. The demographic changes that took 115 years in developed countries such as France (He et al., 2016, p. 12; National Institute on Aging, 2011, p. 4) will take place in Turkey in only a few decades (velocity of ageing). Second, developed countries first developed and then aged. Therefore, they had the chance to accumulate the capital to finance the burden of ageing. Turkey has to manage its development and ageing processes at the same time (sequence of ageing) (Apakan, 2012, p. 2).

Fertility rates have declined markedly in Turkey since the 1960s from 6.30 children to 2.1 in 2015 (World Bank, 2016). In contrast, as a result of improvements in health and living conditions, life expectancy at birth has gradually increased in Turkey. Table 13.2 indicates the increase in longevity between 1970 and 2015. From this perspective, with the falling fertility rate and the increase in life expectancy, Turkey will not long remain a country with a young population. Turkey currently has a relatively low life expectancy at birth, although it has achieved huge gains in longevity over the past few decades (78.1 in 2014) and is quickly moving towards the OECD average, 80.9 in 2014 (OECD, 2016b, pp. 56–7).

Turning to changes in ratios of dependency, the total ratio of individuals dependent on others (ratio of people aged 0–14 and those aged 65 and over to working-age population, 15–64) has been falling gradually, from 84 in 1940 to 78 in 1980 and 48 in 2012 (Eryurt, 2014, p. 96). However, the elderly dependency ratio of people aged 65+ to the working population (Table 13.3) has increased to 12.2 per cent in 2015, and this measure is expected to reach 33 per cent in 2050.

Table 13.2 Life expectancy at birth in Turkey (1970–2015)

	1970[1]	2002[2]	2014[3]
Male	52.9	70.5	75.4
Female	57.3	74.7	80.9
Total	55	72.5	78.1

Source: Adapted by author from: (1) Hamzaoğlu and Ozcan (2006, p. 24); (2) MOH (2015a, p. 17, Figure 2.1); and (3) OECD (2016a, p. 57, Tables 3.1 and 3.2).

Table 13.3 Actual and projected changes in elderly dependency ratio, Turkey, 1940–2075

Years	1940	1950	1960	1970	1980	1990	2000	2010	2015	2050	2075
Elderly dependency ratio (aged 65+)	6.5	5.7	6.4	8.2	8.5	7.1	8.8	10.8	12.2	33	48

Source: Adapted by author from Turkstat (2017b, Table 3); Eryurt (2014, p. 96).

As the ageing population continues to grow, health expenditures are likely to gradually increase, though other factors may have a larger impact than ageing itself (National Institute on Aging, 2011, p. 18).

A crucial question is whether projected gains in longevity will be accompanied by increases in illness, disability and vulnerability. Like other middle-income countries, Turkey is far into the epidemiological transition and has seen major shifts in the main burden of disease away from communicable diseases towards chronic diseases (WHO, 2012, pp. 26–7).

Health and social inequalities in elderly people

While the average proportion of people aged 65+ in OECD countries in 2013 reporting good/ very good health was 43.4 per cent, less than 20 per cent of over-65s in Turkey reported this (OECD, 2015a, Table 11.6). There were strong differences between men (26.1 per cent) and women (12.6 per cent) reporting good/very good health. Findings from the Turkstat Health Interview Survey 2012 indicate that only 13.6 per cent of women and 24.3 per cent of men aged 75+ reported good/very good health, the percentages being lower in rural than in urban areas (MOH, 2015a, p. 35). Compared with the average for OECD countries (50.1 per cent), a higher proportion of Turkish people (56.9 per cent) aged 65+ also reported that they were limited in their daily activities (OECD, 2015a, Table 11.7). Lower income has also been found to be related to poorer health in people aged 60+ (Ergin and Mandiracioglu, 2015).

Changing family structure and increase of living alone

Turkey has become similar to developed countries in family size. Extended families that provided care for elderly family members in the past are being replaced by nuclear families. It was found in the *Research on Family Structure* survey 2011 that 15.9 per cent of older people lived alone, 22.9 per cent of women and 7.5 per cent of men, while 42.7 per cent lived with their spouse alone (Eryurt, 2014, p. 100). However, according to the 2016 *Family Structure* survey, it seems that people aged 65+ are still very keen to co-reside with their children if they become unable to care for themselves, 51.3 per cent giving this as their preference, compared with 27.5 per cent wanting home care and only 7.7 per cent wanting to live in a nursing home (Turkstat, 2017b, Table 15).

Turkish social security system

In the past, Turkey had a predominantly Bismarckian social security system. This is one in which expenditure is funded through social insurance, employees and employers jointly contributing (SSI, 2016). Social insurance programmes were based on occupational groups, with separate schemes for different groups, and those working in the informal economy were excluded.

Turkey's healthcare system

Before the Health Transformation Programme in Turkey in 2003, the organization and financing of healthcare services were fragmented. There were different health insurance schemes for different occupational groups, and from the 1990s a 'green card' non-contributory scheme for people with very low incomes. There were varying benefit packages and premiums for the different schemes (Atun, 2015; Yilmaz, 2013; Agartan, 2012; Barıs et al., 2011). The first major change was the transfer of public hospitals, formerly owned by the insurance funds, to the Ministry of Health, there also being incentives for private health services to play a larger part in public healthcare delivery. Second, under legislation implemented in 2008, the different insurance funds were merged under a single body called the Social Security Institution (SSI). The green card scheme became part of this general health insurance in 2012 (Karadeniz, 2012). Following the healthcare transformation, Turkey has achieved almost universal health insurance coverage (SSI, 2016). Every citizen has to contribute, according to their income, though there is a means test below which those with very low incomes have their contribution paid by the state. Health spending has increased considerably, but at 5.1 per cent of GDP in 2013 (OECD, 2015b) is well below the OECD average of 8.9 per cent of GDP. The share of government spending on healthcare has increased, though, to 78 per cent, above the OECD average of 73 per cent (OECD, 2015b). Since the reforms, reasonably successful and improved health outcomes and high and rising levels of consumer satisfaction have been achieved (WHO, 2012, p. 8). Out of pocket spending by households decreased by half between 2010 and 2013 to 22 per cent. However, there is some evidence that co-payments for hospital visits and medication, and additional co-payments for private providers, may be resulting in income inequalities (Yilmaz, 2013; Agartan, 2012). There are still inequalities in health status, satisfaction levels and access to health services due to differences in healthcare infrastructure, personnel and insurance coverage among different regions and urban-rural settings (Okem and Cakar, 2015, p. 116). The reforms, though, have improved access to healthcare for older people.

Pensions and social assistance for older people

Using data from the TUIK 2009 Household Budget Survey (Karadeniz and Durusoy, 2011, cited by Karadeniz, 2012, p. 11) it was found that nearly 50 per cent of people of pensionable age were receiving a contributory old-age pension or means-tested pension (tax-funded), while 15.4 per cent were receiving a survivor's pension. There were large differences between men and women, with 68.6 per cent of men receiving an old-age pension but only 8 per cent of women doing so. More women (26.3 per cent) than men (13.2 per cent), though, received a survivor's pension. Low labour market participation, low-paid or unregistered work (i.e. not paying pension contributions) and unpaid family work result in many women not receiving a contributory old-age pension.

A means-tested pension scheme was introduced in 1976 (Law Number 2022). People aged 65 and over who have no income or other means of assistance have been entitled to a monthly pension since 1977 (Karadeniz, 2012, p. 9). However, while contributory pension rates have increased above the level of inflation over the last 10 years, this is not the case for the tax-funded pension, and it is still extremely low compared with other minimum pension amounts (Karadeniz, 2012, p. 14).

Policies for older people

As well as the improved healthcare coverage, there have been other recent government policies aiming to improve the position of disabled and older people. The Ministry of Family and Social Policies (MoFSP) was established in 2011. The General Directorate of Services for Persons with Disabilities and Elderly People (GDSPDE) within the structure of the MoFSP was established at the same time. The MoFSP became the sole government body responsible for both carrying out services and coordinating public and private institutions that provide services for elderly people (Karadeniz, 2012; Republic of Turkey, 2012). GDSPDE carries out the following activities with the purpose of fulfilling its responsibilities on social policy implementations towards elderly persons: (a) to plan, monitor, coordinate or audit services that aim at determining socially or economically disadvantaged elderly people or providing them care or protection; (b) to plan, implement, monitor or coordinate for the audit of related activities on establishing and systematically enhancing quality of institutional care settings and widespread community and home care facilities; (c) to plan or ensure implementation of activities aiming at protecting elderly people in social life; and (d) to determine the procedure and rules of establishment, operation or audit of institutions for elderly people to be operated by public institutions, natural or legal entities, and to provide guidance, coordination or monitoring for these institutions. The establishment of the GDSPDE brought a new insight to services for elderly people. A National Plan for Action was to focus on social integration of elderly people, improvement of long-term services and solving healthcare problems of elderly people. The plan was not only to improve the quality of the existing services, but also to introduce new service and care models based on societal realities (Republic of Turkey, 2012, p. 3).

Availability of long-term care for elderly people

Lack of data

There is a lack of information on long-term care in Turkey. Indicators used in *Health at a Glance: Europe* (OECD, 2015c) for the number of care recipients, informal carers, long-term care beds in hospitals or institutions, or long-term care expenditure do not include Turkey, indicating that there is no clear and consistent data collection on long-term care in Turkey. Scheil-Adlung (2015) has pointed out that in the absence of such data, informed decision-making is hardly possible, and issues regarding LTC remain unclear and confusing.

Informal care

Traditional family relationships and ties are still very strong for older persons in Turkey; family and friends are the most important source of care for people with long-term care (LTC) needs. Women, in most cases, are responsible for care within the family (Ozbay, 2014, p. 87; Republic of Turkey, 2012, p. 13, SPO, 2007, p. 110). According to the data from the *Research on Family Structure* study (MoFSP, 2014b), care for elderly people in households is conducted primarily by daughters-in-law (32 per cent). The rate of households where care is given by the spouse is 27 per cent, by the son 22 per cent, and by the daughter 20 per cent. The rate of households with a paid caregiver is only 2 per cent (MoFSP, 2014b, pp. 278–9). Six per cent of households in Turkey were found to have an elderly person in need of care. The Turkish Civil Code and the Turkish Penal Code include certain obligations for the family to look after dependents (Karadeniz, 2012, p. 23). Results from the *Turkish Population and Health* study (2008) show that even when children do not live with their parent, they prefer to either live in the same building or nearby (Koc et al., 2010, cited by Eryurt, 2014, p. 103).

There are no clear and sustainable support services or policies for informal caregivers in Turkey, apart from monetary help to poor families (Ozbay, 2014, p. 87). Often the type of care provided by informal family caregivers is very demanding, particularly if care is needed beyond the activities of daily living such as dressing and eating. As indicated above, it is not easy to obtain data on the number of people caring for family and friends in Turkey.

Migrant care workers

Declining family size, increased geographical mobility and rising participation rates of women in the labour market mean that there is a risk that fewer people will be willing and able to provide informal care in the future in Turkey. The lack of adequate public care services and formal care worker shortages are the main drivers of demand for migrant care workers (Tufan and Seedsman, 2015; Gökbayrak, 2009, pp. 60–1). It is particularly upper- and middle-class Turkish families who counter the lack of formal care provision and high female labour market participation by employing migrant women as domestic care workers.

Migrant care workers in Turkey are mainly women who have migrated from ex-communist countries such as the former Soviet Union, particularly Moldova, Uzbekistan, Turkmenistan, Azerbaijan, Bulgaria and Georgia. Since the mid-1990s, Moldova has become one of the main sending countries, especially for migrants of Gagauz ethnic origin who speak the Turkish language (Tufan and Seedsman, 2015, p. 43; Akalın, 2007, pp. 121–2). Since 2003, new Turkish legislation (Work Permits for Foreigners, Law No. 4817) allows working foreigners to be employed as domestic workers (Official Gazette, 2003).

Formal care workers

One of the challenges in the LTC sector is the lack of skilled formal care workers (Karadeniz, 2012, pp. 4–5). Formal LTC workers per 100 people aged 65 and over in Turkey in 2013 have been reported as 0.1, compared with the average of 6.1 (OECD, 2015c, Table 11.17). Care workers in nursing homes have expressed the need for higher wages, better physical conditions, and psychological support (Öntanc and Tunç, 2011, cited by Karadenuz, 2012, p. 26).

Since 1998, care workers' vocational training in Turkey has been provided by different institutions such as universities (vocational schools), the Ministry of Education (MoE) and the Ministry of Labour (Karadeniz, 2012, p. 26; Oglak, 2008, p. 243). Although the number of relevant faculties at universities, vocational training colleges and the number of courses have increased in recent years, formal care worker shortages have continued. Unfortunately, there is also no law that regulates the work of formal care workers in terms of defining their function and licensing.

Long-term care funding

Turkey does not have a long-term care insurance (LTCI), although this is planned for the future (Karadeniz, 2012, p. 4). A national long-term care insurance system benefits not only elderly people, but also protects the family members and the entire population against much of the financial risk of chronic illness and disability (Geraedts et al., 2000, p. 375). LTCI would provide relief from much of the financial burden of long-term disability and illness, thereby complementing the comprehensive medical services financed by a health insurance fund.

In the absence of an LTC insurance system, however, there are regulations in Turkey establishing a right to financial help with long-term care for low-income families. In order to support families with low incomes that care for disabled people, a tax-financed programme was introduced in 2006 (Karadeniz, 2012, pp. 23–4; Oglak, 2008). Only persons falling under certain income and wealth thresholds enjoy legal coverage for LTC. Thus, older people with income or assets above the thresholds have to first use up their savings and assets (sometimes even support of their relatives is taken into account) before being entitled to services. If a family's income is below the poverty threshold, the MoFSP provides social assistance to family caregivers (domiciliary care allowance) or payments to care homes or day centres. LTC coverage therefore exists but is limited. This system does not provide help to middle- or high-income groups (Karadeniz, 2012, p. 4).

Some older people who have no one legally responsible for looking after them, no pension, no property that would enable them to survive, or where the person legally responsible for them has an income too low to care for them, are entitled to free residential care (Karadeniz, 2012, p. 24). Five per cent of the capacity of private homes is also dedicated to poor older people who cannot afford the fees. The MoFSP local management determines the eligibility of elderly people for free care (Karadeniz, 2012, p. 24).

Provision of LTC

Provision of LTC is carried out by the MoFSP, municipalities, public institutions, NGOs, and minority ethnic groups – Greek, Armenian, Italian (mostly in Istanbul) – and private sector organizations, generally in residential care settings. Municipalities have duties and responsibilities to provide relevant services for 'disabled, elderly, dependent and needy persons' (SPO, 2007, p. 13). The Turkish Red Crescent (Kızılay) is an example of an NGO providing LTC. They provide residential or home-based care to people who have donated real estate to them (SPO, 2007, p. 36).

The changes in social structure have also changed people's needs/demands and expectations of receiving care services from outside of the family. These expectations constitute not only residential care, but also patterns of social care services that do not separate elderly people from their social life, daily routines, friends, neighbours and relatives, allowing them to spend their leisure time effectively and productively. Karadeniz (2012) suggests that there has been a shift in political priority away from institutional care and towards home care.

Due to the lack of care facilities and insurance, many older people have difficulty accessing services, especially in rural areas (Republic of Turkey, 2012; Oglak, 2007, pp. 104–8).

Residential care

As seen in Table 13.4, approximately 38 per cent of residential care homes in Turkey are funded by the government, 6 per cent by the municipalities, and almost half by for-profit organizations. Altogether, there were 29,186 beds based in 353 facilities in 2016. The number of residential facilities has been growing but is still very limited; GDSPDE facilities have increased from 106 in 2012 to 133 in 2016, and for-profit facilities from 123 to 164 (Eryurt, 2014, p. 103; cf. GDSPDE, 2017 p. 15). Given that the population of those 65 years of age and older in Turkey is nearly 6.5 million and the number of elders residing in care institutions is 23,532, the rate of older adults residing in residential care or nursing homes is 0.004 per cent. These very limited capacities are concentrated in certain communities in large cities (GDSPDE, 2017).

Residential care is the least preferred option for older people needing care services, both by family members and older people. Although the number of beds is limited, they are not totally occupied. While the results of several studies show that elderly people are satisfied with the social services and the support in residential care homes, at the same time they describe residential care homes as such places that force them to stay away from the people they love and the environment they lived in; study respondents state that they would never prefer residential care if they had any other choice (MoH, 2015a; MoFSP, 2014b; Oztop et al., 2008).

Applicants to MoFSP residential care homes have to be people over 60 years old who do not have any chronic illnesses or any physical or mental disabilities, but need social, physical or psychological support. They have to be able to perform daily necessities (eating, drinking, using the rest room) independently and not have any contagious disease (Özmete et al., 2016, p. 13). However, these homes also serve elderly people whose physical or mental condition declines after they begin their stay at residential care homes in special care services in a different section of the home (Özmete et al., 2016, p. 14). In addition, those who are in such situations in their homes and whose care has become difficult for their families may occasionally be admitted to special care services in care homes, or they can be admitted to private homes (MoFSP, 2014d). Private nursing homes admit people from the age of 55 (Özmete et al., 2016, p. 6). Their prices are also higher than those of public residential care.

There are also some innovatory forms of residential care for elderly people, such as small homes built in the grounds of residential care homes. Life homes are for more capable people, aiming to allow people to remain integrated in society. They are situated outside residential homes but are affiliated with them (MoFSP, 2017). Another innovation is elderly houses. These houses are ordinary apartment flats around the city that can accommodate up to four elderly persons (Republic of Turkey, 2012, p. 8).

Finally, hospitals are still highly important institutions for elderly people to obtain LTC. The hospitalization rate of people who are 75 years and older is 2.5 times higher than those between 25 and 44 years old (MoH, 2015b). The number of geriatric clinics and hospitals that are prepared for LTC has recently increased, but has still not reached a desirable level.

Home-based care

The provision of home care began quite late in Turkey. Home care services were first provided by private institutions, and since 2001 these services have been followed by some municipalities (MoH, 2015b, pp. 47–8). The first legal regulation in this field was the 'Regulation on Home Care Service Providing by Private Organisations', which was issued by the MoH and came into force in 2005, many years after the onset of care provision. The provision of home healthcare by public hospitals started in 2004, and regulation of this by MoH in 2010 was an important step for the dissemination of these services throughout the country (MoH, 2015b, pp. 47–8; Oglak, 2008; Oglak, 2007, p. 101). In response to most people's preference to receive LTC services

Table 13.4 Number of residential care facilities in Turkey (2016)

	Number		Capacity	Occupancy
Operated by the General Directorate of Disabled and Elderly Services, Ministry of Family and Social Policies	133	37.7	13.602	12.411
Life Homes for Elderly Persons	40	11.3	154	154
Operated by other ministries	2	0.5	570	566
Operated by municipalities	20	5.6	2.871	2.010
Operated by associations and foundations (non-profit)	29	8.2	2.360	1.652
Operated by Minorities	5	1.4	508	355
Operated by for-profit private institutions	164	46.4	9.121	6.384
Total	**353**	**100**	**29.186**	**23.532**

Source: Compiled by author from GDSPDE (2017).

at home, home healthcare services aim to ensure that dependent people in need of healthcare services are treated in their homes in a familiar environment. Delivering the necessary medical care and rehabilitation services outside of a hospital environment whenever possible reduces the number and duration of hospital stays (Karadeniz, 2012, p. 5).

With regard to home-based care, some public services (municipalities, NGOs) exist that are directed to helping people in need of social care with their daily activities. Generally, the availability of home-based care services is fragmented, very limited, and seldom available or affordable for older persons in need of care. Municipalities generally only provide social home care to poor and frail people, although there are plans to transfer government resources to them to develop their services (Özmete et al., 2016, p. 11). Furthermore, public and private home social care facilities tend to be located in the main cities, concentrated in provinces such as Istanbul, Ankara, Kocaeli, Trabzon, Aydın and İzmir (Oglak, 2008).

The MoFSP carried out a number of regulations in this field in 2006. Yet the MoFSP does not directly provide services at home. As indicated above, a means-tested monthly payment of the net minimum wage is paid by MoFSP to the family member caring for the elderly and/or disabled person in need of care living at home (Karadeniz, 2012, pp. 23–4). Means-tested limited public-funded LTC to the poor parts of the population creates extreme inequities in access to LTC. Rather than providing for the right to financial support to access LTC, policymakers have decided to enact legislation that shifts the burden of LTC from the government to families. In the case of insufficient quality or absence of public services, it also forces those in need to purchase services privately. It has been argued that giving support to family members reinforces women's caregiving role and conflicts with their struggle to head out into the public sphere (Ozbay, 2014, p. 87).

Adult day-care services are very limited in Turkey (Özmete et al, 2016, p. 10). Bettio and Verashchagina (2012, p. 74) found reported coverage of semi-residential care provision (e.g respite care, adult day centres) in Turkey to be almost zero (0.02 per cent). There are five public adult day-care centres, affiliated with the MoFSP, and a few organized by NGOs, particularly the Alzheimer's Society (Özmete et al., 2016, p. 12). Recently, a service has been initiated where a care worker can be requested from the nearest nursing home, but very few people are benefitting from this (Özmete et al, 2016, p. 10).

Finally, it should be mentioned that elderly solidarity centres have been set up in several cities throughout the country, designed similar to an ADC for elderly people. They provide several social activity opportunities such as music groups, art classes, educational activities on healthy living, and picnics that bring the elderly together. Older people are able to play an active part in these centres, and take part in their administration. Other than a symbolic membership fee, benefiting from the facilities is free (Republic of Turkey, 2012; SPO, 2007, p. 32).

Concluding discussion

Despite its young population compared with European countries, and relatively low proportion of older people (aged 65+), Turkey is ageing rapidly. This is occurring much faster than it did in the developed countries, and at a stage of lower economic development. The growing proportion of older people has consequences for many aspects of Turkish society, including healthcare and long-term social care. This is especially so because of other changes in Turkish society, similar to those in developed countries, the transition from extended to nuclear families, and a considerable proportion of older people living alone.

Since the 1990s, the reform of the Turkish social security system has been on the agenda. Previously, pensions and healthcare were dependent on social insurance determined by employment status, and many people in the large informal economy were excluded, though some benefitted as dependents of employed people. There is tax-funded social assistance for disabled people and those aged 65 and over for people without a contributory pension, but it is very low. Legislation in 2008 ended occupationally based health insurance and implemented near universal health coverage. However, there is no social insurance for long-term care, although this is under discussion. Long-term care is still predominantly regarded as a role for the family.

The absence of clear and consistent data collection on long-term care at the national level makes planning difficult, mirroring the priority given to this.

The most important step taken by the government in relation to the ageing population was setting up, in 2011, the General Directorate of Services for Persons with Disabilities and Elderly People within the Ministry of Family and Social Policies. Among its responsibilities are the regulation and improvement of quality of residential services for older people, and the introduction of new models of care. However, institutional care at present remains fragmented, provided by a variety of organizations, including various non-profit associations and for-profit entities, and having different eligibility rules. Free care is only available to older people on very low incomes who do not have anyone to care for them. Above all, the availability of residential care is totally inadequate, covering only 0.004 per cent of the population aged 65 and over in 2016.

Home-based care is the least developed, not widely available, and beyond the means of most families. Families mainly provide the care for elderly people needing this, the main support being a means-tested monthly allowance equivalent to the minimum wage to a family member providing care for a disabled or older person. This reinforces family responsibility, and particularly of women as caregivers. Home-based services were first provided by private organizations, then by municipalities. Services provided by the municipalities are limited and only for the poor, though there are plans to develop these.

Additionally, there is an insufficient number of formal care workers. Training is provided by a variety of institutions, but there is no common curriculum, and conditions of work need to be improved.

There are some interesting innovations in care provision for older people in Turkey, but they only cover very small numbers.

Overall, long-term care provision for older people in Turkey is fragmented and uncoordinated, lacking in availability, does not have a high profile, and although there are attempts at improvement, there is a notable lack of a clear policy vision on how to address critical issues.

References

Agartan, T.I., 2012. Marketization and universalism: crafting the right balance in Turkey's healthcare system. *Current Sociology*, 60(4), pp. 456–71. DOI: http://dx.doi.org/10.1177/0011392112438331.

Akalın, A., 2007. Hired as a caregiver, demanded as a housewife: becoming a migrant domestic worker in Turkey. *European Journal of Women's Studies*, 14(3), pp. 209–25. DOI: http://dx.doi.org/10.1177%2F1350506807079011.

Apakan, E., 2012. Population aging and development: opportunities for economic growth. *Council on Foreign Relations Conference*. New York, 7 September.

Atun, R., 2015. Transforming Turkey's health system: lessons for universal coverage. *The New England Journal of Medicine*, 373(14), pp. 1285–9. DOI: http://dx.doi.org/10.1056/NEJMp1410433.

Barıs, E., Mollahaliloğlu, S. and Aydın, S., 2011. Healthcare in Turkey: from laggard to leader. *BMJ*, 342:c7456. http://dx.doi.org/10.1136/bmj.c7456.

Bettio, F. and Verashchagina, A., 2012. *Long-term care for the elderly: provisions and providers in 33 European countries*. Luxembourg: European Union. Available at: http://ec.europa.eu/justice/gender-equality/files/elderly_care_en.pdf [accessed 19.07.2017].

Ergin, I. and Mandiracioglu, A., 2015. Demographic and socioeconomic inequalities for self-rated health and happiness in elderly: the situation for Turkey regarding World Values Survey between 1990 and 2013. *Archives of Gerontology and Geriatrics*, 61(2), pp. 224–30. http://dx.doi.org//10.1093/eurpub/ckv 176.140.

Eryurt, M.A., 2014. Elderly population in Türkiye and preferences for elderliness. In M. Turgut and S. Feyzioğlu, eds. *Research on family structure in Türkiye: findings and recommendations*. Ministry of Family and Social Policies. Research and Social Policies Series No. 08. Istanbul: Çizge Tanıtım Publishing, pp. 88–109. Available at: http://ailetoplum.aile.gov.tr/data/54292ce0369dc32358ee2a46/taya2013eng.pdf [accessed 19.07.2017].

Eurostat, 2015. *Demographic balance, 2015*. Available at: http://ec.europa.eu/eurostat/tgm/table.do?tab=ta ble&init=1&language=en&pcode=tps00001&plugin=1 [accessed 20.06.17].

GDSPDE (General Directorate of Services for Persons with Disabilities and Elderly People), 2017. *Statistical information dealing with the disabled and elderly people*. Ministry of Family and Social Policies, Department of Research and Development, p. 15. Available at: http://eyh.aile.gov.tr/yayin-ve-kaynaklar/arge-ve-istatistik/engelli-ve-yasli-bireylere-iliskin-istatistiki-bilgiler [accessed 19.07.2017]. [In Turkish]

Geraedts, M., Heller, V.G. and Harrington, C.A., 2000. Germany's long-term care insurance: putting a social insurance model into practice. *Milbank Quarterly*, 78(3), pp. 375–401. DOI: 10.1111/1468-0009.00178.

Gökbayrak, S., 2009. Refah devletinin dönüşümü ve bakım hizmetlerinin görünmez emekçileri göçmen kadınlar [Transformation of welfare state and female migrants as invisible care workers]. *Çalışma ve Toplum* [Work and Society], 2(21), pp. 55–82. Available at: http://calismatoplum.org/sayi21/gokbayrak.pdf [accessed 19.07.2017].

Hamzaoğlu, O. and Ozcan, U., 2006. *Türkiye Sağlık İstatistikleri* [Turkey health statistics 2006]. Ankara: Türk Tabibler Birliği Yayınları [Turkish Medical Association Publishing].

He, W., Goodkind, D. and Kowal, P., 2016. *An aging world: 2015*. US Census Bureau, International Population Report, P95/16-1. Washington, DC: US Government Publishing Office. Available at: www.census.gov/content/dam/Census/library/publications/2016/demo/p95-16-1.pdf [accessed 19.07.2017].

Karadeniz, O., 2012. *Annual national report 2012: pensions, health care and long-term care, Turkey*. Asisp (Analytical support on the socio-economic impact of social protection reforms). European Commission DG Employment, Social Affairs and Inclusion. Available at: http://pensionreform.ru/files/13660/ASISP.%20Annual%20National%20Report%202012%20-%20Turkey.pdf [accessed 19.07.2017].

MoFSP (Ministry of Family and Social Policies), 2014a. *Research on family structure in Türkiye TAYA 2006*, M. Turgut ed. Research and Social Policies Series No. 02. Second Reviewed Print. Ankara: Uzerler Matbaacılık Publishing. Available at: http://ailetoplum.aile.gov.tr/data/54292ce0369dc32358ee2a46/taya_2006_eng.pdf [accessed 10.07.2017].

MoFSP (Ministry of Family and Social Policies), 2014b. *Research on family structure in Türkiye TAYA 2011*, M. Turgut ed. General Directorate of Family and Community Services. Research and Social Policy Series No. 05. Second Reviewed Print. Istanbul: Çizge Tanıtım Publishing. Available at: http://ailetoplum.aile.gov.tr/data/54292ce0369dc32358ee2a46/taya2011-eng.pdf [accessed 19.07.2017].

MoFSP (Ministry of Family and Social Policies), 2014c. *Research on family structure in Türkiye: findings and recommendations*, M. Turgut and S. Feyzioğlu eds. General Directorate of Family and Community Services. Research and Social Policies Series No. 08. Istanbul: Çizge Tanıtım Publishing. Available at: http://ailetoplum.aile.gov.tr/data/54292ce0369dc32358ee2a46/taya2013eng.pdf [accessed 19.07.2017].

MoFSP (Ministry of Family and Social Policies), 2014d. *Engelli bakım hizmetleri* [Disability care services]. Department Presidency Briefing Report. Available at: http://eyh.aile.gov.tr/yayin-ve-kaynaklar/engelli-bakim-hizmetleri/engelli-bakim-hizmetleri-dairesi-baskanligi-birifing-raporu [accessed 22.07.2017].

MoFSP (Ministry of Family and Social Policies), 2017. *Yaşlı Yaşam Evleri* [Elderly life homes]. Available at: https://eyh.aile.gov.tr/uygulamalar/yasli-bakim-hizmetleri/yasli-yasam-evleri [accessed 19.07.2017].

MoH (Republic of Turkey Ministry of Health), 2015a. *Health statistics yearbook 2014*, B.B. Başara, C. Güler and G.K. Yentür eds. General Directorate of Health Research. Publication No. SB-SAGEM-2015/3. Ankara: Ministry of Health. Available at: http://sbu.saglik.gov.tr/Ekutuphane/kitaplar/EN%20YILLIK.pdf [accessed 19.07.2017].

MoH (Republic of Turkey Ministry of Health), 2015b. *Turkey healthy aging action plan and implementation program 2015–2020*. Publication No. 960. Ankara: Ministry of Health Turkey. Available at: http://kronikhastaliklar.thsk.saglik.gov.tr/Dosya/Dokumanlar/kitaplar/Saglikli_yaslanma_eylem_plani_22_03_2016.pdf [accessed 19.07.2017].

National Institute on Aging, 2011. *Global health and aging*. NIH Publication no. 11-7737. Available at: www.nia.nih.gov/sites/default/files/global_health_and_aging.pdf [accessed 19.07.2017].

OECD, 2015a. Self reported health and disability at age 65. *Health at a glance 2015, OECDiLibrarys*. Paris: OECD. DOI: http://dx.doi.org/10.1787/health_glance-2015-graph186-en.

OECD, 2015b. *OECD health statistics 2015, country note: how does health spending in Turkey compare?* Available at: www.oecd.org/els/health-systems/Country-Note-TURKEY-OECD-Health-Statistics-2015.pdf [accessed 19.07.2017].

OECD, 2015c. *Health at a glance 2015: OECD indicators*. Paris: OECD.DOI: http://dx.doi.org/10.1787/health_glance-2015-en.

OECD, 2016a. *Social expenditure database (SOCX)*. Paris: OECD. Available at: www.oecd.org/social/expenditure.htm [accessed 19.07.2017].

OECD, 2016b. *Health at a glance: Europe 2016 – state of health in the EU cycle*. Paris: OECD. DOI: http://dx.doi.org/10.1787/9789264265592-en.

Official Gazette, 2003. Labour law on permit for foreigners [Yabancıların Çalışma İzinleri Hakkında Kanun]. Law no. 4817. Accepted date: 27.2.2003. Official Gazette, 06.03.2003, no. 25040. Available at: http://turkishlaborlaw.com/work-permits-in-turkey/work-permit-law [accessed 24.11.2016].

Oglak, S., 2007. Uzun süreli evde bakım hizmetleri ve bakım sigortası [Long-term home care and insurance]. *Turkish Journal of Geriatrics*, 10(2), pp. 100–8.

Oglak S., 2008. *Evde bakım hizmetleri ve bakım sigortası, ülke örnekleri* [Home care services and long-term care insurance, country examples]. Municipality of Iskenderun Culture Publication, No. 6. Hatay: Color Publishing.

Okem, Z.G. and Cakar, M., 2015. What have health care reforms achieved in Turkey? An appraisal of the 'Health Transformation Programme'. *Health Policy*, 119, pp. 115–63. DOI: http://dx.doi.org/10.1016/j.healthpol.2015.06.003.

Ozbay, F., 2014. Relative and neighbor relationships. In M. Turgut and S. Feyzioğlu, eds. *Research on family structure in Türkiye: findings and recommendations*. Ministry of Family and Social Policies. Research and Social Policies Series No. 08. Istanbul: Çizge Tanıtım Publishing, pp. 56–87. Available at: http://ailetoplum.aile.gov.tr/data/54292ce0369dc32358ee2a46/taya2013eng.pdf [accesed 19.07.2017].

Özmete, E., Gurboga, C. and Tamkoç, B., 2016. *Country report: Republic of Turkey*. Available at: www.unece.org/fileadmin/DAM/pau/age/country_rpts/2017/TUR_report.pdf [accessed 26.06.17].

Oztop, H., Sener, A. and Guven, S., 2008. Evde bakımın yaşlı ve aile açısından olumlu ve olumsuz yönleri. [Positive and negative dimensions of home care services for elderly people and family members]. *Yaşlı Sorunları Araştırma Dergisi* [Journal of Research of Ageing Challenges], 1(1), pp. 39–49.

Republic of Turkey, 2012. *Second review and appraisal of the Madrid international plan of action on ageing*. Available at: www.unece.org/fileadmin/DAM/pau/age/country_rpts/2017/TUR_report.pdf [accessed 19.07.2017].

Scheil-Adlung, X., 2015. *Long-term care protection for older persons: a review of coverage deficits in 46 countries*. ESS Working Paper No. 50. Geneva: ILO. Available at: www.ilo.org/secsoc/information-resources/publications-and-tools/Workingpapers/WCMS_407620/lang--en/index.htm [accessed 19.07.2017].

SPO (State Planning Organization), 2007. *The situation of elderly people in Turkey and national plan of action on ageing*. Available at: www.monitoringris.org/documents/tools_nat/trk.pdf [accessed 19.07.2017].

SSI (Republic of Turkey Social Security Institute), 2016. *Social security system*. Available at: www.sgk.gov.tr/wps/portal/sgk/en/detail/social_security_system [accessed 19.07.2017].

Tufan, I. and Seedsman, T., 2015. The case of Moldovan female migrants providing home-based assistance to informal caregivers in Turkey: the impetus for aged care reform. *International Journal of Humanities and Social Science*, 5(2), pp. 40–50. Available at: www.ijhssnet.com/journals/Vol_5_No_2_February_2015/5.pdf [accessed 19.07.2017].

Turkstat, 2013. *Population projections 2013–2075*. Press release, 14 February. Available at: www.turkstat.gov.tr/PreHaberBultenleri.do?id=15844 [accessed 19.07.2017].

Turkstat, 2017a. *Research on family structure, 2016*. Press release, 18 January. Available at: www.turkstat.gov.tr/PreHaberBultenleri.do?id=21869 [accessed 06.07.2017].

Turkstat, 2017b. *Elderly statistics, 2016*. Press release, 16 March. Available at: www.turkstat.gov.tr/PreHaberBultenleri.do?id=24644 [accessed 20.06.17].

Uckardesler, E., 2015. Turkey's changing social policy landscape. *Turkish Policy Quarterly*, 13(4), pp. 149–61. Available at: http://turkishpolicy.com/Files/ArticlePDF/turkeys-changing-social-policy-landscape-winter-2015-en.pdf [accessed 19.07.2017].

WHO, 2012. *Successful health system reforms: the case of Turkey*. World Health Regional Office for Europe (WHO/Europe). Available at: http://dosyasb.saglik.gov.tr/Eklenti/2106,successful-health-system-reforms-the-case-of-turkeypdf.pdf?0 [accessed 27.06.17].

World Bank, 2016. *Fertility rate Turkey*. Available at: http://data.worldbank.org/indicator/SP.DYN.TFRT.IN?contextual=default&locations=TR [accessed 20.11.2016].

World Bank, 2017. *Turkey: country profile*. Available at: www.worldbank.org/en/country/turkey [accessed 25.06.17].

Yilmaz, V., 2013. Changing origins of inequalities in access to health care services in Turkey: from occupational status to income. *New Perspectives on Turkey*, 48, pp. 55–77. DOI: http://dx.doi.org/10.1017/S0896634600001886.

Part V
Asia

14

The emergence of the eldercare industry in China

Progress and challenges

Xiying Fan, Heying Jenny Zhan and Qi Wang

Introduction

Population ageing is a global trend. Yet the speed of population ageing in China has surpassed the rest of the developed world – while it took a century for most developed nations, such as France, Germany and the US, to double the elderly population from 7 per cent to 14 per cent of the nation's total population, it took China only between 25 and 27 years to do so. According to a recent report from the National Bureau of Statistics of China (2015), by the end of 2014 the elderly population (65+) has reached 13.7 per cent (National Bureau of Statistics of China, 2015, Table 2.11). The United Nations (UN) projects that by 2050, the older population (65+) in China will reach 331 million (UN, 2011, Table A.31). Simultaneously, persons aged 80 and above will also increase dramatically, from 23 million in 2013 to 90 million in 2050 (UN, 2013, p. 32).

The rapid growth of the elderly population is directly related to the demographic transition in China that is characterized by its high birth rate during the 1950s to 1970s, low birth rate as a result of the one-child policy during the 1980s to 2010, and relaxed position towards birth rate from 2010 until now. After the Second Word War, women commonly gave birth to five to seven children, creating China's baby boom (Zhan, 2013). In 1979, the Chinese government initiated a nationwide family planning policy, the so called one-child policy, to stimulate the economy and lay the groundwork towards modernization (Zhang et al., 2012). Once the policy was implemented, the birth rate sharply reduced from 5.8 in 1970 to 2.8 in 1979, and the rate continued to decline to lower than 2 in 2010 (Peng, 2011, p. 581). The demographic structure in China has changed from a perfect pyramid shape in 1950 towards a lighthouse shape in the following few decades (Zhang et al., 2012). This shift indicates a shrinking number of working-age adults available to take care of a large number of older persons. Although the Chinese government loosened the one-child policy recently, many families still bear the '4:2:1' (four grandparents, two adults, one child) family structure.

By 2015, large numbers of those Chinese baby boomers born after 1950, the establishment of New China, have entered retirement. Some already need various types of eldercare. The rapid increase in the demand for long-term eldercare has propelled the rapid growth in eldercare facilities. This chapter will offer a general understanding of the background to the development of eldercare, the recent developments, and the major challenges facing the developments. We will also offer discussions related to emerging social inequalities and policy implications for long-term care at facility and individual levels.

Background: concepts and definitions

Before a detailed discussion of recent developments of eldercare facilities in China, we need to spell out the meanings and distinctions in relevant terminologies: those between long-term care, nursing home, and eldercare, and between familial care, home-based and community care, and non-government 'non-profit' and 'for-profit' and private eldercare facilities.

The concept of 'long-term care' is very much a Western or foreign idea in China. Other than in scholarly translated literature, rarely do ordinary Chinese people hear the term 'long-term care'. Most often, people use the term 'eldercare' and eldercare homes. Eldercare refers to any type of long-term care at home or in a facility. Eldercare homes refer to institutional long-term care homes for older adults. However, due to the lack of professionalization and specification in most areas, eldercare in China includes a range of facilities. In this chapter, we refer to our study sample as 'eldercare homes' – which include all those that serve older adults who reside in retirement homes, independent living, assisted living, and nursing home settings.

The distinction between familial care and home-based community care can be vague. In China, familial care comprises all care activities provided by family members, including services provided by an in-home care worker (baomu 保姆 maid) paid for and arranged by adult children. Home- and community-based care, according to Du (2006), is an umbrella term that refers to all public or private services provided to enable elders to age at home, including adult day care and all types of professional care services delivered to the home, such as meals on wheels, house cleaning, hair dressing, nurse and physician visits, etc.

The difference between government, non-government, for-profit and non-profit eldercare institutions is context-specific to China. Because of the solo government ownership and management of all eldercare and welfare institutions until the late 1990s, non-government facilities in eldercare became a new and growing industry in the last two decades. In the process of decentralization and privatization of welfare institutions in the 1990s, all non-government eldercare facilities were encouraged to be registered under the 'non-profit' category at the local Civil Affairs Bureau (民政局). In practice, for-profit and non-profit eldercare facilities are little different in China since there is nearly no distinguishable difference in their mission and financial management. Very few for-profit eldercare facilities are available on the market; they became 'for-profit' mainly due to their earlier registration from the Labour Department (劳动局) rather than the Civil Affairs Bureau (民政局) before the major government promotion of non-profit eldercare development in the 1990s. The major difference, therefore, lies between the government and non-government facilities; non-government-owned facilities can be for-profit and non-profit, managed by individuals or corporations. The focus of this chapter is on the recent development of non-government eldercare institutions.

Chinese culture and eldercare

For thousands of years, the Chinese culture embraced the Confucian doctrine of filial piety, which places great emphasis on the extended network of family and kin, especially parent-child relationships (Tang et al., 2009). As a key cultural ideology, filial piety consists of a set of attitudes and behaviours that entail children's feelings of love, respect, obedience, loyalty, sense of obligation, material provisions, and physical care towards ageing parents (Mao and

Chi, 2011; Lee and Hong-kin, 2005). The concept can be summarized into two dimensions: one is behavioural-based filial piety where children take responsibility or make repayment and sacrifices toward their parents, and the other is emotional-based filial piety, which is counted by children's love, affection, and respect (Sung, 1995).

Filial piety is essential to Chinese people for it sets moral and behavioural guidelines, and it serves as an important goal for formal and informal education in Chinese societies (Chen et al., 2007). When children are young, the ideal of 'being filial' is instilled as a core familial and social value. It is socially expected that when parents grow older, adult children are to take the responsibility to provide financial, emotional, and physical care for their parents (Luo and Zhan, 2012).

Adult children's obligation to their parents is not only a cultural virtue, but also law-based. In 1950, the Marriage Law stressed adult children's duty to care for their parents, and the Constitution of 1954 directly announced that 'parents have the duty to rear and educate their minor children, and the children who have come of age have the duty to support and assist their parents' (Zhang et al., 2012, p. 164). The Criminal Law of 1979 states that individuals who fail or refuse to perform their filial responsibility may be imprisoned for up to five years (Zhang and Goza, 2006). In 1996, the Law for the Protection of Elders' Rights formally regulated adult children's responsibilities towards ageing parents, such as provision of housing, medical support, and property protection (Luo and Zhan, 2012).

Despite the government's efforts of preserving the tradition of filial piety, rapid economic expansion and demographic transformation seemed to pull it in another direction. As a result of the one-child policy, Chinese family structure has shifted from extended family to the nuclear family (Shen and Yeatts, 2013). Many Chinese elders can no longer draw support from multiple children, but only rely on one. It is too demanding for the only child to provide both long-term familial care as well as working outside to support the family financially. Research shows that children from only-child families expressed lower levels of willingness to sacrifice their employment opportunities for the sake of providing parental care, even though they expressed a strong obligation to do so compared to children from multiple-child families (Zhan, 2004).

Moreover, providing in-home care to fragile parents seems to be unfeasible for working-age adults. The accelerated internal migration in the process of urbanization puts elderly parents in a more difficult situation. Once, multigenerational co-residence was seen as a marker of children's filial piety. As many young adults move to cities or more developed regions for better job opportunities, co-residence with children in a stable home environment becomes impractical for many ageing parents (Silverstein et al., 2006). Massive internal migration has resulted in a large number of empty-nest households (Chen and Silverstein, 2000). According to the sixth National Census report (National Bureau of Statistics of China, 2012), by the end of 2010, there were a total of 18,211,000 elders who lived alone, and 40,130,000 elders who only co-resided with their spouses. The empty-nest household takes up to one-third of the total ageing population, accounting for 62 million seniors (Wu and Du, 2012, p. 117).

To respond to the urgent need for eldercare, due to the reduced feasibility of maintaining familial care, in recent years the Chinese government has vigorously promoted eldercare services.

The development of institutional eldercare

Prior to the 1980s, formal eldercare facilities in China were rare and restricted to certain groups of people, namely the 'Three No's' – people with no children, no income, and no available caregivers (Feng et al., 2012). Since the establishment of the People's Republic of China, the government provides welfare services to the most needy older persons. All of these eldercare homes were called *Fuli Yuan* (welfare institutions), they were owned and managed by the central government or collective organizations (Zhang, 2007), and the central and local governments bore the financial burden of providing all formal eldercare services. The deficits of this state and collective-run welfare system were evident; there was a lack of financing sources, a limited number of state-run eldercare homes, and poor care quality (Zhang and Min, 2015). To relieve the government's financial burden and make progress in eldercare, in the mid-1990s, the central government in China promoted the growth of non-government eldercare facilities by decentralization and privatization of former government-owned facilities (Zhan et al., 2006). Consequently, there was a major shift in financing eldercare homes from primarily public funding toward more diversified sources (Feng et al., 2012). Since then, the number of private eldercare facilities in China has rapidly increased, especially in urban areas. In Tianjin, for instance, the number of eldercare homes increased from only 11 state-run welfare homes in 1980 to 19 state-run and 106 non-government facilities in 2010 (Feng et al., 2011, p. 741).

Despite the great improvement in availability of eldercare services in recent years, eldercare homes, especially those run by private sector entities, are still limited in their development. The demand for institutional eldercare far exceeds the current number of available eldercare homes. In 2010, China had over 40,000 running eldercare homes, including state, collective, and privately owned facilities, and that counts for 3.12 million beds (Wu and Du, 2012, p. 426). Either according to the '90:7:3' model from Shanghai (90 per cent familial care, 7 per cent community-based care, 3 per cent institutional care) or the '90:6:4' model from Beijing, the gap between demand and supply is huge.

Based on the number of older people in 2010 (177 million 60+ older adults), the number of available beds in institutions should reach 5.31 million or 7.08 million, according to the model used in the calculation, which surpasses the existing number of beds in eldercare homes (Wu and Du, 2012). In an opinion poll about the willingness to use institutional care in Beijing, results show that 24.5 per cent of people were interested in ageing in eldercare homes, exceeding the government's eldercare plan (Mu, 2012). If nearly a quarter of the elders have expressed interest in using institutional care services, while the government only plans growth up to institutional care for 3–4 per cent of the total elderly population, what are the potential challenges China may be facing?

Challenges facing institutional eldercare

In spite of the shortage of eldercare homes, the actual occupancy rate is very low. Some facilities have an occupancy rate of 60 per cent and some may only have 20 per cent (Mu, 2012). The high cost of living in an eldercare home is one reason. Besides low-income childless elders with 'Five Guarantees' or 'wu-bao hu' in rural regions (i.e. government welfare guarantee on food, clothing, medical care, housing, and funeral expenses) and family members of revolutionary martyrs, the majority of elders need to pay out of their own pockets to access eldercare institutions (Zhang and Min, 2015). Elders have to pull on multiple financial sources to afford the cost, such as their monthly pension, financial support from children or relatives, and insurances. For disabled elders or elders with dementia, the fee is way beyond their affordability. In 2012, for example, the minimum fee for a disabled elder in eldercare homes was about 2 to 3.5 times the size of an elder's average pension (Zhang and Min, 2015). The worst case is that many older people do not even have a pension. As Zhang (2007) noticed, elders who cannot afford to pay are blocked from getting into a facility in the first place, and they might be those needing the most intensive care.

The high cost of non-government homes results in a preference for government-run facilities since they tend to be cheaper, but these are very limited in number. Elders may wait for years

The eldercare industry in China

to get into one. The high cost of high-quality non-government facilities and the preference for government-owned facilities together lead to a low occupancy rate for most private eldercare homes.

Simultaneously, the low occupancy rate in non-government-run facilities often interplays with poor living conditions and low-quality services. Besides initial investments, the operation of non-government facilities depends on elderly residents' fees. The low occupancy rate signifies that many private facilities are under great financial pressure. The government-run facilities can apply for public funds when maintenance is required, and for advancing amenities, expanding the facility, or providing training for care workers (Ye, 2012). By contrast, non-government facilities assume major responsibility for their own profits. To maintain operation, some private eldercare homes cut labour costs, reduce fees and the amount of available services to attract residents (Dan et al., 2013; Mu, 2012). This leads to an unfavourable reputation for non-government-run eldercare homes, which in turn affects the quality of care and the occupancy rate. For instance, in Dan et al.'s (2013) study, a manager from a private eldercare facility said:

> We want to improve the conditions and make our residents more comfortable, but we only have 300 to 400 thousand Yuan to invest in comparison to several million Yuan of invest-ment in government-run facilities. The financial gap is huge. We do receive subsidy from the government, but the amount of money from subsidy is too little to improve anything.
> *(Dan et al., 2013, p. 64)*

The shortage of financial resources among non-government facilities is related to a lack of policy support. In comparison to government-run facilities, the majority of non-government eldercare institutions rely on leasing, and the longest lease agreement only lasts for 20 years (Mu, 2012). Many non-government eldercare homes show no interest or ability to advance their services and amenities because of their limited time in the use of land and the high cost of leasing. On top of these challenges, non-government facilities have to bear water and electricity fees that are much higher than for government-run facilities, forming a major proportion of facilities' operational costs (Ye, 2012). The deficits of financial sources impede private eldercare homes from expanding their scope. With a small size, those private institutions undergo inadequate profits and high prime cost. They are made uncompetitive against government-run facilities.

Additionally, the increased daily expenses among non-government-run facilities becomes a growing problem. As Dan et al. (2013) illustrate, in Gu Lou district in Nanjing, there were about 13 non-government eldercare homes that paid rental fees ranging from 350,000 to 700,000 yuan (roughly £42,000–82,000) yearly, and this number has continued to increase by 5–10 per cent due to the fluctuation of the real estate market. Living expenses are increasing as well. Even though some private eldercare homes raised their monthly fees, this was far behind the rise in living and operation expenses (Dan et al., 2013). The government subsidizes the non-government eldercare homes' expansion on beds, but there is no financial support towards the high cost of food preparation and nursing. Hence, while the total number of beds has increased dramatically, 'empty beds' and elders' inability to afford monthly fees are a common phenomenon (Zhang and Min, 2015). In recent years, many private eldercare institutions have suspended activities due to the increasing operational costs.

Financial difficulty in private institutional care also relates to the shortage of qualified care workers. According to the 2015 Working Paper Series of the Social Development Division of the UN Economic and Social Commission of Asia and Pacific (SDD), in 2013, 37.5 mil-lion older people needed to use eldercare services at least at some point of time (SDD, 2015, p. 14). Based on the ratio of 1:4 (one care worker provides care for four elders), China needs 9 million care workers, but the actual number of care workers was only 320,000 by the end

207

of 2012, and less than 10,000 of them held professional certificates (SDD, 2015, p. 14). Many non-government facilities post advertisements for care workers on their front door, but only a few people would take the job (Dan et al., 2013).

The front-line workers in eldercare institutions often receive low wages, and there is not much social status attached to it (Dan et al., 2013). Most young people from cities are not interested in working in eldercare homes because of the hard work, low wages, and unpleasant reputation of the job. Thus, the majority of eldercare care workers are in their mid-forties and fifties, and come from less developed provinces with very little or no education and skills. These front-line workers rarely receive professional care training. Their busy work leaves them no time to attend any professional training, and their age and low education impede advancement in their careers (Dan et al., 2013).

The turnover rate tends to be very high in non-government-run facilities. Front-line workers rarely consider their jobs as a lifelong career. There is little chance for them to receive a promotion or rise in salary. The high turnover rate of employees in long-term care is also a serious concern in developed countries; for instance, the National Center for Assisted Living (2011, p. 2) found the total turnover rate of long-term care employees in the US in 2010 was 25 per cent, rising to 38 per cent among front-line care workers (no certificate). This turnover affects elderly residents as they need to establish relationships with a multitude of care workers.

We next present findings from a national survey of non-government eldercare facilities in China. The findings and discussions add to the existing literature on recent development of eldercare in China.

Methods of the national survey

This chapter utilizes data collected in a national survey conducted in 2008, completed on 1 September 2008, sponsored by the Chinese National Committee of Ageing.[1] The goal of the survey was to gain a general understanding of the current developments of non-government facilities for eldercare. Even though many changes have taken place, these data are still from the most comprehensive national study, giving a good picture of the recent development of eldercare, especially non-government eldercare facilities. All non-government facilities, for-profit and non-profit, in all 30 provinces in China that registered for business prior to 1 September 2008, were invited and requested to file the survey report. On the date of data collection completion, 4,134 facilities completed the survey, representing roughly 10 per cent of the 40,000 existing eldercare facilities of all types, government, non-government for-profit, and non-government non-profit, in the nation. Since the Chinese government does not yet have a way to control the statistics in the eldercare field, as the US government does by controlling the Medicare and Medicaid funding through the provision of data on facilities, the 10 per cent in the report is all we could gather for the understanding of the facility and residents' situation. Therefore, no generalization is possible. Data were entered into SPSS (version 21 software) and analysed in aggregated fashion. The presentation of the data below is divided into two parts: aggregated characteristics of facilities, and aggregated characteristics of residents.

Characteristics of facilities in the study

Among the 4,134 non-government facilities completing the national survey, there were 411,723 beds and 241,914 elderly residents living in these facilities, and the occupancy rate was 57.8 per cent (see Table 14.1 for detail). Among all participating facilities, 97 per cent of the facilities were registered as 'non-profit'; only 3 per cent were registered as 'for-profit'. Based on the survey, the largest percentage of facilities were small, containing under 50 beds.

Table 14.1 Characteristics of facilities

Facility characteristics	N	%
No. of facilities	4134/40,000	10.3
No. of residents	241,914	
No. of beds	411,723	
Occupancy rate	241,914/411,723	58.8
Time established		
Before 1995	87	2.1
1995–2004	1,476	35.70
2004–2008	2,471	59.77
N/A	100	2.4
Size of facility		
Under 50 beds	1,632	39.47
50–100 beds	1,340	32.41
101–200 beds	807	19.52
200+ beds	320	7.74
N/A	35	.8
Facility type		
Non-profit	4,010	97
For-profit	124	3
Geographic distribution		
Urban	3,141	76
Rural	992	24
Land use		
Designated by government	868	21
Rented	1,488	36
Mixed/unclear	1,653	40+
N/A	125	3.0
Facility housing		
Rented	2,067+	50+
Remodeled	372	9
Newly constructed	1,695	41
*Type of rooms offered**		
One-bedroom suites	248	6
Single room	950	23
Double room	1,736	42
Triple room	826	20
Multi-person room	620	15
Medical facilities available		
Emergency kit	3,224	78
Vehicle for emergency use	742	18
N/A	168	4.0
Self-rated financial standing		
Have surplus	372	9
Can balance the budget	2,067	50.4
Difficult	1,612	39
N/A	83	2.0

(continued)

Table 14.1 (continued)

Facility characteristics	N	%
Gender of care workers	N = 36,645	
Male	9,161	25
Female	27,483	75
Care worker source		
Local	24,552	67
Migrant labourer	12,093	33
Turnover rate		
Care staff hired in the last year	11,729/36,645	32
Care staff left in the last year	5,637/36,645	15.38
Age of care workers	N = 37,011**	
Under 30	3,298	9
31–40	9,528	26
41–50	16,123	44
50+	8,062	22

Source: Created by the authors from data in the survey report.

Notes:

* Facilities could offer more than one type of room.
** Over-counting appears to be related to age 50 in both categories of 41–50 and 50+.

Time of establishment

What stands out, as shown in the data, is the year of establishment of the facilities. Prior to the mid-1990s, there were nearly no non-government eldercare facilities available. The major increase in their growth took off after 1995, and peaked in 2006.

Geographic location

The survey results revealed that the north-east of China had the highest number of recently developed facilities. In Northeast of Helongjiang province, for instance, there were 611 eldercare homes. In the interior west, on the other hand, institutional eldercare was most underdeveloped. In Qinghai, which locates in north-west China, there were no non-profit non-government facilities available for eldercare.

Another major difference in geographic distribution is the urban and rural gap. Based on the survey result, 75 per cent of facilities were located in urban China, and only 25 per cent of them were in rural China. Comparatively speaking, rural population in China accounts for about half (50.05 per cent) of the total population in 2010 (National Bureau of Statistics of China 2015, Table 2.1).

Facility resources

Establishment of a facility requires the most basic utilization of the land, facility housing, facility equipment, and working staff. Based on survey results, 21 per cent of non-government facilities enjoyed the utilization of land designated by the government, 36 per cent used rented property, and 40 per cent had mixed use of land and property – it is unclear what this actually means. Among all non-government organizations, above 50 per cent rented their facility housing, 9 per cent utilized remodeled housing, from former hotels, schools, or hospitals, after making the purchase, and 41 per cent constructed new facility housing specifically for the eldercare facility use.

Based on the self-report of financial standing, half of all facilities reported that they were able to balance their budgets, and 35 per cent reported their facilities had a negative balance. Only 9 per cent reported making any profit. Among the facilities that reported a positive margin, 45 per cent stated that this margin was at 5 per cent or less, 51 per cent reported a margin between 5 and 10 per cent, and only 2 per cent reported a profit margin above 10 per cent.

Services and amenities in the facilities

As shown in Figure 14.1, 93 per cent of facilities have gates or lobbies that checked in visitors and watched over wandering elders with dementia, but around 290 facilities did not have a front gate or lobby area. This indicates that residents with dementia could wander outside the facility without being noticed. Over 80 per cent of facilities had reading rooms, activity rooms, and public toilets. Over half had a public shower space, garden, clinic, and visiting guest space. Having a gym and dinner room was relatively uncommon.

A close look at the available amenities in residents' rooms (see Figure 14.2) shows over 90 per cent had TV sets and closets. Over 70 per cent of rooms have a wheelchair available for use. Over half of facilities installed telephone and electric fans in residents' rooms. Less than half of facilities installed air conditioning and heating in rooms, an emergency call button or switch, and drinking water dispenser. Access to the Internet was still rare in 2009, at 13 per cent in all facilities.

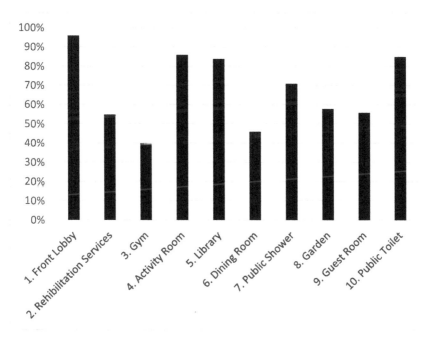

Figure 14.1 Available services and amenities in the facilities

Source: Created by the authors from data in the survey report.

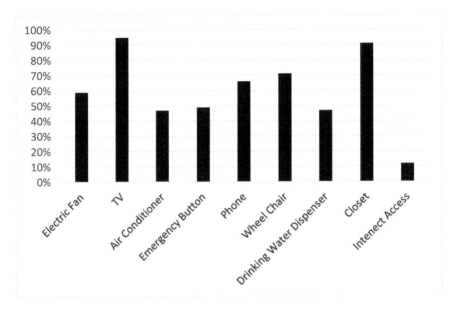

Figure 14.2 Amenities in residents' rooms

Source: Created by the authors from data in the survey report.

Facility staffing

Among all employees in these facilities, over half are front-line workers, taking care of residents. On average, a facility had nine direct care workers, three administrative staff, three other staff (such as drivers, cooks, janitors, lobby/gate security), one physician, and one nurse. Of course, the numbers varied by the size of the facility, small facilities not having a physician or nurse. Overall, administrative staff accounted for 20 per cent, doctors, 6 per cent, and nurses 7 per cent of total staffing in all facilities.

Tasks of front-line workers included bathing, feeding, washing the residents, and helping residents move and turn in their beds. The vast majority of direct care staff were female, the gender ratio being 3:1. Direct care workers were also likely to be migrant workers. Although the majority came from the same city or location, one-third of the care workers were from other cities or provinces. By age distribution, the majority of direct care workers were in their middle ages of 40–50 (44 per cent) and 50+ (22 per cent), and roughly one-quarter (26 per cent) were in their thirties.

Staff turnover rate was relatively high. In the year of the research, 15 per cent of front-line care staff left their post in the last 12 months, while 32 per cent of the employees were new hires in the past year.

Characteristics of residents

Based on the survey, the majority of the residents were between the ages of 70 and 89 (see Table 14.2 for detail). Roughly 25 per cent of residents were suffering from long-term physical or mental disability, and 11 per cent of residents were under the age of 60. Family members were reported to have no ability to provide care on a daily basis. The majority of residents were female (54 per cent). Over half were reported to need full or partial assistance in managing daily life.

The eldercare industry in China

Table 14.2 Characteristics of residents (*n* = 241, 914)

Variable name	N	%
Age of residents	N = 241,914	
Below 60	26,003	11
60–69	41,577	17
70–79	80,093	33
80–89	76,142	31
90+	18,099	7
Gender of residents	N = 237,876	
Male	109,370	46
Female	128,506	54
Health status	N = 240,254	
Can self-manage daily living	109,423	46
Need partial assistance	64,226	27
Need full assistance	66,605	28
Source of payment	N = 223, 602	
By oneself	142,725	64+
By relatives	71,362	32+
By government	9,515	4.2
Reasons for moving in	N = 237,875	
Children unable/unavailable	104,665	44
Facility is better than home	95,150	40
Don't want to bother children	38,060	16
Facility selection criteria	N = 237,875	
Good price	118,938	50
Good service	57,090	24
Good living condition	42,817	18
Close to home	19,030	8

Source: Created by authors from data in the survey report.

When asked about the major reasons for the relocation, residents appeared to be fully aware of the unavailability of their children, and were therefore looking into alternative options of care to avoid 'disturbing' their children. In selection criteria for a particular facility, residents ranked 'a good price' (50 per cent), followed by 'good services' (24 per cent), 'good living condition' (18 per cent), and 'close to home' (8 per cent).

Concluding discussion

Challenges facing eldercare in China

The demographic challenges that China is facing have created enormous needs for the care of the rapidly increasing numbers of older adults. The national survey shows a major growth of eldercare facilities after the mid-1990s, mainly in urban areas along the east and north-east regions of the country. The areas with rapid economic growth also show rapid growth in non-government eldercare facilities. Consequently, this increases the inequalities between rural and urban, and coastal and interior regions of the country.

Another challenge facing the eldercare industry in China is the impact of social policies. Evidently, the rapid growth of (non-profit) non-government eldercare facilities is directly related to the various tax benefits available for the construction and maintenance of eldercare (Feng et al., 2011; Zhan et al., 2008). Taking the land use of the facilities as an example, 21 per cent reported that they had the land 'designated by the government', 36 per cent rented the land, and 43 per cent reported 'mixed use'. Land or real estate is one of the most valued properties in China. The fact that some could have the privilege of using the land with low or no interest rate for mortgage suggests that the market of the eldercare industry was not built on an equal footing. The ones with better government support are bound to have quicker and better return.

Eldercare facilities require a large amount of initial investment in land, housing and equipment, such as beds and bedding. As reported by some facility owners and managers, it takes 9–10 years to make a profit. The fact that some facilities enjoyed free land or subsidized land use suggests that these facilities are far more likely to enjoy benefits or be able to balance budgets compared to those paying for mortgage as well as facility equipment. In the process of transition from all government-owned to non-government-owned eldercare facilities, the lack of transparency in funding and resources may create disparity between facilities and regions. Consequently, this disparity is translated into differing qualities of care.

The key difference between facilities, as shown in this chapter, is the funding source between the government and non-government facilities. Being a one-party system, the central government appears to possess the omnipotent power in policymaking, implementation, and distribution of resources. To what extent can the government balance decentralization and privatization while promoting the market force in the growth of the eldercare industry? Without a doubt, this balance is critically important, because it eventually translates into the quality of life for older adults in government- and non-government-run eldercare institutions.

The workforce challenges

Similar to the workforce of eldercare in other nations, such as the US, China is struggling in the quality of direct care workers. Shown in this study, one-third of the care workers were migrant workers, typically women in their forties or fifties. They are a very transient labour force, with a very high turnover rate, roughly one in three. With such a high turnover rate, the relationship between care workers and care recipients can be challenging. When care providers do not know care recipients' habits, needs, and personalities, the care may be ensured at the most basic level of assistance at best.

Another related issue is language communication. In China, there is a recognizable dialect difference in every 50–100 km distance. If migrant workers were raised in an area over 200 km away from the workplace, the communication between care recipients and care workers may pose challenges. Matching care providers with care recipients who are from similar geographic locations will always be a challenge in eldercare facilities in China.

The composition of nurses is another challenge. Based on this study, the majority of nurses were young females under the age of 30, among them nearly half in their twenties. This age distribution suggests a mismatch between the care providers and care recipients. Fresh graduates from college in contemporary China may not find working with and for older adults satisfying. Furthermore, the lack of career growth in this field may also pose a challenge for retaining the workforce of nurses and care workers. To meet the future needs of eldercare in either community-based care or eldercare facilities, the numbers of visiting or facility nurses will need to grow. Creating career paths accompanied by levels of training or certification, and salary compensation

The eldercare industry in China

for years of experience, may create incentives for care workers and nurses to stay in this field. Maintaining a high-quality workforce is going to be the most important issue for the quality of care, after the need for growth of facilities.

The culture of eldercare

Findings in this study reveal that 55 per cent of residents needed some or full assistance when they moved into an eldercare home. Medical and physical needs clearly are major reasons for the moves. Being aware of the increasing unavailability of adult children, many older adults have chosen to move to an eldercare facility to avoid 'disturbing' their children.

As more and more ageing adults have worked in the public labor force in urban China, more will receive a pension when they retire. With increased financial independence accompanied with increased unavailability of adult children, more elders are likely to make their own choice of moving into a facility. In this process, the traditional expectation for adult children's physical care is becoming internalized by the elderly generation to be a 'disturbance' instead of 'filial piety'. This change is likely to increase as more elderly people enter into retirement with a comfortable pension and comprehensive healthcare. With the high rate of having only one child, the baby boomers in China, those born between 1950 and 1975, are likely to further emphasize independence rather than 'filial piety' in the near future. This shift in interpretation of care behaviour, on the part of the care recipients, may further indicate an increasing demand for community-based neighbourhood eldercare services. When adult children are unavailable or unequipped to provide care for medically or physically dependent elderly parents, professional care services in a neighbourhood, such as adult day care, meals on wheels, and physician visits are increasingly likely to play an important role in the lives of elderly people in China.

Policy implication

Facing all these challenges in institutional care, it is vital for the Chinese government to develop a holistic eldercare system that includes multiple forms of eldercare services. A recent national policy – the Twelfth Five-Year Plan of China – reflects the need for combining and integrating familial, community, and institutional care. The policy specified the role of each form of eldercare: familial care is the 'base', community-based services serve as 'backup', and institutional care provides 'support' (Feng et al., 2012). According to this macro-social project, '90:7:3' or '90:6.4' were its projected designation for eldercare distribution: 90 per cent of care is projected to be provided at home, either 7 or 6 per cent is to be provided in the community, and 3 or 4 per cent is to be provided in eldercare institutions (Wu and Du, 2012, p. 245). The government funding and urban planning in each province and city are supposed to follow this macro-social project. If so, informal home-based care will continue to take the lion's share of eldercare. Yet Chinese families are reduced in size, fewer children are available, many elders, over 50 per cent in some cities, in the next 20 years may have only one child. While many elders may prefer to age at home being cared for by adult children, a large number of them will either choose 'not to disturb children's lives' or children will simply be unavailable for direct care. In these cases, familial care may need to be tied to formal community-based services so that seniors can age in a place where they are able to draw support from both formal and informal eldercare. Providing regular training for front-line care workers will be critical for the quality of care older adults receive. As the large army of Chinese baby boomers are retiring and entering the field of eldercare, institutional eldercare will necessarily need to become the engine of the eldercare service industry, driving up the quantity as well as the quality of eldercare services in China.

Note

1 This Research is funded by China's National Social Science Foundation Grant, entitled *The Impact of Social Economic Conditions on Elders' Health* 国家社科基金项目 "社会经济地位对老年期健康影响的动态整合研究"(14CRK008)阶段性成果. This chapter is largely based on the report written by the National Ageing Committee Career Development Department (11 June 2009), *The Report of Basic Findings Based on National Non-Government Elder Care Services Survey Research* 全国老龄工作委员会办公室事业发展部(2009-6-11) 全国民办养老服务机构基本状况调查报告.

References

Chen, S.X., Bond, M.H. and Tang, D.H., 2007. Decomposing filial piety into filial attitudes and filial enactments. *Asian Journal of Social Psychology*, 10, pp. 213–23. DOI: 10.1111/j.1467-839X.2007.00230.x.

Chen, X. and Silverstein, M., 2000. Intergenerational social support and the psychological well-being of older parents in China. *Research on Aging*, 22(1), pp. 43–65.

Dan, S., Jie, G.Z., Mao, Q., Zhen, G.Z., Jin, W.Y. and Feng, Z.J., 2013. Research regarding the development strategies of private-owned long-term care facilities in China: based on the status quo of private-owned long-term care facilities in Gu Lou district in Nan Jing. *Legal System and Society*, 9, pp. 63–6. 法律与社会. [In Chinese]

Du, C., 2006. *Research on community-based eldercare in China*. Dalian: Dalian Science and Engineering University. 杜翠欣。我国城市社区养老模式研究。大连：大连理工大学2006.5. [In Chinese]

Feng, Z.L., Zhan, H.J., Feng, X.T., Liu, C., Sun, M. and Mor, V., 2011. An industry in the making: the emergence of institutional elder care in urban China. *Journal of the American Geriatric Society*, 59, pp. 738–44. DOI: 10.1111/j.1532-5415.2011.03330.x.

Feng, Z.L., Liu, C., Guan, X.P. and Mor, V., 2012. China's rapidly aging population creates policy challenges in shaping a viable long-term care system. *Health Affairs*, 31(12), pp. 2764–73. DOI: 10.1377/hlthaff.2012.0535.

Lee, W.K. and Hong-kin, K., 2005. Differences in expectations and patterns of informal support for older persons in Hong Kong: modification to filial piety. *Ageing International*, 30(2), pp. 188–206. DOI: 10.1007/s12126-005-1011-1.

Luo, B.Z. and Zhan, H.Y., 2012. Filial piety and functional support: understanding intergenerational solidarity among families with migrated children in rural China. *Ageing International*, 37, pp. 69–92. DOI: 10.1007/s12126-011-9132-1.

Mao, W.Y. and Chi, I., 2011. Filial piety of children as perceived by aging parents in China. *International Journal of Social Welfare*, 20, pp. S99–S108. DOI: 10.1111/j.1468-2397.2011.00826.x.

Mu, G.Z., 2012. Dilemma and strategies of the development of long-term care services in China. *Journal of Huazhong Normal University*, 51(2), pp. 31–8. 华中师范大学学刊. [In Chinese]

National Ageing Committee Career Development Department, 2009. *The report of basic findings based on national non-government elder care services survey research*. 11 June. 全国老龄工作委员会办公室事业发展部(2009-6-11) 全国民办养老服务机构基本状况调查报告. [In Chinese]

National Bureau of Statistics of China, 2012. *2010 China's national census material*. Beijing: National Bureau of Statistics of China Publishing Company. Available at: www.chinayearbook.com/yearbook/item/1/158427.html [accessed 18.07.2017].

National Bureau of Statistics of China, 2015. *China statistical yearbook 2015*. Beijing: China Statistics Press. Available at: www.stats.gov.cn/tjsj/ndsj/2015/indexeh.htm [accessed 18.07.2017].

National Center for Assisted Living, 2011. Findings of the NCAL 2010 assisted living staff, vacancy, retention, and turn over survey: a NCAL study with collaboration from Leading Age, American Seniors Housing Association, and Assisted Living Federation of America. Available at: www.ahcancal.org/ncal/resources/documents/2010%20vrt%20report-final.pdf [accessed 07.04.2016].

Peng, X.Z., 2011. China's demographic history and future challenges. *Science*, 333(6042), pp. 581–7. DOI: 10.1126/science.1209396.

SDD (Social Development Division of United Nations Economic and Social Commission of Asia and Pacific – Working Papers Series), 2015. *Long-term care for older persons in China*. Available at: https://jrgrace.files.wordpress.com/2015/12/long-term-care-for-older-persons-in-china.pdf [accessed 18.07.2017].

Shen, Y.Y. and Yeatts, D.E., 2013. Social support and life satisfaction among older adults in China: family-based support versus community-based support. *International Journal of Aging and Human Development*, 77(3), pp. 189–209. DOI: http://dx.doi.org/10.2190/AG.77.3.b.

Silverstein, M., Cong, Z. and Li, S., 2006. Intergenerational transfers and living arrangements of older people in rural China: consequences for psychological well-being. *The Journals of Gerontology*, Series B, 61(5), pp. S256–S66. DOI: 10.1093/geronb/61.5.S256.

Sung, K.-T., 1995. Measures and dimensions of filial piety in Korea. *The Gerontologist*, 35, pp. 240–7. DOI: https://doi-org.pva.uib.no/10.1093/geront/35.2.240.

Tang, C.S., Wu. A.M.S., Yeung, D. and Yan, E., 2009. Attitudes and intention toward old age home placement: a study of young adult, middle-aged, and older Chinese. *Ageing International*, 34, pp. 237–51. DOI: 10.1007/s12126-009-9047-2.

UN, 2011. *World population prospects: the 2010 revision. Economic and social affairs.* Available at: www.un.org/en/development/desa/population/publications/pdf/trends/WPP2010/WPP2010_Volume-I_Comprehensive-Tables.pdf [accessed 18.07.2017].

UN, 2013. *World population ageing 2013. Economic and social affairs.* Available at: www.un.org/en/development/desa/population/publications/pdf/ageing/WorldPopulationAgeingReport2013.pdf [accessed 17.07.2017].

Wu, C.P. and Du, P., 2012. *Aging society and harmonious society.* Beijing: China Population Publishing House. 邬沧萍和杜鹏 主编：【老龄社会与和谐社会】中国人口出版社。. [In Chinese]

Ye, J.J., 2012. Research of the current development of private-owned long-term care facilities: using Cheng du private-owned facilities as examples. *Modern Economy Information*, 17, 217. 当代经济信息. [In Chinese]

Zhan, H.J., 2004. Socialization or social structure: investigating predictors of attitudes toward filial responsibility among Chinese urban youth from one-and-multiple-child families. *The International Journal of Aging and Human Development*, 59(2), pp. 105–24.

Zhan, H.J., 2013. Population aging and long-term care in China. *Generations*, 37(1), pp. 53–8.

Zhan, H.J., Liu, G., Guan, X. and Bai, H.G., 2006. Recent developments in institutional elder care in China: changing concepts and attitudes. *The Journal of Aging and Social Policy*, 18(2), pp. 85–108. DOI: 10.1300/J031v18n02_06.

Zhan, H.J., Feng, X. and Luo, B., 2008. Placing elderly parents in institutions in urban China: a reinterpretation of filial piety. *Research on Aging*, 30(5), pp. 543–71. DOI: 10.1177/0164027508319471.

Zhang, H., 2007. Who will care for our parents? Changing boundaries of family and public roles in providing care for the aged in urban China. *Care Management Journals*, 8(1), pp. 39–46. DOI: 10.1891/152109807780494087.

Zhang, N.J., Guo, M. and Zheng, X.Y., 2012. China: awakening giant developing solutions to population aging. *The Gerontologist*, 52(5), pp. 589–96. DOI: https://doi-org.pva.uib.no/10.1093/geront/gns105.

Zhang, Y.H. and Min, J., 2015. Long-term care services, problems and public policies in China. *Contemporary Economic Management*, 37(1), pp. 51–6. 当代经济管理杂志. [In Chinese]

Zhang, Y.T. and Goza, F.W., 2006. Who will care for the elderly in China? A review of the problems caused by China's one-child policy and their potential solutions. *Journal of Aging Studies*, 20, pp. 151–64. DOI: https://doi.org/10.1016/j.jaging.2005.07.002.

15

Challenges of care work under the new long-term care insurance for elderly people in South Korea

Yongho Chon

Introduction

To cope with the new social risks associated with the increase in numbers of the ageing population in need of long-term care (LTC), the South Korean government introduced a new long-term care insurance (LTCI) in 2008. To expand the long-term care service providers and care workers in a short period, various policies of marketization of care have been actively implemented. While the concept of marketization of care can be defined in different ways, this chapter refers to it as 'the active use of private sector forces in the LTC market, the promotion of market principles in the provision of LTC and, in particular, competition among service providers and choice rights for service users' (Brennan et al., 2012, p. 379). In addition, 'care workers' refers to those who provide a number of direct social care services to elderly people with LTC needs, such as body assistance and domestic chores. The care worker is not allowed to provide any medical service under the Korean LTCI.

The aim of the chapter is to examine the way in which the increase in numbers of care workers has been produced and the main outcomes with respect to care workers under the new LTCI in Korea. By examining these issues, lessons from the Korean LTCI experience in the process of developing a large care workforce are expected to emerge. It is argued in this chapter that although there has been a rapid increase in the number of service providers and care workers in a short period through the measures for the marketization of LTC, a number of new challenges, such as high turnover of care workers and poor quality of services, have emerged.

In particular, this chapter is based on the author's research on the marketization of care, service delivery systems, and the overall evaluation of the Korean LTCI (Chon, 2012, 2013a, 2013b, 2014, 2015), which were conducted through literature review or qualitative research methods. Other sources for the chapter are existing literature on care workers and LTCI in Korea (particularly Nam et al., 2013; Seo et al., 2012).

This chapter consists of three main parts. The first part presents the modernization of Korean society and the new social risks associated with this, and the second part examines the old and new LTC systems. The last part of the chapter presents the achievements and challenges in developing a new care workforce able to meet the demands of the LTCI system.

The modernization of Korean society and new social risks

Historically, caring work has been perceived as an essential part of women's daily work in the family in South Korea. Caring for elderly parents, disabled people and children was the natural responsibility of women without expectation of payment, and active caring efforts were regarded as a virtue of women (Peng, 2012).

Under the significant influence of Confucianism, filial piety was an important moral duty of adult children, and elderly people were respected in the family and society in Korea (Chon, 2013a, 2013b, 2014). Taking care of frail elderly relatives was one of the unquestionable roles and duties of women in the family. The first daughter-in-law was responsible for looking after the frail elderly relatives living in the same household. This familialism, mainly by women, was possible due to the high male employment rate and the rapid economic growth in Korea until the 1990s (Peng, 2012). Given the caring role of women in the family, the Korean welfare state was very passive in developing social care services for elderly and disabled people.

However, owing to the sudden outbreak of the financial crisis (so-called International Monetary Fund crisis, or Asian financial crisis) in 1997, many large and small businesses went bankrupt, resulting in a huge increase in the number of the jobless and working poor. To cope with the challenges emerging from the financial crisis, the Kim Dae-Jung government implemented both a pro-welfare policy to develop welfare systems, such as the reforms of pension and national health insurance, and a pro-market policy to emphasize the neo-liberal approach, such as the flexibility of labour markets (Chon, 2014). Luckily, Korea was able to successfully overcome the financial difficulties in a short period through the people's sacrifice and government's efforts. Furthermore, the welfare systems were significantly developed, although they were not fully satisfactory.

Despite this, a number of new social risks have emerged since the early 2000s in Korea. Most of all, the low fertility rate and the rapid increase in the ageing population were regarded as serious social problems. Although the proportion of older people was not so high (10 per cent in 2008) compared with other developed countries (Population Reference Bureau, 2008, p. 13), the speed with which the population aged became a problem (Chon, 2012). It has been predicted that Korea will undergo a rapid transition from an ageing society (7 per cent of older people in the population in 2000) to an aged society (14 per cent in 2018) in only 19 years, which is much faster than in other developed countries (Statistics Korea, 2006, Table 3).

In addition, significant changes have been noted in the structure and function of the family (Kim, 2014; Peng, 2012). The dual-earner model instead of the male-breadwinner model became prevalent in many urban areas, as many women worked in the labour market to make their living. Moreover, the deep-rooted culture of filial piety under Confucianism has been weakened (Peng, 2012), and many people believe that the role of caring for elderly people should be carried out by the state rather than by their family members (Kim, 2014). For instance, while the proportion of people believing that elderly parents should be supported by their family members decreased from 89.9 per cent in 1998 to 33.2 per cent in 2012, the proportion of people believing that the society should take care of elderly parents increased from 2.0 per cent to 52.9 per cent during the same period (Kim, 2014, p. 2). Therefore, it was becoming increasingly difficult to expect adult children, especially from some middle- and low-income groups, to care for their elderly relatives (Sunwoo, 2003, p. 15).

The Korean government understood the seriousness of such new social risks and realized that the existing Korean welfare state was not able to meet the new challenges (Chon, 2013a, 2014; Kim and Choi, 2013). In particular, it was found that the LTC system for elderly people was too inadequate to meet their basic long-term care needs in the early 2000s (Sunwoo, 2004). The LTC services were limited only to poor elderly people as a type of social assistance, and the LTC infrastructure was very underdeveloped.

Therefore, in the 2000s, the Korean government restructured the welfare state itself by drastically expanding social care services for elderly people, children, and disabled people (Chon, 2014; Kim and Choi, 2013). In particular, it is notable that the wider coverage of LTC services for elderly people came about via the introduction of the new long-term care insurance (hereafter LTCI) in July 2008. The introduction of the LTCI system entirely changed the existing LTC infrastructure in terms of service providers and care workers (Chon, 2013a).

The inadequate old LTC system

To understand the old LTC system, which was used prior to the introduction of the new LTCI system, we need to examine it in detail. The LTC system was inadequate in terms of having no separate system for LTC services, a number of social and medical LTC services being provided in a fragmented way; until the middle of the 2000s, the former was under the Older Persons Welfare Act and the latter the National Health Insurance Act (Sunwoo, 2004; Seok, 2002).

The old social LTC services were provided mainly by the not-for-profit sector (Sunwoo, 2003). Since the South Korean government did not have experience of developing a public-based LTC service system and the for-profit sector was not allowed to provide the LTC services, the not-for-profit welfare organizations were in charge of providing the LTC service through the government's subsidy.

Three main types of LTC services were provided by not-for-profit organizations. First, under the Older Persons Welfare Act, combined with the social assistance system, nursing homes were allocated primarily to the poorest and secondary poor people, as decided by the local government's officers based on the monthly income of the household. Most of the nursing homes served the poorest elderly people without any payments, while a small number of nursing homes partially supported by the government served the secondary poor elderly people who paid half of the total costs. Owing to the underdevelopment of LTC service providers, there were only a small number of institutional and domiciliary service providers. In 2002, there were 171 nursing homes (general and special nursing homes), out of which 161 were used for poor elderly people (Sunwoo, 2004, p. 56).

Second, a number of domiciliary social care services were provided to the poorest elderly. In 2002, 368 domiciliary service providers were recorded, comprising 165 home visiting services (*Gajeong-bongsawon service*), 155 day-care services, and 48 short-stay services (Sunwoo, 2004, p. 56).

Third, under the National Health Insurance system, medical services were provided to elderly people with chronic diseases or those at the last stage of life. However, in 2002, there were 26 specialized hospitals for older patients and 28 LTC hospitals, with 6,991 beds in total (Sunwoo, 2004, p. 56). These hospitals were available for older people regardless of their incomes, but they were too limited to accommodate the older people in need of LTC.

While only poor elderly people obtained financial support for living in the nursing homes and receiving domiciliary services, the low- and middle-class elderly people did not receive any public support (Sunwoo, 2004). In general, the number of service providers was too small to meet the needs of elderly people. Therefore, only a small proportion of elderly people were able to use the services. This often led to 'social admission' to the hospitals, which became one of the main sources of financial crisis of the existing National Health Insurance (Kwon, 2007). Moreover, although the low- and middle-class elderly people used the nursing homes services, they had to pay expensive fees for these services, between $700 and $2,500 each month (US$1 was equivalent to around 1,000 Korean won in 2008) (Sunwoo, 2003). This was a huge burden for elderly people and their family members.

Due to the significant underdevelopment of the LTC infrastructure and small number of LTC service users, the number of care workers was also very limited. In addition, no public-based training and certification system for care workers existed. Since only 40 hours of training at private providers was required to become a care worker, it was easy to become a personal care worker. Moreover, the care workers working at the home visiting service (*Gajeong-bongsawon-pagyeon service*) centres were voluntary care workers who were required to take only 20 hours of training to work there without any payments (Chon, 2013a; Kim, 2008). Some people volunteered to look after and support frail elderly people since some older people in need of care did not receive care services from their family members. However, owing to the absence of proper training and support systems for care workers, the quality of service was questionable and the voluntary care workers showed high turnover, which negatively affected the quality of services in terms of continuity of care (Chon, 2014; Kim, 2008). Overall, the existing volume of LTC services, service providers, and care workers were too inadequate to meet the basic LTC needs of elderly people in need of the services, and this became one of the main reasons for the introduction of a separate LTCI system in Korea (Chon, 2014).

The implementation of the new LTCI system

The new LTCI system is compulsory for all adults registered with the National Health Insurance (NHI). The NHI is a compulsory social insurance and covers all the Korean people with medical care benefits, but some people, such as those without working ability or with rare disorders, receive medical care benefits as a type of public assistance. Detailed information on the NHI can be obtained at the National Health Insurance Corporation (NHIC, 2017a). The NHI and LTCI have separate systems. The main scheme of the LTCI is presented in Table 15.1 (see the detailed scheme of the new LTCI in NHIC, 2016, 2017b, 2017c).

To implement the new LTCI system for elderly people, the government had to establish a new LTC infrastructure of service providers and care workforce. The government decided to adopt a market-friendly approach for the provision of LTC (Chon, 2013a, 2014). It endeavoured to facilitate this in particular by establishing low entry barriers to the LTC market, that is, small-size office and small number of care workers for the home care services. It endeavoured to attract for-profit organizations to the provision of LTC services in particular by frequently holding briefing sessions about the new LTCI in many local cities, and emphasized the profitability of businesses related to care services (Chon, 2013a, 2014). The government also looked for individuals seeking opportunities to set up new businesses as well as existing organizations. In addition, the ways in which payments are provided to the service providers changed due to the introduction of the LTCI. Prior to its introduction, the service providers for the nursing home and domiciliary services received regularly fixed amounts of subsidies from the central and local authorities, and the number of older people they had to deal with were broadly recommended by the government. However, since the introduction of LTCI, the payments to service providers depend entirely on the number of LTCI beneficiaries they are in charge of and the service time they actually devote to elderly people under the LTCI (Chon, 2013a).

The rapid increase in the number of new care workers was directly related to the government's market-friendly approach. Instead of developing a public-based training system, it assisted the private sector with the establishment of new training organizations for care workers with low entry legal requirements (Chon, 2013a). The government also announced the introduction of a compulsory certification system for care workers (Kim, 2008). The certification

Table 15.1 The main scheme of LTCI for Korea

Aim of LTCI	To improve the quality of life for older people who are not able to manage their daily lives because of old age or chronic diseases, and to reduce the care burden placed on family members by providing social care services
Financing	1 Contributions of LTCI: compulsory for all adults registered under the NHIC 2 Central and local taxes 3 Service users' co-payments: 15 per cent (domiciliary services) or 20 per cent (institutional) of their costs
Kinds of services	Domiciliary services: home visiting, visiting bathing, visiting nurse, short-stay respite care, welfare equipment (e.g. walking stick, bath chair) Institutional services: small nursing home (less than 10 older people), nursing home (more than nine older people)
Roles of insurer	National health insurance corporation (central and local branches): setting and levying contributions, managing finances, assessing and issuing grades, overseeing services, evaluating service providers
Population coverage	Unconditional for those aged 65+ Conditional for adults aged under 65 with age-related diseases (the disabled are registered with the NHI but excluded from the LTCI services, since there is a separate social support service for them)
LTCI beneficiaries	7.07 per cent of older people aged 65 or over (475,382) in 2015
Assessment	Standard assessment of a 52-item questionnaire (body function: 12 items, cognitive function: 7 items, behavior change: 14 items, nursing treatment: 9 items, rehabilitation: 10 items)
Eligibility levels and scores	Eligible benefits grades 1 (critical, 95 or over), 2 (substantial, 94–75), 3 (moderate, 74–60), 4 (low, 59–51), or 5 (lower and the elderly with dementia, 50–45)

Source: NHIC (2016, 2017b, 2017c).

policy aims to improve the level of functional abilities and knowledge of care workers (Han, 2011). Accordingly, only certified care workers who have taken theory and practice training and field training are able to work at the LTC facilities, although a grace period was given to some care workers at the early stage of LTCI implementation. A grade 1 certificate, which is the highest grade, is awarded to any person completing only 240 hours of training comprising 80 hours of theoretical study, 80 hours of learning practical skills, and 80 hours of field practice. There is no prerequisite in terms of age limit, minimum education and care experiences (Chon, 2013a). However, care workers have been required to complete a theoretical examination to obtain the certificate since 2010 due to the criticism of their illiteracy and the limited ability of some certified care workers. Despite this, it has been pointed out that the requirements to acquire the certificate are very low and the contents of the training are poor compared with those of other developed countries, such as Japan, where care workers must take more extensive courses as well as more training hours (1,500 hours of training) (Han, 2011; Kim, 2008).

The achievements and challenges of the developments related to the new care workforce

Since the introduction of the new LTCI, a number of notable developments and challenges with respect to care workers have emerged in the Korean context. Overall, owing to the policies for the marketization of LTC, the numbers of service providers and care workers rapidly increased in a short period. Many women were eager to become certified care workers and work in the LTCI field. However, it has been reported that it is now getting more difficult to acquire and retain qualified care workers in the field (Nam et al., 2013; Seo et al., 2012). The age of care workers is getting older, on average, since young women are reluctant to work as care workers in the LTC sector. They believe that the payments and welfare benefits for care workers are poor given the demanding working conditions, and they are able to find alternative jobs in the labour market. As these changes suggest, the LTC sector has experienced a drastic boom and burst of care workers during the last eight years.

Increased numbers of and better-trained care workers under LTCI

Owing to the policies for the marketization of LTC, the numbers of service providers and care workers rapidly increased.

First, the actual number of care workers who work at the LTCI service providers has increased significantly from 113,756 in 2008 to 294,788 in 2015 (NHIC, 2016, p. 592). Given the inadequate infrastructure in the past, this reflects a notable development in the Korean context (Chon, 2014). This development was possible mainly because of the rapid increase in the number of certified care workers (those who have ever obtained certificates reached 1,030,000 in 2011) and the number of the LTCI beneficiaries increased from 149,656 in 2008 to 475,382 in 2015 (NHIC, 2016, p. xlvi). Many middle-aged women in particular were eager to become certified care workers and expected to get decent jobs (Hwang and Lee, 2012). Many of them were able to obtain the certificate relatively easily due to the easy process and short training period.

Second, the introduction of the new certification and training systems for care workers became an actual foundation for the development of the abilities and practice skills of care workers under the LTCI. The government provides some guidance in regard to training of care workers, such as contents and qualifications of instructors (Han, 2011). Although the systems have a number of limitations, care workers are trained more systematically now compared to previously in the Korean context. Moreover, the training and management of care workers was put on the social agenda and became a policy area for the government after the quality of services by care workers emerged as a social issue.

Third, the increase in the number of care workers is related to the creation of many new care work jobs. Given the early retirement age of around 50 years of age for men due to the unstable labour markets in Korea, many middle-aged women in particular have the opportunity to make their living and compensate for the declining financial contributions of their husbands. As a number of studies suggest, since the financial situations of many care workers was not good (Nam et al., 2013; Han, 2011), such job opportunities provided means to cope with their difficulties and increased work opportunities for women. In addition, although the majority of people have a low perception of care work, the development of formal LTC service and better training for care workers started to contribute to the thought that care work can be paid and care work for elderly people in need of long-term care can be a job. Moreover, a small proportion of people started to recognize the importance of care work, which previously was simply regarded as a natural role for women in the family, and to respect care work (Nam et al., 2013).

Challenges of care work

First, it is believed that the care worker's job is not a 'decent job'. A number of studies (Lee et al., 2015; Nam et al., 2013; Seo et al., 2012) have shown that although doing housework and providing care services is very demanding, care workers receive low wages in Korea. Workers employed by the home visiting service providers earned merely $560 per month, while those at the nursing home service providers earned $1,300 in Korea in 2012 (Seo et al., 2012, p. 112). Specifically, in Seoul, the monthly payment of nursing home care workers was only $1,359, although they worked 206 hours per month on average, which was longer than full-time workers in general (160 hours, 8 hours per 20 working days) (Nam et al., 2013, p. 63). The hourly payment for the nursing home care worker was $6.9 per hour on average, and this amount is lower compared to other related working areas, such as medical assistant ($9.4) or maid and babysitter ($8.9) (Nam et al., 2013). It is notable that for-profit LTC service providers paid a lower hourly wage to care workers ($6.3) compared to not-for-profit providers ($7.2). Since the competition among service providers to increase the number of cases they are in charge of is extremely strong in many areas, care workers' wages remain low (Chon, 2014). Moreover, since care workers cannot climb up the career ladder and progress in their careers, owing to the absence of a career ladder system in the LTCI system, no differences exist in wages between new and experienced care workers. Although in 2013, to cope with this issue, the government started to provide additional payment (maximum $100 per month) for care workers working longer than 160 hours at nursing homes, their wages are still low. As some studies (Lee et al., 2015; Nam et al., 2013; Seo et al., 2012; Han, 2011) indicated, increase of payment is one of the most effective ways to retain care workers in the LTC market. This is because the financial situation of many care workers is not good, motivating them to work longer hours. As Nam et al. (2013) showed, about half of care workers in Seoul are primary breadwinners in the family.

Second, the working conditions and employment status of care workers are also problematic. According to Seo et al.'s (2012, p. 113) study, 49.2 per cent of care workers in the nursing homes (over nine older people) work a double shift, and 44.1 per cent of care workers in small group homes (less than 10 older people) work every other day. These long working hours often violate the Labour Standard Act and become one of the main sources of the high intensity of caring labour (Nam et al., 2013). In addition, the employment status of home care workers is unstable. Over 81 per cent of care workers providing home visiting services worked temporarily in Seoul in 2012 (Nam et al., 2013, p. 57), and home visiting care workers have difficulties in securing fixed working hours (Chon, 2013a, 2014; Nam et al., 2013). The establishment of a great number of home visiting service providers led to severe competition among them, and thus to frequent bankruptcies of service providers. This unstable situation of service providers in the market is one of the main reasons for the difficulties associated with securing a fixed and sufficient number of working hours by the care workers. Moreover, some older people or their family members tend to change their care workers when they feel that their care workers or service providers are not satisfactory in terms of quality of services.

Third, the high turnover and shortage of care workers becomes a significant issue requiring urgent solutions in Korea. Owing to the low wages and demanding working conditions of care workers, around half of them change their working places frequently, and this turnover rate of care workers in Korea is over twice as high as that in countries such as Australia and Japan (Muir, 2016; Korea Employment Information Service, 2012; Seo et al., 2012). There is evidence that more than two-thirds (67.4 per cent) of LTCI service providers experienced difficulties recruiting new care workers, and particularly nursing home service providers (75.6 per cent), rather than domiciliary service providers, were more likely to experience such difficulties (Korea Employment Information Service, 2012, p. 26). Therefore, the difficulties of retaining and recruiting new care workers have become a serious concern for service providers. Seo et al. (2012, p. 230) estimated that in 2012 and 2015, there would be shortages of about 20,000 care workers and 32,000 care workers in the LTC fields, respectively.

Challenges of care work in South Korea

Finally, many researchers have criticized the quality of care services. The low payments and demanding working conditions for care workers negatively affect the quality of services (Lee et al., 2015; Chon, 2013a, 2014; Seo et al., 2012). Moreover, the low social perception of care workers is prevalent and it is also likely to lead to low morale and turnover of care workers. Despite some changes in views of care workers and the understanding of the importance of continuous relationships between care workers and elderly clients in terms of the quality of service, such a situation of care workers seems likely to negatively affect the quality of services (Chon, 2015). In addition, there is a need for the improvement of the inadequate training system (Seo et al., 2012; Han, 2011). The short training hours and poor contents required to acquire the certificate are problematic. It has been argued that the 80 hours of field practice is too short to provide a quality service for elderly people, and that the contents of training should be emphasized in terms of practice training rather than theory (Han, 2011).

Proper training for providing services for elderly people with dementia is particularly needed. Although care workers have to deal with the progressively challenging behaviour of elderly people with dementia, due to the inadequate training system they have little understanding and knowledge of these clients and have difficulties looking after them.

Conclusions

To cope with the ageing population and the LTC needs of elderly people, the South Korean government introduced a new LTCI system. However, to implement the new LTCI at a national level, the Korean government actively used measures for the marketization of LTC. To rapidly develop the number of service providers and care workers, a number of market-friendly and deregulatory policies to facilitate the participation of for-profit service providers were implemented, such as lowering entrance barriers in the LTC markets (Chon, 2013a). In particular, the government facilitated the establishment of new training organizations in the private sector rather than developing public-based organizations. Additionally, although a certification policy for care workers was introduced, acquiring the certificate is relatively easy, requiring only 240 hours of training and taking examinations.

However, because of these government measures, a number of achievements have been brought out in the Korean context. There has been a rapid increase of the number of service providers and care workers, providing an actual foundation for meeting the basic LTC needs of older clients. The new training system also becomes the foundation for improving the abilities and skills of new care workers in terms of provision of services. In addition, many middle-aged women have been able to work as care workers in the field, providing them with the opportunity to cope with their financial issues.

Despite this, a number of serious challenges have emerged. Most of all, the payments and working conditions of care workers are poor, leading to high turnover of care workers and poor quality of services. Although other developed countries face similar problems, the situation of care workers in Korea appears to be more problematic. For example, there is turnover of around half of the care workers in Seoul (Korea Employment Information Service, 2012). To cope with the challenges of care workers, the Korean government and local authorities have implemented a number of policies for care workers, such as the provision of additional payments. However, such policies have not been effective in coping with the issues. Therefore, the research presented in this chapter suggests that more active policies to tackle the problematic situations of care workers should be implemented, such as higher payment and opportunities for career advancement for care workers in the Korean context. These measures would make a contribution to increased recognition for paid care work in society.

References

Brennan, D., Cass, B., Himmelweit, S. and Szebehely, M., 2012. The marketisation of care: rationales and consequences in Nordic and liberal care regimes. *Journal of European Social Policy*, 22(4), pp. 377–91. DOI: http://dx.doi.org/10.1177%2F0958928712449772.

Chon, Y., 2012. Long-term care reform in Korea: lessons from the introduction of Asia's second long-term care insurance system. *Asia Pacific Journal of Social Work and Development*, 22(4), pp. 219–27. DOI: http://dx.doi.org/10.1080/02185385.2012.726422.

Chon, Y., 2013a. A qualitative exploratory study on the service delivery system for the new long-term care insurance system in Korea. *Journal of Social Service Research*, 39(2), pp. 188–203. DOI: http://dx.doi.org /10.1080/01488376.2012.744708.

Chon, Y., 2013b. The development of Korea's new long-term care service infrastructure and its results: focusing on the market-friendly policy used for expansion of the numbers of service providers and personal care workers. *Journal of Gerontological Social Work*, 56(3), pp. 255–75. DOI: http://dx.doi.org /10.1080/01634372.2013.763885.

Chon, Y., 2014. The expansion of the Korean welfare state and its results: focusing on long-term care insurance for the elderly. *Social Policy and Administration*, 48(6), pp. 704–20. DOI: 10.1111/spol.12092.

Chon, Y., 2015. An exploratory qualitative study on relationships between older people and home care workers in South Korea: the view from family carers and service providers. *Ageing and Society*, 35(3), pp. 629–52. DOI: https://doi.org/10.1017/S0144686X13000950.

Han, J., 2011. A research on the rise of care workers' professionalism. *Women's Studies*, 21(2), pp. 197–235. [In Korean]

Hwang, D.S. and Lee, B.-H., 2012. Low wages and policy options in the Republic of Korea: are policies working? *International Labour Review*, 151(3), pp. 243–59. DOI: 10.1111/j.1564-913X.2012.00147.x.

Kim, J.H., 2008. Proposals for the improvement of service quality of long-term care insurance in Korea: focusing on the improvement of personal care workers in terms of the development of the workforce and professionalism. *Journal of Far East Social Welfare*, 4, pp. 49–83 Available at: http://kiss.kstudy.com/journal/thesis_name.asp?tname=kiss2002&key=2744070 [accessed 06.07.2017]. [In Korean]

Kim, J.W. and Choi, Y.J., 2013. Farewell to old legacies? The introduction of long-term care insurance in South Korea. *Ageing and Society*, 33(5), pp. 871–87. DOI: https://doi.org/10.1017/S0144686X12000335.

Kim, Y., 2014. The aspects of the change of family and its policy implications. *Health and Welfare Issue and Focus*, 258, pp. 1–8 Available at: www.kihasa.re.kr/web/publication/periodical/issue_view.do?pageIn dex=2&keyField=myear&searchStat=2014&menuId=50&key=&tid=38&bid=21&searchForm=Y&ai d=349&ano=604 [accessed 06.07.2017]. [In Korean]

Korea Employment Information Service, 2012. *The evaluation on the employment effect in the long-term care insurance for older people*. Gwacheon: Ministry of Employment and Labour. Available at: www.keis. or.kr/user/extra/main/2102/publication/publicationList/jsp/LayOutPage.do?categoryIdx=131&publ dx=1545&onlyList=N [accessed 27.06.2017]. [In Korean]

Kwon, S., 2007. The fiscal crisis of National Health Insurance in the Republic of Korea: in search of a new paradigm. *Social Policy and Administration*, 41(2), pp. 162–78. DOI: 10.1111/j.1467-9515.2007.00545.x.

Lee, J., Lee, H., Han, E., Jang, S. and Kwon, J., 2015. Understanding the perception gap between management and long-term care workers in nursing homes: the strategies for better working conditions. *Korea Social Policy Review*, 22(2), pp. 97–133. [In Korean]

Muir T., 2016. Attracting and retaining workforce in the long-term care sector: an international overview of long-term care workforce challenges. *Paper presented at the International Long-Term Care Policy Network*, 6 September. London School of Economics. *Slides* available at: www.ilpnetwork.org/wp-content/media/2016/10/Muir-ILPN-conference-06-Sep-LTC-workforce.pdf; video available at: www.youtube.com/watch?v=aJrm_cNytqE&feature=youtu.be [accessed 25.05.2017].

Nam, W., Choi, K., Yoon, J., Ryu, I., Chang, B., Lim, J., et al. 2013. *Working conditions and improvement plan for care helpers in Seoul*. Seoul: The Seoul Institute. Available at: www.si.re.kr/node/48796 [accessed 06.07.2017].

NHIC (National Health Insurance Corporation), 2016. *Long-term care insurance statistical yearbook in 2015*. Available at: www.nhis.or.kr/bbs7/boards/B0160/19799?boardKey=37&sort=sequence&order=desc &rows=10&messageCategoryKey=&pageNumber=1&viewType=generic&targetType=12&targetKe y=37&status=&period=&startdt=&enddt=&queryField=&query= [accessed 06.07.2017]. [In Korean]

NHIC (National Health Insurance Corporation), 2017a. *National Health Insurance service program*. Available at: www.nhis.or.kr/static/html/wbd/g/a/wbdga0401.html [accessed 27.06.2017].

NHIC (National Health Insurance Corporation), 2017b. *Long-term care insurance*. Available at: www.nhic.or.kr/static/html/wbd/g/a/wbdga0501.html [accessed 25.05.2017].

NHIC (National Health Insurance Corporation), 2017c. *Long-term care insurance coverage process*. Available at: http://longtermcare.or.kr/npbs/e/e/100/htmlView?pgmId=npee201m05s&desc=CoverageProcess [accessed 13.06.2017].

Peng, I., 2012. Social and political economy of care in Japan and South Korea. *International Journal of Sociology and Social Policy*, 32(11/12), pp. 636–49. DOI: https://doi.org/10.1108/01443331211280683.

Population Reference Bureau, 2008. *2008 world population data sheet*. Available at: www.prb.org/pdf08/08WPDS_Eng.pdf [accessed 06.04.2017].

Seo, D., Kim, W., Moon, S., Lee, Y. and Lim, J., 2012. *Medium- and long-term prediction of supply and demand of care workers and improvements for it*. Seoul: National Health Insurance Corporation. [In Korean]

Seok, J., 2002. On strengthening the facilities and human resources for the long-term frail elderly. *Health and Welfare Forum*, 4, pp. 48–68 Available at: www.kihasa.re.kr/web/publication/periodical/view.do?menuId=48&tid=38&bid=19&searchForm=Y&keyField=myear&searchStat=2002&key=&aid=18&ano=3 [accessed 06.07.2017]. [In Korean]

Statistics Korea, 2006. *Highlights of population projections, table 3*. Available at: http://kostat.go.kr/portal/eng/pressReleases/8/8/index.board?bmode=read&aSeq=273114&pageNo=&rowNum=10&amSeq=&sTarget=&sTxt= [accessed 25.05.2017].

Sunwoo, D., 2003. *The tasks and direction of development of long-term care insurance for the elderly*. Paper presented at the Korean Academy of Health Policy and Management Spring Conference, 30 May. 2003. [In Korean]

Sunwoo, D., 2004. Long-term care policy for functionally dependent older people in the Republic of Korea. *International Social Security Review*, 57(2), pp. 47–62. DOI: 10.1111/j.1468-246X.2004.00187.x.

16

Migrant live-in care workers in Taiwan

Multiple roles, cultural functions, and the new division of care labour

Li-Fang Liang

Introduction

Most elderly people in Taiwan receive care in their homes, either from unpaid family labour (mostly daughters-in-law; Wu, 2005) or paid care workers. The increase in women's participation in the labour market has created a rising demand for care labourers. About 13 per cent of Taiwanese families that include an elderly person aged 65 years old and above in need of long-term care hire migrant live-in care workers (Ministry of Health and Welfare, 2014, p. 239). Immigrants who offer this service, largely from Southeast Asian countries such as the Philippines, Vietnam, and Indonesia, have responded to this need since 1992, when Taiwan began to permit their temporary immigration. They have lower salaries than local care workers and live-in with their employers, making them far more valuable to families with limited budgets and elastic, round-the-clock needs. Taiwan passed the Long-Term Care Service Act in 2015, which stipulates the definition, framework, and care model of long-term care services, and the management of service providers, including individual workers and institutions. But the Act fails to address the insufficiency of resources, both financial and human, in the development of public care services. In addition, Taiwan has not instituted national long-term care insurance, which might cover these expenses. The lack of public services and of an insurance system encourages the commodification of care through the private market and the employment of migrant care workers.

This chapter represents one part of a larger project in which I investigated the social organization of care and migrant care labour in Taiwan. It focuses on those who work in private households, although some migrant care workers work in institutions. Working in private and intimate spaces affects the lives of care workers as well as the duties they perform.

This chapter is organized as follows. First, an ethnographic account shows that migrant live-in care workers contribute to the daily life of the entire family, not just the well-being of care recipients. Second, I present evidence that financial considerations and the limitations on the availability of public care services alone do not shape the decision to hire a migrant live-in care worker. A cultural idea that elderly people are entitled to in-home care and round-the-clock service also plays a role. Third, hiring migrant live-in care workers changes the division of care labour in private households, creating a hierarchy of various forms of care work. This chapter concludes that the incorporation of migrant care labour does not challenge the gender division of care work. Instead, it creates class and ethnic inequalities between different groups of women.

Method and data

I conducted this study in the Taipei metropolitan area and two less urbanized counties, gathering data from October 2007 to December 2008 and from January 2012 to December 2013, using interviews, participant observations, and textual analysis. This chapter draws on data from interviews with 35 employers (10 care recipients and 25 family members), informal talks with migrant workers, and observations. In interviews, I asked how families made the care arrangement, and how care work occurred every day. I conducted participant observation with 10 families once a week over six months, observing interactions between migrant live-in care workers, their care recipients, and care recipients' family members to see how care workers coordinate and organize their work in local settings.

Transformation of the care sector in Taiwan and migrant care workers

The World Health Organization has defined Taiwan as an ageing society since 1993, when 7 per cent of the population was older than 65, and its ageing has accelerated since then. By 2016, 13.2 per cent of the population was over 65 (Ministry of the Interior, 2017, Table 2.01), and official counts suggest it will increase to 17 per cent by 2021 (National Development Council, 2016). This population will increasingly need long-term care.

In spite of the continuing influence of Confucian culture and filial piety within Chinese families (Zhan and Montgomery, 2003), almost 37 per cent of elderly people do not live with their adult children, reflecting a trend toward nuclear family living (Ministry of Health and Welfare, 2014, Table 1.2). Even those who live with their families may not find unpaid care available for many hours, as women, who are affiliated with care work (Glenn, 1992), have increasingly entered the formal employment market.

The Temporary Measure for the Shortage of Family Care Labour for People with Disabilities created the legal foundation for the migration of care workers in 1992. It has enacted bilateral agreements with sending states to facilitate the international flow of labour. This policy reinforces the private nature of care work (Liang, 2013). Thus, the government sustains families' role in providing elderly care, even as it mostly shifts hands-on care from family members to migrant workers. The number of migrant care workers in the country grew from 306 in 1992 to 235,370 by the end of 2016 (Ministry of Labour, 2016, Table 12.2). Migrant care labour has become the major supplement to the insufficiency of long-term care services (Chen, 2011).

The government divides migrant care workers and domestic workers into two official categories. Employers may not legally ask workers of one type to perform duties specific to the other. Domestic work includes cleaning, cooking, providing care to young children, and other relevant work in private households. Live-in care workers provide care to elderly people, disabled people, and sick people in private households or institutional settings (Employment Service Act, 1992). However, my observations suggest that in everyday practice, care workers often do domestic work in private and intimate settings.

Unlike the other care labour receiving countries in Asia (e.g. Singapore and Hong Kong, whose importation of live-in migrant workers responds only to market demand), Taiwan requires a person in need of care to undergo a medical assessment and meet state-stipulated qualifications before a family can employ a migrant care worker. This process also rationalizes the state's passive attitude towards providing care to people needing this and reinforces the responsibility of individual families (Liang, 2013).

Because of the complex bureaucratic procedures involved in employing migrant live-in care workers in Taiwan, most employers rely on recruiting agencies to match workers to private households. Recruiting agencies perform an important role in the processes of recruiting, selecting, training, and placing migrant workers in the gendered-ethnicized segregated labour market (Bakan and Stasiulis, 1995). Recruiting agencies and employers activate a specific gendered-racialized discourse to justify the work live-in migrant care workers perform, to pair workers to particular households, and to rationalize control over workers (Liang, 2011). For example, it emphasizes that women from particular countries are suitable to do care work because of their gender, ethnicity, and their characteristics of submission and obedience. It does this by imposing an image of an ideal live-in maid on them.

Multiple care roles of migrant live-in workers

The conventional approach of gerontology proposes four models to illustrate the linkage between informal and formal care relationships. The models are compensatory (Cantor and Little, 1985), substitution (Greene, 1983), task-specific (Litwak, 1985), and complementary (Chappell and Blandford, 1991). These models portray informal and formal care as two different systems. Most families prefer informal care (Ward-Griffin and Marshall, 2003). However, the conceptual dichotomy between these two systems of care obscures the real commonalities between them. By contrast, Clare Ungerson (1990) argues for analysing informal and formal care on similar metrics, suggesting the presence of these commonalities. Based on empirical evidence, Ward-Griffin and Marshall's (2003) research illustrates the interweaving of these different models, suggesting the presence of dynamic relationships between informal and formal care systems. In addition, the conventional approach fails to recognize the role of gender relations that organize daily care within the family context. Care is associated with women's natural role under the conventional approach of investigation (Ward-Griffin and Marshall, 2003).

The case of migrant live-in care workers provides an example to illustrate the dynamics between formal care and informal care, and demonstrates the blurring categorization between these two care systems. In this section, I discuss the meanings of employing migrant live-in care workers, their multiple roles, and how their employment reinvents the division of care labour in private households.

In many developed countries, as elderly care needs grow, women's workforce penetration increases, local care workers disappear, and migrant labour soars as a way to solve care deficits (Doyle and Timonen, 2009; Browne and Braun, 2008). Research suggests the number of migrant care workers will continue to grow (Browne and Braun, 2008; Pyle, 2006). Countries such as Taiwan, where the ideology of familialism plays an important role in facilitating home-based care arrangements for elderly people, will have particular dependence on migrant care workers (Huang et al., 2012; Bettio et al., 2006) to maintain the practices of family care in two-income households. Francesca Bettio et al. (2006) propose the 'migrant in family' model to describe this arrangement in Mediterranean countries. In these situations, migrant live-in workers are not only ideologically constructed as 'fictive kin' (Weicht, 2011; Ayalon, 2009), but incorporated into the daily coordination and practices of care work. Relying upon critical discourse analysis, Bernhard Weicht (2011) finds that employers construct migrant live-in care workers as ideal carers, distinguished from professional care workers and aligning them with family carers. Ayalon's (2009) research also finds that both migrant live-in workers and family members of care recipients describe these workers as family-like. It also shows that migrant live-in workers have emotional exchanges with care recipients, as well as providing physical care, which encourages this sense of a familial relationship. Ayalon (2009) argues that both workers and family members of care recipients make this analogy in order to justify the excessive nature of the demands on migrant care workers.

In spite of the equation of migrant live-in care workers with family, family carers that employ paid care workers continue to play a significant role in providing care (Ayalon, 2009). However, the work in which they engage changes; live-in migrant workers tend to carry out hands-on care, which some societies consider dirty, while family members manage care work. Hiring migrant live-in workers also significantly diminishes the labour family carers provide (Porat and Iecovich, 2010). It frequently permits them to continue their career (Lan, 2006).

Round-the-clock care: caring for elderly people, caring for the family

Dany is Indonesian. She has been working for a Taiwanese family in Taipei for four years, caring for the father of the four adult sons who employ her. I refer to the man she cares for as 'Grandfather' and his wife as 'Grandmother' throughout, in part because she does, but also because these are terms used for showing respect in Taiwanese culture. Just like myriads of her counterparts working in private households, Dany provides care around the clock, 24 hours a day, 365 days a year. Dany's story represents a typical case shedding light on the situation of migrant live-in care workers in Taiwan. It also demonstrates the particular social-political context where their lived experiences are constrained.

The sleepless night

Dany spends her nights in Grandfather's room while Grandmother sleeps in another bedroom, even though there is a third bedroom in the apartment. Dany has a single bed in Grandfather's room, but seldom sleeps much at night. Grandmother, who sleeps soundly all night, expressed her satisfaction with the arrangement: 'I don't care about [his nocturnal wakings]! He can bother Dany, not me'. Like many dementia patients, Grandfather is active at night. Dany emphasizes the difficulty of these hours. She worked at a garment factory in Malaysia for two years before she came to Taiwan. She says that care work has been far more demanding, largely because of the hours: 24 hours a day, seven days a week. Grandfather's needs, rather than a set schedule, shape the demands she must satisfy.

Dany noted that Grandfather's changing ability to walk has changed her duties. When she first came to Taiwan, he could walk, haltingly, by himself without any assistance. Dany would block the door of the bedroom with her body, but his four sons, who live nearby with their nuclear families, rotated responsibility for sleeping on the couch in order to help her at night, coming around 8 o'clock every night. While hands-on care and care management is typically the responsibility of daughters-in-law, they recognize that their wives are not strong enough to help Dany, and they prevented him from injuring himself or others. The sons expected her to try to keep Grandfather quiet so that they could sleep, as did Grandmother. Thus, Dany managed requests such as asking for water or food and comfort measures such as scratching or massaging his head or back all night. Describing her feelings, Dany said:

I could not help but accept his situation. Sometimes, I was angry with him. But most of the time, I knew that he was sick and now he was like a kid. If I thought this way [of Grandfather as a child], I would feel better. Sometimes, I would laugh at some of his behaviours, too. He was as cute as a little kid.

Dany developed her own strategy to deal with Grandfather's situation and overcome the demanding work of caring. This was how she negotiated the difficulties in her daily work. The majority of the study's migrant live-in care workers cannot sleep all night. Most care for dementia patients, who are often nocturnal. Ambulatory dementia patients such as Grandfather require intensive night care, and Dany made it possible for Grandfather's sons and daughters-in-law to maintain lives of productivity and comfort. Numerous live-in migrant care workers provide similar service.

The endless day

Dany woke at 6 o'clock every Monday, Wednesday, and Friday in order to dress and feed Grandfather and herself before going to a dialysis clinic. The four sons rotated the duty of bringing them to the clinic, and a taxi would bring them home, as the sons had gone to their jobs. The other four days a week, Dany usually slept until 7.30 or 8 o'clock. She often took Grandfather to the park on days when he did not have dialysis.

Dany told me with some pride that she was not responsible for the household chores because she took such a heavy load in caring for Grandfather. Yet I observed that she did almost all household chores for Grandfather and Grandmother. She even told me that she felt uncomfortable sitting down; in rare moments when Grandfather did not need anything, she generally found work to do. The chores to which she referred were housework in the nearby households of her employers, the adult children of her primary charge. While not having to clean his sons' homes might put her at some advantage in comparison to other care workers, unlike some of them Dany had no days off.

Migrant live-in care workers often clean houses, do laundry, prepare meals, wash dishes, and care for children, in spite of the law. Abuse of workers' rights can be rampant when labour takes place in private households (Christensen and Manthorpe, 2016; Lutz, 2002; Stasiulis and Bakan, 1997; Aronson and Neysmith, 1996), and the Taiwanese government does not monitor workers in private households (Cheng, 2003). In addition to housework for Grandfather and Grandmother, Dany attended to some of Grandmother's needs even though she had no official responsibility for Grandmother, who had not undergone medical evaluation to qualify for a care worker. Grandmother was in her early eighties, and her most proximate health crisis was coronary artery bypass grafting surgery a few years before. Yet Dany had to consider Grandmother's needs in order to meet Grandmother's expectations for an ideal live-in care worker, as well as those of her sons. Dany described taking Grandfather to the park as a way to keep the peace between him and Grandmother, and to prevent him from awakening his wife when he was noisy, as she slept late.

On park days, Dany usually took Grandfather home around 10 a.m. She would clean the house and prepare lunch. She had to mop the terrazzo floor every day because Grandfather sometimes napped on it, especially during summer when the weather was hot and humid. The food for lunch was usually simple, such as noodle soup or porridge, from ingredients Grandmother selected at the traditional market close by. In four years, Dany had become familiar with the cooking style and flavor to which Grandmother and Grandfather were accustomed. She combined ingredients and seasoning and used cooking techniques they preferred. She also had to cater to their physical needs. For example, during the period when Grandmother had her artificial teeth put in, Dany cooked mushy food for her. She monitored Grandfather's liquid and salt intake based on the advice of his doctor, navigating the language barrier as her Mandarin is rudimentary.

After lunch, Grandmother usually took a nap in her bedroom. Grandfather might sleep as well after lunch, especially on the days when he went for dialysis, but he would wake up several times. Dany said she might have benefited from a nap, but Grandfather's demands made that impossible. Sometimes Grandfather slept all afternoon, which meant he would be awake all night. By managing Grandfather to maximize Grandmother's opportunity to rest – though not her own – Dany contributed to the maintenance of a regular and quality life for her and her husband.

After Grandfather's nap, Dany might bring him back to the park. This was her most relaxing time of day, because she would meet other migrant live-in care workers and their charges at the park. However, if Grandfather was pettish, he might ruin her only opportunity to socialize with her peers during the day.

Dany's routine suggests, as also found in other research (Dodson and Zincavage, 2007; Dahle, 2005), that care work is not only a series of concrete physical tasks. Care work involves significant emotional labour in which care workers coordinate relations with care recipients and family members (Dyer et al., 2008; Lopez, 2006; Isaksen, 2005). Like Dany, migrant live-in care workers work to sustain the entire family.

Hiring migrant workers to uphold the family care ideal

Scholars writing about the increase of live-in migrant care workers in Taiwan generally consider it a sign of a shortage of care labour available domestically. They also argue that the lower costs of employing migrant care workers than of local care workers drives demand (Cheng et al., 2002). Migrant care workers earn about a third of local care workers' earnings; there are many families who cannot pay more. The government does not subsidize these wages. The fact that migrant workers live-in, while Taiwanese workers do not, also stokes demand. The families I spoke with emphasized this – even if they could afford a local care worker, migrant care workers provided superior care by living in. I argue that this preference goes beyond convenience to partners and adult children, who prefer to sleep at night. It speaks to an ideal of elderly care based on cultural ideas.

Confucianism retains influence in Taiwan. Thus, filial piety (*Xiao*) – the idea that parents merit 'children's respect, obedience, loyalty, material provision, and physical care' (Zhan and Montgomery, 2003, p. 210) – organizes family relationships and interactions between family members, determining the approach of most Taiwanese to the care of elderly parents. The provision of care for ageing parents is expected to be in the context of in-home care, and is defined as individual responsibility based on familial obligation. The society approves of the realization of filial piety as long as care at home is assured (Thang, 2010). Allowing elderly parents to live in nursing institutions would violate filial piety and shame both parents and their adult children. Lee, for example, said about her father-in-law:

> A nursing home was not the choice. Even though I did not ask my husband, I knew that he would not agree [to a nursing home for his father]. I considered applying for in-home care service sponsored by the government, but it provided limited hours of service. It did not work for my situation. At that time, my kids were still very young and I had my own career. After work, besides caring for my father in-law, I had to take care of my two kids

and do all the household chores. What I needed was an all-day helper. It seemed that it might be a better idea to hire a live-in migrant maid.

The in-home care service Lee referenced has been available to all in Taiwan since 2002, but the use rate has been low. Lan, a man in his late fifties, also described a migrant live-in care worker as the best choice for his 81-year-old mother, who has early stage dementia:

In-home care was the best model of care, especially compared to the institutional one. Taking care of my mother was my responsibility as the oldest son in the family. I not only took care for my mother, but offered the best care for her. She lived in our house for [her] entire life. I could not imagine put[ting] her in the nursing home.

Both Lan and his wife worked full-time at a home appliance factory. Before hiring a migrant worker, his wife Yen was in charge of caring for his mother. She worked a triple shift between paid employment, domestic chores, and care work for his mother (Duncombe and Marsden, 1995; Doress-Worters, 1994). When his mother began to wander during the day, this arrangement became untenable, and government-sponsored in-home care would not have provided sufficient hours.

When Wang convinced his mother after a mild stroke to move in with him and his wife, they decided to hire a migrant live-in care worker from Indonesia to care for her through her rehabilitation period:

By the time we hired Bianca, my mother was already almost 90 years old. Although she recovered well from the stroke, we were worried about her living alone. She insisted on staying near her old neighbours and friends and refused to live with us. We looked at in-home care services sponsored by the government, but we found that the service hours provided were too limited. After discussing it with my other siblings, we decided that it's better to hire a migrant maid. We did not want to take any risk of incidents. If someone could watch out for her for 24 hours, we were more comfortable.

The practice of filial piety suggests that serving is the important characteristic of eldercare (Liu, 1998); this affects how the Taiwanese perceive eldercare. The families that hire migrant live-in care workers emphasize that in-home care is a better arrangement for elderly people, as it provides 24-hour attention and a hierarchal relationship between the elderly person and the one providing care. When unpaid family labour is unavailable, migrant live-in care workers become the approximation of family care, acting as 'fictive kin' (Barker, 2002) and sustaining the ideal of elderly care.

The new division of labour: mind work and body work

Under the patriarchal system, parents invest more financial and educational resources in their sons than their daughters; they regard their sons as the successor to the family blood and ancient roots. According to patrilocal tradition, daughters are 'spilled water', given away after marriage. They become 'outsiders' belonging to their husbands' families (Thornton and Lin, 1994). The practice of filial piety depends on sons' marriages (Li and Chang, 2010). Thus, parents expect their sons to take them in, and their daughters-in-law to play a primary role in caring for them. My observations align with others' in that sons take care of financial matters and daughters-in-law perform the daily care or coordinate the arrangement of caring (Holroyd, 2003; Hu, 1995).

Pei-Chia Lan (2002, 2006) proposes the concept of outsourced filial piety to describe the purchase of paid labour care to substitute for familial care. The ways in which care work is organized and practised in the front-line settings reflects a new division of care work within households. Family members continue to participate actively in the processes of organizing care, although they are less involved in providing manual work.

Lee, for example, provided all the care her father-in-law needed before hiring a migrant worker, and she handled all the processes of employment with the recruiting agent, and training and mentoring the worker. She also managed the worker's extra-legal caring for the couple's two elementary school-age children:

> My husband did not know anything about the migrant maid. I was the person dealing with employment as well as taking care of her. When she was new to my family, I had to coach her doing everything. For example, I made the working plan for her. On the sheet, I listed the work item and time scheduled.

Lee described how bringing in a migrant worker had changed her life:

> I did the grocery shopping once a week and made the cooking plan. But now I seldom cooked by myself. I did not have time. I taught the migrant worker how to cook different ingredients and make the combination of them. I told her what to prepare every morning before I went to work. Additionally, I had to remind her of my husband and two kids' preferences as well as to avoid the food my in-law could not have.

Instead of providing hands-on care for her father-in-law, Lee became the care manager in charge of making care plans, training the care worker, and monitoring the quality of care.

Lan's wife, Yen, had similar responsibilities to Lee. She recruited the worker, contacting the labour broker, speaking to candidates, and completing the administrative processes with the broker's help. After the migrant worker came to their family, Yen acted as the liaison between her mother-in-law and the worker. She not only helped the worker adjust to the new environment, but also coached her in caring for the frail elderly woman. At the same time, Yen created the division of care work between herself and the worker. The migrant worker was more involved with hands-on work while Yen, like Lee, focused on logistics.

Chen's family actually violated the custom of having sons and daughters-in-law take primary responsibility for eldercare. In her late forties, she had retired from work after a minor stroke and had remained single while her elder sister and brother were married and had their own families. When her mother needed care, it was Chen who took charge. She explained why she needed a migrant worker:

> I might appear healthy. But I needed to be very careful because of my [chronic] health condition. For example, I was not allowed to exert myself physically. It was dangerous for me. My mother was quite heavy, and how could I carry her by myself? It's difficult for me to move her from the wheelchair to the bed, or to help her with bathing.

Chen still provided care after bringing in Ah-Di, a migrant live-in care worker from Indonesia. The care worker acted as an assistant rather than as a substitute for her:

> My mother had to take various kinds of medicine every day. It was about that Ah-Di would get confused. I used the small boxes to separate the medicine into the daily amount.

Additionally, I made the chart as a checklist to confirm with Ah-Di my mother's proper taking of medicine. The physician said that it was important to monitor my mother's blood pressure and blood sugar. I recorded the numbers every day and paid attention to the trend.

Employing migrant workers creates a new division of care work. Lee, Yen, and Chen were typical in that they took more control of the mind work – planning, coordinating, and nurturance – of caring, leaving body work – including dealing with human waste, negotiating nakedness, and skin-to-skin care (Twigg, 2000) – for the migrant worker. The division implies a hierarchy between different forms of care work. The mind work is considered more dignified than the body work. This division highlights the relational and nurturant dimensions of care work (Jacoby, 2006), but also creates a distinction between spiritual and menial (Duffy, 2011), the latter considered dirty and demeaning by society (Dyer et al., 2008). In addition, the distinction distorts the value of body work, an essential component of performing care work.

Adult children often deny live-in migrant care workers the mind work of determining how they will work. Family members actively arrange and rearrange the work between themselves and the migrant workers based on the 'importance' of work type. Yen, for example, stated:

> Even though we had the migrant maid, we did not ask her to do everything for my in-law. We were also worried about her ability and were afraid of incidents. I considered some things to be my responsibility. For example, I did not have time to cook dinner after work. But I insisted on doing the grocery shopping once or twice a week. It was important to plan what to cook, to buy the fresh ingredients, and to provide enough nutrition.

Yen emphasized the migrant care worker could not replace her role in organizing family care, including providing care for her mother-in-law. She also divided the work into mind work and body work. She perceived the part she was in charge of as more essential and vital to the family. Similarly, Wang emphasized the responsibility of adult children, saying that he or one of his siblings accompanied his mother to her doctor every three months, both because they felt the care worker could not communicate well with her physician and because his mother would feel more comfortable with one of her children or children-in-law present.

Most family members implied they nurtured their relatives by taking tasks the care workers would not perform properly. Care work is physically demanding and most perceived it as 'dirty'. Giving imported workers the dirty work that local workers refuse is common in countries that receive them (Dyer et al., 2008, p. 2035) and constructs a hierarchy between locals and migrants worldwide (Liang, 2011; Browne and Braun, 2008). Personal care is essential to well-being (Christensen and Guldvik, 2014), but day-to-day practices receive little attention from society or academic work (Twigg, 2000).

Lee argued that the migrant worker was more 'professional' in handling faeces and urine for her father-in-law than she would be.

> I was not good at changing the diaper for my in-law. I was always worried that I was too rude to harm him. His skin was very sensitive. It was also difficult for me to change his diaper without another person's assistance. My in-law was too heavy and I was unable to lift his bottom alone. The migrant maids were different [from me]. It was easy for them to do that kind of work, including changing diapers, bathing, and so on.

Lee's claim that the worker was more 'professional' belied the fact that she saw the work as less valuable than the organizational and planning care work she performed. Talking about the period before she hired the worker, Lee acknowledged she was uncomfortable with intimate body contact:

> My father-in-law refused my offer of some specific help, especially with regard to the body. I knew that he felt embarrassed. For example, he did not want me to change his diapers for him. If he and I were alone at home, he would not tell me that he needed to change his diapers. He would wait until my husband came home, although it was very uncomfortable for him . . . . After we hired the migrant maid, the problem was solved. My father in-law did not reject the help offered by the maid with bathing or changing diapers. He could take the help for granted because the maid was paid to do her work. [Thus, hiring a live-in migrant care worker] provided him with a better quality of care.

Lee's father-in-law was typical. Aged parents, especially fathers, felt that receiving help with specific kinds of body contact harmed their status as the patriarch in the family and inverted the relationships between parents and children. It was easier for elderly people to accept intimate care provided by the paid migrant live-in care workers.

Lan pointed to a more general problem with providing care:

> To be honest, I felt uncomfortable in seeing my mother's body. I suddenly found that she was aged. It was hard to accept the truth. I still remembered how she looked when I was young. She was energetic.

Lan's mother's physical decay was painful to Lan. Providing body work for his mother forced him to confront that reality. Family members prefer not to confront the failing bodies of their aged parents for emotional reasons. Taking care of frail elderly people seems to produce the anxieties associated with bodily decay. It also reminds the adult children of the ageing process they have to face one day themselves (Isaksen, 2002).

Conclusion

Migrant live-in workers not only provide care to satisfy physical and emotional needs of elderly people, but improve the well-being of an entire family. Families choose migrant live-in care workers for practical as well as cultural reasons. The migrant workers act as surrogate for the family members, permitting their parents to avoid institutional care while adult children maintain their lifestyles. Hiring a migrant worker alters the daily division of care work, but family members still engage in organizing care. Lan (2002) asserts that the mediation of gender dynamics (from son to daughter-in-law) and market forces (providing non-family home care workers, most of them female) leads to the realization of filial duty. The care duty for elderly people transfers from the son to the daughter-in-law. The general category of family member veils the gender inequality of care. Usually, women organize and provide daily care. Hiring a live-in migrant care worker frees them from the labour-intensive care and gives them the opportunity to maintain their careers without fundamentally changing the gender division of labour within the household. The practices of care shift from one group of women to another through the market mechanism in the context of labour migration.

The increasing number of migrant care workers in Taiwan reflects both families' rising need to outsource care and the fact that government-provided public care services do not serve the needs of many families. The government policies that respond to the increasing needs of elderly care and the rapid growth of migrant care workers continue to evolve.

The Taiwanese case provides an example relevant to global ageing and care deficits. It demonstrates that labour migration does not release female family members from the practices of daily care, although it generally means they oversee it instead of performing it. Migrant live-in care workers are incorporated into the processes of organizing and providing care. The utilization of migrant care labour reinforces the gender inequality of care work and creates class inequality between different groups of women in the transnational context. At the same time, it hinders the visibility and value of paid and unpaid care work alike – much of it performed by women.

References

Aronson, J. and Neysmith, S.M., 1996. 'You're not just in there to do the work': depersonalizing policies and the exploitation of home care workers' labor. *Gender and Society*, 10(1), pp. 59–77.

Ayalon, L., 2009. Family and family-like interactions in households with round-the-clock paid foreign carers in Israel. *Ageing and Society*, 29(5), pp. 671–86. DOI: 10.1017/S0144686X09008393.

Bakan, A.B. and Stasiulis, D.K., 1995. Making the match: domestic placement agencies and the racialization of women's household work. *Signs*, 20(2), pp. 303–35. DOI: https://doi.org/10.1086/494976.

Barker, J.C., 2002. Neighbors, friends, and other nonkin caregivers of community-living dependent elders. *The Journals of Gerontology Series B: Psychological Sciences and Social Sciences*, 57(3), S158–S167. DOI: https://doi.org/10.1093/geronb/57.3.S158.

Bettio, F., Simonazzi, A. and Villa, P., 2006. Change in care regimes and female migration: the 'care drain' in the Mediterranean. *Journal of European Social Policy*, 16(3), pp. 271–85. DOI: 10.1177/0958928706065598.

Browne, C.V. and Braun. K.L., 2008. Globalization, women's migration, and the long-term care workforce. *The Gerontologist*, 48(1), pp. 16–24. DOI: 10.1093/geront/48.1.16.

Cantor, M., and Little, V., 1985. Aging and social care. In R.H. Binstock and E. Shanas, eds. *Handbook of aging and the social sciences*, 2nd ed. New York: Van Nostrand Reinhold Co., pp. 745–81.

Chappell, N., and Blandford, A., 1991. Informal and formal care: exploring the complementarity. *Ageing and Society*, 11(3), pp. 299–317. DOI: https://doi.org/10.1017/S0144686X00004189.

Chen, C., 2011. Management or exploitation? The survival strategy of employer of family foreign care workers. *Taiwan: A Radical Quarterly in Social Studies*, 85, pp. 89–155. [In Chinese]

Cheng, C.Y., Hsin, P.L. and Liu-Huang, L.J., 2002. A preliminary study on the impact of foreign domestic helper and caretaker importation on the labor market in Taiwan. *Journal of Labor Studies*, 11, pp. 69–95. [In Chinese]

Cheng, S.-J.A., 2003. Rethinking the globalization of domestic service: foreign domestics, state control, and the politics of identity in Taiwan. *Gender and Society*, 17(2), pp. 166–86. DOI: 10.1177/0891243202250717.

Christensen, K., and Guldvik, I., 2014. *Migrant care workers: searching for new horizons*. Farnham: Ashgate.

Christensen, K. and Manthorpe, J., 2016. Personalised risk: new risk encounters facing migrant care workers. *Health, Risk and Society*, 18(3–4), pp. 1–16. DOI: http://dx.doi.org/10.1080/13698575.2016.1182628.

Dahle, R., 2005. Men, bodies and nursing. In D.H.J. Morgan, B. Brandt and E. Kvande, eds. *Gender, bodies and work*. Aldershot: Ashgate, pp. 127–38.

Dodson, L. and Zincavage, R.M., 2007. 'It's like a family': caring labor, exploitation, and race in nursing homes. *Gender and Society*, 21(6), pp. 905–28. DOI: 10.1177/0891243207309899.

Doress-Worters, P.B., 1994. Adding elder care to women's multiple roles: a critical review of the caregiver stress and multiple roles literatures. *Sex Roles*, 31(9–10), pp. 597–616.

Doyle, M. and Timonen, V., 2009. The different faces of care work: understanding the experiences of the multi-cultural care workforce. *Ageing and Society*, 29(3), pp. 337–50. DOI: https://doi.org/10.1017/S0144686X08007708.

Duffy, M., 2011. Making care count: a century of gender, race, and paid care work. New Brunswick, NJ: Rutgers University Press.

Duncombe, J. and Marsden, D., 1995. 'Workaholics' and 'whingeing women': theorising intimacy and emotion work – the last frontier of gender inequality? *The Sociological Review*, 43(1), pp. 150–69. DOI: 10.1111/j.1467-954X.1995.tb02482.x.

Dyer, S., McDowell, L. and Batnitzky, A., 2008. Emotional labour/body work: the caring labours of migrants in the UK's National Health Service. *Geoforum*, 39(6), pp. 2030–8. DOI: https://doi.org/10.1016/j.geoforum.2008.08.005.

Glenn, E.N., 1992. From servitude to service work: historical continuities in the racial division of paid reproductive labor. *Signs*, 18(1), pp. 1–43. Available at: www.jstor.org/stable/3174725 [accessed 19.09.2017].

Greene, V.L., 1983. Substitution between formally and informally provided care for the impaired elderly in the community. *Medical Care*, 21(6), pp. 609–19.

Holroyd, E., 2003. Hong Kong Chinese family caregiving: cultural categories of bodily order and the location of self. *Qualitative Health Research*, 13(2), pp. 158–70. DOI: 10.1177/1049732302239596.

Hu, Y.H., 1995. *Three-generation extended family: myths and pitfalls*. Taipei: Chuliu Publisher. [In Chinese]

Huang, S., Yeoh, B.S. and Toyota, M., 2012. Caring for the elderly: the embodied labour of migrant care workers in Singapore. *Global Networks*, 12(2), pp. 195–215. DOI: 10.1111/j.1471-0374.2012.00347.x.

Isaksen, L.W., 2002. Toward a sociology of (gendered) disgust: images of bodily decay and the social organization of care work. *Journal of Family Issues*, 23(7), pp. 791–811. DOI: 10.1177/019251302236595.

Isaksen, L.W., 2005. Gender and care: the role of cultural ideas of dirt and disgust. In D. Morgan, B. Brandth and E. Kvande, eds. *Gender, bodies and work*. Aldershot: Ashgate, pp. 115–26.

Jacoby, D., 2006. Caring about caring labor: an introduction. *Politics and Society*, 34(5), pp. 5–9. DOI: 10.1177/0032329205284753.

Lan, P.C., 2002. Subcontracting filial piety elder care in ethnic Chinese immigrant families in California. *Journal of Family Issues*, 23(7), pp. 812–35. Available at: http://ntur.lib.ntu.edu.tw/retrieve/167883/13.pdf [accessed 17.07.2017].

Lan, P.C., 2006. Global Cinderellas: migrant domestics and newly rich employers in Taiwan. Durham, NC: Duke University Press.

Li, T.S. and Chang, Y.Y., 2010. The intergenerational caregiving relationship: a qualitative inquiry of adult children's experience in urban Taiwan. *Formosa Journal of Mental Health*, 23(1), pp. 99–125. [In Chinese]

Liang, L.F., 2011. The making of an 'ideal' live-in migrant care worker: recruiting, training, matching and disciplining. *Ethnic and Racial Studies*, 34(11), pp. 1815–34.

Liang, L.F., 2013. State and medicalization of care needs: migrant care labor policy in Taiwan. *Journal of Intimacy and Public Sphere*, 2(1), pp. 82–94.

Litwak, E., 1985. Helping the elderly: the complementary roles of informal networks and formal systems. New York: Guilford Press.

Liu, C.T., 1998. *Women and medical sociology*. Taipei: Fembooks Press.

Lopez, S.H., 2006. Emotional labor and organized emotional care conceptualizing nursing home care work. *Work and Occupations*, 33(2), pp. 133–60. DOI: 10.1177/0730888405284567.

Lutz, H., 2002. At your service madam! The globalization of domestic service. *Feminist Review*, 70(1), pp. 89–104. DOI: 10.1057/palgrave.fr.9400004.

Ministry of Health and Welfare, 2014. *Report of Senior Citizen Condition Survey 2013*. Available at: http://dep.mohw.gov.tw/DOS/cp-1767-3586-113.html [accessed 17.07.2017]. [In Chinese]

Ministry of Labour, 2016. *Foreign workers statistics*. Available at: http://statdb.mol.gov.tw/html/mon/c12020.htm [accessed 17.07.2017].

Ministry of the Interior, 2017. *Statistical yearbook of interior*. Available at: http://sowf.moi.gov.tw/stat/year/list.htm [accessed 17.07.2017].

National Development Council, 2016. *Population project for Taiwan: 2016–2060*. Available at: www.ndc.gov.tw/en/cp.aspx?n=2E5DCB04C64512CC [accessed 17.07.2017].

Porat, I., and Iecovich, E., 2010. Relationships between elderly care recipients and their migrant live-in home care workers in Israel. *Home Health Care Services Quarterly*, 29(1), pp. 1–21. DOI: 10.1080/01621424.2010.487035.

Pyle, J.L., 2006. Globalization, transnational migration, and gendered care work: introduction. *Globalizations*, 3(3), pp. 283–95. DOI: 10.1080/14747730600869938.

Stasiulis, D. and Bakan, A.B., 1997. Negotiating citizenship: the case of foreign domestic workers in Canada. *Feminist Review*, 57(1), pp. 112–39. Avaialble at: www.jstor.org/stable/1395804 [accessed 19.09.2017].

Thang, L.L., 2010. Intergenerational relations: Asian perspectives. In D. Dannefer and C. Phillipson, eds. *The Sage handbook of social gerontology*. London: Sage, pp. 202–14.

Thornton, A. and Lin, H.S., 1994. *Social change and the family in Taiwan*. Chicago, IL: University of Chicago Press.

Twigg, J., 2000. Carework as a form of bodywork. *Ageing and Society*, 20(4), pp. 389–411. Available at: https://kar.kent.ac.uk/id/eprint/16688 [accessed 22.09.2017].

Ungerson, C., 1990. Gender and caring: work and welfare in Britain and Scandinavia. Birmingham: Harvester Wheatsheaf.

Ward-Griffin, C. and Marshall, V.W., 2003. Reconceptualizing the relationship between 'public' and 'private' eldercare. *Journal of Aging Studies*, 17(2), pp. 189–208. DOI: 10.1016/S0890-4065(03)00004-5.

Weicht, B., 2011. Embodying the ideal carer: the Austrian discourse on migrant carers. *International Journal of Ageing and Later Life*, 5(2), pp. 17–52. DOI: 10.3384/ijal.1652-8670.105217.

Wu, S.C., 2005. Population aging and long-term care policy. *National Policy Quarterly*, 4(4), pp. 5–24. [In Chinese]

Zhan, H.J. and Montgomery, R.J.V., 2003. Gender and elder care in China: the influence of filial piety and structural constraints. *Gender and Society*, 17(2), pp. 209–29. Available at: www.jstor.org/stable/3594688 [accessed 20.09.2017].

17

Has the long-term care insurance contributed to de-familialization?

Familialization and marketization of eldercare in Japan

Yayoi Saito

Introduction

The implementation of long-term care insurance (LTCI) (*Kaigo hoken*) for eldercare in 2000 in Japan was expected to promote independence for elderly people, choice and a high quality of care service for individuals. The state manages the insurance system but allows the market to establish a network of care providers that are paid for by insurance premiums, which are mandatory for all citizens aged 40 years old and over. People can start to use the LTCI services at 65, and at younger ages if they have age-related disabilities.

The idea was to combine forces in the public and private sectors and create social services of high quality by encouraging competition. The growth of care services has not kept up with the growth of the ageing population because the government has controlled the LTCI budget strictly. As a result, an undesired grey market of private nursing homes has emerged to meet the demand.

The aim of this chapter is to present the changes in the eldercare system since the implementation of LTCI in Japan using the concepts 'familialization' and 'marketization'. This chapter is based on Japanese official LTCI data and OECD data and previous research. This includes the author's research on eldercare and the long-term care insurance in Japan, and the working environment of care workers in Japan (Saito and Ishiguro, 2013).

'Marketization' is a complex and context-bound term, the meaning of which varies with time, place and academic discipline. Anttonen and Meagher (2013) have provided a definitional framework of marketization in eldercare, focusing on two dimensions: whether or not market practices and logics (most notably, competition) are used in organizing services, and whether or not private actors, particularly for-profit companies, are involved in providing services (Anttonen and Meagher, 2013, p. 16). The concept of 'marketization' in this chapter is based on their definitional framework.

Esping-Andersen used the concept of 'de-familialization' to capture policies that lessen the individual's reliance on the family (Esping-Andersen, 1999, p. 45). (De-)familialization is also a complex term with various interpretations. Social/family policy studies from the (de-)familialization perspective are often focused mainly on the state's role in relation to family care responsibilities. Although Esping-Andersen (1999, pp. 63–4) argues that the contribution of the market to reduce the family care burden should be considered, he also points to the limitation of market solutions. He points out that high wage costs may render marketized care services prohibitively expensive for most families without public support. In this chapter, the term (de-)familialization covers the trend to reduce the family care burden through the welfare state and markets, while the term of familialization is used for the trend to increase the family care burden.

In terms of eldercare, the Japanese government was inspired by the Swedish home care model, and they tried to spread it across the country in the mid-1990s (Saito, 2014a, p. 426). This model, providing 24 hours and 365 days care, is expected to allow elderly people to stay at home independently for as long as possible and to reduce the family care burden. The model also had the ambition to give care workers more responsibilities by working closely together in self-governing small groups, in order to make care work more attractive, and thus facilitate the recruitment of workers (Szebehely, 1995, p. 79). The government was interested in the Swedish/Scandinavian model because its introduction could be expected to solve 'social hospitalization' – the use of hospital beds to solve crushing burdens of family care as there were sufficient numbers of hospital beds while nursing home places were very limited in the 1970s and after this time. During the 1980s and 1990s, family caregivers began to organize associations and groups to improve eldercare in Japan, learning from and discussing eldercare systems in Scandinavian countries (Saito, 2010, pp. 50–1), and the government took notice of the civil movement to improve eldercare.

Folling the introduction, this chapter is divided into five main sections. The next section discusses the welfare state in Japan. Next, the ageing society and eldercare system in Japan is outlined. Then the familialistic character of Japanese eldercare is discussed. Following this, the home help transition is outlined. Then the marketization of facilities services is discussed. Finally, the last section discusses whether the LTCI and marketization has contributed to de-familialization, and also presents the challenges of eldercare in Japan.

Unique or hybrid welfare state in Japan?

Only a few studies of welfare states in East Asian countries were available until the 1980s, and the welfare state in Japan was often identified as 'unique' from the following characteristics: small government, company-based welfare systems and strong familial traditions. The welfare state in Japan had also been considered a residual model, as social expenditures in Japan had been quite low, despite GDP per capita being one of the world's highest (Esping-Andersen, 1997).

Esping-Andersen (1997, 1999), however, argued that Japanese society could not be said to adhere simply to a residual model. He explained that the reasons for the low social expenditure were that the population was younger in Japan compared to European countries and unemployment was not a serious social problem due to the success of the lifetime employment tradition. He argued that Japan's welfare system combines key elements of both the liberal-residual and the conservative-corporatist model (Esping-Andersen, 1997, p. 187). The social insurance system in Japan before the Second World War was inspired by German practices, and in the aftermath of the war, social assistance schemes were implemented by the American occupation forces. Occupational welfare forms part of the consensual mode of labour regulation, but it also mirrors a conservative practice. Esping-Andersen (1997) concluded that more time was needed

242

to define the Japanese welfare system of about 20 years ago, because it was in the process of evolution.

The 1990s was an important decade of social care expansion and welfare state restructuring in Japan. The compulsory long-term care insurance was introduced, public child care expanded, new legislation on parental and family leaves was brought in, as well as other supportive measure for workers with family responsibilities, moving away from earlier policies of welfare retrenchment (Peng, 2002, p. 412).

Companies' ability to maintain welfare packages (e.g. pensions and lifelong job guarantee) was under threat after the 1990s. A recent OECD (2015a) report indicated that the level of redistribution was lower in Japan than in most OECD countries. It also pointed out that income poverty concerned around 16 per cent of the population in Japan, a rate that was above the OECD average of 11 per cent in 2013. Across age groups, the income poverty rate was highest among senior citizens (above 66 years of age), affecting about 19 per cent of them, and the age group that has small children was also higher than the others.

GDP per capita on social spending in Japan caught up to the average of OECD in 2007, and the latest figure is 23.1 per cent (2013), which is slightly above the average of OECD countries (21.1 per cent) (OECD, 2016a). However, it could be said that it is still low compared to European countries, given that Japan has the world's most aged population (UN, 2015). Public expenditure on care and pre-primary education per child aged 0–5 is below the OECD average (OECD, 2016b, Chart PF3.1), and there are also tax incentives discouraging women from full-time work.

Japan's ageing society and the eldercare system

Ageing of society and change in family composition

The Statistics Bureau (of Japan) (2017, Table 3) estimates that 27.3 per cent, or 34.6 million, of the total population of Japan is 65 years of age or older (October January 1, 2017, Final estimates). The share will increase to 30.3 per cent in 2025, and to 33.4 per cent in 2035 (National Institute of Population and Social Security Research, 2012, Table 3.4). This situation is known as the '2025 problem' due to looming issues such as increases in medical and LTC expenditures and the approaching limit in contributions by individuals to healthcare and LTCI insurance, as premiums cannot rise too much or pensioners will be unable to pay them.

In Japan, the percentage of elderly people living with their children is higher than in European countries; about 15.3 per cent of elderly people live in three-generation families (2012) (Cabinet Office, 2014, Chart 1.2.1). However, the percentage of three-generation families has decreased significantly from 26.5 per cent in 2000. This trend also suggests a greater need for non-familial care in the future.

Eldercare system: based on the LTCI system

Japan's public expenditure (health and social components) on LTC as a percentage of the GDP is 2.1 per cent, slightly higher than the OECD average (2013) (OECD, 2015b, Table 11.21). Compared to German LTCI, the Japanese system includes assistance for elderly people who need low levels of support – referred to as 'support required' (*yōshien*). Elderly people deemed to require LTC pay 10–20 per cent of the service costs. One half of the public expenditure is covered by general revenue and the other half comes from the LTCI premiums. The LTCI system has contributed to the catching up to the OECD level of public LTC expenditure.

The assessment of care needs (*Yōkaigo Nintei*) is based on a national standardized instrument (with questions about physical and mental status). The LTCI Need Certification Committee (*Kaigo Nintei Shinsakai*), which is comprised of specialists in public health, medical care and social welfare, has responsibility for the final decision on the care need certification level. A care manager makes an individual care plan, which is a combination of several types of services put together in accordance with the LTCI need certification level. Care managers in Japan work as coordinators, and have no authority for the decision on the care need certification level and care services. Care managers are chosen by the users, and they give advice, draw up a care plan with the users, handle the paperwork, monitor performance, and generally coordinate services and people (Campbell, 2014, p. 17). The municipality has responsibility to manage the assessment as insurer, and most care managers are employed by private care providers.

In Japan's LTCI system, contracts are made between service providers and users in the LTC service market. Compared with countries using taxes to fund LTCI, where contracts are made between service providers and municipality, the market character is relatively strong in Japan.

The LTCI system dramatically increased the number of LTCI service users from 2.87 million (2001) to 6.05 million (includes overall users of more than 30 kinds of services, e.g. day-care, short-stay, technical services, as well as home help and LTCI facilities) (2015) MHLW (n.d., 'LTCI care benefit expenditure'). The graph in Figure 17.1 shows the increase in the number of home help users. In 2015, 2.03 million people used home help. 'Preventive home help', which seeks to promote active improvement in functional status of frail elderly people who need a low level of support, was introduced in 2006 to prevent or delay the need for greater support. The increase in the number of LTCI facility users is shown in Figure 17.2. About 1.3 million people used LTCI facilities in 2015. Facility services of the LTCI are formally divided into three types: welfare facilities for the elderly (*rōjin fukushi shisetsu*), healthcare facilities for the elderly (*rōjin hoken shisetsu*) and medical care facilities (*ryōyōgata iryō shisetsu*). Welfare facilities are most similar to Western nursing homes (Campbell, 2014, p. 20), and residents can stay as long as they need. Healthcare facilities are aimed at rehabilitation with shorter stay. Medical care facilities are sanatoria for elderly people who need medical treatment. Figure 17.3 plots the percentage of facility and home help users aged 80 and over. Although the number of facility users and home help users has increased, the overall percentage of facility and home help users is gradually decreasing because of the rapidly increasing numbers of people aged 80 and over.

Eldercare reliance on the family

Pure 'familistic regime'

Ochiai (2009, p. 72) argued in a comparative study of Asian countries that Japan's eldercare system can be described as a nearly *pure* 'familistic regime', the major part of care work being performed by the family. While many Asian and other countries supplement the lack of public-funded home care by using domestic workers from other countries, Japan is an exception. In Japan, a discussion has been continuing on the acceptance of unskilled foreign workers since the 1980s, but there is no clear vision on the direction yet. Actually, substantial acceptance is seen with special treatment for migrant trainees in some industries with a serious labour shortage.

In 1995, 86.5 per cent of bedridden elderly people were being looked after by their co-residing family members, and another 6.3 per cent were being looked after by family members outside their household (MHW, 1998). Only 7.2 per cent of all bedridden elderly people were being looked after by non-family members (Peng, 2002, p. 417).

Familialization and marketization in Japan

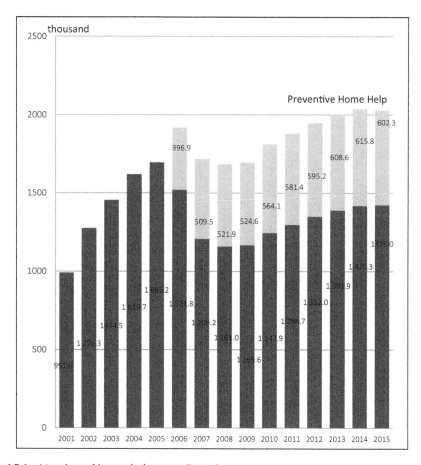

Figure 17.1 Number of home help users (Japan)

Source: Author's compilation from MHLW (n.d., 'LTCI Care benefit expenditure').

Note: 'Preventive home help' was introduced in 2006.

The LTCI system contributes to reducing Japanese people's feelings against care provided by non-family caregivers. However, the burden of family caregivers is still heavy, with growing numbers of caregivers quitting their jobs to provide LTC for their families. In 2015, there were 90,100 family caregivers who left their jobs, almost double the number from five years earlier (not including those who changed to part-time work) (MHLW, 2015, Table 30; MHLW, 2010, Table 30).

In terms of gender, 76 per cent of those caregivers were women, a high number being in their forties and fifties. Re-employment is difficult for such people in the Japanese labour market. Although family caregivers are eligible to use family care leave, many of them hesitate to use it over concerns about how it will affect their career (MHLW, 2012). The family care leave system is regulated by the Child Care and Family Care Leave Law (*Ikuji kaigo kyuugyōhō*): a worker may take family care leave upon application to his or her employer three times for each occurrence of circumstances where the family member falls into a condition requiring constant care, with limits up to 93 days for each family member.

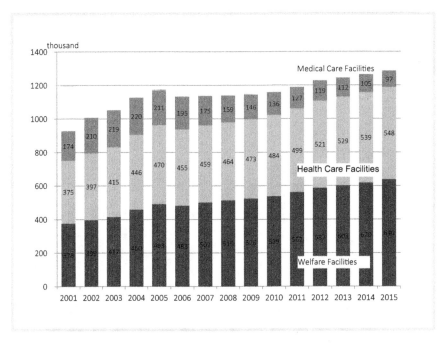

Figure 17.2 Number of the LTCI facility users (Japan)

Source: Author's compilation from MHLW (n.d., 'LTCI Care benefit expenditure').

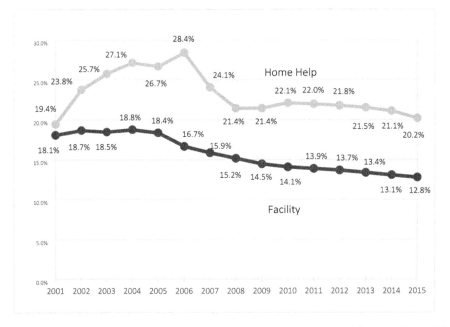

Figure 17.3 The LTCI facility and home help users (Japan) percentage of the population 80+

Source: Author's compilation from MHLW (n.d., 'LTCI Care benefit expenditure').

Note: 'Preventive home help' was introduced in 2006. The users are included in the number of home help users.

From 'Japanese-style welfare society' to LTCI

Why has the eldercare system in Japan traditionally relied on the family? Public eldercare in Japan had already started in the 1960s, which is not that late compared to some European countries. However, the amount of services was restricted until the end of the 1980s (Saito, 2014b, pp. 52–5). After the 1973 energy crisis, the idea of a 'Japanese-style welfare society' (*Nihongata fukushi shakai*) was proposed by the Liberal Democratic Party government that emphasized the role of the family as being the party responsible for welfare (Saito, 2014b, p. 55; Boling, 1998, p. 177; Goodman and Peng, 1996, p. 193). The percentage of elderly people who lived with their children was 69 per cent (1980). The government stated, 'With a high rate of three generations living together, the family is an invisible *capital for welfare services*' (MHW, 1978). Reducing the tax burden serves as an indirect measure of promoting care work within the family: the tax deduction for aged dependents (*rōjin fuyō kōjo*) and the special tax deduction for spouses (*haigusha tokubetsu kōjo*) were introduced in the 1970s (see below).

However, as the ageing of Japanese society advanced, the burden of long-term care by families grew more serious from the 1980s and became a social issue. Because of the absence of home care and the lack of facilities, the number of elderly patients for long periods of time increased. These 'social hospitalizations' began to exert pressure on healthcare costs (Campbell, 2014, p. 10; Christensen, 2010, p. 31).

The so-called 'Golden Plan' (1989), the Ten-Year Strategy for Health and Welfare of the Elderly, was Japan's first national plan for LTC service that had numerical targets – of 100,000 home helpers and 10,000 day-care centres by 2000. Some earnest municipalities tried during the 1990s to introduce home help services operating 24 hours. Following this, the government was inspired by an LTCI system from Germany to secure funds for eldercare. As healthcare and pensions are managed by social insurance in Japan, it was thought that an LTC insurance system would be familiar to Japanese people. In 1997, the LTCI Law was approved by the Diet, and it was introduced in 2000.

Tax deduction for spouse: the family as responsible for social security

The custom of expecting the family to be responsible for eldercare is reflected in the characteristics of Japan's tax and pension systems. The tax deduction for families who live with elderly parents to support them (1979) and the special deduction for spouses (1987) – which is aimed at housewives – indicate the expectations placed on families to be providers of social security and reflect the promotion in social policy of a gender-based division of work within the family. Taxes and insurance premiums in Japan are not used to strengthen finances for public long-term care and family care expenditures, as seen in some European countries. Instead, the method of reducing the tax burden can be said to encourage care work within families (Saito, 2010, pp. 42–4). These characteristics include Japan's public pension system and public health insurance systems. There were 9.15 million people benefitting from the system without contribution, of which 9.04 million were women in 2015 (MHLW, 2017, Table 1). Full-time housewives receive survivors' benefits without ever having contributed to the National Pension Fund (Boling, 1998, p. 181).

This system discourages housewives from full-time work in the labour market and also promotes the minimization of the total work hours of housewives with part-time jobs, as couples obtain a tax advantage when one of them earns below a prescribed yearly amount (Yamada, 2009, p. 206; Boling, 1998, p. 181). In fact, they make up a potential labour market contribution that could support the eldercare system, also through their potential taxpayer roles. These

Yayoi Saito

systems, as well as companies' wage systems, hinder efforts to improve part-time workers' wages (Yamada, 2009, p. 206). Although there are ongoing discussions on the pension and tax systems for spouses, the outcome at present is uncertain.

Home help transition

User-subsidizing type quasi-markets

Since the introduction of Japan's LTCI system, the number of users of home help jumped from 991,600 in 2001 to more than 2 million in 2015 (see Figure 17.1).

Unlike previous systems, under the LTCI system services are provided through contracts between users and service providers. Users choose their services and service providers. Japan's LTCI system can be said to be a type of voucher system (Svensson and Edebalk, 2002), although strictly regulated and controlled by the Ministry of Health, Labour and Welfare. The intention of marketization in the Japanese LCTI system, of competition between diverse service providers, was to increase the availability of high-quality services.

The service choice system is also implemented in some municipalities in Scandinavian countries. However, the Scandinavian system operates 'service-purchasing type' quasi-markets, whereas the Japanese system operates a 'user-subsidizing type' quasi-market. In the service-purchasing type market, the government purchases services in the users' place and makes arrangements so that the services can be chosen and consumed by users (Hiraoka, 2013, p. 196). In contrast, in a user-subsidizing type quasi-market the government (or social insurance) provides users of social services with money to pay for some or all of the social service fees (but only for services allocated by the LTCI system). Marketization is relatively stronger, while the responsibility of the government is weaker in Japan's user-subsidizing type quasi-market.

Service expansion and user choice for home help

Anttonen and Meagher (2013) argue that various market instruments are used to organize provision and that the proportion of for-profit and non-profit provisions varies widely. In the Japanese case, home care services might be said to be 'publicly funded, privately provided'.

The LTCI Law specifies that care services should be provided by a diverse range of care providers. The role of the government is not to produce services, but to manage the LTCI system through certification of LTC need (municipalities), license of service providers (prefecture), and by managing the public finances of the LTCI system as the insurers (municipalities). With the implementation of the LTCI system, new providers such as for-profit corporations (*eiri hōjin*), non-profit corporations (*NPO hōjin*), agricultural cooperatives (*nōgyō kyōdō kumiai*), and consumer cooperatives (*seikatsu kyōdō kumiai*) have set up new home care services. Table 17.1 indicates changes in home help providers. The proportion of for-profit organizations in 2014 was 64.4 per cent, more than double the figure compared to 2000 (in Tokyo: 78 per cent), and public providers have almost disappeared MHLW (n.d., 'LTCI care providers'). Social welfare corporations and medical corporations are traditional welfare service providers in Japan licensed by the MHLW.

Development of the home helper role

In the early 1960s, the work of 'home servants for the elderly' (literally *rōjin katei hōshiin*) consisted of preparing meals for and feeding elderly people, doing laundry, and cleaning. 'Feelings

248

Table 17.1 Changes in home help providers (percentages)

		Public	Non-profit			For-profit
		Municipalities	Social welfare corporations	Medical corporations	Others	For-profit organizations
Home help	2000	6.6	6.6	43.2	10.4	30.3
	2014	0.3	0.3	19.6	6.2	64.4

Source: Author's compilation from MHLW (n.d., 'LTCI Care providers').

of charity' were required for these positions, and home helpers served as daily life counsellors (MHW, 1962). They were expected to provide psychological support for elderly people needing this (Saito, 2010, p. 64). The system also played a role in stimulating the employment of mothers in fatherless families.

Under the Golden Plan in the 1990s, the term 'home helpers' (*hōmu herupa-*) came to be used. Work content was divided into personal care (*shintaikaigo*, literally physical care), practical care (*kaji enjo*, literally housework support) and consultation/advice (*sōdan/jogen*), with emphasis especially placed on personal care (Saito, 2010, p. 64; MHW, 1989). This trend indicates that the number of elderly people who required physical care at home had increased. In the early 1990s, a qualification system for home helpers began, bringing about their professionalization. According to our survey (Saito and Ishiguro, 2013), almost all home helpers had occupational training and occupational licence. However, their training period is relatively short, and about 53.1 per cent of home helpers have less than six months occupational training.

In the LTCI Law, home helpers were given the legal term Visiting Care Worker (*Houmon Kaigoin*). Laws and regulations of the MHLW determine the content of work in the system. The tasks are broadly divided into physical care and housework support. The service fee is paid hourly for providers under the LTCI.

The introduction of a market mechanism into the eldercare system contributed to increase the amount of care services in a short period, but it also resulted in difficulties establishing a comprehensive home care system because of strong competition among providers. In the mid-1990s, some municipalities introduced a round-the-clock comprehensive home care system based on the Swedish/Scandinavian small-district model (see above) (Campbell, 2014, p. 11; Saito, 2010, p. 52). However, only 368 out of 1,579 insurers (municipalities) offering round-the-clock home help services (*24 jikan taiō teikijyunkai-zuijitaiou sa bisu*, literally 24-hour regular home visitation and as-needed visitation services) are available in Japan, and only 20,500 people were benefitting from them in 2015 MHLW (n.d., 'LTCI care benefit expenditure'). It is difficult for those who need help late at night or early in the morning to stay at home, if they do not have family support. The LTCI system cannot support many elderly people wishing to live at home who need intensive care. This is partly the cause of longer stays in hospitals.

Preventive home help, introduced in 2006, is not well understood by users. However, it is officially aimed at keeping people from becoming more dependent, and home helpers are expected to prompt users to do housekeeping by themselves as much as possible. In 2015, the government decided that preventive home help would be excluded from the direct LTCI benefit, and municipalities would have responsibility for its provision. This could provide problems for poorer municipalities. The introduction of preventive home help in 2006, and its move from LTCI to the municipalities, were both major reforms meant to reduce the home help service.

Non-publicly funded home help

While some Asian countries such as Taiwan, Hong-Kong and Singapore have an active market for domestic workers who care for elderly people, Japan had only around 16,430 domestic workers in 2010 (Statistics Bureau, 2013, Table 11.1). They are usually employed privately. There is almost no market of foreign domestic workers because of immigration policies that forbid the entry of unskilled foreign workers, although there have been recent experiments in allowing a limited number of foreign 'housekeepers'. In the 1930s, there were about 510,000 domestic workers, falling to 50,000 plus domestic workers in the 1970s. Some families employed domestic workers when nursing care was needed. In 1990, there were about 50,000 tax-funded public home helpers, and a market of more than 50,000 private domestic workers (Kitaba, 2001, pp. 223–4). In hospitals for elderly people at the time, if patients with dementia showed behavioural and psychological symptoms, an attendant (called a 'chaperone woman', *tsukisoifu*) was summoned by the hospital, the family having to pay for this privately. She would stay by the patient 24 hours a day and sleep in the narrow horizontal space between the patients' beds.

With the introduction of the LTCI system, many housekeeping agencies received certification as home help providers, and domestic workers became qualified as home helpers. This way, the LTCI system contributed to a professionalization of domestic workers and to the integration of a single care worker market.

Facility services transition

Strict provision control

Facility care was provided for around 1.3 million elderly persons nationwide in 2015 (see Figure 17.2). Although the LTCI Law expects a diverse range of care providers, the LTCI facilities are an exception. Only municipalities, social welfare corporations, medical corporations and some others could be licensed as providers by the Social Welfare Law and the Medical Law, a distinctive characteristic remaining from the pre-LTCI system. The total number of LTCI facilities in Japan is strictly managed. The reference standard (*sanshaku hyōjun*) by the MHLW was that 3 per cent of people aged 65 years or older would be served. As with home help, there has been a decrease in public providers (Table 17.2). Focus is also shifting to elderly people with more severe care requirements. As a result of the LTCI Law, in 2015, welfare facility users have been restricted to those requiring higher levels (3–5) of the LTCI's certification, with the aim of reducing the number of users. According to the MHLW (2014), as of March 2014, there were about 524,000 applicants on waiting lists to enter welfare facilities.

Quasi-facilities

The name 'quasi facility' is used here to distinguish 'group living for those with dementia' (*ninchishō taiougata kyōdō seikatsu kaigo*) and 'private nursing homes' (*tokutei shisetsu*) from the LTCI facilities. They are not categorized as LTCI facilities, but they receive monthly fixed payments from the LTCI depending on the level of care need. Although LTCI facilities charge for accommodation, meals, etc., prices are controlled by the government. Quasi-facilities can charge users for room, meals, and additional services freely. Private nursing homes emerged in the late 1980s, but were expensive. As the LTCI covers their care cost, they have been an alternative for elderly people who want to use a facility care. The number of users in private nursing homes has

Table 17.2 Changes in facility care providers (percentages)

		Public	Non-Profit		
		Municipalities	Social welfare Corporations	Medical Corporations	Others
Welfare Facilities	2000	12.7	87.2	0	0.1
	2014	5.9	93.9	0	0.1
Health Facilities	2000	5.4	15.8	73.0	5.7
	2014	4.4	15.6	74.3	5.5
Medical Care Facilities	2000	4.2	0	70.7	25.2
	2014	5.1	0.9	82.7	11.3

Source: Author's own compilation from MHLW (n.d., 'LTCI Care providers').

increased from 19,100 in 2001 to 266,800 in 2014. As of 2014, 67.6 per cent of private nursing homes were owned by for-profit companies (MHLW, n.d., 'LTCI Care providers').

Group living has expanded rapidly, from 22,400 users in 2001 to 231,000 in 2014. As of 2014, 53.1 per cent of group living providers were for-profit companies (MHLW, n.d., 'Care providers').

Emergence of a new facility market

Because the provision of LTCI facilities (including quasi-facilities) has been government-controlled, 'serviced housing' (*sa-bisu tsuki kōreisha jutaku*) has increased rapidly from the beginning, since 2011. The Ministry of Land, Infrastructure, Transport and Tourism (MLIT) and MHLW together promote 'serviced housing' on the basis of the 2011 revision of the Act on Securement of Stable Supply of Elderly Persons' Housing (*Koreisha Sumai Hō*). Construction and remodelling costs of serviced housing for elderly people are supported by grants to a certain extent, based on certain conditions.

As it is not an LTCI service, LTCI need certification is not necessary to live in serviced housing. However, many of the residents use LTCI home help services and LTCI day-care services from providers that are located nearby. About 80 per cent of these facilities are affiliated with offices providing services such as day-care and home help services (MHLW, 2011). This could be considered to be deregulation of LTCI facilities.

Around 218,195 serviced housing units (as of June 2017) had been registered nationwide in a mere 6.5 years (MLIT, 2017). The government seeks to establish 1 million housing units by 2025. More than 50 per cent of providers are joint-stock companies (JARH, 2014, p. 7, Table I.2.9).

The number of staff per resident tends to be relatively low. A quarter of all serviced housing does not have care staff members stationed 24 hours a day (JARH, 2014, p. 75, Table II.1.61). Serviced housing faces the challenge of preparing facilities to respond to the growing severity of the conditions of residents and of worsening dementia.

Unregistered facilities as grey market

The limitation of LTCI facilities has led to the emergence of unregistered facilities (*mitodoke homu*) (Katagiri, 2015, pp. 50–1). These operate without notifying the government because they are not able to satisfy the standards of private nursing homes (for individual rooms, satisfying the Fire Services Act), even though they are supposed to submit notification to the government in advance of establishment. Many elderly people are on the waiting lists of LTCI facilities, especially in urban areas, and the fees for registered private nursing homes may not be affordable. At-home care is not always available in the night and early morning. And it is expensive to obtain sufficient amounts of care services at home within the limits of the LTCI provided payments.

A survey by Japan Broadcasting Corporation indicated there were 1,941 such facilities in 2015 (NHK, 2015). These facilities are based in private homes or condominiums, and there is thus no way for municipalities to grasp the actual situation except by receiving information from neighbours near the facilities. To lower the housing fee, housing providers choose areas with cheap land and cut down on building and labour costs. As a result, there can be serious quality issues. The lack of staff means that incidents such as residents being tied to bedposts and injuries due to accidents have occurred.

The survey revealed that nearly 80 per cent of the residents of unregistered private nursing homes were referred to them by municipalities and hospitals (NHK, 2015). After being hospitalized, an elderly person who cannot face the prospect of being discharged may be referred to an unregistered home by the municipality or hospital. Many residents of unregistered homes do not have relatives or have low incomes. Although unregistered private nursing homes are illegal, the government continues to depend on them. Because regulation of the total number of LTCI facilities is strict, a state of affairs exists in which 'public' LTC facilities, which are strictly regulated, and 'non-publicly funded' LTC facilities with no regulations, coexist.

Conclusions: marketization but not de-familialization

The aim of this chapter is to clarify the transition of eldercare after the LTCI system introduction in Japan in 2000. It is true that the LTCI system has succeeded in outsourcing some part of family-based eldercare to public-financed services and has influenced the traditional family care culture. However, the amount of services has not increased enough to break down its familialistic character. A publicly funded service cannot lead to de-familialization unless other conditions in society are favourable, as in Scandinavian countries.

The number of LTCI home care users is expected to decrease. Preventive home help and preventive day care service will be moved to the municipalities in 2017, and this means that 1.6 million users will not be able to use these forms of LTCI services. The government encourages lower-need home help users to use other kind of private services (e.g. domestic services by private companies or volunteers in the community). As low-income elderly people cannot buy domestic services without family support, the family care burden is expected to increase. Esping-Andersen (1997, p. 183) pointed out the quite low level of the normal public pension in Japan, which amounts to only 40–45 per cent of previous earnings. This situation has not changed, or has changed for the worse, as the OECD (2015b) pointed out.

The biggest challenge in Japan is a lack of human resources. Unlike in other Asian countries, there is no domestic service market of foreign guest workers in Japan, and the working population is shrinking under the low fertility rate. Although some experiments started in 2016 of allowing foreign domestic housekeepers, it will take years to see the result. Discussions on reform of tax deductions for spouses started in 2016. Reform could change around 10 million housewives (including part-time workers) into taxpayers and formal participants in the labour market.

The number of LTCI facility users has not increased as much as the ageing population because of the government's strict limit. As a result, a new market of 'quasi-facilities' and 'serviced housing' has emerged and is expanding rapidly to meet the demand. As services outside of the LTCI system are less regulated, the emergence of unregistered facilities is a serious challenge to care quality.

Various social security reforms in the 1990s made people (especially women) expect a shift towards de-familialization. The Scandinavian-inspired idea of a 24-hour care provided system in small districts has continued. The government is aiming to build a 'community-based comprehensive eldercare system' comprising a network of elderly people, family, care providers, clinics, and voluntary associations and other stakeholders (MHLW, 2016). A serious challenge is how to organize a comprehensive care system when there is severe competition among providers, aiming to attract the most profitable users. Lack of financial resources of the LTCI is another challenge for the comprehensive eldercare system.

Esping-Andersen (1997, p. 187) said that the Japanese welfare state system was still in the process of evolution, and remained elastic and unformed at the end of the 1990s. The trend of developments of eldercare since the 1990s social welfare restructuring in Japan have been in the direction of deregulation and privatization. And marketization does not result in de-familialization under a weak welfare state.

References

Anttonen, A. and Meagher, B., 2013. Mapping marketisation: concepts and goals. In B. Meagher and M. Szebehely, eds. *Marketisation in Nordic eldercare: a research report on legislation, oversight, extent and consequences*. Stockholm: Stockholm University, pp. 13–25. Available at: www.normacare.net/wp-content/uploads/2013/09/Marketisation-in-nordic-eldercare-webbversion-med-omslag1.pdf [accessed 17.07.2017].

Boling, P., 1998. Family policy in Japan. *Journal of Social Policy*, 27(2), pp. 173–90. Available at: http://homepages.wmich.edu/~plambert/boling.pdf [accessed 20.07.2017].

Cabinet Office, Government of Japan, 2014. *Number and percentage of household of people who are 65 and over*. Annual Report on the Aging Society. Available at: www8.cao.go.jp/kourei/english/annualreport/2014/pdf/c1-2-1.pdf [accessed 01.07.2017].

Campbell, J.C., 2014. Japan's long-term care insurance system. In P. Midford, J.C. Campbell, Y. Saito and U. Edvardsen, eds. *Eldercare policies in Japan and Scandinavia: aging societies East and West*. New York: Palgrave Macmillan, pp. 9–30.

Christensen, K., 2010. Between late modern and later modern elderly care in Norway and Japan. In Y. Saito, R.A. Auestad and K. Wærness, eds. *Meeting the challenges of elder care: Japan and Norway*. Kyoto: Kyoto University Press and Trans Pacific Press, pp. 21–3.

Esping-Andersen, G., 1997. Hybrid or unique? The Japanese welfare state between Europe and America. *Journal of European Social Policy*, 7(3), pp. 179–89. DOI: DOI: 10.1177/095892879700700301.

Esping-Andersen, G., 1999. *Social foundations of postindustrial economies*. Oxford: Oxford University Press

Goodman, R. and Peng, I., 1996. The East Asian welfare states. In G. Esping-Andersen, ed. *Welfare states in transition*. London: Sage, pp. 192–222.

Hiraoka, K., 2013. Yōroppa ni okeru syakai sa-bisu no sijyōka to jyun shijō no riron [Marketization of social services in Europe and the theory of quasi-market]. In S. Takegawa, ed. *Kōkyōsei no fukushigaku* [Welfare sociology of the public sphere: what is a fair society?]. Tokyo: Tokyo University Press, pp. 193–213.

JARH (Japanese Association of Retirement Housing), 2014. *Yuryo rojin ho-mu sa-bisu tsuki koreisya jyutaku ni kansuru jittaichosa* [Survey research on private nursing homes and serviced housing]. Supported by funding of the MHLW, Table I.2.9, p. 17, Table II.1.61, p. 75.

Katagiri, Y., 2015. Kōreisya no idokoro hosyō. Mitodoke yuryō rōjin hōmu wo meguru syomondai [Social security of housing for the elderly: challenges of unregistered private nursing homes]. *Syukan Syakaihosyō* [Monthly Journal of Social Security], 2810, pp. 50–5.

Kitaba, T., 2001. Waga kuni ni okeru zaitaku fukushi seisaku no tenkai katei: rōjin hōshiin haken seido no kaihatsu wo chushin ni [The development process of policy concerning in-home care in Japan: with a focus on the evolution of the dispatch system of home servants for the elderly]. *Nihon Shakaijigyō daigaku kenkyu kiyō* [Bulletin of Japan College of Social Work], 48, pp. 207–42.

MHLW (Ministry of Health, Labour and Welfare), 2010. *Koyō dōkō chōsa* [Survey on employment trends]. Available at: www.e-stat.go.jp/SG1/estat/GL08020103.do?_toGL08020103_&listID=000001084943 &disp=Other&requestSender=dsearch [accessed 17.07.2017].

MHLW (Ministry of Health, Labour and Welfare), 2012. *Shigoto to kaigo no ryōritsu ni Kansuru rōdōsya chōsa* [Research of work and care work balance]. Tokyo: MHLW.

MHLW (Ministry of Health, Labour and Welfare), 2014. *Tokubetsuyōgōrōjinhomu no nyusyo moushikomisya no jyōkyō* [Number of applicants on waiting lists to enter welfare facilities]. Press release, 25 March Tokyo: MHLW.

MHLW (Ministry of Health, Labour and Welfare), 2015. *Koyō doko chōsa* [Survey on employment trends]. Tokyo: MHLW. Available at: www.e-stat.go.jp/SG1/estat/GL08020103.do?_toGL08020103_&listID =000001173665&disp=Other&requestSender=dsearch [accessed 17.07.2017].

MHLW (Ministry of Health, Labour and Welfare), 2016. The community-based integrated care system. In *Long-term care insurance system of Japan*. Health and Welfare Bureau for the Elderly, p. 19. Tokyo: MHLW. Available at: www.mhlw.go.jp/english/policy/care-welfare/care-welfare-elderly/dl/ltcisj_e. pdf [accessed 01.07.2017].

MHLW (Ministry of Health, Labour and Welfare), 2017. *Heisei 27 nendo. Kousei nenkinn & Kokumin nenkinn jigyō no gaikyō* [Conspectus of public pension in 2015]. Tokyo: MHLW. Available at: www.mhlw. go.jp/file/06-Seisakujouhou-12500000-Nenkinkyoku/H27.pdf [accessed 20.07.2017].

MHLW (Ministry of Health, Labour and Welfare), n.d., 'LTCI care benefit expenditure'. *Heisei 13–27 nenn. Kaigo kyuhfuhi jittai chōsa houkoku* [LTCI survey report on long-term care benefit expenditure in 2001–2015]. Available at: www.mhlw.go.jp/toukei/list/45-1.html [accessed 18.07.2017]. [It has been published every month since 2001. The number of actual recipients (*nenkan jitsu jyukyusyasu*) is calculated in every fiscal year (from April to March, the following year), and includes the number of recipients who used LTCI services at least once.]

MHLW (Ministry of Health, Labour and Welfare), n.d., 'LTCI care providers'. *Heisei 12–26 nen. Kaigo sabisu shisetsu jigyōsyo tyōsa* [LTCI survey report on long-term care providers in 2000–2014]. Available at: www.mhlw.go.jp/toukei/list/24-22-2.html [accessed 18.07.2017]. [Number of care service providers (*Kaigo sa-bisu sisetsu/ jigyosyo*) on 1 October is calculated every year from 2000.]

MHW (Ministry of Health and Welfare), 1962. *Rōjin katei hōshiin jigyō unei yōkō* [Home help service outline]. Tokyo: MHW.

MHW (Ministry of Health and Welfare), 1978. *Kōsei Hakusyo* [White Paper], Tokyo: MHW.

MHW (Ministry of Health and Welfare), 1989. *Kaitei Rōjin katei hōshiin jigyō unei yōkō* [Revision of home help outline and Golden Plan] Tokyo: MHW.

MHW (Ministry of Health and Welfare), 1998. *Heisei 10-nendo Kōsei Hakusho* [White paper on health and welfare] Tokyo: MHW.

MLIT (Ministry of Land, Infrastructure, Transport and Tourism), 2017. *Sa-bisu tsuki kōreisyamuke jyutaku no tōrokujyōkyō* [Number of registered serviced housing on June 2017]. Available at: www.satsuki-jutaku. jp/system.html [accessed 20.07.2017].

National Institute of Population and Social Security Research, 2012. *Population projections for Japan (January 2012)*. Available at: www.ipss.go.jp/site-ad/index_english/esuikei/h3_4.html [accessed 20.07.2017].

NHK (Nippon Hoso Kyokai – Japan Broadcasting Corporation), 2015. Kyuzō suru Mutodoke Kaigohause no jittai to kadai [Current conditions and challenges of 'non-registered private nursing homes']. *Toshi Mondai* [Journal of the Tokyo Institute for Municipal Research], 106(4), pp. 25–9.

Ochiai, E., 2009. Care diamonds and welfare regimes in East and South-East Asian societies: bridging family and welfare sociology. *International Journal of Japanese Sociology*, 18(1), pp. 60–78. DOI: 10.1111/j.1475-6781.2009.01117.x.

OECD, 2015a. *In it together: why less inequality benefits all in Japan*. Available at: www.oecd.org/japan/ OECD2015-In-It-Together-Highlights-Japan.pdf [accessed 07.06.2017].

OECD, 2015b. *Health at a glance 2013: ageing and long-term care expenditure*. Available at: www.keepeek. com/Digital-Asset-Management/oecd/social-issues-migration-health/health-at-a-glance-2015/long-term-care-expenditure_health_glance-2015-79-en#.WQhF5Mm1uIE#page1 [accessed 17.07.2017].

OECD, 2016a. *Social Expenditure Database (SOCX). Public social spending (Japan and OECD)*. Available at: www.oecd.org/social/expenditure.htm [accessed 17.07.2017].

OECD, 2016b. *PF3.1 Public spending on childcare and early education*. Available at: www.oecd.org/els/soc/ PF3_1_Public_spending_on_childcare_and_early_education.pdf [accessed 01.07.2017].

Peng, I., 2002. Social care in crisis: gender, demography, and welfare state restructuring in Japan. *Social Politics*, 9(3), pp. 411–43. DOI: https://doi.org/10.1093/sp/9.3.411.

Saito, Y., 2010a. Development of home help in Japan: a comparison with Norway. In Y. Saito, R. A. Auestad and K. Wærness, eds. *Meeting the challenges of elder care: Japan and Norway*. Kyoto: Kyoto University Press and Trans Pacific Press, pp. 39–67.

Saito, Y., 2014a. Elderly care transition and welfare state in Japan. In B. Aulenbacher, R. Riegraf and H. Theobald, eds. *Sorge: Arbeit, Verhältnisse, Regime* [Care: work, relations, regimes]. Baden-Baden: Nomos, pp. 419–34.

Saito, Y., 2014b. Care providers in Japan: before and after the long-term care insurance. In P. Midford, J.C. Campbell, Y. Saito and U. Edvardsen, eds. *Eldercare policies in Japan and Scandinavia: aging societies East and West*. New York: Palgrave Macmillan, pp. 51–69.

Saito, Y. and Ishiguro, N. eds., 2013. *NORDCARE Survey in Japan: the everyday realities of eldercare – similarities and differences mirrored by care workers*. Survey report supported by the JSPS (Japan Society for the Promotion of Science).

Statistics Bureau, Ministry of Internal Affairs and Communications (MIAC), Portal Site of Official Statistics of Japan (e-Stat). *Result of the population estimates, time series 2000–2015, Table 3, Population by age and sex (as of October 1 of each year (from 2000 to 2015)*. Available at: www.e-stat.go.jp/SG1/estat/ListE. do?bid=000001039703&cycode=0 [accessed 17.07.2017]

Statistics Bureau, Ministry of Internal Affairs and Communications (MIAC), 2013. *2010 Kaseifu /kajitet-sudai*. [Population Census. E-(26)-99 Number of domestic workers Table 11.1. Employed persons 15 years of age and over by industry, occupation and sex – Japan]. Available at: www.e-stat.go.jp/SG1/estat/List.do?bid=000001050829&cycode=0 [accessed 23.10.2017].

Statistics Bureau, Ministry of Internal Affairs and Communications (MIAC), 2017. *Population estimates by age (5 year age group) and sex: January 1, 2017 (final estimates)*. Available at: www.e-stat.go.jp/SG1/estat/ListE.do?lid=000001184183 [accessed 13.07.17].

Svensson, M. and Edebalk, P.G., 2002. Äldreomsorg och kundsval [Eldercare and consumers' choice]. In Konkurrensverket [Agency of Competition], ed. *Vårda och skapa konkurrens. Vad krävs för ökad konsumentnytta?* Konkurrensverkets Rapportserie. [Control and create competition: what is required for increased consumers' benefit? A report series]. 2, pp. 308–39.

Szebehely, M., 1995. *Vardagens organisering. Om vårdbiträden och gamla i hemtjänsten* [Organization of everyday life: care workers and elderly people in home help]. Lund: Arkiv.

UN (2015). *World population ageing 2015*. Available at: www.un.org/en/development/desa/population/publications/pdf/ageing/WPA2015_Report.pdf [accessed 17.07.2017].

Yamada, K. 2009. Past and present constraints on labour movements for gender equality in Japan. *Social Science Japan Journal*, 12(2), pp. 195–209. DOI: https://doi.org/10.1093/ssjj/jyp020.

18

Care robots in Japanese elderly care

Cultural values in focus

Nobu Ishiguro

Introduction

The utilization of care robots has been proposed in many countries to help older people live independently. Technological solutions are considered breakthroughs for the challenges a steadily ageing society faces. Robots, however, are often controversial and generate anxiety concerning future elderly care. While most medical and health tools and technologies have been widely accepted and are relatively uncontroversial, robots and other automation care technologies are considered exceptions (Coeckelbergh, 2015). However, modern technological development means more advanced technologies will continue to enter the care sector, potentially greatly affecting care work.

Japan, a long-term world leader in the manufacture and use of industrial robots, is often referred to as 'the robot kingdom' (Holroyd and Coates, 2007). It has both the world's largest share of industrial robots and a strong robot culture, including robot-influenced narratives such as manga, animation films and comics, and robot research (Wagner, 2010). In Western countries, robots are often associated with menacing mechanical monsters in contrast to Japan's view of a symbiotic people–robot relationship. The Japanese increasingly consider these machines to be practical and efficient solutions to some of the country's most pressing social and economic challenges (Holroyd and Coates, 2007). Elderly care robot usage has been discussed in Japan and other developed countries for many years. However, despite the Japanese government's enthusiasm, modern assistive technology is infrequently used in elderly care, with the exception of the special bathtub device that allows disabled people to lie on a stretcher in a movable tub.

This lack of usage can be attributed to numerous structural and political factors. While welfare state policies and social structures are interrelated with country-specific cultural systems, culture is often treated as a more marginal issue in the welfare state debate. Cultural values and ideas restrict the spectrum of possible policies and affect the behaviours of individuals and social groups (Pfau-Effinger, 2005). With this in mind, this chapter focuses on the cultural values embedded in the limited use of care robots. First, Japan's demography and care work will be outlined. Next will follow a theoretical framework for understanding care workers' responses to technology in care by contrasting cold technology with warm care. An outline of the factors hindering robot use in Japanese elderly care, through a transfer lift case study, as an example,

256

will follow (a transfer lift is an assistive device for lifting and transferring care recipients). The results of care worker focus group interviews will also be presented. Finally, I will discuss the implications of robots for care work and how to handle them.

Overview of elderly care work and care robots in Japan

The crucial background factor behind care robot use is the ageing population. Japan has the highest proportion of those aged over 65 years in the world – 26.7 per cent in 2015 and an estimated 36.1 per cent in 2040 (Cabinet Office, 2016, pp. 2, 5) – which will further increase demand for long-term care services. A total of 3.7 per cent of elderly people (aged 65+) received care in institutional settings, while 6.2 per cent received care in home settings in 2014 (author's own calculation based on MHLW, 2015a, Table 2). Public long-term elderly care service expenditures (including health and social care components) represented 2.1 per cent of the GDP in 2013, compared to the OECD average of 1.7 per cent (OECD, 2015, p. 208). The majority (94.7 per cent) of the residential homes stipulated in the long-term care insurance (LTCI) scheme are private, mainly non-profit (although private residential homes not stipulated by LTCI, run by for-profit organizations, are increasing), and 99.7 per cent of the home-based care providers were private (mainly for-profit providers) in 2014 (MHLW, 2015b, Table 4). Concurrently, rapid turnover among care workers creates a serious problem, mainly due to precarious working conditions. Care work is considered to be one of Japan's '3K jobs' – unsafe (*kiken*), unclean (*kitanai*), and tough (*kitsui*) jobs – and workers' physical/mental burdens are reportedly heavy (see below). Moreover, care workers have lower wages than other occupational groups; 73.2 per cent of an average worker's wage (author's own calculation based on MHLW, 2016). Japan is projected to suffer a serious care labour shortage in the near future.

One solution proposed by the Japanese government is to use robots in elderly care. Since the robot industry stagnated at the turn of the twenty-first century, the Japanese government has encouraged innovation by relating it to the challenges of an ageing society, expecting the promotion of robots in elderly care to contribute to economic growth. This state initiative began in earnest in 2010, when the government presented its vision for the promotion of the development and implementation of care robots as part of the New Growth Strategy. The Committee on Care/Welfare Robot Dissemination was established, and discussion concerning how to best promote care robot use was generated thereafter. The Ministry of Economy, Trade and Industry (METI) and the MHLW cooperated in creating large-scale funding systems to support care robot projects nationwide. In 2013, the Japan Revitalization Strategy and the Five Year Plan for Development of Care Robots were presented. The term 'robotic assistive technology' was used, indicating assistive devices in which robotics were incorporated. The MHLW sometimes includes the improvement of traditional assistive technology in subsidy schemes for R&D of care robots. The eight focus areas for care robot development promoted by the Japanese government (Robotic Care Devices Portal, 2016) are:

(1) Wearable transfer devices
Worn by the caregiver, these use robot technologies to provide powered assistance to reduce caregiver backload during transfer assistance; for example, from bed to wheelchair or toilet.
(2) Non-wearable transfer aids
Using robot technologies, these provide powered assistance to the caregiver in performing lifting motions, such as when transferring an individual from bed to wheelchair. These are operated by one person.

(3) Outdoor mobility aids

These include mobile support equipment and motorized walking support devices (excluding rideable devices) that provide mobility and luggage assistance to elderly people outside their homes, are capable of stable motion over uneven ground, and are easy to carry.

(4) Indoor mobility aids

These help elderly people stand, sit, and move around their homes. The devices use robot technologies and are specifically designed to assist them in sitting on and standing up from a toilet.

(5) Toileting aids

These should be movable and can be placed anywhere in a room. They should also maximize robot technologies for effective waste treatment.

(6) Bathing aids

These use robot technologies to support elderly people in a series of motions required for getting in and out of bathtubs, and are usable by a single person with or without the help of an assistant.

(7) Monitoring systems for nursing care homes

These include equipment and platforms using sensor and external communication facilities to support the monitoring of the elderly in long-term care facilities.

(8) Monitoring systems for private homes

These are devices and platforms using robot technologies with sensors and external communication functions to monitor the elderly and others in private homes. They can concurrently monitor multiple rooms, including bathrooms.

These devices need humans to be present to operate them; they are not autonomous robots making independent decisions. Some devices are similar to assistive technology already in use. For example, outdoor mobility aids are like rollators (walking frames equipped with wheels). They just have additional motors that enable older people to move more easily along a sloping road. Other devices (e.g. monitoring devices) are somewhat novel and might require further ethical discussions. As many other types of robots will probably be introduced into care work, we must examine how these technologies affect care work.

Industrial robots are used in manufacturing, such as automobile manufacturing and electronic assembly, and have achieved rationalization via labour savings measures and automation. Robots have also freed workers from many unsafe tasks and have contributed to the stabilization of product quality (NEDO, 2014, p. 21). What, then, can be achieved by robots in care work? As manufacturing and care are completely different industries and direct human interaction is indispensable for individual care, care workers must understand the needs and wishes of the care recipient and navigate the social and emotional relationships. If robots are to operate in care work, they must adjust to changing human needs. How can this occur? The scepticism as to whether robots can contribute to care work might lead to reluctance to use them.

Cold care and warm care?

To examine the gap between the government's intention to move robots into care and resistance to this in care workplaces, I will first analyse relevant government documents, and then provide a theoretical framework for understanding care work, focusing on the relational aspects of care, often addressed when discussing care technology.

The government's incentives for introducing care robots

Four care robot discourses in government documents can be identified. First, the 'workload discourse' suggests care robots can reduce the physical/mental burden of care work and can lessen care worker turnover. Government documents note 70 per cent of care workers have backache that can be alleviated by lightening their workloads using care robots (The Headquarters for Japan's Economic Revitalization, 2015; METI, 2013b). According to The Headquarters for Japan's Economic Revitalization (2015), robotic transfer and bath aids are major areas of focus to lighten care workers' loads.

Second, the 'quality discourse' indicates robots will help older people live more independently, thereby maintaining their dignity and enhancing their quality of life. The government's goal is to ensure 'older people with care needs will continue living an independent life in the community' (The Headquarters for Japan's Economic Revitalization, 2015, p. 64). Mobility aids, toileting aids, and monitoring systems for people with dementia will assist older people with maintaining their independence (The Headquarters for Japan's Economic Revitalization, 2015, p. 66). The government also stresses 'care by human hands' – care that only 'human hands' can perform – and the continuance of this 'basic principle' is indicated (The Headquarters for Japan's Economic Revitalization, 2015, pp. 63–4).

The third discourse is the 'robot industry discourse'. The Japanese government wants to enhance the care robot industry and expects overall growth in the domestic robot industry. As the Japanese care robot market size was 16.7 billion yen (£119 million) in 2012 and is projected to be 404.3 billion yen (£29 billion) in 2035 (METI, 2013a, p. 18), the government expects a resulting huge economic growth. This presupposes an increase in the production of *Japanese robots* for use in the care sector.

Fourth, the 'cost-saving discourse' suggests efficiency and productivity should be enhanced to achieve cost containment. Care work is very labour-intensive and is often afflicted with a 'cost disease' (Donath, 2000). The government emphasizes elderly care expenditure will rise from 8.4 trillion yen (£60 billion) in 2012 to 19.8 trillion yen (£141 billion) in 2025, and the number of care workers needed to meet the growing demands will increase from 1.4 million in 2011 to 2.44 million in 2025 (Prime Minister of Japan and His Cabinet, 2013, 6, p. 26), indicating a need to control costs with the help of care robots. There is always tension between providing good care and cost containment pressures, and attempting to raise productivity in care work by increasing the numbers of people cared for at any one time quickly increases the risk of reduced care quality (Donath, 2000).

The nature of care and cultural values

A strong belief exists in Japan that 'human hands' should undertake care (Motegi et al., 2012, p. 82; Tomioka et al., 2007, p. 113). The emphasis on 'care by human hands' (*hitode no kaigo*) can often be found in public discourses, including the government documents mentioned above. Care by human hands is thought to be warm, while care by machines is considered cold, and this may be a consequence of the holistic nature of care. Care robots might perform physical tasks, but they are incapable of meeting emotional and relational care needs. Care is embedded in a set of social relations integral to well-being (Daly, 2001). It consists of two aspects: 'caring for' and 'caring about'. The first involves catering directly to another person's physical and emotional needs; the second involves activity being motivated by others' well-being. Good care will not be successfully delivered unless the person being cared for believes the carer is motivated by genuine concern for his or her well-being (Himmelweit, 1999). Therefore, robots seem incapable of fulfilling some aspects of care, generating a distrust of using technology in care, although some studies suggest increasing numbers of Japanese care workers are interested in using care robots (NCCU, 2015).

The holistic nature of care (as 'caring about') and Japanese culture as a whole can affect Japanese care workers' attitudes towards care technology. As Pfau-Effinger (2005) pointed out, country-specific cultural values can affect how people respond to policies. I will now elaborate on Japanese cultural values, especially the notions of 'self' and features of the resulting interactions with others. Supporting individuals in maintaining autonomy and adjusting/structuring relationships with the environment/others are crucial social work roles (Kuga, 2014, p. 83); therefore, an examination of how self is constructed and how people perceive the care situation as recipients is relevant.

Psychological tendencies involving the self are sustained by the ways in which the attendant social realities are collectively constructed in each cultural context. The Japanese perception of self is interdependently (contextually and socially) construed, while the Western is independently (individually and autonomously) construed. Japanese culture can be traced back to the Buddhist ideal of compassion and the Confucian teaching of role obligation (Shimizu, 2002; Kitayama et al., 1997), as well as the rice farming culture, which consists of arduous cooperative labour requiring people to work hard and steadily together to survive. Conformity and cooperation were cultural prerequisites in this type of community. As a result, collectivism within the community or family has been strong (Ohashi, 2013, p. 2; Herbig and Laurence, 1996, p. 67). Autonomy and self are not well-developed concepts, and self-help and living an independent life are not as important as they are in Western societies.

A contrast between cold care by technology and warm care by human hands might create frictions in care work and care worker resistance to technology. The cold image of care robots reflects, among other things, the government's pursuit of cost containment and care robot industry promotion. Warm care by human hands for older people is a strong value embedded in Japanese care work culture; therefore, the introduction of care robots to alleviate the care work burden or to make older people more independent might enhance the cold perception of technology.

Limited use of technology in care work

In this section, I will discuss why technology is not widely used in Japanese care work, although in other industries most physically heavy tasks have been mechanized.

Limited use of care robots

Even in Kanagawa prefecture, which is a pioneer care robot prefecture, only 3.4 per cent of the residential homes use them (Kanagawa Welfare Service Association, 2014). Residential homes must themselves finance the purchase of often extremely expensive care robots and other assistive technologies. If older people live at home, they can rent some assistive devices by paying 10 per cent of the cost using the LTCI scheme. However, this is mainly for non-robotic assistive devices such as wheelchairs and lifts. Few care robots are currently covered by LTCI. Sufficient information and knowledge about care robots is not provided to residential homes and care workers, nor are they included in care workers' education. Few staff members have the knowledge to instruct and operate care robots. According to a survey, only 0.3 per cent of care workers have used care robots, and 15.9 per cent do not know what care robots are (NCCU, 2015, Table 5). The nature of care can also have an influence. The Kanagawa Welfare Service Association (2012) notes this:

> Work carried out in residential homes is different from work in factories where automation and division of labour is developed .... Efficiency is not always welcomed in care. Moreover, each staff member performs all kinds of tasks such as help with eating, toileting,

bathing, and so on, like a multi-skilled worker. Furthermore, care work is not about doing the same tasks in a repetitive and continuous manner, but adjusting care to the changing conditions and preferences of the care recipient.

This aspect requires special attention to ascertain how (and whether) robots, components of the industrial world, can be applied to care work.

Use of technology for physically heavy tasks in care work

Care work includes heavy person-handling tasks related to increased occupational injuries, such as helping persons with bathing and transferring them from bed to chair. Lifts and other assistive devices can help reduce injury risks (Hignett et al., 2003; Occupational Safety and Health Administration, 2001, 2003). Nevertheless, assistive devices are not often used in Japanese care workplaces, resulting in musculoskeletal disorders among workers. According to our 2012 survey of Japanese care workers (2,440 questionnaires were distributed to care facilities and home help providers nationwide, and the response rate was 43.4 per cent; Saito and Ishiguro, 2013), most (69.1 per cent) almost always or often felt physically tired after a working day, and back pain was almost always or often a problem for 49.5 per cent of the care workers (Saito and Ishiguro, 2012, p. 43). Most (64.6 per cent) care workers responded that they did not have access to adequate equipment for physically heavy tasks (Saito and Ishiguro, 2013, p. 38).

In other industries, occupational health has improved greatly over the last few decades, as most physically heavy tasks have been mechanized. While back pain in general has decreased, back pain among care workers has increased greatly (MHLW, 2013). The MHLW revised the *Guidelines for Back Pain Prevention in the Workplace* in 2013, stating that care workers must not lift persons without technical devices, although manual lifts are still frequently conducted for several reasons. Japanese residential homes often do not offer enough space for the lifts to operate. Furthermore, it takes longer to use transfer lifts, and structural conditions are insufficient for promoting the use of technical devices; for example, no subsidy system exists for purchasing technical devices. The Japanese government has not taken sufficient measures to promote traditional assistive technology use either, including the implementation of transfer lifts, prior to its promotion of care robot use. Arguably, the lack of effective measures to support the use of assistive technology reflects cultural values about machines not successfully accommodating care needs and being unable to provide warm care.

Methods of studies of technology/robots in care work

Central to this section are the focus groups I carried out related to care workers' perceptions of and experiences with technology, in particular transfer lifts in care work. I also briefly refer to surveys of the Japanese public's attitudes towards the use of robots in care work, carried out by the Cabinet Office and the ORIX Living Corporation.

Transfer lift as a case study

To investigate how (and whether) robots can be applied to care work, I will use an analysis of preconceptions about and use of transfer lifts as an example of the absence of technology in care work (even though the MHLW categorizes transfer lift as traditional assistive technology, not as a care robot). The transfer lift is a good example, as it is technology most Japanese care workers have either experience with or knowledge about, even though they are unlikely to have used them; therefore, it is relevant to investigate how the workers perceive it. Moreover, while lifts are widely used in many countries – Europe, for example – they are infrequently used in Japanese elderly care, despite official statements concerning their ability to lighten care workers' physical burdens. Examining the attitudes behind this phenomenon might help us ascertain why technology is unpopular in Japanese care work.

To gain insight into care workers' subjective perceptions of and work experiences with technology, particularly transfer lifts, I conducted three focus group interviews in April 2016. The respondents were staff of three elderly care facilities. Respondents in two groups (four care workers in each) worked for two different residential homes using assistive technologies, and respondents in one group (four care workers) worked for a residential home not using them. All sessions were transcribed, and the data were entered into a database. The researcher discussed the ethical considerations and confidential handling of the data with the respondents. This is an ongoing project on care technology, conducted by a multidisciplinary research team; interviews with care recipients have not been conducted yet, due to the difficulty in finding residential homes allowing this.

Studies of the Japanese public's attitudes toward robots in care work

Japanese adults' attitudes towards the use of care robots in care were assessed in two surveys. The Cabinet Office's (2013) survey investigated the public's attitude toward care robots. It drew its random sample from the general Japanese population aged over 20; 3,000 people were recruited, and 1,842 responses were collected through face-to-face interviews (response rate: 61.4 per cent). The ORIX Living Corporation's (2015) Internet survey investigated the public's attitude toward care; 1,238 people over 40 years of age (456 women and 782 men) responded. However, we must be cautious in interpreting the results of these two surveys given the ages of respondents in these samples.

Results of studies

In this section, I present the findings from the focus groups on attitudes to technology in care work of care workers with and without relevant experience, and from the surveys of Japanese public attitudes to care robots. I discuss these findings in relation to elderly Japanese people's behaviours and feelings towards professional care workers, and how these may affect the introduction and experience of technology in care work.

Care workers' attitudes toward technology

In the focus group interviews, I tried to investigate how care workers perceive the concrete care situations in which technology can be used. Care workers in a residential home not using transfer lifts responded as follows:

Researcher: Are you reluctant to use a transfer lift?
A: Yes. I do not want to use it, and I do not want it to be used for my parents [for example] …. It is like being lifted by a crane truck like an object … I don't like it, because it is not like treating a person.
B: I don't like it because it is like [treating] an object.
C: I don't like it either, and I don't want to get used to that …
B: It must be a strange sight [to see a care recipient transferred using a lift].

Here, the lift is perceived as treating people like an object, associating lifts with industrial robots. They were also reluctant to use special bathtub technology. Although this is relatively widespread in Japanese residential homes, it was not used in the residential home in which they worked. Care workers said:

A: I feel really strange using machines to take a bath …. It is not a real bath – not real bathing.
C: I will never choose to take a bath in that way myself.
A: Because you have to get naked and lie down on the board, and it will automatically sink down into the water in the bathtub.
B: And the shower will come from the side.
A: The water will come, and you are bound by a belt at the waist …
C: Scary. One would not be able to do anything in that situation, you know.
B: You are helpless.
A: Yes, like you are naked and in the machine.
D: It's like an object being washed.

They think providing care with the help of a lift or special bath technology is like treating older people as an object, and using machines is strange and unnatural. The care workers assume older people are placed in a passive role when care is provided with the help of technology:

Researcher: Do you mean older people cannot do anything in that situation while being moved by others?
C: It seems the elderly's wishes are not taken into consideration …. It's like you are being told 'you cannot do anything'.
B: Right. Like, 'I am incapable'.
Researcher: Is it humiliating for older people? Do you think?
A: I think so.
B: It's like they accept it because they have given up.
D: I imagine it would not feel comfortable.
C: Even if it is a lift, if they can operate it themselves and feel they can transfer themselves, then it is okay, I think, but it's not so good if somebody else is operating.
A: It would be better if they choose to use a device in order to be independent, but it is not so good if somebody is telling you, 'you cannot do it yourself, so we will use this'.

When technology is involved, care workers perceive that older people are being treated as objects, regardless of whether the older people accept the treatment. Older people are being treated as powerless, dependent, and passive, because being cared for by technology is a symbol of dependence and passivity, implying that elderly people should be cared for by affectionate, warm, and caring human hands. Cold technology is thought to be incapable of handling vulnerability.

A 'protective' attitude exists in Japan, whereby care workers protect frail, vulnerable older people (Bishu, 2013). Japanese workers express a paternalistic characteristic, as they make decisions in good faith on behalf of frail older people. Care workers speculate older people prefer being lifted manually by warm human hands instead of by transfer lifts. However, some research indicates lifts provide better care to recipients, since manual lifts can feel uncomfortable, and sometimes even painful (Tomioka et al., 2007, p. 120).

Interviews were also conducted with groups of care workers at the residential homes using transfer lifts. Some had anticipated that transfer lift use might feel cold, but these perceptions changed afterwards:

> And we tried being lifted by a transfer lift ourselves, so now we know how it feels for older people. And they say it is comfortable, and therefore it is very good .... There are some people with muscle contracture who feel pain when they are transferred manually by human hands. Using a transfer lift, we have actually been able to avoid that pain.

Another care worker agreed:

> When we transferred them manually, their faces were distorted with pain. But when we use a transfer lift, they smile and say, 'I'm okay'.

In determining whether care robots should be introduced or what kinds of technologies will be applied, care workers and recipients should be given opportunities to speak and be heard (Parks, 2010, p. 109). However, this democratic communication process can be challenging for Japanese care recipients and workers.

The Japanese traditionally have negative attitudes toward speech/words. They are sometimes seen as being obstructive to mutual understanding (Aida, 1972). In this culture, people can communicate by understanding context and relationship without verbally expressing them (Kuga, 2014, p. 115; Kawabata, 1996, p. 211). Silence (*ma*) can express meanings in Japan, and one is expected to 'read the air' and enter into others' feelings (Kuga, 2014, p. 116; Takeuchi, 2013, p. 73; Fukuda, 2009, p. 9). People in need often do not ask for help but prefer to wait until someone comes to assist them, partly because they feel apologetic, and partly because they expect someone to notice it. In this culture, frail elderly people are often passive care recipients who have difficulty expressing their wishes and asking for help (Ohashi, 2013, p. 4). Care workers therefore often take a paternalistic approach and presume that older people prefer human hands to assistive technology, based on the 'caring about' idea.

The Japanese public's attitude to care robots

However, Japanese people are generally willing to use care robots. The Cabinet Office (2013) survey asked Japanese people, 'if you are in need of care, would you like a caretaker to use care robots?', and 65.1 per cent responded, 'yes'. To the question 'what is good about care robots?', 63.9 per cent responded, 'caretaker's physical/mental burden will be relieved', followed by 'you do not have to "*ki wo tsukau*" for caretakers' (41.5 per cent) and 'one can perform more tasks by oneself' (35.8 per cent) (Cabinet Office, 2013, pp. 5, 7). '*Ki wo tsukau*' is a Japanese expression that is difficult to translate into other languages. It literally means to 'use "*ki*" (mind) toward someone', implying one needs to be careful, attentive, and sensitive to someone so as not to cause them trouble. The ORIX Living Corporation (2015) survey showed the same tendency. People were asked, 'when you are in need of care, would you like to receive care by care robots?', and most (69.0 per cent) said, 'yes, if it is recommended', while 9.4 per cent responded, 'yes, very much' (19.3 per cent responded 'no') (ORIX Living Corporation, 2015, p. 12). Concerning their willingness, they responded, 'you do not have to "*ki wo tsukau*" for caretakers' (52.7 per cent), and 26.5 per cent responded, 'care by human hands is preferable, but then you have to "*ki wo tsukau*" for caretakers' (ORIX Living Corporation, 2015, p. 13).

Interaction between elderly Japanese people and professional care workers, and how this affects technology use

Takeo Doi was a leading Japanese psychiatrist who explored behaviour and developed the concept of '*amae*', defined as:

> In the first place, the craving of a newborn child for close contact with its mother and, in the broader sense, the desire to deny the fact of separation that is an inevitable part of human existence, and to obliterate the pain of separation.
>
> *(Doi, 1971, p. 167)*

Doi argues that *amae* is an emotion strongly experienced by Japanese, and to some extent non-Japanese people. According to Doi, '*wo tsukau*' implies a constant feeling of '*enryo*' (consideration) toward the other person as a result of apprehension lest he or she fails to accept his or her own '*amae*' as unreservedly as desired. The fear is that, unless one holds back, one will be thought impertinent and disliked (Doi, 1971, pp. 30, 39). When receiving care, the recipient is grateful to the care worker, as well as apologetic or indebted on the assumption that this was burdensome to the care worker. Japanese individuals would like to avoid such feelings, which are often absent within their 'inner' circle (*uchi*) – immediate family, relatives, or other close relations. In the 'outer' circle (*soto*), they are present, and one has to '*ki wo tsukau*' (Doi, 1971, p. 40). Therefore, if one is cared for by family, one does not need to '*ki wo tsukau*'; if one receives care from a care worker, one may feel apologetic or indebted.

In Japan, family has long been responsible for elderly care. However, more elderly people receive care today from non-family professional care workers, especially after the introduction of the LTCI scheme in 2000. Older people tend to feel apologetic for the trouble they cause others, as they know care work is arduous and can generate heavy physical and mental burdens for care workers. The subjective well-being of Japanese selves may depend on self-appraisals of not having shortcomings and not causing trouble in the context of social relationships (Kitayama et al., 1997). In this regard, care robots have strong possibilities. The alleviation of burdens through the use of robots will be appreciated not only by the care workers, but also by elderly people. Care workers' preconceptions about care robots may also be changed when technology is actually used. This is well illustrated in the case of a Japanese residential home using a transfer lift. Some older residents were reportedly pleased, saying they now did not have to '*ki wo tsukau*' for care workers because they knew the care workers' burdens were alleviated. Care workers were also happy with the technology, as they now recognized the advantages both for themselves and for elderly people (ORIX Living Corporation, 2016, p. 8).

However, caution is needed to not assume older people want to avoid social contact because they do not want to bother others; rather, it reflects their willingness to maintain relationships, using Doi's (1971) perspective. Furthermore, a Japanese social work researcher, Kuga (2014), in his social work theory based on Japanese cultural values, argued the need for heeding Japanese people's tendencies to avoid causing trouble for others. The paternalistic approach is sometimes needed, since appropriate paternalism can mean respecting older people's autonomy (Freudenreich, 2007, p. 228).

Finally, Japanese culture is not unchangeable. We should be aware that culture is a dynamic entity (Erez and Gati, 2004), and generational differences may occur over time.

Concluding discussion

Technology generates pleasure and pain and restructures social relationships in both positive and negative ways. When adopting new systems, such as care robots, a close understanding of their implications is needed (Roberts and Mort, 2009, p. 156; Lehoux, 2006, p. xv).

Nevertheless, the 'robot care' or 'human care' dichotomy makes little sense in the care work discussion; it presupposes all care is provided by either robots or humans. In reality, it is a 'human-technology-human relationship', as Coeckelbergh (2015) noted. Technology can function as part of the care worker-recipient activities. Humans can pursue care provision in a caring, engaging, and attentive way and use robots in care without expecting them to be caring in the same way. The robots the Japanese government wants to promote do not act autonomously or replace humans, so how humans use technology to provide better care is important (Coeckelbergh, 2015).

This is well illustrated by the transfer lift example. The residential home experiences showed that when a care worker conducts a manual lift using their own hands, they hold the care recipient in their arms and cannot see the recipient's face over their shoulder. This is not attentive care, as the care worker cannot see if the recipient is uncomfortable. When a transfer lift is used, the care worker can see the recipient's face from the front, and can thereby provide more attentive care (ORIX Living Corporation, 2016, p. 8). Thus, technology has the potential to enhance the caring situation. How we care for older people – with or without technology – matters, and technology use itself is not necessarily an issue.

Another worry regarding care robots is that they may reduce care worker-recipient interaction hours. While this does not apply to the transfer lift and special bathtub technology, some technologies will reduce the time care workers would otherwise spend with the recipients. Sparrow and Sparrow (2006) stated:

> In many instances, the only regular human contact experienced by frail older people is with those people who provide the physical care for them – who lift, shower, dress, and feed them – and with those who clean their rooms or homes ... the companionship afforded at these times is equally, or even more, important than the actual duties performed.

In Denmark, for example, some municipalities have introduced robot vacuum cleaners as replacements for home care worker cleaning services, leading to debates concerning whether it is fair to reduce elderly people's human contact (Greve, 2011, p. 5). This may be a global issue necessary for consideration when we discuss care robot use, as care is embedded in social relationships, regardless of culture. Wærness (1984) presented the concept of 'rationality of caring', providing a direction when considering the essence of care. Rationality of caring suggests personal knowledge, certain abilities, and understanding the specifics of each situation in which help is required as prerequisites for providing good care (Wærness, 1984, 2005). It also implies that good care can only occur when freedom exists to develop it through dialogue (Christensen, 2008). Providing good care will be problematic if there is insufficient time for care worker-recipient interactions.

Finally, I argue the necessity of discussing the benefits and disadvantages of each specific care robot/assistive technology, in addition to presenting a general discussion on robots/technology. Existing robots are not autonomous entities capable of multiple tasks. Rather, they perform only specialized tasks (Yamauchi, 2015; Nylander et al., 2012, p. 801), with each device having different care implications (Coeckelbergh, 2013; Nylander et al., 2012; Roberts and Mort, 2009). Research into this area is currently lacking, despite the government's enthusiasm for promoting care robots and the abundant research that has been conducted by engineers and robotics professionals. Further cautious discussion is necessary concerning how technology can be integrated into good care practice and what organizational/structural conditions are required before care robot use can increase in an unobtrusive manner in care work.

References

Aida, Y., 1972. *Nihonjin no ishiki kozo* [Structures of Japanese consciousness]. Tokyo: Kodansha.

Bishu, N., 2013. Hokuo kea to wagakuni no koreisha kea no hikaku [Comparative study on Nordic and Japanese eldercare]. In S. Hamauzu, ed. *Ima hokuo kea wo kangaeru*. Osaka: Osaka University, pp. 117–26.

Coeckelbergh, M., 2013. E-care as craftsmanship: virtuous work, skilled engagement, and information technology in health care. *Medical Health Care and Philosophy*, 16(4), pp. 807–16. DOI: 10.1007/s11019-013-9463-7.

Coeckelbergh, M., 2015. Good healthcare is in the 'how': the quality of care, the role of machines, and the need for new skills. In S.P. van Rysewyk and M. Pontier, eds. *Machine medical ethics*. Cham: Springer, pp. 33–47.

Cabinet Office, 2013. *Kaigo robotto ni kansuru tokubetsu yoron chosa no gaiyo* [Overview of the results from the special survey on care robots]. Available at: http://survey.gov-online.go.jp/tokubetu/h25/h25-kaigo.pdf [accessed 17.07.2017].

Cabinet Office, 2016. *Heisei 28 nenban koreishakai hakusho* [Annual report on the aging society: 2016]. Available at: www8.cao.go.jp/kourei/whitepaper/w-2016/zenbun/28pdf_index.html [accessed 17.07.2017].

Christensen, K., 2008. Social capital in public home care services. In S. Wrede, L. Henriksson, H. Høst, S. Johansson and B. Dybbroe, eds. *Care work in crisis*. Lund: Studentlitteratur, pp. 249–71. Available at: www.gbv.de/dms/ub-kiel/572950721.pdf [accessed 17.07.2017].

Daly, M., 2001. Care policies in Western Europe. In M. Daly, ed., *Care work: the quest for security*. Geneva: International Labour Office. pp. 33–55.

Doi, T., 1971. *The anatomy of dependence*. Toyko: Kodansha International.

Donath, S., 2000. The other economy: a suggestion for a distinctively feminist economics. *Feminist Economics*, 6(1), pp. 115–23. DOI: http://www.tandfonline.com/doi/abs/10.1080/135457000337723.

Erez, M. and Gati, E., 2004. A dynamic, multi-level model of culture: from the micro level of the individual to the macro level of a global culture. *Applied Psychology*, 53(4), pp. 583–98. DOI: 10.1111/j.1464-0597.2004.00190.x.

Freudenreich, O., 2007. *Psychotic disorders: a practical guide*. Philadelphia, PA: Lippincott Williams & Wilkins.

Fukuda, M., 2009. Kango ni okeru kyokan to kanjo komyunikeshon [Empathy and feeling communication in nursing]. *The Journal of the Nursing Society of University of Toyama*, 9(1), pp. 1–13.

Greve, B., 2011. Velfærdsteknologi: Buzzword eller løsningsmulighed? [Welfare technology: buzzword or solution?]. *Social Politik*, [Social Policy], 2011(1), pp. 5–9. Available at: http://socialpolitisk-forening.dk/wp/wp-content/uploads/2010/10/Social-Politik-nr.-1-2011.pdf [accessed 17.07.2017].

Herbig, P. and Laurence, J., 1996. Creative problem-solving styles in the USA and Japan. *International Marketing Review*, 13(2), pp. 63–71.

Hignett, S., Crumpton, E., Ruszala, S., Alexander, P., Fray, M. and Fletcher, B., 2003. Evidence-based patient handling: systematic review. *Nursing Standard*, 17(33): 33–6. DOI: 10.7748/ns2003.04.17.33.33.c3383.

Himmelweit, S., 1999. Caring labor. *The Annals of the American Academy*, 561, January, pp. 27–38.

Holroyd, C. and Coates, K., 2007. Robotics in Japan. In C. Holroyd and K. Coates, eds. *Innovation nation: science and technology in 21st century Japan*. New York: Palgrave Macmillan, pp. 105–25.

Kanagawa Welfare Service Association, 2012. *Heisei 23 nendo kaigo iryo bunya robotto fukyuusuishinmoderu jigyo hokokusho* [Report on project of promotion of robots in care and health 2011]. Yokohama: Kanagawa Welfare Service Association.

Kanagawa Welfare Service Association, 2014. *Heisei 24 nendo 25 nendo kaigo robotto fukyusuishin jigyo-hokokusho* [Report on project of promotion of care robots 2012/2013]. Yokohama: Kanagawa Welfare Service Association.

Kawabata, M., 1996. Ibunka rikai to ningenkankei [Cross-cultural understanding and human relationship]. In M. Ishikawa and M. Tanabe, eds. *Sasaeai tsunagariai wo ikiru* [Living in mutual support and relation]. Tokyo: Chuohoki Publishing, pp. 207–25.

Kitayama, S., Markus, HR., Matsumoto, H. and Norasakkunkit, V., 1997. Individual and collective processes in the construction of the self: self-enhancement in the United States and self-criticism in Japan. *Journal of Personality and Social Psychology*, 72(6), pp. 1245–67. DOI: http://dx.doi.org.pva.uib.no/10.1037/0022-3514.72.6.1245.

Kuga, H., 2014. *Sosharu waku niokeru seikatsuba moderu no kochiku* [Establishment of life field model in social work]. Kyoto: Minerva.

Lehoux, P., 2006. *The problem of health technology: policy implications for modern health care systems.* New York: Routledge.

METI (Ministry of Economy, Trade and Industry), 2013a. *2012 nen robotto sangyo no shijo doko* [Market trend of robot industry in 2012]. Tokyo: METI. Available at: www.meti.go.jp/press/2013/07/20130718002/20130718002-3.pdf [accessed 17.07.2017].

METI (Ministry of Economy, Trade and Industry), 2013b. *Robotto kaigokiki kaihatsu donyu sokushin* [Promotion of introduction and development of care robots]. Tokyo: METI.

MHLW (Ministry of Health, Labour and Welfare), 2013. *The 12th occupational safety and health program, February 2013.* Available at: www.mhlw.go.jp/new-info/kobetu/roudou/gyousei/kantoku/dl/040330-8.pdf [accessed 17.07.2017].

MHLW (Ministry of Health, Labour and Welfare), 2015a. *Heisei 26 nendo kaigo kyufuhi jittaichosa no gaiyo* [LTCI expenditure survey in 2014]. Tokyo: MHLW.

MHLW (Ministry of Health, Labour and Welfare), 2015b. *Heisei 26 nen kaigo sabisu shisetsu jigyosho chosa no gaikyo* [Survey of care service institutions and providers in 2014]. Tokyo: MHLW. Available at: www.mhlw.go.jp/toukei/saikin/hw/kaigo/service14/ [accessed 17.07.2017].

MHLW (Ministry of Health, Labour and Welfare), 2016. *Heisei 28 nen chingin kozo kihon tokei chosa* [Basic survey of wage structure in 2014]. Tokyo: MHLW. Available at: www.e-stat.go.jp/SG1/estat/GL08020101.do?_toGL08020101_&tstatCode=000001011429&requestSender=dsearch [accessed 17.07.2017].

Motegi, N., Yasuda, S. and Misawa, T., 2012. Hojogu shiyo to kaigo dosa ni kansuru jikkenteki kenkyu [Experimental study of assistant aids and a new nursing method in nursing care work]. *Rodokagaku*, 88(3), pp. 81–93.

NCCU (Nippon Careservice Craft Union), 2015. *Yotsu to kaigorobotto nitsuiteno anketo kekkahappyo* [The results of the survey about backpain and care robots]. Tokyo: NCCU.

NEDO (New Energy and Industrial Technology Development Organization), 2014. *NEDO robotto hakusho* [White paper on robotization of industry, business and our life 2014]. Kawasaki: NEDO.

Nylander, S., Ljungblad, S. and Villareal, J.J., 2012. A complementing approach for identifying ethical issues in care robotics: grounding ethics in practical use. 2012 IEEE RO-MAN: The 21st IEEE International Symposium on Robot and Human Interactive Communication. 9–13 September, France.

Occupational Safety and Health Administration, 2001. *A back injury prevention guide for health care providers.* Washington, DC: US Department of Labor.

Occupational Safety and Health Administration, 2003. *Guidelines for nursing homes: ergonomics for the prevention of musculoskeletal disorders.* Washington, DC: US Department of Labor.

OECD, 2015, *Health at a glance 2015.* Available at: www.oecd.org/health/health-systems/health-at-a-glance-19991312.htm [accessed 17.07.2017].

Ohashi, K., 2013. *ICF no shiten ni motoduku kea manejimento to fukushiyogu no katsuyou* [Care management by ICF code and assistive products for support of independent living]. Tokyo: Association for Technical Aids.

ORIX Living Corporation, 2015. *Kaigo no hi 11 gatsu 11 nichi ni awase dai 8 kai kaigo nikansuru ishiki chosa.* [The 8th survey on attitudes towards elderly care in honour of Care Day on November 11th] Press release. Tokyo: ORIX Living Corporation.

ORIX Living Corporation, 2016. *Misora vol. 41.* Tokyo: ORIX Living Corporation.

Parks, J.A., 2010. Lifting the burdens of women's care work: should robots replace the 'human touch'? *Hypatia*, 25(1), pp. 100–120. DOI: 10.1111/j.1527-2001.2009.01086.x.

Pfau-Effinger, B., 2005. Culture and welfare state policies: reflections on a complex interrelation. *Journal of Social Policy*, 34, pp. 3–20. DOI: 10.1017/S0047279404008232.

Prime Minister of Japan and His Cabinet, 2013. *Shakaihosho ni kakaru hiyo no shoraisuikei nitsuite* [The estimates of social security expenditure]. Available at: www.kantei.go.jp/jp/singi/kokuminkaigi/dai6/siryou4.pdf [accessed 17.07.2017].

Roberts, C. and Mort, M., 2009. Reshaping what counts as care: older people, work and new technologies. *European Journal of Disability Research*, 3, pp. 138–58. DOI: https://doi.org/10.1016/j.alter.2009.01.004.

Robotic Care Devices Portal, 2016. *Wearable transfer aids.* Available at: http://robotcare.jp/?page_id=29&lang=en [accessed 23.07.2017].

Saito, Y. and Ishiguro, N. (eds.) 2013. *NORDCARE Survey in Japan: The everyday realities of eldercare – similarities and differences mirrored by care workers*, Survey report supported by the JSPS (Japan Society for the Promotion of Science).

Shimizu, H., 2002. Introduction: Japanese cultural psychology and empathic understanding. Implications for academic and cultural psychology. In H. Shimizu and R.A. LaVine, eds. *Japanese frames of mind: cultural perspectives on human development.* Cambridge: Cambridge University Press, pp. 1–28.

Sparrow, R., and Sparrow, L., 2006. In the hands of machines? The future of aged care. *Mind Machines*, 16, pp. 141–61. DOI: 10.1007/s11023-006-9030-6.

Takeuchi, I., 2013. *Yappari mitame ga 9 wari* [Appearance counts for 90 per cent]. Tokyo: Shinchosha.

The Headquarters for Japan's Economic Revitalization, 2015. *New robot strategy: Japan's robot strategy – vision, strategy, action plan.* Tokyo: The Headquarters for Japan's Economic Revitalization.

Tomioka, K., Higuchi, Y. and Shindo, H., 2007. Fukushiyogu no yukosei ni kansuru kaigosagyo futan no hikakukenkyu [A validation study of devices designed to reduce loads in provision of care]. *Journal of Occupational Health*, 49(4): 113–121.

Wærness, K., 1984. The rationality of caring. *Economic and Industrial Democracy*, 5, pp. 185–211.

Wærness, K., 2005. Social research, political theory and the ethics of care in a global perspective. In H.M. Dahl and T. Eriksen, eds. *Dilemmas of care in the Nordic welfare state.* Aldershot: Ashgate, pp. 15–30.

Wagner, C., 2010. The Japanese way of robotics: interacting 'naturally' with robots as a national character? In A. Schad-Seifert and S. Shimada, eds. *Demographic change in Japan and the EU: comparative perspectives.* Düsseldorf: Düsseldorf University Press, pp. 131–54.

Yamauchi, S., 2015. *Kaigo robotto: Genjo to kadai* [Care robots: current status and challenges]. Presentation material for the 2nd meeting at Fukushi senshin toshi Tokyo no jitsugen ni muketa tiiki hokatsu kea shisutemu no arikata kento kaigi [Committee on Community System in Welfare City Tokyo], 30 July.

Part VI
North America

19

Long-term services and supports for the elderly in the United States

A complex system of perverse incentives

Candace Howes

Introduction

In 2016, 15 per cent of the population was over 65 years of age. By 2030, the elderly share of the population is projected to rise to 20 per cent and to make up 25 per cent of the adult population (KFF, 2017a, 2017b; CBO, 2013, pp. 7–8). While as many as 47 per cent of elderly people needed some form of assistance with self-care, mobility or activities of daily living in 2011, less than a quarter received any paid care (Freedman and Spillman, 2014, pp. 518–19).

In contrast to basic health insurance – available to 90 per cent of US residents from employers, the government, or private purchase – widespread coverage for long-term care has never existed (US Census, 2016a). Although the 16.9 per cent of GDP the US spends on healthcare exceeds the share of any other OECD country, US reliance on unpaid family care means it commits a smaller share of GDP (1.3 per cent) to long-term care than the OECD average of 1.7 per cent (OECD, 2015, p. 209; CBO, 2013, p. 4). Elderly people in need of care rely instead on unpaid daily care from friends and family members, many also work in full- or part-time jobs (CBO, 2013, p. 17; Howes et al., 2012).

The US system of long-term services and supports (LTSS) is shaped by a combination of uniquely US institutions. From the beginning, publicly funded long-term care was defined as a means-tested welfare programme for low-income elderly and disabled people. While LTSS provide support both for elderly people and disabled children and working-age people, this chapter focuses only on elderly people.

Much of LTSS is paid for by the Medicaid programme, which is jointly funded by state and federal tax revenue, rather than through a social insurance fund. In 2014, states spent an average 12 per cent of their budgets (including federal contributions) on long-term care programmes, which vie for funding with other priorities (MACPAC, 2016, pp. 15, 53). Budget constraints are chronic and cyclical, and many of the publicly funded long-term services are increasingly outsourced to private for-profit entities whose responsibility to their shareholders may conflict with the interests of their clients.

Depending on public funding sources, the LTSS industry is the creature of federal and state policies. As policymakers expanded the scope of services funded by Medicaid beyond institutional care to home- and community-based care, they spawned new industries, beginning with the private nursing home industry, then home health and home care agencies, adult day services, and large public programmes paying for consumer-directed in-home care. The American model for financing healthcare has, since the 1940s, been dominated by insurance companies paying providers a fee for each medical and long-term care service. Medicaid, in turn, reimbursed the insurance companies for each fee paid. In a new model, many states are substituting managed care for traditional fee-for-service reimbursement schemes. Managed care organizations (MCOs) are paid a maximum, or capitated, fee for each Medicaid-eligible participant. The MCO has the flexibility to arrange the most cost-effective set of services, tailored to each client. While managed care was designed to introduce more flexibility and efficiency into the provision of healthcare, including long-term care, private for-profit MCOs also have a profit incentive to limit services.

Ensuring an adequate, trained workforce to meet the growing demand for paid care has its own challenges, with paid care work having always been undervalued in the US (Boris and Klein, 2012; Howes et al., 2012). But US labour law, which, until recently, excluded homecare workers from basic labour protections, obstructed efforts to improve wages and working conditions. Few are paid less than direct care workers; they have low levels of education, work in female-dominated jobs and have not been supported by the basic labour protections available to other low-wage workers.

This chapter demonstrates that these peculiarly American institutional arrangements have created incentives promoting neither sufficient coverage, high-quality care, nor a sufficient supply of care workers, even as the need for long-term care is expected to double over the next 30 years. The chapter summarizes some of the most important research on long-term care; it also uses federal and state administrative data, as well as various surveys focused on LTSS, to describe trends in policy, programmes, the industry and the workforce. There are no aggregated data for all long-term care services. Much of the data used in this analysis are drawn from multiple surveys conducted between 2011 and 2014, each concerned with discrete types of long-term care services. Existing administrative data are limited to Medicaid-funded services. Even those administrative data do not always separate services for persons over 65 from younger recipients. Consequently, many measures used in this chapter are approximate, often compiled from different sources and multiple years. Nonetheless, the varying sources report roughly similar numbers.

The chapter also reports on the author's work, using administrative data and a large-scale survey, to measure the impact of wages, benefits, and working conditions on the supply of labour (Howes, 2005, 2008).

US long-term care policy

Most social support programmes in the US took their present form during the Great Depression under the Social Security Act, which provided income support for retired workers, disabled persons, the unemployed, children and low-income elderly people. It was not until 1965 that Medicare and Medicaid were added to the Social Security Act. Medicare is the health insurance programme for retired persons who are either over 65 or disabled and who have worked at least 10 years and contributed payroll taxes into the Medicare Trust Fund. Medicaid, in contrast, is a publicly funded, means-tested programme that pays for healthcare services for low-income children, elderly and disabled people. Low-income persons who have worked and paid into the Medicare Trust Fund, and who are either disabled or over 65, may be eligible for both Medicare and Medicaid (Quadagno, 2005).

Importantly, the Medicare Act did not include long-term care for elderly persons with chronic illness or infirmity. Only Medicaid provided public funds for long-term care, and only for very low-income elderly persons and those with disabilities. Those elderly people with incomes above the poverty line have relied on unpaid care from family and friends. A small percentage of higher-income persons use private insurance or pay out of pocket.

The original design of Medicaid as a tax revenue-funded entitlement for low-income people, administered by states, with services delivered by private entities, has defined tensions around which the programme has evolved. As an entitlement, the statute obligates the federal government and states to pay for services to an expanding eligible population, even when tax revenues fluctuate. States and the federal government are rightly concerned that the cost of providing services, estimated to increase from 1.3 to 3.3 per cent or more of GDP by 2050 (CBO, 2013, p. 4), may impose an unsustainable fiscal burden. State legislatures and the federal government constantly try to shift the cost burden between the federal and state governments or to push costs onto families. But features of the programme's design make this difficult.

US LTSS policy has had a strong institutional bias from its beginning in 1965, when states were required to provide institutional care and limited home healthcare to all eligible persons. Home health services are funded only for short-term, intermittent or post-acute care (KFF, 2017a), but I include them in this analysis because they can be an important complement to long-term services for elderly persons with chronic illnesses.

Before the mid-1970s, most elderly people who needed significant levels of support were housed in costly nursing homes. Many eligible people eschewed notoriously bad nursing homes in favour of unpaid family care. Beginning in the 1970s, though, as programme participants demanded home- and community-based alternatives to institutional care, an amendment to the Medicaid Act gave states the option to provide non-medical in-home care and community-based services to nursing home-eligible persons. A second amendment included home- and community-based waiver programmes (HCBS waivers), where states could limit eligibility, giving them more control over demand and costs (Gornick et al., 2012).

The practice of outsourcing service provision to private for-profit firms that are reimbursed for each service has given firms an incentive to provide unnecessary services, at greater cost. In a recent effort to control costs, the Center for Medicare and Medicaid Services designed new managed long-term care waivers. In 2013, 33 per cent of Medicaid LTSS dollars were spent on non-institutional care, up from about 10 per cent in 1995; half was spent on managed care (CBO, 2013, pp. 10, 25).

Long-term care policy shaping the LTSS industry

Over the last 50 years, the LTSS industry has evolved into a highly profitable, rapidly expanding, and increasingly unregulated industry. As fiscal concerns aligned with consumer preferences, most growth has been in the home- and community-based services (HCBS) sector. For-profit firms have overwhelmed the traditional government-owned, non-profit and volunteer nursing homes and agencies. Despite the rising involvement of for-profit firms, public funds continue to pay for the majority of paid long-term care services, raising concerns that the profit motive may reduce costs at the expense of care recipients and care workers.

Six industries, categorized along two dimensions – whether they provide institutional or non-institutional care, and whether they provide medical- or non-medical-based services – comprise LTSS (Figure 19.1). Medical-based long-term care includes skilled nursing combined with continuous personal care services such as assistance with 'activities of daily living' – dressing, eating, bathing, toileting, and transfers. Non-medical long-term care services do not include

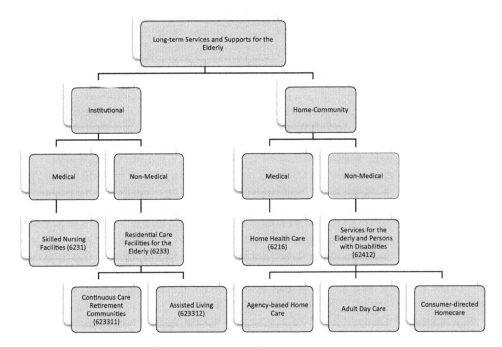

Figure 19.1 Long-term services and supports industries

Source: Compiled by author from US Census Bureau (2017); an earlier version of this figure appeared in Howes (2015).

Note: Numbers in parentheses are North American Industry Classification System (NAICS) codes.

skilled nursing, but may include, in addition to personal care services, help with 'instrumental activities of daily living' – shopping, cleaning, bill paying and trips to medical appointments.

In 2014, just over 4.1 million persons over the age of 65 received paid long-term care services in institutions (1.9 million) and from non-institutional home- and community-based services (HCBS) (2.2 million) (KFF, 2017b; KCMU, 2016; CBO, 2013, p. 19) (Figure 19.2). In 2015, the industry generated an estimated $291 billion in revenue, almost three-quarters in residential services (US Census, 2016b, Table 2). Seventy-five per cent of funding came from public sources, mainly Medicare and Medicaid (CBO, 2013, p. 10) (Figure 19.3). Just under 6 million people, roughly 4 per cent of the entire workforce, were employed in the industry, mainly as certified nurses' aides (CNAs) in nursing homes, or as home health (HHAs) and personal care aides (PCAs or homecare aides) (BLS, 2015, Table 1). Revenue and employment have grown fastest in the non-residential sector of the industry, being among the fastest growing US industries.

Institutional care

While nearly half of paid LTSS recipients get their care in institutions, the mix of institutions is shifting from skilled nursing facilities (SNF) to continuous care retirement communities and assisted living (Harris-Kojetin et al., 2016) (Figure 19.2).

Skilled nursing facilities provide medical-based care, while continuous care retirement communities (CCRCs) provide mainly non-medical residential care to elderly people, including

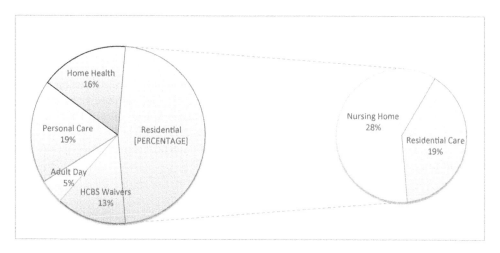

Figure 19.2 Elderly long-term recipients by service, 2014, 4.1 million
Source: Harris-Kojetin et al. (2016); KCMU (2016); KFF (2017b).

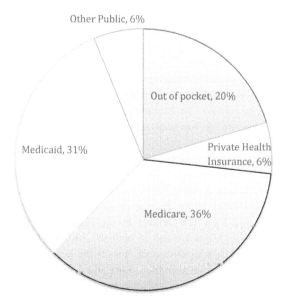

Figure 19.3 Total LTSS spending for elderly people by source, 2011, $191 billion
Source: CBO (2013, p. 18).

personal care services. CCRCs include a separate medical facility for residents when they need a higher level of care.

Assisted living facilities provide a similar range of services but do not offer medical care. The shift from SNFs to CCRCs reflects movement from a medical to non-medical model, as well as ethnic and income differences in cultural practices and long-term care access. Black people are disproportionately served in nursing facilities, black and Latin American people in adult day centres, both venues drawing much of their revenue from Medicaid. Both black and Latin American people are hugely under-represented in CCRCs and assisted living, where white people are over-represented. Medicaid pays a very small share of CCRC and assisted living costs (Harris-Kojetin et al., 2016, pp. 38, 39).

Since 2001, there has been absolutely no growth in the number of skilled nursing facilities or the number of residents (Harrington et al., 2015, Tables 1, 4). Nor has there been growth in employment in nursing homes and residential care. Revenue as a share of total LTSS revenue has fallen from 62 to 51 per cent (BLS, 2017c; US Census, 2016b, Table 4).

Today, almost 70 per cent of SNFs and 80 per cent of residential care facilities operate on a for-profit basis (Harris-Kojetin et al., 2016, p. 102).

Home- and community-based services (HCBS)

Approximately 2.2 million older people are enrolled in publicly funded services in their homes or in the community, either in Medicaid-funded home healthcare services, personal care services or in home- and community-based waiver programmes, including adult day services (KFF, 2017b; Harris-Kojetin et al., 2016, p. 102) (Figure 19.2). Medicaid outsources these services to medically based home health agencies, non-medical home care agencies, adult day service centres, and so-called 'independent providers' who work in two industries – home healthcare services, and services for the elderly and persons with disabilities (SEPD). The shift to Medicaid-managed LTSS should stimulate the already high growth rate of the home health and SEPD industries as for-profit-managed care companies seek lower cost means to provide long-term care services.

Home healthcare services provide short-term, medically based care, including skilled nursing, combined with some personal care services. Although Medicare-/Medicaid-funded home healthcare is not a long-term care service, home healthcare agencies increasingly provide extensive non-medical long-term care services such as personal care assistance, homemaker and companionship services.

Similar to the nursing home industry, this fast-growing industry is dominated by free-standing for-profit agencies, although funded almost entirely by public monies. Employment and industry establishments more than doubled between 2001 and 2015, while revenue increased by 160 per cent (BLS, 2017c) (Figure 19.4). The for-profit share of revenue increased from 60 to 75 per cent between 2001 and 2015 (US Census, 2016b, Table 4). Forty per cent of all funding for home healthcare came from Medicare and 36 per cent from Medicaid (CMS, 2017).

Services for the elderly and persons with disabilities is the heart of home- and community-based services. Home care companies provide non-medical personal care services, including housekeeping and companionship services. Adult day service centres for elderly persons provide personal care services and social, including recreational, services. 'Independent providers', individuals who work outside the agency model in publicly funded, consumer-directed programmes, or who are both hired and paid for privately by consumers, make up a third sector of the industry. Just as home healthcare agencies have moved beyond medical to non-medical services, home care agencies are expanding into medical services. Growth in the SEPD sector has been explosive, from just over 10,000 private establishments in 2001 to 111,000 in 2015 (BLS, 2017c) (Figure 19.4). This industry is still largely funded by Medicare/Medicaid and other governmental agencies.

Adult day centres have evolved over time from a locally funded non-profit industry to a larger, increasingly for-profit Medicaid waiver-funded business, serving almost 300,000

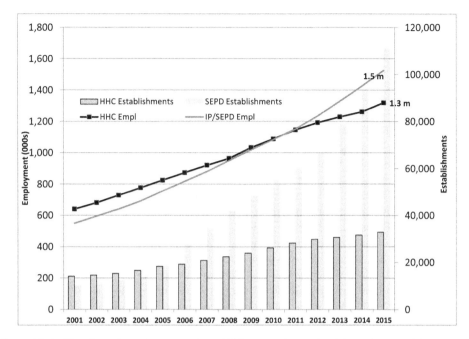

Figure 19.4 Number of employees and establishments, home health services, and SEPD (services for the elderly and persons with disabilities), 2001–2015

Source: BLS (2017c).

Note: SEPD includes independent providers. In 2013, the Bureau of Labor Statistics reclassified independent providers (IPs) from household to SEPD employees and classified each IP as a separate enterprise. With the reclassification, employment in SEPD doubled and the number of establishments increased sevenfold, making it difficult to create a time series. I have estimated SEPD employment, including IPs, retroactive to 2001, and excluded IPs from the count of SEPD establishments. HHC = home healthcare services.

recipients per day (Harris-Kojetin et al., 2016, p. 102). As of 2014, 73 per cent of adult day centres were Medicaid-certified, and Medicaid was the source of payment for 54 per cent of users.

An unmeasured, and possibly immeasurable, grey market serves Medicaid-ineligible persons who pay cash 'under the table' for in-home services complementing unpaid services provided by friends and family members. Family providers, the grey market, and private pay agencies are all that is available to those 80 per cent of elderly people not eligible for Medicaid funded services. Private pay agencies comprise a very small fraction of the industry. Two-thirds of these private home care agencies are for-profit (US Department of Labor, 2013, p. 60514).

The rapidly growing franchise segment makes up 28 per cent of the for-profit, private pay sector. Typically, new franchises are started by middle-aged people who have faced the challenge of finding reliable care for their own parents. A single office of a 'senior care' franchise, as they are called in the industry, requires an average investment of $92,300; it is not uncommon for top franchises to build annual revenue to $1 million with gross margins of 30–40 per cent (Franchise Business Review, 2016, p. 4).

Despite home care agencies playing such a substantial role in the provision of LTSS services, only 30 of the 51 states in 2017 required home care agencies, including private pay home care agencies, to be licensed (Private Duty Insider, 2017). Licensing requirements are determined by states, but are minimal, variable and largely unenforced.

New York City provides a cautionary tale of the challenges that states face as they try to meet the long-term care needs for the Medicaid-eligible population using managed care. Though the culture of managed care varies across states, most managed care organizations (MCOs) are large for-profit insurance companies. New York reports on the extraordinary growth in the number of 'social' adult centres that offer recreational services, after the state moved all Medicaid long-term care recipients out of fee-for-service programmes to mandatory managed care. Apparently, private managed care companies (reimbursed $3,800 per recipient each month) established relationships with hundreds of 'virtually unregulated' pop-up adult day-care centres. These pop-up centres squeezed out non-profit adult day centres, sending potential new 'customers' to managed care companies, which were in charge of determining eligibility. Many new healthy, mobile, and thus low-cost adults were enrolled at Medicaid's expense (Bernstein, 2013). While there may also be a negative impact of managed care on in-home supportive services, no systematic study of the consequences for cost and patient outcomes exists (Bernstein, 2014; Kaye, 2014).

Another fast-growing segment of the industry, consumer-directed home care, is the lowest cost means of providing long-term care services for persons who are able to manage their care. Under this model, which first grew out of California's independent living movement of the 1970s, individuals hire and supervise their own providers paid by Medicaid (Howes, 2014a; Boris and Klein, 2012). Most states now permit recipients to use consumer-directed services (KCMU, 2016). Many states allow participants to hire family members, and a majority of them do (US Department of Labor, 2013, p. 60515; Howes, 2004). While paid care augments unpaid family care, caregivers may give up other jobs to do the work. Since very low-income consumers are generally hiring family members who already work in low-pay jobs, consumer-directed programmes have allowed women to substitute paid care work for other low-wage jobs, such as childcare, factory work or work in food services (Howes, 2008).

Low barriers to entry, high profit margins, the recession-proof nature of the industry, and limited regulation helps explain the rapid growth of the home health and home care sector. As publicly funded care moves to for-profit home health agencies, home care agencies and consumer direction, and out of more regulated nursing homes, these trends can undermine the quality of jobs and the quality of care.

Long-term care workers

Home care and home health aides make up almost three-quarters of the workforce in the home health and home- and community-based care (SEPD) industries, and about 40 per cent in the residential care industries (BLS, 2015). Thus, quality care depends on sufficient numbers of well-trained nurses' aides, home health and home care aides (Table 19.1).

Looking to the next 10 years, demand for these services and their workers will see spectacular growth. Total employment in the home health industry has already doubled, and in SEPD industries tripled since 2001 (BLS, 2017c) (Figure 19.4). Employment growth is driven by spectacular growth especially in the number of personal care (home care) aides (BLS, 2017b) (Figure 19.5). Almost 3.5 million aides worked in the LTSS industries in 2014, 60 per cent in non-residential care (BLS, 2015, Table 1.8) (Table 19.1). Together, these three occupations are projected to add 11 per cent of all new jobs – 1.1 million – between 2014 and 2024. More jobs will be added in these occupations than in retail sales or food preparation and serving (BLS, 2015, Table 1.8).

Table 19.1 Employment in long-term services and supports, 2014 (thousands)

	SNFs	CCRCs & Assis living	Total Residential	HHCS	SEPD	Total Non-Residential	PH, SE & ES	LTSS Industries	Total Empl, by Occupation
Total	1,651.9	343.2	3,261.0	1,262.2	1,470.2	2,732.4		5,993.4	
Healthcare practitioners	427.2	90.2	558.4	308.9	40.4	349.3	361.9	1,269.6	8,236.5
Registered nurses	148.5	31.2	195.0	169.9	20.8	190.7	61.1	446.8	2,751.0
LPNs	1.3	0.7	2.5	3.1	0.3	3.4		5.9	126.9
Heathcare support	677.3	262.5	1,107.4	437.5	260.0	697.5	236.0	2,040.9	4,238.0
Home health aides	27.4	93.7	238.7	351.0	223.2	574.2	55.7	868.6	913.5
Nurses' aides	614.7	157.6	816.2	72.8	33.1	105.9	74.9	997.0	1,569.4
Personal care aides	22.4	112.2	295.8	305.6	760.8	1,606.4	241.6	1,603.8	1,768.4
All aides	664.5	363.5	1,350.7	729.4	1,017.1	1,746.5	372.2	3,469.4	4,251.3
% aides, by industry	0.40	0.43	0.41	0.58	0.69	0.64		0.58	

Source: BLS (2015, Table 1.8); an earlier version of this table appeared in Howes (2015).

Notes:

SNFs – skilled nursing facilities
CCRCs & Ass Living – continuous care retirement communities and assisted living
HHCS – home healthcare services
SEPD – services for the elderly and persons with disabilities, which includes independent providers
PH, SE and ES – private household, self-employed and employment services

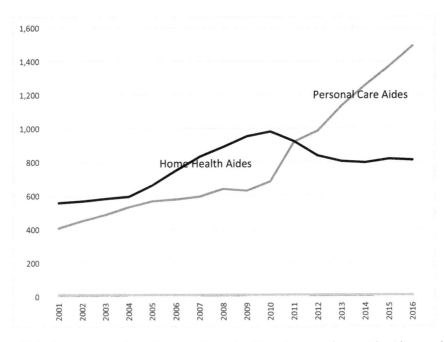

Figure 19.5 Average annual employment, home health and personal care aides (thousands)
Source: BLS (2017b).

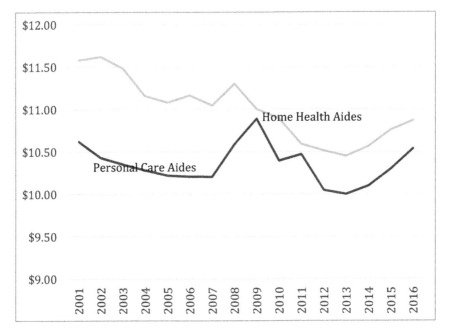

Figure 19.6 Annual median hourly wage, home health and personal care aides (2016 dollars)
Source: BLS (2017b).

Yet as women with low education levels in female-dominated jobs, home health and home care aides rank among the lowest paid in the workforce. Fifty-one per cent of all home health and home care workers received some form of social assistance in 2014 (PHI, 2017b, p. 6). Despite the increase in demand for their labour, real wages fell for both home health and home care workers between 2001 and 2016 (BLS, 2017b) (Figure 19.6).

While many aides find satisfaction in their job, the low pay, poor working conditions, and lack of training and support often push them to leave (Howes et al., 2012; Howes, 2008). Turnover, a generally accepted measure of job quality, is high across all sectors of the industry. Estimates vary dramatically, but all suggest turnover rates well above other industries. A 2005 survey of LTSS reported 40–60 per cent of home health aides leave after less than a year, and 80–90 per cent within two years (IOM, 2008, p. 209). A recent study, measuring leavers and stayers by sector and occupation, found that, on average for all occupations in LTSS industries, 22 per cent of the workforce left every year, compared to 13 per cent for all industries. Exits were highest for personal care assistants, at 26 per cent; exits were highest in the private household sector and the home care (SEPD) sector, where most employees are personal care attendants (Frogner and Spetz, 2015, pp. 14, 26). Interestingly, measured turnover among aides working in consumer-directed home care programmes is lower than in nursing homes or agencies (Howes, 2005).

High turnover (or its converse, retention) among long-term care workers impacts the quality of care. Beyond simply measuring turnover, it is important to understand what draws care workers to the job and drives them away, and why turnover varies across sites.

In several studies of home care aides working in the California in-home supportive services programme, the largest consumer-directed programme in the country, I was able to both measure turnover among consumer-directed homecare workers and to identify factors, including wages and benefits, that were correlated with turnover. The studies covered periods of up to eight years between 1997 and 2005, during which time there were substantial increases in wages and benefits for some workers.

In the early 1990s, through California's in-home supportive services (IHSS) programme, hundreds of thousands of IHSS workers provided virtually all of California's home care services. No IHSS worker was paid more than the state minimum wage, and none received health insurance, retirement or paid sick leave benefits. Worker turnover was exceptionally high under these conditions (Howes, 2004). Since the workers were classified as self-employed, federal labour law prohibited their joining unions that might have helped improve their working conditions. By 1992, several unions had designed a legal strategy in California, making it possible to reclassify independent providers as employees. Reclassification took place incrementally, county by county, only when the workforce in that county was unionized, which meant there was tremendous variation in wages across California's 58 counties.

San Francisco, where newly unionized IHSS workers saw their wages nearly double between 1997 and 2002, provided the ideal environment in which to measure the effect of wages and benefits on turnover. Using a large administrative data set maintained by the state of California to track home care service authorization for Medicaid recipients, I was able to measure entry, exit and retention over a five-year period in San Francisco. As wages doubled and health insurance benefits were added, retention rose from 39 per cent to 74 per cent a year. Retention rose more among some groups of care workers, varying by ethnicity, and by whether the provider was related to or a friend of the care recipient. But for all, the increase was substantial.

In order to explore what other factors might induce consumer-directed home care workers to enter and remain in the workforce, I conducted a large-scale survey of consumer-directed home care providers working in eight California counties in 2005. The counties were both representative of wage and benefit variation within California and of the ethnic composition of the state population. The survey instrument was administered by mail or phone to 5,019 home care workers; 2,260, or 45 per cent, responded. Workers were asked a series of questions, including why they took the job and why they stayed in the job. By far the most important factor that motivated them to enter and stay in home care was attachment to their consumer. The second most important factor was job flexibility. But in counties where health insurance was included in compensation, even for part-time workers, that attractor was ranked above all others. Wages were an important attractor, but only in counties where they exceeded the state average by a significant margin (Howes, 2008).

These studies of consumer-directed home care expand our knowledge of the determinants for retention (or turnover) in the most rapidly growing site for long-term care. They suggest that because care workers' retention is driven by their attachment to their consumer, retention is strengthened when consumers are allowed to choose their own care worker. The studies also show that care workers put a high value on compensation, including health insurance, and the autonomy and flexibility that comes with consumer direction, as compared to working for an agency.

One of the constraints on quality care is that direct care workers receive little training (Frogner and Spetz, 2015; Kelly et al., 2013). Federal mandates require certified nursing assistants and home health aides to receive 75 hours of training, though states can, and some do, set higher standards (Rowe et al., 2016, p. 4; PHI, 2013). But there are no federal training requirements for personal care and home care aides. Only 35 per cent of states have a training hours requirement for PCAs, and most require 40 hours or less (PHI, 2013).

Despite the long history of low wages, benefits and limited training, several developments have improved the quality of long-term care jobs, including unionization of workers in consumer-directed programmes, recent changes in labour laws targeted to home care workers, successful state and local minimum wage campaigns, and the Affordable Care Act expanding health insurance benefits to low-income people.

As the example from California shows, there has been considerable movement among consumer-directed home care workers toward regularizing the terms of employment, raising wages and benefits and reducing turnover. Workers in many California counties have joined unions and seen their wages rise as high as $13.35 per hour plus better benefits (CDSS, 2017; Howes, 2014b; Boris and Klein, 2012). California's in-home supportive services programme, which currently employs 400,000 workers caring for 500,000 consumers, is still the largest, but the model has spread nationwide so that today, approximately 800,000 home care or personal care aides, almost half of all personal care aides nationwide, are employed in consumer-directed programmes, and as many as 625,000 personal care aides, mainly in consumer-directed programmes, belong to unions (PHI, 2017b, p. 4; Becker et al., 2015, p. 14). Many of these unionized workers are earning well above the occupation's national mean hourly wage.

Close to 90 per cent of care workers are women. Twenty-two per cent live in households whose income puts them below the poverty line; median household income is half that of the US median. They are disproportionately older, women of colour, and over half have only a high school education or less (Howes et al., 2012, p. 68). Care workers suffer not only from the systemic discrimination that affects all female-dominated jobs, but from the particular disadvantages of being older, less educated and non-white. But long-term care work, and especially home health and home care jobs, carry a unique stigma, long embodied in federal labour policies. Since the Fair Labor Standards Act (FLSA) was passed in 1938, as part of the New Deal programmes, lawmakers and other interested parties have consistently characterized home care as companionship, rather than work, to justify exempting them from the minimum wage and overtime protections of the Act (US Department of Labor, 2015).

In 2011, the US Department of Labor intended to overturn the so-called 'companionship exemption', which resulted in a new 'homecare rule' (US Department of Labor, 2013). While the process met many challenges, by October 2015 home care workers were, for the first time, brought under the wage and hours protections of the Act. Among the forces that fought to impede regulatory reform and union successes in home care was the newest and most rapidly expanding sector of the homecare industry, for-profit agencies and private pay home care franchises (Howes, 2014a, 2014b).

Exacerbating the problem of low wages in the United States is its dysfunctional system for setting a wage floor. Only Congress can mandate an increase in the minimum wage. Sadly, Congress has not voted to raise the current federal minimum hourly wage of $7.25, which in inflation-adjusted dollars is 30 per cent lower than it was in 1980, for 10 years. At that rate, a single mother with one child at home, working full-time, would earn an income that puts her 10 per cent below the poverty rate for a family of two. With the median wage rate for a home care worker at $10.54 in 2016, the annual income for a full-time worker would be just 130 per cent of the federal poverty level. In most states, a worker with that income is eligible to apply for many social support programmes, including Medicaid, the same programme that pays them to provide care to other low-income people.

Fortunately, numerous states and municipalities, frustrated with Congress' inaction on the federal minimum wage, have voted to increase state or local minimum wages above the federal standard. Some have indexed the minimum wage to inflation (Economic Policy Institute, 2017). Recently, many low-wage care workers have seen their wages rise with increases in local minimum wages.

Finally, the Affordable Care Act, passed in 2011, gave states the option to expand Medicaid-funded health insurance to persons whose income exceeded the federal poverty level. Among the 30 million new people who got health insurance as a result were 500,000 long-term care aides, raising the Medicaid coverage for LTSS aides by 30 per cent (PHI, 2017a). As of this writing, however, the Republican-dominated Congress is writing a bill that would repeal many features of the Affordable Care Act. Along with repealing the Medicaid expansion, the bill would dramatically cut annual federal funding for state Medicaid programmes, forcing states to eliminate services, drop enrollees, or lower payments to healthcare providers.

These several forces – unionization of home care workers, revision of labour laws that excluded home care workers from minimum wage and overtime protections, state and local level increases in the minimum wage and the Affordable Care Act – have raised real wages by 5 per cent and improved working conditions for home care workers in the last three years. Home care wages have now returned almost to the inflation-adjusted level of 2001 (BLS, 2017b) (Figure 19.6).

Nonetheless, under current conditions, the supply of long-term care workers is unlikely to match demand. Over the 10-year period between 2003 and 2013, workers have exited faster than entered the long-term care workforce (Frogner and Spetz, 2015). The Academy of Medicine recommends, as a means to address the workforce shortage, that federal and state governments require minimum training for certified nursing assistants, home health aides and personal care assistants, and that workers be paid a living wage and guaranteed other supports (Rowe et al., 2016, p. 4).

Conclusions

The US long-term care system falls short of providing adequate care for most who need it. With no universal entitlement programme, only very low-income people are eligible for publicly supported care. Higher-income people frequently pay out of pocket for expensive care until they have spent down a lifetime of savings and finally qualify for Medicaid. By far, the majority of people rely every day on an average of three to four hours of unpaid service from family members and friends whose own quality of life may be compromised (CBO, 2013, p. 17).

In the meantime, fast-growing for-profit home health agencies and home care agencies provide most long-term care services. Managed care programmes have given for-profit companies the flexibility to customize individuals' services, on the questionable and unproven theory that they could provide adequate care at lower cost.

Quality care will potentially be compromised by a shortage of well-trained aides unwilling to work for low wages. Only recently have inflation-adjusted wages for home health and home care workers begun to rise after years of decline. Home care workers' wages have increased only where there is collective bargaining or local minimum wage ordinances. In counties, or states, where consumer-directed care dominates long-term care, wage increases in the public programmes can have a significant impact on wages in the private sector. Consumer-directed home care also tends to improve retention, especially when consumers can choose caregivers from among family members and friends.

The same does not hold true in areas where publicly funded home care services are provided by agencies. Capitated reimbursement schemes give for-profit agencies an incentive to limit services and keep wages down. The incentive structure created by reimbursement policies in the absence of unionization helps explain why wages remain low for these workers.

Unless citizens can convince Congress to legislate universal long-term care, financed by a trust fund, families will continue to shoulder the majority of the care burden. Low wages and inadequate training constrain the development of a skilled workforce. For-profit firms will provide variable quality services for the poor, while high-quality continuous care retirement communities serve the needs of the wealthy.

References

Becker, C. et al., 2015. *Brief amici curiae for AFL-CIO, SEIU, AFSCME, and National Domestic Workers' Alliance in support of appellants on review*. 27 February. Available at: https://phinational.org/legislation-regulations/brief-amici-curiae-afl-cio-seiu-afscme-and-national-domestic-workers [accessed 17.06.2017].

Bernstein, N., 2013. Day care centers sprout up luring fit elders and costing Medicaid. *New York Times*, 23 April, p. A1. Available at: www.nytimes.com/2013/04/23/nyregion/day-centers-lure-fit-elders-and-bill-medicaid.html [accessed 31.03.2017].

Bernstein, N., 2014. Pitfalls seen in a turn to privately run long-term care. *New York Times*, 6 March p. A1. Available at: www.nytimes.com/2014/03/07/nyregion/pitfalls-seen-in-tennessees-turn-to-privately-run-long-term-care.html?&under;r=1&_r=0 [accessed 15.03.2017].

Boris, E. and Klein. J., 2012. *Caring for America: home health workers in the shadow of the welfare state*. New York: Oxford University Press.

BLS (Bureau of Labor Statistics), 2015. *Employment projections, 2014–24 industry-occupation matrix data, by industry, December 8*. Available at: www.bls.gov/emp/tables.htm [accessed 23.03.2017].

BLS (Bureau of Labor Statistics), 2017a. *Occupational and employment statistics May 2016: national occupational and employment estimates United States*. Available at: www.bls.gov/oes/current/oes_nat.html [accessed 20.07.2017].

BLS (Bureau of Labor Statistics), 2017b. *Occupational and employment statistics, May 2000–16, OES data.* Available at: www.bls.gov/oes/tables.html [accessed 20.07.2017].

BLS (Bureau of Labor Statistics), 2017c. *Quarterly census of employment and wages.* Available at: https://data.bls.gov/cgi-bin/srgate [accessed 01.03.2017].

CDSS (California Department of Social Services), 2017. *IHSS wages by county, January 2017.* Available at: www.cdss.ca.gov/agedblinddisabled/res/CoIPWages/IPWages.pdf [accessed 20.07.2017].

CBO (Congressional Budget Office), 2013. *Rising demand for long-term care services and supports for the elderly.* June. Available at: www.cbo.gov/publication/44363 [accessed 15.03.2017].

CMS (Centers for Medicaid and Medicare Services), 2017. *National health expenditure data, 2015: national health expenditures by type of service and source of funds, CY 1960–2015.* Available at: www.cms.gov/Research-Statistics-Data-and-Systems/Statistics-Trends-and-Reports/NationalHealthExpendData/NationalHealthAccountsHistorical.html [accessed 25.03.2017].

Economic Policy Institute, 2017. *Minimum wage tracker.* Available at: www.epi.org/minimum-wage-tracker/ [accessed 20.03.2017].

Franchise Business Review, 2016. *2016 special report: top low cost franchises.* Portsmouth, NH: Franchise Business Review.

Freedman, V.A. and Spillman, B.C., 2014. Disability and care needs among older Americans. *Milbank Q*, 92(3), pp. 509–41. DOI: 10.1111/1468-0009.12076.

Frogner, B. and Spetz, J., 2015. *Entry and exit of workers in long-term care.* San Francisco, CA: UCSF Health Workforce Research Center on Long-Term Care. Available at: http://healthworkforce.ucsf.edu/sites/healthworkforce.ucsf.edu/files/Report-Entry_and_Exit_of_Workers_in_Long-Term_Care.pdf [accessed 25.05.2017].

Gornick, J., Howes, C. and Braslow, L., 2012. Care policy in the United States. In N. Folbre, ed. *For love and money: care provision in the U.S.* New York: Russell Sage Foundation, pp. 112–39.

Harrington, C., Carillo, H. and Garfield, R., 2015. *Nursing facilities, staffing, residents, and facility deficiencies.* Available at: www.kff.org/report-section/nursing-facilities-staffing-residents-and-facility-deficiencies-supplemental-tables/ [accessed 18.06.2017].

Harris-Kojetin, L., Sengupta, M., Park-Lee, E. et al., 2016. Long-term care providers and services users in the United States: data from the national study of long-term care providers, 2013–2014. *National Center for Health Statistics. Vital Health Stat*, 3(38). Available at: www.cdc.gov/nchs/data/series/sr_03/sr03_038.pdf [accessed 26.03.2017].

Howes, C., 2004. Upgrading California's home care workforce: the impact of political action and unionization. *The State of California Labor*, 4, pp. 71–105. Available at: http://escholarship.org/uc/item/1h28v106 [accessed 18.06.2017].

Howes, C. 2005. Living wages and retention of homecare workers in San Francisco. *Industrial Relations: A Journal of Economy and Society*, 44(1), pp. 139–63. DOI: 10.1111/j.0019-8676.2004.00376.x.

Howes, C., 2008. For love, money or flexibility: why people choose to work in consumer-directed homecare. *The Gerontologist*, 48, Special Issue 1, pp. 46–59. DOI: https://doi.org/10.1093/geront/48.Supplement_1.46.

Howes, C., 2014a. *Raising wages for homecare workers: paths and impediments.* Department of Labor, Wage and Hour Division, 75 Years of the Fair Labor Standards Act. Available at: www.dol.gov/whd/flsa/75event/index.htm [accessed 13.07.2017].

Howes, C., 2014b. Living wages and the retention of homecare workers in San Francisco. In M. Reich, K. Jacobs and M. Dietz, eds. *When mandates work: raising labor standards at the local level.* Berkeley, CA: University of California Press, pp. 97–122.

Howes, C., 2015. Home care: the fastest growing low-wage industry. *New Labor Forum*, 2015, 24, pp. 98–105. DOI: 10.1177/1095796015579692.

Howes, C., Leana, C. and Smith, K., 2012. The care workforce. In N. Folbre, ed. *For love and money: care provision in the U.S.* New York: Russell Sage Foundation, pp. 65–91.

IOM (Institute of Medicine), 2008. *Retooling for an aging America: building the health care workforce.* Committee on the Future Health Care Workforce for Older Americans, Institute of Medicine. Available at: www.nap.edu/catalog/12089.html [accessed 20.07.2017].

Kaye, S.H., 2014. Toward a model long-term services and supports system: state policy elements. *The Gerontologist*, 54(5), pp. 754–61. DOI: https://doi.org/10.1093/geront/gnu013.

KCMU (Kaiser Commission on Medicaid and the Uninsured), 2016. *Medicaid home- and community-based services: 2013 data update, October 18*. Available at: http://kff.org/report-section/medicaid-home-and-community-based-services-programs-2013-data-update-report-8800-02/ [accessed 15.03.2017].

Kelly, C.M., Morgan, J.C. and Jeanel Jason, K.J., 2013. Home care workers interstate differences in training requirements and their implications for quality. *Journal of Applied Gerontology*, 32(7), pp. 804–32. DOI: http://dx.doi.org/10.1177%2F0733464812437371.

KFF (Kaiser Family Foundation), 2017a. *State health facts: demographics and the economy – population*. Available at: http://kff.org/state-category/demographics-and-the-economy/population/ [accessed 10.05.2017].

KFF (Kaiser Family Foundation), 2017b. *State health facts: providers and service use*. Available at: http://kff.org/state-category/providers-service-use/ [accessed 10.05.2017].

MACPAC, 2016. *MACStats: Medicaid and CHIP data book, December*. Available at: www.macpac.gov/macstats/ [accessed 25.05.2017].

OECD, 2015. *Health at a glance 2015*. 4 November. DOI: 10.1787/health_glance-2015-en.

PHI, 2013. *Personal and home care aide state training program (PHCAST)*. Available at: http://phinational.org/policy/issues/training-credentialing/personal-and-home-care-aide-state-training-program-phcast [accessed 13.07.2017].

PHI, 2017a. *Impact of Affordable Care Act on health coverage for direct care workers*. Available at: https://phinational.org/research-reports/impact-affordable-care-act-health-coverage-direct-care-workers [accessed 20.03.2017].

PHI, 2017b. *U.S. home care workers: key facts*. Available at: https://phinational.org/home-care-workers-key-facts [accessed 25.03.2017].

Private Duty Insider, 2017. *Private duty homecare state licensing laws*. Available at: https://privateduty.decisionhealth.com/StateLaws.aspx [accessed 23.05.2017].

Quadagno, J., 2005. *One nation uninsured: why the U.S. has no national health insurance*. New York: Oxford University Press.

Rowe, J., Fried, L., Fulmer, T., Jackson, J., Naylor, M., Novelli, W., Olshansky, J. and Stone, R., 2016. *Preparing for better health and health care for an aging population*. Discussion Paper, Vital Directions for Health and Health Care Series. National Academy of Medicine, Washington, DC. Available at: https://nam.edu/wp-content/uploads/2016/09/preparing-for-better-health-and-health-care-for-an-aging-population.pdf [accessed 25.05.2017].

US Census, 2016a. *Health insurance coverage in the U.S.: 2015*. Available at: www.census.gov/content/dam/Census/library/publications/2016/demo/p60-257.pdf [accessed 26.03.2017].

US Census, 2016b. *2015 service annual survey: November*. Available at: www.census.gov/services/index.html [accessed 25.05.2017].

US Census, 2017. *North American industrial classification system*. Available at: www.census.gov/cgi-bin/sssd/naics/naicsrch?chart=2017 [accessed 15.05.2017].

US Department of Labor, 2013. *29 CFR Part 552*. Application of the Fair Labor Standards Act to domestic service; final rule. *Federal Register*, 78(190), pp. 60454–557. 1 October. Available at: http://webapps.dol.gov/FederalRegister/PdfDisplay.aspx?DocId=27104 [accessed 13.07.2017].

US Department of Labor, 2015. *Brief of women's rights, civil rights, and human rights organizations and scholars as Amici Curiae in support of defendants-appellants seeking reversal in homecare association of America, et al. v David Weil*. Administrator of Wage and Hour Division, USC.A Case #15-5018, Document #1540062, filed 28 February. Available at: http://phinational.org/sites/phinational.org/files/legislation-regulations/hcavweil-aclu-20150227.pdf [accessed 06.03.2015].

20

Complexities, tensions, and promising practices
Work in Canadian long-term residential care

Pat Armstrong and Tamara Daly

Introduction

This chapter uses ethnographic research of long-term residential care in Canada to explore the complexities and tensions among the full range of actors involved in providing care. It is based on two studies. First, an international study whose researchers also studied nursing homes in the UK, the US, Germany, Norway and Sweden searching for promising practices.[1] For us, this means practices that understand care as a relationship with multiple players; practices that support differences and equity among staff and residents; and practices that promote active, healthy ageing based on the recognition of different capacities of both residents and staff. It also means paying attention to power and the search for profit, recognizing that context matters. Although we focus on Canada, our analysis benefits from our research in other countries. Second, a smaller Canadian study explored the relationship between paid and unpaid care work in nursing homes, focusing on front-line staff relationships to families, paid companions, volunteers and students.[2]

For our purposes, long-term residential care refers to facilities that provide around-the-clock nursing and personal support, are subject to at least some state regulation, and have some form of public funding. Most commonly called nursing homes, such facilities provide residents with nursing care, assistance with activities of daily living such as eating, bathing and dressing, access to physicians and other specialized health professionals, and offer social and recreation programmes, as well as meals, housekeeping and laundry services. The people who live there have chronic conditions – and most have some form of dementia.

We use two particular aspects of residential care to explore women's work and promising practices in Canadian nursing homes, namely food and laundry. Contrasting with the growing emphasis on medical care in these homes, these are the areas that families, residents and the majority of staff see as critical to daily life and care in nursing homes. The determinants of health approach also demonstrate that they are essential components of care (Armstrong et al., 2008). Food and laundry offer a way in to understanding the complexities and tensions involved in care and the forces that shape them, while the homes we visited provide examples of alternatives to many of the negative practices. These are also areas of care work long associated with women, with the skills too often rendered invisible by the assumption that any woman can do this work (Armstrong, 2013). Such an assumption means that women immigrating to Canada often find jobs doing kitchen and laundry work, especially when the work is segregated from other aspects of care and typically requires little English or French language proficiency (Creese et al., 2008).

Theory and method

The evidence for this chapter comes from our seven year project on Re-imagining Long-Term Residential Care: An International Study of Promising Practices, and from a smaller Canadian study, on Invisible Women: Gender and the Shifting Divisions of Labour in Long-term Residential Care. The international project includes academic staff from the US, Canada, the UK, Germany, Sweden and Norway, along with more than 50 students, postdoctoral fellows and research associates. The smaller project focused on the Canadian province of Ontario. Both are guided by feminist political economy, which understands economics, politics, culture and ideologies as integrally related. These are seen as shaped by unequal and uneven forces of power and resistance differently in different historical periods and circumstances. Both are informed by care theory, especially by the understanding of care as a relationship (Williams, 2001), structured by social and material conditions (Baines et al., 1992). Class, gender, race and age – among other intersecting social relations of inequality – are critical to the analysis whether we are looking at international or local forces, forces increasingly characterized by neo-liberal practices that promote market mechanisms, and even for-profit ownership of health services. This means asking which groups are affected in what ways, when and under what conditions. It also means including the full range of actors in nursing home care as well as linking paid and unpaid work because all are considered critical to care (Armstrong et al., 2008).

From this perspective, there are two contradictory tendencies stemming from for-profit managerial practices. One expands the division of labour, carving out tasks and assigning as many as possible to those defined as unskilled in a process understood as simultaneously deskilling and reducing workers' control based on skills (Braverman, 1998). This process can, however, help to protect the skills of those at the top of the hierarchy. Another tendency expands workers' jobs to increase flexibility, often in ways that can further exploit those defined as unskilled (MacDonald, 1991). At the same time, it has the potential to reduce monotony and increase both autonomy and skill under specific conditions. Organizations representing workers simultaneously resisted and supported such strategies, with contradictory results (Armstrong and Armstrong, 2009).

We are searching for new ways to conceptualize and organize long-term residential care, learning from and with each other. We seek to identify promising practices that encourage dignity and respect for both providers and residents. Our theory teaches us to capture rich complexity, tensions and contradictions, rather than focusing on single variables and searching for single causal relationships. Both projects have ethics approval from York University and, where required, from individual institutions.

Our methods are complex, layered, iterative, and reflexive, allowing us to evolve in new ways. They are composed of three basic approaches to developing evidence: analytical mapping that provides descriptions and analysis of what long-term residential care looks like in our jurisdictions, literature reviews of both theoretical and empirical work, and rapid site-switching team-based ethnography. While the mapping and literature reviews are critical to our analysis here, we draw primarily on observational and interview evidence from our rapid site-switching ethnographies conducted in eight facilities in four Canadian provinces for the international project, and in seven facilities in Ontario for the regional project. We also draw on data from 17 sites in the other countries to reflect on what we have found in Canada. For the international project, interdisciplinary teams of 12 members from different countries were paired to observe and interview in a residential facility over three shifts from 7 a.m. until midnight over a week for our primary sites, and an additional day-long site visit at a second, and sometimes a third site, which we call a flash ethnography. The regional project had teams of eight Canadians. We selected homes to study by asking unions, community organizations and policymakers where they would go to learn about promising practices and why they would go there. We also consulted formal, public assessments. Although 44 per cent of Canadian homes are owned by for-profit corporations, and the proportion is even higher in Ontario and British Columbia (BC), only one for-profit organization was selected for this process focusing on promising practices.

For both studies, observations were conducted in public spaces and in private rooms when permission was granted. Field notes and photos were taken for analysis purposes but not for publication. We also conducted interviews with a wide range of participants, including managers, staff, families, residents, volunteers, and union representatives. The international study conducted a total of 530 interviews with 246 in Canadian facilities; the regional study conducted 203 interviews in Ontario facilities. Ontario and BC were selected because they have large populations and governments that embraced neo-liberal approaches, while Manitoba and Nova Scotia (NS) have much smaller populations and have, at least until recently, been more committed to public provision.

For the international study, the teams conducted thematic analysis by discussing key themes over two separate days for each jurisdiction, reflecting on the content of interviews and observations. On an annual basis, presentations to the entire team highlighted emerging themes and the basis to discuss analysis. Presentations and discussions were informed by feminist political economy as well as by the interdisciplinary perspectives of the team of scholars (e.g. medicine, nursing, social work, health services research, sociology, history, cultural studies). For the smaller study, the team spent two afternoons discussing the site, and conducted a thematic analysis using NVivo software that provides the means for handling large data sets.

Long-term residential care in Canada

The Canada Health Act 1984 does not define long-term care as an insured service, and as a result it is not understood that the provinces and territories must provide universal access without fees. In consequence, levels of public funding and private charges, as well as the regulations and ownership structures, vary significantly across the country.

The majority of the population in the nearly 1,200 nursing homes is female, although the number of men is increasing, as are the number from communities Statistics Canada classifies as visible minorities, especially in large, urban centres. Most of the 200,000 residents have some form of dementia combined with other chronic conditions, and acuity levels have grown significantly as admission criteria have become stricter (CIHI, 2017, Table 1).

The overwhelming majority of the staff are women and an increasing number come from visible minorities and/or or immigrant communities. Most of the care is provided by those called healthcare aides or personal support workers (from here on referred to as care aides), with a few resident support assistants in one province. Most are unionized, although they have not been successful in getting much skill recognition, and there is little national consistency in their formal education, even though they are doing increasingly complicated work. The professional organizations representing the smaller number of registered nurses (RNs) and licensed or registered practical nurses (LPNs) have protected their scope of practice while ensuring both that workers have the appropriate skills and that their skills are recognized (Armstrong and Silas, 2014). Especially in larger homes, housekeeping, food, and laundry have been separated out and assigned to those with little if any formal recognized training. Most of these workers belong to unions that have helped improve their wages and benefits while providing some job security but they have had little success in defending these rights when the services are privatized. Indeed, privatization is often based on savings created by lower wages, less job security and fewer staff (Stinson et al., 2005; Cohen, 2001). None of these workers' organizations have been successful in pressuring governments to adopt regulations on the minimum staffing levels research indicates is necessary to provide good care. As staff, family and residents all tell us, 'there are not enough hands' (Armstrong and Daly, 2004).

The ownership structure of long-term care varies depending on the province. Overall, more than half of beds in Canada are owned by proprietary organizations, nearly one-quarter are non-profit, and the remaining quarter are publicly owned. Ontario is the most commercialized province, where just over two-thirds of beds are in the proprietary sector (Daly, 2015).

According to the 2012 Statistics Canada General Social Survey, age-related care needs required the most unpaid care work from Canadians (Sinha, 2013). Although there are no accurate estimates of how much unpaid care is provided in nursing homes, ethnographic research indicates that families are engaged in a range of decision-making and other activities, with female family members in particular contributing unpaid care work or hiring others to provide companion care (Daly and Armstrong, 2016). Families and volunteers try to fill some of the care gap left by the inadequate staffing related to food, laundry and other care. Some families hire privately paid companions, also mostly women, to do the work left undone or done inadequately (Daly et al., 2015). Long-term care thus offers a rich location for a case study of the nature and relations of women's work, as we indicate through our exploration of food and laundry care.

Findings

Food

'For human beings, food is a critical contributor to physical well being, a major source of pleasure, worry and stress, a major occupant of waking time and, across the world, the single greatest category of expenditures' (Rozin et al., 1999, p. 163). In nursing homes, the major activities of the day are centred on food; food consumes a significant amount of staff time, and food accounts for a major expenditure item for the home. The Canadian nursing homes we visited, however, tend to emphasize the physical well-being of residents defined primarily in terms of nutrient amounts consumed, reducing staff time, and facility costs. The pleasure, worry and stress that result for residents and workers are too often ignored.

We saw starkly contrasting approaches to food within and across jurisdictions in western and eastern Canada. We begin by comparing two non-profit homes in BC before moving on to compare two in a Maritime province. Based on neo-liberal assumptions that the for-profit sector is more efficient and that food can be separated from care, the government in BC pressured nursing homes to contract out their food services. In response, one of the large non-profit homes we visited contracted out their dietary work to a major international corporation. The food was still made on the premises but with a new employer. According to the nutritionist:

> A lot of staff . . . switched to [the corporation] so their pay was reduced and just management style is a bit different. I guess with the kitchen staff, they don't feel part of the community . . . they may not feel such a sense of belonging to the residence. So in some

way that may be different because if the cooks or, you know, the staff know them [the residents] before they will make a conscious effort to kind of cater a bit more to the resident. But now for a lot of them it maybe is just a name.

As the food service manager explained, 'It's very confusing but we don't own the equipment so we have to call [the owner of the equipment] and say we need to get this fixed or it needs to be replaced'. The kitchen was in the basement, with a large sign on the door prohibiting entry. The distance from the dining rooms ensured no smells of cooking would tempt residents and no one involved in cooking mixed with residents or other workers. Dietary aides employed by the corporation took carts laden with trays up to the various dining rooms that accommodated the 35 residents on each floor. They:

> pre-set all the cold items onto the tray with the tray ticket . . . in their unit. And then when the hot items come up they then plate the hot. Once the cart is full the care aides [home employees] take it and deliver it to the appropriate resident.

Dietary staff employed by the corporation stood by the carts, adding drinks according to a prescribed list and without consulting residents. A large sign saying 'DO NOT INTERRUPT OUR KITCHEN STAFF WHILE THEY ARE SERVING' made it clear that these women were not to waste time interacting with residents. The floor services manager did not see this as an efficient approach, suggesting instead that dietary aides ask:

> 'Would you like a glass of apple juice? Excellent'. Pour the apple juice versus somebody pouring apple juice hoping 25 people need it and then putting it into a fridge, then pulling it out and putting it onto a tray to then putting it in front of a resident to have it thrown in the garbage. I think dining room service, how we eat at home versus given a tray of everything in front of me is going to be (a) better for the resident and just much more organized.

The food is determined not primarily by resident preferences, but rather outside the home by nutrition experts and by regulations, as she goes on to explain:

> There's lots of guidelines to follow whether it be . . . the diet guidelines, Canada Food Guide, health guidelines depending on what's going on with a resident physically, allergies, their texture type. There's so many things that go into play. We have a system called Compnutrition that we put all the information for the residents and it calculates and tallies and says this person can have this, this or this.

This home has decided to expand somewhat the number of RNs and eliminate the LPNs, leaving most of the direct personal and social care to care aides while RNs focus on medical care. Responsible for a wider range of tasks, these aides have little time left to help people eat. We witnessed numerous bibbed residents sitting with full trays left uneaten, in part because limited assistance was offered and in part because of what food was on offer:

> Right now, they're given everything all at once, which I think is a shame because a lot of elderly tend to look at all the food and go, 'I'm not hungry any more'. And it's just overwhelming, you know. To be able to put their drink in front of them or to ask them, 'Would you like a glass of juice or would you like milk or how about some water?' Just to give them those options I think is going to be so much better for the resident.

Two-thirds of the residents in this home are Asian, and complaints from this population led to the company offering a choice between an Asian and a 'core' menu, although the nutritionist who is Asian said it is not Asian food that most of the community would recognize. Indeed, it does not include soya sauce because it is considered too salty by the experts who plan meals across the province. As a result of both this food and the lack of staff to assist residents in eating, many families, and especially Asian ones, bring food and help their relatives eat. Not surprisingly, most of this food and assistance is provided by women. Wealthier families hire private companions to help with eating, a practice we see as a clear indicator of the failure to provide adequate staffing. Volunteers also help with eating, although they are not available every day and every meal. Like the privately paid companions, these volunteers are women.

Food in the second home we visited in BC contrasted sharply in many ways. A particular history allowed this non-profit home of a similar size to escape the pressure to privatize the food services, and the director firmly believed in food as critical to care. There was an open kitchen, allowing the residents to smell and see food cooking. The shelves in the kitchen held lots of soya sauce as well as other spices and fresh produce. The Asian chef cooked Asian fusion, responding to the needs of the many Asian residents as well as to those accustomed to other kinds of food. The kitchen staff, all employees of the home, took the food to the table in hot carts, asking each resident what and how much they would like to eat. Instead of a list with predetermined meals based on dietary regulations, these employees could consult cards on all of the tables that show residents' names, food likes/dislikes, allergies and whether they need assistance, while a blue dot means they do not want a bib. Unlike the other nursing home, neither the furniture nor the dishes were plastic and the tables had glass tops. Underneath the glass top were decorations made by residents. Residents and aides could develop a relationship that had the potential to reward both, and both could enjoy a space that felt more like a home.

While we were there, a group of women from the Chinese community were preparing food for a Buddhist celebration in the residents' kitchen next to the lounge and the smells wafted over the room, as did the sounds of laughter from the kitchen. However, some privately paid companions were there, demonstrating that here too there were not enough staff to ensure that everyone had enough support eating, even though this home had LPNs who also helped with eating when they had time. We did see family members walking with residents, some assisting with eating, but were told it was unusual for them to bring food regularly for residents.

In a Maritime province, a new non-profit home was built to replace an older one. Although the home is large, it is divided into houses of 12–15 residents. The cook was consulted on the design of the new kitchen and was sent to a cooking school. While some lessons, such as 'cooking broccoli al dente', did not transfer well to a rural nursing home, she did acquire cooking and managerial skills that, combined with her considerable autonomy, allows the kitchen staff to be creative in responding to resident and staff preferences. The spacious and efficient ground-floor kitchen off the main lobby had music and conversation, with the sous-chef proudly displaying the cake he had just made. The dietary staff works with the nutritionist to design menus and buy locally. Food is taken on hot carts by this kitchen staff and served by them to individual residents, allowing each resident to select how much and what they prefer, and allowing kitchen staff to know residents and their preferences. The lone male in the kitchen – a cook – said he worried at first about having to interact with residents, but now he loves it and them. There is little waste, and because the food is freshly made, leftovers can be made into soups and purees. The home purchased coloured plates to help those with vision problems identify food, and special utensils for those with arthritis.

While the kitchen staff deliver hot food at breakfast, resident support assistants (RSAs) arrive early to set tables, make coffee, offer juice, and make toast and cook eggs for residents who come when they feel like it or when they are accompanied by the care aides who also help with dining. The kitchen area is integrated into a large, sunny room with dining tables scattered around, adjacent to a lounge outside the open counters. RSAs' formal job description makes it clear that the objective is to make meals enjoyable, even memorable. These assistants also help with the noon meal, and between meals clean the rooms. They do other cooking in the kitchens located in every house, as evident from the smell of banana bread when we were there. There are no formal requirements for these assistants, who learn by working with an experienced assistant for a short time. All of them are women, and asked if she had training in food handling, one replied, 'I don't handle food. The kitchen staff do. I just do what any woman can do'. There was a flexible division of labour, some autonomy for both residents and assistants and teamwork, especially during the morning meal. With RSAs handling much of the morning meal, care aides who have formal training can focus on getting people up and dressed in ways that allow residents more time and attention. At the same time, RSAs are mainly part-time and low paid, with virtually no recognized skills.

In the same Maritime province, we visited a for-profit home similar in size, also organized into houses of 12–15 and in a new building. This for-profit corporation prepared all its food in one industrial centre characterized by an industrial division of labour, shipping it out mostly prepared and portioned to the nursing homes. Unlike the other home, there does not seem to be any place for visitors or residents to buy food. Each house has a small, hot, crowded kitchen, which, unlike the other home, where the kitchen is integral to the lounge space, is separated off and largely invisible. A turkey was cooked here at Christmas so residents could smell the food cooking. The food is reheated by an RSA working alone. RSAs are supposed to take turns doing this work, but we were told not everyone does a rotation in the server because they hate the job. An RSA working in the server said she 'tweaks the food a little', putting potatoes in the blender or mashing them by hand or adding more water to the beans. 'I'm a mom too and that helps. Sometimes it needs more', indicating this is not part of the formal training or work organization. With meals planned centrally, 'They don't always send what the dietician wants'. 'I have to make it work for [the residents]'. 'Breakfast is a favourite because they get whatever they want', making it clear this is not the case the rest of the day. She also assists in eating, but said, 'I wish we had more time to spend with them'. She is always 'hoping that they get enough. It's very stressful sometimes'. A family member we interviewed complained that choice was severely limited and the food too heavily reliant on carbohydrates. She said her mother kept gaining weight, resulting in the constant need for new clothes and discomfort. The daughter was told the only option was to have a diabetic diet, which she thought had even less taste. Although this RSA also cleaned, we saw little evidence of the teamwork we witnessed in the other home. Food quality was low, giving little pleasure to either residents or staff. The division of labour – also based on an assumption of natural female skills – did not lead to teamwork. This home, unlike the other one in the same province, did not have a union to represent the workers, which may explain some of the failure to reap the benefits of a flexible division of labour.

These examples illustrate the complex and contradictory patterns in the division of food labour. In one BC home, privatization in a not-for-profit home complicated the detailed division of labour, deskilling the work, further separating workers from residents and each other while downloading the work to families or their substitutes. In one Maritime for-profit home, food production was even further separated from the home at the same time as there was a more flexible division of labour in the home. But this flexibility was combined with low staffing, little space for creativity in food preparation, food waste and virtually no food training, further denigrating the skills and intensifying the work. In the two not-for-profit homes with on-site, non-privatized kitchens, a more flexible division of labour and some worker autonomy, care relationships were more possible and injury less likely. However, in these homes, there was still little formal training that recognizes the skills required and staffing did not expand to reflect increased workloads, relying on 'what any women can do' and leading to contradictory results. Menu decision-making based primarily on cost, combined with nutrition and portion rules or government regulations, meant more work for women relatives and few options for residents, as well as more food waste and less autonomy for workers.

Laundry

As Twigg and Buse (2013, p. 327) explain in their study of people with dementia, clothes are critical to care:

> Clothes lie at the interface between the body and its social presentation. They signify to the wider world who and what the person is; and in doing so have the capacity to act back on that individual endorsing their sense of identity at a directly embodied level. They can thus play a significant part in the maintenance, or otherwise, of embodied personhood.

Laundry work is central to keeping those clothes not only clean, but also dignified and personal. Unlike hospital patients, residents wear their own clothes every day, and the condition of these clothes is central to their self-respect. When we met in Manitoba with senior management and some board members of a home, we raised the question of laundry. A board member who had not yet spoken immediately jumped in to tell a story of her mother's sweater, lost for months and returned destroyed. A social worker talked about how laundry had been raised as an issue regularly in resident council meetings. What was particularly interesting was the director's response. He quickly cut off the discussion that ensued, telling us firmly to move on to more important issues.

Many of the homes we visited contracted out the work of cleaning bed and other linens, allowing the work to be done under factory-like conditions. One BC laundry worker had previously worked in an industrial hotel laundry and was pleased to now do laundry work in a nursing home. She received no additional training when the company switched her to a nursing home, in spite of the particular hazards faced from things such as infections and the need to do personal laundry. Although many homes did personal laundry on site, the laundry process tended to be industrial, typically used strong chemicals and high heat that wrecks most clothes, and often mixed colours while creating health hazards for workers. Some of this work too was privatized.

Larger homes tend to have laundry workers, although they may do other work as well. Although one job description of laundry work reduces it primarily to labelling, timely pick-up and completion of laundry, maintaining laundry records, and occupational health and safety requirements, it ends by including responsibilities for the well-being of residents, which is so much more than a series of tasks. Many of those who do laundry work interact with residents on a daily basis and have an impact on their well-being. However, few receive formal training in laundry work beyond minimal health and safety rules, let alone training on other aspects of care, reflecting the notion that this is unskilled women's work.

In some places, the division of labour means some workers do nothing but laundry all day and have very little interaction with the residents. Job rotation and flexibility in the division of labour have the potential to reduce strain, expand skills and allow relationships with residents, but it depends on the conditions. In one Ontario home, the laundry staff was told that an additional evening shift would mean lower electricity costs and help prevent privatization. Two workers were assigned to that shift. A laundry worker's initial reaction was positive:

I thought, 'Oh, wonderful. Wonderful. We'll have time to actually get the job finished to the way we were taught, to the way we expect it to be'. And it's just like, 'oh no, they're going to put the laundry in the evening shift as well and then you're going to have bed-making and then you're going to have stuff that wasn't originally your job'.

Not only was the job expanded to include the bed-making previously done by nursing staff – adding 22–25 beds a day to their workload – but the number of workers was reduced to one who laboured alone. Moreover, the evening shift disrupted her home life:

For the evening shift, I had to rearrange all appointments. I was not there for dinner. I was not there for evening entertainment like movies or what not. I wasn't there for that. That was the biggest complaint. I wasn't there for that. It was only six months but six months too soon when we really didn't . . . it seemed like you're making progress but then part of the progress they make it doesn't seem like they're making progress in some areas. It's just the way they rearrange things and they rearrange our lives.

In this home, housekeeping and laundry work are rotated over relatively long periods of time, again assuming that the jobs are similar and require few if any skills. Although this could mean variety, the laundry work is both heavy and repetitive, often done alone in a hot, windowless room. And workers here have little choice about taking this rotation. A union representative described a woman rotated into laundry from housekeeping:

I knew going in and I'm also a union rep so I was in with her at these meetings where she was trying to get the point across, like, 'My doctor has said I have limitations'. She can do the housekeeping but not the laundry. The employer claimed he could not see the difference and the union could do little to prevent the move. Although 'you have support from the union if you've hurt yourself, but other than that we can't dictate to them how to run their company'. The woman who rotated ended up on disability leave because of her back. According to this worker, when you do laundry 'You aren't so valued by the staff . . . . But residents have always valued us'.

A deskilling strategy may mean, as is the case in this home, that lower-paid workers take over some task previously done by nurses. But the reverse can also happen. McGregor et al. (2005) found slightly lower laundry staffing levels in non-profit compared to for-profit facilities, a pattern that may reflect the attempt in non-profit homes to provide more integrated care through a more limited division of labour. Increases in nursing staff levels have been found to be associated with declining levels of support staff, including laundry workers (Bowbliss and Heyer, 2013), suggesting a possible 'substitution' effect as laundry shifts onto nursing staff. Without support from either laundry workers or nurses, the work of care aides is intensified. The result then can be contradictory, with expanded jobs leaving less time for care.

There were other strategies. In a Manitoba home, a woman delivered and picked up laundry from residents' rooms, stopping to chat while she did so before she returned to her well-equipped laundry room. She was included in training sessions provided in the home, which meant she often received help and recognition from other staff.

Like food preparation and assistance with eating, the laundry work is often shifted onto women family members or privately paid female companions as a way to compensate for low staffing and to deal with delicate fabrics. An Ontario home has washing machines and dryers available on each floor for private use, and made it clear that some clothing would not be the responsibility of the nursing home. People without family or the financial means to hire someone to do the work simply had to give up any clothing that would not withstand the industrial process. Laundry can be an important source of participation for family members, who may perceive doing their relatives' laundry as a way to remain involved in or connected to their care (Habjanic and Pajkinhar, 2013). But Canadian research suggests families are more likely to do so if they have to pay for some laundry services, indicating class plays a role (Keefe and Fancey, 2000). We also saw some cultural differences, with Asian families in particular taking home the laundry. At a residents' council meeting, a woman explained that a daughter in her culture was expected to do this work. However, she also described the multiple strategies she used to ensure that her mother's clothes were not taken away and destroyed in the laundry process. She saw care aides so stressed and so focused on getting tasks done that 'they acted like robots', automatically picking up the clothes regardless of the signs she put on the clothes closet and the seals she put on laundry baskets.

Working only on laundry can be isolating, stressful, and harmful to health, especially when the work is defined as something any woman can do. When it is combined with other care work and appropriate training is provided, some of those hazards can disappear and laundry work can be integral to the care relationship, allowing clothing to contribute to the dignity and respect of both residents and staff. But if laundry tasks are simply added on to other care work, the hazards may increase.

Conclusions

In struggling to protect their skills and to ensure that those providing care have the appropriate skills, Canadian RNs and LPNs have been largely successful not only in gaining state protection for their skills, but also in shedding the tasks long associated with women's work by following the male professions model. Although understandable as a strategy and beneficial in many ways, it has unintended consequences. This approach fits well with both medical models and the detailed division of labour popular especially in for-profit firms, and it can reinforce hierarchies that undermine teams. It also fits well with privatization in whole or in part by allowing aspects of the work to be carved out to be done by those given little formal training, defined as unskilled and employed under precarious and often dangerous, industrial conditions. Especially with contracting out, food and laundry workers in particular are separated from care, with negative consequences for both residents and workers. In every nursing home, the majority of these workers are women, and in urban Canada a significant number are from visible minorities and/or immigrant communities. Most employees in nursing homes have unions that have made important gains in wages and benefits, but unions often cannot protect workers when their jobs are contracted out. Some of this food and laundry work is defined out of care entirely, left to be done mainly by female relatives, volunteers or privately paid companions, who are primarily women from visible minority and/or immigrant communities who have few formal protections.

Not all nursing homes have followed the privatization and/or detailed division of labour strategies. Some rotate laundry, housekeeping and dietary tasks or have RSAs do all three kinds of labour. Some have care aides and even nurses assist with food, laundry and housekeeping. A more flexible division of labour can make care more integrated for both residents and staff, and allow for care relationships to develop. It can also provide more variety for workers and help avoid repetitive work. However, if this flexible work is not accompanied by formal training and some autonomy, particularly as resident care needs become increasingly complex, it can serve both to denigrate skills traditionally associated with women's work and to further intensify labour. This is especially the case if flexible work arrangements are a means of reducing staff or not increasing staff in the face of growing demands from residents. Canadian unions have not been successful in protecting workers by getting governments to set minimum staffing requirements based on the evidence. Nor have they often been successful in resisting management decisions about the division of labour or government decisions about privatization.

In sum, while our research identified various promising practices for organizing women's work in nursing homes in order to provide care that is supportive for both those who need and those who provide care, our research indicates that there are at least three basic conditions required. All staff should be employees of the nursing home and the work should be done on site. There needs to be sufficient and appropriate staffing based on the research. Finally, there must be formal training for all work that recognizes the skills required and the role they play in care, creating conditions that allow workers to practise those skills and gives both residents and workers some autonomy.

Notes

1 Funded by the Social Science and Humanities Research Council of Canada, with additional funding from the European Research Area in Aging and the Canadian Institutes of Health Research. Pat Armstrong, Principal Investigator.
2 Funded by the Canadian Institutes of Health Research.

References

Armstrong, P. 2013. Puzzling skills. *Canadian Review of Sociology*, 53(3), pp. 256–83. DOI: 10.1111/cars.12015.
Armstrong, P. and Armstrong, H. 2009. Contradictions at work: struggles for control in Canadian health care. In L. Panitch and C. Leys, eds. *Morbid symptoms: health under capitalism*. Pontypool, Wales: Merlin Press, pp. 145–67.
Armstrong, P. and Daly, T. 2004. *'There are not enough hands': conditions in Ontario's long-term care facilities*. Toronto: Canadian Union of Public Employees. Available at: http://archive.cupe.ca/updir/CUPELTC-ReportEng1.pdf [accessed 18.07.2017].
Armstrong, P. and Silas, L. 2014. Nurses unions: where knowledge meets know-how. In M. McIntyre and C. McDonald, eds. *Realities of Canadian nursing: professional, practice and power issues*. New York: Walters Kluwer/Lippincott Williams & Wilkins, pp. 158–80.
Armstrong, P., Armstrong, H. and Scott-Dixon, K., 2008. *Critical to care: the invisible women in health services*. Toronto: University of Toronto Press.
Baines, C., Evans, P. and Neysmith, S., 1991. Caring: its impact on the lives of women. In C. Baines, P. Evans and S. Neysmith, eds. *Women's caring: feminist perspectives on social welfare*. Toronto: McClelland & Stewart, pp. 11–35.
Bowbliss, J. and Hyer, K., 2013. Nursing home staffing requirements and input substitution: effects on housekeeping, food service and activities staff. *Health Services Research*, 48(4), pp. 1539-50. DOI: 10.1111/1475-6773.12046.
Braverman, H. 1998. *Labor and monopoly capital: the degradation of work in the twentieth century*. New York: Monthly Review Press.
CIHI (Canadian Institute for Health Information), 2017. *CCRS profile of residents in continuing care facilities 2015–2016*. Available at: www.cihi.ca/en/quick-stats [accessed 18.07.2017].
Cohen, M. 2001. *Do comparisons between hospital support workers and hospitality workers make sense?* Vancouver: Hospital Employees Union. Available at: www.heu.org/.../Comparison_Hospital_Support_Workers_1.pdf [accessed 18.07.2017].
Creese, G., Dyck, I. and Tigar McLaren, A., 2008. The 'flexible' immigrant? Human capital discourse, the family household and labour market strategies. *Journal of International Migration and Integration*, 9(3), pp. 269–88. DOI:10.1007/s12134-008-0061-0.
Daly, T., 2015. Dancing the two-step in Ontario's long-term care sector: deterrence regulation = consolidation. *Studies in Political Economy*, 95, pp. 25–58. DOI: http://dx.doi.org/10.1080/19187033.2015.11674945.

Daly, T. and Armstrong, P., 2016. Liminal and invisible long-term care: precarity in the face of austerity. *Journal of Industrial Relations*, 58(4), pp. 473–90. DOI: http://dx.doi.org/10.1177%2F0022185616643496.

Daly, T, Armstrong, P. and Lowndes, R. 2015. Liminality in Ontario's long-term care homes: private companions' care work in the space 'betwixt and between'. *Competition and Change*, 19(3), pp. 246–63. DOI: http://dx.doi.org/10.1177%2F1024529415580262.

Habjanic, A. and Pajnkihar, M., 2013. Family members' involvement in elder care provision in nursing homes and their considerations about financial compensation: a qualitative study. *Archives of Gerontology and Geriatrics*, 56(3), pp. 425–31. DOI: http://dx.doi.org/10.1016/j.archger.2013.01.002.

Keefe, J. and Fancey, P., 2000. The care continues: responsibility for elderly relatives before and after admission to a long term care facility. *Family Relations*, 49(3), pp. 235–44. DOI: 10.1111/j.1741-3729.2000.00235.x.

MacDonald, M., 1991. Post-Fordism and the flexibility debate. *Studies in Political Economy*, 36 (Fall), pp. 177–201. DOI: http://dx.doi.org/10.1080/19187033.1991.11675447.

McGregor, M.J., Cohen, M., McGrail, K., Broemeling, A.M., Adler, R.N., Schulzer, M., et al., 2005. Staffing levels in not-for-profit and for-profit long-term care facilities: does type of ownership matter? *Canadian Medical Association Journal*, 172(5), pp. 645–9. DOI: 10.1503/cmaj.1040131.

Rozin, P., Fischler, C., Imada, S., Sarubin, A. and Wrzesniewsk, A., 1999. Attitudes to food and the role of food in life in the U.S.A., Japan, Flemish Belgium and France: possible implications for the diet-health debate. *Appetite*, 33(2), pp. 163–80. DOI: https://doi.org/10.1006/appe.1999.0244.

Sinha, M., 2013. *Spotlight on Canadians: results from the general social survey. Portrait of caregivers, 2012.* Catalogue Number 89-652-X. Available at: www.statcan.gc.ca/pub/89-652-x/89-652-x2013001-eng.pdf [accessed 18.07.2017].

Stinson, J., Pollak, N. and Cohen, M., 2005. *The pains of privatization: how contracting out hurts health support workers, their families and health care.* Ottawa: Canadian Centre for Policy Alternatives. Available at: www.policyalternatives.ca/publications/reports/pains-privatization [accessed 18.07.2017].

Twigg, J. and Buse, C.E., 2013. Dress, dementia and the embodiment of identity. *Dementia*, 12(3), pp. 326–36. DOI: http://dx.doi.org/10.1177%2F1471301213476504.

Williams, F., 2001. In and beyond New Labour: towards a new political ethics of care. *Critical Social Policy*, 21(4), pp. 467–93. DOI: http://dx.doi.org/10.1177%2F026101830102100405.

Part VII
Australia

21

Reforms to long-term care in Australia

A changing and challenging landscape

Jane Mears

Introduction

Long-term care (LTC) touches the daily lives of millions of Australians: older people, informal carers and paid care workers. Historically, the primary providers of LTC, referred to as 'aged care' in Australia, were informal carers, mostly families and not-for profit care providers, with governments making a relatively small contribution. However, from the 1980s, the national government started to take on greater responsibility for funding and regulation of LTC, investing particularly in the expansion of home care services.

This expansion of LTC has occurred at a time when New Public Management (NPM) has had considerable influence on policy development, internationally and in Australia. The influence of NPM can be seen on the reforms to LTC since the 1980s, with progressive waves of reform moving towards greater national regulation and increasing marketization and competition. Throughout this period, there have been constant underlying tensions between providing high-quality support and services for older people and demonstrating quantifiable outcomes and balancing budgets (Sidoti et al., p. 8).

This chapter provides an examination of the context and background to LTC in Australia, an overview of reforms from the mid-1980s, and a discussion of the current opportunities and challenges in accessing and providing LTC for older people and informal carers, for care workers and for care provider organizations.

Long-term care in Australia

Australia has a large and growing proportion of older people needing care and support. There are approximately 24.1 million people in Australia with 3.6 million older people (aged 65+) comprising around 15 per cent of the population. By 2054–2055, it is expected that 23 per cent of the population will be over 65 years (ACFA, 2016, p. 18). Approximately 95 per cent of older Australians live in private households, while 5.2 per cent live in residential care facilities (Australian Bureau of Statistics, 2015).

Informal carers provide the bulk of the care to older people and those with a disability. In 2015, almost 2.7 million Australians aged 15 years and over were informal carers. Of these, 856,100 people, 37 per cent of all informal carers, identified as primary carers (Australian Bureau of Statistics, 2015).

In 2015–2016, over 1.25 million older people received some form of LTC, residential care or home care. Around 250,000 older people were living in residential care and over 1 million older people were utilizing home care services. Home care services are provided through the Commonwealth Home Support Programme (CHSP), a programme designed to provide basic services to support older people in their homes and prevent admission to residential care, and the Home Care Package Programme (HCPP), a more intensive programme designed to substitute for residential care (Australian Law Reform Commission, 2017, p. 103).

Government-subsidized home care and residential care services are managed, organized and delivered by not-for-profit and for-profit providers. In 2014–2015, there were over 2,000 providers of home care services, comprising around 1,600 providing home care services under the Home and Community Care Programme (HACC), which became the main programme in CHSP from July 2015 (see below) and 500 providers, providing care packages under the HCPP. There were around 1,000 residential care providers (ACFA, 2016, p. xii).

The majority of providers of LTC were not-for-profit care providers, in residential care (54 per cent), in HACC (74 per cent) and HCPP (69 per cent) (ACFA, 2016, pp. 44, 54, 76). Since the 1990s, with the opening up of the tendering process to include for-profit providers, the for-profit share of the home care market has been slowly increasing. By 2013, the percentage of for-profit home care package providers was 11.9 per cent, and by 2014 this had increased to 12.9 per cent (ACFA, 2016, p. 55).

These not-for-profit and for-profit care providers employ the care workers. In 2016, there were more than 240,317 people working for care provider organizations in direct care occupations (Mavromaras et al., 2017, pp. 12, 70), around 153,854 (of whom 70.3 per cent were care workers) working in residential facilities, and 86,463 (of whom 84 per cent were care workers) working in home care (Mavromaras et al., 2017, pp. 12–13, 70).

Much of what is known about care workers has been collected through National Aged Care Workforce surveys. There have been four National Aged Care Workforce Surveys (NACWS) (2003, 2007, 2012 and 2016). These surveys are commissioned and funded by the Australian Government, Department of Health and undertaken by the National Institute of Labour Studies (NILS) at Flinders University. All provider organizations with LTC funding for residential facilities and home care/home support outlets were invited to participate. The surveys collect demographic information, information about workers' roles, levels of worker satisfaction, training/ qualification levels, and information about the health of the aged care workforce (Mavromaras et al., 2017). To collect these data, a census survey package was sent to all providers of care, one main survey for the manager to fill in and several worker surveys were given to each facility. Interviews with key respondents, managers and care workers were also completed. In 2016, over 4,500 facilities and outlets and more than 15,000 aged care workers were included in the study (Mavromaras et al., 2017).

Around 88 per cent of all care workers were women (Mavromaras et al., 2017, pp. 17, 74), with a third (32 per cent) of residential care workers and 23 per cent of home care workers born outside Australia (Mavromaras et al., 2017, pp. 18, 75). A high percentage of care workers worked part-time, with only around 11 per cent in both residential and home care having full-time jobs (Mavromaras et al., 2017, pp. 25, 84).

In regard to training and qualifications, of those working in residential care, the proportion of care workers with a Certificate III in Aged Care (the standard minimal qualification for working in this occupation) was 67 per cent, and had been around this level since 2012 (Mavromaras et al., 2017, p. 22). However, for care workers working in home care, the proportion with a Certificate III was significantly lower, with only 51 per cent holding a Certificate III in 2016. This had increased slightly, from 48 per cent in 2012 (Mavromaras et al., 2017, p. 79). Of registered nurses (RNs), the proportion of those holding specific qualifications in aged care was even lower, with less than 30 per cent of those working in residential care and less than18 per cent of those working in home care having specific qualifications in aged care (Mavromaras et al., 2017, pp. 22, 82). Residential care workers were more likely to be undertaking further professional development than those employed in home care and community support (58 per cent versus 48 per cent) (Mavromaras et al., 2017, p. 161).

Access to work-related training (short training courses in a specialized area, for example dementia care) by the aged direct care workforce as a whole was high, with 80 per cent of residential care workers and 75 per cent of home care and community support workers undertaking work-related training in the last 12 months. However, much of this training is contracted out to registered training organizations (RTOs), and there is little regulation or uniformity across the sector.

Commonwealth (federal government) expenditure on residential care in 2014–2015 was $A10.6 billion (£6.254 billion), with HACC receiving $A1.9 billion (£1.121 billion) and the more intensive (and expensive) home care programmes receiving $A1.28 billion (£755.2 million). However, although the provision of services is means-tested, and those who are able are expected to pay for services, the fees paid by older people go nowhere near covering the costs of providing the service, particularly in home care. In 2014–2015, the revenue collected from older people made up 27 per cent in the case of residential care (ACFA, 2016, p. xxii), and around 10 per cent of the expenditure for the HACC (ACFA, 2016, p. xvi) and home care programmes (ACFA, 2016, p. xix).

The next section examines the growth and expansion of LTC. Up until the 1980s, LTC mainly comprised residential care. There were very few home care services and little support for older people and informal carers in the community. Further, there was an inequitable and uneven spread of LTC support and services across the nation. Since the 1980s, the system has undergone major reforms. From 2013, the national government has taken on responsibility for managing and regulating all LTC support and services.

Context and background

The development, implementation and management of government-subsidized LTC in Australia is complex and multilayered. Systemic reforms have been shaped by legacies from the past and driven by three tiers of government, the Commonwealth, six state governments (NSW, Tasmania, Victoria, South Australia, Queensland and Western Australia) and two self-governing territories (Australian Capital Territory, Northern Territory), and numerous local municipal governments and significant stakeholders. These stakeholders include older people (the Council of the Ageing [COTA], Alzheimer's Australia), informal carers (Carers Australia) and, more recently, peak bodies for the aged care industry (Aged and Community Services Australia and Leading Aged Services Australia), as well as professional groups representing paid care workers (United Voice, Nurses and Midwives Association) (Jeon and Kendig, 2016, p. 240). The work of these stakeholders has been pivotal in influencing government and transforming care of older people from a primarily private activity, carried out by families in the privacy of their own homes, into a public issue of concern to all Australians.

From the 1970s, the dominant stakeholders were associations advocating for older people and informal carers. These advocates were supported by the not-for-profit care provider organizations (McLeay, 1982; Stevenson, 1976) and lobbied the national government, on behalf of older people and informal carers. These groups have had significant influence in putting these issues onto the political agenda, for example documenting the huge load carried by family carers, work that was hitherto 'hidden' in private homes. Although generally supportive of the government's LTC policies, these stakeholders have consistently contested and critiqued policy initiatives based on NPM principles and have been vocal in their critiques of the government's initiatives to increase the marketization of care services (Fine, 2007a).

In the 1980s and the 1990s, stakeholders directed attention to issues such as the lived experiences of informal carers, their social isolation, emotional investment and the psychological stress that carers experience (Watson and Mears, 1999; Bowman, 1994). Studies on the individual and societal costs of caring complemented this work (NATSEM, 2004; Fisher and Briggs, 2000; Lindsay, 1995). As more informal carers wanted and needed to be engaged in paid work, so the difficulties of juggling paid care and unpaid care came onto the agenda, with studies focusing on the everyday lives of those informal carers engaged in paid work (Watson and Mears, 1999). This work gave further 'voice' to informal carers and brought their stories, needs and concerns into the public and policy domain (Department of Families Housing Community Services and Indigenous Affairs, 2011; House of Representatives: Standing Committee on Family, Community, Housing, Youth, 2009).

As home care services expanded, so the research agenda expanded to include paid care workers. Research was both quantitative (Mavromaras et al., 2017; King et al., 2013; Mears and Garcia, 2011; Meagher and Cortis, 2010; Martin and King, 2008; Meagher and Healy, 2005, 2006) and qualitative (Chesters and Baxter, 2011; Mears, 2007). These studies examined relationships, boundaries and intersections between paid and unpaid care, and the employment and working conditions of care workers (Mears and Watson, 2008; The Benevolent Society, 2008).

At the same time, researchers were also focusing attention on the politics of ageing (Encel and Ozanne, 2007; Fine 2007a, 2007b), particularly the impact of NPM and the marketization of care (Brennan et al., 2012; Davidson, 2009; King and Meagher, 2009; Martin and King, 2008; King, 2007). This work provided new insights into the working lives of care workers and the context of their work, over a period characterized by reform and growth.

Long-term care for older people from the 1980s

This section examines the reform and growth of LTC from the 1980s to the present day. This was a period characterized by ongoing tensions between meeting the demands of stakeholders – older people, informal carers, care provider organizations and professional groups – for governments to invest in high-quality residential and home care services, and governments driven by NPM and imperatives to balance budgets.

In the early 1980s, a committee of inquiry was initiated to:

> establish a framework which allows governments to make cost effective decisions on the provision of both Accommodation (residential care) and Home Care for the Aged and cut public expenditure in attempts to achieve savings in an effort to reduce the growth of the public sector.
>
> *(McLeay, 1982, p. vii)*

The committee recommended that the entire system of LTC be overhauled and that the national government take on the primary responsibility for regulating and funding home care services.

In 1985, the national government took on funding and regulatory responsibilities for home care, through the Home and Community Care Programme (HACC). This programme was jointly funded, 60 per cent by the Commonwealth, and 40 per cent from the states and territories. Most of the Commonwealth funding was granted as block funding to the not-for-profit care providers and to state and local government care providers who were already providing this care. The programme was lauded as:

> a new approach to the planning of community services in Australia, an approach which will hold out the possibility of achieving a more caring and equitable society. Services which are appropriately planned, distributed and financed provide an essential complement to other social policies in achieving social equity and needed support to ensure that our society functions properly.
>
> *(House of Representatives: Standing Committee on Community Affairs, 1994, p. 9)*

The HACC programme provided low-level support services, including home nursing, domestic assistance (home cleaning, showering and dressing), home maintenance and modification, community transport, and some respite services. These services were very thinly spread, with most HACC clients (90 per cent) receiving only two hours of services per week (Productivity Commission, 2011a, p. 21).

In 1992, the national government initiated a new programme, the Community Aged Care Program, and a national assessment and referral programme, the Aged Care Assessment Program. The Community Aged Care Packages (CACP) provided up to seven hours assistance a week for older people assessed as eligible for low-level residential care. In the late 1990s, two further programmes were added, the Extended Aged Care at Home (EACH) and Extended Aged Care at Home Dementia (EACHD) packages. These packages provided up to 23 hours of care per week for older people assessed as eligible for residential care and for EACHD, those with dementia and complex cognitive, emotional or behavioural needs (Productivity Commission, 2011a, pp. 21–2).

Older people were assessed as eligible for services through the Aged Care Assessment Program (ACAP) by Aged Care Assessment Teams (ACATs), multidisciplinary teams of professionals (Fine, 2007a). Once deemed eligible, the older person or his or her carer then initiated contact with a service provider, and if the care provider was able to provide a package, a care manager then conducted a detailed assessment of the older person's needs, drew up an individual care plan, and managed and provided the service. Older people were means-tested, and if deemed as unable to pay, services were provided free. A nominal fee was charged to older people.

By the turn of the twentieth century, there were again calls to overhaul the system. In 2008, the Productivity Commission (the Australian Government's independent research and advisory body on social, economic and environmental issues) advised that urgent reforms were needed so that 'our aged care sector is able to meet these challenges in ways that promote the wellbeing of the oldest generation, while being cost effective for the community as a whole' (Productivity Commission, 2008, p. iii). The Productivity Commission concluded that the current LTC system was unfair, underfunded, fragmented, inefficient, difficult to navigate, and that services and consumer choice were limited, quality of care was variable, and coverage of needs, pricing, subsidies and user co-contributions inconsistent and inequitable. The Commission also found that workforce shortages were exacerbated by low wages, many workers had insufficient skills, and care providers were seen as uncompetitive.

Following this report, the Productivity Commission examined ways to reform not only LTC, but also disability support. After extensive consultation and submissions from major stakeholders, researchers, older people and those with a disability, informal carers, care providers, and professionals working in the ageing and disability sectors, two reports were published, *Caring for Older Australians* (Productivity Commission, 2011a) and *Caring for Australians with Disability* (Productivity Commission, 2011b).

These reports recommended that the government set up a new national system to support older Australians (aged 65+) and those with a disability (under 65 years), regulated and funded by the Commonwealth government. The government responded by introducing a framework for a national system of consumer-directed care (CDC), through two initiatives, the Aged Care Reforms (ACR) and the National Disability Insurance Scheme (NDIS). Under both these schemes, government funding goes directly to individuals, channelled through care provider organizations. Both schemes are underpinned by a rights approach, and recognize the rights of older people and those with a disability to good-quality care and support (Kendig, 2016). Both reform packages were passed through the federal parliament in 2012 with support from all political parties.

Current reforms

The national government now has major responsibility for oversight, funding and regulatory responsibility for LTC. The recommendations from the Productivity Commission (2011a) are being implemented over a 10-year period from 1 July 2012 (Commonwealth of Australia, 2012). The impact of NPM is illustrated by the following quote. LTC has entered an era where:

> Increased consumer choice will be a major change into the future. A fiscally sustainable aged care system that requires consumers to contribute to their care costs where they can afford to do so means that there will be increased consumer expectations for greater choice and control. The ability for consumers to choose who provides care and support will create a more competitive and innovative market. This, accompanied by an aged care sector that has more flexibility to respond to the increasing diversity of consumers' care needs, preferences and financial circumstances will contribute to a sustainable system.
>
> *(Aged Care Sector Committee, 2016, p. 2)*

This section outlines main components of the current reforms to LTC; the creation of the My Aged Care Gateway, the introduction of CDC and opportunities for increased choice for older people, the introduction of mandatory payment for services, and the introduction of a new funding model. The ambition of the government is to reform LTC and create a system where older people and carers 'have access to competent, affordable and timely care and support services, through a consumer driven, market based, sustainable aged care system' (Aged Care Sector Committee, 2016. p. 3).

A central plank of the reforms is the My Aged Care Gateway, a national centralized information and assessment system, to enable equitable and consistent access to information, assessment and services across the country. The My Aged Care Gateway was launched on 1 July 2013. All older people wanting information, services and support are expected to access the My Aged Care Gateway for assessment and referral (ACFA, 2016). Once assessed as eligible, they then choose a care provider to broker the care services. Older people can exit, that is, change care providers if they are not satisfied with the care they are receiving, and transfer their care package funding to a provider of their choice (Low, 2013).

The CDC model was introduced in late 2013 for recipients of home care services. It aims to enable older people to control the type and nature of their home care support by being able to choose their preferred services and service providers and manage their allocated Home Care Package budget (DOHA, 2015). There are plans to introduce consumer-directed care into residential care at an undetermined date.

Two new home care programmes have been set up, the Home Care Package Program (HCPP) and the Commonwealth Home Support Program (CHSP). From August 2013, the Home Care Package Program (HCPP) replaced the Community Aged Care Packages (CCAPs), and from July 2015 the Commonwealth Home Support Program (CHSP) replaced the HACC programme. From July 2018, these programmes are to be amalgamated (ACFA, 2016; Australian Government, 2015).

Mandatory fees have been introduced for all home care services. All older people are expected to pay for services, according to a predetermined sliding scale, based on income. In addition, older people now have the option of paying for extra services and can pay the care provider for more services. They can 'top up' the packages if they choose. Care providers manage the collection of fees for services (ACFA, 2016, p. xxv).

A new funding model was introduced from February 2017 for the CHSP and the HCPP. The funding model changed from a system where government subsidies for home care services were paid as block funding to care providers, to manage and provide services, to a model where the funding goes directly to the older person, who is given the choice of how to spend the payment. Care providers continue to manage the funds, collect fees, and assist in the planning and organization of services. Care workers cannot be employed by the individuals, but must be employed by registered and approved care providers.

While these reforms hold promise, this reform process has occurred over a period where the principles of NPM have been a driving force. The LTC system is now dominated by principles of consumer-directed and market-driven care, with an emphasis on competition, the free market and individual responsibility (ACFA, 2016). This new environment offers some opportunities and many challenges for older people, informal carers, care workers and care providers.

Implications for older people and informal carers

With the introduction of CDC, older people now would appear to have more opportunities to exercise choice in seeking out and managing their home care services. However, older people and their carers have no experience of CDC and little understanding of the reforms, or the operation of the LTC system. Older people experience great difficulties accessing information and finding their way around this complex and fluid system. They also experience difficulties 'choosing' and accessing services and paying the fees required. Further, there are concerns that those older people who already experience difficulties accessing services may well miss out completely, and that with mandatory payment of fees and the opportunity to top up services, existing inequalities will be exacerbated (Day et al., 2017; Productivity Commission, 2017; Australian Law Reform Commission, 2016; COTA, 2016; Simons et al., 2016).

A recent study by COTA, the national peak body representing older people in Australia, found that people did not know where to go to get information. Many had difficulties negotiating the online platform and accessing printed material, and the information provided through the My Aged Care Gateway was not considered to be very helpful. Further, they found that there is no clear information to help make informed decisions about providers and little information available to compare care providers in terms of price and quality of services. Many older people felt they were unable to exercise choice and control of their aged care services, and felt unsupported in navigating this complex system (COTA, 2016, p. 11).

In addition, they experienced challenges accessing home care services due to long waiting lists both for assessment and access to services. At present, the demand for services far outstrips the supply of services. In 2016, the median waiting time for home care services was 73 days, with 43 per cent of people waiting more than three months (Productivity Commission 2017, p. 14). As Fine (2007a) reminds us, care is not like a typical consumer good where the consumer is free to choose or to refuse a particular product. Given there is a shortage of services under the present system, older people in need of services have little choice but to accept the services available.

With the transition to CDC, those older people already receiving home care services were concerned about possible gaps and disruptions to support, fragmentation of care, escalating costs and the lack of information. Even though the packages are now portable, and one may change provider, given the difficulties many older people have procuring a service, older people have said they would be highly unlikely to choose to change providers (Day et al., 2017, p. 166). Also, with the introduction of fees for those receiving government-funded services, some providers are already finding that older people already receiving services, but not at present paying fees, are reluctant to continue to accept care packages for fear that they will not be able to pay the fees, even though the packages are heavily subsidized (Simons et al., 2016).

There are concerns that this system will exacerbate already existing inequalities. Advocates have expressed grave concerns about how particular groups of older people and informal carers will manage under this new scheme (Australian Law Reform Commission, 2016). Different social groups don't have the same capacity to exercise choice, based on their personal resources and command of information. Older people from culturally and linguistically diverse (CALD) backgrounds, those with mental illness and limited or declining capacity already experience difficulties in making informed decisions about care, and may well be unable to access services in the future (Australian Law Reform Commission, 2016). Some older people are able to 'top up' services, with those unable to pay becoming increasingly excluded (Kendig, 2016). Those with high levels of private resources are in the best position to benefit, with others missing out, exacerbating inequality (Brennan et al., 2012).

Implications for care workers

Despite decades of lobbying from professional associations and care providers for extra government funding to improve care workers' employment and working conditions, many challenges remain. Rates of pay are low and remuneration is not commensurate with the qualifications, knowledge and experience care workers bring to their work (Australian Law Reform Commission, 2017, p. 127; The Senate, 2017; Australian Council of Social Services, 2015). Care work is precarious employment, with most care workers employed part-time, and many care workers reporting that they are often not offered sufficient hours of work to earn a living wage. Of those care workers who are thinking of quitting care work, the most common reason given for leaving is the low pay (Mears and Garcia, 2011). This is particularly the case for those working in residential care, where satisfaction in regard to remuneration received a significantly lower overall rating among residential direct care workers, compared with other categories of job satisfaction (Mavromaras et al., 2017, p. 38).

Further, there is little opportunity for career advancement and low staff-client ratios, putting increasing pressure on those providing care. An Australian Nursing and Midwifery Federation

(ANMF) survey reported that 80 per cent of participants who worked in residential aged care considered that staffing levels were insufficient to provide an adequate level of care to residents (Australian Law Reform Commission, 2017, p. 128). Additionally, over the past decade, much of the training for the care workforce has been privatized and contracted to registered training organizations (RTOs). This sector is not well regulated. There is no uniformity across training programmes, courses vary in length, with differing entry requirements, and there are limited opportunities for on-the-job training, resulting in workers who are unprepared for the tasks they are employed to carry out (The Senate, 2017, p. 61).

The impact of funding shortfalls on the care workers in the LTC sector has been well documented over the past decades. Home care workers report being offered fewer hours, through reducing shifts, working split shifts and cutting payment for travel time (Mears and Garcia, 2011). In the residential care sector, there are constant complaints of understaffing, of care workers not having enough time to meet the needs of residents, and reported cases of neglect, abuse and intimidation by care workers towards older people (Australian Law Reform Commission, 2016).

The Australian government has been committed to encouraging people to stay in the workforce as long as possible, through measures such as increasing the age at which one becomes eligible for an old-age pension. This means that for most older people to survive, they will need to continue working for as long as possible (Australian Council of Social Services, 2015). Older workers face a number of barriers, including experiences of ageism in the workplace, and employment rates drop rapidly between the ages of 55 and 65. Discrimination and negative stereotyping make it very difficult for people to find work after the age of 45. There have been a number of significant government inquiries examining this issue and looking at ways of alleviating discrimination against older workers, and ways employers can encourage, attract and retain older workers (Australian Human Rights Commission, 2016).

It would appear that ageism is not generally a problem for care workers. In particular, in home care, older experienced workers are valued, with 72 per cent of home care and home support workers aged 45 years and over, and 55 per cent of residential care workers, compared to only 38 per cent of workers 45 years and over in the workforce (Mavromaras et al., 2017, pp. 16, 73). Many care workers enter the industry as older workers (over 45) having pursued other careers and taken time out of paid work caring for children, those with disabilities and older people (Mears and Garcia, 2011). Around 65 per cent of care workers had in the past cared informally for older relatives or friends with a disability, with 47 per cent currently caring for one or more older people (Mears and Garcia, 2011, p. 18). As one chief executive officer (CEO) of a care provider organization reported, 'the care workforce is our biggest asset. We invest all we can to ensure care workers have decent working conditions and are trained and supported to provide good quality care' (Mears and Garcia, 2011, personal commmunication).

In addition, working through care providers offers care workers some protection. Care workers' working and employment conditions are more highly regulated by the care providers than in the cash-for-care system that is operating in countries such as the UK.

Implications for care providers

For the well-established and larger not-for-profit service providers, the new system offers many opportunities. These organizations have taken a lead role in influencing the direction of change and have many decades of experience providing both residential and home care. Many have maintained their original missions and core values of providing services to the most disadvantaged, and have been, for many decades, developing innovative policies and practices underpinned by person centred care (The Benevolent Society, 2008). They are well placed to compete with the for-profit providers and organize and manage CDC and individualized packages as required under the most recent reforms.

The not-for-profit providers of home care have also had experience in adapting to a competitive market. In the 1990s, with the opening up of competitive tendering for care packages, the allocation of funding became far more competitive. At this time, the smaller, specialized, community-based services with few resources to write the tender applications either disappeared or were taken over by larger not-for-profit operators. They have become increasingly competitive and corporatized, and look and operate in very similar ways to the for-profit organizations (Green and Mears, 2014). By 2000, when the home care market was opened to for-profit providers, the larger not-for-profit care providers had become highly competitive. They are the major providers of LTC (Davidson, 2009).

However, the providers are also facing major challenges, including handling the constraints and shortfalls of government funding and dealing with government regulations that may stifle creative, competitive responses.

Conclusions

There is some optimism from older people, informal carers, service providers, service managers and care workers that the current reforms will deliver, as promised, quality care for older people, and that Australia will create an inclusive, sustainable LTC system supporting all Australians. The principles in these reforms have come about through successful lobbying and some enlightened political leadership. Australia is well placed, with governments and stakeholders having worked together to map out these reforms, underpinned by a rights-based framework. Kendig (2016, p. 277) optimistically suggests that if supported by whole-of-community actions, the reforms have the potential to 'transform Australia into an age-friendly society that realizes the benefits of an older society'.

However, there are many challenges still to be overcome. To meet these challenges, and fulfil the goals of the reforms to LTC, governments need to continue to invest in and adequately fund LTC, in particular investing in the care workforce. To attract workers to the sector and ensure a sustainable long-term future for the care force, care workers need decent employment and working conditions, in particular remuneration commensurate with their skills and experience. Otherwise, with the current reforms and the continual moves towards greater marketization and privatization of care, the research indicates that existing inequalities will be exacerbated, with older people, particularly those with few resources, missing out on care and with informal carers and care workers carrying a disproportionate burden of care. Contrary to meeting the goal of creating a sustainable LTC system, the care sector will become unsustainable.

References

ACFA (Aged Care Financing Authority), 2016. *Fourth report on the funding and financing of the aged care sector: July 2016.* Canberra: Department of Health. Available at: https://agedcare.health.gov.au/sites/g/files/net1426/f/documents/10_2016/acfa_annual_report_on_funding_and_financing_of_the_aged_care_industry_2016.pdf [accessed 12.06.2017].

Aged Care Sector Committee, 2016. *Aged care roadmap.* Department of Health. Canberra: Commonwealth of Australia. Available at: https://agedcare.health.gov.au/sites/g/files/net1426/f/documents/04_2016/strategic_roadmap_for_aged_care_web.pdf [accessed 12.06.2017].

Australian Bureau of Statistics, 2015. *Disability, ageing and carers, Australia: summary of findings, 2015.* Canberra: Australian Bureau of Statistics. Available at: www.abs.gov.au/ausstats/abs@.nsf/Latestproducts/4430.0Main%20Features302015?opendocument&tabname=Summary&prodno=4430.0&issue=2015&num=&view= [accessed 20.06.2017].

Australian Council of Social Services, 2015. *Inequality in Australia.* Available at: www.acoss.org.au/wp-content/uploads/2015/06/Inequality_in_Australia_FINAL.pdf [accessed 28.06.17].

Australian Government, 2015. *Commonwealth Home Support Programme (CHSP) guidelines overview.* Department of Social Services. Canberra: Commonwealth of Australia. Available at: www.dss.gov.au/sites/default/files/chsp_programme_guidelines.pdf [accessed 28.06.2017].

Australian Human Rights Commission, 2016. *Willing to work: national inquiry into employment discrimination against older Australians and Australians with disability.* NSW: AHRC. Available at: www.humanrights.gov.au/sites/default/files/document/publication/WTW_2016_Full_Report_AHRC_ac.pdf [accessed 28.06.2017].

Australian Law Reform Commission, 2016. *Elder abuse: discussion paper.* ALRC Discussion Paper 83. Sydney: Australian Government. Available at: www.alrc.gov.au/sites/default/files/pdfs/publications/dp83.pdf [accessed 28.06.2017].

Australian Law Reform Commission, 2017. *Elder abuse: a national legal response final report.* Sydney: Australian Government. Available at: www.alrc.gov.au/sites/default/files/pdfs/publications/elder_abuse_131_final_report_31_may_2017.pdf [accessed 26.06.2017].

Bowman, D., 1994. *Listen to the carers: the many voices of care.* ACT: Carers Australia.

Brennan, D., Cass, B., Himmelweit, S. and Szebehely, M., 2012. The marketisation of care: rationales and consequences in Nordic and liberal care regimes. *Journal of European Social Policy,* 22(4), pp. 377–91. DOI: https://doi.org/10.1177/0958928712449772.

Chesters, J. and Baxter, J., 2011. Prisoners of love? Job satisfaction in care work. *Australian Journal of Social Issues,* 46(1), pp. 49–67. DOI: 10.1002/j.1839-4655.2011.tb00205.x.

Commonwealth of Australia, 2012. *Living longer, living better: the aged care reform package.* Available at: http://apo.org.au/node/29086 [accessed 28.06.2017].

COTA Australia, 2016. *Submission to the 2016 Aged Care Legislated Review.* ACT: COTA. Available at: www.cota.org.au/lib/pdf/COTA_Australia/publications/submissions/cota-submission-2016-aged-care-legislated-review.pdf [accessed 28.06.2017].

Davidson, B., 2009. For-profit organisations in managed markets for human services. In D. King and G. Meagher, eds. *Paid care in Australia: politics, profits, practices.* Sydney: Sydney University Press, pp. 43–80.

Day, J., Thorington T., Summons, A.C., Van Der Riet, P., Hunter, S., Maguire, J., et al., 2017. Home care packages: insights into the experiences of older people leading up to the introduction of consumer directed care in Australia. *Australian Journal of Primary Health,* 2(23), pp. 162–9. DOI: https://doi.org/10.1071/PY16022.

Department of Families Housing Community Services and Indigenous Affairs, 2011. *National Carer Strategy Action Plan (2011–2014).* Canberra: Commonwealth of Australia. Available at: www.dss.gov.au/sites/default/files/documents/10_2012/ncs_action_plan.pdf [accessed 28.06.2017].

DOHA (Department of Health and Ageing), 2015. *Report on the operation of the Aged Care Act 1997, 2014–2015.* Canberra: Commonwealth of Australia. Available at: https://agedcare.health.gov.au/2015-16-report-on-the-operation-of-the-aged-care-act-1997 [accessed 20.07.2017].

Encel, S. and Ozanne, F., 2007. The politics of ageing. In A. Borowski, S. Encel and E. Ozanne, eds. *Longevity and social change in Australia.* Sydney: UNSW Press, pp. 296–315.

Fine, M., 2007a. Uncertain prospects: aged care policy for a long-lived society. In A. Borowski, S. Encel and E. Ozanne, eds. *Longevity and social change in Australia.* Sydney: UNSW Press, pp. 265–95.

Fine, M., 2007b. *A caring society? Care and the dilemmas of human service in the 21st century.* Basingstoke: Palgrave Macmillan.

Fisher, D. and Briggs., H., 2000. *Warning: caring is a health hazard: results of the 1999 national survey of carer health and wellbeing.* ACT: Carers Association of Australia.

Green, J. and Mears, J., 2014. The implementation of the NDIS: who wins, who loses? *Cosmopolitan Civil Societies: An Interdisciplinary Journal,* 6(2), pp. 25–39. DOI: http://dx.doi.org/10.5130/ccs.v6i2.3915.

House of Representatives: Standing Committee on Family, Community, Housing, Youth, 2009. *Who cares? Report on the inquiry into better support for carers.* Canberra: Parliament of Australia. Available at: www.aph.gov.au/parliamentary_Business/Committees/House_of_Representatives_Committees?url=fchy/carers/report.htm [accessed 28.06.2017].

House of Representatives: Standing Committee on Community Affairs, 1994. *HACC options/discussion paper*. Canberra: Australian Government Publishing Service.

Jeon, Y. and Kendig, H., 2016. Care and support for older people. In C. O'Loughlin, K. Browning and H. Kendig, eds. *Ageing in Australia: challenges and opportunities*. New York: Springer, pp. 239–59.

Kendig, H., 2016. Directions and choices on ageing for the future. In C. O'Loughlin, K. Browning and H. Kendig, eds. *Ageing in Australia: challenges and opportunities*. New York: Springer, pp. 263–79.

King, D., 2007. Rethinking the care-market relationship in care provider organisations. *Australian Journal of Social Issues*, 42(2), pp. 199–212.

King, D. and Meagher, G., eds, 2009. *Paid care in Australia: politics, profits, practices*. NSW: Sydney University Press.

King, D., Mavromaras, K., Wei, Z., He, B.R., Healy, J., Macaitis, K., et al., 2013. *The aged care workforce 2012 final report*. Canberra: Australian Government Department of Health and Ageing. Available at: www.agedcarecrisis.com/images/pdf/The_Aged_Care_Workforce_Report.pdf [accessed 28.06.2017].

Lindsay, M.R., 1995. *Who cares for the carers? The next major focus in social policy*. Canberra: Department of the Parliamentary Library.

Low, L.-F., 2013. Older citizens need information to be good aged-care customers. *The Conversation*, 9 August. Available at: http://theconversation.com/older-citizens-need-information-to-be-good-aged-care-customers-15963 [accessed 03.07.2017].

Martin, B. and King, D., 2008. *Who cares for older Australians? A picture of the residential and community based aged care workforce, 2007*. Adelaide: National Institute of Labour Studies, Flinders University. Available at: www.flinders.edu.au/sabs/nils-files/reports/NILS_Aged_Care_Final%202007.pdf [accessed 11.07.2017].

Mavromaras, K., Knight, G., Isherwood, L., Crettenden, A., Flavel, J., Karmel, T., et al., 2017. *The aged care workforce, 2016*. Canberra: Australian Government Department of Health. Available at: https://agedcare.health.gov.au/sites/g/files/net1426/f/documents/03_2017/nacwcs_final_report_290317.pdf [accessed 28.06.2017].

McLeay, L., 1982. *In a home or at home: accommodation and home care for the aged*. Report October 1982. House of Representatives Standing Committee on Expenditure. Canberra: Australian Government Publishing Service.

Meagher, G. and Cortis, N. 2010. *The social and community services sector in NSW: structure, workforce and pay equity issues*. Sydney: Faculty of Education and Social Work, University of Sydney. Available at: http://handle.unsw.edu.au/1959.4/unsworks_36467 [accessed 03.07.2017].

Meagher, G. and Healy, K., 2005. *Who cares? Volume 1: a profile of care workers in Australia's community services industries*. ACOSS Papers. Canberra: ACOSS.

Meagher, G. and Healy, K., 2006. *Who cares? Volume 2: Employment structure and incomes in the Australian care workforce*. ACOSS Papers. Canberra: ACOSS.

Mears, J., 2007. Paid care workers in the community: an Australian study. In S. Balloch and M. Hill, eds. *Care, citizenship and communities: research and practice in a changing policy context*. Bristol: Policy Press, pp. 211–25.

Mears, J. and Garcia, E., 2011. *Transformations of care: living the consequences of changing public policies in Australia*. School of Social Sciences, Western Sydney University. Available at: www.westernsydney.edu.au/__data/assets/pdf_file/0008/228617/Jane_Mears_article.pdf [accessed 28.06.2017].

Mears, J. and Watson, E., 2008. Boundaries blurred and rigid at the frontline of care: care workers and the negotiation of relationships with older people. In A. Martin-Mathews and J.E. Phillips, eds. *Aging and caring at the intersection of work and home life: blurring the boundaries*. New York: Lawrence Erlbaum Associates, pp. 147–64.

NATSEM (National Centre for Social and Economic Modelling), 2004. *Who's going to care? Informal care and an ageing population*. Canberra: University of Canberra. Available at: www.natsem.canberra.edu.au/storage/care_report.pdf [acccessed 09.07.2017].

Productivity Commission, 2008. *Trends in aged care services: some implications*. Canberra: Commonwealth of Australia. Available at: www.pc.gov.au/__data/assets/pdf_file/0004/83380/aged-care-trends.pdf [accessed 12.06.2017].

Productivity Commission, 2011a. *Caring for older Australians*. Vol. 1, No. 53. Canberra: Commonwealth of Australia. Available at: www.pc.gov.au/inquiries/completed/aged-care/report/aged-care-volume1.pdf [accessed 12.06.2017].

Productivity Commission, 2011b. *Disability care and support*. Canberra: Commonwealth of Australia. Available at: www.pc.gov.au/inquiries/completed/disability-support/report [accessed 29.06.2017].

Productivity Commission, 2017. *Report on government services 2017: Volume F: community services*. Canberra: Commonwealth of Australia. Available at: www.pc.gov.au/research/ongoing/report-on-government-services/2017/community-services/rogs-2017-volumef.pdf [accessed 12.06.2017].

Sidoti, E., Banks, R., Darcy, M., O'Shea, P., Leonard, R., Atie, R., et al. 2009. *A question of balance: principles, contracts and the government-not-for-profit relationship*. NSW: Whitlam Institute, University of Western Sydney. Available at: www.whitlam.org/__data/assets/pdf_file/0020/92090/contracts_paper_final__email_version.pdf [accessed 09.07.2017].

Simons, B., Kimberley, H. and Jones, N.M., 2016. *Adjusting to consumer directed care: the experience of brotherhood of St Laurence community aged care service users*. Fitzroy Victoria: Brotherhood of St Laurence.

Stevenson, C., 1976. *Dedication: a report of a survey on caring for the aged at home carried out in N.S.W., Australia, June–Dec. 1975*. Sydney: NSW Council on the Ageing.

The Benevolent Society, 2008. *Caring for older Australians: care workers and care practices that support and enable good care*. Research to Practice Briefing 1: Social Policy Research Centre in partnership with The Benevolent Society. Available at: www.parliament.nsw.gov.au/committees/DBAssets/InquiryOther/Transcript/9983/Answers%20to%20questions%20on%20notice%20-%20Jane%20Mears%20Associate%20Professor%20-%20Western%20Sydney%20University.PDF [accessed 29.06.2017].

The Senate, 2017. *Community Affairs References Committee: future of Australia's aged care sector workforce*. Canberra: Commonwealth of Australia. Available at: www.lasa.asn.au/wp-content/uploads/2017/06/Report_Future-of-Australias-aged-care-sector-workforce.pdf [accessed 26.06.2017].

Watson, E.A. and Mears, J., 1999. *Women, work and care of the elderly*. Farnham: Ashgate.

Part VIII
Latin America

22

Facing the challenges of population longevity but not being ready

The case of Argentina[1]

Nélida Redondo

Introduction

Argentina lies at the southern tip of South America. Given its territorial extension, it is the second largest country in the subcontinent; politically, it is organized as a federation, with 24 subnational jurisdictions, while its economic growth is intermediate. Argentina is one of the earliest countries in Latin America to experience demographic ageing. It is currently going through the advanced phase of its demographic transition: in 2010, people aged 65 and over accounted for 10.2 per cent of the total population (INDEC, 2012, Table p. 2).

Throughout the twentieth century, progress in living conditions, the urbanization and modernization of the country and technological development, among other factors, were determining factors for the demographic transition being accompanied by an epidemiological transition that transformed the health profile of the population. In the first half of last century, the death rate fell because of the fall in infant mortality and the reduction in the lethal nature of infectious and parasitic disease. Over the last decades of the twentieth century, the fall in the death rate spread to more advanced ages as deaths from cardiovascular illnesses and cancer were brought under control. The result of this process was the continuous increase in the proportion of people over 80 years old in the total population. In other words, the progressive ageing of the elderly was recorded (Redondo, 2007).

The aim of this chapter is to show the inadequacies of social care for the increasing population of older dependent people in Argentina, and particularly the gender inequalities both in providing and receiving care. The next section discusses social and regional inequalities, especially in healthy life expectancy. Following this, it is shown that although Argentina has virtually universal retirement pensions and health coverage, social care relies almost exclusively on the family. The methods of two studies carried out by the author are then described, one of institutions for older dependent people in Buenos Aires and the other a longitudinal study of costs, both financial and emotional, of caring for elderly dependent people with prepayment health plans in Buenos Aires. The next two sections report the findings from these studies. Then the following section is concerned with gender inequalities in providing and receiving care. The chapter concludes with a discussion about the need for affordable long-term care for older people to be put on the public agenda in Argentina.

Social inequality and ageing: a challenge for the health system

Latin America is currently the second region in the world with most social inequality: a Gini coefficient of 52.9, which is close to 56.5, as observed in Sub-Saharan Africa, the first on the list, and significantly more than Asia at 44.7, and Eastern Europe and Central Asia at 34.7 (Gasparini et al., 2014) (0 represents perfect equality in the distribution of income, and 100 represents perfect inequality).

Conditioned by the evident social inequality, the epidemiological transition in countries in the region has followed a unique pattern that Frenk et al. (1989) called a 'prolonged polarized epidemiological transition', characterized by different durations and sequences depending on socio-economic sectors, whether in urban or rural surroundings, and on the geographical regions that make up the country as a whole.

In Argentina, death rates have been reduced throughout the country, but the composition of causes of death is much more complicated; the clear predominance of infectious diseases has been lost in favour of degenerative diseases, although infectious diseases are still a force to be reckoned with in the epidemiological profile. We could add to this growing complexity the deficient health systems, which suffer from significant technological underdevelopment and low productivity in the most backward provinces, and which have not yet solved old problems, but have to take on new challenges in the most deprived zones.

The increase in the percentage of over-80s as part of the total population of the country was slight in the first half of the twentieth century, up to the 1960s. With the census of 1970, a sharp increase became evident in the proportion of people aged over 80, which became even more pronounced in the 1990s and 2000s (cf. Figure 22.1).

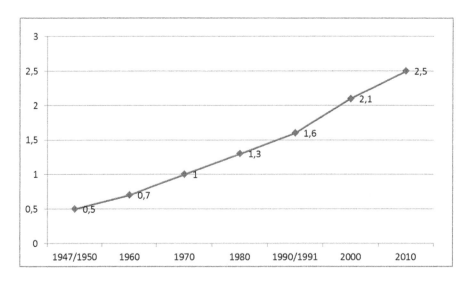

Figure 22.1 Percentage of people aged over 80 in the total population – Argentina – census dates 1947–2010

Source: Drawn up by the author from: National Censuses of Population and Housing 1947, 1960, 1970, 1980 and 1991, National Censuses of Population, Homes and Housing 2001 and 2010, INDEC (2012).

The over-80s age group was the fastest-growing age group in the whole population of Argentina in the decades between the two most recent censuses, from 1991 to 2010 (Table 22.1).

Likewise, the number of people who reach the age of 100 grew by almost 90 per cent from 2001 to 2010 (INDEC, 2012). The increase in longevity is proof of Argentina's success in improving general welfare, but, on the other hand, it implies the challenge of procuring a good quality of life for those who live longer. In Argentina, as in other Latin American countries, social and regional inequality constitutes the main hurdle to overcome in order to reach this goal.

Although there are obvious inequalities, the longevity of the population of Argentina is progressively growing in all the country's provinces and regions. The Healthy Life Expectancy study (HLE – Esperanza de Vida Saludable) (Belliard et al., 2013) shows that the average years of life added to the population of Argentina have not led to similar health situations all over the country.

According to the data provided by the 2010 census, the HLE (free of permanent limitations) at birth for the population of Argentina is 61.2 years for men and 64.3 years for women (Belliard et al., 2013). Polar situations were observed in the city of Buenos Aires, the capital, with the highest HLE, and in the province of Chaco (in the north-east of the country) with the lowest. The difference between the two areas is 11.3 years, in favour of the former (Belliard et al., 2013).

Focusing on the differential impact of disability on total life expectancy, we see that the city of Buenos Aires is the area with the highest HLE in the country and the lowest number of years of life expected with disability and severe levels of disability, while the region with the greatest impact of disability on total life expectancy is Jujuy, in the north-west, as the population here is expected to live the longest with severe levels of disability. While in the wealthy city of Buenos Aires longevity free of disability is growing, in the north-west of the country longevity is increasing, but with years of life expected with disability and severe disability. The north-east of the country, which is the most socially and economically backward region in the country, has not yet shown a clear increase in the longevity of its population, and shows the lowest total life expectancy and HLE.

In this epidemiological context, the country's health systems have not yet transformed their main orientation towards serious illnesses and maternal, newborn and child healthcare programmes. We should not forget, furthermore, that the average overall fertility rate in the country is 2.4 children per woman of fertile age, but the rates are higher in the poorer social strata and regions. Hence, there are more children and young people in poor homes, and they produce a greater demand on the public health services.

Table 22.1 Percentage growth of the population of Argentina between censuses 1991–2001 and 2001–2010 by age groups

Age groups	Relative increase in population	
	1991–2001	*2001–2010*
Total population	11.2	10.6
0–4 years	2.7	−0.3
15–64 years	13.6	15.0
65–79 years	19.7	9.8
80 years and over	43.7	31.9

Source: Drawn up by the author from: National Censuses of Population and Housing 1991, National Censuses of Population, Homes and Housing 2001 and 2010, INDEC (2012).

Nélida Redondo

Furthermore, in 2016, the country underwent a period of counter-transition caused by the serious dengue epidemic, which affected just about the whole country.

The complex health scenario is one of the fundamental reasons why long-term care systems have not yet been developed with a social focus on caring for fragile and dependent elderly people. The Pan American Health Organization (PAHO, 2012) warned that the lack of long-term services for elderly people will increase social inequality, which is already a problem in the region.

The social protection system for elderly people

Argentina's social protection system for elderly people is old and widespread. Retirement and widowhood pensions and old-age pensions are virtually universal for elderly people. Health coverage too is virtually universal by means of social security for people in formal employment and retired persons, the health prepayment plans and the state programmes. Argentina, together with Uruguay, Brazil and Chile, make up the group of Latin American countries known as 'pro aging' in the World Bank report (Cotlear, 2011). The term is a reference to the impact of retirement and pension systems in these countries on the living conditions of elderly people; elderly people suffer less from poverty than the rest of the population. In particular, in these four countries, people aged 80 and more are the least poor. The retirement system in Argentina is efficient in eliminating the risk of poverty in old age, but does not provide high financial income once people stop working. See Tables 22.2 and 22.3.

Likewise, the population of over-65s has more extended health coverage than the rest of the population.

The social protection system in Argentina is the heir to the 'family' tradition (Sunkel, 2006; Esping-Andersen et al., 2002; Esping-Andersen, 1990) characteristic of certain social security regimes in Southern Europe. Hence, the system provides financial income and access to medical coverage for healthcare when people retire from work. Care for disabled and dependent people, however, is practically the exclusive responsibility of families. We should point out that in the 'family' tradition, such as the one in Argentina, inheritance rules oblige adult children, and if

Table 22.2 Country total, population of 65 and over in private homes (or households) by retirement or pension income, according to gender and age group, 2010

Gender and age group	Both sexes		Male		Female	
	Population in private houses	*Receives retirement pension*	*Population in private houses*	*Receives retirement pension*	*Population in private houses*	*Receives retirement pension*
		%		%		%
Total 65 years and over	**3,979,032**	**93.0**	**1,632,039**	**89.7**	**2,346,993**	**95.3**
65–69	1,273,386	85.8	580,090	78.4	693,296	92.1
70–74	999,265	95.1	431,601	94.4	567,664	95.6
75–79	775,667	96.4	310,402	96.3	465,265	96.5
80 and over	930,714	97.7	309,946	97.9	620,768	97.6

Source: Drawn up by the author from: National Censuses of Population and Housing 2010, INDEC (2012).

Note: Homeless are included.

The challenges of population longevity

Table 22.3 Country total, population of 65 and over in private homes (or households) by health

Age groups	Both sexes		Male		Female	
	Number in population	% health coverage through social security or prepayment	Number in population	% health coverage through social security or prepayment	Number in population	% health coverage through social security or prepayment
		%		%		%
Total 65 years and over	3,979,032	95.0	1,632,039	93.2	2,346,993	96.2
65–69	1,273,386	92.2	580,090	88.6	693,296	95.3
70–74	999,265	95.8	431,601	95.2	567,664	96.4
75–79	775,667	96.1	310,402	95.7	465,265	96.4
80 and over	930,714	97.0	309,946	96.7	620,768	97.1

Source: Drawn up by the author from: National Censuses of Population, Homes and Housing 2010, INDEC (2012).

Note: Homeless are included.

there are none, the compulsory heirs to the assets (the law establishes an order of succession), to provide food and care for parents and direct relatives when they reach the age of 60. The state's part in providing long-term services for the fragile and dependent elderly is subsidiary: the state only intervenes in cases in which people have no family help and do not have enough financial resources.

The increase in longevity related to transformations in families and migrations of adult children to places located far from their parents' houses, among other outstanding aspects, questions the continuity of traditional family support models for the fragile and dependent elderly. When domestic help is deficient or there are no relatives, in Argentina almost the only other current alternative for caring for those who cannot care for themselves is putting them in 'geriatric homes' or in institutions addressed to assist the poorest older persons.

The new demographic scenario, and the slow but irreversible changes taking place in families, fundamentally deriving from a lower number of children and the fact that women work, highlight the need for programming integrated community support actions and services for fragile and dependent elderly people, both public and private, profit-making and profit-free, to enable such people to remain in their homes even as their limitations grow. The lack of integral programming in this field is made manifest in the observation of the inappropriateness of long-stay institutions, which in many cases violate elderly people's human rights and lead to gender inequality, which is damaging for women towards the end of their lives.

Methods and data

In order to study the institutional and domestic service models for taking care of dependent people provided in the Metropolitan Area of the City of Buenos Aires (MABA), two empirical research studies were carried out by the author and colleagues. The first was in 2006 under the patronage of the Inter-American Development Bank on a statistically representative sample of 'geriatric homes', the name given to long-stay institutions for elderly people, located in the MABA (Redondo, 2010). The sample was derived from random selection procedures using

323

data provided by the National Population, Household and Housing Census, 2001. Although there was 60 per cent rejection by the original contacts, the sample of 101 establishments eventually achieved appeared to be evenly distributed in the different districts and neighbourhoods and not biased in the services provided, but there may have been a bias towards those meeting legal requirements and offering a higher quality of services. Personal interviews were carried out using mainly structured questionnaires with the managers of the establishments, randomly selected residents from each establishment (304) and family members of residents not cognitively able to take part. A 'life story' interview was also carried out with 10 residents selected on the basis of gender, age and time in the establishment, who had indicated in the questionnaire interview that they would be happy to participate. This focused particularly on the events leading to their admission and daily life in the institutions.

Second, in 2008–2009, research was carried out on health services provided at home (and as hospital in-patients for more complex services) for a number of dependent elderly people in the city of Buenos Aires with a health research grant awarded by the National Ministry of Health (Redondo et al., 2013). One hundred and fifty-three people aged 60+, with average age of 85, who had prepayment health plans from two private hospitals in Buenos Aires were followed up for 12 months. Study participants had to have been dependent on others for basic activities of daily living (ADLs, e.g. feeding, bathing) or instrumental activities of daily living (IADLs, e.g. cleaning, shopping) for at least 90 days, and not receiving palliative care. The sample comprised around 37.5 per cent of people aged 60+ living in Buenos Aires included on the prepayment plans from these two hospitals. Data were obtained on hospital costs and invoices and also for 57 per cent of the sample (66 living at home and 21 in long-stay institutions) on household expenditure and perceptions of welfare.

Empirical evidence for inadequate services for fragile and dependent elderly people: institutional care

The study carried out in geriatric homes in the MABA showed that the highest proportion of elderly people in institutions were taken there because of the need for some kind of help that they could not get when they were living alone in their single-person homes. However, even in these cases, over half of those interviewed said that when they were taken to the home, they were still capable of taking a bath or shower (including getting in and out of the bathtub), getting dressed, eating (including cutting their food), sitting down on and getting up from the toilet, walking across a room and taking their medicine by themselves. By means of detailed interviews, it came to light that it was the situation of fragility or the appearance of permanent limitations in carrying out instrumental activities in daily life, such as going shopping and going out, that led to the family decision to put them in a long-stay home.

Furthermore, the research showed that putting the fragile and dependent elderly people in long-stay homes is financed almost exclusively privately, with the elderly person's own money or that of their relatives. Social work and local governments only put people in this kind of institution if they have social problems, mainly nowhere to live and poverty, whether they are dependent or not.

Being put in a long-stay institution modifies the habits of life for elderly people. The research showed that around 70 per cent of the homes interviewed employ daily physical constraint for residents to stop them from falling, and that psychotropic drugs are the most used by elderly residents, more than high blood pressure medicine, which is next in order. Thirty-five per cent of residents said that they often get bored (Redondo, 2010, pp. 31, 47, 73, 104).

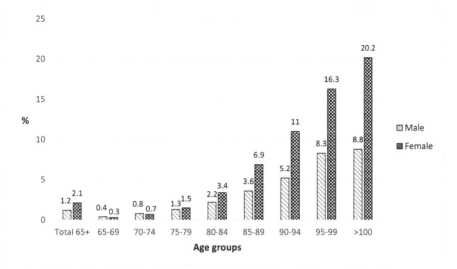

Figure 22.2 Percentage of elderly people put in geriatric homes by gender and age group, Argentina, 2010

Source: Drawn up by the author from: National Censuses of Population, Homes and Housing 2010, INDEC (2012).

The care plan for residents is drawn up in most cases by the home's doctor, or, in second place, by other professionals, but only 15 per cent of the homes let residents have a say in the drawing up of their care plan, while slightly over 20 per cent include relatives in the planning. This way of drawing up care plans shows that they are not designed for rehabilitation, or at least not to slow down the advance of the disability or dependence. In plans that are conceived for functional improvement, the participation and commitment of the patient is essential. The predominant care plan at the institutions researched seems, on the contrary, to be designed for the convenience of the organization's activities and staff.

The detailed interviews showed that when faced with the loss of the capacity to carry out instrumental activities in daily life, such as going shopping and going out alone, families decide to put the elderly in long-stay institutions instead of leaving them in single-person homes, because there are no community support services for dependence. Given their greater life expectancy, a greater proportion of women live in single-person homes, and so the lack of an appropriate care system is damaging for them towards the end of their lives. According to data from the 2010 population census, the rate of women doubles the rate of men put in geriatric homes at the same age (cf. Figure 22.2).

The lack of suitable support services for dependent people generates gender unrest, which harms women's rights to live as they would wish, stay in their own homes and remain part of their community.

Private home care and health services for elderly dependent people

The organization of appropriate services, at reasonable prices, including subsidies for those who do not have enough money, is not one of the priorities in health policies, not even for the local governments in cities with the most aged populations in the country.

Home care health services for fragile and dependent elderly people form part of the medical services that are contracted privately through prepayment plans. The information that came out from the 12-month longitudinal follow-up study of elderly dependent people in Buenos Aires with private prepayment medical plans shows that the right support for dependent people is expensive, and furthermore has to be carried out over a lengthy period of time (Redondo et al., 2013).

The main purpose of the investigation was to analyse the basic structure of services provided at home for elderly people in a situation of dependence, the costs thereof and the results obtained in personal and family welfare, among two populations with such private prepayment medical plans.

The empirical study carried out showed that in the sample observed in the city of Buenos Aires, family expenses, which are mostly paid by the elderly people receiving the service from their life savings, are the only source of financing for home medical services, personal and domestic care, purchasing or renting support elements, medicine, supplies and paying long-stay institutions, among the main items. According to the information brought to light by this research, it is the elderly people themselves or their families who exclusively bear increases in costs as the lack of personal autonomy progresses in the carrying out of tasks in daily life.

The information provided by families showed that the average annual cost of the goods and services in healthcare for elderly people with severe dependence (on the Katz scale) who live in their own homes was around $12,000 in 2008, while for people living in long-stay institutions, the average family expense goes up to $16,000. The composition of the expense is different in each case. The household expenditure of people living in long-term (long stay) institutions does not vary according to the level of dependency: in all dependency levels of activities of daily life (ADL), 70 per cent of the expenditure is directed to pay the monthly instalments of the institution that accounts, on average, to $16,000 per year. Whereas the household expenditure in private households varies significantly according to the levels of dependency of ADL, household expenditure for elderly people with a severe level of dependency can be twice as much as that for those with a slight or moderate level of dependency. The study also demonstrated that in the slight and moderate levels of dependency of ADL, the household expenditure in private households is lower than that of the household expenditure in long-term institutions. On the other hand, the household expenditure for patients with a severe level of dependency in a private household is higher than for patients that live in long-term institutions. This is due to the additional expenses for payment of staff for the personal care and domestic services, which at this level of dependency claims the household expenditure in private households of $6,400 per year, 42 per cent of the total expenditure of $15,324 (including food and housing expenses).

Long-stay institutions seem to be a more economically efficient alternative for caring for elderly people when they have severe levels of dependence or dementia. This observation is confirmed if we look at hospital costs or invoices, which also come down when patients reside in long-stay institutions. The elderly dependent population who live in private homes had greater invoicing and costs in both hospitals in the research study. Non-paid costs, that is, those involving efforts by families, friends and neighbours to do paperwork, accompany people and cover care needs for dependent people, accounted for 3 per cent of family costs in this sample of the population. This value is significantly lower than the 15 per cent (average for all levels of dependence) for paying home carers and domestic workers. One of the characteristics of the population studied, due to their relatively high social class, is the predomination of formal over informal care.

The study provided empirical evidence that enables us to ratify the initial hypothesis that states that family expenses increase for elderly people living in private homes as their dependence increases in carrying out the basic activities of daily life, as the expenses for personal care,

The challenges of population longevity

supplies and first aid articles increase. By way of contrast, according to the information provided by this research, hospital costs and invoices come down when the level of dependence and cognitive deterioration is more severe. Likewise, the costs of caring for patients with cognitive deterioration come down in a relative sense if the patients live in a long-stay institution.

The study produced a significant finding that should be ratified or rectified by further research: chronological age is an independent variable of healthcare system costs in an inverse sense; in other words, the increase in chronological age explains the fall in hospital costs for medical care for the extremely elderly and dependent. This is because technological and aggressive interventions decrease and care is predominantly palliative.

The analysis of the information produced by this investigation shows that dependence has a negative effect on the elderly person's character and state of mind. Even though everything points towards the fact that elderly dependent people forming part of the sample studied receive social and healthcare at home, both formal and informal, which can be considered as 'excellent' or 'very good', their state of health and situation of dependence tends to produce changes in their character towards negative feelings such as sadness, anxiety and pessimism.

The finding is even more significant if we bear in mind that, as the elderly people themselves and their families point out, over 80 per cent of those interviewed have no financial limits when it comes to choosing goods and services in accordance with their own preferences, and that a very high proportion of them say that they decide how to organize their daily lives for themselves, alone or in the company of others, as is the proportion of relatives who prioritize opinions given by people with severe cognitive deterioration, or prioritize their previous tastes and preferences when it comes to taking decisions about the lives of their dependent relatives. Neither could we ratify the initial hypothesis about the constraint exercised by good financial conditions and the control over vital decisions on the adverse effects that cause poor health and dependence.

Finally, we could highlight the fact that stress levels among carers, measured by the Zarit test (Zarit et al., 1986), a self-administered test that measures caregiver burden, were low in the sample studied. From the perspective of this investigation, the low stress levels shown by family carers are due to the sufficient availability of financial resources that characterizes this sample of the population of dependent people in the city of Buenos Aires, which facilitates the hiring of support employees, both for housework and personal care, and lightens the weight of family responsibility.

Likewise, the information revealed by this study enables us to show the statistical association between certain social and demographic characteristics of family carers (gender and age of the carers, whether they have paid employment and the degree of blood relationship that joins them to the dependent person) and feelings of stress. The information revealed enables us to state that family carers who live together with the dependent people they support, mainly couples living alone, who devote over four hours per day on average to assistance and caring, who do not work and are aged over 65, are those who declare most frequently or almost always that it affects them negatively. Hiring people for personal care at home or having dependent people live in long-stay institutions are factors related to fewer feelings of pressure. Furthermore, paid employment of the family carer seems to constitute a protective factor when there are feelings of stress.

The results of this research pose questions about the impact of the ageing of the population of Argentina on the costs of the health system and private health costs for the population.

The figures analysed question the capacity of most families in Argentina and that of the elderly people themselves to bear the costs of long-term private services. Given that the study was carried out on middle-and upper-middle-class families in the city of Buenos Aires, we may very well wonder what the situation of elderly people is in poorer urban sectors with respect to

327

access to this kind of service, and if they cannot enjoy them, what the consequences are on the survival and quality of life of these elderly people and their families. The lack of a state policy in the field could lead to severe inequality in access to care, due to the lack or insufficiency of financial resources to provide support.

One question that arises from the analysis is the magnitude of the non-financial expenses, in personal effort, that have to be made by families with limited financial resources to reduce the financial costs taken on by the families observed in this study, and what the consequences of this effort are in terms of the deterioration of the physical and mental health of those who have to provide support.

Finally, observing family expense according to the level of dependence and the type of place of residence showed that in the case of severe dependence, family expenses are higher in private homes than in long-stay institutions. In the case of elderly people who live in single-person homes, the fixed costs for the upkeep of the house are not shared with other residents, and so on a relative basis are higher.

Social care and gender inequality

In the sample studied, over 75 per cent of family carers were women, a similar percentage to that recorded in the national and international literature on the topic (López-Casanova et al., 2009; Espin Andrade, 2008; Pérez Peñaranda, 2006). Likewise, the costs of dependence are greater for elderly women who live in private homes, because of the increased costs of hiring workers to provide personal care. This is due to two factors associated with gender patterns: (1) the relatively longer life of women, and consequently their tendency to be living in single-person homes when support workers are hired for them; and (2) men do not usually provide personal care, and so if it is the wife who is dependent, workers are normally hired to provide it.

Moreover, the investigation showed that children perceive that they are overloaded if they have to help their dependent parents. This subjective tension of family carers for parents mainly affects elderly women, mostly widows living alone, who had been responsible for familial care throughout their (adult) lives, including during the illness of their husbands, and nobody can provide care for them when they need support because of their own dependence.

All these aspects seem to lie at the root of the higher numbers of extremely elderly women being put in geriatric homes, as can be seen in the table with the latest census data for residents of geriatric homes by gender and age in the city of Buenos Aires (see Figure 22.2).

The question of gender in relation to dependence deserves to be discussed because it brings to light a profound inequality in the later stages of life: women are the main informal carers of dependent people throughout their lives, but they tend not to receive the same care when their own situation of dependence requires it. The research results provide empirical evidence that reinforces the need for including the 'economy of care' in the agenda of public policies in Latin America.

In countries in Latin America, family organization based on the patriarchal hierarchy underlies the clear gender inequality that is still characteristic in the region. In the second half of the twentieth century, Latin American countries established diverse legislations to attain greater equality between the sexes. Without prejudice to this fact, so far the target of democratizing relations between genders has not been reached: problems with domestic violence, inequality with the sharing out of work and asymmetry in the use of time for providing care are just some examples of problems that still require solutions (Anderson, 2011; Aguirre, 2009; Arriagada, 2007).

Diverse surveys on the use of time carried out in Mexico (INEGI, 2004) and Uruguay (Aguirre, 2009) show that tasks such as looking after children and dependent elderly people

The challenges of population longevity

are mainly done by women. However, the improved education level of women, and the consequent increase in the numbers of women employed, lead to a deficit in care, which in the case of children has been covered by the market or by the state. Contrary to this, as Aguirre (2009) points out, care for dependent people has received less attention from both the state and the market or civil society, and has been relegated to the private setting of the family. In consequence, little is known about current deficiencies. The author underlines the fact that due to the different life expectancy of the sexes, extremely elderly people are now mainly women, who require these services more than anyone else. The matter becomes especially controversial in the countries of the Southern Cone – Argentina, Chile and Uruguay – with advanced ageing in their populations, and in particular in their populations of elderly adults. In these countries, as the process of demographic ageing advanced, social protection systems for the elderly were set up, and they are now the oldest and most widespread in the region. As a result of their ample coverage, elderly people are relatively less poor than the younger population (Cotlear, 2011).

And yet so far, the social protection systems do not include policies for intervening in the care of dependent people. Ana Sojo (2007) underlines the importance of the trilogy made up of the state, the market and the family in theories of gender and specific public policies. It is based on the concepts of 'de-commodifying' and 'de-familializing' developed by Esping-Andersen (1999), in reference to the need for care policies that facilitate conciliation between the productive and reproductive fields Latin American women move in. From Sojo's (2007) point of view, 'de-familializing' policies relax the gender tension caused by the growing demand for care generated by the ageing of the population.

As can be seen, the emphasis in the literature in the field lies on the inequality evident in the productive stage of women's lives, as they have to be workers, mothers and daughters all at the same time, which demands a double or triple working day. By way of contrast, the effects of the lack of care policies on the quality of life of elderly women have not been studied at all, as it is these women who require support from third parties given their situation of dependence.

For all these reasons, it is inevitable to talk about the role of the state in the promotion, certification, regulation and eventually the subsidizing of long-term comprehensive services for dependent people who do not have sufficient financial resources.

Concluding discussion

The increased longevity of the population in Latin America generates uncertainty about the capacity of traditional modes of exchanging resources and services among generations to take on the new demographic and epidemiological scenario. Up to now, in all the countries in the region, families have borne the almost exclusive responsibility for looking after and providing support for elderly people suffering from problems related to fragility and dependence.

Argentina is one of the countries with the earliest and most pronounced demographic ageing in the region. Likewise, the social protection system for the elderly is old and provides extensive financial income and healthcare for elderly people. In contrast, care for dependent and fragile people is not sufficiently covered by either the state or the market. There are no basic community services to help elderly people with some kind of permanent limitation from physical or cognitive illness to remain in their own homes. The private supply of long-term services is virtually limited to long-stay institutions, commonly known as 'geriatric homes', which often violate residents' rights to privacy and intimacy, or, even worse, their essential human rights, as they physically restrain elderly people with cognitive deterioration or keep them sedated with daily pharmaceuticals.

In all social sectors, the efforts made by families in the daily care of elderly dependent people are made by women, the main informal carers. In middle- and middle-to-low-class homes, looking after children and elderly people limits women's possibilities of working outside the home, and thereby makes families even poorer.

The diversification of the public and private supply of long-term care services for dependent elderly people, at affordable prices or subsidized by the state, depending on the purchasing power of the family, is an outstanding matter that has not yet been incorporated into the public agenda in Argentina. The prevalence of structural poverty in children and young adults in the country, together with the persistence of infectious and parasitical diseases, leads to a complex scenario for public health and policies. Without prejudice to this, the sustained increase in the longevity of the population imposes the conditions for the development of long-term care services, fundamentally community-based, to help elderly people remain in their own homes with appropriate levels of comfort, safety and welfare.

Note

1 The editors much appreciate Maria Correa's help in translating from Spanish parts of this chapter.

References

Aguirre, R., ed., 2009. *Las bases invisibles del bienestar social. El trabajo no remunerado en Uruguay* [The invisible basis of social welfare: unpaid work in Uruguay]. Montevideo: UNIFEM. Available at: www.inju.gub. uy/innovaportal/file/21713/1/2_las_bases_invisibles_del_bienestar_social.pdf [accessed 10.05.2017].

Anderson, J., 2011. *Responsabilidades por compartir: la conciliación trabajo-familia en Perú* [Responsibilities to share: work-family conciliation in Peru]. Santiago de Chile: Oficina Internacional del Trabajo (OIT). Available at: www.ilo.org/wcmsp5/groups/public/---americas/---ro-lima/---sro-santiago/documents/publication/wcms_179779.pdf [accessed 10.05.2017].

Arriagada I., ed., 2007. *Familias y políticas públicas en América Latina. Una historia de desencuentros* [Families and public policies in Latin America: a history of failure]. Santiago de Chile: Comisión Económica para América Latina y el Caribe (CEPAL). Available at: http://repositorio.cepal.org/bitstream/handle/11362/2504/S0700488_es.pdf [accessed 10.05.2017].

Belliard, M., Massa, C. and Redondo, N., 2013. Analisis comparado de la esperanza de vida con salud en la Ciudad Autonoma de Buenos Aires in Poblacion de Buenos Aires [Comparative analysis of a healthy life expectancy in the autonomous city of Buenos Aires]. *Revista semestral de datos y studios sociodemograficos urbanos* [Magazine of Sociodemographic Urban Data Studies], 10(18), pp. 7–33.

Cotlear, D., 2011. *Population aging: is Latin America ready?* Washington, DC: World Bank. Available at: https://openknowledge.worldbank.org/bitstream/handle/10986/2542/588420PUB0Popu11public10 BOX353816B0.pdf?sequence=1&isAllowed=y [accessed 09.05.2017].

Espin Andrade, A.M., 2008. Caracterización psicosocial de cuidadores informales de adultos mayores con demencia [The psychosocial characterization of informal carers of elderly people with dementia]. *Revista Cubana Salud Pública* [Cuban Public Health Magazine], 34(3), pp. 393–402.

Esping-Andersen, G., 1999. *Social foundations of postindustrial economies,*. Oxford: Oxford University Press.

Esping-Andersen, G., Duncan, G., Hemerick, A. and Milles, J., 2002. *Why we need a new welfare state.* Oxford: Oxford University Press.

Frenk, J., Bobadilla, J.L., Sepúlveda, J. and López-Cervantes, M., 1989. Health transition in middle-income countries: new challenges for health care. *Health Policy and Planning*, 4(1), pp. 29–39. DOI: https://doi.org/10.1093/heapol/4.1.29.

Gasparini, L., Cicowiez, M. and Sosa Escudero, W., 2014. *Pobreza y desigualdad en América Latina: conceptos, herramientas y aplicaciones* [Poverty and inequality in Latin America: concepts, tools and applications]. La Plata: Centro Estudios Distributivos Laborales y Sociales, Nacional Universidad La Plata. Available at: www.depeco.econo.unlp.edu.ar/cedlas/libro-gcse-1/material/Gasparini-Cicowiez-Sosa-Cap1-Cap2.pdf [accessed 10.05.2017].

INDEC (Instituto Nacional de Estadistica y Censos – Institute of Statistics and Censuses), n.d. *Censo Nacional de Población y Vivienda* [National Census of Population and Housing], 1947, 1960, 1970, 1980 and 1991.

INDEC (Instituto Nacional de Estadistica y Censos – Institute of Statistics and Censuses), 2012. *Censo Nacional de Población, Hogares y Vivienda 2010* [National Census of Population, Homes and Housing]. Available at: www.indec.gov.ar/nivel4_default.asp?id_tema_1=2&id_tema_2=41&id_tema_3=135 [accessed 19.07.2017].

INEGI (Instituto Nacional de Estadística, Geografía e Informática), 2004. *Mujeres y hombres en México* [Men and women in Mexico]. Octava edición. Aguascalientes, México. Available at: http://internet.contenidos.inegi.org.mx/contenidos/productos/prod_serv/contenidos/espanol/bvinegi/productos/nueva_estruc/702825075019.pdf [accessed 10.05.2017].

Katz Index of Independence in Activities of Daily Living, 2009. Available at: www.alz.org/careplanning/downloads/katz-adl-lawton-iadl.pdf [accessed 10.05.2017].

López-Casanova, P., Rodríguez-Palma, M. and Herrero-Díaz, M.A., 2009. *Perfil social de los cuidadores familiares de pacientes dependientes ingresados en el Hospital General Universitario de Elche* [A social profile of the family carers of dependent patients at the General University Hospital of Elche]. *GEROKOMOS*, 20(4), pp. 167–71.

PAHO (OPS – Organización Panamericana de la Salud) [Pan American Health Organization], 2012. *Estrategia para la prevención y el control de las enfermedades no transmisibles, presentada en la 28ava Conferencia Sanitaria Panamericana* [Strategy for the prevention and control of noncommunicable diseases, presented at the 28th Pan American Health Conference]. Washington, DC: PAHO.

Pérez Peñaranda, A., 2006. *El cuidador primario de familiares con dependencia: calidad de vida, apoyo social y salud mental* [The main carer of dependent relatives: quality of life, social support and mental health]. Salamanca (España): Universidad de Salamanca. Available at: www.telefonodelaesperanza.org/cuidando-cuidador/download/40 [accessed 10.05.2017].

Redondo, N., 2007. Estructura de edades y envejecimiento [Age and ageing structure]. In S. Torrado, ed. *Población y bienestar en la argentina. Del primero al segundo centenario* [Population and welfare in Argentina: from the first to the second centenary]. Buenos Aires: Edhasa, pp. 139–75.

Redondo, N., 2010. *La internación en instituciones de larga estadía en el Área Metropolitana de la Ciudad de Buenos Aires. ¿Desconociendo derechos o promoviendo autonomía?* [Living in a long-stay institution in the metropolitan area of the city of Buenos Aires: ignorant of rights or promoting autonomy?]. Serie de Estudios No. 10. Buenos Aires: ISALUD. Available at: http://www.isalud.edu.ar/institucional/publicaciones/series-de-estudio [accessed 10.05.2017].

Redondo, N., Manzotti, M. and de la Torre, E., 2013. *¿Cuánto cuesta y quién paga la dependencia en las personas mayores?* [How much does the dependence of elderly people cost and who pays for it?]. Un estudio en la Ciudad de Buenos Aires [A study in the city of Buenes Aires]. Buenos Aires: Ediciones del Hospital. Available at: www.hospitalitaliano.org.ar/multimedia/archivos/noticias_archivos/13/Notas_PDF/13_dependenciacorte.pdf [accessed 10.05.2017].

Sojo, A., 2007. Estado, mercado y familia: el haz del bienestar social como objeto de política [State, market and family: the social welfare bundle as an object of policy] In I. Arriagada, ed. *Familias y políticas públicas en América Latina. Una historia de desencuentros* [Families and public policies in Latin America: a history of failure]. Santiago de Chile: Comisión Económica para América Latina y el Caribe – Economic Commission for Latin America and the Caribbean (CEPAL), pp. 157–70.

Sunkel, G., 2006. *El papel de la familia en la protección social en América Latina* [The role of the family in social protection in Latin America]. Elaborado por Guillermo Sunkel. Serie Políticas Sociales No. 120. Santiago de Chile. CEPAL, 66. Sale No. S.06.II.G.57.

Zarit, S.H., Todd, P.A and Zarit, J.M., 1986. Subjective burden of husbands and wives as caregivers: a longitudinal study. *Gerontologist*, 26(3), pp. 260-6. DOI: 10.1093/geront/26.3.260.

Index

Note: **bold** = tables, *italic* = figures

24-hour care work *see* live-in migrant care work

Act No. 108/2006 Coll., Czech Republic 162, 164, 165
Act on Adapting Society to an Ageing Population, 2015 (*loi d'adaptation de la société au vieillissement*), France 103, 104, 113
active ageing: Norway 17, 21, 23, 25; Poland 173, 176, 181
activities of daily living (ADL) 3–4, 108, **109**, 142, 144, 163, 273, 275–6, 289, 324, 326
Ädel-reform 1992, Sweden 50
adult day care centres: Poland 176; Turkey 196; US 278–9; US 'pop-up' centres 280
adult social care sector, England 76; transformation of 93
Affordable Care Act, US 284, 285
age dependency ratio: Italy 143; Turkey 189, Table 13.3
age discrimination 24, 84, 174, 311
aged care *see* Australia
ageing in place 3, 47, 146, 149, 215
ageing population: Argentina 319, 320, *320*, 321, **321**, 329; Australia 303; China 203; Czech Republic 159; Italy 143, 159, 161; Japan 243, 257; Poland 172, 181; South Korea 219; Sweden 46; Taiwan 229; Turkey 187, 188–9; US 273
ageism 79, 84, 174, 311
Allocation personnalisée d'autonomie (APA) 104, 113; *see also* cash-for-care
Alzheimer's Society 196
Anttonen and Meagher 5, 241, 248

Argentina: carer stress 327, 328; costs of home care 326, 328; family care role 319, 322, 323, 328, 329, 330; gender inequality of care 328–30; healthcare coverage 322, **323**, 329; lack of long-term care 322, 323, 329; pensions 322, **322**, 329; study of 'geriatric homes' 323–4, 324–5; study of home care of people with private prepayment health plans 324
assessment of care needs: Australia 308; Japan 244; Norway, inequality in 24; South Korea 222; Taiwan, to employ migrant care worker
assistenti familiari, Italy 142
Assistenza Domiciliare Integrata (ADI: Integrated Home Care), Italy 142–4
Australia 10; care workers need for improved conditions 310–11; consumer-directed choice 308, 309, 310; current reforms, implications for older people 309–10; current reforms of aged care 308–9; family care role 303, 304, 305, 306; reform of aged care from 1980s 306–308; research agenda on caring issues 306; stakeholder role in transforming care of older people into issue of public concern 10, 305–6
Austria 6; cash-for-care 131, 132, **133**, 136; expenditure on long-term care 132, Table 9.1; family orientation 132, 133, 136; migrant care work, benefits of 136, 137, 138; migrant care work, eligibility criteria 134; migrant care work, intermediaries 134, 138; migrant care work, legal framework 134; migrant care work, means-tested benefit 134; migrant care work, quality assurance 138, 139, 140; migrant care work, risks 137–138, 139–40; migrant care work, self-employment,

144, 137, 139; migrant care workforce growth 135; migrants' country of origin 135, **135**
AWBZ (*Algemene Wet Bijzondere Ziektenkosten*) *see* Exceptional Health Expenditure Law

bankruptcy care organizations 33–4, 36, 37, 42, 67, 224
Barvíková J. and Österle, A. 162, 164, 166
Baumol, W. 62
birth rate: Argentina 321; China 203; Italy 143; Japan 252; Poland 171; South Korea 219; Turkey 189
blurring boundaries: care and domestic work 5, 8, 11, 111–3; professional care work and informal care 3, 6, 8, 11, 103, 111, 118, 230
body work 51, 236, 237 *see also* care work division of labour
brokers, local council-based, England 96
bureaucratization/standardization 4, 21, 25, 49
Canada 9; division of labour 290, 295, 296, 297, 298, 299; ethnographic study of food preparation in nursing homes 292–6; 298; ethnographic study of laundry in nursing homes 296–9; family role in nursing homes 292, 294, 297, 298; flexibility of work 290, 296–7, 298–9; privately paid companions 293, 294, 297, 298; promising practices in nursing homes 9–10, 299; volunteers 292, 294, 298; women's work 289, 290, 292, 296, 298–9
Canada Health Act, 1984 291, Care Act, 2014, England 74–5
'care by human hands', Japan 259–60, 263, 264
care dialogue 9, 266
care drain 6, 143, 151
care leave: Austria 132, 138; Italy 14; Japan 245
care manager: Australia 307; England 89; Japan 244
care plan: Argentina 325; Austria 307; France 104; Japan 244; Sweden 49
care preferences, older people 190, 194, 213, 215
care robots 9, 256; care workers' attitudes to, Japan 262–4, 265; care worker-recipient interactions 265, 266; case study, transfer lift 261–2, 26–24: cultural values, Japan 256, 259–60, 263, 264, 265; lack of usage, Japan 256, 260–1; potential of 266; promotion of, Japan 257–9; public attitudes to, Japan 262, 264
care round-the-clock 65, *see also* live-in migrant care work
care sector: dimensions of, Netherlands 67; exclusion from, Netherlands 69; and flexibility of, Netherlands 67–8; France 102, 104
care, understanding of 2–3
care work: as emotional 50, 79, 233; as inferior, low status 11, 22, 84, 284; as invisible 50, 151, 289; as women's 'natural' role, responsibility 5, 11, 18, 112, 144–5, 196, 219, 223, 230, 237, 290, 295, 296, 298
care work distinction from domestic work 108, 112, 229

care work relationships: Austria 138, 139, 140; Canada 298; Italy 149-50; Japan 265-6
care workers, characteristics of : Australia 304, 311; Canada 291; China 208, Table 14.1; England 76; France 107; Sweden 47; US 284
care workers, conditions of work: Australia 310, 311, 312; Austria 137, 139; China 208; Denmark 38–41, 43; England 77, 78, 79, 84; France 108, Table 7.2, 111, 113; Germany 122, 123, 127; Japan 257; Netherlands 68; South Korea 8, 223, 224, 225; Sweden 49, 51–4; Turkey 193; US 274, 283, 284, 285; *see also* Denmark; stress; training levels; turnover rate; wages
care workers: physical demands on 48, 52, **52**, 53, 54, 261; psychosocial demands on 48, 51-2, **52**, 79–83, 84, 85, 151, 233; satisfaction of 68 84, 283, 310
care workforce, size of: China 207–8; Denmark 33; England 76; France 107; Japan, expected 259; Netherlands 67; Poland 179, 180; South Korea 223; Turkey 193; US 276, 280
'caring for' and 'caring about' 2, 3, 259, 264
'caring states' 30
Caritas 178
cash benefits for disabled/older people, Poland 175
cash-for-care 5, 6, 7, 311; Austria 131, 132, Table 9.1; Czech Republic 162, 166, 167; England 75; France 102, 104, 112–13; Germany 116, 118, 120; Italy 142, 144, 148, 151; Netherlands 63, 65, 70; Norway 15; *see also* direct payments; personal budgets
certification of care workers, South Korea 221, 222, 223
charities role in care 17
children's duty *see* family care obligations
China: 7–8; ageing population; 203; care workers 207–8, **209–10**, 212; characteristics of non-government eldercare facilities 208–13, **209–10**, *211, 212*; characteristics of non-government eldercare facility residents, 212–13, **213**; costs of eldercare 206–7; definitions eldercare in China 204; demand exceeding availability 206; development eldercare 205–6; filial piety 204–5, 215; financial pressures on eldercare 207; geographic distribution 210, 213; impact social policies 214; national survey of non-government facilities 208–15; one-child policy 203
Christensen, K, and Manthorpe, J. 138, 139 232
Christensen, K, and Pilling, D. 5, 75, 93
church, role in care 17, 165, Catholic, Poland 7, 178, 180
cleaning *see* domestic work; home help; household services
class inequality of care 7, 8, 238, 320, 322, 328

Index

commercial care sector, Poland 177–8, 180

commercialism 7, *see also* commodification of care, marketization

commodification of care 7, 9, 11, 104, 162, 165, 167, 228

Commonwealth Home Support Programme (CHSP), Australia 304, 309

communist ideology 6–7, 161, 163, 167

Community Aged Care Programme, (CACP), Australia 307, 309

competition between providers: Australia 303, 309; Denmark, 31; Denmark, by procurement or endorsement 33; England 77, 89, 94, 95; France 111, Germany 116, 120, 123, 127, Netherlands 64; Norway 24; Japan 241, 248, 249, 253; South Korea 218, 224

competitive market: effect on services 42, 224, 253; effect on workers 8, 42–3, 77, 224

Confucianism 7, 204, 218, 219, 229, 233, 260

conservative/corporatist welfare regime 62, 130–1, 242

consumer choice *see* free choice of provider; user (consumer) choice

consumer-directed home care: Australia 308, 309, 310; US 280; and payment to family 280; and survey of job retention 283–4; and unionization 284, 286 *see also* cash-for-care

Continuous Care Retirement Communities (CCRC), US Figure 19.1, 277–8

contracting out work 31, 296, 298, *see also* privatization, marketization

co-payments: Austria 132, 133; South Korea 222; Turkey, for healthcare

co-production 23

cost containment 5; Australia 306; Denmark 31, 33; England 74, 84; France 102; Germany 123, 127; Netherlands 62, 63, 64–5, 66, 69; Japan 259, 260; Sweden 49; US 275

'cost-disease' problem 62–3;

Czech Republic 6–7: caregiving burden 159–60; 163, 167; cash-for-care 162, 166; constraints on consumerism 166, 167, 168; defamilialization under communism, 160–1; eldercare placement agencies 166–7; family as foundation of state 163; family/informal care role 159–60, 161, 163, 164, 167; from de-familialism to familialism 163, 167; health and social care split 165; limited role for-profit organizations 165; residential care remains as major public care provision 164–5, 168

Da Roit, B. 61, 62, 63, 64, 65, 66, 70, 131, 133, 142, 150

Da Roit, B. and Weicht, B. 70, 133, 136

Daly, M. 104, 117, 118, 119

de-caring 48, 49

decentralization 6; China 204. 206, 214; Czech Republic 162, 164-5; Netherlands 62, 64, 69, 169; Norway 20

de-familialism/de familialization 10, 63, 160–61, 167, 242 252, 253, 329

de-institutionalization 20, 30, 47, 162, 164, 165

dementia care 22, 47, 50, 123, 127, 225, 250, 251, 259, 289, 291, 326

Denmark 4; changes in home care provision over time 32; competition models 33; free choice, implications for care workers 36–43; free choice, implications for users 35–6, 42; free choice of provider 31; marketization of care 29, 31, 32, 33, 42; personal vs practical care 33, 34; popularity free choice 31–32; public vs private providers 29, 33–4 35–6, 37–43; quality of care 31, 36, 40; role of municipalities 29, 30, 31, 33, 34, 42; size of workforce 33; universalism 30; user satisfaction 35, 36, 42

dependence, negative effects of 327

de-professionalization of care work 5, 11; Austria 139–40; France 112, 113; Netherlands 65, 68–9

deskilling 112, 290, 295, 297

direct employment, France 106–7, **109**, 111, 112

direct payments, England 75, 76, 89–90, 95, 98

'dirty' work 231, 236

disengagement theory of ageing 17

division of labour 290, 295, 296, 297, 298, 299; migrant workers and women family members 231, 235, 236, 237

documentation of care tasks 21, 25, 41, 49, 51, 53

Doi, T. 265

domestic work 15, 18, 23, 24, 37, 38, 50, 51, 103; as major source of employment, France 105, 111; distinction from care work 3, 69, 112; *see also* blurring boundaries, care and domestic work; household services

domiciliary care allowance, Turkey 193–4, 197

domiciliary services: England 76, 84; South Korea 220, 221, 222; *see also* consumer directed care; direct payments; home care; home help; home nursing, household services, personal budgets

Dutch *see* Netherlands

education of care workers *see* training

elder abuse/neglect 151, 174

elder care placement agencies, Czech Republic 166–7

eldercare; *see* home care; nursing homes; residential care

eldercare China *see* China

elderly care policy, France 104–5

elderly houses, Turkey 195

elderly solidarity centres, Turkey 196

Eliasson-Lappalainen, R. 45, 49, 51

eligibility for long-term care: Austria, for employing migrant care worker 134; Poland 176, 177; South Korea 222; Turkey 197; Turkey, for free residential care 194 *see also* targeting care services

e-market websites 95, 96, 98–9

empty-nest household 8, 205

England 6; adult social care sector 76; contracting, types of 93–5; cost containment 74; increased purchasing of care services by local councils 89; low wages care workers 78, 84; market shaping 95–6; marketization 74, 75, 78, 83–4; migrant care workers 76–8, 77, 84; personal assistant market 97; personal budgets 74–5, 89–90, 84, 95, 96, 97, 99; personalization 74-5, 88; reasons for low wages 78–9, 84; stress social care work 79–93; types of services used by older people 97–8

Esping-Andersen 4, 15, 17, 20, 26, 62, 63, 242, 252m 253, 322, 329

ethnic inequality care work 11 *see also* social inequality

Exceptional Health Expenditure Law, 1968, Netherlands 61, 65, 66, 69

expenditure on long-term care services *see* public expenditure on long-term care services

Extended Aged Care at Home (EACH) package, Australia 307

Extended Aged Care at Home Dementia (EACHD) package, Australia 307

facility services, Japan 244, *246*, 250

Fair Labor Standards Act (FLSA), US, 1938 285

familialism/familistic 7, 160, 161, 163, 167, 219, 230, 244

familialization 9, 62, 160, 161, 167, 241, 242

family care *see* informal/family care

family care homes: Poland, 177

family care legal obligation: Argentina 322, 323; China 203, Norway 20; Turkey 192

family caregiver burden 5, 9, 10, 11, 149, 150, 159–60, 167, 181, 196, 242, 245, 247, 252, 312

family structure changes: China 203, 205; Japan, 243; South Korea 219; Taiwan 229; Turkey 190;

Federal Law on Social Assistance, Germany 119

feminist perspective/approach 9, 20, 45, 46, 104, 290, 291

fertility rate *see* birth rate

fictive-kin 230, 234

filial piety 7, 8, 204–5, 215, 218, 219, 229, 233–4, 237; outsourced 235, 237 financial benefit for family caring: Czech Republic 161; *see also* domiciliary care allowance; tax deductions encouraging family caring

financial incentives to increase care work, France 105; see also cash-for-care, *Plan Borloo*

flexibility of work 68, 290; benefits and disadvantages 296–7, 298–9

food and 29, 298-9; *see also* food in nursing homes; laundry in nursing homes

food in nursing homes 292–6, 208–9

for-profit managerial practices 290

France 5; care providers 106; care work (employment) relationships (prestataire, mandataire and direct employment) 106–112; cash-for-care allowance 102,104, 112–13; elderly care policy103, 104–5, 113; employment policy 103, 104, 105,113; externalization of care tasks 105–6; financial incentives to increase care work 105; formalization care work 102,103, 104–6, 111, 112, 113; numbers and characteristics care workers 107; pathways to care work 107–8; personal services sector 103, 105–6; *Plan Borloo* 106; prioritization home care 104; professionalization and de–professionalization 104–5, 112, 113

free choice of provider 4, 23–4, 31–2, 35, 36, 42–3; *see also* Denmark

gender inequality of caring/care 10, 237, 238, 328–9

gender-segregated labour market 47

gender sensitive perspective 16, 18

General Directorate of Services for Persons with Disabilities and Elderly People, Turkey (GDSPDE) 191–2, 194, 197

'geriatric homes', Argentina 10, 323–4, 324–5; higher numbers women in homes 328, Figure 22.2

Germany 6; care arrangements at home 120–21; expansion professional care system 116; growth professional care workforce 121–2; household-related assistance outside professional care system 124, 126; live-in migrant care workers 121,124, 126, 127; long-term care insurance 116, 110, 120; migrant care workers 116, 123; migrant/non-migrant care worker comparison 124, **125**, 127; migrant worker discrimination 124, 127; paid care top-ups 121; provider access to professional care system 120; role family care 121; qualification requirements care staff 123; training, wages and employment conditions 122–3

'Golden Plan' (1989), the Ten-Year Strategy for Health and Welfare of the Elderly, Japan 247, 249

grandparents: caring by 163, 174; caring for 163

grey market/economy: Austria 138, 139; Germany 124, 126; Japan 9, 241, 251, US 279

group homes; South Korea 224; Sweden 50

healthcare: Argentina, coverage 322, **323**, 329; Czech Republic, provision of long-term care 164–5; Italy, spending on long-term care 148;

Index

Poland, provision of long-term care 175, 176–7; *see also* medical-based long-term care, US

health insurance: Netherlands, for exceptional costs 61, 62, 65; Poland 177; Turkey, reform of 187, 190–1

health problems of older people: Poland 173–4; Sweden 48,; Turkey, health inequalities 190

healthy life years: Argentina 321; Italy 143; Poland 173

historical sociological approach 16

Home and Community Care Programme (HACC), Australia 304, 307

home-and-community programmes, US 275, 278; spending on 275; waiver programmes 275

home care: Australia 303, 304, 307, 309–10; Austria 131, 132; Czech Republic 165–7; Denmark 30–2; England 88–90; France 103, 104, 106–7; Germany 120–1; Italy 143–4; Poland 175–6; Sweden 48–9; Taiwan 233–4; Turkey 196; US 278, Figure 19.4, 279; *see also* consumer directed care; direct payments; domiciliary services, home help; home nursing; household services; personal budgets

home care companies, US 278, 279

Home Care Package Programme (HCPP), Australia 304, 309

home healthcare services: Turkey 195, 196; US 278

home help: Japan 244, 248-9, *245, 246*; Norway 15, 18, 19, 22, 23, 24; Turkey 196; *see also* consumer directed care, direct payments, domiciliary services, home care; home nursing; personal budgets; household services

home nursing: Australia 307; Germany 123, 127, Netherlands 62, 69; Norway 15, 17, 18, 19, 20, 22, 23, 24

home, staying as long as possible at 3, 20, 22, 23, 102

hospitals as long-term care provision: Turkey 195; South Korea 220

hospital-stay problem *see* 'social hospitalization'

household services: France 103, 113; Netherlands 62, 69, 70 ; Germany **120**, 122, 124–4, **125**; Japan 250 *see also* domestic work

house wife substitute, Norway 18

'In Control' scheme, England 90

Indennità di Accompagnamento (IA: Attendance Allowance), Italy 144

individual budgets, England 90

individualization/individualism/individualized services 22, 23, 35, 49, 162

informal care, payment of 65, 148, 280

informal/family care: Argentina 327, 328; Australia 303, 304, 305, 306; Austria 131,132, 133,

136, 138, 139, 140; Canada 292, 294, 297, 298; China 2045; 212, 215; Czech Republic 159–60, 161, 163, 164, 167; Denmark 29, 30; France, 102, 104; 105, 106, 112–13; Germany 116, 119, 120, 121, 126; Italy 142, 144, **145**, 145–6, 148–9, *148*; Netherlands 61, 63, 64, 65, 66, 67, 69–70; Norway 15, 17, 18, 20, 21, 23, 25; Poland 172, 173– 74, 180; Sweden 47, 51; Taiwan, 228, 231, 234–8; Turkey 190, 192; US 273, 275, 279, 280, 286

informal/formal care 69, 103, 111, 112–13, 118, 132, 230; blurring of 3, 6, 8, 11, 111, 118, 230

informalization 68, 69

institutions *see* nursing homes; residential care

instrumental activities of daily living,(IADLs) *see* activities of daily living

Invisible Women: Gender and the Shifting Divisions of Labour in Long-term Residential Care 290, 291

intergenerational relationships 1, 163-4

intermediaries (in recruiting migrant care workers), Austria 134, 138

intersectional analysis 119, 126, 136, 290

Italy 6; ageing 143; caregiving burden 150; caregiving triad 149-50; cash-for-care (attendance allowance, IA) 144,146,148, 151; cash-for-care, other 144, 151; components of long-term care provision 148, *148*; family role care 142, 144, **145**, 145–6, **145**, 148–9, *148*; health and social care split 143; migrant care work challenges 151; migrant care workers 146–151; migrant cohabitation 146; migrants' country of origin 146, *147*

Japan 9; ageing population 243, 257; de-familialization 242, 252, 253; family care role 244, 245, 247, 265; home help transition 248–9; long-term care insurance (LTCI) system 241; LTCI assessment of care needs 244; LTCI changes providers 248, **249**, **251**; LTCI facilities 244, 257; LTCI increase service users 244, *245, 246*, 248; quasi-facilities 250-1; role municipalities 248; serviced housing 251; Swedish/Scandinavian home care model 242, 249, 253; tax deductions encouraging family care 247; unique or hybrid welfare state? 242-3; unregistered facilities 251–2; *see also* care robots

job creation, in care work: France 105, 112; South Korea 223

job rotation 296, 297 laundry in nursing homes, ethnographic study of 296-9; *see also* contracting out work

life homes, Turkey 196

Karadeniz, O. 191, 192, 193, 194, 196

Karasek control demand model 75; and Karasek Job Content Questionnaire (JCQ) 76; and social care workers characteristics 79–81, **80–81**; and job characteristics 81–2, 82

Law on Free Choice of Provider (Denmark) 31
Le Bihan, B. 102, 103, 105, 108, 112
liberal welfare regime 63, 242
life expectancy: Italy 143; Poland 171, 173; Turkey 189, **189**
live-in migrant care work 5, 6, 8, 70, 94, 121, 124, 126, 127, 134–40, 147, 228, 229, 230–38; *see also* migrant care work/ers
local councils (authorities), England 75, 88–9; and types of contract 89
local government *see* local councils; municipalities
loneliness older people 174, 180
Longitudinal Care Work Study (LoCS) 75, 81–2
Long Term Care Act of 2015, Netherlands 62, 64, 65, 69
long-term care insurance: Germany 116, 119, 120, **120**; Japan 9, 241, 243, 244, 247, 248,252; Netherlands 62, South Korea 8, 220, 221, **222**
Long-Term Care Service Act, 2015, Taiwan 228
Long term service and supports (LTSS), US 273, 275, *276*, 275–80
Law on free choice of provider 2003, Denmark 31
Low Pay Commission, England 78

managed care 9, 274, 275. 278, 280, 286
mandataire system, France 106–8, **109**
marketization of care 5, 7, 8, 9, 11, 63, 218, 241; Australia 303, 304, 306, 308, 312; Czech Republic160, 162, 165, 167, 168; Denmark 29, 31, 32, 33, 42; England 74, 75,77, 78, 79, 83–4, 96; France 104, 106, 111, 112, 113; Germany 116, 117, 118, 119, 121, 123, 126, 127; Japan, 248, 249, 253; Netherlands 63, 64, 65, 69–70; Norway 21, 23, 24, 26; South Korea 218, 219, 221, 222–223, 225; Sweden 49, 51; *see also* privatization
Marquier, R. 103, 106, 107, 108, 109, 110, 111
means-test: Australia 305, 307; Australia, sliding scale payments 309; Austria, for migrant worker benefit 134; England 74; Germany, pre-long-term care insurance 119; Turkey, for domiciliary allowance 196, 197; US 273, 274
Medicaid 9, 273–5, 276, 278, 279, 280, 285, 286
medical-based long-term care, US 275 *see also* non-medical long-term care, US
medicalization: prioritizing medical needs 22, 23; of ageing 159, 165
Medicare 274–5, 276, 278
migrant care worker burden 150–1, 231, 233
migrant care worker, legal framework/foundation: Austria 134, 137, 138, 139; Taiwan 228, 229–30
migrant care work/ers 5, 7, 8, 9; Australia 304; Austria 130, 132, 133–139; Denmark 37, 40; Canada 291; China 212; Czech Republic

166; England 76–8, 84, 85; France 107, 108; Germany 116, 119, 121, 123, 124, Table 8.3, 126, 127; Italy 142, 146–51; Netherlands 70; Poland 178–9; Sweden 47; Taiwan 228; Turkey 193
'migrant in the family model' 6, 143, 230
migrant live-in care worker case study 231–233
migration policies 118; Austria 136–7; Taiwan 229
migration source countries: 76–7, *77,* 84, 135, **135**,146, *147;* effects on 137, 151, 178–9, 193, 228
mind work/body work 8, 236
minimum wage legislation US, effects on care workers 285, 286
mixed economy of care 43, 47, 89, 161
modernization of public services/society 5, 21, 219, 220
Možný, I. 160, 163, 164
Municipal Health and Care Services Act of 2011, Norway 20
Municipal Health Service Act of 1982, Norway 18, 20, 26
municipalities' role in service provision: Czech Republic 165; Denmark 29, 30, 31, 33, 34, 42, 49; Italy 143, 144, 148; Japan 244, 247, 248, 249, Table 17,1, 250, Table 17,2, 252; Netherlands 62, 65, 67, 69; Norway 17, 18, 20, 21, 24, 25–6; Poland 176, 177, 178; Sweden 46, 49, 50, 51; Turkey 194, 195, 196, 197; *see also* local councils (authorities)
Municipality Law of 1837 (Norway) 17

National Aged Care Workforce Surveys (NACWS), Australia 304
National Health Insurance system, South Korea 220
National Health Service (NHS), UK 74
National Minimum Dataset for Social Care (NMDS-SC) 75, 77
National minimum wage, UK 78, 79
neo-liberal 64, 66, 219, 290, 292
Netherlands 5; cost containment 62, 64, 65, 66, 69; 'cost disease' problem 62–3; decentralization of care 62, 63; exclusion housework 69; flexibilization strategy 68; integration of long-term care services 62; job losses 66–7; migrant worker possibilities 70; professionalization core care sector 69; shifting responsibility to family 68–70
New Public Management (NPM) 5, 10, 21, 31, 49, 64, 89, 303, 306, 308
NHS and Community Care Act, 1990, UK 89
non-medical long-term care, US 275, *276 see also* medical-based long-term care, US
NORDCARE surveys 30, 37–42, 46, 51–4, 117
Nordic model of long-term care 4, 15, 26, 29, 30, 46, 47, 61; problematization of 4, 42; and women-friendliness 25, 45, 54

Index

nurses: Australia, qualifications of ; Canada, protection by professional organizations 291–2, 298; China, composition of 214; Poland, education of 179

nursing homes: Canada 289, 291–2 ; Czech Republic 163–4, 168; Japan 244; Norway 15, 18, 19, 20, 22, 24; Poland 176–7; South Korea 220–1; Sweden 50, 51; US 275; *see also* old people's homes; residential care

Norway: activity theory of ageing 17, 21, 23, 25; current long-term care services 15;decrease in services 25; home nursing15, 17, 18, 19, 20, 22, 23, 24; housewife substitute service 18–19; individualization 22, 23; institutional care 15, 17; medicalization 22, 23, 25, fig. 1.4; municipalization/municipalities' role 17, 18, 20, 21, 24, 25–6; nursing homes 15, 19, 20, 22, 24; old people's homes 15, 17, 19, 20, 22; separation/tension between social and nursing services 18, 20, 22, 25, *19*; service inequality based on age *24*, 24-25

old people's homes, Norway 15, 17, 19, 20, 22

older people: attitudes to care workers, Japan 265; attitude to care technology, Japan 265; care preferences 148, 190, 194, 213, 215; choice 98, 166; and loneliness, Poland 174

Older Persons Welfare Act, South Korea 220

one-child policy; 203

Österle, A. 6, 131, 132, 161, 162, 163, 164, 165, 166

pay *see* wages

pensions: Argentina, 322, **322**, 329; Turkey 188, 191

personal budgets: England 74–5, 88, 89–90, 84, 95, 96, 97, 98, 99; Netherlands 65, 69

person-centred care 3, 49, 312

personalization 5, 11, 74–5, 88, 90

Pfau-Effinger, M. 103, 112, 256, 259

Pflegegeld 131

Plan Borloo (Social and Cohesion Plan), France, 2005 5, 105–6, 111, 112

Poland 6–7; ageism and loneliness 174; charity and religious care services 178; commercial services 177–8; demand for care 172–3; education care staff 179; family role 172, 173–4, 180; home care 176; imbalance demand and supply 179–81; migrant care workers 178–9; residential care 176–7; supply of services 176

precarious employment 84, 108, 111, 119, 124, 127, 137, 139, 146, 257, 298, 310

prestataire system, France 106–8, **109**, 111,112

Prestation spécifique dépendance PSD 104; *see also* cash-for-care France

preventive home help, Japan 244, *245, 246,* 249, 252

private pay agencies, US 279; licensing of 279

privately purchased (paid) care: Argentina 324, 326; Czech Republic 167; Denmark 31; Germany 121, 124,126; Italy 144, 148; Norway 15; Poland 177–8; Sweden 47; Taiwan 233; Turkey, 196; US 279 *see also* self-funding

privatization 79, 111, 113, 204, 206, 214, 292, 295, 296, 298, 299, 312 *see also* marketization

professionalization of care work 5, 21, 23, 63, 65, 67, 69, 104–5, 113, 127, 131, 162, 249, 250; types of professional development 118; and effects of unregulated migrant care work 139, 140

promising practices 9, 289, 290, 291, 299

providers of long-term care (public, non-profit, for profit): Australia 304; Austria 131; Canada 291; Czech Republic 165; Denmark 29 31–2, 33–4; England 75, 89; France 106; Germany 121, **122**; Japan 248, **249, 251**; Norway 21; Sweden 49, 50; Turkey 194, **195**,195–6; US 275, 278

public benefit organizations (OPP), Poland 178

public expenditure on long-term care: Austria 132, **133**; England 74, 88; France 102; Germany 120; Italy 142, 148; Japan 257, 259; Netherlands 65; Norway 15, 25; Poland 175; Sweden 46; US 273

public social expenditure, Japan, 243; Turkey 188

purchaser-provider split 21, 24, 49

qualifications; *see* training

quality of care services: Austria, 131; China 206, 207, 214, 215; Czech Republic 161, 165, 166; Denmark 29, 30, 31, 33, 35, 42; Denmark, comparison public and private home care providers 36, *37*, 40, *42*; England 79, 83, 85, 95, 97; France 112; Netherlands 65, 69; Norway, 21; Poland 176, 177, 180; South Korea 218, 221, 223, 225; Sweden 49, 50, 51, 54; Turkey, 192, 197; US 283, 284; and unregulated migrant care work 138, 139, 140, 143, 151

quasi-facilities, Japan 250

rationality of caring 16, 21, 23, 25, 266

recruiting agencies (of migrant care workers),Taiwan 230

re-familialization 9, 11, 63, 69–70

rehabilitation (reablement) 21, 23, 25

Re-imagining Long-Term Residential Care: An International Study of Promising Practices 290, 291

reimbursement policies 9, 20, 274, 286

religious organizations 61, 178, 180

residential care: Australia 303, 304, 305, 306, 309; Austria, 131,132, 135; Czech Republic 161, 164; Germany 119, 120, 121, 122, 123, 124, 127; Italy 143; Netherlands 61, 62; Poland

176–8; Sweden 46–7, 49–50 51–54; Turkey 194–5, **195**; US 276–8; *see also* China; 'geriatric homes'; Japan, LTCI facilities, quasi-facilities, serviced housing, unregistered facilities; nursing homes; old people's homes

resident support assistants, Canada 294–5, 298

residualism 6; 131, 163, 242

restricted universalism 131, 133

restricting services 250

risk/social risk 6, 9, 137-8, 140, 159, 218, 219, 259

Rostgaard, T. 31, 36, 70

self care (self help) 23, 65

self employment: Austria, migrant care workers 134, 137, 139; Netherlands 65, 67

self-funding/self funders 75, 84, 98, 99, 144, 191, 206, 324, 326

semi-formal care 103, 112–13

semi-professional activity 61, 112

semi-residential facilities; Poland, 176

sending country: Czech Republic 166; Poland 178; *see also* migration source countries

senior homes, Poland 176

'serviced housing', Japan 251

services for the Elderly and Persons with Disabilities (SEPD), US 278

Servizio di Assistenza Domiciliare (SAD: Home Help Service) 144

sheltered housing 15, 20, 22, 25, 176

Skilled nursing facilities, US: *276*, 276, 277–8

social assistance: Austria 130, 131; France 104; Germany 119; Norway 17; Turkey 188, 191, 197

social assistance homes, Poland (DPS): 175, 176, 177

Social Care Act of 1964, Norway 18, 20, 21

social care definition 3

social democratic welfare regime 4, 15, 63, 69

social health insurance, Poland 177

'social hospitalization' 9, 17, 220, 242, 247

social inequality due to gender, class, or city/rural area 7, 8, 10, 66, 70, 177, 179, 190–1, 196, 213, 238, 286, 298, 310, 319, 320, 322, 323, 328

social perception of care work, South Korea 223, 225

Social Service Law 2013, Denmark 33

Social Services Act No. 102/1964, Czech Republic 161

Social Services Act, 1991, Norway 21

Social Support Act, 2007, The Netherlands 62, 64, 65, 66, 69

social sustainability 10–11

Social Welfare Act, 1923, Poland 176

South Korea 8; ageing population 219; filial piety 219; high turnover care workers 224; inadequate old long-term care system 220–1; increased numbers of care workers 223; long-term care insurance 220, **222**; low wages and

demanding working conditions 223–4, 225; marketization 218, 219, 221, 222–3, 225; new training system and certification 221, 222, 223, 225; quality of care work 218, 221, 223, 225

Sowa, A. 163–4, 165, 172

state, role of the 1, 3, 4, 5, 6, 9, 10 ; Argentina 322, 323, 328, 329, 330; Australia, federal (Commonwealth) 305, 307, 308; Austria 130–131; Canada 289, 298; China (government) 205–6, 214; Czech Republic 161, 162, 163,165, 167; Denmark 30; England 74; France 104, Germany 119, 127; Italy 144, 148; Japan 241, 242, 243, 253, 257; Netherlands 61,63, 64 ; Norway 15, 17, 18. 20, 21–22; Poland 172, 175, 179; South Korea 219, 220; Sweden 46, 47, 48, 51; Taiwan 230; Turkey 191; US, federal 273, 274, 275, 285; AQ: shouldn't this be in 'F' unless there is something missing?

stress and care work 79–83

sustainable long-term care 10, 11, 66, 151, 192, 308, 312

Sweden/Swedish: care workers 4; 47–8; changes in eldercare provision over time 46–7, 49, 51; deteriorating working conditions, residential vs home care 51–54; home care 48–9; marketization 51; residential care 49–50; role of municipalities 46, 49, 50; shift from domestic to bodily (personal) care 51; switch nursing homes from health to social care 50;

Swedish/Scandinavian home care model 242, 249

Szebehely. M. 30, 46, 47, 48, 49, 50, 51, 70, 242

Szebehely. M. and Vabø, M. 30, 46, 49, 51

Taiwan 8; case study migrant-live-in care worker 231–3; division of labour, mind work and body work 234–7; family role in care 228, 231, 234–8; filial piety 23, 23–5, 237; legal framework migrant care work 228, 229–30; recruiting agencies 230

targeting care services/tightening criteria: Denmark 32; England 98; Netherlands 64; Norway 20, 23, 32, 46, 65; Poland 175; Sweden 46, 47, US 275

tax deduction: France 105; Germany 124, 151; Japan 247-8, 252; Poland 179

Taylorization of care work 21, 49, 63, 64–5

Temporary Measure for the Shortage of Family Care Labour for People with Disabilities, Taiwan 229–30

Thatcher government, UK 5, 74

Theobald, H. 117, 118, 119, 161

top-up (supplementary) payments: Australia, 309, 310; Denmark 31; Germany 121

training and qualifications of care workers: Australia 304–5, 311; Canada 296, 297, 298;

China 208; England 83; France 108, 111, 112; Germany 122–4, 127, **122**; Japan 249; Netherlands 61; Norway 21; Poland 179; South Korea 221, 222, 223, 225; Sweden 48, 50; Turkey 193; US 283, 284, 285

training organizations for care workers, South Korea, development of 8, 221–2, 225

Transforming Care Conference, Milan, 2017 10

Turkey 7; demographic outlook 188–190; difficulty accessing long-term care 194; family care 190, 192, 196; financial help, long-term care193–4; funding long-term care 193–4; government policies for older and disabled people 191–2; healthcare insurance reform 190–91; home-based care 195–6; lack skilled care workers 193; migrant care workers 193; residential care 194–5, **195**; shift institutional care to home care 194; social assistance 188, 191, 193–4

Turkish Red Crescent (Kızılay) 194

turnover rate, care workers: China 208, **210**, 212; England 76; Japan 257; South Korea 8, 221, 224, 225; US 283; US, reasons for turnover (or retention) 283–4

Twelfth Five-Year Plan of China 8, 215

Ungerson, C. 2, 104, 112, 230

US 9; adult day centres 278, 280; consumer-directed care 280, 283–4, 286; home-and community based care 278, *279*, 279; home healthcare services 278, *279*; employment growth care workers 280, *282*; improved quality care jobs; 284–5; institutional care 276–7; institutional care, ethnic and income differences in access 277–8; long-term services and supports 273, 275–80; managed care 274, 275. 278, 280, 286; Medicaid 273–5, 276, 278, 279, 280, 285, 286; Medicare 274–5, 276,

278; private pay agencies 279; reasons for high turnover care workers 283–4

user (consumer) choice 5, 23–4, 29, 31, 35, 36, 74, 93, 94–5, 96–7, 132, 248, 308; and older people 5, 98, 99, 166, 167, 168, 309–10; *see also* free choice of provider

user satisfaction 35–6, 42

unions: Canada, limited success of 291–2, 298–9; England, relationship to job stress (Karasek scales) 81, **82**; Netherlands, protest against potential job losses 66, 67; US, effect on wages 284, 286

universalism of services 5, 15, 29, 30, 43, 46, 61, 62, 63, 64, 66, 74, 83, 116, 118, 130, 133, 177

unregistered facilities, Japan 251–2

value (of caring) 79, 84

Van Hooren, F. 6, 70, 117, 118, 133, 136, 143 150

voluntary care workers: South Korea 221; Canada 294

voluntary organizations, Norway 17, 20, 21, 24

Wærness, K. 2–3, 16, 17, 18, 21, 22, 45, 266

wages of care workers: Australia, 310; China 208; England, 78, 84; England, reasons for low wages 78–9, 84; France 111; Germany 122–3, Japan 257; South Korea 224, 225; Sweden, 49, 53; US 283, 284; US reasons for low wages 284–5; US, receipt social assistance/support, 283, 285

welfare triangles 17, 20

women-friendly welfare state 4, 54

women's work 11, 18, 298; *see also* care work as women's 'natural' role, responsibility

younger care users, Norway 24, 25

Zarit test of carer stress 327

zero-hours contracts, England 77, 78, 94